KU-716-434

FROM GRACE TO BOTHAM

FIFTY MASTER CRICKETERS FROM
THE TIMES

CHOSEN AND INTRODUCED
BY KENNETH GREGORY

Published in 1989 by
TIMES BOOKS LIMITED
16 Golden Square
London W1R 4BN

Copyright © 1989
Times Books Limited

British Library Cataloguing in Publication Data
From Grace to Botham: 50 master cricketers from
  The Times
  1. Cricket — biographies — collections
  I. Gregory, Kenneth 1921– II. The Times
  796.35'8'0922

  ISBN 0-7230-0311-4

Typeset by
CRB Typesetting Services
Ely, Cambridgeshire

Printed in Great Britain by
Butler & Tanner Limited
Frome & London

CONTENTS

INTRODUCTION

The reader must first be disarmed. Although personal choice has obviously determined the identity of cricketers presented here, this has, in turn, been governed by certain factors — the ability of sporting editors (as they were once called) of *The Times* to despatch correspondents to the right games, the meagre coverage of matches in far-off days, and what can only be termed misfortune. Consider the South African G.A. Faulkner, who played his finest innings, at least in England, for A.C. MacLaren's amateur side against Armstrong's hitherto unbeaten Australians of 1921 at Eastbourne. The only paper to have a man present was the *Manchester Guardian*, the young Neville Cardus wishing to show his faith in MacLaren. It would be pleasant, too, if *The Times* had published an analytical essay on Arthur Shrewsbury's defensive technique, and on the bowling methods of the off-spinner Hugh Trumble and the googly master from South Africa, A.E. Vogler. It did not. Again, any outstanding performance immediately after the Second World War was apt to be ignored, or confined to a few lines, for reasons of space — sport, now allotted five pages or so, often being confined to a couple of columns. Hence the omission of two opening batsmen, India's V.M. Merchant in 1946 and the cavalier New Zealander B. Sutcliffe three years later. Sir Donald Bradman hailed the 254 by Sobers for the World XI at Melbourne in 1971–2 as the finest innings ever played in Australia. It was not covered by *The Times*, though many of Sobers's triumphs were. Gavaskar's 221 at the Oval in 1979 occurred when the paper was in the ninth month of its historic shutdown.

One text for this book — and it may be revised by readers as they see fit — is to be found in Dudley Carew's *To the Wicket* (1946): "There was some grand cricket played in the period between the wars, and if our children and grandchildren condole with us in having lived in those dreadful times, we can at least answer, 'Ah, but we saw Chapman field, Larwood bowl, Hammond bat, and we are not so much to be pitied as you think'."

Every age has remarkable cricket to watch, the essential difference between Jessop at the Oval in 1902 and Botham at Headingley and Old Trafford in 1981 being the absence of television cameras on the former occasion. Sometimes, of course, the present refrains from paying homage to the past for fear of denigrating itself. Sir Leonard Hutton has written of Hammond's slip fielding: "No diving to left or right, collecting green marks on his immaculate flannels. It was not necessary for Walter to spread himself on the ground as with normal slip fielders." Which asks a further question or two these pages will not answer. How were Jessop, Hobbs, Washbrook and others effective in the covers, and Pellew in the deep, without resorting to the sliding tackle? Similarly, that modern phenomenon, the scientifically placed field: did Spofforth, Barnes, Rhodes and O'Reilly permit their accessories to wander about as they pleased, finishing in some indeterminate spot as the whim took them? That Verity bowled the equivalent of 50.3 six-ball overs in an innings for 79 runs at Melbourne, followed by 49.2 overs for 53 runs at Adelaide, as Bradman twice topped 200, was presumably a reflection on the batsman rather than a tribute to the bowler's accuracy and G.O. Allen's placements. Did the Australians place their fields scientifically when attacking Botham in 1981?

Such questions can at least receive subjective answers; one concerning the Hon. Robert Henry Lyttelton must be asked only of social historians. Why, and how, in 1902 did *The Times* contact Lyttelton? The Fourth Test of that year had been covered by Ernest Ward, who took over the reporting of important matches from George West on the latter's death in 1896. Yet the Fifth Test saw Ward replaced by a solicitor, a partner in the firm of Stow, Preston and Lyttelton, 35 Lincoln's Inn Fields, WC (Holborn 760), and a member of Brooks's Club, St James's Street, SW (Gerrard 3745). Lyttelton's residence was 9 Barton Street, SW, where the telephone had apparently not been installed, though it had at *The Times* office (Bank 581), where many of the staff shunned the instrument as newfangled, a likely exception being the paper's drama critic, Arthur Bingham Walkley, who by day held down a senior post in the Secretary's department of the GPO.

Whether *The Times* rang Lyttelton at his office or club, wrote to him, or simply bumped into him in Piccadilly ("Care to write on the Test match tomorrow? Have to go to the Oval, I'm afraid"), will never be known. What was important was the capacity in which Lyttelton was engaged to perform. According to a letter* from his nephew George to Rupert Hart-Davis on 22 October 1959, he had professional shortcomings: "My uncle Bob was a solicitor — and by far the stupidest of all the eight brothers, sons of the fourth Lord Lyttelton. He did all the family business and cost them thousands of pounds through his blundering." But *The Times* was not seeking a lawyer to represent it at the Oval, being content to leave decisions to the umpires. In any case, the Hon. Alfred Lyttelton, KC, a brother, was better qualified, having once taken four Australian Test wickets for 19 runs when bowling lobs and wearing his wicketkeeping pads. *The Times* was seeking a man of letters.

The Hon. R.H. Lyttelton was such a man. He had written five chapters of the Badminton Library's *Cricket*, including an account of the 1870 University match when Oxford, requiring 179 to win, reached 153 for three and 175 for seven. Whereupon F.C. Cobden prepared to bowl at F.H. Hill, who poked a single, the over being transcribed as 1WWW — the hat-trick balls later being described by Cobden as the three best he had ever bowled. The non-striker Hill recalled them as three half-volleys, the wicketkeeper W. Yardley as a near wide, a half-volley and a long hop. Not having been present, Lyttelton wrote graphically in Cardus vein, concluding "Up went Mr Absolom's hat, down the pavilion steps with miraculous rapidity flew the Rev. A.R. Ward, and smash went Mr Charles Marsham's umbrella against the pavilion brickwork." Lyttelton's earthly reward came in 1925, when Sir Arthur Quiller-Couch immortalized this memory of Cobden's match in the *Oxford Book of English Prose.*

Cricket coverage in *The Times* has changed with the mood and demands of the century. In 1902 county matches were hardly reported beyond an

agency paragraph apiece, whereas by 1930 eight such games merited 4,500 words. Not until 1928 did an annual series of Tests become the norm in England; previously, and excluding the years of the First World War, Tests had graced only eight of the present century's twenty-four seasons. West Indies' win at Lord's in 1950 was only the second by a non-Australian visiting side, the first being South Africa's in 1935. Small wonder, then, that *The Times* related cricket to the social status of its readers — Gentlemen v. Players, the University match and Eton v. Harrow in the foreground:

The Duchess of Newcastle was in cerise-coloured chiffon with a hat to match. Sir William and Lady Noreen Bass were on the Duke of Newcastle's coach. The Countess of Ilchester was in beige lace with a black hat, Lady Annabel Dodds in hydrangea-blue.

That was the Eton v. Harrow match in 1924 when — with a future Eton captain, Henry Edward Hugh Pelham-Clinton-Hope (later Duke of Newcastle) unable to play at Lord's — the honour of *Debrett* was upheld by Lord Hyde with a sound 86. The cricket correspondent of *The Times*, A.C.M. Croome, took it for granted that his readers were as erudite as himself. A former demy of Magdalen, with a first in Moderations and Blues for cricket and athletics, Croome had earlier recognized the existence of Harrow: "Stewart-Brown clearly has a *flair* for wicketkeeping, but he has not yet mastered the Aristotelian doctrine of the Moral Thermometer: Virtue is the Mean between two extremes." No lady in cerise, beige or even hydrangea-blue could quarrel with that.

The Times's appointment of cricket correspondents was for long a canny business. Croome, as already noted, was admirably qualified to cover two sports (three if we include his additional job as golf correspondent of the *Morning Post*), and so were his successors for half a century. Richard Beaumont Vincent was a Cambridge golf Blue — in 1919 *The Times* Golfing Society's top pair were Vincent and Bernard Darwin — Geoffrey Green and John

* *The Lyttelton Hart-Davis Letters,* Vol. IV (1982), p. 148.

Woodcock, respectively, football and hockey Blues at Cambridge and Oxford. Should cancellations suggest a day or two off, the sporting editor had merely to switch their coverage, seasons permitting. Sydney Herbert Pardon was the *grand seigneur*, unique in that he had apparently never played the game, wrote with distinction on music, the theatre, racing and cricket, and acted as cricket correspondent of *The Times* without describing any play, his duty being to preview great occasions. Cardus saw him as "a typical English gentleman, late-Victorian and ripe Edwardian".

The "ripe Edwardian" earned an ideal death. On 19 November 1925 he attended a Royal Philharmonic Society concert at Queen's Hall, where the music was by Elgar: *Enigma* Variations, the 'cello concerto, *Falstaff, In the South*. The composer conducted. As the night was still young, Pardon decided to visit his Cricket Reporting Agency office; he had, after all, been editor of *Wisden* for thirty-five years. And there he died. Among the mourners at his funeral was a former captain of England, C.A. Smith, long since transformed for professional reasons into C. Aubrey Smith.* From the closing hours and after of Pardon's life, only a Derby winner was missing.

John Woodcock's sojourn as cricket correspondent of *The Times* must be put into perspective, lasting as it did from 1954 to 1988 — after which he relinquished his role though still travelling the world in pursuit of cricket. At the end of 1988 he announced his own Test score as "about" 350, a revealing figure considering that prior to 1954 the various countries had participated in these games:

England	310			
Australia	213			
South Africa	122		Tests in	
West Indies	52	386 Tests	England 200	
New Zealand	31			
All India	7		Tests outside	
India	32		England 186	
Pakistan	5			

Of the 386 Tests played, England or Australia (or both) had appeared in 360, spanning 76 years. The

* An even more distinguished film actor-to-be of the Smith family — T.W. Howard-Smith — appeared for Clifton at Lord's in 1932. By the time of *Brief Encounter* (1945) he was Trevor Howard.

next 24 years after 1954 saw an additional 397 Tests, i.e. between 16 and 17 a calender year. It only remains to add that, on account of R.B Vincent's illness soon after reaching Australia in 1950–51, Woodcock was the first *Times* cricket correspondent to write on England abroad. His mileage is awe-inspiring and beyond calculation, his meals consumed at 30,000 feet a warning to all.

The "style" employed in these pages is predetermined, no changes having been made (save for indicated cuts) from the original texts. If the reader is irritated by the insistence on preceding the name of every amateur by "Mr" in pre-1930 days, nothing can be done about it. By the 1930s *The Times* had dropped "Mr", only to indulge in another absurdity — the use of initials to denote amateurs: "K. Farnes and Nichols bowled to P.A. Gibb and Hutton." The objection to both conventions is aesthetic: it is hard to establish the rhythm of a sentence if irrelevant words or signs have to be inserted in front of surnames. Lest any reader compares these pages with a microfilm version of their originals, he will notice that certain paragraphs have been divided into two or three. Indulgent subeditors allowed the Hon. R.H. Lyttelton slabs of 600 words, that is, twice as long as Lincoln's Gettysburg address. If brother Alfred was briefed in like fashion, small wonder he forsook the law for politics.

Statistics sometimes appear in the firmly held belief that they illustrate or add to reports. The miracle of Hobbs's career — and miracle it was — cannot be appreciated until we realize that the First World War really did mark the half-way stage in the number of innings he played. Statistics often translate poetic intuition into fact. Cardus liked to see the Australian Macdonald, Lancashire's great mercenary of the 1920s, as a bowler who was supreme when the mood took him, and who went through the motions when it did not. Macdonald's idea of cricket was attacking Hobbs or Woolley; when the tail-enders came in, he lost interest and slunk away from the bowling crease. He was paid to win matches for Lancashire, which he sometimes did. "A typical Australian," spectators remarked as Macdonald, heaved for six by some village blacksmith, spat — then plucked a blade of grass to chew. (Where he found a blade of grass on the cropped fields of the time is beside the point.) That was Macdonald in the Cardus mythology.

Did it contain a germ of truth? Surprisingly, it was the truth. While we may concede that any fast bowler must have off-days, be obliged to perform on pitches which offer him nothing and be driven to try his hand at medium-pace off-breaks, it is hard to account for Macdonald, say, in 1926, save in terms of "when the spirit moves". First his total county figures, then the revealing division:

Inns	Wkts	Av.	B/W		Inns	Wkts	Av.	B/W
					26	124	12.38	25
51	163	19.04	39					
					25	39	42.79	84

If asked for a justification of such greatness and sloth, Macdonald had the perfect answer: "Lancashire won the Championship."

The presentation of figures also serves to emphasize the difference between cricket today and cricket yesterday. Of late, a touring side's ambition has been to win the Test series and to survive the rest of its programme without injury. County teams have responded by playing numerous reserves, the outcome in many instances being three days of boredom. I.W. Johnson's 1956 Australians used their early games for practice in the middle, not seeking to bolster team morale with victories. Accordingly, when beaten by Laker in the Tests, they were unable to reflect how good they had been when Laker was not among the opposition. Once upon a time, though few under the age of 60 will credit it, a party from overseas included a bowler who took over 100 wickets during the English season but who did not play in a single Test, his skills being considered irrelevant — which indeed they were. He remains a statistician's minor joy, homage of a kind being paid on page 157.

If this book has one particular hero it is because he was the choice of The Times writers between the wars, when words were at their most prodigal. Hobbs, of course, was revered as a national institution; Hammond was the ideal cricketer; Sutcliffe surveyed his subject bowlers with disdain; Hendren was loved; the cunning of Rhodes seemed eternal. The Times could interpret, or pretend to interpret, all these; Woolley it could not. Woolley caused men to doubt the evidence before them, surely nothing could manifest such elegance and magic. As the George Lyttelton, quoted earlier, who wrote on many Eton v. Harrow matches for The Times, said: "When he [Woolley] played a characteristic innings, anyone who saw it was temporarily unbalanced and scorned the very notion of Trumper, Hobbs, Hammond, Macartney amd Bradman. As I heard Charles Fry say, 'But for that hole in his defence, he would have been the greatest of all'." This particular writer recalls him as a disdainful aristocrat to whom bowlers were but children in need of correction. A garbled agency message once informed the world that Woolley had hit Bowes of Yorkshire out of the ground and into the sea — some quarter of a mile distant. This instance of poetic truth was appreciated even in Bradford and Headingley, and by Bowes himself.

From time to time in these pages, over-rates are mentioned, not to snipe at the present but to show one reason at least why certain glories of the past were possible. Not so long ago in a Test match two Indian slow left-arm bowlers took an hour to complete seven overs, thereby suggesting that today Woolley would have to satisfy himself with 25 runs an hour — though hitting the odd delivery at Eden Gardens into the Bay of Bengal. Over-rates have become either a cricketing obscenity or the cause of great hilarity. Any defenders of modern dawdling should consult Wisden on the Headingley Test of 1930, when Australia scored 566 off 168 overs in 460 minutes. They will discover that if Larwood bowled an over in 4 minutes and Tate, Geary and Hammond an over in 3 minutes 15 seconds (highly unlikely today), then the spinners Richard Tyldesley and Leyland completed each of their 44 overs in 45 seconds. As Bradman was swatting the bowling to all points of the compass, this offered solution to the mystery is clearly wrong.

An anthology such as this must depend on the sheer good fortune of correspondents, and the inspired instinct of editors, who chance to be in the right place at the right time — the classic example being Dudley Carew in 1932. On 15 June he journeyed to Leyton to watch Holmes and Sutcliffe create a world's first-wicket record partnership of 555, gleaning the incidental intelligence that the Essex wicketkeeper, J.R. Sheffield, who dropped Holmes when that batsman was three, spent the winter months voyaging up the Amazon in a canoe. A month later Carew encountered another oddity, Verity's 10 wickets for 10 runs in Nottinghamshire's second innings at Headingley. In 1934 Carew was present at Brentwood when Kent reached 623 for two on the first day, before adding 180 in an hour on the second — Essex managing 21 overs to the hour. Woolley's 172 was not one of his best innings, taking just over three hours, though he did once lean on the ball to hit a six.

Two of the funniest accounts of cricket matches are missing from here because they were never written. Alletson's mighty slog of 189 at Hove in 1911* coincided with R.C. Robertson-Glasgow's prep-school days; then the wrong age, "Crusoe" was on the wrong continent in 1926 when Victoria totalled 1,107 against New South Wales at Melbourne. Woodfull should have been run out at 17, but a finely judged — and lobbed — return from mid-on saw the bowler fall over the stumps, then miss the ball. The first wicket later fell at 375. A whimsical Arthur Mailey complained of missed catches in the "outer" by a man in a trilby hat; as Somerset players sometimes took the field in trilby hats, and knew how to drop catches, Robertson-Glasgow would have felt at home. Besides, this laughing philosopher of the game doted on the writings of "Beachcomber". He was also a master of the relevant; obeying an editorial command to report on the previous day's weather, "Crusoe" could oblige with "windy and warm like bottled lemonade".

More dignified correspondents sometimes, and blandly, differ from one another. After England had topped 600 at Old Trafford in 1934, Australia (with

* See John Arlott's monograph, *Alletson's Innings* (1957). After lunch Alletson scored 142 off 51 balls in 40 minutes, though the time seems an over-estimate.

several men, including Bradman, suffering from a throat infection) had nothing but a draw to play for.

The crowd, who had allowed the heat to irritate it into vocal disapproval of the batsmen's methods, gave D.G. Bradman, who did not look himself, a good reception (*The Times*, 10 July 1934).

Now entered Bradman, looking ill and quite worn; he was given a curiously quiet reception — I can only trust that Old Trafford did not know who it was (*Manchester Guardian*, 10 July 1934).

Presumably the *MG* expected Wagnerian trumpets and heard only muted strings. And to show how our own cricket correspondents do not always learn from the past, there is the distant response to some West Indies' fast bowling. At the close of the 1923 season (five years before West Indies were granted Test status) at Scarborough, Leveson-Gower's XI were set 28 to win in the fourth innings. They won by four wickets against the fury of Francis and John. *The Times* accounted for the collapse, in which even Hobbs and Ernest Tyldesley were swept aside, in words to be remembered today: "An inability to play good first-class fast bowling."

Today the history of cricket may be seen as comprising three ages: pre-Bradman, Bradman and post-Bradman. It was not until Sir Donald's 80th birthday in 1988 that the world, at least England, said of him publicly, what many had said privately, long before: "The Greatest Cricketer." This accolade can be disputed but only by those who insist that the greatest cricketer must be an all-rounder; if so, we must compare the impact Bradman had as a batsman with that of Sobers as batsman and bowler, both being superb fielders.

Bradman dominates these pages because of his achievements, the amount that was written about him and the way in which his genius brought out the best in onlookers. He had the advantage of not being an English player; had he been one during the years 1930–48, he would most likely have batted in excess of 500 innings in home games. As it was, his 120 innings in England were spread over 19 years: he never outstayed his welcome — an absurd statement but one which cannot be phrased in any other way. From Worcester 1930 to Scarborough 1948 he made runs: 9,837, average 96.44. Never once, though there was an Australian moral defeat at Sheffield in 1938, did he finish on the losing side in non-Test games and, when he batted, only twice in 18 Tests. Sports editors had merely to send a man to cover Australian matches and, with a greater consistency than any other batsman, Bradman obliged. Bad patches there certainly were: in 1934 he played 13 innings without a century before the floodgates opened again with 140, 334, 244, 77, 19, 149 not out and 132.

As Hobbs said in his interview with John Hartley: "Don was too good; he spoilt the game." Bradman was too good, he did spoil the game for the opposition. Rhodes, who bowled at everyone from Grace, Ranji and Trumper to Hobbs, Macartney, Hammond and Duleepsinhji, placed Bradman on the summit; Laker said that Bradman gave him an inferiority complex. The case rests.

Kenneth Gregory

ACKNOWLEDGEMENTS

I am deeply grateful to Messrs Bill O'Reilly and Alec Bedser for answering questions concerning field placements on certain great occasions.

My thanks are also due to Ann Pigott and Melanie Aspey, Archivists of *The Times*, to Mr Tim Jollands of Jollands Editions, and to the Hampset Cricket Club, Bath.

My editor, Mr James Shepherd, has much to answer for; without his ruthless cutting there would have been even more of Bradman and Woolley in this book. His dedication was, and is, an object lesson.

Kenneth Gregory   1989

WILLIAM GILBERT GRACE
Gloucestershire

The Times celebrated Grace's centenary by calling upon its golf correspondent, Dickensian and supreme stylist, Bernard Darwin (1876–1961). The publication of this article coincided with the start of the Gentlemen v. Players match at Lord's, the two sides captained, respectively, by N.W.D. Yardley and L. Hutton. The Players won by seven wickets, thanks mainly — or so Sir Pelham Warner thought — to an overgenerous declaration by Yardley. "If the shade of W.G. was hovering over Lord's he would assuredly have plucked at his beard — a sign that he was worried or displeased — for he who had taken part in so many victories over the Players would have seen to it that they did not win."

THE GREATEST CRICKETER THAT EVER LIVED OR EVER WILL LIVE

By Bernard Darwin

On July 18, 1848, after an interlude of inconsiderable daughters, a fourth son was born to Dr Henry Mills Grace and his wife (*née* Martha Pocock), of Downend, in Gloucestershire. It was an event destined to change the face if not of England at least of the great English game of cricket; if John Small the elder, of Hambledon, had been the "man who found out cricket," it was William Gilbert Grace who raised it to heights, alike of skill and popularity, undreamed of before his day. At the time it seemed doubtless an event of purely domestic importance and we do not know if Dr Grace, when he came riding home from his long round, praetermitted for once his cricket practice in the evening. It is pleasant to fancy that he did not and that Mrs Grace, who according to Richard Daft knew ten times as much about cricket as any lady he had ever met, was soothed, as she lay in bed, by the familiar sound of bat and ball amid the Downend apple trees.

Since it is primarily the birth of a hero that is being celebrated we may look back to those early years in which the small Gilbert (how impossible it is to fancy him as ever being small!) was first able to take part in the family ritual, with his father and elder brothers and perhaps a cousin or two of the clans of Rees and Gilbert. At intervals there ring out the excited barks of Don, Ponto, and Noble, that immortal trinity, as they pursue the ball into the outfield or oppose to it their dauntless breasts. Mrs Grace is there to look on with serious, appraising eyes and the girls throw up the ball if it comes their way or perhaps bowl one in a little game of their own to the still toddling Fred. And of course there is Uncle Pocock. If anyone watches the centenary matches with exultation from Elysian wickets it should be he. He made Gilbert his peculiar care, insisting that he should not, like his brother E.M., be corrupted into the heresy of the cross bat by being given too early a bat beyond his strength; preaching to him the virtues in life that really matter, the straight bat, the left shoulder forward, defence before hitting, and, above all, patience, that endless patience that was never to desert him and caused the appetite for runs to grow only more insatiable in the making. Uncle Pocock must never be forgotten.

Comparisons between the champions of different generations are nearly always as futile as ungracious. If they are to be made at all it must be by someone with claims to which the present writer has no pretensions whatever. This is a moment when hero-worship may be given free play, and unlearned worshippers at least will accept Mr C.E. Green's* fine, defiant eulogy, "The greatest cricketer that ever lived or ever will live." But perhaps one exception to this wise self-denial is permissible. No one can ever have attained to greatness at so tender an age. The true Infant Phenomenon was not Miss Ninetta Crummles but Master Gilbert Grace. Let those who spill too fervent ink over a promising colt or a schoolboy given a trial for his county eleven, ponder over a line or two of statistics. At ten W.G. played in his first match for the West Gloucestershire Club and at 12 made 51 against Clifton. At 14 he played against the All-England Eleven and faced two famous fast bowlers, Tarrant and Jackson, whom all his life he regarded as among the very best. The bowling had to be changed and Tinley brought on with his crafty lobs before the boy was bowled — for two and thirty runs. At 15 he himself played for the All-England Eleven and not much more than a year later for the Gentlemen against the Players and for England against Surrey. The day of the Australians had not yet come and so, as far as representative honours were concerned, the boy of a little over 17 had become a youthful Alexander with no more worlds to conquer.

He had not yet reached his ultimate pinnacle,

....

* President of MCC, 1905. On 24 August 1909 Green wrote to *The Times*, denouncing the idea of colonial players appearing in English county cricket.

but it was not far off. In 1867, which he deemed his best bowling year, only one professional, Wootton, took more wickets than he did. We think now of a venerable bearded giant beguiling youth with slows of innocent aspect, such as old William Beldham would have called (as he did Tom Walker's) "such baby bowling." So it is worth recalling the thin, lanky boy, with an incipient black scrub on his chin, bowling fast medium round arm, straight at the stumps, with no great guile but trusting to the wicket to do the rest. And, apropos, how bad were the wickets on which W.G. was soon to gather so monstrous a harvest of runs? It is a subject on which it is for ever interesting to speculate and perhaps easy to exaggerate. We have his own word for it that in the sixties many of them, and Lord's in particular, were very rough indeed. There is further Tom Emmett's testimony to his own and George Freeman's "expresses flying about his ribs, shoulders and head." But no doubt there came an improvement and W.G., never anxious to take undue credit, told at least one distinguished batsman of a later era that many of the wickets on which he played in his prime were very good. Good or bad he soon became, according to all previous standards of scoring, thoroughly outrageous upon them, and it was in 1870, when he was still but 22, that Emmett crystallized the general feeling in a memorable sentence: "I call him a non-such; he ought to be made to play with a littler bat."

A non-such he remained from then till that far distant year of 1895 with its crowning glory of 1,000 runs in May and the hundredth 100. And all that time the vast W.G. legend was growing and growing. It is a tribute to his surpassing fame that many fine cricketers of his prime are now only known, save to the more assiduous students of Wisden, because they played with him. Emmett was a great bowler and a great character, but men remember not what he did but what he said of W.G. The first thing recalled about J.C. Shaw is that twice he got W.G. out for a duck in the first innings of a benefit match and paid dearly for such presumption in the second. Their places in the averages are long since lost; their places in the legend make their names secure.

Popular fame is not necessarily evience of real, enduring greatness, and the immensity of the legend is not cited with any intention of making back-handed comparisons, but it does show the extraordinary position which one player of a game attained almost as a boy and never lost. As long as he lived he remained the best known man in England, at whom the inescapable finger would always point, a figure to be instantly pick-ed out even in a Derby Day crowd, unique, not to be mistaken. To be sure this could not have been so had W.G. been merely a supreme cricketer. There were contributory causes. His huge and, as the years passed, almost lumbering frame, his mighty beard growing gradually a "sable sil-vered," marked him as a colossus. Furthermore he was essentially a man of character. His sim-plicity and his guile; his words often spoken in deadly earnest but giving delighted if concealed amusement; his boyish jollity and his occasionally boyish pettishness; his intense keenness, which sometimes led him too far but had in it nothing of rancour or malice; finally his obvious lovableness — these things were all blent in a picture which was a public possession, a picture of one who in some obscure, indefinable way was a great man.

To meet him casually, and there could be no one more friendly, was instantly to be impressed by several things — his kindliness, his true mod-esty which took himself for granted, his complete simplicity of demeanour and perhaps above all his great natural dignity. He was easily approach-able but to take a liberty with him seemed un-thinkable. If that casual acquaintance, desiring to probe further, asked questions of those who really know W.G. and had played with him, there was but one answer. If ever he had a weakness it was an amiable one and no fault was to be hinted, no word heard against him; he was a dear old man. To be thus held in memory is surely something for which any man might be grateful on his birthday.

The young W.G. Grace dominated cricket as no one

else before or since. During the years 1867–76 he played 280 first-class completed innings with an average of 57, the next best figure of 36 being obtained by combining the ten most productive seasons of *seven* other men.

Success in the Gentlemen v. Players matches decided a man's worth before Tests began to hold sway. If the Players won 22 of 24 games from 1850 to 1864 and the Gentlemen 17 of 25 from 1867 to 1876, the change-about was due mainly to the pres-ence of one man. Almost half a century later another batsman would rival, but hardly surpass, Grace's deeds in these games:

1867–76	Grace	Innings 41	Runs 2,540	Average 65
1919–28	Hobbs	Innings 34	Runs 2,281	Average 71

A cricketer's achievements are relative to those of men who play with him. Statistically, Bradman's career dwarfs those of Grace and Hobbs. If both Grace and Hobbs scored eleven hundreds in the Gentlemen v. Players matches of 1867–76 and 1919–28, Bradman scored eleven in 20 Test innings (March 1929–Feb-ruary 1932) and eleven in 22 innings (January 1936–January 1948). But both Hobbs and Bradman had to watch, or field to, many other individual hundreds:

1936–48	Bradman	11 hundreds, other batsmen	31
1919–28	Hobbs	11 hundreds, other batsmen	27
1929–32	Bradman	11 hundreds, other batsmen	18
1867–76	Grace	11 hundreds, other batsmen	4

Those four hundreds by the best professional bats-men in England are readily explained: in the Gentle-men v. Players games in 1867–76 W.G. took 128 wickets with an average of 14 runs per wicket.

The young W.G. Grace *was* cricket.

On 3 July 1876 at Lord's, W.G. scored 169 for the Gentlemen, hitting Tom Emmett for a six and a seven in the same over — to the chestnut tress, all run out. In due course he arrived at Canterbury.

COUNTY OF KENT V. MARYLEBONE CLUB

14 August 1876. In the long list of cricket marvels and curiosities few stand out, or are likely so to do, with greater prominence than those comprised in the last "Week at Canterbury." Three days of sunshine, with only an occasional passing cloud, were considered sufficient to play out the first match on the paper. But it proved otherwise; and with 1,132 runs recorded it was left unfinished. Towards this number Mr Gilbert contributed 143, Mr A.J. Webbe 117, Mr W.G. Grace 100, and Lockwood 99. The second match was more remarkable than the first. Kent began the batting, and occupied the wickets the whole of Thursday. Nine wickets were lost in the meantime for 453 runs. To these 20 were added on Friday morning. Marylebone were singularly unlucky at the start, nor were they much befriended by fortune at any of the subsequent stages, being 329 runs in arrear at the fall of the tenth wicket. A "follow on" was inevitable, and 217 were obtained with four wickets down when play for the day ceased.

Deciding he might as well travel home to Bristol that evening, W.G. announced he would hit out. He did, his share of the 217 for four (made in one hour and 50 minutes) being 133.

No one attempted to forecast the result, and few, if any, dreamt that Mr Grace would rub out the debt of arrears himself. But he did. This feat puts in to the shade that of Mr Ward in 1820, whose score of 278 has till now been regarded as the most wonderful of its kind on record. The enormous total of 344 completed by Mr Grace on Saturday occupied six hours and a quarter, thus giving an average of 57 runs per hour. He had to contend against all the Kent bowlers save one. Three of them went on three times and three twice. In one instance Mr [William] Yardley bowled from the right arm and then from the left.* Never was a more striking exhibition of endurance against exhaustion manifested.

. . . .

* Perhaps a reflection of other skills: he wrote farces and was a drama critic. His 100 for Cambridge in 1870 was the first century made in the University match ("Cobden's"); he made 130 two years later. At this time he was held to be the second-best batsman in England.

The Times omitted to point out that in mid-afternoon W.G. adjourned to the officers' tent and, while the fielders lay prostrate, knocked back much champagne and seltzer. Revived, he returned to work.

To explain the progress it may be well to say that play began at 12 o'clock on Saturday, and in 90 minutes the overnight total of 217 advanced to 323, and ten minutes later the arrears were pulled off. At 4.35 Mr Grace had scored just 300, and at 5 o'clock the figures 500 appeared on the telegraph, of which total Mr Crutchley claimed no ordinary share. Mr Turner, after resisting several changes of bowling, fell to the first ball delivered by Lord Harris. Six wickets 506. Now came the close of Mr Grace's career — caught at mid off, and great was the joy thereat. His score of 344 contained 51 fours, eight threes, 20 twos, and 76 singles. There remained yet half an hour for play. This time was expended partly by Mr Cottrell, caught at square leg for 10. Neither Captain Meares nor Mr Goldney had a favourable opportunity for scoring, and when stumps were drawn 557 runs were announced for the loss of nine wickets; at the same time the match was declared drawn. Mr Absolom delivered 39 overs for 105 runs; Hearne 35 for 91 runs; Mr Foord-Kelcey 40 for 84 runs; Captain Fellowes, 28 for 63 runs; Lord Harris, 19 for 59 runs; Mr Thomson, 20 for 52 runs; Mr Shaw, 4 for 14 runs; Mr Penn, 7 for 25 runs; Mr Yardley, 8 for 27 runs, and Henty 2 for 7 runs. Umpires — Willsher and Hearne.

KENT 473 (Lord Harris 154, G. Hearne 57 not out) drew with MARYLEBONE Club 144 (Capt Fellowes 5 for 50) and 557 for 9 (W.G. Grace 344, P.C. Crutchley 84).

From Canterbury on the Saturday, Grace won the toss against Nottinghamshire at Clifton on the Monday and in just over three hours made 177. In the visitors' second innings he took eight wickets for 69, Gloucestershire winning by 10 wickets.

As the defeated Nottinghamshire side crawled home, they met the Yorkshire team on a railway platform, and were mocked. On Thursday, 17 August, Gloucestershire batted first against Yorkshire at Cheltenham: close of play — 353 for four, Grace 216 not out. Lockwood, the Yorkshire captain, found it difficult to get anyone to bowl.

On Friday, 18 August, Grace carried his score to 318 not out. His 839 in a week, made out of 1,336 while he was at the wicket, occupied seventeen and a half hours, and included two sevens, four sixes, four fives and 103 fours. In the three matches he also took 15 wickets for 20 runs apiece.

Grace was unable to play in May 1879 due to the demands of his studies. Bristol Medical School, and later St Bartholomew's and Westminster hospitals, saw him through, and in November he obtained his LRCP at Edinburgh as well as the MRCS of England. Thirty-one years of age is perhaps an indication of his being a mature student; on the other hand, few men on becoming qualified can point to 20,158 first-class runs (average, 50.41) and 1,419 wickets.

A THOUSAND RUNS IN MAY

Prior to the game between Kent and Gloucestershire at Gravesend which began on 23 May 1895, Grace had scored 499 first-class runs in six innings since 9 May. He was two months short of his 47th birthday.

27 May 1895. Dr W.G. Grace seems to have taken a fresh lease of his cricket life, and on Saturday afternoon at Gravesend he followed up his batting triumph of Friday with another brilliant innings, which won the match against time for Gloucestershire. His play was as fine as ever, and the manner in which he forced the game brought out an increase in the power of hitting as compared with his cricket of Friday. In this match at Gravesend Dr Grace was in the field for the whole of the three days, for he played right through Gloucestershire's first innings and was not out in the second. His record for the match was 330 for once out. Dr Grace never played better in his 30 years experience than in these

three days at Gravesend, and with nearly a week of May left he has the wonderful aggregate of 829 runs for eight times at the wicket (once not out), giving him an average up to date of 118. This season promises to equal in excellence Dr Grace's great years of 1871, 1873 and 1876.

The fortunes of Gloucestershire have always been more or less bound up with the success or failure of Dr Grace, and this fact was never more patent than on Saturday, when Gloucestershire beat Kent after a finish which was almost sensational. That a side which makes over 400 in the first innings of a match should be beaten is without precedent in English cricket. There have been some near approaches to such a result, but the rarity of its occurrence in England is naturally caused by the three days' limit for an important match. On Friday evening the whole doctrine of chances pointed to a draw, for Gloucestershire had got within 115 of the opponents' great score and had still three wickets in hand. In the end Kent were left with a lead of only 27. Dr Grace, who had gone in first, was the last to leave; he did not quite get hold of a ball from Alec Hearne, and was well caught in the long field. His stay at the wicket had been seven hours and a half, and his only mistakes* were those mentioned on Saturday; he maintained his vigour and finish of play throughout, and he hit 24 fours, five threes, and 23 twos. The Kent fielding was remarkably good throughout.

The natural thought at the end of the innings was that the great events of the match had occurred, and most of the spectators must have settled themselves down for a quiet finish as a draw. None could have expected the startling incidents that made up the closing stages of the game. That on a hard and true wicket the Kent men failed before the bowling of Painter, whom Dr Grace put on because Murch, the chief bowler of the Gloucestershire team, had, in view of the prospective draw, been allowed to leave for the

....
* *The Memorial Biography* says he gave one chance (to the wicketkeeper) when 80.

West of England; that Painter kept a good length and was pretty straight; and the misfortunes which overtook Kent made up a remarkable chapter in the match. Changing the "order" has often been disadvantageous to a side, and the alteration wrought in the state of the game on Saturday was not unallied with Mr Marchant's falling into this error. It was in the two hours after luncheon that all the mischief was done for Kent, whose wickets went down with startling rapidity.

A. Hearne kept up his end, but his companions' coming and going furnished something of a procession. Kent had virtually lost the match in an hour and a quarter, when nine wickets were down for 53. Martin and A. Hearne made a spirited attempt to check the misfortunes. They were together 40 minutes and added 23 runs. Painter,* who is not a regular bowler in the team and, indeed, seldom goes on, took seven wickets for 25. Gloucestershire had 104 to get to win in an hour and a quarter. They lost Wrathall at 15; but then Dr Grace was joined by Painter, and the Kent bowling was completely mastered. Dr Grace forced the game in a wonderful way, and got his 50 out of 76 in three-quarters of an hour. The hitting continued, and in 12 minutes 30 more runs were added, Painter making the winning stroke — a drive for four — and Gloucestershire were hailed the victors at a quarter past six† by nine wickets. Dr Grace sprinted for the pavilion to avoid the crowd, but there was great enthusiasm. He hit 11 fours, two threes, and five twos, and Painter six fours.

KENT 470 (A. Hearne 155, G.J.V. Weigall 74) and 76 (Painter 7 for 25) lost to GLOUCESTERSHIRE 443 (W.G. Grace 257) and 106 for one (Grace not out 73) by nine wickets.

Grace made his 330 runs against such good bowlers as J.R. Mason, Alec Hearne, Walter Wright and Fred

. . . .

* John Richard Painter, a right-arm fast bowler, took only 46 wickets, average 26.78, in first-class cricket.

. . . .

† Half an hour earlier, Oscar Wilde had been sentenced to hard labour for two years.

Martin. His season's aggregate was now 829 when he took part in a revival of the Surrey v. England match for W.W. Read's testimonial. After scoring 18 rather freely, he was bowled by Tom Richardson. As the game ended in an innings victory for his side, he had no second opportunity to bat.

On 30 May Grace brought a weak Gloucestershire side to Lord's to play Middlesex. He won the toss.

31 May 1895. At Lord's yesterday, the scene of so many of Dr Grace's great cricket triumphs, the most wonderful player of our time achieved another feat marked by all his old excellence. From noon until nearly half-past six he was at the wicket, and then, being a little wearied by his hard work under a hot sun, in a declining light, he was beaten by a ball from Dr Thornton, which kept low and which he played outside. It must be something of a record even for Dr Grace to make over a thousand runs in the first month of the season. By his 169 yesterday his aggregate for the ten innings played by him in a little over three weeks reaches 1,016. The champion seems to have taken a fresh lease of his cricket life. He seemed determined to make a big effort yesterday to get the thousand runs, and this and the fine bowling and fielding caused an unwonted steadiness in his play. Before luncheon he batted beautifully; but afterwards he was a little slow in getting back his game — in fact, for a few overs he played Mr Nepean's slows very badly, and once or twice put the ball up dangerously towards the fieldsman. Still, the exercise of more care and his anxiety to reach the four figures did not make his cricket less attractive. There was all the old power in the drive and the cut, while few balls to leg escaped unpunished. Dr Grace has played many a quicker innings; but the bowling and fielding were very good, and Hearne and Rawlin were especially difficult to score from. He made some bad strokes and narrowly escaped being run out midway through the innings. He was batting altogether for a little over five hours, and was ninth out at 362. An idea of his rate of scoring will be gathered from the fact that he made 50 out of 108 in an hour and a half; his 100 was scored out of 198 in three hours, and his last 69 occupied two hours and a half. He hit 21 fours, 5 threes and 11 twos. At the different landmarks, so to speak, of the innings the crowd of 7,000 who had come up to Lord's were very enthusiastic, and when at last it was over the champion had a wonderful reception, the members in the pavilion rising to applaud him.

GLOUCESTERSHIRE 366 (W.G. Grace 169, Capt. A.H. Luard 64) and 46 for 5 (G. Thornton 5 for 20) beat MIDDLESEX 200 (G.F. Vernon 62; G.L. Jessop 5 for 88) and 208 (J.T. Rawlin 83, R.S. Lucas 70; J.R. Painter 8 for 67) by five wickets.

When Grace was on 149 — four runs short of his 1,000 aggregate — Nepean gave him a friendly long-hop on the leg-side which was hit to the boundary. Thirty-five years and one day later, D.G. Bradman was similarly treated. Requiring 46 for his 1,000 by the end of May, he opened the Australians' innings at Southampton (the only time in 120 first-class innings in England) and was 28 at tea when rain intervened. A resumption just before the close saw him advance to 39 — still seven runs short — when rain again set in. Lord Tennyson, the Hampshire captain, had a word with Jack Newman, who thereupon bowled a full toss followed by a long-hop, both hit for four.

Scorers of 1,000 runs by the end of May

		Age	Innings	Average
1895	W.G. Grace	46	10	112.88
1900	T.W. Hayward	29	13	97.63
1927	W.R. Hammond	23	14	74.42
1928	C. Hallows	33	11	125.00
1930	D.G. Bradman	21	11	143.00
1938	D.G. Bradman	29	9	150.85
1938	W.J. Edrich	22	15	84.16
1973	G.M. Turner	26	17	78.30
1988	G.A. Hick	22	11	101.90

A thousand runs in May is somehow considered more meritorious than a thousand runs by the end of May: the latter includes runs made in April. This is clearly a nonsense: in 1895 Grace played 10 innings in 22 days, in 1988 G.A. Hick 11 innings in 43 days.

What made Grace's feat the more remarkable was his age, the accumulation of runs in large quantities generally being considered a young man's prerogative.

When Grace began his tenth innings of 1895, and Hick his eleventh innings of 1988, both needed 153 to reach their 1,000 runs.

"GRACE. — On the 23rd Oct., suddenly, WILLIAM GILBERT GRACE, the dearly-loved and loving husband of Agnes N. Grace, and father of Captain H.E. Grace, RN, and Captain C.B. Grace, KFRE, of Fairmount, Mottingham, Eltham SE, aged 67. No flowers, by request. Funeral at Elmers End Cemetery, Beckenham, 3 pm, Tuesday" (*The Times*, 25 October 1915).

THE GREATEST OF CRICKETERS

By Sir Arthur Conan Doyle

27 October 1915. The world will be the poorer to many of us for the passing of the greatest of cricketers. To those who knew him he was more than a great cricketer. He had many of the characteristics of a great man. There was a masterful personality and a large direct simplicity and frankness which, combined with his huge frame, swarthy features, bushy beard, and somewhat lumbering carriage, made an impression which could never be forgotten.

In spite of his giant West-of-England build, there was, as it seemed to me, something of the gipsy in his colouring, his vitality, and his quick, dark eyes with their wary expression. The bright yellow and red cap which he loved to wear added to this Zingari effect. His elder brother, the Coroner, small, wizened, dark, and wiry, had even more of this gipsy appearance. I speak, of course, only of the effect produced, for I have no reason to think that such blood was in his veins, though, following Borrow, I am ready to believe that there is no better in Europe. There was a fine, open-air breeziness of manner about the man which made his company a delight and added a zest to the game. He was, of course, a highly educated surgeon, but he had rather the fashion of talk which one would associate with a jovial farmer. His voice was high-pitched, considering the huge chest from which it came, and it preserved something of the Western burr.

His style and methods were peculiar to himself. In his youth, when he was tall, slim, and agile, he must have been as ideal in his form as in his results. But as this generation knew him he had run to great size and a certain awkwardness of build. As he came towards the wicket, walking heavily with shoulders rounded, his great girth outlined by his coloured sash, one would have imagined that his day was past. He seemed slow, stiff, and heavy at first. When he had made 50 in his quiet methodical fashion he was somewhat younger and fresher. At the end of a century he had not turned a hair, and was watching the ball with as clear an eye as in the first over. It was his advice to play every ball as if it were the first — and he lived up to it. Everything that he did was firm, definite, and well within his strength.

I have had the privilege of fielding at point more than once while he made his hundred, and have in my mind a clear impression of his methods. He stood very clear of his wicket, bending his huge shoulders and presenting a very broad face of the bat towards the bowler. Then, as he saw the latter advance, he would slowly raise himself to his height, and draw back the blade of his bat, while his left toe would go upwards until only the heel of that foot remained upon the ground. He gauged the pitch of the ball in an instant, and if it were doubtful played back rather than forward. Often he smothered a really dangerous length ball by a curious half-cock stroke to which he was partial. He took no risks, and in playing forward trailed the bottom of his bat along the grass as it advanced so as to guard against the shooter — a relic, no doubt, of his early days in the sixties,

when shooters were seen more often than on modern grounds.

The great strength of his batting was upon the off side. I should not suppose that there was ever a batsman who was so good at controlling that most uncontrollable of all balls, the good-length ball outside the off stump. He would not disregard it, as is the modern habit. Stepping across the wicket while bending his great shoulders, he watched it closely as it rose, and patted it with an easy tap through the slips. In vain, with a fast bumpy bowler pounding them down, did three quivering fieldsmen crouch in the slips, their hands outstretched and eager for the coming catch. Never with the edge of the bat but always with the true centre would he turn the ball groundwards, so that it flashed down and then fizzed off between the grasping hands, flying with its own momentum to the boundary. With incredible accuracy he would place it according to the fields, curving it off squarely if third man were not in his place or tapping it almost straight down upon the ground if short slip were standing wide of the wicket.

In no shot was he so supremely excellent, and like all great things it seemed simpicity itself as he did it. Only when one saw other great batsmen fail did one realize how accurate was the timing and the wrist-work of the old man. When he was well on towards his 60th year I have seen him standing up to Lockwood when man after man was helpless at the other wicket, tapping those terrific expresses away through the slips with the easy sureness with which one would bounce a tennis ball with a racket. The fastest bowler in England sent one like a cannon-shot through his beard with only a comic shake of the head and a good-natured growl in reply.

The Australian fast bowler Ernest Jones started the Lord's Test of 1896 with a deliberately short ball at W.G. Lord Harris commented: "I saw the incident. W.G. was not quite quick enough. The ball grazed his beard, touched the top of the handle of the bat, ricocheted far over the wicketkeeper's head and went to the screen for four. I did not notice his being at all upset, and I was told that the remark he made to Jones as he ran up the wicket was: 'Whatever are ye at?'" At all events, W.G. then took it out on Jones.

Of his bowling I have very clear recollections. He was an innovator among bowlers, for he really invented the leg-theory a generation before it was rediscovered and practised by Vine, Armstrong, and others. Grace's traps at leg were proverbial in the seventies. His manner was peculiar. He would lumber up to the wicket, and toss up the ball in a take-it-or-leave-it style, as if he cared little whether it pitched between the wickets or in the next parish. As a matter of fact this careless attitude covered a very remarkable accuracy. His command of length was absolute, and he had just enough leg spin to beat the bat if you played forward to the pitch of the ball. He was full of guile, and the bad ball which was worth four to

you was sent, as likely as not, to unsettle you and lead you on.

Those who knew him will never look at the classic sward of Lord's without an occasional vision of the great cricketer. He was, and will remain, the very impersonation of cricket, redolent of fresh air, of good humour, of conflict without malice, of chivalrous strife, of keenness for victory by fair means, and utter detestation of all that was foul. Few men have done more for the generation in which he lived, and his influence was none the less because it was a spontaneous and utterly unconscious one.

London County Club v. MCC and Ground
Played at Crystal Palace, 24 August 1900

LONDON COUNTY
Second innings

Dr W.G. Grace c Storer b Conan Doyle 110

FREDERICK ROBERT SPOFFORTH

New South Wales

Spofforth achieved immortal fame on 27 May 1878, when the touring Australians beat MCC in a day by nine wickets, his match figures 10 wickets for 20 runs. On 29 August 1882 at the Oval he entered cricket's mythology by taking seven wickets for the second time in the Test against England, an unlikely Australian victory giving rise to the famous *Sporting Times*' "obituary":

In Affectionate Remembrance
of
ENGLISH CRICKET
which died at the Oval
on
29th August, 1882.
Deeply lamented by a large circle of
Sorrowing Friends and Acquaintances
R.I.P.
N.B. — The body will be cremated, and the
Ashes taken to Australia.

A century and more later there are still mysteries, hitherto unexplained, concerning the game. Did a spectator drop dead from excitement in the closing stages? The late Ian Peebles (*Barclay's World of Cricket*, 1980) found this "a picturesque but unsubstantiated story". Why, as the interval between innings had been one of 16 minutes on the first day, was there one of 25 minutes on the second day? Did C.T. Studd, who had twice scored hundreds against these same 1882 Australians, walk round the pavilion covered by a blanket (C.I. Thornton's testimony) as England collapsed in the second innings? And if so, why? As Spofforth bowled the first over of this innings and Boyle the last, how are we to account for the individual overs bowled — Spofforth 28, Garrett 7 and Boyle 20? Should not Spofforth's overs equal those of Garrett and Boyle combined? Did Spofforth bowl round the wicket? This question was asked by Neville Cardus (*The Summer Game*, 1929), the answer to be found in the 1927 *Wisden*, where Lord Darnley (the former Ivo Bligh) contributed some recollections of Spofforth: "A long delivery stride coming down with great force and damaging effect on a very awkward spot for a breaking-back ball bowled from the other end." In the same *Wisden* Lord Harris wrote of Spofforth following up "straight down the wicket, thus, left foot on or about the popping crease, right foot well on to the half volley pitch, and then both feet plump on the awkward pitch; and when wickets were soft, he undoubtedly made a mess of the pitch." This would suggest that both Spofforth and Boyle bowled round the wicket in 1882 at the Oval, pitching the ball in one another's footmarks. Umpires Thoms and Greenwood probably took this ploy for granted, though today it would be the cue for terpsichorean antics from umpire Bird, with an accompanying declamation of the relevant section of Law 42.

On the first day of the Test — 28 August — Australia made 63 and England managed 101 from 71.3 four-ball overs — a first innings lead of 38.

30 August 1882. Our Colonial visitors have added another match to their long roll of victories obtained during the present season, and this, too, the most coveted of them all. Few of the 20,000 spectators on Kennington Oval yesterday were prepared for such a result, even within less than an hour of its accomplishment. In spite of the fact that the rain, which had been falling at intervals during the early morning, had increased to a heavy downpour by 10 o'clock, there was at this hour almost a complete belt of spectators round the field of play, who, protected by umbrellas, macintoshes, &c. maintained their positions throughout all discomfortures. Before 11 there was a break in the clouds, and the rain ceased. It was fortunate for the Australians that they had to go in first, as the wicket played far easier than it otherwise would have done. They did not obtain so many runs, however, as was expected of them. Mr Massie hit vigorously, and his performance was very praiseworthy, in spite of his escape at the hands of usually so reliable a fieldsman as Mr Lucas. Mr Murdoch batted in his usual finished style, and Mr Bannerman hit with great care. Beyond these none of the team did much. Mr Hornby seemed to know the bowling which would most baffle the batsmen, and varied it accordingly, while he altered the disposition of the field with great judgment. Peate's bowling was again excellent.

The small total of 85 which England had set them to win caused the match to be regarded by most people as a foregone conclusion for them, and this confidence was increased when the third wicket fell for 51. Thus there remained seven batsmen to be dismissed and only 34 runs to get. The Australians, however, although defeat stared them in the face, played with that thoroughness which we pointed out yesterday as being one of their most admirable characteristics. Two more wickets speedily fell. Yet, with five to go down and only 19 to get, it seemed almost impossible even in the game noted for its surprises that the home team should not be able to get them. Every ball was watched with the keenest interest; but batsman after batsman succumbed with a

rapidity that soon caused great anxiety on the part of the on-lookers, and at length, after victory appeared to be almost within their grasp, the English Eleven found themselves beaten by seven runs. Mr Spofforth sustained the reputation which secured for him the title of the "demon" bowler, as in the double innings he claimed 14 wickets for 90 runs. It is needless to say that the excitement was intense, and that the winners were warmly congratulated on their success. True, they had the best of the wicket, which played very treacherously during the English innings. Still the gallant manner in which they played an uphill game when there seemed no hope of success will cause their victory to be a subject of lasting admiration.

With 38 runs on the wrong side of their account, the Australians started batting again at 12.10. Messrs Bannerman and Massie were their representatives. Barlow bowled the opening over from the Pavilion end. Mr Bannerman cut the first and last balls for two each. Ulyett conducted the attack from the other end. His second delivery Mr Massie drove to the off. Read saved the ball from reaching the boundary; but a possible, though difficult, opportunity of running Mr Massie out, was missed, owing to the ball being returned, in the opinion of many, to the wrong end. This player then secured seven runs in two overs of Barlow's by a cut and a square-leg hit. Each batsman having made a single, a very fine hit round to long leg by Mr Massie for four caused 20 to be registered as the result of a quarter of an hour's play. This feat he speedily supplemented with a square-leg hit to the boundary, and at 25 Peate superseded Ulyett, and Mr Studd displaced Barlow. Some very lively batting was now shown by Mr Massie. The first ball of Mr Studd's he hit finely to the on for four, and then drove Peate on either side of the wicket for like amounts, which caused the arrears to be rubbed out at 20 minutes to 1. Having secured another four from Mr Studd by driving him to the boundary, that gentleman gave way to Barnes. The first ball sent down Mr Massie raised to long-on, but Mr Lucas failed to hold it. Mr Bannerman made a cut for two, which brought the total up to 50 at ten minutes to 1. Mr Massie continued his free hitting, and having obtained six runs by on and off drives from Peate, Mr Steel was tried in lieu of the Yorkshireman.

For a few overs these variations did not seem to disconcert the batsmen. Mr Massie, however, having sent a ball of Mr Steel's to deep square leg for four, was clean bowled by the next, the leg stump being knocked out of the ground. One for 66, as many as 55 having been obtained by the retiring batsman, whose chief hits were nine fours, two threes, and three twos. Those who expected to see some of Mr Bonnor's tall hitting must have been sorely disappointed. Ulyett resumed again in place of Mr Steel, and the change proved most happy, as the fourth ball struck Mr Bonnor's middle stump right out of the ground. Mr Murdoch came in, but did not long have the society of Mr Bannerman, who before another run had been obtained was easily caught at mid-off. Mr Horan remained while nine were obtained, but then played a ball tamely into the hands of Dr Grace at point, while from the next ball Mr Giffen, who supplied the vacancy, was served in the same manner. Half the wickets for 79 runs. Messrs Murdoch and Blackham were associated, the most notable hit for a little time being one to leg for four by the latter. The total having reached 99, rain fell somewhat heavily, and an adjournment for luncheon was made a quarter of an hour earlier than usual.

The interval over, Peate and Barlow proceeded with the attack against Messrs Blackham and Murdoch. Ill-fortune attended the colonists at the outset. From the last ball of the opening over from Peate Mr Blackham was well taken at wicket. Six for 99. Mr Jones supplied the vacancy. A square-leg hit for a single by the Australian captain caused the three figures to be signalled at ten minutes to 3. Mr Jones made six by cuts for two and four in an over of Barlow's. During the next nine overs Mr Murdoch monopolized the little run-getting that was shown. Seven were gained by him, all by on drives, the most important being

one for three off Barlow. With the score at 113, Mr Murdoch hit a ball to leg, which was fielded by Mr Lyttelton, who threw it at the wicket; the object was missed, and the ball went to Dr Grace, who as Mr Jones was out of his ground, put the wicket down, the batsman being adjudged run out. Mr Spofforth's stay was brief and valueless — clean bowled. Eight for 117. Mr Murdoch next had the companionship of Mr Garrett, and at 25 minutes past 3 120 runs were registered. After this the innings speedily terminated, both the remaining wickets being taken in an over of Mr Steel's. Mr Murdoch was run out in attempting a third run, while Mr Boyle was bowled, leg stump. Total, 122; time, 3.20.

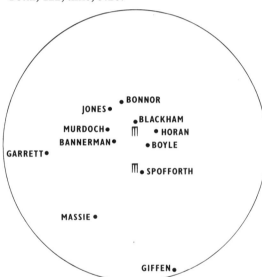

Spofforth's field at the Oval, 1882

"Sudden Death at the Oval. — At the close of the Australian innings Mr George Eber Spendlove, of 191 Brook Street, Kennington, collapsed and died, his body being removed to a room adjoining the pavilion" (*The Times*, 30 August 1882, page 10).

With the apparently easy task of getting 85 to win, England started on their second venture at a quarter to 4.

As Mr Spendlove died at 3.20, or soon after, why did it take 25 minutes to remove the corpse?

Dr Grace and Mr Hornby were placed in opposition to Mr Spofforth (gasometer end), and Mr Garrett. The opening over was a maiden, but a single by each batsman resulted from the second and the third overs. This moderate rate of run-getting was relieved by Mr Hornby driving a ball of Mr Spofforth's to the on for four, while in the same over he made a lucky "snick" to leg for two. Two overs subsequently, however, his off stump was struck, while Barlow, who followed, had his wicket upset by the first ball he received. One and two for 15. Dr Grace and Ulyett were partnered, and for a time all went well. At ten minutes past 4 an off-drive for two caused 20 to be signalled. Dr Grace then made seven in an over of Mr Spofforth's by two on-drives. A change was consequently deemed desirable and this bowler crossed over, while Mr Boyle went on at the gasometer end.

In 1882 Law VIII stated that "No bowler shall bowl more than two overs in succession". After Garrett had bowled his seventh over (14th of the innings), Spofforth bowled his eighth, then changed ends to bowl his ninth (16th of the innings), Boyle taking over at the gasometer end. From now on, even at the conclusion of a Boyle over, Spofforth's total overs were one more than those of Garrett and Boyle combined.

This alteration in the attack did not bear fruit for a considerable time. Besides minor hits, Dr Grace and Ulyett were each accredited with one to deep square leg for four. The "50" was attained at 4.35. One only had been added to this number when Ulyett was splendidly caught at wicket. Three down. Mr Lucas came in, but without having much opportunity to score, he was separated from Dr Grace, who was easily caught at mid-off. Four for 53. The Hon. A. Lyttelton came in, and started by scoring a single and three in an over of Mr Spofforth's. Two maidens followed, and then the new arrival obtained two somewhat luckily and supplemented this by a very clean leg-hit to the boundary. Now followed a great display

of patience on the part of the batsmen. Twelve overs were sent down without result and a single only was obtained in 17. The 18th proved fatal to Mr Lyttelton, whose wicket fell to an excellent ball of Mr Spofforth's, which struck the top of the middle stump. Half the wickets for 66.

And where was Studd,* who had gone in No. 6 in the first innings? In a letter to a friend, the Reverend Robert Hindle, in 1926, Studd denied the Thornton-inspired story of his wandering round the pavilion covered by a blanket. "We sat in the committee room with the windows closed because of the cold... When we had made over 50 for two wickets everything was over bar the shouting, as they say... Then came a time when the best English batsmen played over after over and never made a run... Then these got out. Hornby, on his own account, began to alter the order of going in. I believe he did ask me if I minded." What Studd did not mention was that Hornby had altered the order from the start, the only men to occupy the same place in the second innings as in the first being Grace, No. 2, and Peate, No. 11.

There we still, therefore, five to fall, and only 19 to get for victory. Mr Steel joined Mr Lucas, and the latter elicited considerable applause by a late cut from Mr Boyle which yielded four runs. This, however, was soon followed by misfortunes. The first ball of Mr Spofforth's next over Mr Steel returned to him, while Read, who succeeded, had his mid and off stumps struck by the third. Six and seven for 70. Only five runs were added, three of them byes, when Mr Lucas played the ball on. Eight for 75. Mr Studd and Barnes joined partnership, when only ten runs were required — a task which such batsmen as these would have been expected to accomplish without difficulty. The professional, however, was speedily caught at point. Nine for 75. Peate, the last man, sent the first ball he received to square leg for a couple.

....

* C.T. Studd (Eton, Cambridge University and Middlesex) died on 16 July 1931. His last entry in *Who's Who* revealed him to be the founder of the Worldwide Evangelization Crusade and he had served in the China Inland Mission. There was no mention of cricket.

This hopeful start was not followed up, and in the same over he was clean bowled. Total, 77. The Australians thus won by seven runs.

The last six overs of England's innings went thus:

SPOFFORTH   BOYLE   SPOFFORTH   BOYLE   SPOFFORTH   BOYLE

.W-   4-   W. W2   .... W   W2. W

LYTTELTON   LUCAS   STEEL / BARNES   3 byes   BARNES   PEATE
                            READ   LUCAS

ENGLAND v. AUSTRALIA
The Oval, 28 and 29 August 1882

AUSTRALIA

1st innings

A.C. Bannerman	c Grace b Peate	9
H.H. Massie	b Ulyett	1
W.L. Murdoch	b Peate	13
G.J. Bonnor	b Barlow	1
T. Horan	b Barlow	3
G. Giffen	b Peate	2
J. McC. Blackham	c Grace b Barlow	17
T.W. Garrett	c Read b Peate	10
H.F. Boyle	b Barlow	2
S.P. Jones	c Barnes b Barlow	0
F.R. Spofforth	not out	4
Extras	(b 1)	1
Total		63

2nd innings

A.C. Bannerman	c Studd b Barnes	13
H.H. Massie	b Steel	55
W.L. Murdoch	run out	29
G.J. Bonnor	b Ulyett	2
T. Horan	c Grace b Peate	2
G. Giffen	c Grace b Peate	2
J. McC. Blackham	c Lyttelton b Peate	7
T.W. Garrett	not out	2
H.F. Boyle	b Steel	0
S.P. Jones	run out	6
F.R. Spofforth	b Peate	0
Extras	(b 6)	6
Total		122

ENGLAND

1st innings

R.G. Barlow	c Bannerman b Spofforth	11
W.G. Grace	b Spofforth	4
G. Ulyett	st Blackham b Spofforth	26
A.P. Lucas	c Blackham b Boyle	9
Hon A. Lyttelton	c Blackham b Spofforth	2
C.T. Studd	b Spofforth	0
J.M. Read	not out	19
W. Barnes	b Boyle	5
A.G. Steel	b Garrett	14
A.N. Hornby	b Spofforth	2
E. Peate	c Boyle b Spofforth	0
Extras	(b 6, lb 2, nb 1)	9
Total		101

2nd innings

A.N. Hornby	b Spofforth	9
W.G. Grace	c Bannerman b Boyle	32
R.G. Barlow	b Spofforth	0
G. Ulyett	c Blackham b Spofforth	11
A.P. Lucas	b Spofforth	5
Hon A. Lyttelton	b Spofforth	12
A.G. Steel	c & b Spofforth	0
J.M. Read	b Spofforth	0
W. Barnes	c Murdoch b Boyle	2
C.T. Studd	not out	0
E. Peate	b Boyle	2
Extras	(b 3, nb 1)	4
Total		77

Fall of wickets: 1–6, 2–21, 3–22, 4–26, 5–30, 6–30, 7–48, 8–50, 9–59, 10–63.

Second innings: 1–66, 2–70, 3–70, 4–79, 5–79, 6–99, 7–114, 8–117, 9–122, 10–122.

Fall of wickets: 1–13, 2–18, 3–56, 4–59, 5–60, 6–63, 7–70, 8–96, 9–101, 10–101.

Second innings: 1–15, 2–15, 3–51, 4–53, 5–66, 6–70, 7–70, 8–85, 9–75, 10–77.

ENGLAND BOWLING (4-ball overs)

	O	M	R	W	O	M	R	W
Peate	38	24	31	4	21	9	40	4
Ulyett	9	5	11	1	6	2	10	1
Barlow	31	22	19	5	13	5	27	0
Steel					7	0	15	2
Barnes					11	5	15	1
Studd					4	1	9	0

AUSTRALIA BOWLING (4-ball overs)

	O	M	R	W	O	M	R	W
Spofforth	36.3	18	46	7	28	15	44	7
Garrett	16	7	22	1	7	2	10	0
Boyle	19	7	24	2	20	11	19	3

AUSTRALIA WON BY 7 RUNS

SPOFFORTH   He once attended a fancy dress ball as Mephistopheles.

The inquest on Mr George Eber Spendlove was held in the Crown Tavern, Church Street, Lambeth on 31 August. The East Surrey coroner, Mr William Carter, returned a verdict of "natural causes", noting the deceased had been attended on the field of play by Dr W.G. Grace, "the well-known cricketer", who directed that the body be removed to a room above the pavilion. Whether waiting to bat beneath a corpse — the unhappy Spendlove had suffered a haemorrhage — demoralized England will never be known; certainly the only man to bat at anywhere near his best (George Giffen described Grace's innings as a "masterpiece") was a medical practitioner. The 25-minute interval between the innings on the second day was surely due to an England opener being professionally engaged.

Mr Spendlove was not the only person treated by Dr Grace on the field of play. Five years later, the patient's life was saved. Had it not been, Arthur Capel Molyneux Croome could never have become cricket correspondent of *The Times*.

It is, in all human probability, due to W.G. Grace that I survive to write my reminiscences of him, for he saved my life at Manchester in 1887.* I ran into the railings in front of the Old Trafford pavilion while trying to save a boundary hit, and fell on to the spikes, one of which made a deep wound in my throat. They had to send out for a needle and thread to sew it up and for nearly half an hour W.G. held the edges of the wound together. It was of vital importance that the injured part should be kept absolutely still and his hand never shook all that time. I should have known it if there had been any twitching of finger and thumb, for I was conscious most of the time and the nerves of my neck and face were severely bruised. It would have been a remarkable feat of endurance under any circumstances, but the Old Man had been fielding out for over four hundred runs and had done his full share of the bowling. I have two reasons for mentioning this incident. One is obvious; the other is that it affords evidence of W.G.'s amazing stamina — *The Memorial Biography of W.G. Grace* (1919).

---

* Late on 22 July: a "regrettable" incident, according to *Wisden*.

KUMAR SHRI RANJITSHINHJI
Sussex

THOMAS RICHARDSON
Surrey

OLD TRAFFORD, 1896

George Henry West's literary style suggested a minor late Victorian novelist of either sex. West was cricket correspondent of *The Times* from 1880 to 1896. Where his successors might decide that a batsman who kept playing and missing outside the off stump was lucky, West preferred "Fortune did in no sense frown on him, for his innings was not wholly faultless". West was also capable of the unlikely conclusion — which, after almost a century, we are in no position to question — offered with the authority of Printing House Square: "[England's] fielding yesterday was good generally; but not quite up to the standard of this year's Oxford Eleven, or even that of Winchester and Eton." That "even" mystifies. West could, when necessary, fall back on the blandly vague, leaving readers to interpret as they pleased. "Mold, whom Mr A.N. Hornby [the Lancashire captain] sent to London last week to see Mr Atkinson about an injured limb, was unable to play." Mold had four limbs, as did A.D. Pougher, another bowler unable to play at Old Trafford in 1896. But whereas Pougher was "lame", Mold had an "injured limb". Perhaps the right leg, perhaps the left: or could it have been his right arm? As Mold was what we should now call a "chucker" — the most famous of all time — he may conceivably have been sent south to have his right elbow massaged. The lips of West were sealed. Not so those of the great Surrey bowler, George Lohmann, who reported to

W.G. before the same Old Trafford Test: "Doctor, I don't feel myself today."

The background to Old Trafford 1896 was unusual. The Australians began their tour well, winning seven and drawing two of their first nine games. Then at Lord's against MCC, and on a difficult wicket in reply to 219, they lost their first three men for 18 runs, and their last six for 0 runs — one man absent ill. J.T. Hearne's figures (5-ball overs) were 11–9–4–4, and Pougher's 3–3–0–5. Ten days later in the first Test at Lord's, and this time on a perfect pitch, they collapsed for 53 before Richardson (6 for 39) and Lohmann (3 for 13). A fine second innings recovery could not prevent England winning by seven wickets.

The Lord's Test of 1896 was also memorable for a variation on what Lady Bracknell (*The Importance of Being Earnest* was one year old) would have called an act of violence. "Lord's has scarcely before been the scene of so much noisiness and rowdyism as were displayed yesterday when the crowd encroached on the ground, shortening the boundaries to an alarming extent, and when those whose view was obscured by the people in the field of play had recourse to such methods as throwing missiles of every kind at the people in front of them" (*The Times*, 23 June 1896).

Missile throwing was not confined to the spectators, Lord's in 1896 witnessing the most famous delivery in cricket history. By way of introduction we should note *The Times'* preliminary observation:

The fairness of Mr Ernest Jones's bowling has been widely questioned ever since the opening match at Sheffield Park, and the first ball which he sent down to Dr Grace quite startled the members in the pavilion by its near resemblance to throwing. Mr Jones mended his ways after a while, but the umpires do not seem to lend much attention to the rule which says that the ball must be bowled, "not thrown or jerked".

The delivery itself — Jones's first in the England innings — was, of course, the "beard" ball. Reference has already been made (page 18) to Lord Harris's memoires; here is a selection from numerous accounts:

The ball grazed his beard, touched the top of the handle of his bat, ricocheted far over the wicketkeeper's head and went to the screen for four (Lord Harris).

It shot through W.G.'s beard hard to the screen for four byes (*The Memorial Biography of W.G. Grace*, 1919).

Very short and very fast, and got up quickly. J.J. Kelly, the Australian wicketkeeper, lost sight of it in Grace's beard, and it went to the screen (Sir Pelham Warner, who was playing for Oxford University at the Oval, Lord's, 1946).

I collaborated with W.G. Grace in writing his *Cricketing Reminiscences and Personal Recollections*, and in 1899 spent hundreds of hours with him... He never mentioned the "ball and beard" incident (Arthur Porritt in a letter to *The Times*, 10 August 1944).

Ever afterwards Grace was wont to speak of Jones as "the fellow who bowled through my beard". (*Memorial Biography*).

W.G. Grace and Stoddart went in for England at 1.35. Jones started the bowling from the pavilion end, and from a short and fast ball Grace got a two through the slips. In this same over there were a bye and a four and a two by Stoddart through the slips (*The Times*, 23 June 1896).

The first day at Old Trafford saw a complete reversal of form, Australia scoring 366 for eight wickets. England were singularly unfortunate: the Lancashire executive, as West called it, had presented W.G.

with a list of 14 players to choose from, but as three — Mold, Pougher and Lohmann — were unfit, the side chose itself and England went into the field at least one bowler short:

As to the presence of the young Indian Prince in the side, it may be interesting to mention that he stipulated that he would play if the choice were unanimous, and if the Australians raised no objection. Mr Trott, the Australian captain, openly expressed a wish to see Ranjitsinhji in the English side.

After Frank Iredale had snicked the first ball of the innings through the slips for four — Richardson's opening over cost 11 runs — Australia settled down to their strokes:

Mr Iredale has an easy method of batting which compares well with that of any other member of the side; but on a true wicket he does not get forward enough to please the keen upholder of what might be termed the Stoddart or MacLaren form. Apparently he has yet to learn the art of scoring off a good ball in the way practised by the school referred to, and his game often becomes dull by his indomitable patience in waiting for the bad ball from which to score.

As Iredale's hundred came out of 229 in three and a half hours, England must have bowled many bad balls.

"Richardson" [after lunch taken at 130 for one] continued to bowl with bad luck, and often only just missed the stumps by a hair's breadth." F.S. Jackson, on the other hand, "seemed in no bowling form, and, with only an indifferent length, he was severely punished". Later in the day, Jackson bowled again, failing "to find his length, and both batsmen scored freely from him". Which, considering that after Iredale had struck him for three fours in one over, Jackson bowled 15 overs for 22 runs, was harsh criticism on West's part.

Historically, the day's most memorable feature was Grace's twelfth bowling change, when Australia were nearing 300 for the loss of only Darling, Giffen and Iredale. "'W.G.' decided to give a chance to

RANJI   He never played a Christian stroke.

Lilley, whose place at wicket was taken by Brown. This newest change quickly brought about the dismissal of Trott who was caught at the wicket off a 'long hop'." Lilley later wrote: "I had taken my only wicket in a test match* and I naturally expected to continue bowling, but W.G. came to me and said, 'Put the gloves on, Dick, I shall not want you to bowl again; you must have been bowling with your wrong arm'."

ENGLAND V. AUSTRALIA

By G.H. West

Second day

18 July 1896. It was a grievous spectacle at Old Trafford yesterday to see so many fine English batsmen, players of the highest class, fail before the keen Australians, who, having once got a

....

* Eighty years later — on 12 August 1976 — A.W.T. Greig, confronted by a rampant I.V.A. Richards at the Oval, used nine bowlers as West Indies scored 373 for three in a day, though ignoring his wicketkeeper, A.P.E. Knott.

game in hand, have shown over and over again the great aptitude they possess for the retention of their advantage. England fared very badly yesterday, and their present position promises nothing short of defeat unless a long day's rain should come to their aid. Their comparative failure came even after the realization of their wishes as to the wicket's remaining true and the weather fine. But on this fine piece of turf 14 of the Englishmen were dismissed for 340 runs, leaving the home side still 72 runs in arrear, with Dr Grace, Mr Stoddart, Mr Jackson and Abel all out in the second innings. There is still some batting talent left; but the odds against which the Englishmen have to fight are extremely heavy, and their sole hope must be a draw. K.S. Ranjitsinhji played two fine innings, the second yet unfinished, and got his runs in that inimitable style of finish and quickness which is so much his own, and in which the wonderful stroke on the leg side was as prominent as ever. Already he has scored over 100 in the match, and has once more demonstrated the skill which was acquired by him in the few years of his residence at Cambridge.

Close: AUSTRALIA 412 (T. Richardson 7 for 168), ENGLAND 231
(K.S. Ranjitsinhji 62, A.A. Lilley 65 not out) and 109 for 4 (Ranjitsinhji 41 not out).

Third day

20 July 1896. At the end of the second day of the great test match at Old Trafford the English eleven appeared to be in a hopeless position; but on the third afternoon they almost had the game in their hands, and were beaten by only three wickets. It was a great victory for the Australians, and every one will be ready to congratulate them. Englishmen, with their rich resources of cricket, can well afford to be generous to their colonial friends in the matter of congratulation; for in matches, recognized as representative, the English eleven have a great preponderance of victories [now 11 to 3 in England, though 13 to 12 in

Australia]. K.S. Ranjitsinhji's batting and the bold attempt subsequently made by England to pull the match out of the fire made Saturday the greatest day of the match and the five or fix thousand people who went up to the Manchester ground instead of seeing the expected easy win for Australia had a splendidly keen fight over which to grow enthusiastic. And the end might have been closer had a catch not been dropped when there were yet nine runs to win. The man who did most to rescue England from ignominious defeat was K.S. Ranjitsinhji, who in his not-out innings of 154 played in the course of a stern uphill fight, exceeded all the many other brilliant feats in his comparatively brief career as a cricketer. Some cricketers were, on principle, against the inclusion of Ranjitsinhji in the English side. The Marylebone Club committee thoroughly weighed the matter, and, while recognizing the wonderful ability of that cricketer, thought it scarcely right to play him for England against Australia. And Mr Perkins, on behalf of the MCC, sent a letter to K.S. Ranjitsinhji explaining the reason why the MCC did not choose him. But the Lancashire committee did not follow the MCC precedent, and their policy proved immensely successful. Ranjitsinhji is playing cricket this season in a way that recalls to many Grace's great years in the seventies. The easy precision of his batting is wonderful, and he has developed that short-arm stroke on the leg side to a degree never before attained by any one. Brown, of Yorkshire, practises it at times; but with nothing like the consistency or success of Ranjitsinhji. In an innings of over three hours the Indian Prince scarcely made an ill-timed hit, and he contributed 154 to a total of 305, while in the double innings he was credited with 216. These figures fully demonstrate how ill England would have fared without him. He and Mr Stoddart and Lilley were in fact the only English batsmen who can be said to have played up to their form. But on Saturday nothing could be said against the manner in which the Englishmen by their fielding and bowling strove to win the game.

The fourth innings even with only 125 to score is a trying ordeal when there is so much at stake. And on Saturday, the Australians, who had so far been playing a winning game, almost suddenly became involved in a hard fight for victory. How well Richardson and the others bowled, and how excellent was the fielding may be gathered from a simple statement of fact — at the end of two and three-quarter hours the Australians found themselves with seven men out for 100 runs and 25 more wanted. Fortune then fluttered back to the visitors, whom she never forsook for any lengthened spell in this match; and a dropped catch and a few small hits followed and the match was over. Richardson's pace and pitch were worthy of the great Surrey bowler, and were sustained for the three hours and 10 minutes which it took the Australians to make their 125. Throughout the match he did nearly all the hard work with the ball. The Lancashire executive should have made a much greater effort to have another good bowler in the side, and the fact that Lohmann, Mold, and Pougher were all too unwell for cricket does not wholly exonerate them from blame. It was the Australians' third victory over England since the institution of this particular match in England, played for the first time in 1880. The third and last of the test matches will be decided at Kennington Oval on August 10 and following days. It may be pointed out that the English score of 305 is the highest so far made against this season's Australian team as K.S. Ranjitsinhji's 154 is the first three-figure innings played against them.

The morning was dull, and rain threatened, when at 11.35 England renewed their second innings, in which four wickets were down for 109. So that 72 were still necessary to save the innings defeat. Ranjitsinhji, not out 41, and Brown started steadily to the bowling of Giffen and Jones. Brown soon began to score freely; but in his attempts to force the game he did not show much of that fine, clean batting for which he has grown famous, and, having made 19 out of 23 added for the partnership, he was easily caught in the slips. Five for 132 was the record when MacLaren joined Ranjitsinhji, who by careful batting ran to his 50 after a stay altogether of an hour and a half. Having got thoroughly set, Ranjitsinhji began to force the game in great style. He was very severe on Giffen, four of whose overs yielded 26 runs.

But just when there was a prospect of a long stand MacLaren hit too quickly at a ball from Trumble and gave an easy catch on the off-side. With only four men left England were still two runs behind, so that their prospect was very bad. However, a change was at hand. Lilley, finding Ranjitsinhji doing so well, contented himself with steadiness. Ranjitsinhji when nearing his 100 went straight along, and he hit the bowling all

ENGLAND v. AUSTRALIA
Old Trafford, 16–18 July 1896

AUSTRALIA
1st innings

F.A. Iredale	b Briggs	108
J. Darling	c Lilley b Richardson	27
G. Giffen	c & b Richardson	80
G.H.S. Trott	c Brown b Lilley	53
S.E. Gregory	c Stoddart b Briggs	25
H. Donnan	b Richardson	12
C. Hill	c Jackson b Richardson	9
H. Trumble	b Richardson	24
T.R. McKibbin	not out	28
E. Jones	b Richardson	4
Extras	(b 6, lb 8, w 1)	15
Total		412

2nd innings

F.A. Iredale	b Richardson	11
J. Darling	c Lilley b Richardson	16
G. Giffen	c Ranjitsinhji b Richardson	6
G.H.S. Trott	c Lilley b Richardson	2
S.E. Gregory	c Ranjitsinhji b Briggs	33
H. Donnan	c Jackson b Richardson	15
C. Hill	c Lilley b Richardson	14
H. Trumble	not out	17
Extras	(lb 3)	3
Total	(7 wkts)	125

Fall of wickets: 1–41, 2–172, 3–242, 4–294, 5–294, 6–314, 7–325, 8–362, 9–403, 10–412.

Second innings: 1–20, 2–26, 3–28, 4–45, 5–79, 6–95, 7–100.

ENGLAND
1st innings

Dr W.G. Grace	st Kelly b Trott	2
A.E. Stoddart	st Kelly b Trott	15
K.S. Ranjitsinhji	c Trott b McKibbin	62
R. Abel	c Trumble b McKibbin	26
F.S. Jackson	run out	18
J.T. Brown	c Kelly b Trumble	22
A.C. MacLaren	c Trumble b McKibbin	0
A.A. Lilley	not out	65
J. Briggs	b Trumble	0
J.T. Hearne	c Trumble b Giffen	18
T. Richardson	run out	2
Extras	(b 1)	1
Total		231

2nd innings

Dr W.G. Grace	c Trott b Jones	11
A.E. Stoddart	b McKibbin	41
K.S. Ranjitsinhji	not out	154
R. Abel	c McKibbin b Giffen	13
F.S. Jackson	c McKibbin b Giffen	1
J.T. Brown	c Iredale b Jones	19
A.C. MacLaren	c Jones b Trumble	15
A.A. Lilley	c Trott b Giffen	19
J. Briggs	st Kelly b McKibbin	16
J.T. Hearne	c Kelly b McKibbin	9
T. Richardson	c Jones b Trumble	1
Extras	(b 2, lb 3, w 1)	6
Total		305

Fall of wickets: 1–2, 2–23, 3–104, 4–111, 5–132, 6–179, 7–154, 8–166, 9–219, 10–231.

Second innings: 1–33, 2–76, 3–97, 4–109, 5–132, 6–179, 7–232, 8–268, 9–304, 10–305.

ENGLAND BOWLING (5-ball overs)

	O	M	R	W	O	M	R	W
Richardson	68	23	168	7	42.3	16	76	6
Briggs	40	18	99	2	18	8	24	1
Jackson	16	6	34	0				
Hearne	28	11	53	0	24	13	22	0
Grace	7	3	11	0				
Stoddart	6	2	9	0				
Lilley	5	1	23	1				

AUSTRALIA BOWLING

	O	M	R	W	O	M	R	W
Jones	5	2	11	0	17	0	78	2
Trott	10	0	46	2	7	1	17	0
Giffen	19	3	48	1	16	1	65	3
Trumble	37	14	80	2	29.1	12	78	2
McKibbin	19	8	45	3	21	4	61	3

Umpires: J. Phillips and A. Chester

AUSTRALIA WON BY 3 WICKETS

over the field. He ran to his 100 in two hours and ten minutes, his last 50 having been obtained in 40 minutes. Lilley had a single increased to five by an overthrow; but soon afterwards, with Giffen back again, he hit a ball hard to short leg, where Trott brought off a wonderful catch; he knocked the ball up and caught it at the second attempt. Fifty-three had been obtained during the partnership. Ranjitsinhji went on forcing the game, and had some assistance from Briggs and Hearne; but the side were all out by a quarter to 2 for 305. Ranjitsinhji had a great reception on his way back to the pavilion. In his brilliant innings of 154, not out, he gave no chance whatever; he was batting rather more than three hours; and he hit 23 fours, five threes, and nine twos.

On their previous form the Australians, it was thought, would easily make the 125 necessary to win. But the fourth innings is nearly always a very difficult one to play. Iredale and Darling started to Richardson and Briggs. Neither batsman seemed very confident; but Darling got some lucky strokes away through the slips. Indeed, the runs were only scraped together. Hearne, who came on for Briggs, had a beautiful pitch, and could not be hit, and Richardson was bowling in great form. A ball from the Surrey man struck Iredale, whom he directly afterwards bowled. The first wicket fell at 20, and six runs later Giffen was beautifully caught in the slips by Ranjitsinhji, while at 28 a fine catch at wicket on the leg side by Lilley standing back got out Trott. England, with a prospect of winning, bowled and fielded with great brilliancy. The Australians played with care, and the score went to 45, when Darling also fell to the wicket-keeper. Gregory and Donnan stayed together some time; but the bowling was too good to be hit. Eleven overs by Hearne were actually sent down for four runs. The 50 had gone up in an hour and 20 minutes. Briggs came on again for Hearne, and at 79 he got Gregory caught at short leg for 33, a very fine score under the conditions of the cricket. With five men left, the Australians wanted 46 runs. Donnan was out at 95, and at 100 Hill was caught

by the wicket-keeper. Only three wickets remained and 25 runs were wanted. Trumble and Kelly very slowly secured these; but when 12 of them had been made Lilley missed Kelly standing back at the wicket off Richardson. It was an irreparable blunder. So by 6 o'clock the Australians had won the match by three wickets.

THE GAME ANCIENT AND MODERN

INFLUENCE OF THE JAM SAHIB

By A.C.M. Croome

9 August 1930. It is always difficult, sometimes impossible, to date the birth of an idea which has introduced an observed change into the manners, customs, fashions of civilized society, or to name the father of it. J.H. Taylor has been dubbed the Father of Modern Golf by a writer of repute. With at least equal propriety H.H. the Maharajah Jam Sahib of Nawanagar, hereinafter called "Ranji" in token of affectionate admiration, may be selected as the man mainly responsible for the difference between Ancient and Modern Cricket. Following on that selection it is necessary to set the date when the difference became determinate, somewhere between 1895 and 1900. Ranji taught both by example and by precept. He was the first man to make 3,000 runs in a season, and he wrote the *Jubilee Book of Cricket*, a book packed with wisdom from cover to cover.

Deeds are proverbially more arresting than words. Therefore, it is tolerably certain that Ranji's influence impressed itself most strongly on those who watched him bat either from the ring or from coigns of greater vantage out in the middle. Bowlers in particular were shaken by him to the very core of their being. The printed word was supplementary to the done thing. Ranji sums up the art of batsmanship in three direct imperatives. "Find out where the ball is. Go there. Hit it." These imperatives appear in the order of their importance: it is an accident that this order coincides with the order of chronology. Judgment of pace, length, direction, and the correct positioning of the body by means of footwork are more valuable than the minutiae of technique as taught to schoolboys. The main doctrine preached by those who determined the character of the teaching given at the Public Schools in pre-Ranji days was that the forward stroke is the foundation of batmanship. The historical records show that a disappointingly small proportion of those who have been selected as batsmen for the chief representative matches have acquired their technique at the great Public Schools. Lord Harris is the only Etonian who has played as a batsman pure, if not precisely simple, against Australia in this country.

And he, it is pertinent to remark, never stood at the crease as if he believed that the whole duty of man consited in advancing the left foot and thrusting a perpendicular bat at the good-lenght ball with a long fluent motion ending in a pose of statuesque grace. The weakness of that stroke as a means of defence is that the executant of it must to some extent lose sight of the ball at the critical moment. If he has "found out where it is" his knowledge may cease to be useful to him. One of the chief lessons taught in the *Jubilee Book of Cricket*, and by the example of its author, is that the batsman should never come on to his left foot unless he means to drive an overpitched ball for 4. In fact, on most fine days it is possible to meet an ageing cricketer at Lord's who with a little judicious prompting will tell how he once bowled for 10 minutes in a net to Ranji and was complimented because in that short time "you got me on my left foot once."

Of course there were quick-footed batsmen in pre-Ranji days, notably Arthur Shrewsbury and Sir Timothy O'Brien, the two whom W.G. singled out for special recommendation when he was asked to name the batsmen whom he reckoned second to himself. 'Give me Arthur," said the Old Man, "though that Tim was a pretty good 'un." O'Brien quite often came on to his left foot. When he did the ball rattled up against the pavilion rails unless some untoward accident happened. Shrewsbury could drive amazingly hard for a man of his size. He seldom chose to do so because he recognized the obvious fact that the avenues of the drive are better policed than those of any other intentional stroke. There are at least three men, mid-off, the bowler, and mid-on, ready to make catches off the driving stroke, and there may be one or two on the boundary behind them. W.G. rated Shrewsbury and O'Brien as peers. Shrewsbury's average is considerably higher than O'Brien's. The moral is obvious. To point it still more sharply: Ranji for several seasons after he had taken his degree at Cambridge drove hardly at all. He did not thereby disobey his own injunction to hit the ball. When he walked in front of all three stumps and turned a slightly over-pitched ball to the boundary at fine-leg he "hit" it as well and truly as if he had driven it first hop against the sight-screen.

RICHARDSON   A record without parallel.

As soon as other batsmen discovered that the glancing of straight balls was not a feat of extraordinary difficulty, especially if they had a bit of break-back on them, bowlers were compelled to alter their tactics. In the autumn of his career J.T. Hearne ceased to rely entirely on his capacity to make the ball break back quickly at a notably sharp angle, and cultivated the out-swing and the ball that runs away. Hearne's experience was typical. Bowlers, who did nothing but keep a good length and bring the ball back, found their efficiency diminishing as the mobility of batsmen increased. It is frequently suggested that there are no bowlers nowadays like Spofforth and Turner, Lohmann and Hearne, Lockwood and Richardson. The suggestion is perfectly true. It does not follow that those great men, if they could be brought back into cricket today, would bowl precisely like themselves. If they did they would be less effective than their records prove them to have been, for the simple reason that they must deplete their off-side field in order to save the numerous runs which would be scored on the leg side from some of their quite respectable balls. The post-Ranji bowlers are constantly up against problems seldom presented to their illustrious predecesors. Due allowance must be made for that fact. When it has been made it must be admitted that the standard of bowling is not very high at the present moment. But it would be great fun, if only it were possible, to uncage Barnes and Foster, Hirst and Faulkner, against William Gunn and others of the static, forward-playing school, who were very highly esteemed in pre-Ranji days.

The method of batting, of which Ranji is the eponymous hero, has the defect of its quality. The merely painstaking exponent of it, concentrating on footwork, is liable to make insufficient use of his arms and wrists. Consequently he omits the preliminary movement which is the basis of all really good batting. He does not "support the head of the striking implement." The phrase is borrowed from Tennis. But its use is appropriate to all games from cricket down to golf. Many batsmen, especially those who habitually face the new ball, consider it necessary to curtail the back lift of the bat as much as possible. They are wrong always and all the time. They would be able to cope with the swerve and skid of the new ball just as well, probably better, if they would lift the bat freely enough to get their wrists under the blade of it. It is not Ranji's fault that so many of his pupils are reduced to taking the cheap runs offered to them. He himself set the example of a notably free back lift. That example has been more consistently followed in Australia than in England. In this connexion the records of post-Ranji Test Matches are worth perusal.

VICTOR THOMAS TRUMPER
New South Wales

In the Imperial Cricket Memorial Gallery at Lord's are a cap and blazer worn by Trumper and presented by his widow, Sarah Ann, who outlived him by almost 48 years: "He remains a legendary figure in Australia, one whose fame rests not only on his greatness as a batsman but also on his qualities as a man."

Trumper was a batting genius who, one feels, would not get chosen for a modern Test side. "Unlike most other batsmen," wrote M.A. Noble, "he never played himself in before trying to score." C.B. Fry described him as having no style but being all style; the South African C.B. Llewellyn preferred bowling to him on perfect wickets — "He tries too hard on a 'sticky'". To quote M.A. Noble again: "I know of no stroke in cricket of which Trumper was not absolute master."

Trumper's most famous innings was played in the Old Trafford Test of 1902, when he won the game for Australia before lunch on the first day. This, it will be noted, was a dismal summer of wet wickets, in spite of which Trumper scored 2,570 runs and 11 centuries — the highest, 128. Once he had reached three figures, Trumper felt it was someone else's turn.

By Ernest Ward

25 July 1902. There was a fine day's cricket at Old Trafford, Manchester, yesterday. The game opened badly for England both in the field and in bowling. Once after luncheon, when Rhodes was difficult, they looked to have a good chance, but all the luck was with the Australians. Mr Trumper played a grand innings, and made his sixth century for the team. His innings was marked by splendid hitting on the leg side, and his placing on the off side was remarkable. He is certainly the finest cricketer on all wickets that we have had from Australia since Mr Massie and the late Mr Percy Macdonell. It was an easy and slow wicket at starting, but by the time the Englishman went in the ball was aiding the bowlers tremendously, and just suited Mr Trumble. In the early hours the ball came along quite truly, and Mr MacLaren was unable to put on Lockwood until the score was advanced towards a good total. There had been some rain in the early morning, but the wicket was considered playable by the usual hour of starting, and the long day at the wicket was followed with interest by a crowd of quite 20,000. The dull morning was succeeded by a gloriously fine afternoon, and it was the effect of the sun on the pitch that turned the game, and Mr Darling was fortunate in winning the toss. England have a poor chance of saving the game, seeing that they are 299 behind with half the side out.

It was just after 11.30 that the game began. The Australians, who won the toss, quickly grasped the advantage of batting first on the wet wicket, and made a splendid start. The Old Trafford wickets are very good this season, and the ball came along quite easily. Rhodes and Mr Jackson began the bowling. They kept a nice length, but Mr Trumper and Mr Duff scored quickly and at a wonderfully even rate, and at 70 the score was 35 all. After a change of bowling, Braund was played easily and well, and Tate could never get a length. Mr Trumper cut him severely, and 13 were made in one over from him. The fielding was excellent, but the batting was so true that the score mounted quickly. Mr Trumper got his 50 in 55 minutes, and Mr Duff reached 50 just inside the hour.

After the century had gone up inside the hour, the batting was more brilliant than ever. Mr Trumper was particularly strong. The wicket was so soft that Mr MacLaren did not put on Lockwood until 129, and his first two overs were full of incidents. Braund made a big attempt to catch Mr Duff at short slip. He lunged out with his right hand, but fell and lost the ball. Then Mr Trumper was nearly thrown out by Rhodes from cover-point in going for a second run. With the score at 135 the first wicket fell, Mr Duff being caught at the wicket in Lockwood's second over. It had been a wonderful partnership of only 80 minutes' duration. Mr Hill came next. Mr Trumper completed his century in 100 minutes out of 168, and the score at luncheon was 173 for one wicket.

After lunch there was a check to the Australians' success. Rhodes found his length at once, and, the wicket helping him, he got three wickets in his first four overs. Mr Trumper was cleverly caught at the wicket, and Mr Noble gave a return catch that Rhodes only just held as he fell in taking it. The striker appealed, and Moss, at the bowler's end, referred to Mycroft, umpire, and the batsman was given out. Mr Gregory was caught at the wicket in feeling for an off break from Rhodes. Mr Trumper got his runs in less than two hours. He played beautiful cricket, and made 14 fours. Four for 183. The wicket was now helping the bowlers, and there seemed just a chance of the game changing. Rhodes was bowling very well, but Mr Darling and Mr Hill soon put the Australians in a good position again. Mr

Darling made most of his forcing powers. His driving was very strong, and he hit one half-volley from Rhodes straight out of the ground for six and drove the same bowler over the ring twice. Mr MacLaren varied his bowling, but Tate, Braund, and Mr Jackson were of no effect. Lockwood came on again, and when 73 had been added in three-quarters of an hour he got Mr Hill cleverly caught by Rhodes at mid-off. Five for 256.

Thereafter the Australian innings subsided, Darling being caught at mid-off after making 51 — two sixes and five fours — in 90 minutes.

England went in at a quarter past 5. Mr Palairet and Abel started briskly with some good hits in front of the wicket. Mr Saunders and Mr Trumble were the bowlers, and their length and break were excellent. Abel was caught in the slips with only a dozen runs on the board, and Mr Palairet was secured at point, while a break-back from Mr Trumble spreadeagled Mr MacLaren's wicket. Mr MacLaren entirely mistimed the ball which was coming in, and which he tried to meet on the crease. Three for 14. Tyldesley and K.S. Ranjitsinhji made a short stand, but the Australian bowling and fielding were tremendously keen. K.S. Ranjitsinhji was out in trying to turn a ball off his leg stump and Tyldesley was caught at third man through hitting forward at a short ball. Five for 44. Mr Jackson and Braund played steadily, and the bowling was good to the end. The score was left so that England require another 80 runs to save the follow-on.

Close: AUSTRALIA 299 (V.T. Trumper 104, R.A. Duff 54, C. Hill 65, J. Darling 51; W.H. Lockwood 6 for 48). ENGLAND 70 for 5 (F.S. Jackson 16 not out, L.C. Braund 13 not out).

Second Day

26 July 1902. It was a wonderful day's cricket at Manchester yesterday. The English Eleven retrieved the game, and now, with only two wickets left, the Australians are but 123 runs on. There were three great features of the day's play — Mr Jackson's batting, Braund's stand with him, and Lockwood's bowling. But above everything else, the batting of Mr Jackson was the feat of the match. Mr Jackson was always, from his Harrow days, a great batsman, full of resource, courage, and nerve, but in his long series of successes he has never done better than he did yesterday. He forced the game at the proper time; he went in when England were in an almost hopeless position, and he got his runs without a bad stroke. His late cutting was wonderful, and his shortened off drive just beyond cover point was worthy of Dr Grace. Braund, too, played beautiful, steady, cricket. When the Australians went in a second time, Lockwood's bowling was very good; the ball came back at a great pace, and his five wickets have so far cost only 28 runs. There was a crowd of 25,000 people, and the weather was beautifully fine. The present condition of the match holds out a fine prospect for an exciting finish today.

On Thursday night it was generally expected that the wicket, after its cutting up in the morning, would not last, for the sun had baked the pitch, as was observable throughout the afternoon. However, there was a heavy dew, and in the early hours of yesterday, although there had been no more rain, the ball came along quite easily. Mr Trumble and Mr Noble found their length at once, but Mr Jackson and Braund, the overnight not-outs, played steadily and well. Mr Jackson was particularly good, being very strong in his play on the leg side. Mr Saunders soon came on for Mr Noble. The Australians fielded keenly, Mr Gregory at deep cover and Mr Noble at point doing some splendid work. There was a great cheer when the hundred went up, but how great the difficulty of scoring was can be seen from the fact that the runs had taken more than an hour and three-quarters to make. The bowling was wonderfully true. Mr Trumble sent down 30 overs for 24 runs and two wickets. Braund and Mr Jackson batted so strongly on the leg side that the bowlers altered their field. Mr Jackson gave Mr Saunders a very hot return to his right hand when 41, but this bowler soon gave way to Mr Noble. The field was splendidly placed, but Braund managed to get a clever four through the slips, while Mr Jackson pulled a bad ball from Mr Trumble for four.

Mr Jackson and Braund were now thoroughly set, and with the score at 124 Mr Darling at last took off Mr Trumble, who had been bowling altogether two hours and a quarter at a stretch. The batting triumphed, and there were many cheers for the 150, which meant the saving of the follow-on. The batsmen continued to score, and the many bowling changes troubled them not a whit. Mr Darling did his best, and had Mr Trumble and Mr Saunders back. There was one great attempt by Mr Darling to catch Mr Jackson at mid-off from Mr Saunders, but he just failed to reach the ball with his left hand. Mr Noble and Mr Trumper were tried at the ends at which they had not originally bowled. Just before luncheon, with the score at 185, Mr Noble deceived Braund with a slow one that whipped back off the pitch at a great pace. Braund went forward to it, but was completely beaten. The partnership thus dissolved had yielded 141 runs. Braund had a splendid reception for his very fine innings, made at a critical moment. Lilley came in, and the score was 186 before luncheon.

At 214 Lockwood was run out, sacrificing his wicket after he and Jackson had contemplated a single for a misfield by Duff.

With eight men now out, both Mr Noble and Mr Trumble gave Rhodes some short stuff to hit. Rhodes, however, kept up his end, and at last, with a cleverly judged single, Mr Jackson got his century, amid a wonderful scene of enthusiasm. The total was then 222, and he had made his hundred out of 192 put on while he was in...At last Mr Jackson was caught in the long field, Mr Duff bringing off a fine running catch. His grand innings had lasted four hours and a quarter, and he hit 16 fours and seven threes. The innings was over just before 4 o'clock, and England were only 37 behind. Mr Jackson had a wonderful reception on his way in, the crowded company on the pavilion rising to greet him.

The Australians went in again at a quarter past 4. Mr Trumper and Mr Duff were the batsmen, and Braund and Lockwood the bowlers. In Lockwood's second over, when the score was only seven, Mr Trumper was cleverly caught in the slips. Then, in Lockwood's third over, Mr Hill and Mr Duff were out. The former was clean bowled, and the latter cut a ball into his wicket. Thus three wickets were down for ten runs. Next Mr Darling and Mr Gregory were together, and the score was only 16 when Mr Darling was badly missed at deep square-leg, almost on the boundary, by Tate, who, after judging the ball well and making it look an easy catch, dropped it.

Tate's missed catch would never be forgotten. Ernest Ward's account of the Old Trafford Test must now give way to one by P.F. Warner — 21 June 1919.

[It was] the turning point of the match. Mr Darling was in with Mr Gregory, Braund bowled the fifth ball of the over to Mr Gregory, who scored a single off it, and Mr Darling faced Braund. Now Mr Darling was a very fine left-handed hitter, and a bowler like Braund — slow leg break — required a fieldsman at deep square leg. Unfortunately Tate was placed in this position, Mr Darling hit him a catch, and he dropped the ball. Had this catch been caught four wickets would have been down for 16 runs. As it was, 54 runs were added for the fourth wicket.

Now it is impossible to blame Tate. Never had he been a long-fielder; his place was near the wicket, slips or mid-on, and I do not suppose that in all his career he had ever fielded in "the country." It was an instance, on Mr MacLaren's part, of neglect of detail. There was only one more ball to the over to go, and the odds seemed heavily against that particular ball being hit a catch to that particular fieldsman; but in cricket, as in war, nothing should be left to chance. The

story goes — I do not vouch for it — that both Mr Jackson and K.S. Ranjitsinhji offered to drop out into the long field, but that their offer was not accepted. Poor Tate! One can realize his bitter feelings, and one can only sympathize with him, for he was the victim of bad captaincy.

A.C. MacLaren, breathing fire, wrote to *The Times* (4 July 1919):

> … Ranjitsinhji was dead lame, and consequently was useless as an outfielder, and for that reason I refused his offer to fall back. As Darling was hitting out at every ball I felt that, with the great amount of what became off break to the left-hand batsman Braund was getting on the ball, the spin would most likely cause Darling's hit to carry behind rather than in front of the square leg boundary, and I accordingly placed L. Palairet in that position with Tate in front. Braund then asked me if he might not have L.C.H. Palairet in front where Tate was fielding … so Tate was allowed to take the fine leg position and Palairet came in front to occupy the position in which he usually fielded for Somerset … The Hon. F.S. Jackson, a fine infield, on the contrary asked to be allowed to retain that position.

MacLaren went on to say he had felt sore when the selectors would not allow him Jessop at Old Trafford, MacLaren's theory being that if Jessop played in all five Tests he would run out Trumper at least once. He did — at the Oval. To make matters worse, in Gloucestershire's game coincidental with the Old Trafford Test, Jessop made a century against Notts; after a slow 50 in 50 minutes, the next 50 came in 15 minutes.

It merely remains to be emphasized that Warner did not see the Old Trafford Test — he was playing against Kent at Beckenham; that Braund might have done well to try a straight ball on Darling; and that the answer to MacLaren's problems would be given on 15 August when Bosanquet destroyed Notts with leg-breaks and googlies, one of the latter causing William Gunn to be comprehensively stumped. Australia struggled for the remainder of the day.

Close: AUSTRALIA 299 and 85 for 8, ENGLAND 262 (F.S. Jackson 128, L.C. Braund 65).

By Ernest Ward

Third day

28 July 1902. Australia won an extraordinary match at Old Trafford, Manchester, on Saturday, by three runs. The result was the more surprising as at one period the Englishmen seemed to have the match in hand. But the Australians played a fine uphill game, and their bowlers were supreme. Mr Trumble's length and Mr Saunders's pitch and break were wonderful. England had the game in their hands before luncheon, and the 100 went up with only five men out. But then the side collapsed. The wicket certainly helped the bowlers, but it looked as if the Englishmen should have won quite easily. Mr Darling seemed to upset the whole English side by the placing of his field. He got his men close in, even for such forcing players as Mr Jackson and Mr MacLaren, and his bowlers kept up too good a length to be hit. The Englishmen seemed to become afraid. Instead of going forward and hitting the bowlers off their pitch, they played back cautiously at everything. Mr Trumble and Mr Saunders were remarkable in their break and length, and the Englishmen, having once dropped their game, could not recover it. The occasion was too much for them, and it was quite pitiful to see such a splendid side going to pieces in the way they did. In fact, England failed as they did at the Oval 20 years ago in the game of 1882. They made a splendid start, and, after getting the game quite in their hands, lost it. The Australians have now won the rubber of the test matches, but no doubt the Oval match in August will attract great attention. The executive of the Lancashire County Club are to be congratulated on the excellent arrangements they made for the comfort of the 20,000 spectators of the match on Saturday.

After the heavy night's rain the umpires, Moss and Mycroft, considered the pitch unplayable for an hour after the arranged time. The game was renewed at mid-day, when Mr Trumble and Mr Kelly, the not-outs, went on with the batting. The wicket was very soft, and a foothold was difficult to get. Rhodes sent down a maiden to Mr Kelly, and then from the last ball of Tate's first over at the other end Mr Trumble was leg-before, a decision of Moss's that met with much apparent dissatisfaction from the batsman. Nine wickets were down for 85. Mr Saunders joined Mr Kelly, and after four maidens had been sent down Mr Kelly got a single, and then Rhodes got Mr Saunders caught in the long-field by Tyldesley, a beautifully judged catch. Rhodes had immediately before appealed for a return catch, but Moss, umpiring at short-leg, gave the batsman in. The balance of the innings had lasted 20 minutes for the odd single. Lockwood's bowling figures were unaltered from those given in *The Times* of Saturday, but Tate finished with a good analysis, making amends to some extent for missing Mr Darling on Friday.

England wanted 124 to win, and went in at 20 minutes to 1. Mr MacLaren and Mr Palairet started with great care. The English captain soon seemed at home and got rid of some very difficult bowling. Mr Noble and Mr Trumble bowled superbly, and the score was still only 12 at the end of half an hour. Mr Noble once quite beat Mr Palairet, the ball coming along at a great pace and just missing the off stump. In the next over from Mr Trumble, Mr Palairet made a bad stroke to short-leg (Mr Gregory just missed it) and Mr MacLaren, after being appealed for leg-before, drove Mr Trumble almost to the boundary, but the ball was well fielded by Mr Duff just in front of the screen. After this there was no particular incident in the cricket for a few overs. The score was up to 24 at the end of half an hour, when Mr Darling changed his bowling and put on Mr Saunders at Mr Noble's end. There were some clever short runs. The wicket was helping the bowlers tremendously and Mr Trumble and Mr Saunders were keeping a fine length and getting much work on the ball. Mr Palairet was nearly caught at short-leg by Mr Gregory, who made a great effort to get to the ball with his right hand and fell in making the attempt. Mr MacLaren and Mr Palairet showed courage and resourcefulness, and, although constantly beaten, they struggled on to 36, as the result of 50 minutes' batting before luncheon. With the weather threatening, England still wanted 88 to win.

After luncheon Mr Trumble started the bowling from the lower end, and from the fifth ball of the over Mr MacLaren made a drive to the boundary. At 44 Mr Palairet was bowled by a break-back from Mr Saunders. Tyldesley came next, and then Mr Trumble, who was getting a lot of work on the ball, nearly got Mr MacLaren caught at short-leg by Mr Gregory. Tyldesley made a beautiful cut for four from Mr Saunders, and got a clever single on the leg side. The 50 was reached in just over an hour, by means of a clever stroke by Tyldesley to leg. Mr MacLaren made a grand drive for four from Mr Saunders, and was then twice beaten without the ball hitting the wicket. Mr Trumble overpitched one to Tyldesley that was promptly hit for four. But with the field well placed on the leg side there were some narrow escapes. Tyldesley was caught at short-slip at 68, getting forward to a short one. There was a great cheer for K.S. Ranjitsinhji, but almost directly Mr MacLaren, who had been batting for more than 75 minutes, was out to a well-judged catch at long-on. Three for 72. Abel was next in and the score was speedily taken to 76, when a sharp shower drove the cricketers to the pavilion for a quarter of an hour.

England had now only 48 to get with seven wickets left, and the wicket was scarcely affected by the rain. Mr Trumble and Mr Saunders were the bowlers. Abel got a couple of pretty strokes on the leg side for two each, and then getting to the other end he got two nice hits from Mr Trumble, who, with a beautifully placed field, tried to get him at long-on. Abel hit hard, and the ball each time cleared Mr Duff. K.S. Ranjitsinhji was not at home, and shortly afterwards was leg-before to Mr Trumble at 92. Mr F.S. Jackson had a splendid reception. At 97 Abel hit across at a break-

back from Mr Trumble and was bowled. Five for 97. The pitch was now obviously helping the bowlers and the fielding was strong. The 100 had gone up, but the ball was very difficult to get away. Mr Saunders sent down a couple of maidens and then came a lucky three through the slips to Braund. The score reached 107, and then Mr Jackson hit too quickly at a full pitch and gave mid-off an easy catch. Lilley came in next, England wanting 27 to win. Braund got a fluky three in the slips that fell just short of Mr Armstrong. At 109 Braund was beautifully stumped. Rain then began to fall. Mr MacLaren had been saving Lockwood for emergencies; and the famous old Surrey player was very much cheered when he went in. Mr Trumble, after an ineffectual appeal for leg-before, bowled him completely, leg stump, with the third ball, and eight wickets were down for 109. Rhodes came next, and hit a short one from Mr Saunders over the ropes. Lilley was missed being run out through a bad return by Mr Hill, but in the same over the latter secured him by a grand catch at deep square-leg.

Warner again (21 June 1919), less controversially: "I remember Mr Hill telling me he only just reached the ball with both hands outstretched, and that after he had caught it he turned deathly pale, and that his heart beat fast for a few minutes."

Nine for 116. A heavy shower drove the players to the pavilion, and there was no more play for three-quarters of an hour. Tate, the last man, hit the first ball he had from Mr Saunders for four, but in the same over his off stump was bowled down, and amid great excitement Australia won the game by three runs.

THE DEATH OF VICTOR TRUMPER

29 June 1915. Mr Trumper was born on November 2, 1877. He had been in bad health for some little time, and the latest accounts of his condition

ENGLAND v. AUSTRALIA
Old Trafford, 24–26 July 1902

AUSTRALIA
1st innings

V.T. Trumper	c Lilley b Rhodes	104
R.A. Duff	c Lilley b Lockwood	54
C. Hill	c Rhodes b Lockwood	65
M.A. Noble	c & b Rhodes	2
S.E. Gregory	c Lilley b Rhodes	3
J. Darling	c MacLaren b Rhodes	51
A.J. Hopkins	c Palairet b Lockwood	0
W.W. Armstrong	b Lockwood	5
J.J. Kelly	not out	4
H. Trumble	c Tate b Lockwood	0
J.V. Saunders	b Lockwood	3
Extras	(b 5, lb 2, w 1)	8
Total		299

2nd innings

V.T. Trumper	c Braund b Lockwood	4
R.A. Duff	b Lockwood	3
C. Hill	b Lockwood	0
M.A. Noble	c Lilley b Lockwood	4
S.E. Gregory	lbw b Tate	24
J. Darling	c Palairet b Rhodes	37
A.J. Hopkins	c Tate b Lockwood	2
W.W. Armstrong	b Rhodes	3
J.J. Kelly	not out	2
H. Trumble	lbw b Tate	4
J.V. Saunders	c Tyldesley b Rhodes	0
Extras	(b 1, lb 1, nb 1)	3
Total		86

ENGLAND
1st innings

L.C.H. Palairet	c Noble b Saunders	6
R. Abel	c Armstrong b Saunders	6
J.T. Tyldesley	c Hopkins b Saunders	22
A.C. MacLaren	b Trumble	1
K.S. Ranjitsinhji	lbw b Trumble	2
F.S. Jackson	c Duff b Trumble	128
L.C. Braund	b Noble	65
A.A. Lilley	b Noble	7
W.H. Lockwood	run out	7
W. Rhodes	c & b Trumble	5
F.W. Tate	not out	5
Extras	(b 6, lb 2)	8
Total		262

2nd innings

L.C.H. Palairet	b Saunders	17
A.C. MacLaren	c Duff b Trumble	35
J.T. Tyldesley	c Armstrong b Saunders	16
K.S. Ranjitsinhji	lbw b Trumble	4
R. Abel	b Trumble	21
F.S. Jackson	c Gregory b Saunders	7
L.C. Braund	st Kelly b Trumble	3
A.A. Lilley	c Hill b Trumble	3
W.H. Lockwood	b Trumble	0
W. Rhodes	not out	4
F.W. Tate	b Saunders	4
Extras	(b 5)	5
Total		120

Fall of wickets: 1–135, 2–175, 3–179, 4–185, 5–256, 6–256, 7–285, 8–292, 9–292, 10–299.

Second innings: 1–7, 2–9, 3–10, 4–47, 5–74, 6–76, 7–77, 8–79, 9–85, 10–86.

Fall of wickets: 1–12, 2–13, 3–14, 4–30, 5–44, 6–185, 7–203, 8–214, 9–235, 10–262.

Second innings: 1–44, 2–68, 3–72, 4–92, 5–97, 6–107, 7–109, 8–109, 9–116, 10–120.

ENGLAND BOWLING (6-ball overs)

	O	M	R	W	O	M	R	W
Rhodes	25	3	104	4	14.4	5	26	3
Jackson	11	0	58	0				
Tate	11	1	44	0	5	3	7	2
Braund	9	0	37	0	11	3	22	0
Lockwood	20.1	5	48	6	17	5	28	5

AUSTRALIA BOWLING

	O	M	R	W	O	M	R	W
Trumble	43	16	75	4	25	9	53	6
Saunders	34	5	104	3	19.4	4	52	4
Noble	24	8	47	2	5	3	10	0
Trumper	6	4	6	0				
Armstrong	5	2	19	0				
Hopkins	2	0	3	0				

Umpires: J. Moss and T. Mycroft

AUSTRALIA WON BY 3 RUNS

received in this country were so discouraging as to prepare his friends for the worst.

It is impossible in a short notice to give an adequate account of Mr Trumper's career as a batsman. With a sinewy, lissome figure he had a delicate constitution, and this was probably the cause of his career lasting at its extreme brilliance only for a short time from 1899 to 1903. In 1902, when he visited England for the second time, he was unquestionably the greatest batsman in the world. He scored in a wet season 2,570 runs for an average of 48, and nothing finer in the history of batting, on slow wickets, has been seen than Mr Trumper's during that season. In the memorable three-run Australian victory at Manchester he scored 104 by most brilliant batting, and altogether in the season made 11 centuries.

In his first visit, in 1899, he firmly established his reputation by a grand 135 not out in his second Test Match at Lord's, but his great season in England was 1902, and in Australia, 1903–1904. His highest score in England was 300 against Sussex in 1899, but the regularity with which he scored in 1902 was marvellous. Mr Warner has eloquently described how in the Test Match at Sydney Mr Trumper went in when his side were 101 runs behind in the second innings with three wickets down. He made 185 not out, and only Rhodes kept him tolerably quiet. Probably an even better performance was in the same season in Australia in the second Test Match. The wicket was difficult and Australia's combined total in the two innings was only 233, but Mr Trumper made 109 of these and made his colleagues appear very small fry by comparison.

Mr Trumper made four visits to England, but after 1902 he was not the same batsman. He played some grand innings, but he was uncertain.

He injured his back in 1905 in the first Test Match at Nottingham, made a few splendid hits in the second at Lord's, and failed in the other three. After this season he did not play regularly in Australia, and on one occasion made a pair of spectacles against Mr A.O. Jones's MCC team.

Mr Trumper's hitting was unique in its boldness. He hit all round the wicket and seldom left a ball alone. His off drive was superb, and so was his power of stepping almost on the wicket and forcing the ball anywhere. It was necessary for Mr Trumper's style of play to succeed that the batsman should be in the best of health and in the fullest possession of physical power. His constitution being delicate his prime soon passed, but while it lasted, from 1899 to 1903, Mr Trumper was the greatest batsman Australia has ever possessed; on a slow wicket nobody could equal him as a rapid scorer, and he was a fine deep field.

On 24 June 1919 P.F. Warner had this note in *The Times*: "Mr Clem Hill wrote to me at the time of his death:-'Poor Victor is gone. I don't know who was the next best batsman, but he was the best I ever saw. You know what a splendid fellow he was, and how modest. He had a wonderful funeral. The streets of Sydney were lined five and six deep, and an enormous crowd followed the coffin. He was carried to his grave by Australian XI men, and I can tell you we all of us, without exception, broke down. We shall not see a batsman like him again.'" The pall-bearers at Waverley Cemetery were:

W. Bardsley	C.E. Kelleway
A. Cotter	C.G. Macartney
S.E. Gregory	M.A. Noble
H.V. Hordern	J.A. O'Connor
F.A. Iredale	C.T.B. Turner

GILBERT LAIRD JESSOP
Gloucestershire

THE CORONATION TEST, 1902

King Edward VII and Queen Alexandra were crowned in Westminster Abbey on Saturday, 9 August 1902, the event having been postponed from earlier in the summer due to the King's sudden illness and operation for appendicitis. Two days after the coronation the Fifth Test between England and Australia began at the Oval.

By R.H. Lyttelton

12 August 1902. The last test match of the season began yesterday, in fairly bright but very cold weather [61°F max.], before a huge crowd of about 20,000 spectators at Kennington Oval.

The excitement might have been greater if England had won the great match at Manchester and honours had been easy at the end of the fourth match; but there was no lack of enthusiasm, and the Australians had no reason to complain of any partiality of the crowd. An appreciable number of Australian soldiers in their picturesque uniforms formed an attractive group at the south-east corner of the pavilion, and the hitting of Mr Kelly at the end of the day gave great delight to these gallant Volunteers. Though during the last week plenty of rain had fallen, the cold wind had prevented the wicket from becoming difficult, and, if there is no change in the weather and the English batting does not com-

pletely break down, there is every probability of a draw. The wicket was a very easy one to bat on, and might be described as an impossible wicket for bowlers. Not many balls broke, and not one got up — all came easily, half stump high, and it was no fault of either the bowling or fielding that when the tenth Australian wicket fell the large score of 324 had been made. The Australians again showed their capacity to score almost down to the last man, but for most of the time none of them had any apparent desire to force the pace, except Mr Trumper at the beginning and Mr Kelly at the end of the day.

Mr Darling won the toss, and Mr Trumper and Mr Duff began the batting for Australia. They played good and fast cricket, and 45 runs were scored in half an hour. Not even Lockwood could make the ball get up, nor Rhodes make it break. But Hirst, who took up the bowling at Rhodes's end, met with considerable success. He bowled admirably, and got all the first five wickets. Mr Trumper played, as he has done all the season, most attractive and excellent cricket, and so in a less degree did Mr Duff; but neither Mr Hill nor Mr Darling ever got set. Although Mr Noble was not too comfortable at first, still he and Mr Gregory stopped the fall of the wickets and brought the score at the luncheon interval to 107 for four wickets.

The scoring after the fall of Mr Darling's wicket was extremely slow, one hour's play producing only 38 runs. Soon after luncheon Mr Gregory was clean bowled by a rather short ball of Hirst's that he tried to cut. Mr Noble now began to play a free game, but after receiving some valuable help from Mr Armstrong, who was clean bowled by Mr Jackson, was himself caught by the same bowler off a hot return. Mr Noble went in at a critical time for Australia and played a thoroughly sound and good innings. His style was far more attractive than was the case in 1899. He took some time to play himself in, but he had the best of the bowling to play. Much depended on him, and he took two hours in compiling his score. Six wickets were now down for 174, by no means a large score in these days on such a very easy wicket. The troubles of England began when Mr Trumble and Mr Hopkins came together. Mr Hopkins had only scored four when a very confident appeal for lbw, off Rhodes, was given in his favour, but from behind the bowler's arm in the pavilion he certainly appeared to be out. In the next over from Mr Jackson, Mr Trumble was missed at the wicket.

After these two events everything went in favour of Australia. By extremely slow and accurate play the two batsmen gradually wore down the English bowling. It was no doubt the right game to play, and it certainly answered. The fielding never became slack, and the batsmen took not the slightest risk. In fact, Mr Trumble, whose play is entirely in front of the wicket, seldom attempted to play Rhodes's bowling when outside the off stump. The two men added 81 runs, and the whole aspect of the game was altered. Rhodes had not the best of luck, for though the almost painful easiness of the wicket prevented him from getting much work on the ball, he kept an admirable length, and Hirst, not unnaturally, seemed to tire. At length Mr Hopkins was caught off Lockwood after an excellent innings of 40. Mr Kelly then came in, and, after some slow play, began to hit in a most refreshing manner, scoring 39. At the end of the day's cricket the Colonials were in an almost impregnable position. Mr Trumble had, no doubt, most to do with this result. He seemed to set himself the solo task of wearing the bowling down, and he succeeded. He was batting for two hours and a half, and only gave one chance. Mr Hopkins, who most ably assisted him, looks as if he might be lbw every over, for he gets in front more than any player now before the public; but he hits the ball, and his second line of defence is not therefore called upon. Mr Kelly played an exceedingly good game, and, altogether, is a most valuable man to go in tenth.

The extremely easy wicket was too much for the English bowlers. The earlier Australian batsmen played a fairly free game, and when this is the case, though runs may come freely, there is a chance of getting wickets. And this happened yesterday. But the later batsmen concentrated their efforts on keeping their wickets intact, and the lack of sting in the wicket made their task comparatively an easy one. The Australians are to be congratulated on the way in which they again demonstrated their capacity to take advantage of their opportunities. Even on such an easy wicket their total of 324 was an excellent performance, having regard to the fact that only one chance, and that at the wicket, was missed during the whole day.

Close: AUSTRALIA 324 (M.A. Noble 52, H. Trumble 64 not out; G.H. Hirst 5 for 77).

13 August 1902. At the end of the first day's play in the fifth test match England had the worse position, but there was every prospect of a good score and a drawn match. Again, however, did the eccentricities of the English climate overthrow all calculations, for rain fell in the night, and the result was a wicket in favour of the bowlers. This was the case more or less all day yesterday, but very much so in the morning. This was ill-luck for England. But the cricket was far more interesting than on Monday, and the impartial spectator had much to admire in the bowling, batting, and fielding. The wicket was most difficult in the morning, and it would have surprised nobody if England had fared even worse than she did. The bowling of Mr Trumble could not have been surpassed, and he took every advantage of the wicket. The fielding was accurate, and the field was judiciously arranged. Mr Saunders bowls a very difficult ball, but some very bad ones also, and Tyldesley and Mr Palairet made some beautiful strokes. No discredit is imputed to the English batting in stating the fact that it was not good enough for the bowling on such a wicket. The ball hung, got up, and turned. Indeed, some judges of the game thought that the match would be finished during the day, and that the Colonials would win in one innings. When the sixth wicket fell the score was only 83, but after a few overs, in the course of which there were some remarkable performances with the ball, the luncheon interval came with Braund and Hirst not out.

The interval of 45 minutes brought a change in the condition of the wicket, which gradually improved, and during the rest of the day, though it was always rather in favour of the bowlers, it presented no insurmountable difficulty to a really good bat. To Hirst is mainly due the credit of saving England's position, though Braund and Lockwood both played well and helped to avert the follow-on. Hirst never played a pluckier innings. He did not take undue liberties, but pulled Mr Saunders from the off to leg with great success, and hit most vigorously. On one occasion he hit a ball from Mr Trumble into the pavilion. He gave no chance, and, out of a total of 54 runs obtained since he went in, scored no fewer than 43. Lockwood then joined Braund, and played good cricket; but, fortunately for him, and England, too, he was missed when he had got 11 runs in the deep field by Mr Hill. The catch was not exactly an easy one, but it ought to have been held; and, if it had been, there would have been a probability of England's following on and having more than two hours' play on a rather difficult wicket. The follow-on was then saved, and the total after all came to 183, which was far better than appeared probable at lunch time. Braund only scored 22, but he played the bowling for some

considerable time, and had a large share in saving the follow-on. Mr Trumble bowled all through unchanged from the Pavilion end, and again proved himself to be a bowler of the highest class.

The wicket was obviously improving, though the light was by no means good, when the Australians began their second innings; but it cannot be said that they batted up to their reputation. Messrs Trumper and Duff began, and Mr Duff was badly missed by Hirst, off Rhodes, in the first over. Mr Trumper then played a ball tolerably hard to Mr Jessop's left hand and started to run; Mr Duff refused to go, and Mr Trumper, who slipped in trying to return, was easily run out. He would probably have been run out in any case, for Mr Jessop is the last fieldsman in the world to run risks with. The fall of their great batsman may have had a depressing effect on the Australians. At all events, at no time during the rest of the day did they display their real form. Mr Hill, who was in for nearly an hour and a half, played in a cramped style and not like the great batsman he undoubtedly is. Mr Darling began well, though he was missed at the wicket off Lockwood, but only scored 15. Mr Noble, Mr Gregory, and Mr Hopkins did nothing remarkable, and when stumps were drawn eight wickets were down for 114. Mr Saunders, who was sent in early, was finely caught by Tyldesley in front of the pavilion. Hirst, who is usually a very safe field, missed two catches, but Mr MacLaren made a fine catch at extra short slip when Mr Hill was disposed of. Lockwood, Braund, and Rhodes all bowled well, but it seemed strange that Hirst was not put on earlier after his success in the first innings.

The Australians are now 255 runs on with two very useful wickets still to go, and have no doubt by far the best position; but considering the circumstances England may be congratulated on the form shown in the second day's play, in which, independently of the first day, they fairly held their own. If no rain falls and they can get rid of the last two Australian wickets cheaply, they will still have a difficult task to win, but not an absolutely impossible one. The Englishmen have had so much the worst of the luck this season that it would seem to be only natural to expect more rain tonight and a bowler's wicket tomorrow, but if this is not the case a good finish may be hoped for.

There is only one other point to which attention ought to be drawn, and that is the inordinate extent to which leg play was indulged in. Some of the English batsmen get very much in front of the wicket, but they play at the ball with the bat. But several of the Australians, notably Mr Armstrong and Mr Gregory, and in a lesser degree Mr Noble and Mr Hopkins, continually got in front of the wicket to Braund's leg-breaks and made no attempt to play the ball.* This is not cricket, and the hope that such play was a thing of the past has been ruthlessly dispelled this season. It may, however, produce a change in the laws, which will be a point gained. There was again a very large crowd, about 20,000 spectators being present.

Close: AUSTRALIA 324 and 114 for 8, ENGLAND 183 (H. Trumble 8 for 65).

14 August 1902. Whatever may be said about the unsatisfactory weather that cricketers have experienced this season, the year has produced two struggles that can never have been surpassed for excitement. England has lost the rubber, but her defeat at Manchester and her victory at the Oval will never be forgotten, and both were much to her credit.

Every batsman on his way to the wicket yesterday felt that on his success or failure depended the fate of the match. In other words, the match was always in a critical position, and every run had to be fought for. The bowling of Mr Trumble could not have been better. Every variety of pitch and break back seemed to be at his command, and he never sent down a ball of bad length. In

....

* Lyttelton was presumably offended by the blatant pad play of Armstrong and Gregory; in 1928 he published *The Crisis in Cricket and the Leg-Before Rule.* Coincidental with the 1902 Test, a masterly hundred by Arthur Shrewsbury, aged 46, for Notts v. Derbyshire won a game. Shrewsbury's pad play to off-breaks was legendary — and maybe more stylish.

this he was a very different bowler from Mr Saunders, who bowls a very difficult ball, but many very bad ones — of such bad length that a child would score from them. Mr Trumble bowled from the pavilion end from half-past 11 in the morning until 4 in the afternoon. He was never taken off, nor was his bowling once collared in an innings of 263.

At the end of the second day's play Australia were 255 runs ahead with two wickets in hand. No rain had fallen in the night, but it was generally thought that the wicket would be slow and easy. There was, however, a heavy dew, and the wicket up to luncheon time was very difficult and never became easy all day. Only seven runs were added to the Australians' score. Indeed, the Australians may be said to have lost the match chiefly by their failure in batting on the second day when the wicket was not difficult. As at Manchester, they collapsed in a way that was unworthy of a strong batting side. Lockwood's five wickets cost only 45 runs — a very good performance.

At 11.35 England began the last innings on a wicket that appeared made to suit the Australian attack, and the first three wickets fell for ten runs. The chances were quite four to one on Australia at this stage, and six to one when the fifth wicket fell at 48. The batsmen did not play well, but there was every excuse on such a wicket and against such bowling. But Mr Jackson was still in, and wonderfully free was his play. To him is due, to a very large extent, England's victory. On five occasions in the last five test matches has Mr Jackson had to go in at a critical moment for his side, and only once did he fail. There is no batsman in the world whose nerve is so surely to be relied on. When he was joined by Mr Jessop the great stand that paved the way for victory was made. Up to lunch time the wicket was so difficult that nobody could have felt surprised if either batsman had got out; but they stayed in and brought the score to 87 [Jackson 39, Jessop 29], though Mr Jessop appeared to give a chance of stumping, and was missed by Mr Trumper off a difficult chance in the long field.

Runs came far faster after luncheon, Mr Jessop putting in some of his finest work, while Mr Jackson was content to take things steadily. Too much use was made of Mr Saunders, who was now bowling a very bad length and was freely punished by Mr Jessop. Three full pitches and one long hop were bowled consecutively, and 17 runs were scored from one over. Mr Jackson was then caught and bowled by Mr Trumble for 49, after an hour and 40 minutes' first-rate batting [Jessop then 83]. The match appeared to be lost when he left. Hirst came in next and he, Mr Jessop, and Mr Jackson were the three heroes of this famous innings. It must, however, be confessed that Hirst looked very like being lbw to Mr Trumble almost immediately after he went in. Mr Jessop continued his hitting, and sent Mr Trumble twice in an over into the pavilion. Mr Armstrong relieved Mr Saunders, and was vigorously hit by Hirst. But Mr Jessop must have longed for Mr Saunders again. He could not hit Mr Armstrong's leg balls with a little break on in his usual style, and the new bowler got him caught at short leg. Seven wickets were now down for 187, and 76 runs were still wanted.

Mr Jessop has accomplished several very wonderful performances in his life, but has frequently, both here and in Australia, failed against the colonial bowling. But as long as cricket history lasts will this great performance be remembered. He ran risks, as every man must who makes more than a run a minute, but he only gave two chances, and one of them was very difficult. He completely demoralized Mr Saunders. His wonderful success must have been a great cause of rejoicing to those who, in spite of so many failures, have urged his claim to represent England; and all these failures will be forgotten long before this great feat of fierce hitting against first-rate bowling and fielding and on a difficult wicket. Out of 139 runs scored while he was in 104*, came from his bat.

On several occasions during this innings the prospects of England looked well, but, as so often happens, at a critical moment a wicket fell. Mr Jackson, Mr Jessop, Lockwood, and Lilley all got out just when the chances might have veered round in England's favour. Seventy-four runs were wanting when Lockwood went in, 49 when Lilley succeeded him, and 15 when Rhodes, the last man, came out of the pavilion. All these men played with nerve, but Hirst was the real hero. Nothing seemed to put him out. Indeed, he played with more confidence than in the first innings, and his hits were hard and along the ground. Lockwood stayed while 27 runs were scored, but his share was only two. Lilley got 16 out of 34 by good batting, but was dismissed by a good catch by Mr Darling at mid-off. Rhodes then came in, and it is not likely that he will ever again have to face a more trying ordeal.

Nobody could have risen to the occasion better. Hirst went on the even tenor of his way, and Rhodes stopped the straight balls and judiciously left alone the rising off balls from both Mr Trumble and Mr Noble. And thus the runs were slowly hit off, Rhodes making the winning hit amid a scene of excitement that can never be forgotten. Mr Darling is so experienced a captain that it may seem presumptuous to wonder why he was so unwilling to make use of Mr Noble's bowling, but he undoubtedly was wise to keep on Mr Trumble all the time. In the whole match Mr Trumble bowled 65 overs for 12 wickets at a cost of 14 runs each — a splendid performance.

When all the conditions under which these last two test matches were played are considered, it must be conceded that it was a wonderfully fine feat of England's to lose the first match by only three runs and to win the second by one wicket.

....

* Jessop's 104 included one five, 17 fours, two threes, four twos and 17 ones — that is, he scored from 41, and did not score from 34, of the 75 balls he received. Jessop scored at 83 runs an hour and 138 runs per 100 balls.

The Croucher (1974), Gerald Brodribb's biography of Jessop, gives the Oval innings thus:
1 2 4 1 1 . . 4 4 1 . 4 . . . . 1 4 1 . 1 1 1 . 4 1 . . .
1 . 3 . 1 . 3 5 1 (50 off 38 balls in 43 minutes)
4 . . 4 4 4 4 1 . . . . 1 . . . . . 1 2 . . . . . . 4 . .
4 1 . 4 2 . 2 4 4 (second 50 off 38 balls in 32 minutes/100 off 76 balls in 75 minutes)
. 4 . W

ENGLAND v. AUSTRALIA
The Oval, 11–13 August 1902

AUSTRALIA
1st innings

V.T. Trumper	b Hirst	42
R.A. Duff	c Lilley b Hirst	23
C. Hill	b Hirst	11
J. Darling	c Lilley b Hirst	3
M.A. Noble	c & b Jackson	52
S.E. Gregory	b Hirst	23
W.W. Armstrong	b Jackson	17
A.J. Hopkins	c MacLaren b Lockwood	40
H. Trumble	not out	64
J.J. Kelly	c Rhodes b Braund	39
J.V. Saunders	lbw b Braund	0
Extras	(b 5, lb 3, nb 2)	10
Total		**324**

2nd innings

V.T. Trumper	run out	2
R.A. Duff	b Lockwood	6
C. Hill	c MacLaren b Hirst	34
J. Darling	c MacLaren b Lockwood	15
M.A. Noble	b Braund	13
S.E. Gregory	b Braund	9
W.W. Armstrong	b Lockwood	21
A.J. Hopkins	c Lilley b Lockwood	3
H. Trumble	not out	7
J.J. Kelly	lbw b Lockwood	0
J.V. Saunders	c Tyldesley b Rhodes	2
Extras	(b 7, lb 2)	9
Total		**121**

Fall of wickets: 1–47, 2–63, 3–82, 4–82, 5–126, 6–174, 8–256, 9–324, 10–324.

Second innings: 1–6, 2–9, 3–31, 4–71, 5–75, 6–91, 7–95, 8–114, 9–115, 10–121.

ENGLAND BOWLING

	O	M	R	W	O	M	R	W
Lockwood	24	2	85	1	20	6	45	5
Rhodes	28	9	46	0	22	7	38	1
Hirst	29	5	77	5	5	1	7	1
Braund	16.5	5	29	2	9	1	15	2
Jackson	20	4	66	2	4	3	7	0
Jessop	6	2	11	0				

ENGLAND
1st innings

A.C. MacLaren	c Armstrong b Trumble	10
L.C.H. Palairet	b Trumble	20
J.T. Tyldesley	b Trumble	33
T. Hayward	b Trumble	0
F.S. Jackson	c Armstrong b Saunders	2
L.C. Braund	c Hill b Trumble	22
G.L. Jessop	b Trumble	13
G.H. Hirst	c & b Trumble	43
W.H. Lockwood	c Noble b Saunders	25
A.A. Lilley	c Trumper b Trumble	0
W. Rhodes	not out	0
Extras	(b 13, lb 2)	15
Total		**183**

2nd innings

A.C. MacLaren	b Saunders	2
L.C.H. Palairet	b Saunders	6
J.T. Tyldesley	b Saunders	0
T. Hayward	c Kelly b Saunders	7
F.S. Jackson	c & b Trumble	49
L.C. Braund	c Kelly b Trumble	2
G.L. Jessop	c Noble b Armstrong	104
G.H. Hirst	not out	58
W.H. Lockwood	lbw b Trumble	2
A.A. Lilley	c Darling b Trumble	16
W. Rhodes	not out	6
Extras	(b 5, lb 6)	11
Total	(9 wkts)	**263**

Fall of wickets: 1–31, 2–36, 3–63, 4–67, 5–67, 6–83, 7–137, 8–179, 9–183, 10–183.

Second innings: 1–5, 2–5, 3–10, 4–31, 5–48, 6–157, 7–187, 8–214, 9–248.

AUSTRALIA BOWLING

	O	M	R	W	O	M	R	W
Trumble	31	13	65	8	33.5	4	108	4
Saunders	23	7	79	2	24	3	105	4
Noble	7	3	24	0	5	0	11	0
Armstrong					4	0	28	1

Umpires: C.E. Richardson and A.A. White

ENGLAND WON BY 1 WICKET

Several good judges yesterday said that for England to get 200 runs on the wicket would be a very fine performance, and they got 263. The Australians threw no chances away, and their fielding and throwing were magnificent, Mr Hopkins especially doing grand work.

But Englishmen may justly claim for their side superiority in batting on a bowlers' wicket, though, with the exception of Mr Jackson, no batsman shows the skill of Shrewsbury and other great batsmen of former years. Until this season the Colonials have not had much practice on

JESSOP   Bowlers do ask for it, you know.

Trumper on both these occasions demoralized the side; and this need not be a matter for surprise, for such things are common, and Mr Trumper is the greatest bat in the world.

In this last match Australia had the advantage of occupying the wickets the whole of the first day, the only period when run-getting and batting were easy. Notwithstanding this fact, the English side, who never once in the match had anything but a difficult wicket to bat on, won the match; and this more than redeemed their reputation. The Australians, however, have won the rubber, and hearty congratulations must be given to them. They may have had the best of the luck, but this is part of the game, and every true sportsman will give them the credit of being the better side.

bowlers' wickets, but the blot on their escutcheon is their collapse in batting on the second day both at Manchester and at the Oval. In both cases the Englishmen had the same wicket to play on; perhaps it was a trifle more difficult, but their batting was better. It may be that the fall of Mr

C.B. Fry, covering the match for the *Daily Express*, mentions that when Trumble dismissed Lockwood lbw he was bowling round the wicket. As the pitch was easing after lunch, it may be fair to assume that Trumble bowled round the wicket throughout the England innings, as Spofforth and Boyle had done at the Oval in 1882.

When the game was over, the Australians produced an autograph book and politely asked if members of the Press Box would sign.

WILFRED RHODES
Yorkshire

Rhodes was born in 1877 and died in 1973, his career so unlikely that it needs to be put in some sort of perspective. A right-handed batsman, Rhodes bowled slow left-arm.

12 May 1898: debut for Yorkshire v. MCC, captained by W.G. Grace, at Lord's; ends season with 154 wickets.

1 June 1899: debut for England at Trent Bridge, batting at No. 10; in second Test at Lord's assumes rightful position of No. 11.

1902: 1,000th wicket; helps Hirst see England home by one wicket in the Oval Test.

1903: double of 1,000 runs and 100 wickets for the first time.

1903–4: still at No. 11, with R.E. Foster adds 130 for 10th wicket in the Test at Sydney.

1907: 10,000th run.

1908: 2,000th wicket. 27 August: birth of Donald George Bradman.

1909–10: opens England innings in South Africa with Hobbs.

1911–12: 20,000th run. Hobbs and Rhodes in first-wicket partnership of 323 at Melbourne.

1919: Aged 41, resumes career after First World War: leading bowler in 1919, 1920–23 and 1926.

1920: 3,000th wicket.

1921: 30,000th run; plays at Trent Bridge in apparently his last Test.

1926: two months short of 49th birthday is recalled to England side for the Oval Test; dismisses Woodfull, Ponsford, Bardsley, Collins and A.J. Richardson, the last-named twice; Ashes regained. Performs double for the last time.

1929: 4,000th wicket; 100 wickets in a season for the last time.

1929–30: plays against West Indies; while Headley averages 87 in series, bowls 256 overs at 1.76 runs an over.

11 September 1930: playing for H.D.G. Leveson-Gower's side at Scarborough, has Bradman missed first ball, twice more in that batsman's innings of 96; takes a wicket with his last delivery in first-class cricket. Career record:

39,802 runs   4,187 wickets   708 catches

1948: Bradman retires from Test cricket in Grace's centenary year.

HOBBS AND RHODES AT MELBOURNE, 1911–12

12 February 1912, Melbourne. At the close of play on Saturday the MCC had made 370 for the loss of one wicket. As the game stands, therefore, with nine wickets still in hand, they hold a lead of 179 runs on the first innings.

Hobbs and Rhodes, who had made 30 and 23 respectively when stumps were drawn on Friday, were not separated today until 323 runs had been scored. This easily the best partnership for any wicket in a Test Match, and both batsmen played fine cricket, although both gave chances. One of the features of the partnership was the fine judgment displayed in running between the wickets, which showed the thorough understanding that existed between the two players...The weather was gloriously fine and the pitch had recovered from the recent rain when Hobbs and Rhodes continued the Englishmen's first innings with the score at 54 for no wicket. Dr Hordern and Mr Cotter were the bowlers, and the former began with two maiden overs. Both batsmen found the "googlies" very troublesome, and treated them with the utmost respect. Rhodes, when he had scored 37, should have been caught off Dr Hordern's bowling, but Mr Trumper at square-leg, anticipating the stroke, jumped in and thus missed an easy chance. The Yorkshireman scored at a much slower rate than yesterday. A double change in the bowling was soon tried, Mr Armstrong going on for Mr Cotter at 82 and Mr Kelleway for Dr Hordern one run later.

Rhodes, when he had made 31, gave a difficult chance at the wicket off Mr Kelleway's bowling, but the ball went to the boundary. Hobbs played in his usual beautiful style; he took the total to 100 with a leg-hit for four, all run, off a no-ball from Mr Kelleway. Rhodes continued to do very little, and when his score had reached 39 he hit up a ball from Mr Kelleway; the bowler made a great effort to reach the ball but failed. The ground fielding of the Australians was very smart, Mr Trumper and Mr Matthews being really brilliant. There was a burst of cheering when Mr Matthews was put on to bowl for Mr Kelleway at 121. One run later Mr Cotter relieved Mr Armstrong, but neither of these changes met with any success, and the luncheon interval was taken with the total at 137, Hobbs having made 86 and Rhodes 48.

Dr Hordern and Mr Cotter were the bowlers after luncheon. Rhodes was now much more aggressive and there were cheers when he reached his fifty. Soon afterwards Hobbs, with a straight drive off Dr Hordern for a single, completed his hundred when he had been at the wicket for two hours and twenty-three minutes. He was heartily cheered and the Australian players joined in the applause...Hobbs, with his score still at 100, gave a difficult chance of stumping off Mr Matthews's bowling, and the crowd appeared to be very indignant with Mr Carter. Mr Minnett was sending down some loose balls, and the spectators were disposed to be ironical at the expense of the home eleven. Hobbs, with a drive for a single, made England's score level with the Australian first innings total, amid cheers, and then, with two beautiful square cuts to the boundary off Mr Minnett's bowling, sent up the 200.

The batsmen were now giving a masterly display and changes in the bowling made no difference to them. Mr Armstrong relieved Mr Kelleway at 243, and Rhodes, with a square cut off the new bowler, completed his hundred, having been batting for three hours and forty minutes. This is Rhodes's first century in a Test Match, and he was heartily cheered. At the tea interval the total stood at 249, Hobbs having made 138 and Rhodes 102. The two batsmen were enthusiastically cheered as they returned to the pavilion.

Mr Cotter and Mr Armstrong continued to bowl after tea, but both batsmen scored rapidly and stole singles cleverly. Indeed, the bowlers were quite helpless and runs were scored all round the wicket. Hobbs, when he had made 176, gave an easy chance to Mr Cotter at square-leg off Dr Hordern's bowling; the fieldsman missed the catch, but the mistake was not expensive, for Hobbs was out, caught at the wicket, off the next ball sent down by the "googlie" bowler. Hobbs played a magnificent innings. Eighty-eight of his runs were scored by boundary strokes; he was batting for four hours and 23 minutes, and he hit splendidly all round the wicket. He met with a fine reception from the crowd.

MCC [sic]

1st innings

Hobbs	c Carter b Hordern	178
Rhodes	not out	157
Gunn	not out	22
Extras		13
Total	(for one wkt.)	370

Mr J.W.H.T. Douglas, Mr F.R. Foster, Woolley, Hearne, Mead, Vine, Smith and Barnes to go in.

At least *The Times* did not report that Hobbs had been caught by Mr Carter from the bowling of Dr Hordern.

AUSTRALIA 191 (R.B. Minnett 56; F.R. Foster 4 for 77, S.F. Barnes 5 for 74) and 173 (J.W.H.T. Douglas 5 for 46) lost to ENGLAND 589 (J.B. Hobbs 178, W. Rhodes 179, G. Gunn 75, F.R. Foster 50, F.E. Woolley 56) by an innings and 225 runs.

WILFRED RHODES REACHES 90

By A.A. Thomson

28 October 1967. Mr Wilfred Rhodes, who celebrates his ninetieth birthday tomorrow, is one of the surviving great figures of cricket's golden age. He has lived long, travelled widely, and has always been a shrewd observer of the human scene, but it is fair to say that cricket has been his life.

He and his lifelong friend, the late George Herbert Hirst, came from the same tiny hillside village in the West Riding and when, in their heyday, the question arose, "Who is England's greatest all-rounder?", the local worthies would nod sagely, murmuring enigmatically: "He bats right and bowls left; and he comes from Kirkheaton". No two men, in character and outlook, could have been more different — Hirst, dashing, exuberant; Rhodes, cool, relentless, technically a perfectionist — but, together, for Yorkshire and England, they were the consummate pair.

Rhodes's career reads like that of the industrious apprentice, blessed with a fairy godmother. In 1898 he came into the first class game as heir to Yorkshire's line of slow lefthanders, Peate and Peel; he retired 32 years later, after taking his regular 100 wickets up to the age of 50 and, more astonishingly, after enjoying a middle period as England's No. 2 batsman, opening with Hobbs, England's greatest No. 1. In the historic tour to Australia in 1911–12 these two set up a first-

wicket Test record, only surpassed by Hutton and Washbrook 37 years later.

The old Yorkshire cricketers called W.G. Grace a "nonesuch" and, by any standard, Rhodes has been a nonesuch, too. In cricket there has hardly been a prize that he has not won, an objective he has not attained; 16 doubles, over 4,000 wickets, nearly 40,000 runs. His first Test match in 1899 was W.G.'s last. In his year of retirement he bowled against Bradman, who, he thinks, was the finest of all batsmen.

His career has touched the high peaks of cricket history. In the first match of the epic rubber of 1902 he and Hirst crushed the Australians for 36, and in the last — Jessop's match — he joined his fellow-Yorkshireman when 15 runs were needed. Whether they "got them in singles" or not, get them they did in an electrifying finish which brought triumph to England by one wicket.

His exploits in Warner's Australian tour of 1903–04 ranged even higher. In the second Test he exploited a Melbourne "glue-pot" to take fifteen wickets, while in the first, at Sydney, he had shared what is still a record last-wicket stand with R.E. Foster and bowled all day on a billiard-table pitch at the brilliant Victor Trumper, who hit 185 not out, but not many of them off Rhodes. Before the day's last over Trumper begged, with a rueful smile: "Now, Wilf, give us a bit of mercy."

Whereupon Rhodes bowled him the most diabolical maiden over of the day, which no one but Trumper could have survived.

Heads were shaken when in county cricket Rhodes started to score runs. "Now, Wilfred", said Lord Hawke, "no more than 20". But his scores multiplied; soon he was opening for Yorkshire and then for England. That perfect understanding between partners which we associate with Hobbs and Sutcliff sprang to life with Hobbs and Rhodes. Asked to explain the secret of this remarkable harmony, Rhodes replied with his own gruff humour: "Here's the secret: if I'm coming I say Yes; if I'm not, I say No."

In the 1914–18 War he worked on munitions, playing League cricket at the weekend. When county cricket restarted he was over 40 and the Leagues tried hard to entice him away. ("They sat on my doorstep with their contracts," he told me.)

But Yorkshire retained his allegiance, and, season after season, in devastating fashion, he headed the first class bowling averages until in 1926, another Australian year, he was dramatically recalled.

"Can you", he was anxiously asked, "still pitch them there?"

"There", he replied, "or thereabouts".

He was two and a half months away from his forty-ninth birthday and three members of the England side, including his captain, had not, at the time of Rhodes's first Test, been born. Yet it is history that in the last Test at the Oval England won the rubber and regained the Ashes. It is also history that in Australia's second innings Rhodes clinched the issue by taking four for 44.

Thirty years later he told me: "The pitch was improving. They should have put me on sooner."

That was the last of his 58 Tests [he appeared in four Tests against West Indies in 1929–30], but he went on four seasons longer, taking 100 wickets in both 1928 and 1929. After his retirement in 1930 he played a season with a Scottish county and here the shadow of tragedy fell.

"I got bowled by a slow full toss", he said, "and I knew something was wrong with my eyes".

Twenty years passed before total blindness overtook him. Its onset was a double blow, for his keen, clear eyesight was the envy of all cricketers.

"Is it true", he was asked, "that when you batted with Jack Hobbs you could see the seam on the ball?"

"Ah", said he, "you should have played with Ranji. He could see the stitches."

In the years following the Second World War his sight grew worse but he faced the enemy indomitably. Seeing the ball as a small white blur, he played a remarkable game of golf. ("I've no trouble keeping my head down. I don't have to watch the ball.")

In the 1950s I watched him tending his garden. "It's no trouble", he said, "I can work between those two big white stones".

For many Septembers his friends have greeted him at the Scarborough Festival, and apart from the war years I do not think that, as player or patron, he has missed a trip to Scarborough between 1898 and 1966. He sits on the bench outside the Yorkshire dressing-room, "watching" the play by ear, criticizing the sound of an edgy stroke, holding court among old admirers.

In his blend of inflexibly firm character and splendid skills, he has been the complete cricketer. No bowler before or since has matched his classic art, his rhythmic action, his supreme command of length and flight. To the impatient batsman he was the subtlest tempter since the Serpent of Eden. His batting lacked the sheer beauty of his bowling. ("The cut was never a business stroke.") It was utilitarian, but massive, and you cannot score 39,797 runs without gifts of the highest order.

In old age and blindness there is pathos, but in Wilfred Rhodes at 90 there is no pathos, but something far, far from it. He has attained the highest reaches of his profession, which happens to be an English way of life; he retains his dry humour, his acute intelligence, his delightfully youthful complexion and, above all, the un-affected dignity of a life well lived. No pathos, indeed, but a kind of human grandeur.

Inevitably, the "legendary Rhodes" (as Cardus called him) will appear again in these pages.

SYDNEY FRANCES BARNES
Warwickshire, Lancashire and Staffordshire

Barnes made his only home Test appearance as a member of a first-class county, Lancashire, at Sheffield in 1902. Thereafter he was Barnes of Staffordshire. Not that "thereafter" meant much. From Sheffield until the outbreak of the First World War — and Barnes would be aged 48 in 1921 — England met Australia sixteen times at home; Barnes bowled in only six of those Tests. Yet before the Sheffield game, *The Times* could write: "It seems strange to find such a great bowler so little known to the English public."

However, Barnes began his Test career in England most auspiciously. Brought on at 38, he took two wickets in his first over, and before long had figures of 3–0–7–3; catches went down so that he finished with 20–9–49–6. Eventually, with England requiring 339 to win, Jessop was promoted to open and scored 55 in 45 minutes; MacLaren contributed 63, the rest of the side 70 between them. For the fourth Test at Old Trafford Barnes was dropped, as were Jessop and Hirst.

In a review of the season, *The Times* stated that Barnes was "somewhat unsound in limb and, if report speaks truly, rather lacking in grit".

BARNES AT MELBOURNE
30 DECEMBER 1911

The captaincy of the 1911–12 MCC side to tour Australia was offered to C.B. Fry, the vice-captaincy to P.F. Warner. The latter accepted, the former preferred to remain with the Training Ship *Mercury;* Warner was thereupon promoted. In the first game at Adelaide Warner made 151 but was then taken seriously ill and removed to a nursing home. From there he decided that J.W.H.T. Douglas should assume command, though he might have chosen F.R. Foster; both were all-rounders, and leaders of their respective counties, Essex and Warwickshire.

At Adelaide Warner had given the new ball to Foster (left-arm round the wicket with four short-legs — three behind the wicket — a long leg and a mid-on) and Barnes. Against New South Wales and Queensland, Douglas — with Barnes and Foster also playing — opened the bowling with Foster and himself. In the first Test at Sydney, Foster started England's attack — with Douglas. Barnes raged, Hobbs tried to pacify him, so did Woolley: "Why am I here?" Australia won the match by 146 runs, and the world knew why. A fortnight later Warner received Douglas at his sick bed: "Open the bowling with Barnes."

30 December 1911, Melbourne. Some sensational cricket was witnessed today in the second Test Match of the MCC tour, the first six Australian wickets falling for 38 runs. After this, however, the "tail" saved the side from a bad collapse, and the last four wickets added 146 runs to the total. Barnes bowled magnificently throughout, and in the early stages of the game he was almost unplayable. At one time he had secured five wickets for six runs. He kept a perfect length, swinging in from the off and turning back. Hitch bowled below form, and Mr Douglas and Mr Foster, although accurate, were not particularly dangerous.

The Play

The weather was overcast and the prospects uncertain when Mr Hill, who won the toss, decided to go in first. Mr Kelleway and Mr Bardsley opened the innings against the bowling of Mr Foster and Barnes. In spite of rain overnight the wicket appeared to be in good condition. After the former had sent down a maiden over, Mr Bardsley played Barnes's first delivery on to his wicket.

Later accounts suggest Bardsley missed an in-swinger which bowled him off his pads; had it not done so, he would have been out lbw.

Mr Hill came in, but runs were very difficult to get, and the batsmen frequently examined the wicket, which appeared to be playing trickily. With only five runs scored Mr Kelleway was out leg-before-wicket off Barnes's bowling.

Kelleway missed an in-swinger which straightened.

A slight shower was falling when Mr Hill was joined by Mr Armstrong. After adding two runs to his score off Mr Foster, Mr Hill was bowled by Barnes with the total at eight.

Hill received a ball which pitched on his leg stump and hit the top of the off.

Up to this point Barnes had taken three wickets for one run. Rain fell rather more heavily for a few minutes, but play was not interrupted. Mr Trumper went in next, but with only three runs added Mr Armstrong was caught at the wicket off Barnes's bowling.

AUSTRALIA

C. Kelleway	lbw b Barnes	2
W. Bardsley	b Barnes	0
C. Hill	b Barnes	4
W.W. Armstrong	c Smith b Barnes	4
V. Trumper	not out	0
Extras		1
Total	(4 wkts)	11

After Mr Ransford came in a slight delay was caused by Mr Trumper being struck by a rising ball from Mr Foster, but he was soon able to continue. With the total at 14 for four wickets — Mr Trumper having made two and Mr Ransford one — play was stopped for ten minutes owing to rain. A small section of the crowd hooted, and on the umpires coming out again they were met with ironical cheers.

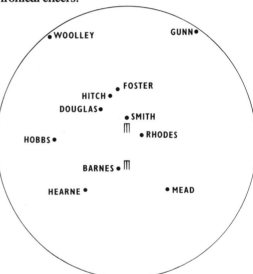

Barnes's field at Melbourne, 1911

When he had made three, Mr Trumper was twice beaten by Barnes, but he scored the first four of the match with a beautiful square cut off a short ball from Mr Foster. The first change in the bowling was tried at 29, Hitch going on for Mr Foster, and three runs later Mr Douglas relieved Barnes, whose analysis then stood at

O	M	R	W
9	6	3	4

With the total at 32 for four wickets the luncheon

interval was taken, Mr Trumper then having made 13 and Mr Ransford eight.

When play was continued the weather had improved considerably. Mr Foster and Barnes were the bowlers, and the former with his second delivery clean bowled Mr Trumper, who had been batting nearly three-quarters of an hour for his runs. With half the side out for 33, Mr Ransford was joined by Mr Minnett. Three runs were scored off Barnes in his first over...

Other accounts say that in this over Minnett was missed at third slip. If Barnes's field was as it had been at the start of the Australian innings, third slip was Douglas; Barnes doubtless suspected a conspiracy of incompetence.

...but he got Mr Minnett caught at cover point by Hobbs off the first ball of his next.

O	M	R	W
10.1	6	6	5

Six wickets were now down for 38 and Dr Hordern came in. The score was taken to 50 after the innings had lasted just under an hour and a half. Runs were now coming rather more freely. Hitch went on for Mr Foster at 62, and at 71 Mr Douglas relieved Barnes whose analysis then read:-

O	M	R	W
15	6	19	5

Mr Ransford scored at a steady rate and Dr Hordern made runs occasionally, but the former was caught at the wicket off Hitch's bowling, and seven wickets were down for 80 runs. Mr Cotter, the next man in, opened by hitting Hitch to the boundary and he repeated the stroke three balls later. There was a scene of enthusiasm when he got Hitch's fifth delivery to the leg boundary and followed with a similar stroke off the sixth, which, however, Hearne saved from going to the boundary. The fieldsman sent in a fast return to Woolley at mid-on...

The field clearly had been changed since the start of play.

...and the latter threw down the wicket before Mr Cotter could complete the third run.

With the total at 97 for eight wickets, Mr Carter joined Dr Hordern. Runs came steadily, and at 117 Mr Douglas and Barnes resumed bowling. Barnes was applauded on taking the ball, but after Mr Carter had scored a single off his first delivery Barnes took some time to change his field and the crowd grew noisy.

Barnes's dictum is here recalled: "When I'm bowling, there's only one captain. Me!" Douglas probably offered moral support. Barnes heard the crowd's noise.

He threw down the ball and refused to bowl, and thereupon the crowd made a variety of noises mingled with cheers and hoots. When Barnes continued each run scored off him evoked great enthusiasm, and there was much cheering when Mr Carter glanced him for two. The tea interval was taken with the total 129 for eight, each batsman having made 20.

Barnes's frustrations were not yet over.

There was a peculiar incident at 140 for nine wickets when Mr Whitty, the last man, joined Dr Hordern. The former had scored three and was then apparently bowled by Barnes. He was leaving the field with the Englishmen when the umpire Crockett called out, "No, no." It appears that the ball came back on to the wicket from Smith's pads.

The last wicket fell to Woolley, who thereby achieved 0.1–0–0–1. Barnes's figures for the innings were 23–9–44–5.

AUSTRALIA 184 (S.F. Barnes 5 for 44) and 299 (W.W. Armstrong 90; F.R. Foster 6 for 91) lost to ENGLAND 265 (W. Rhodes 61, J.W. Hearne 114) and 219 for 2 (J.B. Hobbs 126 not out).

The sweetest irony of the series which England won by four games to one occurred in the fifth Test at Sydney. The Australian selectors chose Macartney as a left-arm bowler, adding he might also be useful as a stonewalling batsman.

BARNES V. SOUTH AFRICA, 1912

The year 1912 was a season of absurdity. Against Staffordshire Monmouthshire were dismissed for 39 and 87, Glamorgan for 78 and 62; Kent 2nd XI managed 89, Durham 65 and Cheshire 41. On a higher level against England, South Africa totalled 41 from the bat in the first innings at Lord's and 84 and 72 at the Oval. The common factor was Barnes. The other England bowlers against South Africa included F.R. Foster, Walter Brearley, Harry Dean of Lancashire, Woolley, Rhodes and J.W. Hearne.

THREE TESTS v. SOUTH AFRICA
Barnes

Overs	Mdns	Runs	Wkts	Av.
128	38	282	34	8.29

Balls/wkt 22.58

Others

Overs	Mdns	Runs	Wkts	Av.
170.1	46	396	24	16.50

Balls/wkt 42.5

Had not three of the summer's Tests in the Triangular Tournament clashed with Staffordshire games, Barnes's figures for his minor county would doubtless have seen an increase in the number of his wickets.

FOR STAFFORDSHIRE

Overs	Mdns	Runs	Wkts	Av.
191	75	376	70	5.37

Balls/wkt 16.37

Barnes passed his Saturdays lucratively playing in the North Staffordshire League.

BARNES AT LORD'S

By E.B. Noel

11 June 1912. There are many disappointments in watching a first-class cricket match; there are many delights, and there is none in present-day cricket to surpass the pleasure of seeing Barnes bowl.

A fine figure of a man, whether in rest or action; a run up to the wicket lithe and "springy," in which not a step is wasted; a beautiful action with the arm right over the head, and then the ball is made to go away or to come back; and there is always that inexorable length, the life off the pitch, and the subtle changes of pace. It is the perfection of the bowler's art, and there is no question that Barnes is the greatest bowler of this generation, and is to be classed with the greatest of all time. He is not really fast, and yet he can bowl with no man out. He was not hit yesterday for a single four in front of the wicket, though there were two snicks off him to the boundary. He hardly bowled more than one really bad ball. It makes the bowler of modest attainments realize what bowling really can be.

The South African batsmen had a thankless task, and better batting sides than they might well have failed. There was no peace for them. If they got away from Barnes, they had to face Mr Foster from the pavilion end, which was nearly as bad. For the first few overs Mr Foster did not look as if he would be very difficult to play, only that he would be very difficult to score from. But after a bit the ball began to come quicker off the pitch, and then he was much more deadly. The South Africans certainly did not bat well, and there is no doubt that they have not many "class" batsmen on the side. Mr Nourse was bowled by a "yorker" just as he looked likely to overcome the difficulties; and Mr Faulkner, on whom they rely so much, got a very good ball from Mr Foster which came quickly off the pitch and seemed to come back instead of going with the arm. It seemed mistaken policy for some of the later batsmen not to have a hit. They were not likely to get many runs if they stayed on the defence, and "three fours and out" is more useful in such conditions than 15 minutes' inglorious batting for about two.

In his second over Barnes got Mr Hartigan caught at slip off a slow ball that went away quickly; in his next he got Mr Taylor leg-before-wicket with a ball that came up the hill. Mr Llewellyn joined Mr Nourse, and a short stand followed. Mr Nourse made two fine fours off Mr Foster — one a well-timed placing stroke to leg, the other a good, old-fashioned off-drive — and there was no man out. But with the score at 28 Mr Foster bowled Mr Nourse with a "yorker"; at 35 Mr Llewellyn, who also had batted well, made a thoroughly bad stroke, trying to hit a straight ball to leg; and worse was to come, for with one more run added Mr Faulkner was out. For the rest of the innings the bowlers were absolute masters of the situation, and the highest score after Mr Faulkner was out was four. Mr Foster hit the wicket five times and came out with a better analysis than Barnes, but the latter looked the more difficult. Mr Foster caught the only two catches at slip, and so he and Barnes alone figured on the score in every wicket. It was essentially a case of good bowling making use of its chance, and reaping its full reward against batsmen who could not cope with it. Extras were easily top score.

SOUTH AFRICA 58 (F.R. Foster 5 for 16, S.F. Barnes 5 for 25) and 217 (G.C.B. Llewellyn 75; Barnes 6 for 85) lost to ENGLAND 337 (R.H. Spooner 119, F.E. Woolley 73; S.J. Pegler 7 for 65) by an innings and 62 runs.

BARNES AT THE OVAL

As the Third Test was over by lunch on the second day, it seems likely that none of the modern sponsors would volunteer their services were Barnes playing for England.

By E.B. Noel

14 August 1912. England beat South Africa at the Oval yesterday by ten wickets. On Monday each side had played an innings, and England held the long lead of 81 runs. After about ten minutes' play yesterday it was obvious that this had, for all practical purposes, meant victory, for the wicket once more gave the bowlers great help, and it was seen that the batsmen would have another grim struggle against Barnes's bowling. Once more Barnes used his wicket as only a great bowler can. The ball was not getting up so high or so straight as on Monday, but it was doing its work more quickly, and Barnes got every possible ounce of help out of the pitch. The South Africans just saved themselves from defeat by a single innings, but England were left with only 13 runs to make, and these were scored by Hobbs and Hearne without loss. By half-past 1 the game was over.

Barnes yesterday took eight wickets for 29 runs, and in the whole match 13 for 57 — a great performance on any wicket, and he had the greatest share in the victory. His accuracy of length, his "life" off the pitch, and his variations of pace and break yesterday were a delight to watch for any intelligent spectator...

Mr Fry started his bowling with Woolley and Barnes, the latter again from the Gasworks end. Before a run had been scored Mr Tancred was stumped off Woolley's bowling, and with the total at ten two more wickets fell; Mr Taylor was out leg-before-wicket in trying to get a ball from Barnes round to leg, and from the next ball Mr Stricker was caught at point; Mr Spooner fumbled the ball at the first attempt but caught it at the second. Then came the stand between Mr Faulkner and Mr Nourse, and with byes to the boundary off Barnes's bowling twice in the same over — the first time the ball went over Mr Nourse's shoulder and the second close to his wicket — and a five off Woolley's bowling to long leg runs came fairly fast. But just when Mr Faulkner seemed to be settling down, he was bowled by Barnes. Mr Llewellyn was unlucky enough to get a ball that jumped quickly. He was caught off his glove, and half the side were out for 54 runs. Mr White was caught at the wicket, and Hearne held rather an awkward high catch at mid-on to dismiss Mr Snooke, who mis-hit the ball. Mr Beaumont helped Mr Nourse to save the side from defeat by an innings, but with the total at 89 he got a ball that turned like a flash of lightning, and was clean bowled, Barnes having

now taken seven wickets in succession. Four runs later Mr Nourse's fine innings came to an end. Mr Foster had gone on some time before at Woolley's end, but his bowling had not looked very difficult. In having a hit at a ball from him Mr Nourse mistimed it and was easily caught and bowled. No addition to the score had been made when the last wicket fell, and the innings was over for 93.

It was a great piece of bowling by Barnes, and

ENGLAND v. SOUTH AFRICA
The Oval, 12 and 13 August 1912

SOUTH AFRICA

1st innings

L.J. Tancred	b Barnes	0
H.W. Taylor	c Foster b Woolley	23
A.D. Nourse	lbw b Woolley	8
G.A. Faulkner	c Hayes b Barnes	9
L.A. Stricker	b Barnes	5
G.C.B. Llewellyn	c Rhodes b Woolley	0
G.C. White	b Barnes	4
S.J. Snooke	c Foster b Woolley	23
R. Beaumont	c Hearne b Barnes	3
S.J. Pegler	c Hitch b Woolley	3
T.A. Ward	not out	6
Extras	(b 8, lb 3)	11
Total		95

2nd innings

L.J. Tancred	st Smith b Woolley	0
H.W. Taylor	lbw b Barnes	6
A.D. Nourse	c & b Foster	42
G.A. Faulkner	b Barnes	10
L.A. Stricker	c Spooner b Barnes	0
G.C.B. Llewellyn	c Hitch b Barnes	0
G.C. White	c Smith b Barnes	1
S.J. Snooke	c Hearne b Barnes	7
R. Beaumont	b Barnes	6
S.J. Pegler	b Barnes	0
T.A. Ward	not out	0
Extras	(b 18, lb 3)	21
Total		93

Fall of wickets: 1–2, 2–31, 3–38, 4–47, 5–50, 6–53, 7–76, 8–86, 9–86, 10–95.

Second innings: 1–0, 2–10, 3–10, 4–54, 5–54, 6–58, 7–70, 8–89, 9–93, 10–93.

ENGLAND BOWLING (6-ball overs)

	O	M	R	W	O	M	R	W
Foster	6	2	15	0	7	2	19	1
Barnes	21	10	28	5	16.4	4	29	8
Woolley	15.3	1	41	5	9	2	24	1

ENGLAND

1st innings

J.B. Hobbs	c & b Faulkner	68
W. Rhodes	b Faulkner	0
R.H. Spooner	c Nourse b Llewellyn	26
C.B. Fry	c Snooke b Faulkner	9
E.G. Hayes	b Faulkner	4
F.E. Woolley	b Pegler	13
J.W. Hearne	lbw b Faulkner	20
F.R. Foster	st Ward b Faulkner	8
E.J. Smith	b Faulkner	9
S.F. Barnes	c Taylor b Pegler	0
J.W. Hitch	not out	0
Extras	(b 10, lb 1)	11
Total		176

2nd innings

J.B. Hobbs	not out	9
J.W. Hearne	not out	5
Extras		0
Total	(0 wkts)	14

Fall of wickets: 1–4, 2–65, 3–85, 4–89, 5–111, 6–127, 7–135, 8–163, 9–176, 10–176.

SOUTH AFRICA BOWLING

	O	M	R	W	O	M	R	W
Pegler	19	2	53	2				
Faulkner	27.1	4	84	7	2	0	4	0
Llewellyn	10	1	28	1				
Nourse					2.3	0	10	0

Umpires: A.A. White and W. Richards

ENGLAND WON BY 10 WICKETS

the fact that neither Mr Foster nor Woolley looked really difficult showed in a sense how well he must have bowled. Only two fours were hit off his bowling yesterday, a beautiful stroke by Mr Nourse past cover-point and a cut by Mr Snooke.

In 1913–14, with Douglas's side in South Africa, Barnes took 49 wickets in the first four Tests but did not play in the fifth. On Monday, 16 March 1914, this news item appeared in *The Times;* in essence, it sums up the career of Sydney Francis Barnes.

THE MCC TEAM DEPARTURE FOR ENGLAND

14 March 1914. The members of the MCC team, with the exception of Barnes, left here today in the Union-Castle liner *Kinfauns Castle* for England. They were accorded a hearty send-off by a large crowd, which included many prominent people in the cricket world. Mr J.W.H.T. Douglas once again reiterated his great admiration for South African hospitality.

Barnes is sailing for home on Monday in the Union-Castle liner *Guildford Castle* (Reuter).

TEST CAREER

In England
v. Australia

Overs	Mdns	Runs	Wkts	Av.
249.3	93	561	29	19.34

v. South Africa

128	38	282	34	8.29
377.3	131	843	63	13.38

In Australia

Overs	Mdns	Runs	Wkts	Av.
708.4	171	1727	77	22.82

In South Africa

Overs	Mdns	Runs	Wkts	Av.
226	56	536	49	10.93

v. Australia

Overs	Mdns	Runs	Wkts	Av.
958.1	264	2288	106	21.58

v. South Africa

Overs	Mdns	Runs	Wkts	Av.
354	94	818	83	9.85

Total

Overs	Mdns	Runs	Wkts	Av.
1312.1	358	3106	189	16.43

EIGHTIETH BIRTHDAY TRIBUTE TO S.F. BARNES

By John Hartley

14 April 1953. Sydney Barnes, the former England Test cricketer, will be 80 on April 19, and to celebrate his birthday he will bowl at the beginning of a match in his honour at Stafford on April 26. As the tall, erect figure runs slowly up to the wicket and delivers the ball from the outside edge of the crease, cricket lovers will be seeing one of the greatest cricketers of all time.

It is many years since Australian mothers frightened naughty children with the name of Sydney Barnes. It is years since Australian and South African crowds sat stunned into horrified silence as Barnes shattered the might of their batsmen on their own perfect wickets.

But Barnes's reputation has lived on. It tells of devastating bowling; of an attack that came like summer lightning, impersonally destroying wherever it struck.

In 1901, when Barnes was 28, A.C. MacLaren dropped a bombshell into the cricket world when he announced that S.F. Barnes would go on the next Australian tour.

Yet after two Tests the Australians were hailing him as the finest hard wicket bowler ever sent from England. Six years later, after another tour, M.A. Noble was describing him as the finest bowler in the world, and P.F. Warner said that Barnes was the best bowler he had played against.

But Barnes did not reach his peak for another six years — during tours of Australia and South Africa in which his performances have moved into legend. He was then widely acclaimed as the finest bowler the world had ever seen.

At 80 Barnes is neither frail nor infirm. Anyone seeing him striding easily and quickly each day up the long flight of steps to his office in the Shire Hall, Stafford, must be impressed by his vigour.

His manner is courteous and gentle. It is only when an incautious word is uttered that one realizes that the internal fires are not completely banked down, that age will never entirely mellow this rock of a man. The fateful, kindling word is "batsmen." At its sound a frosty look overtakes the bright blue eyes, and a hard edge comes into the Staffordshire accent. Mention of the ancient enemy takes Barnes back in his memory through the stages by which his attack was built up.

He began as a fast bowler, playing occasionally, but without much success, for Warwickshire. He was taught the off-break, but decided that the ball moving away from the batsman was more difficult to play. He developed a leg-break which was spun with the third finger so that it could be whipped down from the same height as the off-break. "It is speed off the pitch that counts." The "Barnes ball" was a leg-break that pitched on the leg stump and came off very fast to hit the top of the off stump. The action was very similiar to that of the off-break, and Barnes never bowled googlies — "I did not need to."

He learnt much about swing in his first Test tour, and on a later tour Charles Macartney, in his first innings for Australia, saw Barnes bowl Victor Trumper. The ball was fast on the leg stump, but just before it pitched it swung suddenly to the off. Then it pitched, broke back, and took Trumper's leg stump. Macartney said afterwards: "It was the sort of ball a man might see if he was dreaming or drunk."

Barnes could make the ball swing one way and break the other and he could do it for both off-and leg-breaks. What is more, through variation of pace and flight alone, he could change both the spot at which the swing would become effective and the amount of the break. Finally he decided to bowl from the outside edge of the crease to make the line of flight of the ball more deceptive.

He was accurate and kept a perfect length. His bowling was directed against the weaknesses of batsmen. "I never bowled at the wickets: I bowled at the stroke. I intended the batsman to make a stroke, then I tried to beat it. I tried to make the batsman move. The time a batsman makes mistakes is when he has to move his feet."

Barnes's field was meticulously set. He would stand impassively, sometimes being barracked for delay, with long forefinger flicking every

BARNES   His brain an icicle and technique supreme; the scourge of batsmen — and his own captains.

fielder to the exact spot. After a few balls he might move a man just a yard and a half — where he would take the catch straight to him.

The bowling today makes him impatient. "The lbw rule is mainly responsible. It has shut out the lovely off-side strokes; there is too much defensive bowling outside the leg stump and too much playing off the back foot. If you are going to get wickets you must attack the batsman."

Barnes thinks we have one good bowler — Bedser — and a very promising bowler — Trueman — and that we can beat the Australians. "We should have beaten them years ago if we had attacked them." He would like to have bowled at Bradman. "He did not like one going away."

Barnes could bat, and once, with a 38 not out, including the winning hit, saved a Test for England. But he often threw his wicket away. "Why don't you try to make runs?" asked C.B. Fry. "If I make a century and took no wickets, would the selectors pick me for my batting?" was the reply. He once undertook to make 50 if allowed to go in first. He opened against Tasmania, but made only 47.

Barnes is not prepared to say who he thinks was the best batsman of his day — "there were so many really good men then." He would sometimes "just plug them down at Jack Hobbs and hope he would have a fit or something." Clem Hill was probably the most difficult to get out.

Although he had an immensely long playing career — from 1893 to 1936 — Barnes played little first-class cricket. After his Test *début* he played two seasons for Lancashire — 1902 and 1903 — and thereafter played no first-class cricket except representative matches. In 22 seasons for Staffordshire he took 1,432 wickets for an average of 8.03 runs, and in 38 seasons of League cricket he took 3,741 wickets for an average of 6.68 runs.

The battles with the Australians provide his most treasured memories. Of these the most vivid is the classic occasion at Melbourne in 1911 — one of the finest feats of bowling in Test history. Australia with a powerful, triumphant side had won the toss and went in first on a perfect wicket. The crowd settled back happily in expectation of a huge score. F.R. Foster bowled the first over, then Barnes, who had been ill all week and was scarcely recovered, took the ball.

His first ball swung in to Bardsley, hit him on the toe and went on to the wicket. "He would have been lbw if it had not." Shortly afterwards Kelleway stepped in front of the wicket and did not attempt to play a ball going past his legs. "It dipped into him and he was lbw." Clem Hill, the left-hander, was next. "I gave him one that was an off-break to him and then an in-swinger. Then I sent him one going away and he let it go. The last ball of the over pitched on his leg stump and hit the off. Clem said afterwards he had never had such an over."

The crowd was thunderstruck. But worse was to follow. Trumper and Armstrong, grim and determined, seemed to be making a stand. "Then a leg break to Armstrong went across nicely and very quick off the pitch. He played back, snicked it, and was caught at the wicket. I turned to Douglas, who was captain. Everything was going round. I said: 'I'll have to chuck it. I can hardly see the other end.' " He came off, having bowled nine overs with six maidens and taken four wickets for three runs. He did not bowl again until after lunch.

Then, in his first over, three runs were scored. In the next Minnett played forward to a leg-break, did not get it in the middle, and was caught by Jack Hobbs at cover-point. Barnes had taken five wickets for six runs.

In spite of his successes Barnes was not a popular idol. He was then too stern, too reserved, and he played too little first-class cricket. There was never any national tribute paid him, and though the game on Sunday comes for his eightieth birthday it is gratifying that Barnes is now as able as at any time in a distinguished career to appreciate the feelings of regard that cricket lovers everywhere will feel for a very great player.

Barnes died on 26 December 1967 in his 95th year.

HERBERT WILFRED TAYLOR
Natal

Taylor was a great theorist, quite indifferent to the span of oceans or — as befitted one who had won a Military Cross in the First World War — to the thought of blood. One Taylor pronouncement merits inclusion in a book of quotations: it concerned the way to play the body-line bowling practised by Larwood and Voce in Australia, 1932–3. An agency man in South Africa, 6,000 miles from the battle zone, consulted the great theorist, then informed *The Times:* "H.W. Taylor says there is no danger if the batsmen play forward."

Taylor was a batsman whose fame was established during the visit to South Africa in 1913–14 of an MCC side captained by J.W.H.T. Douglas. Its bowling consisted of Douglas himself, M.W. Booth of Yorkshire (who had just been chosen by *Wisden* as one of its Cricketers of the Year and who would be killed in action before he was 30), A.E. Relf, J.W. Hearne, Woolley, Rhodes and S.F. Barnes. The last-named proved virtually unplayable on the matting wickets save by Taylor, who, applying logic, solved the Barnes problem to the extent that, in the ten innings when they were in opposition, he averaged 57. Taylor's scores for South Africa (italics when Barnes was not playing) were 109 and 8, 29 and 40, 14 and 70, 16 and 93, *42* and *87;* for Natal v. MCC 83 not out and 42 not out, 91 and 100. So while Barnes took 49 wickets (average 10.93) in the first four Tests, and 56 wickets (average 11.60) in games against South Africa and Natal, Taylor's record against the Englishmen was 14 innings, 2 not out, 824 runs, 68.66 average. A.D.

Nourse, senior's average for 13 innings was 28.90. In the five Tests and two games for Natal Taylor scored 34 per cent of runs from the bat.

GREAT INNINGS BY MR TAYLOR

15 December 1913. The English cricket team in South Africa have established themselves in a strong position in their first Test Match, which began at Durban on Saturday. The feature of the first day's play was undoubtedly the innings of 100 by Mr H.W. Taylor, the South African captain. To score 109 out of a total of 182 in a Test Match is a performance which speaks for itself, and the fact that Barnes was one of the bowlers opposed to him makes Mr Taylor's feat the more remarkable. Mr Douglas, at the banquet given in honour of the English team on Saturday evening, described Mr Taylor as one of the greatest players South Africa has produced, and the tribute is well merited.

As we remarked in Saturday's issue of *The Times*, the performance of Hobbs and Barnes are awaited with especial interest in this country, and both have already distinguished themselves in this match. Barnes took five wickets for 57 runs, and can now claim 145 wickets in Test Matches, more than any other bowler has secured. Hobbs has made 59 runs in England's first innings, and is not out.

A motor-car accident, in which Hobbs, Strudwick, and Booth were involved — though all three fortunately escaped injury — is reported on another page.

Strudwick, Hobbs and Booth had embarked on a motor excursion to Amanzimtote, 17 miles from Durban. On approaching a level crossing at Umbito, and trying to pass a trap, the car ran into a bank, smashed an open gate and turned completely over, imprisoning its occupants, who had a few scratches and a miraculous escape. Motoring continued to be a hazard for cricketers in South Africa. As a member of A.P.F. Chapman's MCC side in 1930–31, Sandham was hurt and played no more on the tour; in 1949–50 W.A. Johnston of A.L. Hassett's Australians suffered similarly, an SOS being sent to K.R. Miller, mysteriously omitted from the party in the first place.

The Play

Play began at 12 o'clock in fine, cool weather. The attendance at the start numbered about 2,000, including many visitors from all parts of the country. As was expected, Hearne and Smith were omitted from the English side.

South Africa, having won the toss, batted first on a perfect pitch. Mr Taylor and Mr Hartigan opening the innings to the bowling of Barnes and Booth. Mr Taylor made the first scoring stroke of the match off a ball from Barnes, and he had scored the five runs on the board when Mr Hartigan was smartly caught at the wicket by Strudwick off the first ball of Barnes's second over. Mr Hands came in next, and Mr Taylor hit two successive balls from Booth to the leg boundary. Barnes was trying the "leg theory," and with the total at 20 Mr Taylor was missed off his bowling by Woolley. Two runs later Booth sent down a kicking ball from which Mr Hands was caught at third man by Barnes. Mr Nourse came in, and with the score at 37 Woolley took the ball from Booth. The scoring was slow, and consisted chiefly of singles, but 17 overs had been sent down before there was a maiden. Relf relieved Barnes

at 48, and the total reached 50 after 70 minutes play. Mr Douglas put himself on instead of Woolley at 60, and two runs later Rhodes was tried for Relf. The English captain soon met with success, dismissing Mr Nourse for 19 at 62, and at this point the luncheon interval was taken.

Mr Lewis accompanied Mr Taylor to the wicket after luncheon, while Barnes and Mr Douglas shared the bowling. Mr Taylor very nearly pulled Barnes's first delivery on to his wicket — it was a very narrow escape, and with only three runs added to the luncheon total Mr Lewis was magnificently caught in the slips off Barnes's fourth ball by Woolley, who fell over in securing the catch. Mr Cooper ccame in next and finished the over by driving the fifth ball to the boundary and scoring a couple off the sixth; he was clean bowled, however, by the first ball of Barnes's next over, the fifth wicket falling with the total at 73. Mr Tapscott was the next batsman, but after having scored four he was bowled by the fifth ball of the same over. Six wickets were now down for 77, and Mr Taylor, who had scored 40, was joined by Mr Ward. Mr Taylor was heartily cheered when he reached his 50, after having been two hours and five minutes at the wickets. Mr Douglas gave way to Rhodes at 95, and in the latter's first over the century went up, the innings then having lasted just under two hours and a quarter. At 104 Booth was put on again instead of Barnes, and at 113 Mr Ward was caught off his bowling by Woolley for nine, Mr Taylor's score at this point being 67. Mr Baumgartner, who came in next, was cheered for scoring 12 off one over from Rhodes, who gave way to Woolley at 140, Relf having relieved Booth four runs earlier. With the total at 144 Mr Baumgartner was out leg before to Woolley for 16. Mr Taylor had then made 82, and his next partner was Mr Blanckenberg, who was content to keep up his end while his captain hit brilliantly all round the wicket. Barnes was put on again for Relf at 146, Rhodes for Woolley at 156, and 13 runs later Mr Douglas himself took the ball from Rhodes. Mr Taylor, however, passed his century, and with a huge drive lifted a ball from Mr Douglas out of the ground. When 37 runs had been added for the ninth wicket the tea interval was taken with the score at 181 for eight wickets, Mr Taylor having made 109 and Mr Blanckenberg 6.

Before a run had been added Mr Taylor was caught at the wicket off the second ball sent down by Mr Douglas. Mr Cox, the last man, survived a most confident appeal for a catch at the wicket in the same over, and Strudwick actually started for the pavilion. Only a single had been added, however, when the new batsman was clean bowled by Barnes, and the innings closed for 182. Mr Taylor was batting three hours and 18 minutes for his splendid innings of 109, and he hit a 6 and eleven 4's. He played an orthodox game, and made less use than usual of his characteristic pull.

SOUTH AFRICA
1st innings

Mr H.W. Taylor	c Strudwick b Douglas	109
Mr G.P.D. Hartigan	c Strudwick b Barnes	0
Mr P. Hands	c Barnes b Booth	3
Mr A.D. Nourse	b Douglas	19
Mr P.T. Lewis	c Woolley b Barnes	0
Mr A.H.C. Cooper	b Barnes	6
Mr G.L. Tapscott	b Barnes	4
Mr T.A. Ward	c Woolley b Booth	9
Mr H. Baumgartner	lbw b Woolley	16
Mr J.M. Blanckenberg	not out	6
Mr J.L. Cox	b Barnes	1
Extras	(b 6, lb 1, nb 2)	9
Total		182

Fall of wickets: 1–5, 2–22, 3–62, 4–65, 5–73, 6–77, 7–113, 8–144, 9–181, 10–182

ENGLAND BOWLING

	O	M	R	W
Barnes	19.4	1	57	5
Booth	10	0	38	2
Woolley	7	0	24	1
Relf	5	2	9	0
Douglas	8	2	19	2
Rhodes	7	0	26	0

ENGLAND
1st innings

Hobbs	not out	59
Rhodes	c Tapscott b Cox	18
Relf	c Baumgartner b Cox	1
The Hon L.H. Tennyson	not out	6
Extras		10
Total	(2 wkts)	94

Fall of wickets: 1–24, 2–40

England went on to score 450 (Hobbs 82, Tennyson 52, Douglas 119, M.C. Bird 61) before winning by an innings and 157 runs. The only time when South Africa presented a real challenge was in the Fourth Test, when England, batting last, were 154 for five, still 159 runs short of victory.

It is part of cricket's folklore that Barnes once grew so tired of bowling to Taylor that he threw down the ball and refused to operate any more. The date was 10 February 1914, the occasion, Natal v. MCC at Durban. In old age, Taylor related details of the Natal second innings to Chris Greyvenstein;* read with Bernard Hollowood's† memories of playing alongside Barnes for Staffordshire as a companion piece, they are surely true to character. The great theorist explained his method: "I kept my eyes glued to the ball in his hand as he ran up to the wicket. And just before he delivered it I would switch my eyes to about a yard above his head to catch any finger movement as the ball left his hand."

At the close of the first day's play, Natal were 95 for four wickets (Taylor 53, Arbuthnot 4, the not-out batsmen) in reply to MCC's 132; at the close of the second day, MCC were 210 for eight wickets in their second innings, Natal having been dismissed for 153. So far in the match MCC men had gone 21 times to the crease scoring 307 runs, while ten men of Natal had scraped together 45 runs.

THE ENGLISHMEN'S FIRST DEFEAT

11 February 1914. The MCC team met with their first defeat of the tour at Durban yesterday, when Natal beat them by four wickets. Natal lost two wickets in their second innings for 27 runs, but a splendid partnership between Mr Taylor and Mr Nourse placed them within 43 runs of victory.

It is true that Hobbs was not playing in this match, but the victory of Natal is nevertheless a fine achievement. Mr H.W. Taylor, who made 91

* *Masters of South African Cricket.*

† *Cricket on the Brain.*

and 100, Mr A.D. Nourse, who made 59 in the second innings, and Mr C.P. Carter, who took four wickets for 32 in the first MCC innings and six for 58 in the second, played the most important parts in the success of their side. Mr Taylor and Mr Carter were both members of the last South African side to visit this country, in 1912. Mr Nourse came with the team of 1907 as well.

It will be remembered that the Englishmen have won all the three Test Matches played during the present tour, and thus have already won the rubber. Two more Test Matches remain to be played, the first of which is due to begin at Durban on Saturday.

Overnight the game had been left in a very interesting position, the Englishmen being 189 runs ahead with two wickets of their second innings still in hand. The remaining batsmen were disposed of for the addition of 23 runs, and Natal were thus set to make 215 to win. The weather was fine when Booth and Smith, the not-outs, continued the MCC second innings with the total at 210 for 8 wickets. After 22 runs had been added, Smith was bowled by Mr Carter, and three runs later Booth got in front of a straight ball from the same bowler, the innings closing for 235.

Natal began their second innings with Mr Chapman and Mr Taylor. Barnes and Mr Douglas shared the bowling, and with only eight runs on the board the latter dismissed Mr Chapman with a fast ball which broke in on to the wicket. Mr Pearse, the next man, made four runs and was then brilliantly caught low down in the slips by Mr Douglas from Booth's bowling. The second wicket fell at 27, and Mr Nourse came in, but before any addition had been made to the total the luncheon interval was taken, Mr Taylor's score then being 17.

"Herby," said Nourse at lunch, "I can't play this blighter [Barnes]." Taylor told his partner to keep his head down; *he* would take Barnes as far as possible.

Both batsmen played carefully and occasionally with some hesitation for a time after luncheon,

but the score rose steadily, and they soon appeared to have settled down comfortably. Mr Douglas bowled well, but Barnes was not at his best, and gave the batsmen far less trouble than Woolley. Mr Taylor's batting was consistently good and he hit all round the wicket, but with his score at 46 he was badly missed by Smith. Very soon after this escape he hit three successive balls from Barnes to the boundary.

"Barnes's wrath was something to behold" (Taylor). Was it here that the Taylor–Barnes duel entered folklore? Probably not.

Mr Nourse hit the first 6 of the match, a fine pull off Woolley's bowling. The partnership put on a hundred runs in an hour and 25 minutes, and with the total at 131 for two wickets, the tea interval was reached, Mr Taylor having made 73 and Mr Nourse 37.

After tea Mr Taylor hit 13 runs off one over from Barnes, who was taken off in favour of Hearne.

More likely here. Taylor claimed that as he was about to take strike for another over Barnes took his cap from the umpire, threw the ball to the ground, made some rude remarks about Taylor — and stalked off. Apologies to Taylor from Douglas. "We were later told that Barnes had stormed into the dressing-room, whipped off his shirt and had a nice wash-up. Then he stretched himself out and drank several whiskies!"

Mr Taylor scored 8 off the new bowler's first over and continued to hit freely as he approached his century. He had made exactly a hundred when he was smartly caught in the slips by Woolley at 172. In his splendid innings he hit eleven 4's and three 3's. Twelve runs later Mr Nourse was caught for a fine innings of 59. With the score at 194 Mr Carter was caught off Barnes's bowling, and at 209 Mr D Taylor was dismissed also by Barnes, but with Mr Arbuthnot and Mr Tuckett together the remaining runs were hit off without further loss.

NATAL v. MCC
Durban, 7, 9 and 10 February 1913

MCC

1st innings

Mr M.C. Bird	b Cox	4
Rhodes	b Carter	7
Hearne	lbw b Tuckett	12
Mead	lbw b Carter	15
Mr J.W.H.T. Douglas	b Tuckett	24
The Hon L.H. Tennyson	b Tuckett	34
Woolley	lbw b Carter	23
Relf	b Cox	4
Booth	lbw b Cox	0
Smith	b Carter	1
Barnes	not out	1
Extras		7
Total		132

2nd innings

Mr M.C. Bird	c Arbuthnot b Carter	27
Rhodes	c Nourse b Carter	28
Hearne	c Tuckett b Chapman	7
Mead	b Easterbrook	29
Mr J.W.H.T. Douglas	lbw b Easterbrook	23
The Hon L.H. Tennyson	lbw b Carter	19
Woolley	b Chapman	20
Relf	c Arbuthnot b Carter	4
Booth	lbw b Carter	22
Smith	b Carter	15
Barnes	not out	1
Extras		30
Total		235

NATAL BOWLING

1st innings

Cox 3 for 29, Nourse 0 for 14, Tuckett 3 for 26, Taylor 0 for 1, Carter 4 for 32, Chapman 0 for 13, Easterbrook 0 for 10

2nd innings

Cox 0 for 43, Nourse 0 for 26, Carter 6 for 58, Tuckett 0 for 16, Chapman 2 for 34, Easterbrook 2 for 28

NATAL

1st innings

Mr H. Chapman	c Smith b Relf	11
Mr H.W. Taylor	c Mead b Bird	91
Mr D. Pearse	c Woolley b Barnes	0
Mr A.D. Nourse	c Woolley b Relf	3
Mr D. Taylor	lbw b Barnes	8
Mr Arbuthnot	c Rhodes b Barnes	7
Mr C.P. Carter	c Rhodes b Relf	8
Mr J. Easterbrook	c & b Barnes	2
Mr D. Nicol	c Douglas b Barnes	0
Mr L.R. Tuckett	c Bird b Relf	6
Mr J.L. Cox	not out	0
Extras		17
Total		153

2nd innings

Mr H. Chapman	b Douglas	6
Mr H.W. Taylor	c Woolley b Hearne	100
Mr D. Pearse	c Douglas b Booth	4
Mr A.D. Nourse	c Tennyson b Woolley	59
Mr D. Taylor	b Barnes	23
Mr Arbuthnot	not out	3
Mr C.P. Carter	c Woolley b Barnes	0
Mr L.R. Tuckett	not out	6
Extras		15
Total	(6 wkts)	216

MCC BOWLING

1st innings

Barnes 5 for 44, Relf 4 for 59, Woolley 0 for 9, Douglas 0 for 3, Hearne 0 for 15, Bird 1 for 9.

2nd innings

Barnes 2 for 70, Douglas 1 for 27, Booth 1 for 6, Relf 0 for 28, Hearne 1 for 37, Woolley 1 for 24, Bird 0 for 9.

NATAL WON BY 4 WICKETS

In old age Taylor likened the pace of Barnes in 1913–14 to that of E.J. Barlow, the South African all-rounder of the 1960s. Taylor's mastery on home wickets was never in doubt; by the end of his career he had played 36 innings against England, facing bowlers such as A.E.R. Gilligan, Kennedy, Jupp, Fender and Macaulay in 1922–3, Geary, Peebles, Astill, Freeman and S.J. Staples in 1927–8 and Voce, Tate, Peebles and J.C. White in 1930–31 — with an average of 51.45. If not as successful in England, where South Africa did not win a Test until 1935 (after Taylor's retirement), he still impressed. At Headingley in 1924 he made 59 not out and run out 56 from the bowling of Gilligan, Tate, Macaulay, Richard Tyldesley, Hearne and Woolley.

MR TAYLOR IN HIS BEST FORM

15 July 1924. Having put four men out for 34, England were in a position to play the winning game, and played it well, although Mr Taylor and Mr Catterall batted extremely well and made a useful stand. The stroke which Mr Taylor played to the first ball bowled to him showed that he was in his best form. Tate pitched the ball on the off stump, a few inches short of the ideal length; Mr Taylor drew himself up and, with a long back stroke, forced it at amazing speed past cover-point to the boundary. He did not repeat this particular stroke, but he showed us all the others, executed as all the books, both ancient and modern, prescribe. The moderns might, perhaps, suggest that some of them should not be attempted early in an innings, but, as made by Mr Taylor, they were as safe as they were graceful and edifying.

Five years later at the age of 40, he faced, among others, Geary, E.W. Clark and Freeman at the Oval.

By A.C.M. Croome

20 August 1929. The appearance of the telegraph board, three for 20, was not encouraging, and H.W. Taylor did not start his subsequently magnificent innings as if he were destined to improve it. Like Catterall, he shortened his usually free back-lift for the occasion while watching for the specially dangerous ball. Consequently he jabbed at two, if not three, outside his off stump, making a stroke which schoolboys are told can only be profitable by accident, and may be a means of suicide. However, he escaped disaster. Deane, as usual, prepared to prefer the interests of his side to his own convenience, came in himself at the fall of the third wicket, and cracked his duck before luncheon.

After the interval we were privileged to watch an exhibition of batting which, whatever criteria be adopted, must be described as altogether admirable. The technical excellence of the strokes made and the judgment which inspired the selection of them were so faultless that in the course of a stand which put on 214 runs and lasted for nearly 2½ hours the ball was only twice lifted off the ground by the bat.

The courage of the batsmen was as impressive as their technique...The Taylor seen in the afternoon was the Taylor whom Barnes is said to have selected as about the best batsman to whom he has ever bowled, confident, free, and masterful. Deane, if not quite so polished, was certainly not less determined and discreet. The pair dealt with every ball sent to them strictly on its merits. They rarely employed the hook stroke because, with the exception of Freeman, no bowler was guilty of the long-hop, and Freeman did not exceed the slow leg-breaker's fair ration. They did little cutting, since the ball suitable for the cut did not come their way, and they did not send the over-pitched ball crashing into the boundary behind the bowler. But they scored persistently on the leg side by extraordinarily deft placing of pushes and glides. They kept deep third man busy by back strokes played at the last possible moment, and when they came forward, the swing of the fluent bat was long enough and firm enough to beat the in-fielders at frequent intervals and yield a satisfactory crop of driven 4's.

Taylor's theorizing on the subject of body-line may have been due to his experiences the previous season, 1931–2, when the South Africans toured Australia and lost all five Tests. Taylor made 78 and 84 in the Adelaide match with Grimmett and O'Reilly in harness. But 42 was no age for chasing strokes made by Bradman — 806 runs with an average of 201.50. Possibly Taylor felt out of sorts when Australians were mentioned; the thought of them playing forward to Larwood's short-pitched deliveries was an intriguing one.

SIR JOHN BERRY HOBBS
Surrey

Hobbs was often regarded as the perfect batsman. "Those who played with and against him," wrote John Arlott, "generally considered him — in all conditions, on all pitches and against all types of bowling — the finest batsman." D.R. Jardine called him "The Master". His extraordinary career can perhaps best be explained by a remark of Learie Constantine's, that the great English professional batsmen of the inter-war years (Hobbs, Woolley, Mead, Hendren, Ernest Tyldesley, Sutcliffe, *et al.*) reached their peak at 35 and, so consummate was their technique, remained there for at least another seven years. (Hammond was about to confirm this contention when the Second World War intervened.) Hobbs celebrated his 35th birthday on 16 December 1917, and made the last of his 197 hundreds on 28 May 1934. Because the First World War divided his career with rare precision into two halves — 647 innings before 1914, 668 innings after 1918 — an analysis of the Hobbs miracle, or absurdity, is in order.

CAREER 1905–34 (aged 22–51)
1315 innings   106 NO   61,237 runs   50.65 av.
Pre-1914–18 (aged 22–31)

	Innings	NO	Runs	Av.
Total	647	43	25,587	42.36
Home	565	38	21,085	40.00
Abroad	82	5	4,502	58.46

Post-1914–18 (aged 36–51)

	Innings	NO	Runs	Av.
Total	668	63	35,650	58.92
Home	614	60	32,899	59.81
Abroad	54	3	2,751	53.94

100s
197 (1 in 6.67 innings):
in England 175 (1 in 6.73 innings)
abroad 22 (1 in 6.18 innings)

Pre-1914–18

Total	65 (1 in 9.95 innings)
Home	52 (1 in 10.36 innings)
Abroad	13 (1 in 6.30 innings)

Post-1914–18

Total	132 (1 in 5.06 innings)
Home	123 (1 in 4.99 innings)
Abroad	9 (1 in 6.00 innings)

CAREER IN TESTS 1907–30
(aged 25–47)
102 innings   7NO   5,410 runs   56.94 av.
Pre-1914–18 (aged 25–31)

	Innings	NO	Runs	Av.
Total	49	6	2,465	57.32
Home	15	2	519	39.92
Abroad	34	4	1,946	64.86

Post-1914–18 (aged 38–47)

	Innings	NO	Runs	Av.
Total	53	1	2,945	56.63
Home	25	1	1,416	59.00
Abroad	28	0	1,529	54.60

100s in Tests
15 (1 in 6.8 innings):
in England 5 (1 in 8 innings)
abroad 10 (1 in 6.2 innings)

Pre-1914–18

Total	5 (1 in 9.8 innings)
Home	1 (1 in 15 innings)
Abroad	4 (1 in 8.5 innings)

Post-1914–18

Total	10 (1 in 5.3 innings)
Home	4 (1 in 6.25 innings)
Abroad	6 (1 in 4.66 innings)

Hobbs, with his customary modesty, would dismiss his mounting success after the First World War; the bowling was not as good as it had been before 1914, and he scored his runs increasingly from the back foot. Although both contentions were undoubtedly true, modesty can be carried too far.

HOBBS AND "OLD AGE"

	Innings	NO	Runs	Av.	100s
Before 40	817	59	34,796	45.90	99 (1 in 8.25 innings)
After 40	498	47	26,441	58.62	98 (1 in 5.06 innings)
Before 45	1,057	80	47,456	48.57	146 (1 in 7.23 innings)
After 45	258	26	13,781	59.40	51 (1 in 5.05 innings)

Lest the before and after 45 figures are deemed misleading, one would merely point out that Hobbs really did become even more effective with the passing of years — that during his age span 36–44 he played 410 innings (average 58.63), whereas between the ages of 45 and 50 he played 240 innings (average 61.19).

HOBBS AND W.G. ALL SQUARE

By E.H.D. Sewell

18 August 1925. There was a thoroughly interesting day's cricket at Taunton yesterday, when a huge crowd assembled in the hope and expectation of seeing Hobbs score his 126th hundred and so equal Dr W.G. Grace's record of centuries. Hobbs had made 91 not out on Saturday and at 11.37 yesterday morning he duly accomplished this feat after play had been in progress for 12 minutes. Surrey's first innings ended at 2.35 for 359 and, making light of their deficit of 192, Somerset made 256 for three wickets by the close of play, Mr MacBryan playing a magnificent innings.

J.C.W. MacBryan played once for England, against South Africa at Old Trafford in 1924. Rain prevented the home side from batting. MacBryan's father, Dr Henry MacBryan, was almost certainly the model for P.G. Wodehouse's looney doctor, Sir Roderick Glossop.

The best cricket of the day and the match came in the afternoon, when Mr MacBryan, playing England cricket, and Young were making 184 for Somerset's first wicket in their second innings. The late start was due to the fact that the authorities wished to give as many spectators as possible a chance of witnessing Hobbs's feat, if it was to be done.

At 11 o'clock the queue at the gate was nearly half-a-mile long. In obtaining the necessary nine runs Hobbs had 17 balls bowled to him in the course of five overs. With three singles, a 4 off a no-ball, and two more singles he reached his hundred. The crowd gave him a very warm reception and the Somerset players crowded round to congratulate him. After Mr Fender had taken him out a drink, the exact nature of which was not disclosed, the game proceeded, Hobbs playing the next six balls from Mr Robertson-Glasgow without scoring. Three overs later he was very well caught on the leg-side by Mr Hill.

It is as well to give the complete details of this historic innings. Hobbs batted for two hours and 50 minutes and scored off 59 of the 192 balls bowled to him, hitting eight 4's, two 3's, 12 2's, and 39 singles. He gave only one catch, when he had made 14, but narrowly escaped being run out at 87, when Mr Knight sacrificed his wicket for him, and again at 90. By scoring this hundred Hobbs equals the late W.G. Grace's total of centuries, but has now to make 19 more to equal Dr Grace's total of hundreds in first-class cricket in this country. He also equalled the 13 centuries in a season scored by Mr C.B. Fry, Tom Hayward, and Hendren. He received a great ovation on retiring to the pavilion to cope with a deluge of telegrams.

After the tension of Hobbs's hundred, the dismissal of Mr Jardine, who might have been caught in the slips twice in one over off Mr Robertson-Glasgow when he had made 32 and 34 respectively, came as a slight relief. Mr Fender, hitting at everything, skied a ball towards square leg. Mr Hill started for the impossible catch, doffing his hat in the first few yards. Having run ten yards he flung away one glove and a little farther on he flung away the second one, thus blazing his trail with articles of attire. He was, however, unable to grab the ball as it fell. In the meanwhile Mr Fender and Mr Jardine were ambling up and down the wicket; at last Mr Hill got to the ball, and returned it to mid-on; the batsmen attempted a fourth run, but Mr Ingle's return to the bowler being accurate. Mr Jardine was run out. Mr Fender made several glorious strokes during his stay of 50 minutes, his straight and off driving being magnificent. He was mainly responsible for the third hundred being scored in 40 minutes.

Peach was striking frequently and well when he turned a ball on to his wicket at 322, and Mr Fender, in the following over, was well stumped at 325. At the luncheon interval the score was 331 for eight wickets. The Surrey innings ended soon after the interval. Somerset's out-cricket was splendid, the ground fielding and throwing-in both being good, and the bowlers were very wise to keep the ball so straight for Hobbs.

It is noteworthy in concluding this description of a day's cricket that will become historic that it was against Somerset at Bristol in May, 1895, that Dr Grace scored his hundredth century. He made 288 out of 474, and the Somerset wicket-keeper, the Rev. A.P. Wickham, said that during Dr Grace's innings he had only four balls to take. In this respect there is parity between Dr Grace's 288 and Hobb's 101, for it is probable that Mr Hill did not have more than 12 balls to handle behind Hobbs.

Next day Somerset left Surrey 182 to win. Sandham, though scoring well himself, saw to it that Hobbs received a generous share of the bowling; The Master reached his second hundred of the match in 2 hours 25 minutes (his first had taken ten minutes longer), thus beating W.G.'s number of centuries.

SOMERSET 167 (A. Young 58) and 374 (J.C.W. MacBryan 109, A. Young 71, G. Hunt 59; P.G.H. Fender 5 for 120) lost to SURREY 359 (J.B. Hobbs 101, P.G.H. Fender 59) and 183 for none (J.B. Hobbs 101 not out, A. Sandham 74 not out) by 10 wickets.

JACK HOBBS AT 70 NOT OUT

By John Hartley

16 December 1952. John Berry Hobbs is 70 today. This astonishing fact has come as a surprise to many lovers of cricket for whom the memory of this legendary figure is still as green as the Oval table in the days, not so long ago, when he stood slim and erect in the middle and the runs flowed in an effortless stream from his bat.

To Hobbs himself the achievement of three-score years and 10 has come as no less of a surprise. But for the publicity it has aroused and the requests for interviews — such as the one he gave to your Correspondent — the date might have passed unnoticed. For at 70 he is still slim, still alert and nimble; there is scarcely a line of his face and his hair is not, as he claims, "picked up eleven-a-side."

As a batsman Jack Hobbs was always a delight to watch. He attacked the bowling, scored freely and fast, except when occasion demanded he should just stay there, and he delighted in short runs. He had a zest and passionate enjoyment for cricket as a game which was transmitted to the crowd. He has always been modest, but, having decided to delve into the past as a form of birthday celebration, he has brought up memories and comments all reflecting a love of the game.

From his early days he was a natural batsman. His father was groundsman at Jesus College, Cambridge, and in Jesus Close he used to practise hitting the ball. He would set up a stump as a wicket, and with a stump as a bat would get a friend to bowl to him with a tennis ball — "and stumps were thin in those days, too."

His trial and acceptance for Surrey came on Tom Hayward's recommendation after an unofficial trial on Parker's Piece, where a wicket was set up and Hayward and Reeves (of Essex) bowled to him. In his first game for Surrey, against the Gentlemen, Hobbs came up against Dr W.G. Grace. "I had never seen him before, except at a distance. It was a very proud moment for me when I faced up to him. He bowled those donkey drops of his. I cannot say I found him difficult; but I did not take any liberties with him, I must admit."

In his next match — against Essex — he made a century. "I thought I knew it all then. Later I found I did not. Opening with Tom Hayward, I learned what balls to leave alone and what to go for. I learned the scoring strokes to improve and those to drop." Later he came to prefer other partners. "Poor old Tom, he did not like the short run, he was too heavy. It was lovely with Wilfred Rhodes when we started the short run business. Sutcliffe and Sandham liked cheeky runs, too. I think a lot of short runs are missed these days."

Jack Hobbs looks on the period 1910–14 as his most brilliant. He could attack the bowling with zest when he felt like it. "You could play cheeky shots and make 50 or 60 and feel life was worth living. Then came the exasperation when they started counting your hundreds, publishing averages, and it was all figures. They think too much of figures these days." This from the man who made more runs than anyone else has ever done — 61,237 — and whose 197 first-class centuries is also a record.

Batsmen today have all Hobbs's sympathy. Bowling has become defensive and wickets are slower. In-swingers across the wicket from outside the leg-stump do not give batsmen a chance. "If you try to glide them now you get caught, and all the beautiful shots on the off-side that one used to see have been shut up. An off-drive by Hutton or Compton is something to admire, but you no longer get much wristy cutting. It is much easier to stay in now, but not so easy to score runs. Players like Hayward would have adapted themselves to it, but Hayward would have been a bit better than most today. I think I might have adapted myself. I do not see why I should not also have scored runs."

There was fast bowling in the old days. "A fast bowler today is an event. They tell you the wicket is too easy paced, but a fast bowler is a necessity; he is always likely to get a wicket at the beginning of an innings. Pace bowlers are still the same type, but they have lost a bit of their devil. If Trueman keeps free from injury he should 'make the grade.'"

The game is more commercialized now, he says. There must be good gates and lively cricket is necessary. Surrey played lively cricket last summer and had some handsome gates. He did not want to compare the team of last year with that in which he played when Surrey last won the county championship in 1914. "I do not think we were inferior, but they played magnificently last summer and gave me a thrill or two. There is such a good spirit in the side."

The difference between players then and now is not so much of quality as of quantity. "There were more stars then; many good amateurs are lost now because of high costs and taxes." But English teams have been improving since the war. "With young Len Hutton as skipper we have the best chance of beating the Australians next summer than we have had for years. The Australians seem to be in the doldrums now; with an even break in the luck, we should win. They do not seem to have as many good players as in the Bradman era.

"Bradman was a team in himself. I think Don was too good; he spoilt the game. He got too many runs. The pot calling the kettle black? No, I was human; he got hundreds every time he went in. I did cheer the hearts of the bowlers even in my most palmy days. He was mechanical; he was the greatest run-getting machine of all time. I do not think we want to see another one quite like him. I do not think we ever shall."

Hobbs spoke of his favourite strokes. "We always liked to hook a good ball. Then I liked a good square cut, you could get a lot of power into it, it was a beautiful shot to make. I liked a cover drive, but..." he paused and gave a slow smile, "you like them all when you can hit them hard."

Of all the bowling he faced he preferred the googlies above all. "They put you on your mettle and there is always a loose one — and then you crack it." Sydney Barnes was perhaps the best bowler of all and would have been even better on present wickets.

Hobbs qualified two comments that have been made on his game — his improved fielding, and a tendency to be lbw.* It was said that he developed suddenly from a comparatively poor fielder into the most brilliant cover-point of his generation. He denies he was ever poor. "I had a minor injury — I had thrown my arm out — and nobody knew about it at the time." The way he used often to be out he explains on the ground that to play a straight bat he had to stand behind the flight of the ball. Sometimes he missed it. "If you miss a straight ball, you get out. Some people get bowled, I was lbw."

He really enjoyed the Tests, but it is not always the big occasions that are fixed in his memory. His most enjoyable innings was in a private match in 1921 when he played for Lionel Robinson's XI against a side captained by MacLaren which included Australians. Everything went right and he felt he could not get out. After making 87 [85] he retired hurt, having pulled a muscle going for a desperate run.

Hobbs remembers every innings he played on a bad wicket. There was the terrible "sticky" at Melbourne on the 1928–29 tour when he and Sutcliffe put on over 100 for the first wicket after people had prophesied that England would be out for under 70. England won by four wickets. He considers his most valuable innings was that at the Oval in 1926 when he and Sutcliffe each made centuries on a bad wicket and England won the rubber against Australia for the first time for 14 years.

....

* One might as well be lbw as bowled; the outcome is the same. Consider these dismissals, percentage figures based on completed first-class innings:

	Grace	Hobbs	Bradman
Bowled	31.63	23.66	26.44
LBW	3.89	10.34	9.15
Total	35.52	34.00	35.59

He will never forget the game against Kent at the Oval in 1919 when he and Jack Crawford, batting against the clock, made 90-odd in 35 minutes and the crowd went mad. He remembers the excitement when he needed a hundred to equal Grace's record of 126 centuries. It was a long time coming; then he scored 91 one day at Taunton and had to make nine the next morning. "We started a quarter of an hour late while they let the crowd in. I remember feeling a bit jittery waiting." He recalls his highest score, 316 not out at Lord's in 1926 at the age of 43. "I did not get tired. I never got tired batting, though cricket is a game of intense concentration."

When Jack Hobbs retired in 1934 after making 197 centuries, regret was expressed universally; but he was certain then, as now, that he was right. "I gave up before my 200th century because I thought I had outstayed my usefulness with the Surrey side. You cannot go on for ever keeping people out of the side. Also I did not want to be an object of sympathy. Some people said I was playing as well as ever, but I knew how I felt, what I could and could not do. Looking back, though, it is a pity I did not get the 200; I should like to have been the first."

Jack Hobbs was a cricket idol then. Today he is a sporting legend.

Hobbs was knighted in the Coronation Honours of 1953.

MASTER AT THE WICKET

23 December 1963, leading article. Sadness at the death of SIR JOHN HOBBS is of the mellow, reflective kind that so often came over an Oval crowd at the drawing of stumps on a Saturday after the master had given of his best. Lord's is not the only ground over which Father Time broods with his scythe; every innings must close and that of the great cricketer who has now gone from us was played through to the end with unfailing sense of style. On and off the field, in the

HOBBS & SUTCLIFFE   The old firm sartorially here, as ever in practice, in mourning for bowlers.

Reminded recently that he had been top of the first-class bowling averages in 1920, he replied with a typical glancing shot: "I had bowled a bit for Cambridgeshire, you know, and got a few wickets as a young chap." Nobody ever heard HOBBS boast. He looked back on the four seasons before the First War as his happiest. But those who saw him only in the twenties and later would not exchange their memories of him at the wicket or at cover-point with those of watching any other player. He was an artist in every movement. He gave delight whether he was making one of those daring strokes that would have been suicide for a lesser batsman or gliding rhythmically to gather a ball that most fielders would have let go to the boundary. To see him on an easy wicket sending the ball at all angles to the boundary was good and to be there on a testing day for batsmen even better. HOBBS was never greater than in militant defence, while his partners followed one another in procession to the pavilion.

He has died just after his eighty-first birthday in dark December. The aptest tribute to him is to say that all who once watched him have only to close their eyes today to see him, a never-to-be-forgotten figure, white-flannelled, moving at his ease in the sunshine. The great ones of his day who have paid their personal tributes recall a golden age of cricket. HOBBS was the gold standard itself.

brilliance of youth, in towering prime, and on into old age HOBBS naturally, and unaffectedly rose to the occasion. When he retired in 1934 after making 197 centuries and murmurs were heard because he did not hang on for the 200th he remarked, "I thought I had out-stayed my usefulness with the Surrey side."

HERBERT SUTCLIFFE
Yorkshire

Sutcliffe was a great moral force among opening batsmen. Because of the First World War, he was 24 when he made his debut for Yorkshire; because of the paucity of Tests, it was another five years before he played for England. Thereafter he reigned. More than a thousand innings for Yorkshire saw him average 51, but in 46 Test innings against Australia (when that country provided the sternest opposition) he averaged 66.

W.J. O'Reilly summed him up: "A tremendously difficult bloke to get out. He would do things that would annoy you, turn the ball off the middle of his bat to gully, for instance. He had a magnificent temperament and was virtually unrattlable. You could leave him for dead with a ball and he'd almost leer at you."[*]

Sutcliffe believed in the divine right of Sutcliffe; it so happened that his first partner for England was Hobbs. Here chronology is ignored, Hobbs and Sutcliffe at Melbourne 1928–9 taking precedence over Hobbs and Sutcliffe at the Oval, 1926. The aim is to pave the way for another appearance by Rhodes, the hero — or near-hero — of any book whose pages he graces.

MIRACLE AT MELBOURNE 1929

At the close of the fifth day (3 January 1929) of the Third Test at Melbourne the scores were Australia 397 and 347 for eight, England 417.

4 January 1929, Melbourne. A thunderstorm broke in the early hours of this morning, and was followed by a heavy shower at half-past 11. Although the sun came out soon afterwards, the gates were not opened until a few minutes before noon. After the two captains disagreed about the conditions at 12.30 p.m., the umpires decided play should begin at once. White then took the two remaining Australian wickets, the home side being out for 351, so leaving England to score 332.

4 January 1929, Melbourne. No finer exhibition of batting in such special circumstances than that given by Hobbs and Sutcliffe today has been seen for very many years. Called upon to begin a task which in favourable conditions demanded the exercise of great skill and determination, these two famous batsmen had to put England on the way towards obtaining no fewer than 332 runs on a really treacherous wicket. The Melbourne sticky wicket is a nasty affair; the ball not only turn but gets up almost straight, and like a flash. Indeed, it may be said to do everything but keep straight.

No Englishman on the ground, and certainly not one of the little band of men who, after quickly getting down two outstanding Australian wickets, saw Hobbs and Sutcliffe from the dressing-room windows, expected other than a beating. The hot sun on a rain-damaged pitch,

....

[*] *Time of the Tiger*, R.S. Whitington, p. 203.

which in England would have been considered unfit for cricket at the time the match was continued, had brought joy to the bowlers' hearts. Had England been out for 100 no one would have been surprised, but now, with the probability of a splendid wicket on which to bat tomorrow, they have to score less than half the required runs, and still have nine men to be dismissed. To Hobbs must be awarded the palm. It must be said at once that he enjoyed one piece of luck when Hendry missed him at slip, but that was the only mistake in a truly magnificent display. Here was a case of the old, experienced player fighting against trouble and coming out on top. He could not be caught by any tricks; his footwork was superb; and he showed younger and possibly more active players how it was possible to change the stroke almost at the last minute and still make it technically correctly. He managed cleverly to get most of the bowling, just as he had done at the Oval two years ago in less agonizing circumstances.

Sutcliffe, for his part, rose to the occasion wonderfully, playing easily his best innings of the tour, and the little doubts that were being expressed as to whether the two were still the great opening pair that they used to be are now ended for good. The fact that the Australians had no one able to take full advantage of the wicket does not detract from what was, to those who saw it, one of the most remarkable batting performances ever seen.

The Play

Soon after lunch, taken with England's score at three, Hobbs caused a thrill by giving a chance off Hendry in the slips, which was missed by a'Beckett. Blackie, who displaced Hendry at 19, began by bowling over the wicket, but, finding the ball was breaking too much, he changed to round the wicket after the first over and had three men placed close in on the leg-side in addition to the usual deep fieldsmen. Sutcliffe nearly fell into the trap, making a big hit on the on-side off Blackie,

which Woodfull just failed to reach. Off the next ball Hobbs took a very foolish risk in attempting a sharp run for a hit to mid on. Sutcliffe would most certainly have been run out if a better return had been sent in.

Oxenham bowled at a'Beckett's end at 24, and caused the batsmen a good deal of trouble by making the ball get up nastily close to their left elbows...At 39 he retired in favour of Hendry. In the new bowler's first over, Hobbs, when he had made 17, was nearly caught at fine-leg by Bradman who dived after the ball but failed to reach it. The 50 was sent up in an hour and a quarter...The wicket was doing all sorts of fancy tricks, and whatever the result of the match may be, the magnificent defensive methods of Hobbs and Sutcliffe will long be remembered as a wonderful performance.

While the pair were seeking England's salvation by diligence, Hobbs signalled to the pavilion for a new bat. Having tried it, he kept the one already in use; Hobbs was sending a message to his captain — if a wicket falls, Jardine should come next; save Hammond for the morrow. The Master clearly felt that England had a chance.

Ryder [fast-medium] replaced Oxenham at 70, and Hobbs, in trying to hit a rising ball from the Australian captain, was struck on the back of his head. Fortunately he was not much hurt, and was able to continue batting at once. At the tea interval 78 runs had been scored in an hour and 50 minutes, of which Hobbs had made 36 and Sutcliffe 32.

...The 100 went up in just under two hours and a quarter, this being the eighth three-figure opening partnership btween Hobbs and Sutcliffe in Test Matches between England and Australia. Blackie bowled again for Grimmett at 105, and Hobbs in playing forward to his fourth delivery missed the ball and was given out leg-before-wicket.

P.G.H. Fender's reaction was that Hobbs was most certainly out if the umpire felt the ball in question would have behaved differently from all previous balls and *not* risen over the stumps.

He had given a grand exhibition in the most difficult conditions, and the partnership will go down as one of the greatest in the history of the game. Hobbs scored his 49 in two hours and 18 minutes, and hit one 4.

Sutcliffe, who was then 42, was joined by Jardine. The ball was now not turning so much as

AUSTRALIA v. ENGLAND
Melbourne, 29 and 31 December 1928, 1–5 January 1929

AUSTRALIA
1st innings

W.M. Woodfull	c Jardine b Tate	7
V.Y. Richardson	c Duckworth b Larwood	3
H.L. Hendry	c Jardine b Larwood	23
A.F. Kippax	c Jardine b Larwood	100
J.S. Ryder	c Hendren b Tate	112
D.G. Bradman	b Hammond	79
W.A. Oldfield	b Geary	3
E.L. à Beckett	c Duckworth b White	41
R.K. Oxenham	b Geary	15
C.V. Grimmett	c Duckworth b Geary	5
D.D.J. Blackie	not out	2
Extras	(b 4, lb 3)	7
Total		397

2nd innings

W.M. Woodfull	c Duckworth b Tate	107
V.Y. Richardson	b Larwood	5
H.L. Hendry	st Duckworth b White	12
A.F. Kippax	b Tate	41
J.S. Ryder	b Geary	5
D.G. Bradman	c Duckworth b Geary	112*
W.A. Oldfield	b White	7
E.L. à Beckett	b White	6
R.K. Oxenham	b White	39
C.V. Grimmett	not out	4
D.D.J. Blackie	b White	0
Extras	(b 6, lb 7)	13
Total		351

Fall of wickets: 1–5, 2–15, 3–57, 4–218, 5–282, 6–287, 7–373, 8–383, 9–394, 10–397.

Second innings: 1–7, 2–60, 3–138, 4–143, 5–201, 6–226, 7–252, 8–345, 9–351, 10–351.

ENGLAND BOWLING (6-ball overs)

	O	M	R	W	O	M	R	W
Larwood	37	3	127	3	16	3	37	1
Tate	46	17	87	2	47	15	70	2
Geary	31.5	4	83	3	30	4	94	2
Hammond	8	4	19	1	16	6	30	0
White	57	30	64	1	56.5	20	107	5
Jardine	1	0	10	0				

ENGLAND
1st innings

J.B. Hobbs	c Oldfield b à Beckett	20
H. Sutcliffe	b Blackie	58
W.R. Hammond	c à Beckett b Blackie	200
A.P.F. Chapman	b Blackie	24
E. Hendren	c à Beckett b Hendry	19
D.R. Jardine	c & b Blackie	62
H. Larwood	c & b Blackie	0
G. Geary	lbw b Grimmett	1
M.W. Tate	c Kippax b Grimmett	21
G. Duckworth	b Blackie	3
J.C. White	not out	8
Extras	(b 1)	1
Total		417

2nd innings

J.B. Hobbs	lbw b Blackie	49
H. Sutcliffe	lbw b Grimmett	135
D.R. Jardine	b Grimmett	33
W.R. Hammond	run out	32
E. Hendren	b Oxenham	45
A.P.F. Chapman	c Woodfull b Ryder	5
M.W. Tate	run out	0
G. Geary	not out	4
G. Duckworth	not out	0
Extras	(b 15, lb 14)	29
Total	(7 wkts)	332

Fall of wickets: 1–28, 2–161, 3–201, 4–238, 5–364, 6–381, 7–381, 8–385, 9–391, 10–417.

Second innings: 1–105, 2–199, 3–257, 4–318, 5–326, 6–328, 7–328.

AUSTRALIA BOWLING

	O	M	R	W	O	M	R	W
à Beckett	37	7	92	1	22	5	39	0
Hendry	20	8	35	1	23	5	33	0
Grimmett	55	14	114	2	42	12	96	2
Oxenham	35	11	67	0	28	10	44	1
Blackie	44	13	94	6	39	11	75	1
Ryder	4	0	14	0	5.5	1	16	1

Umpires: D. Elder and G. Hele

ENGLAND WON BY 3 WICKETS
....

* Bradman's first Test hundred came in his fourth innings for Australia. Thereafter he improved — a hundred every 2.71 innings.

previously, but its pace off the pitch was quicker, Blackie in particular making it rise very sharply...The close of play was reached with the total 171 for one — Sutcliffe 83 and Jardine 18.

Next day, after many trials and tribulations, England struggled to an historic victory.

THE OVAL TEST, 1926

The first day of the final Test was one of the most eccentric in the annals of England–Australia games. Because the previous Tests had the two sides level, that at the Oval would be played to a finish. In spite of this, England got themselves out in four and a quarter hours on a perfect pitch, their scoring rate being 66 runs an hour. The Australian bowling rate was almost 23 overs an hour.

By A.C.M. Croome

16 August 1926. In spite of rain during the week, the wicket at the Oval was in first-rate order on Saturday when the fifth and deciding Test Match was begun. At the close of play England had scored 280 and had dismissed four of their most dangerous opponents for 60.

On the first day of the "Go as you please" Test Match they were pleased to go at the gallop: 340 runs were scored and 14 wickets fell. The figures speak for themselves. They indicate truthfully that the play was crammed with incidents. It is not easy to account for all those seen and noted, except by supposing that the Imp of the Perverse decided to take a hand in the game. It was his whim that the run of the luck should persistently favour the fielding side. Here is the tale of events which support that theory set out in chronological order.

Hobbs batted divinely for an hour and then missed a slow full pitch directed at his leg stump and was clean bowled. I know this thing happened, because I saw it myself. Hendren, as soon as he had taken guard, started at once to deal

with each ball strictly on its merits. He did not wait till he had "got a sight of the ball" before retiring in the direction of short leg and testing the quality of Mr Mailey's off-side fielders. But in the last over before luncheon he cut at a long hop of rather more than medium pace and dragged it into his stumps. After the interval Mr Chapman played the innings of the day and put his side in the ascendant. I have never before seen him watch the ball so closely in making his defensive strokes or pick the one to hit with such wise discrimination. Yet at the critical moment he jumped short at a ball 2ft wide of his off stump, and was out, stumped through an error of judgment committed on a day when he was unprecedentedly judgmatical. Mr Stevens, definitely a Test Match player, was re-establishing the temporarily lost ascendancy when he, too, fell to an error of judgment. He hit Mr Mailey high into the pavilion for 6. The next ball, to all appearance, was identical with its predecessor, and Mr Stevens pushed it gently to silly mid-off. It looked as if, before the ball was bowled, he had made up his mind to apply a defensive stroke to it. Geary was batting like a No. 1 when he was run out through a misunderstanding that would not occur once in a month.

The Australians can also cite two instances in which their batsmen were victimized. Mr Macartney had apparently begun one of his match-winning innings, and was just reaching the stage when he, not the bowler, determines the length and direction of the ball. He turned one which was not very far short of a length into a long hop, and pulled it into his stumps, not, as was his intention, to the boundary in front of square-leg. Mr Ponsford was batting comfortably when he called his partner for a desperately short run, and failed to recover his crease when justifiably ordered to return to it.

If further proof that the Perverse informed the play is required it can be supplied. The top score was made by the man who obviously was in less good form than all, save one, of his successive partners. To say that is to pay Sutcliffe a very high compliment. Neither he, nor any other Yorkshireman, can take offence if a Southerner affirms that one of his second-best innings saved England. The termination of it was unlucky, for he tapped himself on the nose with his bat in playing the ball next before that which defeated him. He wasted no time before resuming his stance at the wicket. It may be that his eyes were still watering, and it was ordained that Mr Mailey should send down one of his best leg-breaks, which beat the tentatively offered bat. The only batsman who enjoyed a palpable piece of luck was Rhodes. Probably he was unprepared for the demonstration of affectionate good will which welcomed him. He played at his first ball as one completely unnerved by the occasion, and spooned it gently over silly mid-on for a single. However, a sergeant-major of the Old Guard does not make two mistakes on parade. Rhodes subsequently batted extremely well. He was always looking for runs, and made 28 in little more than half an hour, a pace which he does not always attain when there is a time limit.

These incidents occurred on a pitch which must have been a batsman's paradise. Mr Gregory could not make the ball rise more than stump high. Mr Richardson and Mr Macartney came straight on to the bat, however much their actions in delivery might portend a break back. Mr Mailey and Mr Grimmett turned the ball appreciably, and Mr Mailey gave as fine an exhibition of slow bowling as we have seen or are likely to see for many a long day. Mr Grimmett's efforts, admirable as they were, might have gone unrewarded had Mr Collins done the obvious thing and put on Mr Gregory after the fall of the seventh wicket...

Close: ENGLAND 280 (H. Sutcliffe 76; A.A. Mailey 6 for 138), AUSTRALIA 60 for 4 (W.M. Woodfull 22 not out, H.L. Collins 1 not out).

On the second day Australia recovered from 122 for six to 302, England in their second innings were 49 for none (J.B. Hobbs 28, H. Sutcliffe 20).

HOBBS AND SUTCLIFFE
Third Day

18 August 1926. The Prince of Wales visited his Oval [should his great-nephew, Prince Charles, visit the Oval, it will not be his but the spiritual home of an Australian brewery] yesterday and lunched with the contending teams. He saw part of an extraordinarily good batting performance by Hobbs and Sutcliffe, and when he had to leave the ground at 3 o'clock, England were on the way to victory. Before the close of play, however, the pertinacity of the Australians was rewarded. They have got down six of our wickets and are now 353 runs in arrear. It may be that today and tomorrow they must tackle a heavy, but not a hopeless, task. In the last quarter of an hour yesterday Sutcliffe, having batted since 5.30 p.m. on Monday, was bowled by Mr Mailey, and England's expectation of 500 runs became a hope for 450.

The story of the third day's play begins with the tropical rain which fell in the small hours of Tuesday morning and awakened thousands of England's supporters to blasphemy. For the first hour of play the sky was cloudy and the light dull. Hobbs and Sutcliffe were fairly comfortable during this period. Then the sun came out, and the pitch from noon to half-past 1 was horrid. Mr Grimmett, Mr Macartney, Mr Richardson, and Mr Mailey, to name them in the order of their going on, bowled on it each of them as well as he knows how. But our two opening batsmen remained masters of their fate throughout. Their artistry in manipulation of the bat was consummate, their judgment infallible, their patience inexhaustible. Before they started their performance I should, if I had been given my choice of all the pairs who have ever gone in first for England, have selected Dr W.G. Grace and Shrewsbury to bat for my side in the existing circumstances. Now I consider reincarnation unnecessary. I also consider that I have done my best to render to Hobbs and Sutcliffe the gratitude due to them from the community of English cricketers.

Mr Grimmett and Mr Macartney started bowling to them, and in the former's first over third man was called up to stand at second slip rather wide, an eloquent manoeuvre. For both bowlers the offside was practically blocked, and Mr Andrews at silly mid-off prevented the stealing of short singles. Hobbs twice hit Mr Grimmett to leg for 4, but 40 minutes passed before Sutcliffe scored. With the score at 80 Mr Richardson went on at the Vauxhall end. He placed Mr Andrews at forward cover-point, Mr Woodfull at mid-off, Mr Bardsley and Mr Ponsford at long leg. The rest of his fielders stood on a line from leg-slip to mid-on. Mr Richardson took a couple of overs to find his length, although he bowled a couple of trial balls to cover-point while his short legs were sorting themselves. Hobbs hooked him twice for 4, and with other clever strokes brought up the hundred* just before noon.

Then Mr Richardson went round the wicket, mid-on came up within six yards of the bat and two of the short legs went not twice that distance away. The inference was that the ball was expected to pop. And pop it did. Moreover, an occasional ball kept low and came on quickly. It was decreed that Hobbs should take eight consecutive overs from him. Mr Richardson is not the bowler that Mr Hugh Trumble was, but he is not palpably inferior to him in capacity to keep a length. He hammered away yesterday at the "blind" spot with an excellent persistency. Nearly every ball cut out a little fid of turf when it pitched. Hobbs, for his part, showed that it is almost a misuse of language to speak of any spot as "blind" when he is keyed up to give of his best. Runs were less important than time at this period of the match. What mattered was that no wicket should fall until the pitch had had a chance to dry. So it is no wonder that the pace of scoring was little more than 40 per hour. The most critical two hours were outstayed.

* Hobbs and Sutcliffe opened for England on 38 occasions, and passed 100 for the first wicket 15 times. Their average partnership was 84 against Australia and 98 against South Africa and West Indies.

It was very instructive to note the way in which Hobbs dealt with Mr Richardson. He stood nearly a foot wide of his leg stump, so that the bowler could not range on his pads. Then, when he had detected the length and pace of the ball, he glided — sometimes ran — into position for the appropriate stroke. Mr Macartney, when he came on at the Pavilion end, was very difficult. Half a dozen times or more he made the ball whip back at least the breadth of the stumps. Since it is now certain that he will lack opportunity to profit by the implied advice, it can do no harm to ask why a left-hander, when he can do that, should decline the advantage derivable from bowling round the wicket. Our openers came in to luncheon unparted, and they had put their side more than 120 ahead in what had become a single-innings match. After the interval Mr Gregory, to the general surprise, was put on at Mr Richardson's end. The spot which Mr Richardson had worn was too far on the leg side to be of any use to him, and his first two overs were easily and profitably played. But the event justified Mr Collins's tactics. Hobbs completed his hundred by laying down "chase better than the wicket-keeper," and the game was interrupted while the crowd applauded, finishing by giving him three formal cheers. In Mr Gregory's next over he was bowled by a ball which seemed to come back fast to graze his leg and flick the off-bail.

Woolley leant on the next ball and drove it hard to the on boundary. He obviously liked the fast bowling, which he found several opportunities to drive straight. So at 187 Mr Richardson came on again. Woolley at once snicked him over slip's head, a lucky stroke, but shortly afterwards brought up the second 100 with a grand leg hit off Mr Mailey. He continued to deal adequately with the leg-breaks but was never comfortable when facing Mr Richardson. At 220 he covered up and missed the ball. He was ruled out leg-before-wicket and retired. Hendren was Sutcliffe's next partner, and the pair did some very smart running between wickets. Hereabouts Sutcliffe became quite aggressive. He actually took a risk with Mr Richardson and mowed him very hard for four to long leg. Mr Gregory relieved him at 241 and a new ball was requisitioned. Sutcliffe promptly hit it twice to the leg boundary, and Mr Richardson was soon back again. Hendren put us 250 ahead by driving him straight for four, but he was not quite comfortable with the slow stuff. He had not begun to step back and slash it on the off-side when he barely touched Mr Grimmett's googly and was bowled. Mr Oldfield caught the ball and possibly a bail or two as well, but could not be credited with the wicket.

Mr Chapman, like Woolley, hit his first ball for 4 and, also like Woolley, skied one in the slips; Mr Gregory reached it, but slipped in the effort and failed to hold it. He made some other powerful hits and Mr Woodfull in the effort to reach one of them, strained a leg and had to retire. Unfortunately Mr Chapman was shortly afterwards deceived by the pace of Mr Richardson's fast ball. Mr Stevens came in and for the better part of an hour played exactly the right game. He knew, none better, how nice it would be if he and Sutcliffe could start afresh on the morn's morn. Nor could he have a better model to imitate than his partner, whose mental stamina enabled him, after nearly six hours' batting, to resist the temptation to score off any ball which could not be hit with absolute safety. All was for the best in the best of all possible worlds when Mr Stevens suddenly tried to hit Mr Grimmett's slowest into the Ladies' Pavilion and gave an easy catch to cover-point. Worse was to come. In the last over of the day Sutcliffe misjudged Mr Mailey's performance, if not his intention. He played as a googly a ball which came straight on and disturbed his stumps.

I find I have omitted to enumerate Sutcliffe's brilliant scoring strokes. They constitute the least important feature of his innings. What every one who saw it will remember to his dying day is the graceful solidity of his defence, his subordination of self to side, and his almost uncanny wisdom.

The Australians have a fine batting side, but I am inclined to think that England has already made a winning score. I am the more encouraged to this belief because the law did not allow the Australians to use the heavy roller last night. In the absence of rain they will bat today on a faster wicket. But some of the top has been knocked off it, just at the places which will suit Rhodes, at least. Perhaps also the faster bowlers.

Close: ENGLAND 280 and 375 for 6 (J.B. Hobbs 100, H. Sutcliffe 161), AUSTRALIA 302.

...AND RHODES

Fourth Day

19 August 1926. We have won! And after all the lean years we were more than half-pleased. We began to cheer when the Australians' innings was little more than half over, and at the finish we charged, ten thousand of us, across the ground, and massed ourselves in front of the pavilion, where we shouted for the 11 men who had won the game, and for the Chairman of the Committee which selected them. We shouted even more loudly for Mr Collins and the members of his team. We wanted them to know that we appreciated the high standard of keenness and honourable conduct which they have set up and maintained in this and all their other matches.

This final Test match has been an extraordinarily interesting game. There were grounds for fearing that England had missed a golden opportunity by omitting to make at least 400 on the first day, after Mr Chapman had won the toss on a perfect Oval wicket. But the Australians declined the offered chance. In fact their later batsmen had to extricate the side from a nasty hole. Still it seemed likely that we should have to pay for Saturday's comparative failure in batting. The thunderstorm of Monday night, followed by hot sunshine on the following morning, produced a wicket on which 200 was a remarkably good score against first-rate bowling. Hobbs and Sutcliffe made more than that number between them and raised the aggregate of their combined scores in the last ten Test matches against Australia to something like 2,300. Every moment that has passed since they were parted has emphasized the magnitude of their performance. England's last nine wickets fell at rather frequent intervals and when the Australians went in to make 415, they were put out for 125.

The explanation is simple. We had Rhodes on our side. Larwood, Tate, Geary, and Mr Stevens all bowled well. Larwood, in particular, rendered valuable service by getting rid of Mr Woodfull and Mr Macartney. But these bowlers might possibly have been worn down. From the moment that Rhodes went on the match was over. Rhodes has learnt no new tricks since he used to bowl one end for nearly half the time that England were in the field, and his length is not so regular as it was. Yesterday he sent down a full toss and two long hops to leg, balls which he could not bowl in his palmiest days. The unbowlable ball has had some very distinguished victims in this match. Hobbs, Mr Macartney, Mr Bardsley, and Mr Andrews have all given away their wickets to it. The specimens released by Rhodes were all properly hit for four. Otherwise they found themselves playing forward when they would fain have played back, and he used the spin which his fingers impart to the ball to make it break back sharply, leaving those who will to swerve. On a biting pitch the best batsmen in the world cannot take root against a flighty left-hander who places a man at silly mid-off, another not quite square with the wicket at the point of the bat, and pitches the ball well up on the leg stump, making it break back to hit the top of the off, unless it is stopped by the bat; for there is no second line of defence to this form of attack. Only the two left-handed strikers, Mr Bardsley and Mr Gregory, were even moderately comfortable when facing Rhodes. And he took Mr Bardsley's wicket. In this he was fortunate, for the fatal ball must be included in the category of the unbowlable.

The Australians have been beaten and even in the moment of defeat they are generously glad of it. They think that the result will do much good to the game of cricket "at home." It will, if English batsmen have learnt the lesson of wise conservatism which Australian example can teach. I do not myself think that the rain which interrupted play between 1.15 and 3 o'clock made the Australians' task more impossible than it already was. At no time yesterday was the pitch so difficult as it had been on Tuesday morning, when Hobbs and Sutcliffe were — Hobbs and Sutcliffe. Rhodes needed no rain; the faster bowlers might even have preferred that none should fall. What is not matter of opinion is that Mr Collins may have chanced giving away as many as 20 runs by consenting to resume play so promptly after the shower ceased. But he and his men have come many thousands of miles to play cricket, and have fulfilled their purpose.

The concluding stages of the game were watched by the Prime Minister and an important section of his Cabinet. Some, at least, of them must have been late for their afternoon appointment.

A few spots of rain fell just before noon, but the weather seemed set fair when Rhodes and Geary took guard against Mr Mailey and Mr Gregory, the latter bowling for the first time from the pavilion end with no screen behind his arm. Mr Gregory soon had Geary caught at the wicket and Rhodes played him a trifle diffidently, though he drove an over-pitched ball in great style to the pavilion, and once and again condescended to cut the short one. Tate hit very hard and with discrimination, but Rhodes was out leg-before to Mr Grimmett, who superseded Mr Gregory. The fatal ball kept low. Larwood stayed a while and watched Tate make four extremely ponderous hits to the on boundary. He himself brought off a glorious drive for 4 through Mr Andrews and then was bowled by a googly. Strudwick stayed for nearly two hours while the rain fell and then was caught at silly mid-off.

Mr Collins sent in Mr Ponsford with Mr Woodfull this time, and the bowlers were Larwood and Tate. The heavy roller had been used for the full time allowed, but Larwood at once made the ball fly and might have had Mr Ponsford out if Geary

ENGLAND v. AUSTRALIA
The Oval, 14, 16–18 August 1926

ENGLAND
1st innings

J.B. Hobbs	b Mailey	37
H. Sutcliffe	b Mailey	76
F.E. Woolley	b Mailey	18
E. Hendren	b Gregory	8
A.P.F. Chapman	st Oldfield b Mailey	49
G.T.S. Stevens	c Andrews b Mailey	17
W. Rhodes	c Oldfield b Mailey	28
G. Geary	run out	9
M.W. Tate	b Grimmett	23
H. Larwood	c Andrews b Grimmett	0
H. Strudwick	not out	4
Extras	(b 6, lb 5)	11
Total		280

2nd innings

J.B. Hobbs	b Gregory	100
H. Sutcliffe	b Mailey	161
F.E. Woolley	lbw b Richardson	27
E. Hendren	c Oldfield b Grimmett	15
A.P.F. Chapman	b Richardson	19
G.T.S Stevens	c Mailey b Grimmett	22
W. Rhodes	lbw b Grimmett	14
G. Geary	c Oldfield b Gregory	1
M.W. Tate	not out	33
H. Larwood	b Mailey	5
H. Strudwick	c Andrews b Mailey	2
Extras	(b 19, lb 18)	37
Total		436

Fall of wickets: 1–53, 2–91, 3–108, 4–189, 5–213, 6–214, 7–231, 8–266, 9–266, 10–280.

Second innings: 1–172, 2–220, 3–277, 4–316, 5–373, 6–375, 7–382, 8–425, 9–430, 10–436.

AUSTRALIA BOWLING

	O	M	R	W	O	M	R	W
Gregory	15	4	31	1	18	1	58	2
Grimmett	33	12	74	2	55	17	108	3
Mailey	33.5	3	138	6	42.5	6	128	3
Macartney	6	3	16	0	26	16	24	0
Richardson	7	2	10	0	41	21	81	2

AUSTRALIA
1st innings

W.M. Woodfull	b Rhodes	35
W. Bardsley	c Strudwick b Larwood	0
C.G. Macartney	b Stevens	25
W.H. Ponsford	run out	2
T.J.E. Andrews	b Larwood	3
H.L. Collins	c Stevens b Larwood	61
A.J. Richardson	c Geary b Rhodes	16
J.M. Gregory	c Stevens b Tate	73
W.A. Oldfield	not out	33
C.V. Grimmett	b Tate	35
A.A. Mailey	c Strudwick b Tate	0
Extras	(b 5, lb 12)	17
Total		302

2nd innings

W.M. Woodfull	c Geary b Larwood	0
W.H. Ponsford	c Larwood b Rhodes	12
C.G. Macartney	c Geary b Larwood	16
W. Bardsley	c Woolley b Rhodes	21
H.L. Collins	c Woolley b Rhodes	4
T.J.E. Andrews	c Tate b Larwood	15
A.J. Richardson	b Rhodes	4
J.M. Gregory	c Sutcliffe b Tate	9
W.A. Oldfield	b Stevens	23
C.V. Grimmett	not out	8
A.A. Mailey	b Geary	6
Extras	(lb 7)	7
Total		125

Fall of wickets: 1–9, 2–44, 3–51, 4–59, 5–90, 6–122, 7–229, 8–231, 9–298, 10–302.

Second innings: 1–1, 2–31, 3–31, 4–35, 5–63, 6–83, 7–83, 8–87, 9–114, 10–125.

ENGLAND BOWLING

	O	M	R	W	O	M	R	W
Tate	37.1	17	40	3	9	4	12	1
Larwood	34	11	82	3	14	3	34	3
Geary	27	8	43	0	6.3	2	15	1
Stevens	29	3	85	1	3	1	13	1
Rhodes	25	15	35	2	20	9	44	4

Umpires: F. Chester and H. Young

ENGLAND WON BY 289 RUNS

had not been too far forward at third slip. Geary was moved to the left, and in Larwood's next over caught Mr Woodfull, whose stroke was not one of his best. Mr Macartney came in, the man for whom only himself can determine the limits of the possible. He took a couple of minutes to look at the bowling, and then set himself to spoil it. He off-drove Tate, forced a fast rising ball from Larwood off his chest to the leg boundary, and cut him splendidly, though he only got a single for the last stroke of the three. But to the intense relief of every Englishman present, from Mr Chapman and the Prime Minister downwards, he shortly afterwards cut an almost similar ball to Geary at third slip. Mr Chapman had a special reason to be elated, for a moment before he had strengthened the field behind the wicket on the off side for Larwood's bowling. Rhodes was called up to stand in the gully and Geary placed precisely where the decisive chance went. The dismissal of Mr Macartney was of such vital moment that it has caused me to anticipate the order of events. Rhodes had previously been put on in place of Tate, and without another run scored he had Mr Ponsford caught at backward point. A ball of perfect length broke back the breadth of the wicket and reared up sharply. No first-rate batsman's back stroke can be certain to keep that ball down, though the village blacksmith might mow it to square-leg for 6. Larwood actively and intelligently dived forward from backward point and got a hand under it as it fell. Mr Collins and Mr Bardsley were now partnered, but not for long. Mr Collins got something like Mr Ponsford's ball, and snicked it to short slip.

Mr Andrews batted as freely as if the pitch were fast and true. He made some delicious strokes off Rhodes on the off-side, most of which were stopped with apparent ease by Hobbs, and he hit a couple of his loose balls very hard to the on boundary. Since the match was practically won I could with equanimity have watched Mr Andrews play a long innings in the manner of his opening. But it was not to be. He hooked a short ball from Larwood quite well, but not with the driving part of his bat, and Tate at short leg took a nice catch with his right hand. Mr Gregory made some powerful strokes before hitting rather recklessly at Tate and getting himself caught at mid-off. Mr Bardsley dealt with Rhodes better than anybody else, but his efforts at the off balls of the faster bowlers were not convincing. Ultimately Rhodes got his wicket with a long hop which Mr Bardsley skied to short leg.

As in the first innings Mr Oldfield and Mr Grimmett played first-class cricket. Rhodes could deceive neither with his flight and gave way to Mr Stevens, who bowled for this turn medium pace. His first over was expensive, but in his second he made Mr Oldfield play a yorker on to his stumps. Mr Mailey made one slashing cover-drive off Geary, but was clean bowled by him and, catching Strudwick napping, was able to pocket the ball.

Each of our bowlers got at least one wicket. The fielding was exuberantly keen and Strudwick kept wicket splendidly on a pitch which constrained Mr Oldfield to let 19 byes. It was pleasant to see Mr Chapman captain his side so ably — and alone he did it. No doubt he had discussed strategy and tactics in the pavilion with his staff officers, but on the field he relied on his own judgment. The demeanour of his colleagues indicated clearly their absolute approval of his direction.

SUTCLIFFE AND HOLMES

Steady Progress by Yorkshire

Soon after the start of the game between Essex and Yorkshire at Leyton on 15 June 1932 the visitors should have lost Holmes to a catch at the wicket when his score was three. Thereafter Yorkshire spent the remainder of the day plodding at 70 runs an hour.

YORKSHIRE
First innings

P. Holmes	not out	180
H. Sutcliffe	not out	231
Extras		12
Total	(0 wkt)	423

A FIRST-WICKET RECORD

by Dudley Carew

17 June 1932. At Leyton, at exactly 1 o'clock yesterday, Sutcliffe, by hooking a short ball of Eastman's to the boundary, broke, in partnership with Holmes, the record first-wicket stand of 554 runs set up by two other Yorkshiremen, Brown and Tunnicliffe, in 1898. Sutcliffe promptly got out to the next ball, but the excitement was not yet over, for, as soon as A.B. Sellers had declared the innings closed and the players had reached the pavilion, the figures 555 on the score board, which meant that the record had been broken, were changed into 554, which meant it had only been equalled, and it was not until half an hour later that the new record passed into cricket history.

YORKSHIRE
First innings

P. Holmes	not out	224
H. Sutcliffe	b Eastman	313
Extras	(b 13, lb 3, nb 2)	18
Total	(1 wkt dec.)	555

ESSEX BOWLING

	O	M	R	W
M.S. Nichols	31	4	105	0
A.G. Daer	40	5	106	0
P. Smith	46	10	128	0
J. O'Connor	23	5	73	0
L. Eastman	22.4	2	97	1
L.G. Crawley	3	0	7	0
R.H. Taylor	4	0	14	0
C. Bray	1	0	7	0

Umpires: E.J. Smith and F. Field

It would have been the cruellest ill-fortune had a mistake of one run on the score-board robbed the batsmen of the full fruits of their triumphs, for their respective innings were so consistently and unfailingly sound that the strokes which sent the ball to any direction other than that which they intended could be counted on the fingers of two hands. The pitch was, of course, perfect — the record could hardly have been broken had it not been — but the secret of Holmes and Sutcliffe's success lay not in the pitch nor in the shortcomings of the Essex bowling but in their endurance, their unfailing patience, and their vast technical resources.

Sutcliffe's 313 was his highest individual score, and it enabled him to reach his 1,000 runs for the season, but Holmes has six times exceeded the 224 he made yesterday and on Wednesday. When Essex went in, Verity, who took five wickets for eight runs, and Bowes consolidated the work Holmes and Sutcliffe had begun and got the home side out for 78 runs. Following on, Essex

lost five wickets for 92 runs, and so finished up the day needing 385 runs to save the innings defeat with five wickets in hand.

The weather was fine and sunny and a large crowd was present when Holmes and Sutcliffe went in to bat again yesterday morning. Nichols and A.G. Daer opened the bowling for Essex, but the batsmen began as they had left off, and soon after Holmes had driven Daer beautifully past mid-off to the boundary Sutcliffe beat the 456 made by E.R. Mayne and W.H. Ponsford in Australia with a square-cut for 4 off Nichols. After an hour's play the score had been raised to 500, and it was becoming more and more obvious that only time stood between the batsmen and the world's record. What happened at 1 o'clock has already been described, and, when everything was finally reduced to statistics, it appeared that Sutcliffe gave no chance and hit one 6, one 5, and 33 4's, and that Holmes, who might have been caught at the wicket when he had made three, hit 19 4's.

Yorkshire's progress throughout this marathon was impressively methodical:

First hundred	105 minutes
Second hundred	95 minutes
Third hundred	75 minutes
Fourth hundred	50 minutes

By the close on the first day, 423 runs had been scored in 355 minutes:

Fifth hundred	90 minutes
Last 55 runs	30 minutes

Yorkshire had therefore scored 555 runs in 445 minutes, that is, 75 runs an hour. Essex obliged with about 23 overs an hour.

After the declaration, Yorkshire — in their best 1930s style — then dismissed Essex twice in a day, for 78 (Bowes four for 38, Verity five for 8) and 164 (Nichols 59 not out; Bowes five for 47, Verity five for 45), thus winning by an innings and 313 runs. The partnership between Holmes and Sutcliffe was the

65th time the pair had opened with 100 or more runs for Yorkshire.

Lest the Essex over-rate of 23 an hour is held to be a vital factor, it should be mentioned that Yorkshire would still have had time to win the game had Essex achieved a more realistic 17 overs an hour as Yorkshire made their 555 runs.

MR HERBERT SUTCLIFFE

23 January 1978. Mr Herbert Sutcliffe, one of the famous cricketers of his time, has died at the age of 83.

From Hirst, Rhodes and Jackson to Leyland and Hutton, Yorkshire has always provided England with cricketing backbone and at no time was the old saying, "When Yorkshire is strong, England is strong", so true as when Herbert Sutcliffe stood, in the words of his autobiography, "...For England and Yorkshire". His playing career spanned almost exactly the period between the two world wars and by any standard his figures were massive. In all, he scored over 50,000 runs, including 149 centuries. His England caps were 54, though he was seldom seen to wear one, and, of his 16 Test hundreds, half were taken off Australian bowling. In each of 21 home seasons and on three tours he made his thousand runs, a dozen times 2,000 and three times 3,000. Four times he scored two hundreds in a match and twice four successive hundreds. His records flowed opulently like the bequests of a generous millionaire.

He was born on November 24, 1894, in Pudsey, the West Riding hometown of his predecessor John Tunnicliffe, and his eminent successor, Sir Leonard Hutton. In his teens he caught the eye of the Yorkshire authorities and had already made an appearance or two for the county's second eleven when the First World War broke out. He enlisted in The Sherwood Foresters and later was commissioned. In the first post-war season Yorkshire called on him at once and after an attractive innings in the first game against MCC at Lord's,

he found himself in possession of his county's No. 1 batting position. By the end of the summer he had established himself so firmly that he was named as one of Wisden's Cricketers of the Year.

Each season saw him steadily advancing and his first 2,000 runs came in 1922. Two years later his selection for England against South Africa marked the beginning of his long association with Sir Jack Hobbs, the most impressive and prolific partnership that English batting has known. Their first stand produced 136 runs, the second 268 and the third 72, and this initial success brought Sutcliffe an invitation to tour Australia where, though the rubber was lost, his personal performance was magnificent, producing four successive hundreds and a Test average of over 80.

With that gayest of good companions, Percy Holmes, he broke virtually every Yorkshire batting record. Their century partnerships numbered 69 for Yorkshire (74 in all) and their highest was the record-breaking 555, scored at Leyton in 1932 at a rate of 74 runs an hour. This was Sutcliffe's richest season, bringing him 3,336 runs and keeping him at the head of the first class averages, a place he had held in 1928 and 1931. His three-figure partnerships with Hobbs totalled 26, of which 15 were against Australia. The understanding which inspired their almost uncanny running between wickets — daring, but safe — was foreshadowed in the days when Rhodes was Hobbs's prewar partner and was brought to perfection with Sutcliffe's intelligent cooperation. Of their combined exploits two at least are outstanding. In the fifth Test of 1926, with the rubber still undecided, England began their second innings 22 runs behind. In poor evening light Hobbs and Sutcliffe scored 19, but a thunderstorm in the night made the morning's pitch at first dead-slow and then as the sun came out, vilely treacherous. If either Hobbs or Sutcliffe had succumbed, England could have been out for a hundred. As it was, the pair batted valorously, adding 112 by lunchtime and after Hobbs had been bowled for exactly 100, Sutcliffe stayed till the last over of the day. His share was

SUTCLIFFE   A foundation stone laid, and speeches made, the alderman departs for his next engagement.

161 and sharply rising deliveries had bruised him all over. Connoisseurs of his batting speak with even greater awe of his innings for Chapman's side of 1928–29 on a Melbourne "sticky dog". In hideous conditions the two Englishmen fought their way to a total of 105, when Hobbs was out, and afterwards Sutcliffe went serenely on to take his individual score to 135, bringing England within sight of victory.

Sutcliffe's success sprang from his personal character, based on tenacious courage and unshakable concentration. In an age when bat dominated ball, he was among the giants; Hobbs, Hammond, Bradman and Woodfull at one end and Hutton, his own disciple, at the other. Though he fell short of the consummate artistry of Hobbs or the sheer brilliance of Hammond, he was a handsome batsman with an armoury of powerful on-side strokes and a defence that was a bowler's despair. He could score steadily or swiftly, as he judged the situation, and once, with Leyland, hit 102 off six overs against Essex.

As a mark of respect to his famous England first-wicket partner, Sutcliffe named his son, who was later to captain Yorkshire himself, William Herbert Hobbs. Sutcliffe's wife, Emily, died in 1974.

His appearance at the crease, from elegant buckskin boots to perfectly smoothed black hair, was as immaculate as his defence. His quiet voice masked a tremendous combativeness. Congratulated on his superb innings at the Oval in 1926, he replied softly: "Ah, Mr Warner, I love a dog fight". And after his equally valiant effort at Melbourne Sir Jack Hobbs observed: "There was Herbert, black and blue, and not a hair out of place". Under the harshest of stresses, he was unruffled and unrufflable.

It was once said of Yorkshire's opening batsmen that, while Holmes looked as if he was off to the races, Sutcliffe had the air of an alderman about to lay a foundation stone. There was truth in the jest, for a characteristic innings by Sutcliffe formed the foundation of many a Yorkshire and England victory. Though he looked young all his playing life, he was England's "Old Imperturbable".

JACK MORRISON GREGORY
New South Wales

EDGAR ARTHUR MACDONALD
Victoria and Lancashire

If English cricket was inevitably weak after the First World War, was it as weak as Armstrong's 1921* Australians made it appear? Since the Tests of that year were each limited to three days, and those of 1948 were played over five, it is impossible to compare Armstrong's side with Bradman's at the highest level. Even the county matches were different, the Australian Board of Control having insisted on a five-hour day in 1921; to complicate matters, if Armstrong felt in a dark mood, he would refuse to start until 2 p.m. Here it may be noted that Armstrong was himself a remarkable cricketer, performing the "double" of 1000 runs and 100 wickets in an English season three times. He scored more first-class runs than would Macartney or Ponsford, and took more wickets than O'Reilly or Lindwall.

One myth survives concerning the 1921 Australians: Gregory and Macdonald were guilty of intimidatory bowling. True, they often pitched short, but if Armstrong was right when he argued that English batsmen could not play rising balls on, or outside, the off-stump, the charge must be qualified. The field placings of Gregory and Macdonald in 1920–21 (when Australia won all five Tests) and in

* After England had lost the final Test of 1920–21 Douglas met the press. The Australian party chosen for the tour of England was "a fine selection, though Gregory is not as fast as he was...Much work will fall on Macartney and Collins as spin bowlers".

During the tour of England, Gregory, Macdonald, Mailey and Armstrong would take 284 wickets against county sides — Macartney eight and Collins one.

1921 were similar to those employed by Tom Richardson in the 1890s and by Larwood when bowling to Bradman at Headingley in 1930: a wide mid-on and long leg, and everyone else on the off side of the wicket. One concludes that in the absence of Hobbs, first through injury and then illness, England's batsmen would have been sorely troubled by very fast bowling, regardless of its direction.

At the start of the Trent Bridge Test, the Australian attack suggested three parts maturity; if Gregory was only 25, Macdonald was 30, Mailey 35, and Armstrong on the verge of retirement at 42. Macdonald was mature only in years. Most fast bowlers have hinted at their potential by the age of 24 — not so Macdonald, whose Sheffield Shield haul of wickets was then two. By his 30th birthday he had taken 101 first-class wickets, by his 34th, 386. Thereafter, as one of the abiding joys on English cricket fields, he took 1,009 wickets. "So shrewd a judge as D.R. Jardine," wrote Ian Peebles, "observed that all the fastest bowlers attained a common maximum speed, but that Macdonald's fastest *ball* perceptibly exceeded it."

The year 1921 was not a one for English patriots — for seeing was disbelieving and hateful — only for those in search of entertainment. It was a year when the Australian opener Bardsley was constantly reproached for slow scoring as, on occasions, Boycott would be half a century later.

30 April v. Leicestershire. Macdonald bowls out home side for 136: "Not a great bowler but has pace" (*The Times*). Australians lose Collins for 2, Macartney reaches 50 in half an hour. After two hours Australians 243 for one, Bardsley 97, Macartney 140.

6 June v. Gloucestershire. Armstrong in dark mood, 2 o'clock start; Bardsley and Mayne struggle to 134 in 85 minutes. Macartney and Bardsley add 147 in an hour (Bardsley out for 132), Macartney and Andrews 121 in 40 minutes. At 422 for three Armstrong announces dinner.

15 June v. Hampshire. Bardsley and Andrews open with 62 in half an hour, the former treating the bowling "with considerable respect" (*Wisden*). Enter Macartney, 105 in 85 minutes; Bardsley plods to 209, his last 100 runs made in an hour. 569 for five at the close, 708 for seven at lunch next day.

22 June v. Northants and 25 June v. Notts. Two Australian innings total 1,296 runs, four by the counties 295 runs. Macartney warms up at Northampton with 193 at 75 an hour before annoying Trent Bridge with 345 at 88 an hour; four England bowlers — past, present or future — Barratt, Richmond, S.J. Staples and John Gunn returning 95–9–484–5.

30 June v. Warwickshire. Tenth-wicket stand by Oldfield and Mailey realizes 124 in 40 minutes.

The Australians did not, of course, always perform in the above manner, but in 21 matches against the counties their first innings averaged 443 made at 85 runs an hour.

The irony of the season was indeed sweet: in late August a team of amateurs assembled by A.C. MacLaren beat the Australians at Eastbourne. MacLaren was aged 49, his old friend Walter Brearley 45; they made six runs, and Brearley did not bowl. In fact 19 individual innings by the amateurs realized 88 runs, with Gilbert Ashton's second innings taken into account, 20 innings amounted to 124 runs. MacLaren's heroes were three in number: Michael Falcon, who took six wickets in the Australian first innings; Clement Gibson, who took six in the second innings; and Hubert Ashton, who made 75. There was also the superhero G.A. Faulkner — six wickets and a second innings of 153. Falcon passed his cricketing life with Norfolk, Gibson in the Argentine, Hubert Ashton was lost to the first-class game after

leaving Cambridge. Faulkner was the South African master who had punished Armstrong severely in 1910–11 and who did so again in his fortieth year.

J.M. Gregory, E.A. Macdonald, A.A. Mailey and W.W. Armstrong in 21 matches against counties

	Innings	Wkts	Av.	Balls/wkt
Gregory	1st	42	12.76	28
	2nd	25	11.72	27
	Total	67	12.37	27
Macdonald	1st	47	12.61	29
	2nd	27	14.07	29
	Total	74	13.14	29
Mailey	1st	31	21.48	37
	2nd	44	13.29	26
	Total	75	16.88	31
Armstrong	1st	44	12.97	41
	2nd	24	11.16	41
	Total	68	12.33	41

	Wkts	Av.	Balls/wkt
1st innings	164	14.59	34
2nd innings	120	12.71	30
Total	284	13.70	31

Had these four bowlers been used exclusively, the counties' average first-innings total would have been 146 from the bat off 57 overs and 127 off 51 overs in the second innings.

TRENT BRIDGE, 1921

H.L. Hendry batted at No. 10 for Australia in the Trent Bridge Test of 1921, an event of small significance were it not that seven years later at Sydney he went in first wicket down and made a century off the bowling of Larwood, Tate, Geary, White and Hammond. Stranger things happened in 1921; in the six innings of the first three Tests, England did not once last 100 overs. Any who marvel at, and resent, the spectacle of four West Indies fast bowlers attacking England today must divide that number (though not their resentment) by two, and then marvel the more at the impact of Gregory and Macdonald in 1921.

The Trent Bridge Test of 1921 was the eleventh to be completed in two days, though its 1,241 balls was far from being a record. The Oval game between England and South Africa in 1912 required only 815 balls to produce a result — S.F. Barnes returning 37.4–14–57–13.

By A.C.M. Croome

28 May 1921, Nottingham. The Australian cricketers have come a long way to play five Test Matches and to fulfil more or less punctually upwards of 30 other engagements. Naturally, their fighting form is not to be estimated by their performance on occasions when the results are regarded as matters of secondary importance. Their exhibitions on afternoons previous to today had suggested that they had plenty of power in reserve for a crisis, and the absence of Hobbs and Hearne from the English team in this, the first Test, diminished the probability that they would be obliged to exercise the whole of it. It is a noteworthy fact that this morning Mr Gregory bowled faster than he has done since he landed in England, although the wicket was not of the kind that suits fast bowling.

There had been a good deal of rain at Nottingham overnight, and the appearance of the sky indicated that shower-dodging would be one of the day's pastimes. Before the showers began the wicket played easily. It was of such pace that a good-length ball from a medium-paced bowler could be played either forward or back at will. The omission of Mr Mailey, the googly bowler, indicated that, in his captain's opinion, the pitch was unlikely at any period of the match to suit his bowling. Such conditions are almost equally unsuited to the fast bowlers who form Mr Armstrong's battery of heavy artillery, and for the first hour Mr Gregory and Mr Macdonald kept the batsmen quiet and got an unpleasantly large number of them out by sheer good bowling, and not by mere pace. During that time, Mr Carter, standing back, was only once obliged to jump in order to reach a bumper, and two or three times he was yorked on the second bounce by balls which came on from the pitch with unexpected mildness. The comfort of the wicket-keeper is a pretty good criterion by which spectators may estimate the character of the pitch. It was a different story after luncheon when the sun was shining on the ground dampened by morning showers. Then Rhodes in particular had a most unpleasant time. A ball from Mr Macdonald grazed the peak of his cap, and thereafter neither bowler showed excessive consideration for his feelings.

The first ball of the match was bowled by Mr Gregory, and Mr Knight should have hit it for four. Admittedly one does not go in to bat in a Test Match expecting a half-volley to leg, but it was soon apparent that Mr Knight's timing was less accurate than it was in 1919. His partner, Holmes, was clearly in better form, and the latter made no mistake with his first ball, a full-pitch outside the off stump, which was sent past cover-point to the boundary. Eighteen runs were made in a quarter of an hour, and then Mr Knight played weakly forward at a ball well pitched up outside the off stump. A tail-end batsman might have missed it altogether, but Hobbs or Mr Macartney almost certainly would have tested cover point's ability to save four runs. Mr Knight just touched it and was easily caught by the wicket-keeper. The very next ball was a good one, and it beat E. Tyldesley. Certainly he got almost the full face of his bat on to it, but his stroke was late, and did no more than knock the ball down on to the base of his stumps. A third wicket fell without the addition of a run. Hendren saved the hat trick, but, in Mr Gregory's next over, he got one which might have bowled W.G. Grace himself. It came back several inches, and so quickly, that Hendren could not follow the break with his bat, and saw his off stump turn cartwheels.

The captain came next, and his partnership with Holmes was destined to become the longest of the innings. Colonel Douglas has recently acquired the knack of selecting bats that will drive, and on this occasion he showed an inclination to increase the pace of the scoring. The fielding, however, prevented his well-intentioned efforts from producing boundary hits, and Mr Pellew in particular was brilliant at long leg. When 34 runs had been scored, Mr Armstrong relieved Mr Macdonald at the Pavilion end. In his first over Colonel Douglas made a most uncharacteristic stroke at a ball delivered with a leg-break action, and pitching, if anything, short of a length outside the off stump. The result was an easy catch to slip.

Woolley and a couple of showers tided over the remaining time before luncheon, and, after the interval, things looked like improving. Holmes was quite comfortable, and Woolley several times brought off the left-hander's off-drive. Mr Armstrong had a man out to turn the fours into singles, and it was not very long before Woolley mistimed the stroke and was grandly caught at third slip. The ball came to Mr Hendry with a bit of bat behind it, as they say; somehow, Mr Hendry got both hands to it after it had passed his left side. Almost immediately afterwards, Holmes was yorked, and this was the beginning of the end.

Mr Jupp started confidently, but cut a long hop straight to third slip — a bad stroke. More was expected from Rhodes now than when he first played for England at Nottingham 22 years ago. He did not exactly disappoint, but an excessive number of his scoring strokes were made with the edge of his bat. Richmond hit a brave four off a short ball, which reached him shoulder-high, but, otherwise, the batting of the tail was more amusing than profitable.

There is no getting away from the fact that the English batting was unworthy of the occasion. Holmes proved that the bowling could be met with the middle of the bat but no one else looked like staying for long. Mr Gregory bowled magnificently, and Mr Macdonald well, but none the less, 112 was a poor score, as the Australians immediately proceeded to demonstrate. Howell could not make the ball bump or break as Mr Gregory had done from the far end, and Colonel Douglas soon found the other end unsuitable to him. Both Mr Collins and Mr Bardsley seemed to have plenty of time in which to make their defensive strokes.

They were not obviously anxious to make runs, yet the scoring was faster than it had previously been. Nor did the ball go so frequently to the slip fielders, but the ordinary off-side strokes produced a useful crop of singles to the right or left of cover-point, in spite of the excellence of Mr Jupp's work there. Neither batsman missed anything on the leg side, and Mr Bardsley made several nice cuts.

At 29 Richmond [leg spin] went on for Colonel Douglas. His first over was expensive, but, after that, he began to puzzle both batsmen, and he soon had Mr Collins out palpably leg-before. We were then treated to about 20 minutes of Mr Macartney at his best. Mr Macartney is sometimes found to be in an unorthodox position at the finish of a stroke which has failed to find the ball, but his bat is always perfectly poised in time for the stroke and it must be a matter of pure guesswork for the bowlers to discover where he will be when the ball pitches. His footwork enabled him to make Howell seem slow, and to cut Richmond as if the ball had considerable pace on it. Colonel Douglas did his side a good turn when he went on at the far end and got him out leg-before-wicket.

He also persuaded Mr Taylor to drive a slow ball, and so send an easy catch to cover-point. Mr Armstrong had the satisfaction of putting his side ahead before failing to stop Mr Jupp's fast one. In the same over, Mr Armstrong had delighted ageing spectators [Croome was a mere 55] by forcing a good length ball to the boundary between mid-on and short-leg, just like "W.G." or Walter Read.

Mr Gregory then came in, and the two left-handers looked very likely to play out time. However, Woolley, who had relieved Richmond, got Mr Bardsley leg-before for an eminently respectable 66. Mr Bardsley had been in two hours and a half without once putting the ball in the air. In the same over, Woolley saved four by stopping a hard return from Mr Pellew with his right hand at full stretch; an even taller man might have caught it. Colonel Douglas wisely gave Richmond a turn at the far end before the finish, and had his reward, for Mr Gregory walked in front of all three stumps and missed the ball.

The position at the finish was better than had at one time seemed probable, but the events of the day are not specially pleasant to remember or encouraging as a basis of prophecy.

Close: ENGLAND 112 (J.M. Gregory 6 for 58), AUSTRALIA 167 for 6 (W. Bardsley 66).

The second day of the Trent Bridge Test was promoted to the main news page of *The Times*, which meant that, strategically placed, the column had three headings:

TEST MATCH DEBACLE

AUSTRALIA WINS BY TEN WICKETS

ENGLAND'S INGLORIOUS DISPLAY

30 May 1921, Nottingham. Australia beat England here to-day by 10 wickets.

It is a cold-blooded proceeding to resume on a Monday a match which had started during the last week; so many things can happen in the interval. At Nottingham the chief incident was a heavy storm of rain on Sunday night. The sun shone out with some power this morning, and the state of the wicket may be judged by Colonel Douglas's decision to start the bowling with Woolley and Rhodes. Both of them had the batsmen in trouble when they pitched the ball correctly. The ball was liable to get up pretty straight, and to come back sharply from the leg.

Rhodes got Pellew out as he has done hundreds of others. The ball pitched on the leg stump or thereabouts, whipped back quickly and struck the edge of the bat to fly straight up in the air. Once at each end the batsmen tried an off-drive, and the ball went shoulder high past short slip. It looked as if Colonel Douglas at second slip might

have reached the first one, but apparently he lost sight of the ball against the telegraph board. Woolley made a lot of ground to the other, but, for all his length of reach, he was a foot short.

There were other hopeful moments. Twice Mr Carter, in trying to drive Woolley, dropped the ball just short of cover-point. But there is another story to tell; on such a pitch it was a crime to pitch short. Woolley and Rhodes are not habitual criminals, but in the first half-hour's play to-day they gave Mr Pellow, Mr Carter, and Mr Andrews four opportunities to employ the hook stroke, with the result that 16 superfluous runs were added to the score. Mr Andrews tried the stroke at a ball which was a trifle too far up for his purpose, and Rhodes had another easy return catch. Possibly the wicket was worse at the Pavilion end, towards which Rhodes was bowling, than at the other. Whether that be so or not, he was obviously more difficult to play than Woolley, off whom Mr Carter managed to make several clever strokes on the leg side behind the umpire. As there was no man there, he did not bother to keep the ball down, but his scoops* were worth, on the average, two apiece...

...On such a wicket, a deficit of 120 was likely to develop into bankruptcy. Colonel Douglas had the heavy roller on the pitch, and Mr Armstrong gave an order for sawdust, indicating an intention to start with his fast bowlers. Sure enough Mr Gregory and Mr Macdonald began the bowling. Neither seemed to find much difficulty in getting a foothold, and either, when he can stand, is a good bowler.

Mr Knight and Holmes played the first few overs easily, with the exception of one ball which cocked up. Mr Gregory may have strained himself in a strenuous attempt to catch Mr Knight, who could not keep the ball down. Anyway, he was immediately relieved by Mr Macartney, and, simultaneously, Mr Macdonald moderated his

* Carter's famed "shovel" shot was fondly remembered by Jack Fingleton (*Batting from Memory*, 1981, p.53): "We on the outer were inclined to believe he had learnt the shot in his undertaking business."

pace and moved one of his slips across to short leg. Holmes was playing as well as he did on Saturday, and Mr Knight had recovered his timing. There were no cheap fours to be had, except when Mr Macartney gave Mr Knight a no-ball and the first 20 runs took well over half-an-hour to collect. Mr Macdonald then still further reduced his pace, until he was now little faster than Mr Jupp. The manner of the batsmen indicated that he was liable to break back. He got Holmes caught at mid-on, but Tyldesley played him easily, although he was an unconscionable time in saving his "pair." When he got to the other end, he shaped very badly at Mr Armstrong, who had gone on for Mr Macartney. Mr Gregory had two more overs from the Pavilion end before luncheon, but he hardly bowled his fastest. At the interval 28 runs had been made in an hour for one wicket. On continuing, Mr Gregory and Mr Armstrong bowled, with Mr Collins posted at short mid-off.

Mr Gregory bowled very fast, but Mr Knight played him delightfully. He made one magnificent square cut, and scored infallibly on the leg side, however high the ball bumped. Tyldesley was less quick in dealing with a long hop that flew up at his head; he missed it, and received a stunning blow. He was assisted to the Pavilion, and later was informed that the ball had carried on to break his wicket. The batsman was more to blame than the bowler for the accident, and neither the advice tendered by the crowd to Mr Armstrong, nor the cheering when he took it, was justified. After all, he merely substituted Mr Macdonald for Mr Gregory, and the frying-pan is proverbially cooler than the fire.

In Mr Armstrong's next over Hendren made a costly mistake. He played a ball back to the bowler, who half stopped the ball; Hendren started to run and Mr Knight responded; Hendren sent him back, but Mr Macartney, dashing in from mid-off, ran Mr Knight out by yards. Hendren, himself, hit across a half volley two overs later, and four of our eight batsmen were out with only half the arrears cleared off. Woolley

joined Colonel Douglas, and for several overs nothing happened except some screen shifting, due to the fact that Mr Macdonald went round the wicket to the left-hander. At last Colonel Douglas drove him for four, but neither batsman could do anything with Mr Armstrong, who was keeping a wonderful length and making the ball turn appreciably. But slowly over after over was met by defensive forward play. The duel was interesting to watch, though the cricket was monotonous. No doubt the slow scoring suited Mr Armstrong's book, for there was a prospect that the ground would get faster and livelier as the afternoon wore on, and at the proper moment he could unleash Mr Gregory once more.

At about 4 o'clock Mr Macdonald made a ball kick up, and Colonel Douglas was caught at second slip off the shoulder of his bat. Before the tea interval Woolley got his first overpitched ball and drove it past cover to the boundary. Mr Jupp also got a half-volley from Mr Armstrong, which he vainly tried to drive through Mr Pellew at silly point. Otherwise they could do nothing but place the accurate bowling accurately to the accurately placed fieldsmen.

When Mr Gregory went on again, there was an unseemly display of ignorance and bad manners from a section of the crowd. After Woolley, of all people, had been in nearly an hour for eight runs, he almost doubled his score by leaping out at Mr Armstrong, and hitting him over long-on's head for six.

After the tea interval, Mr Armstrong, who had bowled unchanged since luncheon, keeping the number of his overs almost equal to the number of runs scored off them, gave up his end to Mr Hendry. Naturally Mr Gregory bowled from the other end. In his first over Mr Jupp edged him through the slips for four, and then, trying an off drive with his feet wrongly placed, was easily caught at mid-off.

Mr Hendry made an occasional ball go quickly from the pitch, and Rhodes, practically England's last hope, had a narrow escape of being caught off him at first slip. Mr Gregory got his hands to the ball, and that generally suffices. The wicket by this time had manifestly improved, for the slips had less work to do, and both Woolley and Rhodes found it comparatively easy to place the ball for singles with strokes primarily defensive in character. They had put their side 18 runs ahead when Woolley was caught at the wicket. It must have been a very good catch, for the contact of bat and ball was audible all round the ring. One ball sufficed for Strudwick. Mr Gregory will do no unnecessary work this summer, and Mr Macdonald went on to get the last two wickets. His third ball bumped and Rhodes just touched it. The innings ended five minutes later.

The out cricket of the Australians was of the highest class. Possibly none of their bowlers

ENGLAND v. AUSTRALIA
Trent Bridge, 28 and 30 May 1921

ENGLAND

1st innings

D.J. Knight	c Carter b Gregory	8
P. Holmes	b Macdonald	30
E. Tyldesley	b Gregory	0
E. Hendren	b Gregory	0
J.W.H.T. Douglas	c Gregory b Armstrong	11
F.E. Woolley	c Hendry b Macdonald	20
V.W.C. Jupp	c Armstrong b Macdonald	8
W. Rhodes	c Carter b Gregory	19
H. Strudwick	c Collins b Gregory	0
H. Howell	not out	0
T.L. Richmond	c & b Gregory	4
Extras	(b 6, lb 6)	12
Total		112

2nd innings

D.J. Knight	run out	38
P. Holmes	c Taylor b Macdonald	8
E. Tyldesley	b Gregory	7
E. Hendren	b Macdonald	7
J.W.H.T. Douglas	c Hendry b Macdonald	13
F.E. Woolley	c Carter b Hendry	34
V.W.C. Jupp	c Pellew b Gregory	15
W. Rhodes	c Carter b Macdonald	10
H. Strudwick	b Hendry	0
H. Howell	not out	4
T.L. Richmond	b Macdonald	2
Extras	(b 4, lb 3, nb 2)	9
Total		147

Fall of wickets: 1–18, 2–18, 3–18, 4–43, 5–77, 6–78, 7–101, 8–107, 9–108, 10–112.

Second innings: 1–23, 2–41, 3–60, 4–63, 5–76, 6–110, 7–138, 8–138, 9–145, 10–147.

AUSTRALIA BOWLING

	O	M	R	W	O	M	R	W
Gregory	19	5	58	6	22	8	45	2
Macdonald	15	5	42	3	22.4	10	32	5
Armstrong	3	3	0	1	27	10	33	0
Macartney					5	2	10	0
Hendry					9	1	18	2

AUSTRALIA

1st innings

W. Bardsley	lbw b Woolley	66
H.L. Collins	lbw b Richmond	17
C.G. Macartney	lbw b Douglas	20
J.M. Taylor	c Jupp b Douglas	4
W.W. Armstrong	b Jupp	11
J.M. Gregory	lbw b Richmond	14
C.E. Pellew	c & b Rhodes	25
H. Carter	b Woolley	33
T.J.E. Andrews	c & b Rhodes	6
H.L. Hendry	not out	12
E.A. Macdonald	c Knight b Woolley	10
Extras	(b 8, lb 5, nb 1)	14
Total		232

2nd innings

W. Bardsley	not out	8
C.G. Macartney	not out	22
Extras		0
Total	(0 wkts)	30

Fall of wickets: 1–49, 2–86, 3–98, 4–126, 5–138, 6–152, 7–183, 8–202, 9–212, 10–232.

ENGLAND BOWLING

	O	M	R	W	O	M	R	W
Howell	9	3	22	0				
Douglas	13	2	34	2				
Richmond	16	3	69	2	3	0	17	0
Woolley	22	8	46	3				
Jupp	5	0	14	1	3.1	0	13	0
Rhodes	13	3	33	2				

Umpires: J. Moss and H.R. Butt

AUSTRALIA WON BY 10 WICKETS

would be anxious to take the wicket about with them. But none of them bowled anything like badly. It would not be surprising if Mr Knight and Woolley, the two men best qualified to give an opinion, should place Mr Armstrong first and Mr Gregory second, but Mr Macdonald adapted his style to the varying conditions quite admirably, and deserved his pleasing analysis.

The fielding was superb, and Mr Carter is still a great wicket-keeper. The discipline of the side was clearly in evidence; any fieldsman may throw at the stumps with full assurance that some other fieldsman will prevent an overthrow, and neither wicket-keeper nor bowler is ever obliged to take unnecessary exertion in gathering a return when no run has been attempted.

Mr Collins had damaged his finger, and Mr Mailey had fielded for him; but, in any case, it is likely that Mr Macartney would have gone in first. The Australians' programme is so full, and so uncomfortably arranged, that the chance of a whole holiday is not to be missed. The necessary runs were made easily and surely in a quarter of an hour.

In the column to the left of Croome's final paragraphs was printed a letter from the Archbishops of Canterbury and York: "Never in our history was it more necessary at this hour to call upon all Christian people to be instant in prayer." The letter referred not to the Trent Bridge Test but to the prevailing social conditions.

E.A. MacDONALD

By R.B. Vincent

23 July 1937. The death of E.A. McDonald (*sic*), who was killed in a motor accident near Bolton yesterday morning, will be mourned all the world over where cricket is played. His career was short — all too short — in first-class cricket, but during that time he had established himself as one of the greatest fast bowlers of all time. No man in so brief a period can have achieved such great things or have granted such pleasure as he did.

The great men of this, or even of a previous, generation who bowled habitually and successfully at more than a fast-medium pace are few in number, McDonald was one of them. The horrors which England suffered in the summer of 1921, when Armstrong's team conquered the best that an after-War England could offer, was attributed to a great extent to the combination of Gregory and McDonald, and of the two, with all due respect, I believe McDonald to have been the greater match-winner. Gregory was fiercely, ferociously fast; McDonald was the more restrained, the more accurate, and the more dependable. He had above all the ability, such as Lockwood had, to bowl at his full pace when the wicket was slow, and sawdust was poured into the foot-holes. He was a bowler — and a man — of moods.

It was said by the ungenerous cricketer that he bowled short to intimidate the batsman. That I am sure he would never have done. He said to me once on the Aigburth ground that if the batsman walked away from his wicket the ball had a habit of following the batsman. A fairer comment could not be made, for above all he was a fast bowler. Whatever his record may be, of his technique there can be no question.

Once there was shown in a cinematograph exhibition a slow-motion picture of McDonald which well might have been distributed to every club and every school. The slow, almost lazy, arrival from the take-off of his run, like an animal which peeps its head from rushes; the gradual acceleration of pace; and then, with the left shoulder full to the bowler's bat, an action which was perfect and joyous to watch.

...His record, whether it be for Australia, for Lancashire, or in League cricket can never explain the bowler that he was. Those that saw him bowl will never forget.

CHARLES GEORGE MACARTNEY
New South Wales

Macartney was a batsman of such brilliance that in an Australian XI of the ages he might claim the position of first wicket down, with Bradman to follow. R.C. Robertson-Glasgow played against both:

His batting suggested a racket player who makes winners from any position. Length could not curb him, and his defence was lost and included in attack...No Australian batsman since him, not even Bradman at his best, has approached Macartney for insolence of attack. He made slaves of bowlers.

Macartney toured England four times between 1909 and 1926 at the ages (in mid-season) of 23 and 40. In Tests before the age of 35 he played 42 innings, average an unimpressive 31.28; after the age of 35 he rounded off his career with 13 innings, average 75.91. The irony is to be found in *Wisden*, which selected him as one of its Five Cricketers of 1921; his success was "largely dependent upon extraordinary quickness of eye, hand and foot". His great contemporary, Hobbs, mellowed with age but Macartney became more impudent, devoting himself to the seemingly impossible in stroke play. According to the chronicler one reads, he was both modest and clear-headed. One account has him — like A.C. MacLaren — insisting he was not worthy to tie Trumper's laces, another has him listening to a eulogy of the same batsman, then asking in amazement: "What could he do that I can't?"

Small wonder that Macartney's cricket gave birth to myths. Inspired by Neville Cardus, who, at various times, saw Macartney as D'Artagnan and Rossini's Figaro, Jack Fingleton in his last book, *Batting from Memory*, retold Cardus and did Macartney wrong:

He [Cardus] told the story of Macartney coming down to breakfast on a sunny morning in his London hotel, the day a Test was to begin at Lord's, rubbing his hands together and saying: "I feel sorry for the poor cove who has to bowl at me today." And it was so. Charlie made ninety-nine in two hours and forty minutes.

Macartney batted in four Tests at Lord's, twice before the First World War when Cardus most certainly was not staying in the same hotel. The occasion was clearly 1926. However, Macartney did score 99 in the Lord's Test of 1912 — not, as Fingleton wrote, in 2 hours and 40 minutes but in 2 hours and 12 minutes. Even more remarkable was the quality of the England bowlers Macartney put to the sword, after he had informed his team-mates that he intended to hit Barnes for six. The other England bowlers were F.R. Foster, Harry Dean (the Lancashire left-hander, second only to Blythe as the summer's most prolific wicket-taker), J.W. Hearne and Rhodes.

The Lord's Test was ruined by rain, the Australian first innings being delayed until 5 minutes to 12 on the third day after England had declared at 310 for seven wickets — Hobbs 107. Macartney went in at 27 after the dismissal of C.B. Jennings.

27 June 1912. Mr Macartney began a beautiful innings at once, so to speak, as if he had been batting an hour. If a pull can ever be a graceful stroke it is when Mr Macartney makes it, with a flick of the wrists in a bright and sparkling style; and no player in the world has a prettier cut. He faces the bowling in a way that would have been very dangerous to life and limb at Lord's 40 years ago, but his great quickness of movement both of wrist and feet makes it almost impossible for any bowler on a slow wicket to keep runs down when bowling to him...The bowlers after luncheon were Barnes and Dean. Mr Macartney rattled away in fine style and looked as if nothing would get him out...Barnes, bowling from the pavilion end, did not seem able to make the ball spin — in other words, the wicket did not suit him — but he was bowling a trifle too short, and from one of these short balls Mr Macartney made a splendid pull for six...At this stage it really looked as if England's total might be passed, so harmless was the English bowling on the slow easy wicket, and so completely set was Mr Macartney. With his score at 99, however, he just touched a ball from Mr Foster outside the leg stump and was caught by the wicketkeeper. Mr Macartney was batting for two hours and twelve minutes. He never made a mishit and never looked anything but thoroughly at home to all the bowlers. He hit a 6 and 13 4s.

At the close Australia were 282 for seven wickets, C.E. Kelleway's 61 occupying 256 minutes; after the First World War he improved on this run-rate, his 147 at Adelaide in 1920–21 taking only 420 minutes.

Barnes conceded 74 runs in the Lord's Test of 1912 without taking a wicket, but in all games of the Triangular Tournament (for which the Australians Armstrong, Carter, Cotter, Hill, Ransford and Trumper absented themselves) his 39 wickets cost only 10.35 runs each, a wicket every 30 balls.

Macartney paid tribute to Barnes's bowling, emphasizing that he was in his 60s before hitting the great man for six.

27 June 1921. The Australians had little difficulty in piling up the huge score of 608 for seven wickets on a perfect pitch at Trent Bridge on Saturday. They certainly lost Mr Bardsley for a cypher, but afterwards the Nottinghamshire bowlers had a dreadful time.

Mr Macartney went in when Mr Bardsley had been bowled by the first ball sent down by Richmond with only one run on the scoreboard. He made his runs in 4 hours [235 minutes the official time], out of 540 scored while he was in. Finally he was out leg-before-wicket to Hardstaff. When he had scored nine, he had a great piece of luck, being missed in the slips [neither *The Times* nor *Wisden* says by whom; could it have been A.W. Carr who did miss Macartney five years later in the Headingley Test?], and, at 213, he gave a hard chance to mid-on, but these were the only blemishes in a really dazzling innings, in which he revealed in the most brilliant fashion all his wonderful footwork, together with extraordinary accuracy in cutting and power in driving and leg hitting. His hits included four 6's, 47 4's, three 3's, and 30 2's. One remarkable feature of the innings was the pace at which the runs were obtained [100 in 95 minutes, 200 in 145 and 300 in 205].

The Notts ground fielding was excellent. There were more than 10,000 spectators [one of whom, according to Jack Fingleton, summed up Macartney's innings as "bloody monotonous"].

---

25 June 1921

AUSTRALIANS

W. Bardsley	b Richmond	0
T.J.E. Andrews	c Oates b Barratt	29
C.C. Macartney	lbw b Hardstaff	345
J.M. Taylor	c Whysall b Barrett	50
C.E. Pellew	c Oates b Staples	100
J.M. Gregory	c G. Gunn b Hardstaff	19
J.S. Ryder	b Hardstaff	20
H.L. Hendry	not out	20
W.A. Oldfield	not out	14
Extras		11
Total	(7 wkts)	608

Carr tried eight bowlers, himself one of the least successful: 1–0–24–0. On the Monday the Australians were out for 675, then dismissed Notts for

58 (26.4 overs) and 100 (41.5 overs), so winning by an innings and 517 runs.

HEADINGLEY 1926

By A.C.M. Croome

AUSTRALIA

W. Bardsley	c Sutcliffe b Tate	0
W.M. Woodfull	not out	134
C.G. Macartney	c Hendren b Macaulay	151
T.J.E. Andrews	lbw b Kilner	4
A.J. Richardson	not out	70
Extras	(b 2, lb 2, nb 1)	7
Total	(3 wkts)	366

Fall of wickets: 1–0, 2–235, 3–249

J.M. Gregory, J.M. Taylor, J.S. Ryder, W.A. Oldfield, C.V. Grimmett and A.A. Mailey to bat.

ENGLAND:
J.B. Hobbs, H. Sutcliffe, F.E. Woolley, E. Hendren, A.W. Carr, A.P.F. Chapman, R. Kilner, M.W. Tate, G. Geary, G.G. Macaulay, H. Strudwick.

Umpires: W. Reeves and H. Butt

12 July 1926. The third Test match was begun in Leeds on Saturday, when Australia, having been sent in to bat first, scored 366 runs for the loss of only three wickets.

An inspection of the pitch late on Friday afternoon revealed that the unprotected part of it was almost marshy. Nevertheless, two of the English selectors showed no signs of an intention to pass a sleepless night. This was encouraging, because on the morrow they would have to face one of the most horrid problems which has ever confronted persons in authority. They must have their teams finally chosen before the captains tossed and without fore-knowledge of the possible vagaries of the weather, and they must choose three out of five bowlers to assist Kilner and Woolley. The suggestion made by superficial students of cricket that they would omit a batsman was, of course, ignored. Mr Bardsley was not similarly perplexed; at least he was not embarrassed by wealth of choice in respect of bowling. It was finally decided to omit Root, Larwood, and Parker.

The preliminaries to the match were more than normally interesting. First, another pitch than that specially prepared for the match was chosen; then Mr Carr held a consultation in the middle of it at which two local experts, Leyland, the groundsman, and Sutcliffe, assisted. A few minutes later the captains tossed, and Mr Carr sent Australia in to bat. If ever in the last 20 years appearances have justified that policy this was the occasion. The sun was shining fiercely on a damp marled wicket, and the weather seemed to be set fair, but there would seem to have been some lack of co-ordination between the captain and his colleagues of the selection committee, for it was illogical to omit Parker and subsequently put the other side in.

Great responsibility was thus thrown on the shoulders of Macaulay. Tate and Geary like to hear their feet rattle and to see the dust fly; Kilner does not now spin the ball after the manner of his predecessors in the Yorkshire eleven, Peate, Peel, and Rhodes, but Macaulay girds up his loins gleefully when the boy brings out the sawdust. The sawdust was plentifully spread on Saturday morning, but Mr Macartney very soon transformed Macaulay's glee into gloom. The estimate of the probable behaviour of the pitch, by whomsoever it was formed, turned out to be ludicrously inexact, for not a ball popped, not a ball broke sharply all day. Batsmen other than Mr Macartney, who is to be judged by standards applicable only to himself and George Gunn, found conditions ideal for run-getting. They did not need the protection of batting gloves [nevertheless Macartney wore them; Woodfull on his bottom hand], and the ball rarely gathered pace from the pitch, but yet came on to the bat fast enough for the purposes of all the scoring strokes. Consequently the area of the "blind spot" was reduced to the minimum, and Strudwick, who was keeping wicket well, had very little to take.

Mr Bardsley flicked at Tate's first ball, and Sutcliffe, at slip, picked it up off his toes — a beautiful catch. Mr Macartney placed the next ball behind point for two runs, but then was forced to play a hurried stroke, and gave Mr Carr a difficult catch at third slip. A less vigilant fielder would have reached the ball with his left hand only, and it might have struck. Had that catch been made the two best Australian batsmen would have been out for two runs, and yet the policy of declining first innings would not have been justified. Both strokes were of the kind which gives Tate his wickets at Brighton in fine weather. After his escape Mr Macartney completely dominated the English bowlers. Nothing like it has been seen since Mr Victor Trumper made 100 before luncheon for Australia against England at Manchester in 1902. Only Tate looked capable of bowling him a good ball. If I describe his batting as insolent or contemptuous I do so with the desire to pay the highest possible compliment to his technique, not to impugn his sense of proportion. They could not set the field for him on Saturday. His twinkling feet and the telescopic reach of his arms enabled him to meet two similar balls at different stages in their careers, and to send them to points in the boundary separated by fifty yards. One remembers, too, that he scored several 4's by getting up on his toes, and playing the back strokes as Dr W.G. Grace used to play them.

To carry the comparison between a large man and a small one a stage further, Mr Macartney's ordinary forward stroke counted 4, and the bowler acquired merit if he could oblige him to play half-cock to the ball. Kilner had to keep four men in the outfield for him, and Macaulay was reduced to complete impotence in two overs. He would overpitch a ball by a foot or so, and see Mr Macartney step out of his ground to hit it first hop against the sight screen. When he avoided that particular form of punishment he was hooked unmercifully to the square-leg boundary. Tate and Geary were not so regularly driven and hooked, but they could seldom tell when a ball of good length on the middle stump would not be turned to fine leg or alternatively forced past cover-point.

I do not remember that Mr Macartney every found it expedient to leave the off ball alone, but I do recall a fluent strain of delightful cuts, and three impudent attempts to slice yorkers through the slips. There is a certain satisfaction to be derived from the attempt to detect flaws in a masterpiece. I shall therefore note that Mr Macartney declined a number of singles which Hobbs would have taken at the trot, but if a batsman can stand and hit 4's at will he cannot be seriously blamed for conserving his physical resources. Mr Macartney reached his 100 in an hour and 40 minutes, was not out 112 at luncheon time, passed 150 three-quarters of an hour after the resumption of play, and then gave his wicket away.

Mr Woodfull kept up the other end all day. His stroke is short compared with that of the great artists, but his defence is extremely stubborn, and he does watch the ball. For the first two hours he was content to stay there and take such cheap runs as were offered, but in the concluding stage of his partnership with Mr Macartney he did his full share of the scoring...

The rain robbed England [play stopped at 5.20] of the opportunity to use three new balls in a single day, and when we left the ground we had to derive such satisfaction as we could from the fact that Mrs Pelham Warner's MCC flag, now faded and darned, was nailed to the mast near the entrance. It has never yet flown at a ground in which England has suffered defeat.

AUSTRALIA 494 (W.M. Woodfull 141, C.G. Macartney 151, A.J. Richardson 100) drew with ENGLAND 294 (G.G. Macaulay 76; C.V. Grimmett 5 for 88) and 254 for 3 (J.B. Hobbs 88, H. Sutcliffe 94).

The two sides averaged 21 overs an hour.

MAURICE WILLIAM TATE
Sussex

Tate was aged 26 in 1921 when England sorely needed an opening bowler of class to reply — even if in gentler vein — to Gregory and Macdonald. (In due course, Larwood, Statham and Trueman would make their debut for England at 21 and Farnes at 22.) But Tate in 1921 was only a promising county player; sometimes he opened the bowling for Sussex, on occasions he was used as fourth or fifth change. Then, in mid-1922, after surprising his captain Arthur Gilligan at nets with some lethal faster deliveries, he was ordered to bowl in his new style against Kent at Tunbridge Wells. The outcome was eight wickets for 67 runs, including Woolley for 0. Tate increased his season's victims from 70 to 119, reducing his average by nine points to 17. In 1923 his haul was 219 wickets, by 1924 he was regarded as the finest bowler in England; Tate had turned himself from a slow-medium off-spinner into one of the three great medium-pace masters of the century, chronologically after Barnes and before Bedser.

Sir Donald Bradman, who first faced Tate in 1928–9 when the bowler was 33, said later that he found Bedser more difficult to play, which prompted Ponsford to retort that Bradman had not met the Tate of 1924–5. Here we should note that Tate was basically an out-swing bowler who could also bring the ball back sharply from the off (at a time when the lbw law permitted batsmen to play deliveries pitching outside the off stump with their pads) and Bedser basically an in-swing bowler with full command over the leg-cutter.

Tate bowled in 38 Tests for England, the games being neatly divided — the first period ending with the Sydney game of 1928–9 for which Bradman had been dropped:

38 TESTS			
155 wkts	26.13 av.	81 B/W	
19 TESTS			
100 wkts	21.43 av.	63 B/W	
19 TESTS			
55 wkts	34.69 av.	111 B/W	

Of the latter 19 games, eight found Bradman in opposition (with Larwood Tate's opening partner in five; in a sixth Larwood was incapacitated by gastritis), and eleven without Bradman in opposition.

John Woodcock has often observed how Bedser would report at Trent Bridge for the first Test of a series having already bowled 600 overs. Tate's acceptance of hard labour would have made even Bedser blink. From May 1923 to September 1928 Tate's figures per calendar year averaged

10,764 balls   3,522 runs   217 wickets   16.23 average

He also scored 10,000 runs, performing the "double" of 1000 runs and 100 wickets in a season seven times in six years,* an unprecedented "double" during the MCC tour of India (1926–7)

. . . .

* Or nine times in eight years, 1922–9, with a total of 11,800 runs and 1,502 wickets.

often being overlooked. Tate's equivalent of 10,585 six-ball overs from May 1923 to September 1928 prompts comparison with the efforts of three slow left-arm bowlers: Rhodes 1898–1903, Parker of Gloucestershire 1921–6 and Lock of Surrey 1955–60.

Tate in 1923–8 exceeded Rhodes's balls by 12,000, and the balls bowled by Parker and Lock in England, respectively, by 12,000 and 22,000.

Freeman, a slow leg-break bowler, in the seasons 1928–33 took 1,673 wickets. He averaged a mere 35 overs a season more than Tate did in one place and another from 1923 to 1928.

There is the inevitable comparison with Barnes, who, during the whole of his first-class career *and* his years for Staffordshire 1904–34, bowled only 122 more overs than Tate did from 1923 to 1928.

Tate's action was perfect for its purpose (Robertson-Glasgow saw his approach to the wicket as "a short galumphing run, like some policeman easing his conscience in a token pursuit of the uncatchable"), but it seems logical to suppose that the bowler must have lost something by the time he first confronted Bradman in a Test and, incidentally, got him lbw for 18 at Brisbane in 1928–9.

Tate's Test debut at Edgbaston in 1924 was memorable. The South African side was not a strong one but after England had batted on the first day and for a few overs on the second, none expected to see South Africa following on before lunch.

By A.C.M. Croome

17 June 1924. The cricket before luncheon at Edgbaston yesterday was quite remarkable...The batting [in South Africa's first innings], it may at once be admitted, was not masterly, but it would be most unjust to Mr Gilligan and Tate to attribute the responsibility of their record-breaking achievement entirely, or even mainly, to the weakness of the opposition. There was something definitely terrific about their bowling. It was not that they made the ball bump. Neither of them hit a single batsman on the fingers, but they did impart some abnormal

ENGLAND v. SOUTH AFRICA
Edgbaston, 14, 16, 17 June 1924

ENGLAND 438
(J.B. Hobbs 76, H. Sutcliffe 64, F.E. Woolley 64, E. Hendren 74, R. Kilner 59; G.M. Parker 6 for 152)

SOUTH AFRICA
1st innings

H.W. Taylor	b Tate	7
R.H. Catterall	b Gilligan	0
M.J. Susskind	c Kilner b Tate	3
A.D. Nourse	lbw b Gilligan	1
J.M. Commaille	not out	1
J.M. Blanckenberg	b Tate	4
H.G. Deane	b Gilligan	2
E.P. Nupen	b Gilligan	0
S.J. Pegler	b Tate	0
T.A. Ward	b Gilligan	1
G.M. Parker	lbw b Gilligan	0
Extras	(b 2, lb 7, nb 3)	11
Total		30

2nd innings

H.W. Taylor	c & b Tate	34
J.M. Commaille	c Hendren b Tate	29
M.J. Susskind	b Gilligan	51
A.D. Nourse	c Wood b Gilligan	34
R.H. Catterall	c Hobbs b Tate	120
J.M. Blanckenberg	c Chapman b Gilligan	56
H.G. Deane	run out	5
E.P. Nupen	lbw b Tate	5
S.J. Pegler	c Hobbs b Gilligan	6
T.A. Ward	b Gilligan	19
G.M. Parker	not out	2
Extras	(b 4, lb 18, w 1, nb 6)	29
Total		390

Fall of wickets: 1–1, 2–4, 3–6, 4–14, 5–20, 6–23, 7–23, 8–24, 9–30, 10–30.

Second innings: 1–54, 2–101, 3–152, 4–161, 5–275, 6–284, 7–295, 8–350, 9–372, 10–390.

ENGLAND BOWLING (6-ball overs)

	O	M	R	W	O	M	R	W
Gilligan	6.3	4	7	6	28	6	83	5
Tate	6	1	12	4	54.4	19	103	4
Parkin					16	5	38	0
Kilner					22	10	40	0
Fender					17	5	56	0
Woolley					10	2	41	0

Umpires: H. Butt and W. Reeves

ENGLAND WON BY AN INNINGS AND 18 RUNS

quality in its flight, they did cause it frequently to break back at an extraordinarily sharp angle, and they most certainly did develop pace off the ground to an amazing extent. Very likely the acceleration of pace was the more disconcerting to the earlier batsmen because Mr Parker at the start of the day, had not foreshadowed the possibility of it.

Even Mr Taylor, one of the world's great batsmen, had to hurry his stroke, although it happened that he did not get a ball until he had seen three of his colleagues dismissed, and had had an opportunity to note what the wicket was doing. Tate made a collapse probable by finding an exceptional ball to beat the visitors' captain; it pitched on the blind spot and came back like lightning from the line of the off stump to make the leg turn cartwheels. Mr Gilligan turned probability into certainty by getting Mr Nourse leg-before in his next over. Mr Nourse plays the back-stroke as well as any living man. He could not, however, get his bat down in time for that one, but he had placed his feet early and correctly, and so the appeal was a mere formality.

Before these decisive events happened the innings had started dramatically. Mr Gilligan opened with a no-ball. His first counting delivery beat Mr Catterall for pace and knocked his leg stump out of the ground. The total was only 14 when Mr Taylor and Mr Nourse were sent back. Only eight more runs were made off the bat, but several balls, which beat it, went for leg-byes. The two bowlers took their wickets alternately until they were all square with two to go. Then Tate deserved to get dormy, but Parkin, who somehow had strayed into the slips, dropped an easy chance offered by Mr Commaille. In his next over Mr Gilligan finished off the innings. He gave Mr Ward a fast break-back, even more vicious than that which beat Mr Taylor, and, though the forward stroke which he opposed to it was executed admirably, perfect attack beat perfect defence, as it always has done and always will do. Thus the English captain was able to achieve a "record" analysis in his first Test Match at home.

Tate, after bowling more than 3,000 overs in two years, spent 1924–5 in Australia where his 38 wickets, average 23.18, in a series persuaded both batsmen and spectators that here was a worthy successor to Barnes. A virtual passenger through injury in the third Test, Tate bowled 2,304 balls for 36 wickets in the others, besides being called upon to perform against Goldfields Association, Toowoomba and Northern Districts. In 1911–12 Barnes had F.R. Foster at the other end in 1924–5 Tate was gloriously alone — Gilligan's blow over the heart in the Gentlemen v. Players match the previous summer having put an end to his career as a fast bowler.

Back in England, Tate went on bowling, so that at the close of 1925 his toil for three years could be expressed as

32,657 balls   729 wickets   14.75 average

plus minor efforts against Toowoomba, Northern Districts and the Goldfields.

Tate's misfortune was Bradman. The two Test series when they were in opposition predated body-line, after which (in the opinion of many) Bradman was a different player. In the series of 1928–9 and 1930 Tate just went on bowling at Bradman, his deliveries to that batsman exceeding those of Larwood by 500, Geary by 493, Hammond by 350 and J.C. White by 321. In 1930 Tate bowled 20 more balls at Bradman than did Larwood, Geary, White and Peebles combined. In the first game of each series Tate dismissed Bradman for a low score; by the fifth he had been worn down — 0 for 180 at Melbourne and one for 153 (the Australian No. 11) at the Oval. It was suggested above that Tate's Test career could be divided into two periods: 19 games before, and including, Sydney 1928–9, and 19 games afterwards. The latter must now be subdivided:

8 v. sides with Bradman	23 wkts	46.21 av.	142 B/W
11 v. sides without Bradman	32 wkts	26.40 av.	87 B/W

The year 1930 was, of course, one of destiny not only for Bradman and Tate but for the game of cricket, its outcome being body-line. Tate's misfortune to have predated body-line in his encounters with Bradman may be simply shown; Bradman's age span being v. Tate 20–21, v. Larwood 20–24, v. Verity 24–29, v. Bedser 38–39.

	Wkts	Ave.	B/W
Tate	5	71.40	149
Others	8	135.62	239
	13	110.92	204
Larwood	5	65.00	86
Others	13	95.69	180
	18	87.15	154
Pre-body-line			
Larwood	1	209	255
Others	10	96.40	200
	11	106.63	205
Body-line			
Larwood	4	29.00	44
Others	3*	93.33	116
	7	56.57	75
Verity	8	50.12	116
Others	19	99.68	134
	27	85.00	129
Bedser	6	43.83	84
Others	8	115.62	223
	14	84.85	163

Tate's third, and final, trip to Australia has often been regarded as a mistake. He was in his 38th year and, with body-line a reality in Jardine's mind, his presence would hardly be relevant. If, however, body-line failed, Tate was still the finest medium-pace bowler in England. He had just enjoyed a splendid domestic season (when Sussex were runners-up to Yorkshire in the Championship), finishing fourth in the national averages after Larwood, Verity and Bowes.

TATE'S DEADLY BOWLING

By G.J.V. Weigall

1 August 1932. The Bank Holiday match between Sussex and Middlesex, which was begun at Hove

* Two of these wickets were taken by Verity, so suggesting that the 1932–3 tour was essentially Larwood versus Bradman.

on Saturday, was dominated by the bowling of Tate, who came out with the following analysis:

O	M	R	W
21.3	6	28	7

one of the best he has ever had in his illustrious career. Up to luncheon he had taken only two of the five wickets that had fallen, but afterwards in seven overs and three balls, the rest fell to him for 13 runs.

When N. Haig won the toss he must have been exercised in his mind whether or not to bat first. The pitch was soft, and there were indications that the sun would shine strongly. Haig decided to bat, and set in the Rev. E.T. Killick and J.L. Guise,† and, curiously enough, the pitch was at its most difficult in the 45 minutes before luncheon, and it was during that 45 minutes that Hearne and Hulme were in together and Sussex did not get a wicket. The pitch, at any rate, cannot be blamed for the early Middlesex disasters. With the total at 22 the Rev. E.T. Killick was lbw to Tate, but Guise and Hearne brought the score to 44 before Guise was caught close in on the leg side by Wensley off a stroke made with the middle of the bat. Hendren, in going for a third run off a stroke to third man played by Hearne, was well run out by Bowley, and at 49 Allen jumped wildly down the pitch to Langridge, missed the ball, and was stumped. Twelve runs later H.J. Enthoven, who played a memorable innings in this match two or three years ago, was beaten and bowled by Langridge, and Middlesex, with half their wickets down for 61 runs and the pitch beginning to take spin with real enthusiasm, were in a desperate position.

Hearne remained, however, and Hulme came in to play an admirable little innings, which showed him quick on his feet [as became Arsenal's

† Whose finest cricketing moment had occurred on 24–5 June 1921 at Agar's Plough after G.O. Allen bowled out Winchester for 57 in their first innings, Eton replying with 255. Except for one man, Winchester did not do much better at their second attempt: Guise run out 278, the other batsmen 0, 21, 2, 13, 6, 9, 5, 9, 0, 0 not out. Eton won by seven wickets.

outside-right] and resolute in his punishing of any ball which gave him the slightest chance. Langridge gave both batsmen some uncomfortable overs, but they survived, and Hulme, indeed, hit him off his right foot through the covers to the boundary. K.S. Duleepsinhji might well have put on A. Melville [who bowled leg-breaks of a kind] to get the wicket Sussex wanted so badly before luncheon; but he did not, and at the interval 104 runs were on the board, of which Hearne had made 42 and Hulme 23.

Afterwards came Tate's triumph on a pitch which had become firmer. At 111 Hulme was bowled by a beautifully flighted ball at which he played far too soon, and one over later Hearne under-estimated the venom of Tate's speed from the pitch, and was caught close in at square-leg. Haig drove Tate and Scott for 4's, and then skied a ball of Tate's to Melville deep at mid-off, and soon afterwards Melville took another catch in the same position, this time off a hard, low drive by Price. Three runs later Durston gave K.S. Duleepsinhji a catch at first slip, and the Middlesex innings was over.

Sussex had an hour's batting before tea, and during that time Bowley and J. Parks scored 47 runs together. Those 47 runs were very valuable to Sussex, for the bowling of Allen and I.A.R. Peebles after tea reached a high standard. Only four runs had been added when Bowley, who seemed for a fraction of a second to lose sight of the ball, had his off-stump knocked out of the ground by Allen, and at 64 Parks, who played inside a ball that went away a little, was out in exactly the same way. Middlesex soon had another success, for Peebles, who was using his leg-break [odd phrasing: years of bowling the googly gradually deprived Peebles of his leg-break. Had it now been restored?] and bowling as well as he has done this season, got Cook caught at the wicket after that batsman had scored three. When Durston eventually came on for Allen K.S. Duleepsinhji, who played well and carefully for his 29 runs, hooked him for 4, but both he and H. Parks were out by the time the score had reached

112, and the fall of another wicket would have seen the game evenly balanced. Melville and Langridge, however, batted coolly during the last critical 20 minutes, and Sussex finished up with a substantial advantage. The fielding of both sides added not a little to the joys of a thoroughly interesting day.

Close: MIDDLESEX 140 (M.W. Tate 7 for 28), SUSSEX 137 for 5
(James Langridge 15 not out, A. Melville 15 not out.)

Second Day

2 August 1932. The Bank Holiday match at Hove between Sussex and Middlesex which ended at

TATE   He never bowled a no-ball.

5.50 yesterday in a victory for Sussex by an innings and 37 runs was a personal triumph for Tate. He followed up his feat of taking seven Middlesex wickets in the first innings for 28 runs by scoring 50 runs and then taking six wickets for 30 runs in the second innings. In the whole match he bowled 46.3 overs, including 17 maidens, for 58 runs and 13 wickets.

Tate owed a little of his success to the state of the pitch, a little to the weakness of the batting, and more than a little to the excellence of the fielding, but most of all to the fact that he was continually producing that extra pace off the pitch which beats the soundest stroke of the soundest batsman.

[Sussex carried their overnight 137 for 5 to 191 for 8] Langridge all this time was defending soberly and correctly, and then Tate came in to provide the perfect contrast. At the beginning he played with all the conscious rectitude of a Test Match No. 1, but then the old, delightful instincts asserted themselves and Tate became the formidable

SUSSEX v. MIDDLESEX
Hove, 31 July and 1 August 1932

MIDDLESEX
1st innings

Rev. E.T. Killick	lbw b Tate	3
J.L. Guise	c Wensley b Tate	17
J.W. Hearne	c Wensley b Tate	44
E. Hendren	run out	0
G.O. Allen	st Cornford b Langridge	3
H.J. Enthoven	b Langridge	6
J. Hulme	b Tate	25
N. Haig	c Melville b Tate	17
W.F. Price	c Melville b Tate	3
T.J. Durston	c Duleepsinhji b Tate	6
I.A.R. Peebles	not out	0
Extras	(b 12, lb 3, w 1)	16
Total		140

2nd innings

Rev. E.T. Killick	lbw b Tate	5
J.L. Guise	c J. Parks b Tate	7
J.W. Hearne	c J. Parks b Scott	3
E. Hendren	c Duleepsinhji b Tate	32
G.O. Alien	lbw b Tate	11
H.J. Enthoven	b Wensley	1
J. Hulme	b Wensley	19
N. Haig	b Wensley	0
W.F. Price	b Tate	2
T.J. Durston	not out	10
I.A.R. Peebles	c Bowley b Tate	0
Extras	(b 5, lb 2, w 1)	98
Total		98

SUSSEX
1st innings

E.H. Bowley	b Allen	25
J. Parks	b Allen	23
K.S. Duleepsinhji	c Guise b Durston	29
T. Cooke	c Price b Peebles	3
Jas. Langridge	not out	57
H. Parks	run out	9
A. Melville	b Haig	24
R.S.G. Scott	c Hulme b Peebles	9
A.F. Wensley	c Hulme b Durston	7
M.W. Tate	lbw b Peebles	50
W. Cornford	c Hearne b Peebles	4
Extras	(b 18, lb 10, w 2, nb 5)	35
Total		275

MIDDLESEX BOWLING

	O	M	R	W
Allen	34	10	72	2
Durston	22	7	37	2
Haig	17	9	29	1
Peebles	41.4	12	86	4
Hearne	6	1	16	0

Umpires: W. Hitch and W.A. Buswell

SUSSEX BOWLING (6-ball overs)

	O	M	R	W	O	M	R	W
Tate	21.3	6	28	7	25	11	30	6
Scott	10	1	32	0	9	4	13	1
Wensley	11	6	19	0	18	6	31	3
Langridge	15	3	36	2	7	2	11	0
Bowley	3	0	9	0	1	0	3	0
Melville					1	0	2	0

SUSSEX WON BY AN INNINGS AND 37 RUNS

batsman who can take liberties with all the canons of orthodoxy and yet hit the ball hard and uncommonly accurately. There were a few more or less hilarious mis-hits, of course, but the pull that earned him six runs to square-leg off Peebles was a noble stroke and there was nothing in the least fortuitous about an off-drive to the boundary off Haig, who had the new ball after the interval.

Tate had scored 41 to Langridge's 48 and afterwards Langridge reached his 50 after he had been batting for three hours and Tate immediately followed him by means of a stroke off Peebles which defies analysis, after batting only 45 minutes. He was leg-before-wicket to the next ball, however, and at 2.40 the innings came to an end with Langridge not out for a patient 57.

When Middlesex went in they had not only a deficit of 135 runs to depress them, but also the fact that during the end of the Sussex innings the ball bowled to the north tended to pop. They made a bad start, the Rev. E.T. Killick being leg-before-wicket to Tate with the score at seven, and Tate for some time continued to bowl intimidatingly enough for the silly mid-off and mid-on he brought in to field in their perilous positions with complete equanimity. At 16 two major disasters befell Middlesex. First Hearne touched an outswinging ball from Scott and was caught low down by J. Parks close in at third slip, and then J.L. Guise snicked a ball from Tate, which beat him by its pace off the pitch, on to his pads, from whence it went to backward point. The pitch had not been guilty of giving Sussex any unfair help, and when Allen, at 30, was leg-before-wicket to Tate, Tate was only realizing on the score card the moral claim to a wicket his bowling had already established. H.J. Enthoven, after scoring a single, was bowled by Wensley, who had come on for Scott, but after that Hendren and Hulme stayed in together until they had raised the score to 53.

...This stand, small as it was, gave a definite check to Sussex. The sixth wicket partnership added in all 48 runs before Hulme was bowled in playing forward to Wensley. Any hope Middlesex might have had of saving the innings defeat vanished when Hendren was beautifully caught at first slip by K.S. Duleepsinhji off Tate. Durston hit a brave 4, but at 98 Tate bowled Price with a ball that was not only admirable in itself, but which suggested that the spot at the north end would have caused Sussex some anxiety had they been called on to make 200 runs in the fourth innings. In the same over Peebles was brilliantly caught at second slip by Bowley and the match was over.

FRANK EDWARD WOOLLEY
Kent

His style, certainly, is ideal both to watch and to try to copy. Whatever he does when batting is most graceful. He is the modern-day Palairet. The grace and ease of his attack and defence is unsurpassed, and unlike many present-day players, he is never guilty of making an unorthodox stroke, and his timing of the ball when driving is the perfection of what timing should be. In all that he does while he is batting there is a simplicity of method which is the essence of correctness and which gives the onlooker ample time to recognize the stamp of a really great batsman. Although popularly supposed to be almost a hitter Woolley's defence and back play are actually his strongest weapons, so correct are his methods (G.J.V. Weigall, 7 August 1922).

Woolley probably caused more spectators to ignore the scoreboard than any other batsman in history. (He played almost four times as many innings as Victor Trumper.) He was a cult figure much as B.A. Richards was in the 1970s, persuading rational men that a felicitous hour spent in the company of the hero — whatever the outcome of the game — was preferable to a ground-out win. Just as Richards played some of his greatest innings in limited-overs cricket, we may be certain that Woolley would have justified this form of entertainment.* "There was all summer in a stroke by Woolley and he batted as is sometimes shown in dreams," wrote R.C. Robertson-Glasgow. When Woolley was in form,

bowlers waited upon him; he was also an artist–batsman and therefore frowned upon by those who seek to invest in a player. In nineteen Tests against Australia after the First World War — and before being omitted from the 1928–9 MCC party ("the worst crime since the Crucifixion," said Weigall) — Woolley played 33 innings, average 36 — only ten times reaching 50, with one century and five "ducks".

On the occasion of Woolley's eightieth birthday in 1967 Sir Donald Bradman paid tribute to "one of the most majestic and classical innings I have seen, with every stroke in the book played with supreme ease". Sir Donald was referring to a match long since forgotten save by its few survivors and onlookers, one hardly noticed in England at the time, between New South Wales and A.H.H. Gilligan's MCC side on its way to New Zealand in November 1929 at Sydney. For the connoisseur of contrasting styles, it was a re-enactment of MacLaren, Spooner and John Tyldesley pitted against Ranji and Fry or Trumper and Duff. At Sydney the very young McCabe showed more than promise, Archie Jackson and his mentor Alan Kippax made hundreds, Duleep enchanted,

* The August Bank Holiday game between Kent and Gloucestershire at Canterbury in 1932 ended early after Hammond, 136 in 95 minutes, had been severe on Freeman, 18–0–135–3. A.P.F. Chapman and B.H. Lyon then arranged an each side bat for an hour contest; as the fielding was "brilliant", it may be assumed the bowling was not contemptible. Gloucestershire 194, Kent 201 for five in 45 minutes: Woolley, "not exerting himself", 86 in half an hour.

while Bradman butchered the bowling. Surpassing them all was Woolley — 219 in four hours, without a sponsor in sight.

Perhaps the key to the Woolley personality is to be found in the 1939 *Wisden*, to which he contributed some thoughts on his career. This had begun in 1906, a year when Kent won the Championship, Woolley's first hundred coming in 90 minutes. It was the summer when Tom Hayward scored 3,518 runs, when George Hirst's "double" consisted of 2,385 runs and 208 wickets, when Arthur Fielder of Kent took all ten Gentlemen's wickets in the first innings at Lord's before N.A. Knox bowled as fast as anyone P.F. Warner had seen. Henry Martyn of Somerset stood up to Knox for a while, taking the ball "with ease and certainty". Woolley was a product of this age, his response manifesting itself in 1939: "Before 1914 there were something like 30 players up to his [Hammond's] standard and he would have been in the England team only if at the top of his form."

On the face of it, this statement is absurd; not so if we amend it to become "30 players looked as good as Hammond". Similarly with Warner's view that the pre-1914 Hobbs batted just like an amateur, meaning surely that some amateurs batted just like Hobbs while they were at the wicket.

A further key to the Woolley personality is also to be found in that 1939 *Wisden*: "The time may arrive when the third day of county games will be abolished…I think if the counties played matches of two days' duration with a day's rest between each for travelling, it would be a step towards better cricket."

As Woolley had batted with K.L. Hutchings before 1914, and with A.P.F. Chapman and L.E.G. Ames after 1914, his suggestion made sense, bearing in mind that he generally progressed at 50 runs an hour.

Cricketing wordsmiths may care to ponder the meaning of "leisurely", and see if they agree with the *Shorter Oxford English Dictionary's* "proceeding without haste". On 1 August 1922 Woolley batted for Kent against Surrey at the Oval.

Woolley took 101 minutes to make his 100. He went leisurely along, never seeming to be dis-turbed by anything, and, as usual, his fours looked effortless; nor was he ever in difficulties with any of the bowling.

A perfect description of the great aristocrat at the wicket.

GREAT INNINGS BY WOOLLEY

Kent won the toss against Middlesex at Canterbury on 8 August 1923.

By G.J.V. Weigall

Woolley's hitting roused the large crowd to a high pitch of enthusiasm. [He] was driving the ball to the boundary on either side of the wicket, pulling 6's from wide balls or placing and forcing the ball off his body to square leg. There was grace and wonderful timing in all his scoring strokes, and his late cutting, which was used only at rare

WOOLLEY   The slightest hint of being amused.

intervals, was the perfection of elegance. Nor must we forget his defence in such a brilliant innings; there is no living player whose body balance and methods of execution are so effective from a scoring point of view. He has made a habit and study of always having his back foot facing point when he plays back, so that his body is sideways when he is naturally playing the ball and not facing the bowler with both shoulders...[After the interval] Woolley was batting with tremendous power and actually made 105 runs off his own bat in the first hour.

KENT 445 (F.E. Woolley 270, W.H. Ashdown 44, G.J. Bryan 26).
The Middlesex bowlers included J. Durston, G.T.S. Stevens and the very young G.O. Allen.
A week later, against Somerset, Woolley made 105 in 100 minutes.

WOOLLEY V. MACDONALD
Old Trafford, 15 August 1928

By Dudley Carew

The match between Lancashire and Kent — the match that will in all probability decide the championship — was begun at Old Trafford yesterday. At one time Kent had actually 262 runs on the board with only three wickets down, but yet they were all out for a total of 277.

If Kent do not win the championship — and that they will now do so seems very improbable — they will have the austere consolation of knowing that their batting yesterday, with the illustrious exception of Woolley, was nothing like good enough to deserve it. As was right and proper, the day was a triumph for the two outstanding cricketers of the match, Woolley and Macdonald. Woolley, playing magnificent cricket, scored 151 runs, and Macdonald not only took seven wickets, but, once Woolley had gone, swung the game decisively and dramatically over in favour of Lancashire.

Except for ten minutes, in which Hardinge, always less than a first-class batsman when there is a fast bowler about, died a dozen moral deaths before he actually snicked a ball to Duckworth, the story of the morning's play is the story of the brilliance of Woolley. Ashdown looked like getting runs before he fell to a catch at the wicket off a good lengthed ball from Macdonald, and Ames, coming in with two wickets down for 43, proved in everything except the not unimportant matter of running between the wickets an able and discreet partner in a stand that put on 128 runs.

Macdonald was bowling extremely fast when Woolley went in, and Woolley immediately, with a nonchalance that amounted to an act of positive cruelty to a determined and potentially destructive bowler, proceeded to take three yards off his pace; four times he got on top of a rising ball and cut it for a boundary that half a dozen slips would not have been able to stop. When Hopwood came on the partnership was thrown for a moment out of its stride, for Ames could have been run out off his first ball, and Woolley might possibly have been caught at short slip. Things after this once more proceeded to go according to plan — Woolley's plan. Whenever Macdonald was off the Lancashire bowling sagged badly. Neither R. Tyldesley, Iddon, nor Hopwood would keep a length, and Iddon and Hopwood, both of whom normally rely on the ball that goes away from the batsman, found it obviously awkward to bowl against a left-handed batsman as inconsiderately determined to use his height and reach as Woolley.

After he had reached his 50, Woolley straight-drove Hopwood for a lovely and effortless 6, and he then hit two consecutive balls from Tyldesley to the boundary. Ames also hit two quick 4's off loose balls from Iddon, and before luncheon J.R. Barnes brought Macdonald back, but Woolley showed no sign of faltering in the first duty of every great batsman — that of making the bowling look easy. He made another beautiful square cut, and at luncheon he had made 80 out of a total of 148 for two wickets. Ames was then 38.

Rain fell during the interval, and a further

shower just as the players came on the field prevented a start from being made until after 2.30. With the sun coming out the ball was inclined to fly, and Ames was hit on the hand by a ball from Macdonald that came back sharply. The blow was a nasty one, and Ames, playing irresolutely at the next ball, had his middle stump knocked out of the ground. Woolley, who throughout his innings gave a thrilling exhibition of the way rising balls can be cut off the middle, and even the leg stump, took his score past the hundred with two square cuts off Macdonald that were 4's every yard from the bat. The 200 came on the board, but Barnes did not have the new ball. The wicket was taking spin, and for a time the left-handed bowlers kept down the scoring. Woolley, however, hit a 6 and a 4 off Iddon in one over, and at 242 Barnes decided that the tide in the affairs of three-day cricket demanded that the new ball should be taken, and Macdonald and Sibbles were put on.

Woolley immediately cut Macdonald for a 4 and a 3, and soon afterwards pulled him to the boundary to complete his 150. In the same over however, he gave Iddon at square leg an easy catch. He had batted for just over three hours and had hit three 6's and sixteen 4's.

KENT 277 (F.E. Woolley 151; E.A. Macdonald 7 for 101) and 113 (Macdonald 8 for 53) lost to LAN-CASHIRE 478 for 5 declared (F. Watson 56, C. Hallows 184, E. Tyldesley 159) by an innings and 88 runs.

Lancashire won the Championship for the third year in succession, winning 15 matches out of 30 (as did Kent), but losing none to Kent's five defeats.

Woolley's county season:
Innings 47   TNO 3   Runs 2,582   HS 198
Av. 58.68
Macdonald's county season:
Overs 1,173   Mdns 252   Runs 3,443
Wkts 178   Av. 19.34

Macdonald, in four full seasons for Lancashire, had so far taken 666 wickets, average 19.92.

A DAY AT THE OVAL, 1924

Yorkshire won the Championship four times in a row from 1922 to 1925, and, truth to tell, were getting somewhat arrogant. It was hardly surprising therefore that when things did go wrong for them cricket correspondents representing papers outside Yorkshire tended to rejoice, albeit in mannerly fashion. Certainly the county's attack in 1924 — Emmott Robinson, Waddington, Macaulay, Kilner and Rhodes — strikes our eye as pretty formidable.

By A.C.M. Croome

16 September 1924. Yesterday at the Oval the Rest of England greatly increased the advantage that they had gained over Yorkshire on Saturday. They began with 165 for two wickets against Yorkshire's score of 166, and had made 524 for eight wickets by tea time, when they declared their innings closed. Yorkshire then made 103 for the loss of Holmes and Sutcliffe.

The Rest made light of the best county attack in the country, and that on a wicket which did not strike the spectator as specially easy and with the outfield slow. Degenerates as these moderns are they yet managed between them to hit eight 6's from a wicket pitched in the middle of the Oval... Mr Chapman drove home an advantage in a way to prove himself an invaluable batsman in a three-day match. While he was in with Woolley there was a period of 30 minutes during which the two left-handers treated the Yorkshiremen as if they were country-house bowlers, and drove them for 4's and 6's — a most agreeable spectacle.

But the treat of the day was the batting of Woolley, who added 156 to his Saturday's score of 46 in three hours and a quarter. He was not slogging; his ease was as remarkable as his power; he was so quickly in position when playing back that his arm movement was deliberate and his driving was done from his full height with a smooth unhurried sweep; he played the innings of the batsman that old gentlemen write about — the batsman who drives fast bowlers over the in-fields and whose strokes cannot be blocked because he has too many of them. One rejoiced at his driving Rhodes over and through his deep-fields for three 4's in one over; but a more delicate titbit was the left-hand batsman's late cutting of the left-hand bowler Kilner with the field arranged to stop driving. Yorkshire let him off several times, but that was no fault of Woolley's, and one left it at that. Rhodes's analysis — 0 for 124 — testified to resolute batting.

Woolley, after his first stroke [which almost resulted in a caught and bowled to Kilner] had been timing the ball perfectly and making runs quickly, and for some minutes one was a little sorry for Mr Chapman, in that he had to stand comparison with such perfect left-handed batting; it looked as if the ball was hesitating too much between pitch and bat to suit Mr Chapman's optimistic stroke. Then Mr Chapman made a straight drive for 4, and after that he hit the ball before it could hesitate and banged it exactly where he pleased. One over from Rhodes must have reminded that bowler of the incalculable insolence of Mr Jessop. Mr Chapman hit his third ball over the ropes at long-on for 6, the fourth he hit out of the ground slightly squarer — a huge hit; the fifth he drove hard and straight, but as the ball travelled slowly on the wet outfield he got only a 3; thereupon Woolley showed he could do that sort of thing, and with less effort, and he hit the last ball for 6 square, as if it had been teed — 21 from four balls.

Mr Chapman's most remarkable stroke was yet to come — a 6, a little to the on of straight, from a full pitch of Waddington's. He was out from his next drive to a good, plain catch by Sutcliffe at extra cover. He had made his 74 in 52 minutes, and that though he started slowly. Woolley, though temporarily outpaced, had been doing his part, and the wicket had added 124 in those exhilarating 52 minutes, at one time 50 runs having been scored in seven minutes...At lunch the score was 362 for five. Afterwards Woolley hit out as if a deep field was merely a bunker to be carried, and he reached his second hundred

serenely and without altering his gait with a confident on-drive from Macaulay. He was then stumped.

THE REST beat YORKSHIRE by an innings and 124 runs.

AGAIN THE OVAL, THIS TIME 1926

Lancashire won the Championship in 1926, the deciding factor being the fast bowling of MacDonald. When it came to Lancashire's match against The Rest, the selectors paid Lancashire — and spectators — the compliment of picking *en bloc* the same side which had beaten Australia in the Fifth Test. In spite of this, Lancashire dismissed The Rest on the first day for 217, only a hundred by Hendren, a superb hooker, offering much challenge to Macdonald, who was admirably supported by Sibbles and Richard Tyldesley. By the close Lancashire were 84 without loss, and in a commanding position.

On the Monday Lancashire collapsed, all ten wickets falling before Larwood and Tate for 93 runs.

By A.C.M. Croome

14 September 1926. When the Rest went in again Hobbs's innings was a lesson in timing the ball. With him you are not struck with the power in the stroke, except when he lets all Hobbs go into a leg hit; the ball hurries off of its own accord. There was one on-drive of his from a ball that seemed to be pitching out of reach. Hobbs did reach forward — and smoothly; he kept it down and with no more than a push sent it between two fieldsmen to the on boundary. Equally unintelligible to the ordinary player is the meditative stroke of his which places the short ball behind the wicket with the angled face of an upright bat. But yesterday even Ovalites had to allow that he was overshadowed by Sutcliffe. The bowlers, especially R. Tyldesley, were generous to Sutcliffe with leg balls, and he hit 4's off them superbly; but what was more interesting because it demanded more initiative, was the powerful thrust in his back play. The short balls from Macdonald that came at a dangerous height were revealed as long hops.

A fast bowler who keeps the ball short is never an object of sympathy, and the crowd made it clear in the usual way that the trouncing of Macdonald by Sutcliffe was entirely to its taste. Off or on, if the ball was short — and it usually was — it was banged with a full bat. Later on it was the turn of Sibbles, from whom Sutcliffe hit 20 in five balls. In the end he was caught from a big drive in the deep field for as exhilarating an innings as one could hope to see; he made his 136 in just over two hours; they came in a very large proportion from big hits; among them were a 6 and 23 4's. His wicket, the second, fell at 225. Hobbs, who gave two hard chances, had been caught from a skied mis-hit at 157. After that Woolley hit the tired bowlers all over the field.

The Rest were now 291 for two, the runs scored in 155 minutes.

15 September 1926. Woolley, with 65, and Hendren, with 15, continued the England innings in a position of no responsibility. Woolley showed his appreciation of this freedom by hitting out at the fresh bowling from the start, as he had hit out overnight when the sting had been forcibly extracted from it by Sutcliffe. He had some luck with his strokes, but as he was deliberately hitting under the ball and across it to make the pace, it was not to be counted against him. He kept the ball out of harm's way by hitting it hard, and his range of strokes was so extensive that he made it look as if Lancashire were two men short in the field. Anything pitched up he drove; the short ball to the off was forced anywhere between third man and mid-off; and if it came near his legs gliding was too tame for him; he hit it hard with an upright bat. He took his own score from 65 to 100 in less than 20 minutes. Hendren to begin with was modestly content to play Remus, but after a little he asserted himself, and towards the end of

the partnership he was scoring the faster of the two...In 70 minutes the pair added 177 runs. If cricket must be played on wickets that favour the batsmen, this was the way to bat, and with the fourth day available some disappointment was expressed when the innings was declared closed at 468 for two — 508 on.

Tate and G.T.S. Stevens then bowled Lancashire out for 134, The Rest winning by 374 runs.

Woolley's 172 not out in 125 minutes was the more remarkable in that he hit only two sixes and 17 fours — 80 runs in boundaries. There must have been relatively few "dot" balls bowled to him. During The Rest's innings Lancashire averaged 20.4 overs an hour.

15 August 1938. Twenty-nine years less four days after making 68 for Kent v. M.A. Noble's Australians at Canterbury, Woolley played against Bradman's side. His first-class record to date was 58,715 runs, 2,055 wickets and 1,010 catches. The first ball of Kent's innings proved fatal; patting it up the pitch, Woolley embarked upon a single [Woolley, run out 0].

The countryside for miles around was shocked into a stricken and incredulous silence...[Kent followed on]. There was no repetition of the first innings' fiasco; so much the reverse, indeed, that in under 40 minutes Woolley had completed a 50 which included a 5, thanks to an overthrow, and 10 4's. He started off with two boundaries off Waite, and then two drives off White which confirmed that the old ease of timing wrist and foot-work were still there. He took two 4's in one over off White — pull is too vulgar and utilitarian a word to describe the gentle process by which Woolley persuaded the ball to the mid-wicket boundary — and then, when Fleetwood-Smith came on, he hit successive balls through the covers and to mid-wicket for 4's, the second of which gave him his 50.

After scoring 81 in 66 minutes, Woolley checked his stroke to Ward and was caught low down at mid-on by Bradman.

On 26 May 1939 a Kent XI played King's School, Canterbury, and managed to draw, replying with 89 for eight wickets to the School's 245. Among those appearing for the Kent XI were P.R. Sunnucks, the first victim of the 1935 revised lbw law; J.G.W. Davies; T.W. Spencer, a future Test umpire; three Kent stalwarts-to-be in B.R. Edrich, R.R. Dovey and N.W. Harding; and a wicketkeeper, T.G. Evans.

J.C. Corben opened for the School and made 31, ten other batsmen contributing 44; in that sense the Kent XI won the game. However, King's School were permitted to include their coach, F.E. Woolley, who — as *Wisden* had long been in the habit of pointing out — inflicted heavy punishment on the bowlers, on this occasion, 148 runs.

On 23 May 1946 King George VI was present at the Oval to see Surrey play Old England, the latter represented by H. Sutcliffe, A. Sandham, F.E. Woolley, E. Hendren, D.R. Jardine, P.G.H. Fender, D.J. Knight, M.W. Tate, E.R.T. Holmes, M.J.C. Allom and E.W. Brookes — with A.P. Freeman to help out with the bowling. The umpires were J.B. Hobbs and H. Strudwick. R.B. Vincent noted that the start of Old England's innings (in reply to Surrey's 248 for six declared) was

...tragic, the great Sutcliffe, saviour of England in many a hard-fought match, being leg-before-wicket and Sandham caught high up in the slips with but two runs on the board. And so, after all these years, Woolley, greeted as ever he was all over the world, and Hendren batting together in the sunshine at the Oval. Could the heart of a cricket lover ask for more? Woolley with his elegant ease lofting the ball over the bowler's head or placing it with exquisite timing to the on: and Hendren, still nimble of foot, advancing out to tame the bowling. Together they had added 102 runs in a partnership glorious to watch before Woolley was out to a hero's death, caught in the deep.

OLD ENGLAND 232 for 5 (E. Hendren 94, F.E. Woolley 62, D.R. Jardine 54). Match drawn.

Woolley was aged 59, Hendren 57 — and Jardine wore his Harlequin cap.

LORD CONSTANTINE (SIR LEARIE NICHOLAS)
Trinidad

The summer of 1928 saw West Indies lose all three Tests to England by an innings, a result hardly surprising in view of Australia's fate the following winter, and a match with Wales by eight wickets. Larwood and Tate were among those who bowled for England, and the West Indians deemed them good. But the man who impressed them most of all was a "Welshman" born in Smethwick, one S.F. Barnes, then in his 56th year, whose match figures (in spite of sundry missed catches) were 48–14–118–12. In support of Barnes was the American Frank Ryan.

With George Challenor past his best at 40 — and C.L.R. James ranked the Challenor of earlier years as the equal of Worrell, Weekes and Walcott — Constantine was West Indies' outstanding player of 1928, scoring 1,381 runs, average 34.52, and taking 107 wickets, average 22.95 in first-class games.* If, on his record, an inspirational cricketer, Constantine had no superior as an entertainer.

By R.B. Vincent

11 June 1928. The West Indies made their second appearance at Lord's on Saturday, when Middlesex kept them in the field all day to score 313 runs for the loss of six wickets. The score, as scores go in these days, was not an unusually large one on an easy paced wicket, and the West Indies must be credited on the whole with having done quite well on the day's play. Had their fast bowlers been granted that shade of good luck which fast bowlers quite rightly expect but so seldom get, N. Haig would have scored 100 runs less than he did, but the West Indies can console themselves with the knowledge that by allowing Haig to stay in — he was missed twice in the slips very early in his innings — they escaped the pain of a Hearne–Hendren partnership, Hearne being out before his comrade came in. Individually they are, to be sure, hard enough to get out, but when they are in together they are twice as difficult to shift.

It is no depreciation of Haig's valuable innings to say that what the Saturday afternoon crowd enjoyed more than anything was the magnificent fielding of the West Indies team, and if among a thoroughly keen team L.N. Constantine attracted the most favour it must be on the score that the ball followed him round the field. It is doubtful whether at the moment there is a better all-round cricketer in this country than Constantine; he is a match-winning batsman of the most adventurous type; a definitely fast bowler, and as a fieldsman not even Robinson of Yorkshire, has more original ideas of getting a batsman out. At one time on Saturday the fielding was so keen, and the ball came back so unexpectedly fast, that the batsmen were afraid to move a foot. The pitch never

* Other touring players to perform the "double" during the present century were W.W. Armstrong (1905, 1909, 1921), G.A. Faulkner (1912), H.L. Collins (1919) and J.M. Gregory (1921). V. Mankad would in 1946.

played quite fast enough to suit the West Indies' fast bowlers, and they never seemed quite firm in their run up to the wicket, but both G.N. Francis and Constantine pegged away courageously. Of the two Francis remained the more accurate, but Constantine on occasions bowled the faster and more dangerous ball.

The heavy rain in the early morning had no effect on the pitch itself, which had been covered, but there had already been enough rain earlier in the week to prevent it from having much life. Constantine, from the pavilion end, and Francis, however, must both have had some hope of sending back Haig, whose idiosyncracies of footwork — the left foot is very errant at times — invited a sudden fast "yorker." One such "yorker" did hit him on the foot, but the appeal for leg-before-wicket was not allowed. Haig, however, has a wonderful eye, and, having had his escapes, settled down to hit the ball about in the most confident manner. He lost Lee, caught at short leg off a full pitch, when fewer than 20 runs had been scored, and Hearne himself put the ball up dangerously near to square leg when he had scored only three runs. After that Hearne showed the bowlers nothing but the full blade of the bat with two legs behind it, and at luncheon the total had been taken to 37.

After the interval the slower bowlers had even less effect on the rate of scoring than the fast bowlers had done, but when the partnership had produced 153 runs in about two hours Hearne suddenly played, for him, a most loose stroke, and was caught off a skier on the leg-side by the wicket-keeper. Hendren from the first showed very little inclination to rub home the opportunity which Hearne had prepared for him, and towards the end of the day, when F.T. Mann clearly showed him what the state of the game demanded, became even more strangely subdued. Haig, on the other hand, did his utmost to keep up the rate of scoring, until, having scored his second century of the season, he was bowled with the total at 227. E.T. Killick was obviously never comfortable, and G.O. Allen was sacrificed to an injudicious call for a run by Hendren to an extremely alert cover-point. Mann required no more than three overs to loosen his shoulders, and then treated the spectators, who had shown a tendency to be exasperated with Hendren's batting, to some glorious hitting. He scored a 6 and two 4's in one over from Roach, but in trying to hit Francis over the pavilion was bowled, and the day ended with Hendren still there and the West Indies fieldsmen still greedily looking for the leanest chance of running him out.

Close: MIDDLESEX 313 for 6 (N.E. Haig 119, J.W. Hearne 75, E. Hendren 62 not out).

Second Day

12 June 1928. The play in the match between the West Indies and Middlesex at Lord's threatened at one time yesterday to be disastrous to the touring team, but a truly great innings by L.N. Constantine and an eventful half-hour's play at the end of the day left them full of life and hope to fight again to-day. As the game now stands, Middlesex, with two wickets down in their second innings, are 162 runs ahead.

Everything else in the day's play was entirely put in the shade by Constantine's batting, and it is not flattery to remark that when once he was out cricket seemed to be a dreary game. He went in to bat when five wickets were down for 79 runs, against a Middlesex total of 352, with the bowlers no doubt in thoroughly good conceit with themselves; but half an hour of Constantine entirely changed the outlook of the game.

The cricket-going public have been lucky in that these last two touring sides in this country have possessed cricketers such as C.C. Dacre and Constantine. Whether it be Dacre [qualifying for Gloucestershire for whom he played in the 1930 tie with the Australians] or Constantine who hits the ball harder, or more often, is open to question. Possibly Dacre could make the ball travel off the bat a little more viciously, but no one living could have shown a more pleasurable intent to score off every ball sent down to him than did Constantine yesterday. Moreover, he tried, so far as he could, to adopt the most orthodox, though now frequently unexploited, method of dealing with each particular ball. Some of his scoring strokes were a revelation to those who had forgotten where runs could be made, and memorable in an innings which must rank among the very best played at Lord's this year were the way in which he hit the fast bowling over mid-wicket's head, a remarkable 6 over cover-point's head which landed high up in the new grand stand, and his straight driving of short-pitched balls. Altogether, after his magnificent fielding on Saturday and the perisistent threat of his fast bowling, Constantine established definite claims to be considered an ideal number eight in a World team. . .

Close: MIDDLESEX 352 for 6 declared (E. Hendren 100 not out) and 40 for 2, WEST INDIES 230 (L.N. Constantine 86).

Third Day

13 June 1928. The West Indies, after a match which was a continuous triumph for Constantine, beat Middlesex at Lord's yesterday by three wickets.

Constantine's fielding on the first day, his batting on Monday, and his bowling and batting yesterday definitely established his claim to be considered as the most determined match-winning cricketer in the world. It is seldom that the Pavilion at Lord's twice rises to a player in one day; but yesterday Constantine was accorded that honour — and it is a very considerable one — first, before luncheon, when he had rattled out the Middlesex batsmen, and towards the end of the match, when he had won the match for his side by a gloriously daring display of batsmanship. If further proof is needed of what he can reasonably be expected to do, the unusually large amount of people who left their work unaccoun-

tably early was clear testimony, and he did not fail them. Moreover, it is difficult to see how he will fail his admirers. As a fieldsman he may be inclined impetuously to overrun the ball, as a bowler he may not always be able to persuade batsmen to withdraw so obviously as some Middlesex batsmen did yesterday, and as a batsman he may be deceived by a persistent spin bowler, but his record in the match in question was triumphant. In the first Middlesex innings he saved a quantity of runs, and in the West Indies' first innings he for the first time clearly saved his side from defeat. He followed that by giving his team a chance of winning the game by hitting the stumps five times and getting two other batsmen caught in the slips, and he then rounded off a truly wonderful achievement by scoring 103 runs out of 133 [in 60 minutes] for the sixth wicket, when the balance of play was overwhelmingly against his side — a match of which any cricketer may well be proud, and which the spectators at Lord's were fully appreciative. Such compliment as he was paid by every one at Lord's yesterday, spectators, card-sellers, groundsmen, gatemen, and all the others who should have been attending to their particular business, probably not even excluding the umpires and the scorers, and most certainly including the beaten side, was remarkable, but no more than he deserved.

When play was continued in the morning Middlesex were in the comfortable position of being 163 runs ahead with eight wickets yet to fall. Hearne and Hendren seemed well set to avoid any possibility of defeat, but there followed a curious turn in the game. Constantine, bowling from the practice ground end, all but bowled Hendren and hit him a wicked blow on the chest in one over. He was taken off, and J.A. Small, who relieved him, did the necessary by sending back Hearne leg-before-wicket. N. Haig then came in, and the West Indies captain very wisely put Constantine on again, this time at the Pavilion end. That decision by R.K. Nunes won the match for his side. Constantine bowled as a fast bowler will do when his tail is up [in his second spell, six wickets for 11 runs off 45 balls], and Middlesex were all out for 136, and the West Indies required no more than 259 runs to win the match.

After luncheon G. Challenor and M.P. Fernandes, keeping well apace with the clock, for a time established a winning mood, but when at 63 Challenor was bowled the game was apparently nearly won by Middlesex. W. St Hill was also soon out, and although the diminutive E.L. Bartlett played courageously and attractively, five wickets were down with 138 runs still required for victory.

Fernandes, however, had in the meantime been batting most surely, and no enthusiastic laudation of Constantine must be allowed to belittle what he, too, did for his side. He, in fact, never looked like getting out, and while the crowd stood on their seats to cheer Constantine's audacious hitting [including two sixes and twelve fours], contended himself with playing well

MIDDLESEX v. WEST INDIES
Lord's, 9, 11, 12 June 1928

MIDDLESEX
1st innings

N.E. Haig	b Small	119
H.W. Lee	c Martin b Constantine	11
J.W. Hearne	c Nunes b Roach	75
E. Hendren	not out	100
E.T. Killick	b Francis	6
G.O. Allen	run out	4
F.T. Mann	b Francis	32
I.A.R. Peebles	not out	0
T.J. Durston		
W.F. Price	did not bat	
J.A. Powell		
Extras	(b 2, lb 4, nb 3)	9
Total	(6 wkts dec.)	352

2nd innings

G.O. Allen	c & b Francis	7
H.W. Lee	b Constantine	15
J.W. Hearne	lbw b Small	28
E. Hendren	c Francis b Constantine	52
N.E. Haig	b Constantine	5
E.T. Killick	c Francis b Constantine	4
F.T. Mann	b Small	4
I.A.R. Peebles	b Constantine	0
T.J. Durston	not out	9
W.F. Price	b Constantine	3
J.A. Powell	b Constantine	1
Extras	(b 3, lb 2, nb 3)	8
Total		136

WEST INDIES BOWLING (6-ball overs)

	O	M	R	W	O	M	R	W
Francis	35.5	4	107	2	10	3	30	1
Constantine	20	1	77	1	14.3	1	57	7
Browne	11	2	21	0				
Small	29	5	72	1	11	3	36	2
Martin	13	0	30	0	3	0	5	0
Roach	7	0	36	1				

WEST INDIES
1st innings

G. Challenor	c Hendren b Durston	23
C.A. Roach	c Lee b Durston	0
M.P. Fernandes	c Hearne b Allen	29
W.H. St. Hill	c Hendren b Peebles	5
E.L. Bartlett	st Price b Powell	13
F.R. Martin	not out	26
L.N. Constantine	b Peebles	86
J.A. Small	c Hendren b Haig	7
R.K. Nunes	b Durston	17
C.R. Browne	c Allen b Durston	0
G.N. Francis	lbw b Haig	1
Extras	(b 18, lb 3, nb 2)	23
Total		230

2nd innings

G. Challenor	b Haig	33
C.A. Roach	run out	10
M.P. Fernandes	c Allen b Haig	54
W.H. St. Hill	b Durston	5
E.L. Bartlett	lbw b Hearne	26
J.A. Small	c & b Peebles	5
L.N. Constantine	c Haig b Lee	103
F.R. Martin	not out	1
C.R. Browne	not out	4
Extras	(b 18)	18
Total	(7 wkts)	259

MIDDLESEX BOWLING

	O	M	R	W	O	M	R	W
Durston	21	10	16	4	15	3	32	1
Haig	24.4	7	32	2	22	5	80	2
Hearne	11	4	25	0	15	3	51	1
Peebles	18	2	51	2	11	2	45	1
Allen	8	2	43	1				
Powell	7	1	40	1	1	0	6	0
Lee					4.4	0	27	1

Umpires: J.W. Day and W.R. Parry

WEST INDIES WON BY 3 WICKETS

within himself and taking the runs as they came along. The running between the wickets of this pair was in itself an education. Constantine, like all batsmen with a quick brain, is very sure of his own runs, and he is also amazingly quick in backing up the striker. A difficult man to run out.

Unfortunately this pair, who had done so well by their side, were not together when the winning hit was made, Constantine being out first, with only five runs more required, and Fernandes following before another of those five runs had been scored.

WALTER REGINALD HAMMOND
Gloucestershire

Hammond in the 1930s was the noblest sight ever seen on a cricket field. Two masters must be quoted, first Sir Leonard Hutton:

I think Walter Hammond was the finest cricketer I played with or against. He made batting so easy, graceful and effortless…As a slip fielder, he was second to none — no diving to left or right, collecting green marks on his immaculate flannels…His bowling action was just as graceful as all his cricket, the perfect sideways-on delivery which any aspiring bowler should copy…Walter was the complete cricketer, and I never tired of watching him.*

W.J. O'Reilly thought Hammond:

easily the best English stroke-player, the best-equipped English stroke-player, I bowled against. He was magnificent. He was also a magnificent slips field and a very good bowler, at a pinch.†

In 1923, a fortnight after his twentieth birthday, Hammond made his first appearance in the Gentlemen v. Players match — at the Oval: c Jeacocke by Fender 46 and b Falcon 19. Oddly, in this series of matches his batting average of 38.16 was 13 points lower than in Tests against Australia, and 20 points lower than in all Tests.

....
* Foreword to *In Celebration of Cricket* (1978).
....
† *Time of the Tiger*, by R.S. Whitington (1972 edition).

6 July 1923. This is a most interesting player. He obeys exactly the canons of nineteenth century orthodoxy. His right foot is firm; his left shoulder points straight down the pitch; to balls of doubtful length he plays forward rather than back; he tries to score by his defensive strokes, and the leaving of the off ball alone is no more part of his scheme of tactics than the use of his pads as a second line of defence. He even has a suspicion of "flourish" at the top of his free backlift…he missed nearly everything sent down to him on the leg side. Hammond has something to learn about footwork, much in judgement, but it is to be hoped that in learning he will not radically alter his methods of stroke-production.

Just over five years later, Hammond was batting for MCC and England in Australia where, according to P.G.H. Fender, he went down the wicket to the spinners in defence before thrashing them off the back foot. After Hammond's death in 1965, Sir Donald Bradman said "I have never seen a batsman so strong on the off-side"; which explains why W.J. O'Reilly insisted on bowling on Hammond's leg stump.

A CELEBRATION

A dinner in celebration of the 150th anniversary of the MCC was held at the Savoy Hotel, London, on 15 July 1937. Major the Hon. J.J. Astor (President of the

Club and proprietor of *The Times*) presided and over four hundred were present.

The Duke of Gloucester read a telegram from the King; the Rt Hon. S.M. Bruce, CH, High Commissioner for Australia, proposed "Lords and MCC". Colonel the Hon. Sir Stanley Jackson, GCSI, GCIE, proposed the toast of "Cricket", coupled with the name of G.O. Allen; responding, Mr Allen urged that wickets should redress the balance between bat and ball — the bowler must be given a fair chance.

Lord Hawke, who had played in the Centenary Match of 1887, proposed the health of "The Chairman". Major Astor replied.

Some weeks earlier, as part of the celebrations, North had played South at Lord's, the occasion dominated by one man, Hammond. On 22 May — a day afflicted by occasional rain — Hutton made a gracious hundred for North, who closed at 246 for five. They were soon all out on the second day and South 51 for two at lunch.

FIVE DAYS AT CHELTENHAM

GLOUCESTERSHIRE v. SURREY
15–17 August 1928

GLOUCESTERSHIRE

1st innings

A.E. Dipper	c & b Garland-Wells	7
R.A. Sinfield	b Peach	0
W.R. Hammond	c Shepherd b Peach	139
Mr B.H. Lyon	c & b Fender	6
Mr F.J. Seabrook	c Gregory b Fender	0
Mr W.L. Neale	c Ducat b Garland-Wells	10
H. Smith	c Fender b Shepherd	56
Mr C.J. Barnett	c Garland-Wells b Peach	0
Capt M.A. Green	c Sandham b Fenley	37
C. Parker	c Brooks b Fender	19
P. Mills	not out	7
Extras	(b 12, lb 10, nb 1)	23
Total		304

2nd innings

A.E. Dipper	c & b Peach	41
R.A. Sinfield	lbw b Shepherd	22
W.R. Hammond	c Gregory b Fenley	143
Mr B.H. Lyon	c Hobbs b Shepherd	27
Mr W.L. Neale	b Fender	5
H. Smith	b Shepherd	0
Mr C.J. Barnett	c Ducat b Fenley	45
Capt M.A. Green	not out	21
C. Parker	c Shepherd b Fenley	11
P. Mills	b Shepherd	2
Extras	(b 2)	2
Total	(9 wkts dec.)	319

SURREY BOWLING

	O	M	R	W	O	M	R	W
Fender	24.3	10	57	3	25	6	55	1
Peach	27	6	68	3	26	9	71	1
Fenley	12	2	44	1	18	2	83	3
Shepherd	15	4	43	1	32.4	5	74	4
Garland-Wells	22	5	65	2	14	3	34	0
Gregory	2	0	4	0				

SURREY

1st innings

J.B. Hobbs	c Seabrook b Hammond	96
A. Sandham	c Smith b Sinfield	0
A. Ducat	c Dipper b Parker	6
T. Shepherd	c Barnett b Parker	52
T.H. Barling	c Hammond b Parker	4
R.J. Gregory	c Hammond b Parker	7
Mr P.G.H. Fender	c Hammond b Sinfield	55
Mr H.M. Garland-Wells	c Hammond b Parker	6
H.A. Peach	b Mills	5
E.W. Brooks	lbw b Parker	2
S. Fenley	not out	0
Extras	(b 27, lb 7)	34
Total		267

2nd innings

J.B. Hobbs	c Smith b Parker	2
A. Sandham	c Hammond b Sinfield	10
A. Ducat	c Hammond b Parker	55
T. Shepherd	c Hammond b Parker	17
T.H. Barling	c Hammond b Parker	2
R.J. Gregory	c Hammond b Parker	3
Mr P.G.H. Fender	c Hammond b Parker	20
Mr H.M. Garland-Wells	st Smith b Sinfield	49
H.A. Peach	c Smith b Parker	1
E.W. Brooks	run out	0
S. Fenley	not out	0
Extras	(b 1, lb 7)	8
Total		167

GLOUCESTERSHIRE BOWLING

	O	M	R	W	O	M	R	W
Hammond	22	3	71	1				
Sinfield	9	4	10	2	27	9	59	2
Parker	38.4	6	117	6	32	10	80	7
Mills	24	11	35	1	6	0	20	0

Umpires: W. Bestwick and H. Young

GLOUCESTERSHIRE WON BY 189 RUNS

GLOUCESTERSHIRE v. WORCESTERSHIRE
18, 20 August 1928

WORCESTERSHIRE

1st innings

Mr J.B. Higgins	b Hammond	2
L. Wright	st Smith b Hammond	8
Mr B.W. Quaife	c Hammond b Parker	2
W.V. Fox	c Lyon b Hammond	1
H.H. Gibbons	c Stephens b Hammond	4
F. Root	c Seabrook b Hammond	0
C.V. Tarbox	b Hammond	6
J.W. King	not out	0
J.J. Bowles	c Lyon b Hammond	4
Mr D.V. Hill	c Parker b Hammond	0
F.T. Summers	b Hammond	0
Extras	(b 5, lb 3)	8
Total		35

2nd innings

Mr J.B. Higgins	c Lyon b Parker	35
L. Wright	b Parker	1
Mr B.W. Quaife	c Seabrook b Hammond	19
W.V. Fox	c Lyon b Hammond	1
H.H. Gibbons	c Lyon b Parker	9
F. Root	lbw b Hammond	1
C.V. Tarbox	c Barnett b Hammond	29
J.W. King	c Seabrook b Hammond	4
J.J. Bowles	hit wkt b Parker	20
Mr D.V. Hill	st Smith b Hammond	17
F.T. Summers	not out	0
Extras	(b 21, lb 10)	31
Total		167

GLOUCESTERSHIRE BOWLING

	O	M	R	W	O	M	R	W
Hammond	10.2	2	23	9	33.3	5	105	6
Sinfield	2	1	3	0				
Parker	8	7	1	1	33	22	31	4

GLOUCESTERSHIRE

A.E. Dipper	c Quaife b Wright	77
R.A. Sinfield	c Hill b Wright	30
W.R. Hammond	c Summers b Wright	80
Mr B.H. Lyon	b Tarbox	38
Mr F.J. Seabrook	b Hill	29
H. Smith	lbw b Hill	6
Mr W.L. Neale	not out	51
Mr C.J. Barnett	not out	34
Extras	(b 15, lb 9, nb 1)	25
Total	(6 wkts dec.)	370

WORCESTERSHIRE BOWLING

	O	M	R	W
Root	37	10	82	0
Hill	20	1	71	2
Bowles	17	3	49	0
Tarbox	30	5	88	1
Wright	20	4	55	3

Umpires: W. Bestwick and H. Young

GLOUCESTERSHIRE WON BY AN INNINGS AND 168 RUNS

Hammond's record for Gloucestershire in championship matches in 1928:

Innings 35 NO 5 Runs 2,474 HS 244 Av. 82.46
Overs 538.2 Mdns 137 Runs 1,393 Wkts 63
Av. 22.11 Catches 58

By R.B. Vincent

25 May 1937. Afterwards Hammond provided cricket which was a joy to watch. He may not be the most prolific run-maker in the world, but on a sunny day he gives a pleasure which is unsurpassed. Voce once made a ball rear quickly; Hammond contrived to stop it with a dead bat; and from that moment attacked all the bowlers with a quiet but sustained severity. He made many full-blooded hooks to leg, drove in his own incomparable manner straight and to the off with the variation on occasions of perfectly timed tickles to fine long leg, from one of which he was made to run four times up and down the pitch. To stop this Leyland was brought up to an almost suicidal position at short leg. Later he was moved to safer territory.

Hammond and Ames, in together, promised cricket of a high order until Ames stretched too far forward to be well stumped. Hollies had stuck to his work magnificently, but Hammond still attacked him, hitting vehemently to leg, once with a glorious hook with his right knee on the ground and once forcing the ball away at an immense pace to the off. Todd did not last long before he was caught at the wicket, and the splendour of Hammond carried the score to 182 before he was out to a magnificent left-handed catch very low down to the left hand by Voce [off A.V. Pope]. A worthy ending to a great innings.

Youth took over.

Then came an interesting and encouraging stand by the two Middlesex hopefuls, Compton and Edrich. Compton had more of the bowling and so scored the faster of the two, which probably he would have done in any case. He was particularly quick to seize any chance of scoring on the leg side, and was offered many such opportunities by Hutton, who bowled rather untidily from the Pavilion end. A change obviously had to be made in the bowling, so back came Verity and Hollies — and it was remarked at that time that the North's bowling, good as they were individually, was a little slender.

Compton [19 years old and one day] hit at them both with joy, confidently but with vigour. The score was creeping up to within easy distance of the North's score when suddenly Edrich, who had played unobtrusively but well, was caught at cover-point...There was still some more trouble for the North from Compton when he was joined by Robins, the two of them playing just that type of cricket for a sunny day which should for ever silence the perpetual grumbler who asks for "brighter" cricket. Compton had been employing the short-armed hook, the North's score had been comfortably passed, when Verity, tempting him, pitched the ball just a shade farther up and the hook failed.

26 May 1937. The first match of the anniversary week at Lord's finished on the highest note possible yesterday, when the South beat the North at two minutes to 6 by six wickets...

It was a beautiful summer day, when cricket could be watched lusciously, and the play was well worthy of the occasion. I refuse to think of it as anything so banal as a Trial Match; rather was it a game of two excellently balanced teams, one from the North and the other from the South. No particular reputations were made, and more assuredly none was lost, for the game from beginning to end was sheer delight. It was cricket at its best. A game such as this, with amateurs and professionals alike striving benignly, explains the spirit of cricket which can be seen at Lord's and all the other lovely grounds the country through. It was a noble start to a big week.

Farnes bowled greatly in the North's second innings, leaving the South 156 to win. Gimblett was soon caught at the wicket.

So in came Hammond to join Barnett in a partnership which killed the Northern bowlers. Hammond was at his very best. No words can explain his innings more aptly. Not only did he attack the bowlers to drive the ball furiously on the off-side or wide of mid-on, but he found it his fancy to lie back and to follow the ball through, more especially when Hollies was bowling to the finest of fine legs. He was once to be sure all but out leg-before-wicket to Verity, who was given a long spell from the Nursery end. His command over the bowling was complete, both when he walked out to the pitch of the ball or waited to force it either to the off-side or place it away to leg. It made one to wonder why when, as yesterday, he had such a variety of bowling to play it is so often said that his on-side play is comparatively weak — comparatively that is for a "world batsman". Nothing could have surpassed the manner in which he dealt with Hollies, who once again, undeterred by rough treatment, kept pitching his leg-breaks well up with the chance of a catch from a mis-hit. Yesterday Hammond refused to mis-hit the ball. When he did not drive it to the off he knelt down to hook it with a ring off the bat to deep square-leg.

Barnett did not have so much of the bowling and he was out just before tea, caught at the wicket off Hollies, with the score at 67. Ames, too, was out soon afterwards, and so the South had some way to go with not much time to spare. The game was held up for a few minutes after Hammond had injured the ball* so severely by hitting it straight into the Pavilion that another of a similar shape had to be found, but the South were always just ahead of time. Compton played his part nobly by refusing to waste time in getting out; Hammond did his best to get the bowling whenever possible; and so a great match ended with Hammond reaching his century and a thoroughly well-earned victory for the South.

NORTH 271 (L. Hutton 102, J. Hardstaff 71) and 184 (E. Paynter 51; K. Farnes 5 for 43) lost to SOUTH 300 (W.R. Hammond 86, D.C.S. Compton 70) and 158 for 4 (Hammond 100 not out) by six wickets.

HAMMOND THE MASTER

A DAY AT LORD'S, 1938

ENGLAND
1st innings

L. Hutton	c Brown b McCormick	4
C.J. Barnett	c Brown b McCormick	18
W.J. Edrich	b McCormick	0
W.R. Hammond	not out	210
E. Paynter	lbw b O'Reilly	99
D.C.S. Compton	lbw b O'Reilly	6
L.E.G. Ames	not out	50
Extras	(lb 12, w 1, nb 9)	22
Total	(5 wkts)	409

To bat: A.W. Wellard, H. Verity, D.V.P. Wright, K. Farnes.

Fall of wickets: 1–12, 2–20, 3–31, 4–253, 5–271.

AUSTRALIA:
J.H. Fingleton, W.A. Brown, D.G. Bradman, S.J. McCabe, C.L. Badcock, A.L. Hassett, A.G. Chipperfield, B.A. Barnett, W.J. O'Reilly, E.L. McCormick, L.O'B. Fleetwood-Smith.

Umpires: E.J. Smith and F. Walden

. . . .

* This blow landed in the Press room, leaving one to conclude that Major Vincent — ignorant of the drive's true destination — was watching from the comfort of the Long Room.

By R.B. Vincent

25 June 1938. The first day's play in the second Test Match at Lord's yesterday will be remembered by all those who were lucky enough to be there for a display of batting by Hammond which can seldom have been surpassed. He has done great things in Australia, but it is certain that in a Test Match in this country he has never approached such grandeur. At the close of play England had scored 409 runs for the loss of only five wickets, which is pretty reading on paper, but without Hammond one shudders to think what the total would have been.

The fact that he scored more than half the runs speaks for itself; it was the combination of batting technique and cricket brain, supported by physical endurance, which was so amazing. He took command from the moment that he went in, never put a foot wrong; refused to be tempted to achieve the brilliant; and patiently waited for the game to swing round in England's favour. It was an innings which many years hence will be referred to as a classic example of a batsman's elegant triumph over difficulties. The King arrived at the end of the luncheon interval, and both teams were presented to him in front of the Pavilion before the game was continued.

The scene was set, the sun was shining, the ground already packed to capacity, with St John's Wood Road holding another army of optimists who were hoping to gain admittance, when Hammond, having won the toss, decided to bat first. This he obviously had to do taking into account what might happen during the four days of the match, but it is a doubtful privilege to have first use of the Lord's wicket for the first hour or so. And yesterday's happenings were no exception to the rule. There was obviously some moisture on the pitch, and McCormick bowling from the Pavilion end at once made the ball stand up, although he had to bowl decidedly short to do so.

His first ball was a no-ball, and as soon as he had found his registration it was clear that he intended to attack the leg stump. He had three slips, placed there perhaps as a matter of formality, but the really important people were two short-legs and a long-leg, placed fairly wide. McCabe, to return the compliment to McCormick, started off with a wide. Hutton and Barnett had done little more than form an appreciation of Australia's attack before Hutton played a very short ball into the hands of backward short-leg, and that with only 12 runs on the board.

Barnett had found time to make some lovely strokes on the off-side, generally giving the appearance of bright things to come, but he lost Edrich at 20. Again it was a rather short ball, but straight, and Edrich must be found guilty of taking a liberty in trying to hook the ball before he had had time to get a sight of it. It was a mistake which no doubt he will grow out of.

It was five minutes before noon that Hammond swept through the Long Room and strode to the wicket, face black as thunder — or so we are told.

Hammond, therefore, entered at a most gloomy period, which was to become even darker when at 31 Barnett played a rising ball down on to his thigh, from where it bounded into the hands of a crouching short-leg. He was certainly unlucky, for he had played the ball down well enough, but for all that McCormick had done his duty nobly as a fast bowler — not that he is particularly fast — in taking these three quick wickets. Paynter at first seemed a little uneasy, both to McCormick and McCabe, but left-handed batsmen, even the best of them, are liable to give that impression at the beginning of the innings.

Hammond nursed Paynter carefully, he himself finding no difficulty in playing any kind of ball. Fleetwood-Smith was soon put on at the Nursery end, and O'Reilly, who had a short-leg and three other men on the on-side when bowling to Hammond, gave Paynter two more uncomfortable overs. Gradually the precept and dominance of Hammond gave his partner the encouragement he required, and the Australian bowling sagged. O'Reilly bounded away, but the life had

left the wicket. McCabe could do little more than bowl the ball into the middle of Hammond's bat, and Chipperfield's leg-breaks lost their break in Hammond's mastery. Hammond still had to fight after that miserable start, and never for one second was his technique at fault. His batting lost nothing of the glamour associated with his name, but behind it there was a security which killed even O'Reilly's normal venom. Hammond in one over hit him away to the square-leg boundary, which he followed with a gorgeous off-drive, also for four.

Paynter had one more piece of luck when he snicked a ball off Fleetwood-Smith over the head of slip. McCormick, when he came on again, looked to have lost all his pace and ferocity, and he was still further tamed by Hammond. Paynter also found plenty of time to cut him square, and was making runs almost as quickly as Hammond at one time. Fleetwood-Smith continued to tempt Paynter with balls outside the off stump, but Paynter had learned his lesson. Hammond just before luncheon unloosed a battery of strokes and the interval score of 134 for three was a sign of the first stage of a recovery.

Hammond was 70 at lunch, made out of 114.

Fleetwood-Smith began the bowling after luncheon from the Nursery end. Hammond greeted him with a grand delayed drive to the boundary past third man and a sweep, following the break, to long leg. Hammond reached his century at 3 o'clock, a century which might have been marked on the score card from the moment he went in. Fleetwood-Smith was bowling untidily, offering far too many cheap runs, but there was always the danger that his unorthodoxy might gain an unexpected wicket. Hammond, still scoring at a rate of nearly a run a minute, never played the semblance of a loose stroke, while Paynter was hitting the ball with immense power for so small a man on the off side, lying right back and disengaging his left leg to give himself plenty of room in which to make the stroke.

Bowling changes were made every few overs, with O'Reilly moving from one end to the other until he can scarcely have known which way he was facing. The attack by all the bowlers except McCabe was concentrated on the leg stump, with a bunch of short legs, but Hammond was not to be drawn into the error of attempting to play balls which went a foot wide of the wicket. The balls which were straight he forced off his legs away to parts of the field where there was no green cap to be seen, although it must be admitted that the field was very tightly placed to save runs. The new ball had come and had lost its polish without having in the least perturbed Paynter, who had attacked O'Reilly as if he were no better bowler than the rest. He seemed certain to make a century when, only one run short, he missed the ball in trying to hook it and was leg-before-wicket. If anyone had deserved that wicket it was essentially O'Reilly.

Compton survived only a few overs, which he had devoted to playing himself in before, in trying to put the ball away past mid-wicket, he too was leg-before-wicket. That was five wickets down for 271 runs, which was by no means a good score, and England can indeed be considered lucky to have such a batsman as Ames to come in at No. 7. The fall of these two quick wickets had put new spirit into the Australians: O'Reilly appeared in stature more like a giant, and McCabe, at the Nursery end, bowled steadily and well, making the ball go away down the hill from the middle stump. That was no good against Hammond, who, still without taking any risks, played every ball he meant to with the full blade and force of the bat.

As with Paynter he preferred that Ames should

HAMMOND   An umpire wishes he could appreciate Hammond's glory from a position at square cover.

not at first have too much of the bowling until he had had time to have a look at it. When once Ames was settled down he allowed him his full share, Hammond himself on a hot day [72°F] no doubt being glad of some respite so long as he knew he had a trustworthy partner. Ames played in the manner which has always delighted the crowds on Kentish grounds, the free forward stroke, the adroit turn to leg, and the firm defensive stroke. Like Hammond he was having no nonsense with balls which passed harmlessly behind his body, waiting for the ball which could be safely played and taking runs whenever and wherever they were offered.

Small wonder that by 6 o'clock the Australian bowling wilted, although towards the end of the evening O'Reilly rose in his might and bowled as good an over as he had done all the long and tiring day. Hammond reached his 200 still batting as he had done before luncheon, and Ames had scored 50 before the Australians were allowed the solitude and restfulness of their dressing room.

Hammond's was a symmetrical innings: 70 runs before lunch, 70 between lunch and tea and 70 after tea, though his hourly run rate for the three sessions was, respectively, 44, 31, 40. After Hammond's entry at the fall of the second wicket, England scored at 70 runs an hour for the rest of the day.

On the second day England were out for 494, Australia replying with 299 for five, Brown 140 not out. Three hours were lost to rain on the third day, Australia's first innings closing for 422 made in six and a quarter hours.

After a fine innings by Compton, England declared their second innings, setting Australia a target of 315 in two and three quarter hours. Bradman reached his hundred in 140 minutes.

ENGLAND 494 (W.R. Hammond 240, E. Paynter 99, L.E.G. Ames 83) and 242 for 8 declared (D.C.S. Compton 76 not out) drew with AUSTRALIA 422 (W.A. Brown 206 not out, A.L. Hassett 56) and 204 for 6 (D.G. Bradman 102 not out).

KUMAR SHRI DULEEPSINHJI

Sussex

Duleepsinhji batted like the prince he was. He sometimes failed but he never bored. Ranji's nephew, he acquired C.B. Fry as guardian on coming to England to enter Cheltenham College; occasional coaching by G.A. Faulkner helped him to become the best player of googly bowling in English cricket between Hobbs and Denis Compton. (The head professional at Cheltenham was the now long-forgotten William Woof, a slow left-arm bowler from Gloucestershire, who must have taught his charge something and therefore merits a mention.) Duleep was greatly loved; when acting as 12th man for England at Trent Bridge in 1930 a minor chore demanded of him was to convey a sweater — probably adorned with the Six Martlets of Sussex — to his county colleague Maurice Tate in the middle. The Nottingham crowd applauded warmly, though this may have been both a show of affection and also criticism of the Test selectors, who had omitted the Indian from the England side in spite of two recent hundreds in a match against Middlesex when the bowlers bemused were G.O. Allen, N.E. Haig, R.W.V. Robins, G.T.S. Stevens and J.W. Hearne.

Duleep — "Smith" to fellow-undergraduates at Cambridge — liked feasting off the best. In 1925, aged 19, he scored 53 and 70 for the university against the Yorkshire of Waddington, Robinson, Kilner and Rhodes. Two years later, with that attack augmented by Macaulay, he made 101 in just over two hours. In 1928 his 150 for Sussex v. Yorkshire came at 50 runs an hour as he danced out to Wilfred

Rhodes as he must once have done to William Woof. Duleep three times made 100 before lunch in a county match; on 7 May 1930 at Hove he went in with one run on the board and was out five and a half hours later for 333, the Northamptonshire bowlers including E.W. Clark, V.W.C. Jupp and A.D.G. Matthews, who all played for England. The essence of K.S. Duleepsinhji was well expressed by G.A. Faulkner: "It isn't a question of how to get Duleep out: the question is, how to stop him scoring." Duleep didn't appear to mind getting out, so inevitably he scored.

As a slip fielder for England, he would stand next to Hammond, neither suffering in comparison with the other.

K.S. DULEEPSINHJI'S GREAT INNINGS

By Dudley Carew

Close on the second day: CAMBRIDGE UNIVERSITY 231 (E.W. Dawson 53) and 45 for one (Duleepsinhji 30 not out), MIDDLESEX 344 (H.W. Lee 52, Hendren 68, E.T. Killick 94; R.G.H. Lowe 5 for 71).

11 May 1927. The match at Fenner's between Cambridge University and Middlesex ended in a draw. K.S. Duleepsinhji, in his innings of 254 not out, made more runs than any Cambridge cricketer batting at Fenner's has ever made. The previous record was held by Mr Hubert Ashton with 236 not out against the Free Foresters in 1920. While it would not be true to say that his innings was faultless, it was nevertheless full of magnificent cricket. He scored his runs at an exhilarating pace but even when he was hitting out almost at anything his strokes were nearly always made with classic correctness. Strong, as always, on the on-side, he made most of his runs between fine-leg and mid-on, but his cutting was beautiful to watch, and in his driving the ball was hit hard and cleanly, and kept on the ground into the bargain. It was altogether the innings of a man who, in a few years, may be the greatest batsman in England.* It is a remarkable fact that the next highest score on the side was 32. . .

Yesterday morning he batted as though he had the bowling more or less at his mercy. . .It may seem ungenerous to dwell on his weakness, which from time to time persists on raising its head, with the short off ball, but when a batsman has his genius, his faults are of even more interest and importance than his merits. He reached his 50 with a magnificently firm cut off Durston, the best stroke of his innings, and went on to gather runs quickly and surely all round the wicket, risking an occasional stroke with an audaciously crooked bat.

When Hearne came on to bowl he made many runs by jumping out to him, getting him on the full pitch, and sweeping him round to square-leg. Finally he reached his 100, made out of 146 in two hours, by forcing a short ball from Lee wide of mid-on to the boundary, and, hitting out ferociously at Powell, he scored another 43 runs before luncheon, when the score was 209 for three wickets. Afterwards K.S. Duleepsinhji made two lucky strokes off Mr Haig and then went on his way in a blaze of 4's. There was no time to take note of individual strokes, all one's appreciation was drowned in mathematical calculations. He

....

* Duleep, aged 21, was two years younger than Hammond, who had already impressed as a future master batsman.

reached his 200 in 3½ hours out of the 285 runs made, which was in a truly staggering proportion.

When Mr Dawson eventually declared with the total 366 for five wickets, he had made 254 not out. Altogether he was in for four hours, scored his runs out of 362, and hit 34 4's. Figures are supposed to be cold impersonal things, but no highly coloured superlatives could so vividly describe the brilliance of his very great innings.

Middlesex in their second innings scored 123 for three.

Shortly after this innings Duleep caught a chill on a bitterly cold day at Fenner's and — as Sir Pelham Warner noted in his biography Long Innings — "pneumonia following, at one time his life was despaired of. Prayers were offered for his recovery in his college [Clare] chapel, and his uncle, Ranjitsinhji, wrote a beautiful and touching letter in appreciation of this to the college authorities."

After spending the winter of 1927–8 in Switzerland, Duleep returned to cricket belatedly at Fenner's (early June) and did not show his previous season's form until joining Sussex. 1928 was, in many ways, a remarkable summer. 414 individual first-class hundreds were scored, Freeman took 304 wickets, England won all three Tests with West Indies by an innings (at Lord's the tourists, with three fast bowlers in their ranks, achieved 20 overs an hour), while the 55-year-old S.F. Barnes worked his usual wonders for Staffordshire — 55 wickets, average 7.34.

Whether 1929 was as fruitful a year as 1928 is a matter of opinion. In 1928 the St Edward's, Oxford captain, century-maker and leading bowler was D.S.R. Bader, soon to join the Royal Air Force, while for Lancing a successful bowler was P.N.L. Pears, one day to create the title role in Britten's opera, Peter Grimes. 1929 had to suffice with the Harrow batsman T.M. Rattigan; in due course The Winslow Boy had in a supporting role a once-brilliant cricketer faded into the routine of a middle-aged solicitor.

On 10 August 1929 at Lord's the Young Amateurs concluded their match with the Young Professionals in a win by 50 runs. Appearing for the former were J.G.W. Davies (Tonbridge) and G.A.R. Green (Shrewsbury). Two decades or so later Green was briefly cricket correspondent of *The Times*, though lasting fame came to him as chronicler of Association Football. For Geoffrey Green, life's heroes were Matthews, Finney, Bobby Charlton and the Hungarians of 1953.

Two columns away from the Young Amateurs at Lord's a more serious game was reported.

BRIGHT BATTING BY SUSSEX

By Major Campbell

12 August 1929. The Kent eleven proved a big attraction at Hastings on Saturday, and at the end of a good day's cricket were 388 runs behind Sussex with nine wickets in hand...

Wright and Ashdown opened the bowling [to Bowley and A.H.H. Gilligan], and after making three singles Bowley was clean bowled in playing back to a half volley that went away slightly. K.S. Duleepsinhji and his captain, after carefully and quickly playing themselves in, gave as delightful an exhibition of free hitting as it is possible to see...The first hour produced 118 runs, K.S. Duleepsinhji making 50 in 40 minutes. He was particularly severe on Freeman and C.S. Marriott.* No batsman this season has shown such complete mastery in dealing with Freeman. K.S. Duleepsinhji's quick-footed on-drives, which were for the most part pulls, and his delightful wrist play when placing the ball to leg or when cutting, were a very great joy to watch. He played the same sort of innings last year at Eastbourne, when he made over 100 against Glamorgan before luncheon, but Saturday's innings against the very varied Kent attack was, if possible, as fine. He was at the wickets just over an hour and a half [for 115] and he showed almost every stroke known in the game.

....

* Whose only Test appearance was against West Indies at the Oval in 1933: eleven wickets for 96 from 41.1 overs.

Duleep's innings against Glamorgan on 18 July 1928 invited the inevitable anti-climax. Opening with H.W. Parks, J.H. Parks was out for 22 at 47 scored in 55 minutes. Duleep hit six boundaries during his first ten minutes at the crease, and was 102 out of 137 in 65 minutes at lunch. He was out at 2.30 for 121, the Sussex score 218 for two.

Close: SUSSEX 428 (A.H.H. Gilligan 56, K.S. Duleepsinhji 115, James Langridge 80, Wensley 61, R.L. Holdsworth 69 not out; Freeman 6 for 131), KENT 40 for one.

On the second day Kent made 398; Woolley, batting with care, took 65 minutes to reach his 50, and C.H. Knott, after a shaky start, reached his 100 in two hours.

13 August 1929. When stumps were drawn at Hastings yesterday evening Sussex, with seven wickets in hand, were leading Kent by 245 runs. A record crowd, in glorious weather, saw 573 runs scored in the day; saw Sussex repeat their feat of Saturday by scoring over 200 runs in two hours; and last, and best of all, saw a Sussex batsman score his second century of the match in perfect style.

Superlatives are dangerous, but they can be applied to K.S. Duleepsinhji's innings. From the moment that he went to the wicket until a proudly smiling constable piloted him through an openly adoring throng he was master of his bat and of whatever Kent bowler J.L. Bryan chose to put on. Not only that, he was master of the field, and nothing demonstrated the power and pace of his hitting more clearly than to see two deep-fields stand stock still, and rightly so, watching the ball crash against the boards between them and rebound for the nearest of them to pick it up and return it to the bowler.

Sussex went in again at 20 minutes past 4, Bowley and A.H. Gilligan opening the innings to the bowling of Ashdown and Wright. They seemed to be settling down well when, with the total at eight, Gilligan was out to a wonderful catch by Ashdown in the gully off Wright. Gilligan meant to hit the ball, which was well pitched up, through the covers; however, it got up quickly, and as a result it travelled like a flash to the left of Ashdown and shoulder high. Ashdown made a jump for it, and then, when most of the spectators were looking towards the boundary, Ashdown produced the ball out of his left hand just as a juggler produces a rabbit out of a hat. That brought in K.S. Duleepsinhji, and, in spite of Freeman, some delightful batting followed. The 50 went up at 5 o'clock, and 25 more were added before the next wicket fell. The way of it was interesting, and showed clever captaincy. Freeman was not proving effective at his end, so he was taken off and C.S. Marriott was given one over at the other end to bring Freeman on there. The change met with an early reward, for Bowley stepped in front to a googly, and was out leg-before wicket.

That brought in R.L. Holdsworth instead of Cook, who was unable to bat owing to his having

damaged an old injury to his right wrist while fielding. Holdsworth gave K.S. Duleepsinhji, who again batted like a master, just the assistance he required. K.S. Duleepsinhji completed his 50 out of 80 after batting just under an hour, and the 100 went up five minutes later. With the total at 115 Woolley missed Holdsworth at short slip. The third wicket fell at 130, when Holdsworth was out leg-before-wicket to Marriott, having batted 35 minutes for eight runs. Langridge followed, and K.S. Duleepsinhji crept nearer and nearer to his second century, scoring two delightful 4's — one a cut and the other a glide off Woolley — and he eventually completed his 100 with a glorious 6 off Woolley. He had scored his 100 in 90 minutes, and out of a total of 152, and never a shot was mistimed. So it went on until the end, K.S. Duleepsinhji gathering runs in the late sunshine like a bee gathers honey.

Close: SUSSEX 428 and 215 for 3 (K.S. Duleepsinhji 149 not out), KENT 398 (F.E. Woolley 58, W.H. Ashdown 63, C.H. Knott 140 not out; M.W. Tate 6 for 136).

14 August 1929. Sussex won a fine victory at Hastings yesterday, beating Kent just before 5 o'clock by 167 runs, after three days of as great and interesting batting as even the many old and experienced cricketers who remained glued to their seats from first to last can remember.

Towards the end, after K.S. Duleepsinhji had completed his wonderful second innings, and while Ames and Todd were making their gallant effort to save Kent, little gusts of conversation could be heard from the deck chairs in front of the members' tent, of which, "What did Ranji make against Surrey here?" and "This must be nearly a record," seemed to be the leit motif.

Ranji scored 234 not out for Sussex v. Surrey at Hastings in 1902. After C.B. Fry and J. Vine had opened with 238, there was a minor collapse; at the

DULEEPSINHJI   Master England batsman of his time.

close Sussex 419 for six, Ranji 54 not out. Next day, Ranji and George Cox, senior, added 192 in 100 minutes, Sussex declaring at 705 for nine. Ranji's 234 occupied 205 minutes — 68 runs an hour.

Certainly there was every reason for those with leanings towards statistics, for rarely can 1,451 runs have been scored in three days for the loss of 37 wickets, and K.S. Duleepsinhji himself now joins the little band of batsmen who have scored 100 or over in one innings and more than 200 in another.* The players are: —
1900. — C.B. Fry, 125 and 220, Sussex v. Surrey.
1921. — Hardinge, 207 and 102 not out, Kent v. Surrey.
1921. — W.W. Armstrong, 157 not out and 245, Victoria v. South Australia.
1929. — K.S. Duleepsinhji, 115 and 246, Sussex v. Kent.

Again, Duleepsinhji only failed by three runs to score 100 on three successive days, his figures being 115, 149 not out and 97, and this was in the same match.

K.S. Duleepsinhji, not out 149, and Langridge, not out 18, continued the Sussex innings under a blazing sun. In the 65 minutes K.S. Duleepsinhji remained at the wickets 144 runs were added, of which he himself made 97. With the early start, the dew, and the hot sun, it was expected that the pitch might "do" a little, and so it proved, for both Ashdown and Wright made the ball nip quickly and sharply, and K.S. Duleepsinhji was a little more human, and actually gave two hard, but possible, chances. None the less, his innings was one of the finest ever seen on the Hastings, or any other, ground, and definitely places him among the great batsmen of all time.

Duleepsinhji completed his 150 off the first ball of the morning from Ashdown, but at 158 he gave

....

* A feat since performed on 20 occasions, most notably in county cricket by Zaheer Abbas (four times) and M.R. Hallam (twice); in Tests by G.S. Chappell and K.D. Walters (Australia), and on his debut for the West Indies by L.G. Rowe. A.E. Fagg's 244 and 202 not out for Kent v. Essex in 1938 remains unique.

his first chance, a possible catch to mid-off which, however, did not go to hand as the fielder was obviously unsighted by a building. The score mounted quickly to 252, when Langridge, who had played his part admirably, was well caught by Ames off Ashdown for 32. This partnership had realized 122 runs in 65 minutes, and the next, when Wensley came in, put on 66 in 30 minutes. During it K.S. Duleepsinhji gave his second chance, a high dropping catch off a miss-hit over mid-on's head, to which Bryan just got his right hand running hard, and he sent up the 300 with an on-drive off Freeman, who had just relieved Ashdown. Five minutes later K.S. Duleepsinhji passed his 200 with a beautiful square cut to the pavilion off Wright. At 318 Wensley was well caught by Ashdown on the square-leg boundary for 33, which included five 4's. It was about this time that K.S. Duleepsinhji went berserk, and 4's spiced with an occasional 6, came almost too quickly to tally. When at length the end came — a catch on the boundary by Blunden (who was substituting) — off Freeman — he had just hit two 6's in successive balls, and was trying to hit a third in order to pass his 250. He had made 246 runs, which included five 6's and 31 4's, in 195 minutes and out of a total of 359. He had also made cricket history and thousands of people supremely happy, and on coming in he received the ovation he had so well and truly earned.

In spite of a brilliant innings by Ames, who reached 100 in two hours, Kent were defeated. A.P.F. Chapman did not bat in either innings, having withdrawn from the game early on the first day with water on the knee.

SUSSEX 428 and 381 for 8 declared (Duleepsinhji 246) beat KENT 398 and 244 (L.E.G. Ames 118; M.W. Tate 7 for 58) by 167 runs.

For statisticians:
Day 1: Sussex 428 at 85 runs an hour, Kent 21 overs an hour.
Day 2: Kent out for 398 at 88 runs an hour, Sussex 25

overs an hour; Sussex 215 for 3 at 96 runs an hour. *Day 3:* Sussex declare at 381 made at 105 runs an hour, Kent bowling 22 overs an hour; Kent 244 at 80 runs an hour, Sussex bowling 22 overs an hour.

"Grouse shooting in Northern Ireland has been well up to expectations. There is almost no disease" (News item on the same page as the game at Hastings).

THE TEST TRIAL MATCH

The respective captains of North and South were R.E.S. Wyatt and D.R. Jardine, the latter destined to lead the MCC side in Australia the following winter, with Wyatt as his deputy. Jardine had toured in 1928–9 and knew the pace of Australian wickets; he doubtless watched Voce with keen interest.

By R.B. Vincent

20 June 1932. Test trial matches do not always provide information which is not already at the disposal of a selection committee and its critics. On Saturday, at Old Trafford, when the South scored 384 runs for the loss of six wickets against the North, we were reminded of the beauty of the batting of K.S. Duleepsinhji and Woolley, and those who have not been to Australia were given a demonstration by Hammond which explained which strokes are to be used and which are to be discarded on occasions of importance in Sydney or Melbourne.

...K.S. Duleepsinhji survived a most confident appeal, a hearty mixture of Nottinghamshire and Lancashire, for leg-before-wicket before he had scored, and altogether took some time to settle down but, once he had got going, he was truly wonderful. The temptation to cast idle comparisons will be resisted. I will just say that K.S. Duleepsinhji during his innings on Saturday gave me a whole summer's enjoyment. Larwood was not too sure of his length, and Woolley had scored 50 runs in less than an hour when, suddenly, he

hit a full-pitch from Mitchell straight into the hands of deep mid-wicket.

Woolley had earlier, in the same over from Voce, "made an exquisite late cut and a glorious straight drive. He continued to play in his grandest manner, once standing up viciously to his full height and driving Larwood with tremendous power to long-off. He actually played this stroke robustly." Once, the recipient of some Larwood bouncers, Woolley is reputed to have looked sternly down the pitch: "Are you trying to hit me, Harold?" The bowler looked sheepish.

During the next hour before luncheon, Hammond batted as if he were having a quiet knock up in a net, meeting every ball full in the middle of the bat and sending it straight to the particular fieldsman placed for the purpose. On two or three occasions he lay back and hit the ball with intent, and that counted four runs each time; and there were a few strokes by which he put the ball here and there away on the leg-side, but, for the most part, it was grimly admirable Australian Test Match cricket, perfect in its execution, and certain in its results. And so it went on after luncheon, Hammond being perfectly content to allow K.S. Duleepsinhji to do the scoring, and offering the bowlers not the least encouragement of taking a wicket.

Among the many lovely strokes played by K.S. Duleepsinhji, I remember best two late cuts in one over off Larwood, the second excelling the first, which already had suggested perfection. Voce, first at one end and then at the other, was bowling well, and at least twice had the minor satisfaction of hitting Hammond's pads, but, for an hour or so, Duckworth might as well have been sitting in comfort in the Pavilion, so seldom did the ball pass the bat. Some two or three times, to be sure, he had to throw himself at his full length to gather a ball from Voce wide on the leg-side, which he did admirably and which brings one to the point that "Tiger" Smith used to stand up to F.R. Foster, and that was why Smith was chosen for that victorious Australian tour.

Both K.S. Duleepsinhji and Hammond deflected a ball from Voce very late and very fine on the leg side, and both hit a short-pitched ball from the same bowler hard at the head of a short leg, but, with the total at 247, K.S. Duleepsinhji seemed to be caught in two minds playing a ball from Voce which must have come back, and gave a simple catch to the bowler. It was indeed a great innings, and his third consecutive three-figure score.

Close: SOUTH 384 for 6 (F.E. Woolley 50, K.S. Duleepsinhji 128, W.R. Hammond 130).

The match was drawn. SOUTH 447 for eight declared (J. O'Connor 51 not out, W. Voce 5 for 108) and 25 for no wicket, NORTH 242 (H. Sutcliffe 96) and 307 (Sutcliffe 110 not out, H. Larwood 67).

Immediately underneath Vincent's match report was a Reuter despatch from Duncan (British Columbia) where V.Y. Richardson's touring Australians had scored 503 for eight declared, and beaten Cowichan Club by 319 runs. It was an altogether successful invasion of the New World: Bradman made 3,782 runs, average 102.21, Fleetwood-Smith took 235 wickets, average 7.60, and Mailey 202 wickets, average 8.98. McCabe was the side's all-rounder — 2,360 runs and 187 wickets. Whether this tour was the best preparation for Jardine's impending form of warfare was debatable; unlike Voce at Old Trafford, Hollywood's demon bowler — Boris Karloff — did not bowl to a battery of short-legs, something unlikely to have been permitted by his captain C. Aubrey Smith (Charterhouse, Cambridge University, Sussex, The Gentlemen and England).

GENTLEMEN V. PLAYERS

Two Great Innings
By R.B. Vincent

On the first day The Players scored 301 (Hammond 110 in 125 minutes, G.O. Allen 5 for 71) and The Gentlemen were 17 for one when bad light stopped play a few minutes after six o'clock.

The cricket in the match between the Gentlemen and Players at Lord's yesterday was of the highest class, good bowling countered, and eventually mastered, by supreme batsmanship, and a wisely distributed field saving every run possible, with the encouragement of the best wicket-keeper in the world.*

When K.S. Duleepsinhji and the Nawab of Pataudi were batting to Tate, Larwood, Voce and Freeman, with Hammond thrown in, every stroke played was of comprehensive interest. Of the two K.S. Duleepsinhji was the more exuberant, but there was a soundness and perfection of stroke production in his partner's play which developed from being a mere support into a fierce aggression. Each, in fact, played his part superbly for his side, and if the Nawab of Pataudi is the more generously rewarded by the score card, it was K.S. Duleepsinhji who made such things possible.

...Tate in the morning bowled only a few overs from the Nursery end before he was relieved by Voce and transferred to the other end, from which Larwood had bowled one ball short enough for K.S. Duleepsinhji to hook for 4. Voce in one over to the batsman made the mistake of bowling three balls short and outside the leg stump, which between them cost 10 runs, and with the total at 54 there occurred a matter of importance. K.S. Duleepsinhji, in Freeman's first over, attempting a perfectly correct stroke, just failed to clear mid-off's head, and the catch should have been held. He had then made only 24...[After Hazlerigg's dismissal] the Players never could have seen a glimmer of hope while K.S. Duleepsinhji and the Nawab of Pataudi remained together until the luncheon interval, when the total had swollen to 143.

Some may say that after luncheon, with the Gentlemen already in a happy position, the rate of scoring might have been increased [for the rest

....

* Duckworth was not always preferred to Australia's W.A. Oldfield or South Africa's H.B. Cameron.

of the day it was only 71 runs an hour], but a strict analysis of the bowling shows that 75 per cent. of the balls sent down which offered runs were accepted. The bowling for two hours after the interval was genuinely good, but not good enough either to tempt the batsmen to indiscretions or to make them play their normal strokes quicker or later than they intended...K.S. Duleepsinhji played Freeman exquisitely, with a quick step down the pitch and his bat perfectly straight to the flight of the ball. Voce he cut or put away to leg with a short-armed hook, and when Hammond came on he gave us the pleasure of the straight drive which hit the sight screen first bounce, or was yards too fast to the on for an out fieldsman to gather.

The Nawab of Pataudi was for a long time content to make most of his runs on the leg side, and when later in his innings he produced strokes which left the fieldsmen on the off side one was made to think how difficult he must be to set a field for him. K.S. Duleepsinhji was the first to be out when the partnership had added 161 runs, and it was a wicket well deserved by Voce, who in desperation had moved the last available man over to fill the area at short-leg.

Close: PLAYERS 301, GENTLEMEN 430 for 8 wickets (K.S. Duleepsinhji 132, Nawab of Pataudi 165, D.R. Jardine 64).

The Gentlemen declared at this total. On the third day the Players made 320, the second highest individual score Woolley's 31. They were saved by Hobbs, now in his 50th year, who took out his bat for 161.

Immediately after the match, five names were announced as vanguard members of Jardine's Australian party: Hammond, Sutcliffe, Ames, Duckworth and K.S. Duleepsinhji. But a month later, after making 90 for Sussex v. Somerset at Taunton, Duleep left a cricket ground for the last time. He was 27 years and two months old. Instead of visiting Australia, he spent the winter in Switzerland trying in vain to repair his health. He later served his country with distinction as Indian High Commissioner in Canberra, and died in Bombay on 5 December 1959. He was aged 54 years.

Sir Jack Hobbs paid tribute: "He was an extremely popular personality and did not have an enemy on the field. He was a brilliant player." Herbert Sutcliffe said even more: "He was a real joy to watch and was, above all, a first-class man."

HAROLD LARWOOD
Nottinghamshire

Body-line was a restrictive practice, its aim to allow only one productive stroke — the hook. The field for body-line contained as many as six short-legs with two men deep behind them. A batsman could either play protective dabs (for the benefit of the short-legs) or a hook (for the benefit of the long-legs). The reason for body-line was not far to seek. During the Tests of 1928–9 and 1930, when Larwood was in opposition and, for the most part, bowling off-theory, four Australian batsmen — Woodfull, Ponsford, Kippax and McCabe — had between them played 35 innings for an average of 39. Bradman's ten innings averaged 115.

As a restrictive practice, body-line worked. Although a comparison of one innings with another may mean little or nothing, the two highest individual Australian scores of 1930 and 1932–3 certainly invite comparison. At Headingley Bradman's 334 included 113 runs (34 per cent) made in front of the wicket on the off side; at Sydney McCabe's 187 included a mere 16 runs (9 per cent) made in front of the wicket on the off side. McCabe was a great driver as well as a great hooker. If it be argued that any bowler has the right to pitch the ball so as to deprive a batsman of certain strokes, then it must be pointed out that body-line not only restricted strokes but also bruised many of the batsmen facing it.

Larwood denied that he was bowling to hit the batsman, a denial accepted by all cricketers. But he was bowling to compel batsmen to play either a protective dab or a hook, both strokes accompanied by great physical danger to balls travelling at 90 mph. One Australian response to Larwood came from V.Y. Richardson, a player none could intimidate. Having taken leg-stump guard, Richardson found ball after ball directed at his body; he then took guard a foot outside the leg stump — with the same result. Hence "body-line".

The 1932–3 series suffered in England not so much from being under-reported as under-interpreted. Tens of thousands of words appeared in print but none by a Vincent or a Cardus who might (or might not) have reacted differently to body-line had he witnessed it and not been obliged to rely on Reuter. *The Times* prefaced Reuter with a daily summary from "Our Own Correspondent", who would seem not to have been a cricketer. On the opening day of the first Test at Sydney, he dismissed Voce as having "sent down many long-hops, but he was never hostile", an opinion which clashed with Reuter's "the next four balls [from Voce, who had conceded two fours to McCabe] bounced head high and brought forth the disapproval of some of the spectators". At what pace does a long-hop have to be bowled to become a bouncer? To confuse *Times* readers further, the paper's own correspondent described McCabe's innings of 127 on the first day as "chance-less", Reuter having him missed in the gully early in his innings [Fingleton, *Cricket Crisis:* when five].

It was on the second morning that McCabe's batting became incandescent.

3 December 1932, Sydney. McCabe played an amazing innings this morning, making 60 out of the 70 runs scored in 55 minutes, his stand for the last wicket with Wall adding 55 runs in 33 minutes. He cut, hooked and drove with equal certainty and power. One over from Voce produced 14 runs and the next eight, and the over between from Larwood cost nine runs. His is the highest score which has been made by a batsman for Australia at Sydney since S.E. Gregory made 201 in 1894. He was twice dropped wide in the slips, and while he was battering the attack the English team appeared to be rattled. He scored freely off the leg-theory bowling, and proved that it is possible to hit that type of bowling.

The outcome of this Test — O'Reilly's first against England — was never in doubt.

AUSTRALIA 360 (S.J. McCabe 187 not out; H. Larwood 5 for 96) and 164 (Larwood 5 for 28) lost to ENGLAND 524 (H. Sutcliffe 194, W.R. Hammond 112, Nawab of Pataudi 102) and 1 for none by ten wickets.

Australia scored at about one run a minute in the first innings, Larwood and Voce between them took 16 wickets, and with Allen were responsible for 72 per cent of the balls bowled by England.

The second Test at Melbourne must have confused those MCC members who read *The Times*. It is tempting to add that the result — a win for Australia thanks to great bowling by O'Reilly and a second-innings hundred by Bradman — was less significant, in view of what would happen at Adelaide, than two sentences written by *The Times*' own correspondent, here presented as they appeared:

Fingleton, who is a worthy opening batsman, maintained a solid defence [while making 83], and, although battered and bruised, he played the bowling unflinchingly. The Australians were unable to cope with a highly concentrated attack, which included much leg theory, *used in the fairest manner* [editor's italics].

The Adelaide Test began on 13 January 1933, Australia's first innings the following afternoon. From now on the chronology of events is important.

14 January 1933, Adelaide. Larwood began by bumping the ball disconcertingly [wrote *The Times* special correspondent] and after Fingleton had been dismissed by Allen he switched over to leg-theory...The crowd made hostile demonstrations when the batsmen ducked. Vehement protests followed when Woodfull was hit over the heart and had to leave the ground in order to receive massage.

Reuter's order was correct. After Fingleton's dismissal,

Woodfull took a nasty blow over the heart which shook him badly [in Larwood's second over]. Larwood then began to bowl to a leg field in his third over, and the crowd booed him as he sent down each ball.

16 January 1933, Adelaide. [*The Times*, now back with its own correspondent, reported]

mild demonstrations early today...when Ponsford was hit on the body, but when Oldfield was struck on the head [having made 41] by a ball from Larwood the crowd of over 35,000 gave vent to their feelings. Larwood was then bowling to an orthodox off field, and Oldfield swung at a rising ball which seemed to fly off the edge of the bat on to Oldfield's temple. Oldfield staggered away and collapsed and after receiving treatment had to retire. The indignant crowd abused Larwood and Jardine...

18 January 1933, Adelaide. In a little over an hour Bradman showed his best form [in making 66]. He hit the bowling hard at a critical period, and he made it look playable, which other Australians have hitherto failed to do. The crowd applauded heartily while Jardine kept his bowlers to the off theory, but when he reverted to leg theory against

Bradman, who seemed to be getting the better of the bowling, they howled and hooted loudly.

This same day a message reached Lord's from Adelaide. Its appearance in *The Times* (on the main news page) is the more piquant when the two hyphenated words in the heading are compared with the first two hyphenated words of the message:

"LEG-THEORY"
BOWLING

AUSTRALIAN PROTEST
FROM OUR OWN CORRESPONDENT
ADELAIDE, JAN. 18

The Australian Cricket Board of Control has sent the following telegraph to the MCC —

Body-line bowling has assumed such proportions as to menace the best interests of the game, making protection of the body by the batsmen the main consideration. This is causing intensely bitter feelings between the players as well as injury. In our opinion it is unsportsmanlike. Unless stopped at once it is likely to upset the friendly relations existing between Australia and England.

HEADINGLEY 1930, Australia about 480 for 3; Larwood bowls to McCabe, Bradman the non-striker. Duleep, a specialist slip, is at mid on; Chapman in a Quidnuncs cap is socially divisive.

On the opposite page a majestic article sought to put matters in some kind of perspective.

"BODY-LINE BOWLING"

19 January 1933, leading article. In due time, no doubt, the MCC will send a considered and courteous reply to the cable of protest against what has begun to be called "body-line bowling" which they received yesterday from the Australian Board of Control. Meanwhile an attempt to give some idea of how the matter strikes the average Englishman may not be amiss. First of all there is nothing new in the kind of bowling to which exception is now taken. Really fast bowlers are as rare as truly great statesmen. But they do every now and then spring up, both here and in the Dominion, and have been known before now to hit the batsman as well as the wicket. English players who some years ago suffered many a shrewd knock from the bowling of McDONALD and GREGORY — not to speak of JONES in still earlier days — have the right to recall their own experiences to those who are now criticizing the tactics of LARWOOD and his Captain. Australians know as well as our men that the game of cricket is not played with a soft ball, and that a fast ball which hits a batsman on the body is bound to hurt. They also know that, so long as a "shock" bowler is not deliberately bumping down short-pitched balls or purposely aiming at the batsman,

his bowling is perfectly fair. It is inconceivable that a cricketer of JARDINE's standing, chosen by the MCC to captain an English side, would ever dream of allowing or ordering the bowlers under his command to practise any system of attack that, in the time-honoured English phrase, is not cricket. To do the Australians justice the grievance at the back of their complaint is probably neither the pace nor the direction of LARWOOD's deliveries. What they apparently do object to is the array of leg-fielders — corresponding to the closely packed posse in the slips and the gully when the bowler exploits the off-theory — on whom the English captain relies to increase the effectiveness of his fast bowlers. But in that policy there is nothing dishonourable or unsportsmanlike or foreign to the spirit of the game. After all, the object of every fielding side is to get their opponents out for as low a score as possible. If with that aim in view JARDINE has made more use of the "leg-theory" than other Captains before him the development is largely due to the fashion of the two-eyed stance and the modern batsman's habit of covering the stumps with his legs, thereby preventing the bowler from getting a clear view of the wicket, and incidentally making it more likely that he himself will be hit.

In the opinion of the Australian Board of Control bowling of this type has become a menace to the best interests of the game, is causing intensely bitter feelings between players, and unless stopped at once is likely to upset the friendly relations between Australia and England. Their protest, which is at once a warning and an appeal, is the direct outcome of the Adelaide Test Match. Apart from the skilful bowling that in the first innings sent back to the pavilion seven such batsmen as SUTCLIFFE, JARDINE, HAMMOND, AMES FINGLETON, McCABE and BRADMAN for an average of fewer than five runs apiece, the game was remarkable for the dogged pluck with which the batsmen of the two teams that followed them retrieved for the time being the fortunes of their side. Those first two innings were a constant succession of ups and downs, brimful of excitement, as English and Australian players in turn, fighting with their backs to the wall, upset all the calculations of the prophets. Under normal conditions these fluctuating changes and chances would have been enough in themselves to win for the Adelaide match a niche of its own in the annals of Test Match cricket. Unfortunately it will be remembered rather as a game in which good-humoured barracking degenerated as the play went on into angry booing on the part of the spectators, irritated by the failure of their idols, and to acrimonious comments in the pavilion and elsewhere on the particular style of bowling which was one of its causes. On the other hand let it be remembered that the crowds on the mounds, in spite of their disappointments, showed that they could cheer as well as barrack their English visitors, and that OLDFIELD and other Australian batsmen who were hurt by our fast bowlers were the first to own that the bowlers were not to blame.

Any breach in the mutual good will and friendliness between the players of the two countries which have survived the ordeal of many a desperate encounter over a period of more than half a century would be a cricketing disaster of the first magnitude, and the MCC may be trusted to do everything in their power to prevent the dismal forebodings of the Board of Control from coming true. It is difficult to conceive the possibility of their placing a ban on any particular type of bowling or to see by what authority they could instruct the captains of Test teams or any other eleven how to place or not to place their men in the field; but no doubt the common sense of the two great governing bodies of the game will be able between them to hit upon some means of coming to a satisfactory agreement. In all probability the present delicate and difficult position would never have arisen but for the irresponsible chatter of elderly critics in the pavilion and in the Press, and the craving in some quarters for sensational news-stories which has magnified words or incidents natural enough in the heat of a hard-fought battle.

The ensuing correspondence excited the nation, an unusual point of view being offered by A.A. Milne.* "It is definitely the laugh of the year that, season after season, batsmen should break the hearts of bowlers by protecting their wickets with their persons, and that, when at last the bowler accepts the challenge and bowls at their persons, the outraged batsmen and ex-batsmen should shriek in chorus that he is not playing cricket." Students of Milne recalled that when Eeyore lost his tail it was recovered and nailed on.

The Times's cricket correspondent attempted a summing-up.

LEG-THEORY AND BODY-BOWLING

A Word for the Bowler
By R.B. Vincent

1 February 1933. The text of the reply of the Australian Board of Control to the message sent to them on January 23 by MCC was announced yesterday, and will be found in full on page 10. For the moment the important fact is that the remainder of the programme is not to be cancelled and the English captain is free to employ whatever bowling tactics he considers suitable in the two remaining Test matches. If, however, there is any recrudescence of the disorderly behaviour which marred the third Test Match at Adelaide it is possible that MCC, without further discussion, may issue orders for the abandonment of the tour.

So long as tactics of the English bowlers remained the despair of the Australian batsmen and the butt of Australian criticism the matter could be regarded as little more than as a passing incident in Test Match history. But when once a formal protest had been made to MCC the situation became serious. The MCC Committee quite

. . . .
* Who in 1900 had played for Westminster School as an allrounder, and proved himself a more destructive bowler than P.G. Wodehouse of Dulwich College.

naturally refused to believe that their captain could have been guilty of any action which could be considered "unsportsmanlike" — an unfortunate word that for the Board of Control to have used — and since then every one interested in the welfare of the game has been trying to probe the rights and wrongs of the case.

An analysis of the whole matter has not been helped by a confusion between three quite different types of bowling — "bumping" bowling, "leg-theory" bowling, and this new specimen called "body-line" bowling. The fact that fast bowlers have always been liable and tempted to bang down a short ball has nothing to do with this present discussion, and the retort that McDonald and Gregory when bowling to a normally placed field occasionally hit our batsmen is not properly a comment on "leg-theory" as such. Nor can "leg-theory" bowling, as it has been accepted in the past, be considered a sufficient cause for complaint.

There have been at least three types of "leg-theory" bowling to which batsmen have become accustomed. First there is the left-handed bowler, such as F.R. Foster or Voce, who makes the ball go away with his arm and must of necessity rely upon a carefully placed field on the leg-side, and who straightens up the ball to hit the stumps. Foster was able to exploit this to the full by bowling round the wicket, but Voce cannot bring the ball back sufficiently and therefore bowls over the wicket; hence, no doubt, the accusation against him of "body-line" bowling. When he bowls round the wicket the ball travels diagonally from a point outside the return crease to fine long leg, which even if it is a "straight" line certainly is not a "body" line.

In the Tests of 1932–3 Voce bowled round the wicket for five or six overs while the shine was on the ball, then changed to over the wicket with short-legs in position. But "Voce had a short spell [starting in the 8th over of Australia's second innings], during which he bowled round the wicket, and had four short-legs" (Reuter, 18 January 1933).

Secondly, there is the medium-paced right-handed "in-swinger," a type of bowling employed most thoroughly by Root,* against whom there has never been a charge of unfairness. Thirdly, there is the case of the normal medium-paced right-hander who either because the state of the pitch or the habits of a particular batsman affords an opportunity changes from bowling over the wicket to round the wicket and brings his men on to the leg-side. Macaulay, who is one of the most intelligent and accurate of our bowlers at the present time, frequently does this successfully, and no one could regard this as anything but good bowling.

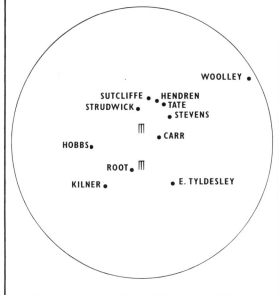

Leg-theory: C.F. Root's field at Old Trafford, 1926. Root's analysis says everything about his method: 52 overs, 27 maidens, 84 runs, 4 wickets. In P.F. Warner's words, "last-minute in-swerve"

None of these three types of bowlers has been regarded as unfair, even if a persistence of such bowling is liable to make the watching of cricket a dull affair in that it must mean the loss of many of the most beautiful strokes in cricket. I have in

. . . .

* Bradman faced Root only once — Worcestershire v. Australians, 1930. Towards the end of his 236, he was driving in-swingers from the leg stump past extra cover. At least, such was Root's testimony in the *Daily Mail*, 13 January 1933, quoted by Irving Rosenwater.

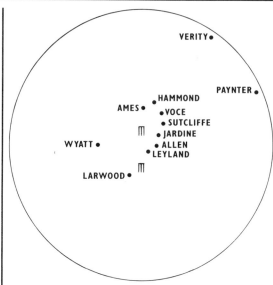

Body-line: Larwood's field at Adelaide, 1932–3. Larwood bowled 151 balls at Bradman in 1932–3, conceded 115 runs and dismissed him four times

recent years been exasperated with continually having to make a note that a batsman was caught at "forward short leg," "backward short leg," or "fine leg," but that does not mean that the bowling has not been both good and effective. Over and above that there has been employed a purely negative form of "leg-theory," in which the ball is pitched consistently outside the leg-stump to waste time. It has been bowled by Australians, and deserves no comment. But now suddenly a definitely fast bowler has taken it into his head to bowl to a field placed on the leg-side, and at once "leg-theory" has become "body-line," not because Larwood is doing anything different from what has been accepted as normal in the past, but because he is doing it fast.

In the opinion of Australians the "leg-theory" has ceased to be clever or amusing and has become dangerous. If this type of bowling, now called "body-line," is to be deemed unfair or contrary to the spirit of the game, then it can only be controlled by limiting the pace of the bowler, or else by destroying the whole theory of bowling to a leg-side field, which has been evolved by previous bowlers of a lesser pace. And surely, when everything is being done to readjust the balance between batsman and bowler, it would be utterly reactionary merely to tell bowlers that they must go back 50 years and start all over again in an effort to find a way of curtailing a batsman's fun?

It was strange the writer's mind did not go back less than six months to the Surrey v. Yorkshire match at the Oval.

By R.B. Vincent

22 August 1932. The strength of their [Yorkshire's] out cricket was evident on Saturday, but its splendour was to some extent marred by the tactics of Bowes, who pitched the ball so short that he not only incurred the displeasure of spectators, but finally moved Hobbs, who must have been wondering what manner of cricket match he was playing in, to make a protest himself. Bowes is not a good fast bowler, but surely he is not such a poor one that he has to rely upon such feeble devices, which are valueless in effect and which are unworthy of the traditions of so great a side.

The irony of that occasion will continue to delight cynics. P.F. Warner, who had denounced Bowes's bowling in the *Morning Post*, would soon, as joint-manager of the MCC party, find himself unhappily involved in the body-line controversy. The Surrey captain, D.R. Jardine, and captain-elect for Australia, apparently saw great merit in Bowes's attack, the Yorkshireman being one of the final selections.

England won the series of 1932–3 by four matches to one, Larwood's 33 wickets each costing 19.51 runs. Four years earlier under A.P.F. Chapman he had taken 18 wickets at 40.44 each. (When Larwood landed in Australia for the 1932–3 series he and his captain doubtless recalled that in his last seven Tests against Australia he had taken 14 wickets, average 68.42.)

Sutcliffe and Hammond both averaged 55 for England, five and three points, respectively, below their career Test averages. Bradman managed 56.57, some 43 points below his final figure. Body-line had therefore succeeded.

Fifty-six years after the body-line tour John Woodcock was in Australia for a series against West Indies and the World Series Cup, "the hyped-up one-day competition". Two paragraphs merit quotation:

5 December 1988. What has been a wonderfully eventful Test match at Perth, in which Australia have batted no less enterprisingly than West Indies, was marred yesterday when Geoff Lawson, coming in at No. 10 for Australia, had to be carried off on a stretcher after being hit a crippling blow on the face by Curtly Ambrose. Lawson was taken to hospital and operated on for a multi-fracture of the jaw.

31 December 1988. Bill O'Reilly was at the Adelaide Oval on Saturday, to rename the North Gate after his old cobber and bowling partner, Clarrie Grimmett. He blames today's trade in unprovoked aggression on the failure of administrators to face up, adequately, to the lessons of the bodyline series in 1932–3.

GEORGE ALPHONSO HEADLEY
Jamaica

Headley's greatness did not coincide with that of West Indies among the cricketing countries. His Test career, in effect concentrated within the decade prior to 1939, saw him without a master batsman at the other end. While he made eight hundreds against England and two against Australia, his colleagues made four and one. Bradman, for his part, scored 15 pre-war hundreds against England and two against West Indies, his partners 19 and three. Bradman was supported by, and sometimes supported, Woodfull, Ponsford, Ryder, Jackson, Kippax, McCabe, Brown, Fingleton and Badcock. What Headley meant to West Indies is hinted at here: his, Bradman's and Hammond's figures are pre-Second World War, those of the rest are complete:

Percentage of side's runs		Side's average total
29	Headley v. England	267
27	Bradman v. England	339
19	Hutton v. Australia	290
19	May v. Australia	247
18	Hobbs v. Australia	324
18	Hammond v. Australia	350
17	Worrell v. England	321
15	Weekes v. England	318
15	Harvey v. England	261
14	Compton v. Australia	296
13	Walcott v. England	327

The last season in England before the Second World War was, and will probably for ever remain, the freak when the eight-ball over was used. The idea was to give it a two years' trial, reverting perhaps to the six-ball over in 1941. Wise men at Lord's also insisted that pitches were too good. However, more serious matters prevailed in 1939. The day after the Oval Test ended on 22 August, the Nazi–Soviet Non-aggression Pact was signed. The West Indies' tourists made for home, arriving en route in Montreal on 3 September; had they waited a few days, they would have been on board the *Athenia*, sunk by a German submarine with the loss of 112 lives. The war in Europe progressed: on 4 September the Polish Pomorska Brigade of cavalry counter-attacked enemy tanks.

The year 1939, as had the previous six summers, saw Hammond at the peak of his powers. Such was his consistent mastery that, but for the war, he must have topped within five years or so Hobbs' 61,237 runs and 197 centuries, though, of course, Hobbs had lost four years to 1914–18. After 1939 West Indies would not visit England again for eleven years, by which time Headley had passed 40, leaving only Hutton, Compton (when his knee permitted), Wright and Gimblett for England, and J.B. Stollmeyer for West Indies, of those who had appeared at Lord's in 1939 to reassert their prowess. Stollmeyer at Lord's was the then second youngest Test debutant, his 18 years 105 days surpassed only by the 17 years 122 days of J.E.D. Sealy at Bridgetown against England in 1929–30. England's young men at Lord's were mature in comparison: Hutton one day past his 23rd birthday, Compton 21 years 32 days.

The Tests at Lord's and the Oval – that at Old Trafford was ruined by rain — saw the two sides manage the equivalent of just under 20 six-ball overs an hour. For this the English professionals' match fee was £27 10s, plus third-class rail travel — and hotel accommodation less drinks. Man of the match awards and bonus payments were all in the future.

HEADLEY AT LORD'S, 1939

By R.B. Vincent

26 June 1939. The first day's play in the Test Match between England and the West Indies at Lord's on Saturday produced cricket well worthy of the occasion, although the weather was almost too cold to be endurable. Lord's dries wonderfully quickly these days, and yet even so the pitch after the recent heavy rain was as nearly dead as a wicket can be.

England did well to be rid of the West Indies for 277; on the other hand it is a handy score to have in the score-book, with the possibility of rain during the week-end. Both sides in fact can be fairly well satisfied with the day's work, although the West Indies, with 225 runs on the board before the fourth wicket fell, might have been expected to pass the 300 in spite of their known tendency to let wickets slip away when once a big stand has been broken. G. Headley took the opportunity to score another century — the seventh he has contributed to Test Match cricket against England, and if it was not one of his most brilliant it was certainly one of his most valuable. His strokes had the appearance of being forced upon him, whereas when he is at his best he dictates the run of the play to the bowlers.

Both Bowes and Copson bowled splendidly, doing their utmost to get something out of a sullen and grassy wicket, and time after time Bowes failed only by a hair's breadth to find the edge of J. Stollmeyer's bat. Wright, I shall always think, bowls too fast, for he does not give himself the chance to make the ball do anything in the air before it touches the ground. Verity could make

nothing of the wicket, and in the circumstances it was remarkable that, at a time when the score was mounting threateningly high, no use was made of either Compton or Hutton. On so cold a day nothing could have been better than the fielding of the whole English side, or the wicket-keeping of Wood, and a crowd of 21,000 frozen people seemed thoroughly to enjoy everything that they saw.

...Twenty-nine runs had come when Grant, without relaxing his grip, played a ball to silly mid-wicket, where Compton leaned forward to hold it with his left hand.

Headley was in for a quarter of an hour before he scored a run, chiefly because he had only about half a dozen balls to play, and he must have considered himself once to have been very lucky not to have been given out leg-before-wicket. A double change with Wright and Verity on kept the scoring down so successfully that only 46 runs had been ticked up in the first hour. Stollmeyer once put Wright away to the square-leg boundary, but in the same over he was well and truly beaten. He seemed, however, to be guardian of his own fate so long as the ball was pitched on his middle or leg stump, and one over which Wright bowled to Headley was very expensive.

Stollmeyer had by now settled down to play with very much more confidence, but it was Headley who, in a sudden burst of lying back and thumping the ball off his back foot, was scoring at a far greater pace after the interval, when the score had been 95, Stollmeyer then being 44 and Headley 28. The bowling, more especially that of Bowes, was still good, and once Headley had been tamed down again to something like reason there was never a time when the game became in the least uneven. Headley reached his 50 with a stroke to leg off Copson which was not very far wide of Verity, who was standing at short-leg, and soon after that he hit a ball backwards which all but knocked Wood's head off and went to the boundary, where a respectable long-stop would be standing. The partnership had added 100 runs, Headley had made a perfect straight drive off

Bowes, and things were looking more than a little awkward for England when Bowes made a ball swing very late and hit Stollmeyer's off-stump. He had been in for nearly three hours, during which time he had shown, for so young a man, promise of great things to come in Test match cricket. His indeed was the success of the day.

There followed what for England was to be their main test — to prevent J.E.D. Sealey, a most dangerous batsman, from helping Headley to take charge of the game. Luckily Sealey solved the problem for them, for after having attacked the bowling ferociously he seemed to become a little too impetuous, and paid the price for it when he was caught at the wicket. The English captain no doubt was relieved, but he still had to rid himself of K.H. Weekes, who can produce many of the left-hander's scoring strokes. Headley sent the 200 up with a straight drive off Copson, who was still bowling fast and economically, and Weekes was a trifle hesitant in his stroke play, although he made some pleasant enough strokes on the leg-side. Bowes, when he was given the new ball, swung it all over Lord's in the most extravagant manner, suddenly seeming to lose all sense of direction. Headley was still walking right across his wickets with apparently all the time in the world to spare in which to play the ball either to the off or even drag it back across to the on. Weekes in the end was out to a truly magnificent catch by Gimblett, who ran back from cover-point, chased the ball when it was still in the air, and eventually held it with one hand outstretched. That was good, and it gave the crowd something really to clap about and keep their hands warm.

There was a deal more cheering when the great Constantine arrived; he twiddled his bat, hooked a ball to the boundary, more elegantly glided another, and made one grand propulsive stroke from a ball of reasonable enough length before he was leg-before-wicket to one of the few balls during the day which kept low. J.H. Cameron was out in the next over, caught by the faithful Hutton off Bowes in the slips, and then came the longed-for wicket of Headley, who hit rather wildly at a ball outside the off stump but did no more than snick it into Wood's gloves. He had batted for four hours like a great player who knows that he is not really in his best form, but who has to make the best possible out of it. Regarded in that light, it was a noble innings...

HEADLEY   Headley on his way to a first innings 116 not out at Chelmsford, 1939. Ten other West Indians scratched 96.

WEST INDIES 277 (J.B. Stollmeyer 59, G.A. Headley 106; W.H. Copson 5 for 85) off 81.4 eight-ball overs, i.e. 109 six-ball overs, England 11 for no wicket.

Second Day

27 June 1939. The Test Match between England and the West Indies, in spite of bad light, a non-committal wicket, and the general impression that three days are not sufficient for a game between two swagger sides, is by no means dead. It is, in fact, very much alive, and those people who thought that Hutton batted too slowly yesterday morning may yet find that he has laid the foundation of a victory for England...

...Later in the day when troubles had been overcome Compton came in to consummate Hutton's good work. His innings was sheer delight; the bowling was made to look easy; but it was Hutton who had done the ground work. Throughout the day the out-cricket of the West Indies was well worthy of any Test Match. Their bowling was accurate, generally on the wicket, and their fielding suffered only from an occasional anxiety to run a man out. They relied to a great extent on a wicket which was a shade easier and firmer than it had been on Saturday on their fast bowlers, but they put even greater faith in J.H. Cameron.* When at Cambridge, and afterwards when he played in county cricket, he was not a remarkably successful bowler, but yesterday he bowled so well, so accurately, and so sensibly with just sufficient spin to make even Hutton pay respect to the bounce of the ball, that for hours he controlled the play.

There were interruptions because of bad light, but whenever they went out again Cameron was bowling from the Pavilion end, and for hours he kept England's batsmen quiet. It was indeed a great achievement, and even if he had not gained

....

* Son of Dr J. Cameron, who had toured England with the West Indies team of 1906. J.H. Cameron was educated at Taunton School; playing for The Rest v. Lord's Schools in 1932, he had a first innings analysis of 19.1–3–49–10.

the wickets he so well deserved he had at least made a day of it.

The West Indies captain when play was begun in the morning believed that the wicket was still docile enough to place the fieldsmen with their toes almost treading on the prepared wicket at silly mid-on to the bowling of Martindale and Hylton. Hutton knows all the tricks of the dead-bat; Gimblett for his part allowed the balls to pass by on the leg side, waiting for the ball which he can drive to the off. He took one opportunity to score four runs away to square leg off Martindale, but then had a hard over to suffer from Hylton, who was able to make the ball rise. Gimblett again attacked in the manner of an opening batsman to cut Martindale and then lying back on his back foot to force him away to long off. Hutton was paying attention to all this, waiting his time, and always moving so that the bat was well on the line of the ball. This is the secret of Hutton's technique; he never allows himself to be in a position when he cannot play a full stroke from the uplift of the bat to its full continuation. He made two strokes off Hylton, which if one had not recognized his sense of timing might have been considered lucky; but the West Indies knew that the blade was well over the ball.

Forty-five runs were on the board when Constantine came on to bowl, and it is difficult to guess exactly what he was trying to do. His first few balls were so slow, so long in the air, that it was excusable to look again to the score-card to see that this was indeed the fierce Constantine. Also came on Cameron, and he in his first over bowled Gimblett so completely that consequent argument as to whether the ball came up or down the hill did not matter. In fact it was straight, well pitched up, and Gimblett was utterly late. Constantine bowling to Hutton had two slips, but when Paynter was batting to him he wanted all the men he could spare on the leg-side, for Paynter can make balls of good length look short, and yesterday he was inclined to hook.

When it became dark Paynter lost some of his patience, flicked at Martindale and consequently found the slips reinforced by another fieldsman. Hutton apparently can bat in the dark; he has been subject to moments of obscurity at Headingley and Bramall Lane, but even so the umpires had to call cease at half-past 12, when the score stood at 71, Hutton then having made 31 and Paynter 11. When they went out again after half an hour the light was still yellow, but Hutton at once flew at Martindale with two lovely strokes on the leg side, while Paynter played the short-armed left-handed batsman's stroke which sends the ball through holes in the field. Cameron was by this time well installed as the bowler, and neither batsman could dare to take a liberty from a length which was inviting a false stroke and a valuable wicket.

Paynter had one chance from a ball which pitched just a shade short of a length and that counted four runs, but he made a great mistake when, with the score at 119, he lashed at a ball wide of the off stump and was caught at the wicket. There was another break for bad light, but W.R. Hammond making little of these inconveniences hit the ball hard past Cameron's boot to the boundary with all the suggestion that runs had better be made before the light became even worse. He was out, trying to force the pace after he had made some glorious strokes off the back foot which for the most part were intercepted by a well-placed field, when he skied the ball to a position best described as silly extra-cover-point.

That was three wickets down for 147, and the West Indies well might have had another very valuable scalp in the next over when Compton edged a ball very close to first slip. Again a chance went very near to hand when Hutton played a ball from Cameron which dropped very near to the feet of short slip. The bowlers were then attacking, Martindale almost ferociously and Cameron quietly but competently. Compton after two or three overs became master of the situation. Hutton could be relied upon to see that the bowlers were allowed no licence. They were both very severe on Constantine, who when he bowled his slow ball was altogether too short and when he

bowled his faster ball outside the off-stump could be ignored. Compton, with that short-arm punch of his, it can be called a swat, hit Cameron away to leg without moving his arms from his body, and Hutton, gradually finding that the runs were coming, allowed us to see some of his strokes. He started with a full blow to long leg off Cameron, who in the end had to be taken off. He was greeted with a full cheer of recognition for a fine performance of bowling against some exceedingly good batting. Clarke came on only late in the proceedings and he offered very little trouble, while Compton was dealing most severely with Constantine, whom he hit in one over for three 4's — a jab to leg, a grand off-drive, and a thrust away past all fieldsmen to long-on.

All lost time had been recovered, the changes in bowling were becoming no more than suggestive, when Compton, who was beginning to make runs at an almost indecent rate, flung his bat at the ball and was caught at deep square-leg. While he had been in he had given the game every encouragement, and soon afterwards Hutton, who had seen to it that runs should come without wickets falling, could stand the strain no longer and was caught at long-on. This then left the game, which has so far seen good bowling, good fielding, and plenty of batting appropriate to the occasion, in a very interesting state, with England having had the better of yesterday's play.

Close: West Indies 277, England 404 for 5 (L. Hutton 196, D.C.S. Compton 120) made off 95 eight-ball overs — 89 on the second day, i.e. 118 six-ball overs.

Third Day

28 June 1939. England beat the West Indies in the first Test Match at Lord's yesterday by eight wickets, but with only half an hour to spare. If ever a case were required to be made for the three-day Test Match in preference to more prolonged exhibitions this was an outstanding example. England no doubt were the better side; they held the advantage throughout the game; yet there was a time yesterday when the West Indies fought back so well that it seemed that they were likely to deprive England of sufficient time in which to win the game.

Had they succeeded it would have been a drawn game, and many people would have talked of the futility of a game which has no definite result, but for all that it would have been a great achievement. As it was, three remarkable catches meant three quick wickets, and England in the end had all the sunny evening to spare. The day was made historic by G. Headley, who followed his century in the first innings with yet another in the second, a feat which has been accomplished seldom before in a representative match. He is the first to have done so in a Test Match at Lord's. Headley has long established himself as one of the three best batsmen now living; yesterday he did all that a man could do to make good bowling look easy, but in fact that bowling was always just a little too good for the other man.

There was a buzz of argument in the morning as to whether W. Hammond should declare England's innings closed with a lead of 127 runs or whether it would be better to gain some quick runs, with Hardstaff still there, and attempt to force an innings victory. Hammond decided to send the West Indies in again at once, even if it did mean that he might lose some wickets in the evening in a rush to score the necessary runs in the fourth innings. Events proved that he was wise, but some of these West Indies batsmen were very stubborn, and it wanted all the luck of the game to be rid of them.

The wicket was still good, fast and true, in the morning when the West Indies started their innings. Bowes bowled an over from the Pavilion end, and when Copson came on at the other end in his first over he had J. Stollmeyer caught in the gully off an unpleasantly rising ball which flew quickly off the bat into the air. Copson is economic in his run, but he makes great pace in his delivery, and yesterday he made the ball fly off the pitch. Headley was not impressed by his array of slips, nor by the three short legs, for he at once

cut him superbly, drove him to long on, and then made yet another late cut which whizzed past Hammond's feet at second slip. R.S. Grant entered into the argument by forcing a ball from Copson with a cross-batted blow straight to the sight screen, but he was missed at short slip when Wright, who yesterday seemed to be bowling slower, came on with the score at 41. It was only a temporary release, however, for soon afterwards Bowes unloosed a ball of perfect length, a little faster than usual, which came down the hill and flattened Grant's off-stump.

Headley's answer to this was to attack Wright, while Verity at the other end bowled to two short slips with the suggestion that the wicket would take spin if he could persuade it to do so. Actually he bowled very straight, but he succeeded in dragging Headley out occasionally with some deception of flight. Bowes, who was taking his time over his business and not bursting himself in an exertion for pace, bowled one splendid over to Sealy, who, in the next over, jumped in the air and thrashed the ball away to the off. The runs were hard to find, for England's fielding was as clean as could be, with Paynter at cover-point and Hardstaff, away on the leg side, particularly energetic. The returns of Gimblett, too, in this match deserve more than passing mention. Once Bowes tried his slow ball; so slow and so tamely obvious that Headley hit it into the tavern.

Compton then was given a short experimental spell, Headley cutting him square, but perhaps higher than he intended, and then making a stroke which was definitely false in the direction of third man. Bowes tested him with two yorkers in one over, which were stopped in a cloud of dust, but his worst anxiety came when he had made 44 and was utterly beaten and confused by Wright. The hundred was up when Copson came on again to have Sealy caught wide at the wicket, and K.H. Weekes was no sooner in than he put a ball from Bowes only just short of Hammond at first slip. Some say it was a catch; if so it must have been a very sharp one, or Hammond would have caught it.

At the luncheon interval the West Indies score stood at 117 for three wickets, Headley then having made 54, and every prospect of leaving England some few runs to make before half-past 6. Bowes afterwards tried bowling round the wicket, which was of little use against Headley, who is so quick on his feet that he can play the ball which comes across the wicket and yet force it away on the on side. Wright he treated with respect until he found a ball which he considered to be short of a length, and he then thumped it away to mid-wicket, while Verity bowled a series of overs which quietly met the middle of the bat and provided mid-off with some not over-anxious fielding and stooping practice.

Weekes had done well, even if he had been a

ENGLAND v. WEST INDIES
Lord's, 24, 26, 27 June 1939

WEST INDIES

1st innings

R.S.Grant	c Compton b Copson	22
J.B. Stollmeyer	b Bowes	59
G.A. Headley	c Wood b Copson	106
J.E.D. Sealy	c Wood b Wright	13
K.H. Weekes	c Gimblett b Copson	20
L.N. Constantine	lbw b Copson	14
J.H. Cameron	c Hutton b Bowes	1
I. Barrow	lbw b Copson	2
E.A. Martindale	lbw b Wright	22
L.G. Hylton	not out	2
C.B. Clarke	b Bowes	1
Extras	(b 3, lb 9, nb 3)	15
Total		277

2nd innings

R.S.Grant	b Bowes	23
J.B. Stollmeyer	c Verity b Copson	0
G.A. Headley	c Hutton b Wright	107
J.E.D. Sealy	c Wood b Copson	29
K.H. Weekes	c Wood b Verity	16
L.N. Constantine	c Hammond b Verity	17
J.H. Cameron	c & b Wright	0
I. Barrow	not out	6
E.A. Martindale	c Bowes b Wright	3
L.G. Hylton	c Hardstaff b Copson	13
C.B. Clarke	c & b Copson	0
Extras	(b 6, lb 4, w 1)	11
Total		225

Fall of wickets: 1–29, 2–147, 3–180, 4–226, 5–245, 6–250, 7–250, 8–261, 9–276, 10–277.

Second innings: 1–0, 2–42, 3–105, 4–154, 5–190, 6–199, 7–200, 8–204, 9–225, 10–225.

ENGLAND BOWLING (8-ball overs)

	O	M	R	W	O	M	R	W
Bowes	28.4	5	86	3	19	7	44	1
Copson	28	2	85	5	16.4	2	67	4
Wright	13	1	57	2	17	0	75	3
Verity	16	3	34	0	14	4	20	2
Compton					3	0	8	0

ENGLAND

1st innings

L. Hutton	c Grant b Hylton	196
H. Gimblett	b Cameron	22
E. Paynter	c Barrow b Cameron	34
W.R. Hammond	c Grant b Cameron	14
D.C.S. Compton	c Stollmeyer b Clarke	120
J. Hardstaff	not out	3
A. Wood	not out	0
Extras	(b 8, lb 6, w 1)	15
Total	(5 wkts dec.)	404

2nd innings

L. Hutton	b Hylton	16
H. Gimblett	b Martindale	20
E. Paynter	not out	32
W.R. Hammond	not out	30
Extras	(lb 2)	2
Total	(2 wkts)	100

D.V.P. Wright, H. Verity, W.H. Copson and W.E. Bowes did not bat.

Fall of wickets: 1–49, 2–119, 3–147, 4–395, 5–402.

Second innings: 1–35, 2–39.

WEST INDIES BOWLING (8-ball overs)

	O	M	R	W	O	M	R	W
Martindale	20	2	86	0	7.7	0	51	1
Hylton	24	4	98	1	7	1	36	1
Constantine	13	0	67	0	3	0	11	0
Cameron	26	6	66	3				
Clarke	6	0	28	1				
Sealy	3	0	21	0				
Grant	3	0	23	0				

Umpires: E.J. Smith and F. Walden

ENGLAND WON BY 8 WICKETS

shade lucky, until he was caught at the wicket, and the game, which had become almost closed once again, became very much alive, for the West Indies were then only 27 runs ahead, and there were still 3½ hours left for cricket. Constantine decided that this was the occasion to play sedately — not even Sutcliffe could have been more tolerant to bowling. Suddenly he changed his mind, his old impulse regained possession, and he swept a ball from Wright which was pitched well outside the off stump, away to the square-leg boundary. A few more eccentricities and he paid the penalty by cutting a ball off the leg stump into Hammond's hands at short slip. That was a very queer thing to do, and when J.H. Cameron played a shade too soon to be caught and bowled six wickets were down for 199 runs.

Worse was to come, for one run later Headley himself hit a ball straight to silly mid-off, and a great innings was at an end. If this match will be remembered for nothing else one will think of Headley's batting; the ease with which he could move his feet to good and threatening bowling and make Bowes and Copson look half pace.*

Then came the first of three catches when Bowes elegantly held his right hand out at mid-on to hold a ball which Martindale hit hard enough to pass any fieldsman. It is in no spirit of disrespect to the fielding of Bowes that I state that it was one of the most surprising events of the match. A few more runs and then Hardstaff held another amazing catch from a hard slash low down on his boots at cover-point, and to keep the keenness alive Copson, off his own bowling, followed up down the wicket to hold a catch as near the bat as the ball had pitched.

All of which meant that England had to score 99 runs to win in 110 minutes.† The start was

terrific; Gimblett hit a full pitch from Martindale for 4, which he followed with a full-blooded blow over the square-leg boundary for 6. Hutton then treated himself to a hook for 4, and with Gimblett making a grand on-drive off Martindale 35 runs had been scored in 20 minutes. At that score Hutton played outside and late to a ball and was bowled, and when Gimblett, rather impertinently, tried to hit a yorker away to leg two wickets were down.

Hammond was in no mood for the loss of another wicket, although he once all but dragged a ball from Martindale on to his wicket. Paynter neglected the invitation to play the left-handed batsman's stroke into the hands of slip, but when the ball was pitched a shade shorter he lashed it square and hard to the boundary. Hammond took matters leisurely enough, with an occasional forcing stroke which makes him look to be a better batsman than anyone else in the world, while Martindale, Hylton, and Constantine bowled their hearts out in an effort to take at least one more wicket. They were denied that pleasure, but they at least knew that their bowling had been not the least distinguished feature of a splendid game.

At the end of the 1939 West Indies tour of England, Headley had scored 1,745 runs, average 72.70. The next man averaged 30.83.

WEST INDIES' FINEST BATSMAN BORE HIS BURDENS LITHELY

By Alan Gibson

14 December 1983. I once took part in a television programme with Lord Constantine and Harold Pinter. We were asked to play the old game of

. . . .

* The batsmen who had made two separate hundreds in a Test were then W. Bardsley (Australia v. England, 1909); A.C. Russell (England v. South Africa, 1922–3); H. Sutcliffe (England v. Australia, 1924–5 and England v. South Africa, 1929); W.R. Hammond (England v. Australia, 1928–9); G.A. Headley (West Indies v. England, 1929–30 and 1939); and E. Paynter (England v. South Africa, 1938–9).

. . . .

† England made the required runs in 75 minutes while three West Indies fast bowlers got through the equivalent of 19 six-ball overs an hour.

choosing an all-time cricket XI. An odd selection committee, you will agree, but we enjoyed ourselves, whatever the viewers thought. We settled on Hobbs and Trumper for the opening pair, and then considered batsmen to follow.

"Headley", said Learie, at once. "Bradman?" suggested someone. "Yes," agreed Learie, "we will have Bradman as well, because after all, he was the white Headley." This was a reference to the constant description of Headley by English and Australian journalists as "the black Bradman", a description which did not altogether please Headley or his fellow West Indians.

George Headley, whose recent death we mourn, was not perhaps quite so good as Bradman, but had to bear heavier burdens. He was probably the best West Indian batsman there had ever been, despite the magnificence of Worrell, Weekes, Walcott, Sobers and Richards. None of the others was so unsupported as Headley.

When he began, shortly after West Indies Test cricket began, it was usually a case of "Headley out, all out". He had no comparatively easy Tests to boost his figures: his opponents were England and Australia. Nevertheless, he scored 10 centuries in 40 innings in 22 Tests. His Test average was 60.83: in all first-class matches, from 1927 to 1954, it was 69.86.

He played his first Test in 1930, when he was 20. England sent a side to the West Indies. It was not a full Test side (another "England" team was playing in New Zealand at the same time), but a strong one, including Hendren, Ames, Wyatt, Sandham, Voce, Gunn (aged 49) and Rhodes (aged 52). Rhodes took Headley's wicket in the second innings of the first Test, but only when he had scored 176, one of four centuries in the four-match series. Rhodes played his first Test in 1899, Headley his last in 1954; it must have been an interesting confrontation.

In 1930–31 West Indies made their first tour of Australia. Headley was then almost entirely an off-side player and the Australians tied him down

for a while, as they did Hammond, by attacking his leg stump. He realized an extra dimension was needed, with the result that Grimmett, who had been causing him problems, later said that he was the greatest master of on-side play whom he had met.

Headley toured England twice and was particularly effective on wet pitches. His record in such conditions was, as C.L.R. James points out in his remarkable book, *Beyond a Boundary*, much better than Bradman's. He had a successful series at home in 1934–35, ending with 270 not out in a Test which West Indies won by an innings. After the war he was not quite the same force again. He mostly lived in England. He was the first black man to captain West Indies, when England toured in 1947–48, but had to retire after the first Test because of a back injury. In 1953 the Jamaican public subscribed to bring him home for the next England series, but he played only in the first Test and Lock got him twice, for 16 and 1.

I saw Headley bat before the war. I have quite a clear recollection of his innings at the Oval in 1939. He scored 65 and a century seemed sure, when he was run out. The culprit was Victor Stollmeyer, and it must have been a horrifying moment for him in his first and, as it proved, only Test, although he made amends with a brave 96. What impressed me about Headley was his lightness of foot, his litheness. You would have to say that he was primarily a back-foot player, as Bradman was, but he always seemed to be dancing.

I saw him again after the war, indeed I saw what I think must have been his last first class match, in 1954, when he played in the Torquay Festival, batted beautifully for an hour or so for 64, and capered happily around the field. He seemed as nimble, as lithe, as ever. The circumstances were not, of course, testing, but I remember I was sitting next to Jack Walsh, one of the best Australian spinners of the day, and Jack said: "I'd love to be bowling to that blighter, just for the pleasure of watching him carve me about."

ARTHUR ALFRED MAILEY
New South Wales

CLARENCE VICTOR GRIMMETT
South Australia

WILLIAM JOSEPH O'REILLY
New South Wales

H.V. Hordern was the first of the great Australian googly bowlers. He toured England in 1907 with a side from Pennsylvania University (where he was studying dentistry), and in 1908 with the Gentlemen of Philadelphia. His Test career was brief — a year from February 1911 — though remarkable, his 32 wickets against England coming in a series which Australia lost 4–1.

Hordern and Mailey were confined to Tests against England and South Africa; Grimmett and O'Reilly did not play against India and Pakistan, the former against New Zealand, the latter against West Indies. Australia did not play New Zealand during Benaud's career.

VERSUS ENGLAND AND SOUTH AFRICA

Bowler and age span	Wkts	Av.	Wkts	Av.
Hordern (27–28)	46	23.36	In Australia 46 (v. England 32/24.37; v. South Africa 14/21.07)	23.36
Mailey (34–40)	99	33.91	In Australia 60 (v. England 60/32.41)	32.41
			In England 26	38.07
			In South Africa 13	32.53
Grimmett (33–44)	183	25.34	In Australia 72 (v. England 39/36.71; v. South Africa 33/16.87)	27.62
			In England 67	29.95
			In South Africa 44	14.59
O'Reilly (26–32)	136	23.68	In Australia 59 (v. England 52/25.23; v. South Africa 7/24.85)	25.18
Benaud (21–33)	135	30.03	In England 50	26.16
			In South Africa 27	17.03
			In Australia 80 (v. England 58/28.43; v. South Africa 22/34.31)	30.05
			In England 25	39.72
			In South Africa 30	21.93

Averages can be deceptive. The most successful of the above, in terms of finishing on the winning side, was Mailey — 10 wins to two defeats when permitted to bowl. Hordern 3–4; Grimmett 15–9; O'Reilly 13–8; Benaud 12–10.

Mailey's good fortune as a googly bowler lay in his side's batting strength, the No. 8 and 9 positions being occupied at one time or another by C.E. Pellew, J.S. Ryder, C.E. Kelleway, H.L. Hendry and J.M. Gregory, who all scored centuries against England, and T.J.E. Andrews, whose top score was 94.

In the ten games when Mailey finished on the winning side and Australia batted twice, he had an average aggregate of 855 to bowl against. His figures were something like (6-ball overs) 30–3–96–3 and 32–3–117–4.

A.A. MAILEY

A Note

Mailey bowled Hobbs with a full toss in the Oval Test of 1926 (as he had at Melbourne in 1924–5), causing *The Times* to write "I know that this thing happened because I saw it myself". Mailey's explanation was that when one of his leg-breaks or googlies reached the batsman without pitching, the spin he had imparted — and no one spun the ball more than Mailey — made it swerve. Ignoring such freak instances, we may agree that neither individually nor collectively were Hobbs, Woolley, Hendren, Rhodes, Makepeace, A.C. Russell, J.W. Hearne, Douglas and Fender negligible batsmen. Yet in 1920–21 they all succumbed to Mailey who, six months later, would be regarded by many English cricket correspondents as a purveyor of rubbish. Mailey played in all five Tests of 1920–21 but did not bowl in the second, presumably because Armstrong thought his googly bowler was irrelevant after rain had fallen — though two specialist batsmen, R.L. Park and C.E. Pellew, were allowed to try. In spite of which, in the other four Tests, Mailey took 36 wickets. Macdonald appeared in only the last three of the series, but the most devastating bowler throughout was Mailey. The batsman's completed innings are given after his name.

		Gregory	Kelleway	Macdonald	Ryder	Armstrong	Mailey
Hobbs	(8)	3	–	1	–	1	3
Woolley	(8)	2	2	1	1	–	2
Hendren	(8)	2	2	–	1	–	3
Rhodes	(6)	1	1	1	–	–	3
Makepeace	(6)	–	1	1	–	1	3
Russell	(5)	1	1	–	–	1	2
Hearne	(2)	1	–	–	–	–	1
Douglas	(7)	1	–	–	–	–	6
Fender	(6)	–	2	2	–	–	2
	(56)	11	9	6	2	3	25

Mailey's 25 wickets against specialist batsmen or allrounders were variously acquired: *Bowled:* Hendren, Russell. *LBW:* Hobbs, Makepeace, Douglas. *Caught and bowled:* Hobbs, Douglas 2. *Caught wicketkeeper:* Hendren. *Caught slip:* Hearne, Russell, Makepeace, Rhodes 2. *Caught covers:* Douglas, Makepeace, Fender. *Caught deep field:* Rhodes, Fender, Hobbs. *Stumped:* Douglas 2, Woolley 2, Hendren.

As bowling of Mailey's kind will certainly never be seen again in first-class cricket, his figures and field placings in 1920–21 are given here — the absurdity of one reflected by the other and vice versa.

The "other bowlers" consisted of J.M. Gregory, E.A. Macdonald, C.E. Kelleway, W.W. Armstrong and J.S. Ryder.

Mailey

	O	M	R	W
1st Test	23	4	95	3
	24	2	105	3
3rd Test	32.1	3	160	5
	29.2	3	142	5
4th Test	29.2	1	115	4
	47	8	121	9
5th Test	23	1	89	2
	36	5	119	5
	243.5	27	946	36

Av. 26.27   B/W 40.50   R/100 B 64

Others

	O	M	R	W
1st Test	36.1	6	88	6
	78.5	15	167	7
3rd Test	100	21	269	4
	77	7	221	5
4th Test	70	11	163	5
	70	17	180	1
5th Test	47	12	107	8
	65	12	150	4
	544	101	1345	40

Av. 33.62   B/W 81.15   R/100 B 41

Mailey, Gregory and Macdonald played together only in the last three Tests of 1920–21. Mailey's 30 wickets averaged 24.86 apiece, the 15 wickets of Gregory and Macdonald each averaged 48.06.

C.V. GRIMMETT

Grimmett was born in Dunedin on 25 December 1891 and died in Adelaide on 2 May 1980. He bowled right-arm. *The Times* confirmed this intelligence on 2 March 1925, though Grimmett had first bowled against an MCC side on 5 February 1921: "Grimmett is not a left-arm bowler." His career was unusual in other ways. When he took the first of his 216 Test wickets he was only two months younger than Benaud when that player took his 248th and last Test wicket. Grimmett was ignored at one end of his cricketing life and prematurely discarded at the other; between times he taxed the resources of the

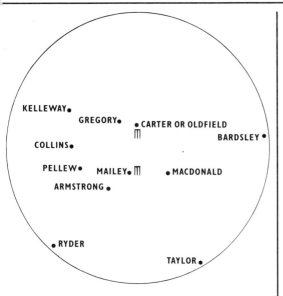

KELLEWAY •

GREGORY • • CARTER OR OLDFIELD

Ⅲ

BARDSLEY •

COLLINS •

PELLEW • MAILEY • Ⅲ • MACDONALD

ARMSTRONG •

• RYDER

TAYLOR •

Mailey's field in Australia, 1920–21. His 36 wickets were: three bowled, three lbw, 21 caught, nine stumped

best, so that at his death Sir Donald Bradman could acclaim him as "the finest of all leg-spin bowlers", a verdict none has challenged.

A schoolboy fast bowler, Grimmett, aged 22, left his native New Zealand for Sydney where he played Grade cricket. Three years later he went to Melbourne where, at 29, he was picked for Victoria v. MCC.* He bowled at Hendren on 96, had him missed first ball, then suffered: Hendren 271, Grimmett 20.3–0–110–1, his solitary wicket being that of MCC's No. 10, Parkin. After six years in Melbourne he received overtures from Adelaide, where a job had been found for him with Harry Lyons, a firm of sign-writers. Making his third appearance for Victoria (ironically, against South Australia) Grimmett took eight for 86 in the second innings. Victoria now saw the light but too late: Grimmett departed.

The 1924–5 season — during which Grimmett celebrated his 33rd birthday — was noteworthy on

. . . .

* Warwick Armstrong, a leg-spinner of sorts, had been purged by the State selectors for dropping out of the Victorian side on the morning of a Shield game at Sydney. The national selectors were more sensible; they picked Armstrong for the Fourth Test and he obliged with 123 not out. This was not the occasion when Armstrong, suffering from malaria, downed several neat whiskies before wandering out to make a hundred.

several counts: the superb bowling of Tate, the mastery of Hobbs and Sutcliffe and the optimism of the England selectors who despatched three googly bowlers. In the event, Hearne, Freeman and Richard Tyldesley combined to take 19 Test wickets, average 58. Meanwhile Grimmett was settling in nicely:

South Australia v. Victoria	42	–10–	97–	5
	50	– 6–	170–	4
South Australia v. MCC	26	– 4–	87–	4
	1.1–	0–	2–	1
South Australia v. Victoria	33.6–	4–	97–	5
	15	– 2–	43–	0
South Australia v. New South Wales	26.7–	1–	137–	5
Australian XI v. MCC	36	– 3–	176–	4
South Australia v. New South Wales	13	– 1–	43–	3
	23	– 3–	103–	6
	266.6–	34–	955–	37

Av. 25.81

After which Grimmett was chosen for the Fifth Test at Sydney.

GREAT BOWLING BY MR GRIMMETT

2 March 1925. England gave a very disappointing display here today in the final Test match, as, after dismissing the Australians for the comparatively small total of 295, they could score no more than 167 in their first innings. Mr *C.E.* [sic] Grimmett, the South Australian slow bowler, who is making his first appearance in a Test match, was chiefly responsible for the sensational collapse of the Englishmen. He bowled with splendid judgment and took five wickets at a cost of only nine runs apiece.

England had never recovered from the dismissal of Hobbs to the fifth ball of Gregory's first over, miraculously caught by Oldfield wide on the leg side. Sandham was run out by a smart stop and throw by Grimmett at cover: "Mr Gregory sprang for the ball and fell towards the wicket, which he broke with Sandham out of his crease. In falling, Mr Gregory dislocated the third finger of his right hand, but, with Woolley in, he completed the over and then retired for treatment. He was able, however, to return in time to take up the bowling without having missed an over [presumably a jerk of the finger by the physiotherapist...]." At tea England were 89 for four wickets.

Mr Grimmett and Mr Gregory bowled when play was continued, and, after seven runs had been added, the former bowler completely beat and bowled Woolley...Hearne was next partnered by Whysall. The partnership, however, was short-lived, as at 109, Hearne was out leg-before-wicket to Mr Grimmett...At 122 Whysall was also out leg-before-wicket to Mr Grimmett, whose figures at this point were three for 17.

Tate and Kilner then scored at a good pace, 30 runs being added in ten minutes...It was Mr Grimmett who captured the next wicket by getting Kilner stumped at 157...Tate was bowled by Mr Ryder at 164, and soon afterwards Mr Gilligan was caught at the wicket* [off Grimmett]. Thus England, who were batting for only 3¼ hours, found themselves 128 behind on the first innings.

Elucidation followed:

Mr Grimmett is a slow right-handed bowler — not a left-hander, as has been stated in some quarters — and bowls a shade faster ball than Mr Mailey. He has no tricks, seldom attempts the googly in serious cricket, and relies mainly on his spin and accurate length.

There are certain questions unlikely now to be answered:

1. If some quarters genuinely believed Grimmett was a left-arm bowler, was the matter finally settled by asking Grimmett himself?
2. As Hearne and Whysall were both out lbw to Grimmett, is it not likely they were trapped on the back foot by his top-spinner? If so, does the top-spinner not rank as a "trick"?

. . . .

* The scoresheet, *Wisden* and posterity has him stumped; no matter, the bowler was Grimmett.

3. When Grimmett had the left-hander Kilner stumped, was not the googly probably the agent of destruction, as it would be with the bowler's first ball to Woolley, stumped, at Trent Bridge in 1930?

Australia made 325 in their second innings, leaving England 454 to win.

4 March 1925. At 14 Mr Grimmett came on at Mr Kelleway's end...With the score at 32, Hobbs jumped out to a tempting ball from Mr Grimmett: he missed it, and before he could regain the crease, Mr Oldfield broke the wicket. One more run had been added when Sandham, who had been joined by Woolley, was out leg-before-wicket to Mr Grimmett, whose figures were then two for 2.

Woolley was next partnered by Hendren, and at the tea interval they had each scored two, the total standing at 35 for three. Mr Grimmett and Mr Gregory continued to bowl after the interval, and, though Hendren did not appear any too comfortable against Mr Grimmett, Woolley soon settled down. He was warmly cheered for a magnificent drive past cover point for four† off Mr Gregory, who himself joined in the applause. Woolley had made 19, when Hendren was caught at the wicket off Mr Grimmett, whose analysis was then three for nine. With four wickets down for 60, Woolley was joined by Hearne, and eight runs later Mr Gregory, whose one wicket had cost 51 runs, gave way to Mr Kelleway. When bowling to Hearne, Mr Grimmett had Mr Mailey at silly mid-on, Mr Taylor at long-on, Mr Kelleway and Mr Collins in the neighbourhood of mid-on, and Mr Kippax at square-leg, with the other fieldsmen on the off-side.

This is surely an odd field for a leg-spin bowler who does not attempt the googly in serious cricket. At

. . . .

† "I shall never lose a boyish memory I have of Woolley crashing Gregory through the covers at Sydney for a matchless boundary" — Jack Fingleton, writing of his 16-year-old self in *Cricket Crisis*, p.214.

the close on the fourth day England were 88 for five, the match ending shortly after one o'clock the next day in a win for Australia by 307 runs. Grimmett's later victims were Hearne again lbw, Whysall stumped and Strudwick caught at short-leg.

Grimmett's first-innings figures were 11.7–2–45–5, in the second innings 19.4–3–37–6, though the latter analysis in *The Times* rounded off the overs to 20.

The Englishmen in 1924–5 played their last game against South Australia at Adelaide. They lost by ten wickets after setting the home team one run to win. Grimmett took seven for 85 in MCC's second innings.

GRIMMETT TAKES ALL TEN WICKETS

By R.B. Vincent

11 May 1930. The day's play in the match between the Australians and Yorkshire at Sheffield on Saturday was a personal triumph for C.V. Grimmett, who took all 10 Yorkshire wickets for 37 runs, with the result that Yorkshire were dismissed for the small total of 155. When bad light stopped play at a quarter past 6 the Australians had scored 69 for the loss of only one wicket, and so start to-day in a strong position.

Grimmett was not put on to bowl until the score was 46, with Holmes and Sutcliffe well set for one of their customary big partnerships, but after he had dug the first three batsmen out he did very much as he liked with the rest of the side, his last seven wickets costing him only 16 runs. He bowled throughout his spell from the Football Ground end, and certainly did not have anything to help him from the pitch, which was quiet and easy. He made the ball turn, however, even if he could not make it do so quickly, and by varying his flight had batsman after batsman either going out or going back to the wrong ball. He was supported magnificently by C.W. Walker,* who is very quick and neat in his work. Only twice

before has an Australian bowler taken all 10 wickets in an innings in this country, W.P. Howell against Surrey at the Oval in 1899 — that being his first match in this country — and A.A. Mailey against Gloucestershire at Cheltenham in 1921.

Woodfull started his bowling with Wall, from the Pavilion end, and à Beckett, but after Holmes and Sutcliffe had scored 16 quiet runs Hornibrook relieved à Beckett, who in turn came on at Wall's end. Richardson came in to silly-point to Hornibrook's bowling, but even that could not stop the batsmen, who throughout showed an inclination to hit the ball hard in front of the wicket. In one over Sutcliffe hit a 6 over long-on's head and a 4 past mid-on off Hornibrook, and things were looking so bad that Grimmett was sent for. The 50 went up after 70 minutes' batting, and nine runs later Grimmett got his first scalp, Holmes playing a ball on to his wicket. Luncheon was taken with the score at 67 for one wicket, and although Grimmett continued to bowl after the interval Oldroyd showed signs of settling down to play one of those innings of his which may not be beautiful to look at but which have been of such great service to his team.

At 84, however, Grimmett, who had beaten him two balls before, deceived him in the flight and had him leg-before-wicket. Sutcliffe was by this time playing splendidly, his driving past extra cover and one or two squarer strokes and his hooking being beautiful. When he had made 59 he did mistime a pull, but the ball went safely over the wicketkeeper's head for 4. Leyland started steadily enough, but at 120 Sutcliffe, playing a chop shot, was magnificently caught by Walker, and five runs later Grimmett completely deceived Leyland, who went out to the ball much too soon. One run later and A.T. Barber may be excused for thinking that the age of miracles is not passed. He played a non-committal, covered-up stroke to

....

* Flying Officer Walker, RAAF, was killed in the Second World War. He toured England twice—in 1930 as understudy to W.A. Oldfield and in 1938 to B.A. Barnett—but never played in a Test.

a ball outside his legs, and having missed the ball found that he had been stumped. He had never actually moved out of his ground, but Walker with amazing speed took his chance when Barber for the fraction of a second had his right foot off the ground. The crowd did not quite appreciate this decision, but it was a wonderful piece of stumping. Robinson hit a ball into long-on's hands after an attempt to brighten up the game, and Macauley, leaning out, was another to be well stumped. Wood batted bravely for a time, but after he had hit a ball round to leg for four, was easily caught by Richardson at silly-point. Nobody took a wicket from the other end, and when Grimmett bowled Bowes first ball the honour and well-merited congratulations were his. His fingers were probably a little sore towards the end, but he pegged away, hardly ever bowling a loose ball and sending down many very good ones.

At the close on the first day the Australians were 69 for one (W.M. Woodfull 37 not out, D.G. Bradman 24 not out). Rain prevented any play on the second day until after lunch; the Australians were dismissed for 320 (Woodfull 121, Bradman 78). There was no play on the third day. The umpire who gave Barber out, stumped Walker, was either Tom Oates or George Beet. Grimmett took his 100th wicket of the season in the return game with Yorkshire at Bradford, his record for the two matches there and at Sheffield being 71 overs, 17 maidens, 170 runs, 21 wickets. The second Yorkshire game was the tourists' 16th of the season, and the 13th in which Grimmett had played. The extent to which the Australians depended on Grimmett in those 13 games was apparent:

	Overs	Maidens	Runs	Wickets	Average
Grimmett	606.4	170	1,403	102	13.75
Others	1,235	341	2,807	123	22.82

1930 will always be remembered as Bradman's *annus mirabilis*. However, at the end of the summer, the sagacious Woodfull could point out that the Australians could have got by without Bradman. Without Grimmett…

GRIMMETT v. HAMMOND

	Balls	Runs	Wkts	Av.	B/W	R/100 balls
In Australia 1928–9	627	281	0	–	–	44.81
In England 1930	325	102	5	20.40	65	31.38

YORKSHIRE v. AUSTRALIANS
Sheffield, 10, 12 and 13 May, 1930

YORKSHIRE
1st innings

Holmes	b Grimmett	31
Sutcliffe	c Walker b Grimmett	69
Oldroyd	lbw b Grimmett	2
Leyland	st Walker b Grimmett	9
A.T. Barber	st Walker b Grimmett	1
Mitchell	b Grimmett	3
Robinson	c Bradman b Grimmett	2
Wood	c Richardson b Grimmett	17
Macaulay	st Walker b Grimmett	1
Rhodes	not out	6
Bowes	b Grimmett	0
Extras	(b 4, lb 9, nb 1)	14
Total		155

AUSTRALIANS BOWLING

	O	M	R	W
Wall	16	3	42	0
à Beckett	12	6	11	0
Hornibrook	12	4	49	0
Grimmett	22.3	8	37	10
McCabe	3	2	2	0

W.J. O'REILLY

O'Reilly was neither a spectator's nor a critic's bowler, at least until they had been watching him for some time. His flailing arms and high-stepping legs offended those who thought a bowler's action should be an aesthetic joy. He was never "fun" to watch because it was not apparent how any batsman would manage to score from him. On helpful pitches he was devastating, on those which offered no help he was simply the finest run-controller of his time. The ultimate tribute came from the ultimate source, Bradman, who said to E.W. Swanton in March 1947:

To my mind there has never been a bowler to equal O'Reilly. To play with him was an education — to play against him usually a lesson.

From every conceivable angle, theoretical, technical and practical, he stands supreme. Moreover, his figures are a monument to his skill and they were achieved in an era of high scoring and good wickets.

His control of length was marvellous, his direction always designed to use his fieldsmen to the utmost, and his subtle variations of break and flight were so admirably handled as to be a constant source of mental hazard to the batsmen.

In support of his natural talents was an outstanding cricket brain which enabled him to achieve a perfection beyond that of any contemporary.*

O'Reilly bowled leg-breaks, top-spinners and high-bouncing googlies at medium-pace, or just under. He was not a late developer in the Grimmett sense, but because he was a schoolmaster teaching up-country he had the remarkable record of taking his first Sheffield Shield wicket the day before his 26th birthday. A few weeks later he made his debut for Australia at Adelaide against South Africa, his Shield wickets to date 15. The following season he appeared in all five Tests in the body-line series when his figures were 383.4 overs, 144 maidens, 724 runs, 27 wickets, 26.81 average.

W.M. Woodfull's 1934 Australians included three wrist-spin bowlers, all of whom took 100 first-class wickets on the tour: O'Reilly 109, Fleetwood-Smith 106 and Grimmett 109. This oddity merits closer examination.

1934

C.V. Grimmett, W.J. O'Reilly and L. O'B. Fleetwood-Smith in 18 matches against counties

	Wkts	Av.	B/W
Grimmett	55	17.67	43
O'Reilly	68	13.44	41
Fleetwood-Smith	74	17.37	41
Wkts 197	Av. 16.10		B/W 42

....

* Quoted from *Sir Donald Bradman*, by Irving Rosenwater, p.291.

Two of the three spinners appeared in each of 17 matches, Fleetwood-Smith alone against Derbyshire: 30–4–86–6.

The Spinners in Partnership

Matches		Wkts	Av.	B/W
4	Grimmett	29	15.51	38
	O'Reilly	20	19.65	45
	Wkts 49 Av. 17.20 B/W 41			
6	Grimmett	26	20.07	49
	Fleetwood-Smith	24	18.66	44
	Wkts 50 Av. 19.40 B/W 47			
7	O'Reilly	48	10.85	39
	Fleetwood-Smith	44	17.09	40
	Wkts 92 Av. 13.83 B/W 40			
Wkts 191	Av. 16.15 B/W 42			

The new ball was variously shared on these occasions between T.W. Wall, H.I. Ebeling, S.J. McCabe and L.S. Darling.

	Wkts	Av.	B/W
Wall	19	22.57	51
Ebeling	38	21.28	66
McCabe	13	29.15	68
Darling	1	100.00	258
Wkts 71	Av. 24.18		B/W 65

The two accredited fast bowlers of the party, Wall and Ebeling, played together against five counties, when they achieved the commendable figures of 30 wickets, average 16.76, 43 balls/wkt.

W.J. O'REILLY AT LEICESTER, 1934

By R.B. Vincent

7 May 1934. Grimmett did not play, and in his absence O'Reilly took the wickets and provided the instruction of the day. Leicestershire have some batsmen who are experienced players, not easily to be diddled out, and the pitch, in spite of some rain in the morning, was remarkably fast for the time of year; but O'Reilly, who makes the ball run rather than spin across from leg, clearly bowls better the faster the wicket. He does occasionally bowl a ball which turns from the off when it might be expected to go the other way, but it is no more a googly than his normal ball a leg-break because neither really comes out of the back of the hand. He is obviously going to cause trouble, if for no other reason that whenever he gets a wicket he invariably gives the incoming batsman a horribly aggressive ball for his first.

O'Reilly's figures in the Leicestershire first innings were 24–10–39–7.

O'REILLY AND GRIMMETT AT TRENT BRIDGE, 1934

At the start of the fourth and last day at Trent Bridge in 1934 Australia were 265 runs ahead of England with seven second-innings wickets to fall. The pitch was taking spin. When would Woodfull declare? In short, how long would Grimmett and O'Reilly take to bowl out England? If England survived with half their wickets in hand, the moral triumph was theirs; if they survived with one or two wickets standing, Woodfull had made too late a declaration.

By R.B. Vincent

13 June 1934. With Australia's score at 244 [the lead 350] and the time 10 minutes past 12, W.A. Brown was caught at the wicket off Verity. This was surely the occasion for Woodfull to declare his innings closed, but instead there was some pottering along by Grimmett and Oldfield, and it was a quarter to 1 before England went in again.

England accordingly were left 380 runs to make in order to win, and Australia four hours and three-quarters in which to take their wickets. Let us now ignore the runs and concentrate on time, the Australian attack and the English

O'REILLY   Should it be the googly, it will bounce like a tennis ball and hit the splice.

defence. Woodfull started again with Wall from the City end, Sutcliffe being hit four times on various parts of his body in this first over. That was an indication of how Sutcliffe was facing the situation. Actually more runs were scored off pleasant strokes in the first few overs than the occasion demanded, Walters driving McCabe past cover-point for 4 and twice putting him away to leg.

McCabe was allowed to bowl only while 16 runs were scored before Grimmett came scurry-

ing on in his place, and from that moment, roughly about half an hour before luncheon, until the tea interval and a little afterwards Grimmett was apparently winning the game. His method of attack is not to take wickets one after another in haste with the possibility of a "hat-trick," but at regular intervals of half an hour, with never a bad ball bowled during those intervals. Yesterday afternoon he was truly magnificent, making the most of the wicket and bowling equally well when moved from one end to the other,* the limit of rest which his captain in these strained relations could allow him. Luncheon was taken fairly hopefully by England's supporters with the thought to help their digestion that neither Sutcliffe nor Walters [captain of England in this game owing to R.E.S. Wyatt's injury] was yet out and there was only another four hours for Grimmett to take 10 wickets. [This last sentence shows how cricket writers tended to under-estimate O'Reilly's powers at this stage of his career.] Australian supporters, however — and there were some few of them in Nottingham during these last few days — were still hopeful, and there was a perfectly legitimate roar of pleasure from their enclosure half an hour after the interval when Sutcliffe, the one man whom most they would like to see walk back to the pavilion, was caught in the slips after feeling forward to the kind of ball which hitherto he had played well with the middle of the bat. So long as Sutcliffe had been there the match had seemed to be saved, but the situation thereafter gradually changed. Hammond did his utmost to play a defensive innings, a role which does not come naturally to him, while at the other end Walters was splendid. Hammond took the opportunity twice to drive Grimmett to long-on for 4. For the rest of the time he had to lean forward in order to smother Grimmett's break and to delay for as long as possible the fall of the next wicket. He was

....

* This was the occasion when Grimmett got it wrong. Having noted a spot at O'Reilly's pre-lunch target area, Grimmett persuaded Woodfull to turn the bowlers round—only to discover that O'Reilly now had the "better" end. The latter's greater pace decided the issue.

lucky once to flick a ball from Wall only just wide of second slip, but at 25 minutes to 4, just when things did look better for England, he was beautifully stumped playing forward to a break from Grimmett which beat the bat. Ten minutes later Walters was bowled and Australia were quite definitely on top.

The Nawab of Pataudi and Hendren surely could last until the tea interval, but first Pataudi was caught at long-off, hitting the ball to Ponsford of all people, and at 20 minutes past 4 Hendren was caught at short slip. That was five wickets down and an hour and three-quarters to go. After tea, with Grimmett spinning the ball so furiously as to raise spurts of dust and the Australian fieldsmen crowding in on the leg-side, Ames stayed stolidly with Leyland, each being content to push his bat down the wicket. Once again it was agreed that the match was to be left drawn, more especially when the dreadful Grimmett and the equally terrible O'Reilly were taken off for the comparatively innocuous Wall and Chipperfield.

Leyland, the adventurer, was as stolid as could be — calm, with the peak of his cap high in the air, but he lost Ames at a quarter to 6, bowled by a ball from O'Reilly, who had just been put on at the pavilion end. The manner in which Woodfull rested his spin bowlers just so long but no longer than was necessary was the admiration of foes and friends alike. For England there followed another disaster when Geary was caught at short slip, and Chipperfield certainly is as good there as his friends in Australia had said he would be.

Leyland, with his feet firm and still quite imperturbable, played back to O'Reilly's slow or to his fast ball. There was a roar of bewildered excitement when he hit the ball only just short of short-leg, and at 6 o'clock Verity was there, but only just there, to Grimmett, who was bowling with all his great heart. He played another over comfortably enough to O'Reilly, but Leyland, with an appropriate single to the last ball of Grimmett's next over, spared his partner any more immediate distress. Once he refused to run twice in the next over, only himself to be caught at the wicket. It had been a great innings, but there was still 20 minutes to go and now only two wickets to fall.

Like many another I could hardly stand the strain. There was another roar: Farnes had been caught at the wicket and Mitchell alone stood for England's honour, with a quarter of an hour to go. Someone in front of me said "He's out"; someone else said "We are going to play out time," and four runs were rather politely thrown back from long-leg. Then, off the next ball, Mitchell was leg-before-wicket. A better cricket match I shall never see.

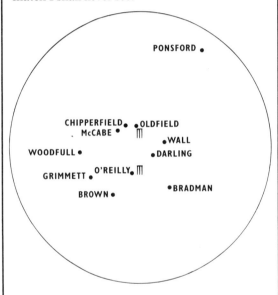

O'Reilly's field at Trent Bridge, 1934

The field set at Trent Bridge in 1934 differs from that discussed in Sir Donald Bradman's *The Art of Cricket* (1984 edition). This consisted of two short-legs very close in, a wide mid-on, two men 25–30 yards from the bat behind the wicket on the leg side, slip, point, short extra-cover and mid-off.

A letter from Mr O'Reilly (12 May 1988) put matters in perspective: "The two-man leg trap was not set until the South African tour of 1935–36 when the presence of two specialists — Fingleton and Richardson — made it wise for peace sake to expand business in the area."

This two-men leg trap would appear to date from

AUSTRALIA
1st innings
374 (W.H. Ponsford 53, S.J. McCabe 65, A.G. Chipperfield 99; K. Farnes 5 for 102).

2nd innings
273 for 8, declared (W.A. Brown 73, McCabe 88; Farnes 5 for 77)

ENGLAND
1st innings

C.F. Walters	lbw b Grimmett	17
H. Sutcliffe	c Chipperfield b Grimmett	62
W.R. Hammond	c McCabe b O'Reilly	25
Nawab of Pataudi	c McCabe b Wall	12
M. Leyland	c & b Grimmett	6
E. Hendren	b O'Reilly	79
L.E.G. Ames	c Wall b O'Reilly	7
G. Geary	st Oldfield b Grimmett	53
H. Verity	b O'Reilly	0
K. Farnes	b Grimmett	1
T.B. Mitchell	not out	1
Extras	(b 5)	5
Total		268

2nd innings

C.F. Walters	b O'Reilly	46
H. Sutcliffe	c Chipperfield b O'Reilly	24
W.R. Hammond	st Oldfield b Grimmett	16
Nawab of Pataudi	c Ponsford b Grimmett	10
M. Leyland	c Oldfield b O'Reilly	18
E. Hendren	c Chipperfield b O'Reilly	3
L.E.G. Ames	b O'Reilly	12
G. Geary	c Chipperfield b Grimmett	0
H. Verity	not out	0
K. Farnes	c Oldfield b O'Reilly	0
T.B. Mitchell	lbw b O'Reilly	4
Extras	(b 4, lb 3, nb 1)	8
Total		141

Fall of wickets: 1–45, 2–102, 3–106, 4–114, 5–145, 6–165, 7–266, 8–266, 9–266, 10–268.

Second innings: 1–51, 2–83, 3–91, 4–103, 5–110, 6–134, 7–135, 8–137, 9–137, 10–141.

AUSTRALIA BOWLING (6-ball overs)

	O	M	R	W	O	M	R	W
Wall	33	7	82	1	13	2	27	0
McCabe	7	2	7	0	2	0	7	0
Grimmett	58.3	24	81	5	47	28	39	3
O'Reilly	37	16	75	4	41.4	24	54	7
Chipperfield	3	0	18	0	4	1	6	0

Umpires: F. Chester and A. Dolphin

AUSTRALIA WON BY 238 RUNS

the Transvaal v. Australians match at Johannesburg on 7 December 1935, when the tourists' captain, V.Y. Richardson, invited J.H. Fingleton to join him close to the bat. Bradman missed this tour on medical advice as he was still recovering from a serious illness.

"At Nottingham in 1934," continued Mr O'Reilly, "Ponsford and Bradman had roving commissions, deep or close according to the run of play. I invariably used two slips when the pitch was taking a drop of turn."

Grimmett did not play against England again after 1934, though his career lasted for a further seven seasons, during which he took 353 first-class wickets, average 20.43. However, his partnership with O'Reilly continued in South Africa (1935–6), when his Test wickets numbered 44 at 14.59 runs each, O'Reilly's 27 at 17.03, the Australians winning four Tests and being undefeated on the tour.

The extent to which Australia relied on the pair during 1934 in England and 1935–6 in South Africa was considerable.

	Overs	Mdns	Runs	Wkts	Av.
Grimmett	742.4	288	1,310	69	18.98
O'Reilly	583.5	240	1,158	55	21.05
Total	1,326.3	528	2,468	124	19.90
Others	691	134	2,015	45	44.77

In spite of this, Grimmett was not chosen to play against England in 1936–7, nor to tour England in 1938. The latter decision seemed incredible at the time, and even more so now, though it was matched by the omission of Tallon as one of the wicket-keepers. The outbreak of war found Grimmett at his peak, nine first-class games in 1939–40 bringing him 73 wickets, average 22.65 — this at the age of 48, when he was perfecting his new googly.

He was still trundling in his garden at 70, though admitting that his leg-break had lost some pace from the pitch.

O'REILLY AT HEADINGLEY, 1938

At the start of the third day of this four-day Test, England were 30 runs ahead with all their second-innings wickets intact. The first wicket then fell at 60, the last nine adding only 63 so that England were out by lunch. As this was a bowler's game, those who made victory possible for Australia shall here be accorded precedence in the story of events, the second day's play being taken out of context — indeed, thrown in at the end as a tribute to genius.

By R.B. Vincent

23 July 1938. England in the fourth Test Match at Leeds yesterday were spared shame only by the runs scored late in the innings by their bowlers. As it was a total of 223, on a wicket which normal preparation, recent rain, and quiet wind between them had made comfortable and of an easy pace, was meagre, and cannot be attributed to any remarkable quality in the Australian bowling.

W.J. O'Reilly certainly bowled well — he always does — but there was more than a suggestion that the early batsmen, in an attempt to build up a big score which would make their side at least secure during the rest of the match, overlooked the rather important matter of scoring runs. It was an object lesson in how not to do it. Possibly England's bowlers will further retrieve the situation to-day, for last night before the close of play they did have the satisfaction of taking one Australian wicket for only 32 runs.

Australia began their bowling in the morning with McCormick from the Football Ground end and Waite. McCormick had what wind the covered stands allow to pass by them to help him, and he started off with four slips and two short-legs. The pace of the pitch was not encouraging to a catch behind the wicket, two of the slips accordingly being moved wider, but the men on the leg side remained expectant. Waite, who bowled an excellent length, making the ball go away late, had his two slips and a gully, but the occasional offer which was made of a stroke suggested a deflection or a prod to leg.

Barnett was anything but the gay and thrustful opening batsman he can be, but Edrich, playing with more certainty and more time in which to make his stroke, looked the man appropriate to the occasion. It was not long before Waite was put on at McCormick's end and O'Reilly at the other. O'Reilly, be the wicket ever so tame, can wring some life out of it, and he has always that variation of flight and length which worries a batsman of indecision.

So it was with Barnett, who seemed unable to decide whether to go forward to the ball or to wait to see what it would do. He was badly missed at second slip off Waite, and the first hour's play produced only 29 rather indeterminate runs. At the end of that hour Edrich, playing forward, was beaten and bowled by an off-break from O'Reilly, and soon afterwards England suffered an accident which never should have been. Barnett played a ball in the direction of mid-on, Hardstaff backed up unnecessarily vehemently and failed to get back, although he flung himself on to the ground, and was run out. So entered Hammond, and on went McCormick again. It was no fault of Hammond's that two wickets had fallen so cheaply and consequently he was forced to exercise some caution. This he did, no doubt to his own satisfaction and to the pleasure of the crowd while Barnett was gradually shaking off the qualms from which he had been suffering.

Runs were not often noticeable, and there was no manner of doubt that this was a Test Match, for there could have been no other explanation for such sterility. The spectators at the far end of the ground were kept physically and mentally on the move by the sight screen being moved from side to side every few overs, and there was an almost flippant cheer when Hammond hit a full pitch from Fleetwood-Smith straight for 4. Luncheon arrived with the total at 62, a not very liberal score as the result of two hours of cricket.

Hammond must have had a talk to himself during the interval, for the tempo of the game altered entirely afterwards, an attack and a genuine desire to score runs succeeding a policy which had been negative to the point of being suicidal. Hammond led the way by driving McCormick to

the off, and then hitting a no-ball into the lofts of the Grand Stand. There were hopes of a revival, for such was needed, when Barnett flicked at a ball outside the off stump and was caught at the wicket.

Hammond and Paynter together was more like an English combination of merit. Fleetwood-Smith bowled particularly well to Hammond, a batsman whom he might well fear more than any other on earth.* He pitched the ball perpetually to that length which made Hammond stretch, and he twice beat him with the spin. O'Reilly, when bowling to Paynter, who started much more confidently than he sometimes does, had a very silly mid-off, but the ball was played well down, and never a chance was missed of tickling it away to leg. Hammond, for half an hour or more, was the true majestic Hammond, reaching his 50 with two exquisite drives wide of extra cover-point.

Fleetwood-Smith kept Paynter quiet, although one short ball was cut square for 4, and Waite was given a short spell to rest O'Reilly before Hammond had become too insolent. The first ball Waite bowled to Hammond came back off the bat so violently that there would have been fears for the umpire's life had he not thrown himself on the ground. In any case there was a spare umpire on the ground. Paynter again cut Fleetwood-Smith, and in the first hour after luncheon 63 runs were added, a much more suitable rate of scoring, even if there was a deal of lost time to recover. There was a check, in fact almost a dead halt, when at 142 Hammond's off stump was hit by a ball from O'Reilly which came back sharply. Hammond's had been a good and valuable innings and the end of it must have been joy to the Australians.

Compton was no sooner in than he had a lucky escape, a ball from O'Reilly passing from the edge

....

* Hammond had destroyed Fleetwood-Smith in the MCC v. Victoria game of 1932–3, so perhaps delaying the bowler's entry into Test cricket. Fleetwood-Smith's revenge came a tour later at Adelaide when, in the first over of the sixth day, he bowled Hammond, so extinguishing any hopes England had of winning the match.

of the bat between the wicketkeeper and first slip. This partnership between Paynter and Compton was regarded as vital to England, for with all due respect to those that were to follow a line could be drawn across the scorecard under Compton's name. Paynter was as comfortable as O'Reilly would allow him to be, and he was content to allow the ball which was breaking away past the off stump to go on its way neglected.

Then, just before tea, came utter disaster to England. Paynter, in attempting to hit the ball ferociously, lost his balance, swung himself off his feet, and was stumped. This was a good wicket for Fleetwood-Smith, who deliberately tossed up this ball to invite indiscretion. Compton was out at the same total, 171, bowled by a beautiful ball which he lost when it left the pitch, and Price, who batted in anything but the manner generally associated with one who has opened the innings for Middlesex, was caught at short slip, or perhaps it would be more accurate to say played the ball into the hands of short slip.

...When Australia went in Farnes from the Grand Stand end gave a splendid exhibition of fast bowling. Three times he beat a batsman utterly and completely, but the ball went over the stumps. In his very first over he well might have bowled Fingleton for all that batsman knew of the ball, and in his next over the ball seemed to pierce Brown's bat and body without even the wicketkeeper knowing that it had passed him. Bowes at the other end, without striving for pace, was bowling steadily, while Fingleton and Brown were collecting runs here and there without any marked certainty of execution. With the score at 28, Wright was put on in place of Bowes, a happy thought on the part of Hammond, for Wright, with his first ball hit Brown's leg stump. Barnett was sent in to play out time, which he achieved after he had just, and only just, brought his bat down on to a yorker from Wright.

Close: ENGLAND 223 (W.R. Hammond 76; W.J. O'Reilly 5 for 66), AUSTRALIA 32 for one wicket.

Third Day

26 July 1938. Australia beat England in the fourth Test Match at Leeds yesterday by five wickets, and so the bogy was laid that four, or even more, days are essential to a definite result. Actually the winning hit was made at a quarter-past 4 on the third day, and that, in spite of some stoppages during the game for rain or bad light.

Sure enough the wicket was taking spin yesterday, a phenomenon which was proved in Australia's second innings, but that cannot fully explain the fatuity of some of England's batting earlier in the day. They had finished the day on Saturday in such a good position that no one could have expected an advantage so hard earned so recklessly thrown away. O'Reilly and Fleetwood-Smith, both of whom bowled magnificently, are not the men to miss an opportunity of rubbing it in, and there can be no doubt that Hammond's failure fell on the side like a pall. Paynter, the saviour of lost causes, struggled nobly, as he always does, but for the rest bats were little more than luxuries.

Rain had fallen on Sunday all round Leeds, but never a drop fell at Headingley, where the pitch remained dusty and threatening. People gazed at it goggle-eyed, as if expecting to see its surface tremble. McCormick, when he began the bowling, did not make the ball rise particularly sharply, but O'Reilly, at the other end, made it turn, both quickly and acutely, and the placing of his field close to the batsmen threatened danger. Barnett hit a no-ball away to the long-off boundary, but Edrich missed two heaven-sent long hops on the leg side which certainly should have counted eight runs.

When the score had been taken from 49 to 60 Barnett played an ill-timed, and ill-judged, stroke to a ball on the leg side, for the wicketkeeper to hold a skier. The subsequent faults of others cannot be laid on Barnett's shoulders, but later there was a feeling that this stroke had opened a way for Australia's attack. Edrich was batting with some degree of composure, although

O'Reilly's spin made the crowd gasp, and the umpire inquiringly trot when a ball from the bat rested against the stumps without moving the bails.

By this time it had been observed that the end further from the Pavilion was playing the more uncomfortably. O'Reilly consequently changed ends, and Fleetwood-Smith was put on at the other. At once O'Reilly made Edrich appear as if he were not timing the ball properly, although he contrived either to stop it or to push it away for an occasional run or two. Edrich survived a confident appeal for leg-before-wicket by Fleetwood-Smith, but it was Hardstaff, who had just hit a no-ball for 4, who was next out, utterly confused, and bowled, by O'Reilly. The score was then 73, which was neither good nor bad, but it was positively terrible when Hammond played the first ball he received into the hands of short-leg.

The joy of the Australians could be both seen and felt, but possibly not even they could predict how near they were already to winning the match. The field crowded so close to Paynter that it was difficult to see him from a distance. What one did see of him, however, was good. No sooner had he come in than he had lost Edrich who, playing forward to a ball which he expected to be an off-break but turned the other way, was stumped. It was a neat piece of work by Barnett, who throughout the match kept wicket excellently. At last a stroke was made which carried with it a ring of confidence when Paynter cut O'Reilly square to the boundary, and, encouraged, he hit the next ball to square-leg. Compton also scored two 4's in one over off O'Reilly, one off a no-ball and the other off a good ball, before in trying to sweep the ball to leg he was caught at the wicket off his glove.

Half England's side now was out and they were only 77 runs ahead. Paynter, to be sure, was still there, but the crowd recognized the danger of the situation so clearly that any purely defensive stroke was greeted by an applause born of relief. Paynter took what chances were offered him of scoring runs, although they were few and far between. Price hit one ball with a flick to the leg boundary before he was leg-before-wicket with the score at 116. Two more wickets fell without the total having been altered, Verity being bowled and Wright caught at backward point to the first ball he had.

It was too late for anything more serious than a gesture by Farnes, who first drove Fleetwood-Smith for 4 and then turned him to leg for 3. O'Reilly soon put an end to that nonsense and Bowes was bowled first ball. That was all out for 123 and luncheon.

The rigours of the match can be best explained by the fact that some people seriously questioned the ability of the Australians to score the 105 runs they required to win, and it was freely stated that 150 almost certainly would have been beyond their limit. Close reckoning, but subsequent events proved that these suggestions were not utter nonsense. Fingleton and Brown began in the approved manner by tucking both Bowes and Farnes away to leg for singles, and the bowlers replied by introducing a maiden over to demonstrate how serious the affair in hand was. A no-ball, especially when it was hit for 4, as one was hit by Brown from Bowes, was greeted by plaintive moans from the crowd, who rose on their feet with a roar when Brown, at 17, was leg-before-wicket to Farnes.

There arrived Bradman, who, in the opinion of many, was to provide the answer one way or the other. He had to smother one ball from Bowes which kept improperly low, and then was tested by a very good over from Farnes, who once got a ball past the great man's bat and hit him on the pads. The crowd unanimously supported Farnes's appeal, but the umpire disagreed with them all.

Bradman then gleaned two runs from the direction of long-on and turned a ball to leg for 4, which brought Verity on. In his first over he had Fingleton leg-before-wicket, and so Australia still wanted 73 runs. Fourteen of these were provided in one over of Verity's, four of them from an overthrow, and four more because Bowes at mid-on allowed a ball to pass him without apparently noticing its whereabouts. This disgusted the crowd, but they had something to cheer about in the next over when Bradman, having edged one ball from Wright for 2, chopped the next into the hands of second slip — 50 for three and Bradman out.

Hassett increased the score by four from a no-ball off Wright, but he played the next very close to second slip. McCabe now was the chief danger, and when he was caught at mid-wicket off a short ball at 61 tremendous possibilities occupied the mind. Australia might win by one wicket, they might lose by a few runs, or it might even be a tie. Hammond switched his bowlers about, relying most, however, on Farnes and Bowes. Hassett now became the centre of attraction. He took as much of the bowling as possible, and ran every run which he deemed in the least reasonable to attempt. Once in running the third run Badcock was only just home in time, and Verity was tried again, with no third man, and the field placed for a catch near the wicket or a mishit on the off. Hassett, to whom great credit must be given at this moment of crisis, swept a ball from Bowes away to square-leg for 4: nor was he worried when the light suddenly turned from a murky grey to a subdued yellow. He took two 4's off Verity, a drive to the on and a firm push to leg. He was helped on his way by another no-ball from Wright, who had, oh, so nearly, bowled Badcock, and the score had mounted to 91 before Hassett was caught off a skier at point.

That was the last wicket which Australia was to lose, but the game was not to be finished before the players left the field because of a drizzle which came with the darkness. When they were out again Australia wanted only nine more runs, which came quickly, as if the fates were exhausted of thrills and a match which in truth had deserved the title of Test Match.

Second Day

25 July 1938. There was a remarkable day's play in the fourth Test Match at Leeds on Saturday, and as a result of it all England have pulled themselves out of a position which on Friday evening looked desperate, almost to the point of being fatal, and are now 30 runs in front with all their second innings wickets yet to fall.

It was certain that, if the game were to remain evenly balanced, England's bowlers would have to toil not only manfully but successfully, and that the terrible Bradman would have to be dismissed cheaply. The bowlers did their part magnificently, and they were well supported by the fieldsmen and ably directed by their captain. As to Bradman, I can say no more than that I consider that he was dismissed cheaply. Such prodigious scores are expected of him, and he has given such trouble before on the Headingley ground, in particular, that a mere century can be regarded as a comparative failure.

At 87, Verity bowled Fingleton which

...brought in Bradman, a Bradman who was not only at first subdued but rather uncomfortable when playing Verity. This period of indecision lasted no more than two overs, and from then onwards Bradman batted with an ease which even for him was almost ridiculous. He drove two consecutive balls from Bowes to the off so fast that a ring of fieldsmen could not have intercepted the ball, and Barnett, to show what he could do, twice struck Farnes away to long leg. Barnett had reached and passed a most valuable 50 when, slashing at a ball on the off stump, he was caught at the wicket. Three wickets were now down for 128. Luncheon over and the light now very bad, England was granted a great mercy, for the great McCabe was late to a ball from Farnes and had his off stump knocked out of the ground. When the illustrious depart it is as well that the business should be done thoroughly.

Bradman must now have felt rather lonely, and, having turned Farnes elegantly to leg, he was still more desolate when Badcock, offering no sort of a stroke, was bowled by Bowes. Australian wickets indeed were falling, and Farnes, in a desperate attempt to dislodge Bradman with a yorker, bowled himself off his feet and landed in the middle of the pitch. This diversion had little effect on Bradman, who, although he was late to one ball from Bowes, batted in the manner of Bradman at his best. He deflected the ball to leg with all the time of a murky afternoon to spare, for it must be fully realised that the Australians were certainly batting in an atrocious light. Twice Bradman went down on his right knee to sweep the ball away to leg, while Hassett at the other end was going through agonies of perplexity. Bradman took all the bowling that he could, but he could not prevent Hassett, who was batting in the manner of a No. 11 holding his end up, from being caught in the slips. A combination of bad

ENGLAND v. AUSTRALIA

Headingley, 22, 23, 25 July 1938

ENGLAND

1st innings

W.J. Edrich	b O'Reilly	12
C.J. Barnett	c Barnett b McCormick	30
J. Hardstaff	run out	4
W.R. Hammond	b O'Reilly	76
E. Paynter	st Barnett b F-Smith	28
D.C.S. Compton	b O'Reilly	14
W.F. Price	c McCabe b O'Reilly	0
H. Verity	not out	25
D.V.P. Wright	c Fingleton b F-Smith	22
K. Farnes	c Fingleton b F-Smith	2
W.E. Bowes	b O'Reilly	3
Extras	(lb 4, nb 3)	7
Total		223

2nd innings

W.J. Edrich	st Barnett b F-Smith	28
C.J. Barnett	c Barnett b McCormick	29
J. Hardstaff	b O'Reilly	11
W.R. Hammond	c Brown b O'Reilly	0
E. Paynter	not out	21
D.C.S. Compton	c Barnett b O'Reilly	15
W.F. Price	lbw b Fleetwood-Smith	6
H. Verity	b Fleetwood-Smith	0
D.V.P. Wright	c Waite b F-Smith	0
K. Farnes	b O'Reilly	7
W.E. Bowes	lbw b O'Reilly	0
Extras	(lb 4, w 1, nb 1)	6
Total		123

Fall of wickets: 1–29, 2–34, 3–88, 4–142, 5–171, 6–171, 7–172, 8–213, 9–215, 10–223.

Second innings: 1–60, 2–73, 3–73, 4–73, 5–96, 6–116, 7–116, 8–116, 9–123, 10–123.

AUSTRALIA BOWLING

	O	M	R	W	O	M	R	W
McCormick	20	6	46	1	11	4	18	1
Waite	18	7	31	0	2	0	9	0
O'Reilly	34.1	17	66	5	21.5	8	56	5
F-Smith	25	7	73	3	16	4	34	4
McCabe	1	1	0	0				

AUSTRALIA

1st innings

J.H. Fingleton	b Verity	30
W.A. Brown	b Wright	22
B.A. Barnett	c Price b Farnes	57
D.G. Bradman	b Bowes	103
S.J. McCabe	b Farnes	1
C.L. Badcock	b Bowes	4
A.L. Hassett	c Hammond b Wright	13
M.G. Waite	c Price b Farnes	3
W.J. O'Reilly	c Hammond b Farnes	2
E.L. McCormick	b Bowes	0
L.O'B. Fleetwood-Smith	not out	2
Extras	(b 2, lb 3)	5
Total		242

2nd innings

J.H. Fingleton	lbw b Verity	9
W.A. Brown	lbw b Farnes	9
D.G. Bradman	c Verity b Wright	16
S.J. McCabe	c Barnett b Wright	15
A.L. Hassett	c Edrich b Wright	33
C.L. Badcock	not out	5
B.A. Barnett	not out	15
Extras	(b 4, nb 1)	5
Total	(5 wkts)	107

Fall of wickets: 1–28, 2–87, 3–128, 4–136, 5–145, 6–195, 7–232, 8–240, 9–240, 10–242.

Second innings: 1–17, 2–32, 3–50, 4–61, 5–91.

ENGLAND BOWLING

	O	M	R	W	O	M	R	W
Farnes	26	3	77	4	11.3	4	17	1
Bowes	35.4	6	79	3	11	0	35	0
Wright	15	4	38	2	5	0	26	3
Verity	19	6	30	1	5	2	24	1
Edrich	3	0	13	0				

Umpires: F. Chester and E.J. Smith

AUSTRALIA WON BY 5 WICKETS

light and a natural desire for tea then held up the game for 20 minutes.

When play was started again Bradman, with his score at 88, edged a ball from Bowes through the slips, and with that stroke England's total was passed. Waite, because he had little of the bowling, stayed in for some time before he was caught at the wicket, and in the next over Bradman reached his century, having scored 100 of the 148 runs made while he was in for two hours and three-quarters. Suddenly he seemed for a moment to relax his concentration, made a swish at a ball on which he cannot have kept his eye, and was bowled. All Bradman's innings are great, but this one perhaps will be remembered longer than some others, for he had received little support. The rest of Australia's innings was uninteresting except for a beautiful catch by Hammond in the slips, a catch of which even the best slip fieldsman in the world might well have been proud.

Close: ENGLAND 223 and 49 for no wicket (W.J. Edrich 25, C.J. Barnett 20), AUSTRALIA 242 (B.A. Barnett 57, D.G. Bradman 103).

After the match was over, R.B. Vincent summed up.

That no more time was spent idly on Saturday was due to the perseverance of the Australians, who continued their first innings in a truly appalling light. No doubt Bradman, batting as he was with absolute confidence, preferred semi-darkness to the possibility of rainstorms later in the match. If the wicket was to wear, and it was confidently anticipated that it would do so, he worked to make the best of a bad job, and his deserved reward was a victory, to which his innings in itself had contributed by far the greater share. Had he faltered — an almost unbelievable proposition — England might well have gained a reasonable lead on the first innings; their second, in turn, would not have been fraught with such anxiety, and experience has shown that the Australians who bat in the middle of their side are not faultless. All these problematical events Bradman killed with his own bat, and only when the match was all over and the Headingley ground was strewn with waste paper was the significance of his innings seen in true perspective.

There was also W.J. O'Reilly.

SIR DONALD GEORGE BRADMAN
New South Wales and South Australia

Bradman played his last first-class game (4–8 March, 1949) 21 years after his debut (16–20 December, 1927), a long career for an overseas cricketer. He stands alone on the summit as a run-maker (which is the purpose of batting) because he succeeded abundantly against bowling which often either contained or dismissed others. Bradman could work wonders at the crease more frequently than other great batsmen.

THE GREATEST TEST MATCH*

The Lord's Test of 1930 was the first to be played in England over four days and on a perfect wicket. Hitherto Tests had lasted three days — that at the Oval in 1926 had gone to a finish, in the event four days — causing Australians to wonder if their journey half-way across the world was justified. Five-day Tests did not become the norm until 1950; during the years 1930–49 there was one series of five-day games, four of four days, and nine of three days. England lost at Lord's in 1930 for several reasons, the most important being a selectorial blunder or two and A.P.F. Chapman's inability to recognize that his side was not participating in a three-day game.

Prior to 27 June there were doubts over Larwood's fitness, though none over Sutcliffe's. The

. . . .

* Not necessarily the most exciting—see Brisbane, 1960. Lord's 1930 did have the greatest of batsmen playing his greatest Test innings—and much else.

batsman had split a thumb hooking at Wall in the Trent Bridge game, and would definitely be unavailable. Sandham, Hobbs' Surrey partner, was therefore summoned to Lord's but did not play; Woolley, who had failed twice in the first Test at No. 4, opened with Hobbs and achieved the feat of batting gloriously but failing again this time in the context of a four-day game. To make matters worse, Larwood withdrew shortly before the game, his place being taken by G.O. Allen, who had so far played very little cricket and whose season's overs for Middlesex would total only 163. (In 1932 Allen bowled as few overs but was chosen for Australia, where he was a conspicuous success, on the assumption that once there he would soon be match-fit.) Probably Nichols of Essex or Clark of Northants should have replaced Larwood.

The abiding lesson of Lord's 1930 was Bradman — a batsman who could score fast without taking risks.

By A.C.M. Croome

First Day

28 June 1930. There was plenty of the dramatic at Lord's yesterday. The final selection of the England team was definitely an incident. Then came the cheap dismissal of Hobbs. This disaster was redeemed by the altogether admirable batting of Woolley, Hammond, K.S. Duleepsinhji, and Hendren. They fairly dominated C.V. Grimmett, though he bowled with all his normal accuracy and cunning. And they made the other bowlers, with the exception of A. Fairfax, look very ordinary. Fairfax deserves full marks. He had to come on at short intervals, now at this end, now at that, and always he bowled dangerously. Every now and again he brought the ball off the pitch unusually fast, and made it run away. If it had been his lucky day he might have had several batsmen caught at the wicket, for W.A. Oldfield was magnificent and missed nothing.

The Australians missed a couple of catches — some would say three, since on one occasion the ball had not touched ground when Richardson saved four by an effort of acrobatics at second slip. But their ground fielding was very good. The men saved numerous runs by intelligent anticipation, and the ball, however hard hit, went to hand as a bullet into a pot of wet clay. Nevertheless they could not prevent the English batsmen from scoring 400 in the day. Speaking from memory one thinks that this feat had not previously been accomplished in a Test Match.* K.S. Duleepsinhji also put up a family record by beating at his first attempt his illustrious uncle's highest score against Australia [Ranji had scored 175 at Sydney in 1897–8]. It was a good, even a very good, innings, distinguished by cutting which was brilliantly certain, and certainly brilliant. But there have been many occasions when Duleepsinhji has found batting an easier business. Therefore he earns the greater credit for the courage and discretion which enabled him to choose the right strokes for the occasion and to avoid the others. Once again Woolley showed that he does right to put himself in first when he is captain. Hammond was more like his old self. Hendren's innings was technically the best of the lot. There were two brief periods during which a breakdown seemed possible. But on the whole the play of the England team indicated the influence of the superiority

* Australia scored 448 against South Africa (16 for one) at Old Trafford in 1912. More remarkable was Australia's 494 for six in a *five-hour* day at Sydney in 1910–11 at the opening of the Test against South Africa.

complex, which is not so salient a feature of the national character as it used to be.

Chapman, acting on the advice tendered to him in *The Times*, won the toss and elected to bat. T. Wall, running at least 27 yards, and getting surprisingly little pace through the air for his mountainous labour, opened the bowling to Hobbs from the Pavilion end. Fairfax had charge of the other. Hobbs would do nothing but play back, but Woolley started as if he had been in for an hour or so and was seeing the seam on the ball as it came down the wicket. Wall offered him a half volley in his second over, and an apparently effortless stroke sent the ball up against the pavilion rails at a surprising pace. But in the next over disaster occurred; Hobbs, playing back to a ball pitched well up, which presumably swung away late, was inside it. He must have turned it appreciably, but Oldfield had his hands in the right place. Woolley and Hammond declined to accept the situation as critical, but dealt with the bowling on its merits, which both, but conspicuously Woolley, seemed to regard as small. In quick succession Woolley hit three off-drives for 4 apiece that must have felt perfectly delicious. Hammond was just as ready as his partner to drive, but less successful in finding the openings, and Grimmett, V.Y. Richardson, and D. Bradman stopped everything within reach accurately and easily. Moreover, wise anticipation made their reach telescopic.

The first change of bowling was made at 38, when Grimmett went on for Fairfax. Wall had one more over from the Pavilion end, which provided Woolley with another 4, and then Fairfax relieved him. Grimmett found his length, and began to exploit all his tricks immediately. It was noticeable that he bowled much slower to Woolley than to Hammond. Woolley was not always comfortable when facing him, and was twice beaten by slow balls deliverd with the arm palpably below the level of the shoulder. From the Pavilion it was extremely difficult to follow the motions of his flickering wrist or to guess what the result of them would be. But, dangerously as Grimmett bowled, the next wicket fell to Fairfax, who had relieved Wall. He sent down a short ball wide of the off stump which got up rather sharply. Woolley cut it hard and truly, but was brilliantly caught, ankle high, by Wall in the gully. The value of his innings was not to be measured solely by the tale of his runs. He had made all the bowling, except one over from Grimmett, look very ordinary stuff, which surely was comforting to those who came after him.

K.S. Duleepsinhji was becomingly nervous at the start of his innings. But nervousness did not affect his judgment nor depress his spirits. If it caused him to abstain from attempting the driving strokes it did not impair the freedom and rhythm of his cutting nor the variety and delicacy of the rest of his off-side play. Hammond was in capital form, and the pair brought up the hundred soon after one o'clock. But a few minutes later Hammond ran yards out of his ground to drive Grimmett, unaccountably missed the ball, and was bowled.

Once again Hendren* had to face a crisis and that 20 minutes before the luncheon interval. In the past it has been suggested that he lacks the Test Match temperament. The suggestion can never be made again. Hendren was destined to stay in little more than an hour, and then to be caught at long-leg off a stroke which few know how to attempt. But in that time he definitely grasped the advantage for his side. Well as K.S. Duleepsinhji batted, admirably as Tate played the part of First Tailender, England might have had the worst of the position if it had not been for Hendren. The occasion was too grave for him to run in and hit Grimmett for 6, but he used his twinkling feet to play him with consummate ease. The two batsmen provided a very interesting contrast. K.S. Duleepsinhji could not be persuaded to leave anything cuttable alone. Hendren cut not at all, but dared greatly by walking in front

. . . .

* It was a private joke between Croome and Neville Cardus that whereas the latter never (hardly ever) saw Woolley save in terms of perfection, the former felt exactly the same about Hendren. Hendren's Test average was 47, Woolley's 36—which must make Croome eternally unbearable wherever the two men are.

to straight balls and hitting them to leg. It was off a straight ball only just short of a length which rose sharply, that he was finally caught at long-leg. Hard luck! If a man has the capacity to make that stroke he gets 4 for it 99 times out of 100.

Chapman made one of the off-side strokes in which he and Woolley specialize. But he was not quick enough to leave alone a fast, bumping ball outside his off stump and was caught behind the wicket. He turned the ball several feet, and a lesser artist than Oldfield would have made the catch look quite difficult. G.O. Allen, yorked by Fairfax, also failed, and with six out of 239 England were doing none too well. As a fact they might have been in a much worse position, for just before the 200 was telegraphed K.S. Duleepsinhji, with his score at 65, had made a bad stroke off a thoroughly bad ball from McCabe, a longhop on his pads, and had hit it straight to W.M. Woodfull at short-leg, who missed the catch.

Tate deserves immense praise for his share in the stand for the eighth wicket, which finally established the ascendancy of England. He hit the short or overpitched balls with marked power and certainty, and his defensive strokes, if not precisely models of grace, applied the centre of the bat to the ball. Moreover, his running between wickets worried bowlers and fieldsmen, which was just what was wanted at that time in the afternoon. He seemed to get more than his fair share of bumping balls. First McCabe hit him on the fingers, and then in one over from Fairfax he snicked over slips' heads two balls that rose shoulder-high, and took another on the back of his left hand. These incidents made one wonder whether the wicket was really so easy as Woolley, Hammond, K.S. Duleepsinhji, Hendren, and Wall had made it appear to be. We should learn more when Tate gets bowling on it.

K.S. Duleepsinhji, when needing only two for his hundred, also received from McCabe a ball which reared up awkwardly. He cut it hard and high to Wall at third slip, who omitted to catch it. He quickly collected the two valuable singles, and then began to hit out. His last 73 runs came at a great pace, and were made by every known stroke, including the straight drive. He finally died gloriously,* caught in the long field shortly before the close of play.

ENGLAND
1st innings

Hobbs	c Oldfield b Fairfax	1
Woolley	c Wall b Fairfax	41
Hammond	b Grimmett	38
K.S. Duleepsinhji	c Bradman b Grimmett	173
Hendren	c McCabe b Fairfax	48
A.P.F. Chapman	c Oldfield b Wall	11
G.O. Allen	b Fairfax	3
Tate	c McCabe b Wall	54
R.W.V. Robins	c Oldfield b Hornibrook	5
J.C. White	not out	14
Duckworth	not out	7
Extras	(b 2, lb 7, nb 1)	10
Total	(9 wkts)	405

Fall of wickets: 1–13, 2–53, 3–105, 4–209, 5–236, 6–239, 7–337, 8–363, 9–387.

Second Day

30 June 1930. On Saturday Australia batting for approximately six hours made 404 runs. On Friday England in about the same time exceeded that total by one. But resemblance between the first two acts of the drama begins and ends with the symmetry of the figures. On Friday we saw a series of incidents which caused the advantage to shift from one side to the other and then back again. On Saturday the game was played strictly according to plan. And the plan, it must regret-

. . . .

* Another way of looking at Duleep's end is to be found in P.G.H. Fender's *The Tests of 1930*, p.53:

> White, on his arrival [at 363 for eight], managed to get a bigger share of the bowling to Duleepsinhji…It was here, however, that I think Chapman forgot he was playing a *four* day game, not a three day one. Soon after six, with the 400 almost reached, a conference took place between White and Duleepsinhji. It was obvious that instructions were being delivered by White…After the conference Duleepsinhji lashed out at the first ball of Grimmett's over, but it was fielded. The second he hit for four, the third for two, the fourth for four, and he was caught on the boundary off a straight drive off the fifth.

Had Chapman intended to declare overnight? Ironically, with Duleep out, he did not do so.

fully be admitted, was drawn by the Australian O.C. and his staff. Its objective is to get a lead of 300 or so by the time in the afternoon when all the pavilion seats at Lord's are in shadow, and then to put England in with nothing but a draw to play for, and plenty of time in which to play for it.

So far W.M. Woodfull's tactics have been completely successful. To some extent he has been helped by circumstances. Unless we allow that A.G. Fairfax is in a different class from Maurice Tate as a bowler, we must conclude that the wicket was more nearly a batsman's paradise on the second day than on the first. At the start of the game the dark marks made by the bowlers' feet showed that the surface was a trifle damp, and all day long an occasional ball would fly up dangerously. On Saturday batting gloves† were no more useful than they are ornamental. The ground had dried completely and two applications of the heavy roller had crushed the last remnant of spitefulness out of it. Another point is that the absence of Larwood relieved Woodfull of any necessity, which he might otherwise have felt, about his batting order. W.H. Ponsford is a remarkably efficient batsman when he can move in front of his wicket equanimously to play his defensive strokes. Ponsford has, however, been badly knocked about by fast bowlers in his time, and not unnaturally is inclined to leave the line to his off stump open when facing one who can produce that extra yard or two of pace which makes so much difference. G.O. Allen set his field menacingly, placing five men behind the wicket on the off side, and only one, Hobbs, in front of it. But Ponsford, though twice hit on the thigh, was not to be deterred from walking in to the fast bowling. Twice in the first half-hour he got well across to slightly over-pitched balls outside his off stump, at which it was hoped he would flick a speculative bat, and drove them firmly through the gap left by the absence of a mid-off. These

. . . .

† A photograph of Bardsley and Woodfull going out to bat in the Lord's Test of 1926 shows both batsmen gloveless on the top hand. J.M. Gregory, of course, did not wear a glove on either hand. Among the bowlers was Larwood.

were the only aggressive strokes attempted during the first hour of play, but they were significant of the fierCeness with which the counter-attack would be delivered later if opportunity occurred.

During that first hour no more than 38 runs were scored off Allen, Tate, and White, who were supported by brilliantly accurate ground fielding. The rate of scoring improved when Robins came on. He seemed to be running up to the wicket a trifle faster than he usually does and to be bowling with a trajectory slightly lower than normal. Neither batsman attempted to drive him, but when he pitched short, as he not infrequently did, both of them forced him for runs either through the covers or past short leg. It was ordained that Ponsford should receive most of the loose balls sent down, and the natural result was that for the first hour and a half he scored nearly twice as fast as his captain. He also looked the more likely of the two to get out, for his bat was not as straight as the text-books say it should be when he played forward in defence, nor was his cutting, when he could be induced to cut, quite safe; once White almost made him play on with a cleverly bowled faster ball outside the off stump. No other salient incident than this occurred between 11.30, when the Australian innings started, and the luncheon interval, at which time the score was 96, and Tate, always a very demonstrative bowler, was beginning to show what he thought of the situation. The gesture which indicates expectation that "that one" would get through was very rarely in evidence. No doubt it was a disheartening job to bowl to two batsmen of limitless patience on a wicket from which the ball would neither make pace nor break, but, to tell the truth, some of the English bowlers seemed to lose heart inconveniently early in spite of Chapman's unceasing efforts to inspire them by his example of hostility in the field.

After luncheon the batsmen were at no special pains to dig themselves in. They just went on as if there had been no interruption at all. If the pace of the scoring improved to something over one run a minute the chief reason was that they were offered a larger number of runs for the taking. A contributory cause was that Woodfull, without appreciably increasing his exiguous backlift of the bat, began to put more power into his strokes and so "made" a few runs by forcing the ball through the fieldsmen in front of the wicket. Once he ran in to drive a ball from Robins which broke sharply from leg and went high behind the wicket off the edge of his bat. Hammond jumped quickly in an attempt to catch it, but it passed at least a foot above his hands. Woodfull had almost caught up his partner when the players were called in to have the honour of presentation to the King, who arrived on the ground shortly after 3 o'clock. Almost as soon as play was resumed Ponsford got himself out by making a clumsy attempt to cut a ball from White which seemed to hang a trifle as it rose. Previously when playing in Test Matches in this country he has been unsuccessful, but on this occasion he gave himself plenty of time in which to play his strokes, and his innings, if not distinguished by any marked grace of style, was eminently sound. He should derive some consolation for his failure to make his 100 from the knowledge that the King was thereby enabled to see more of an innings which must be destined to be famous as long as the game is played.

To do justice to D. Bradman's batting it is necessary to use the language of superlatives and compare it with the acting of Miss Marie Tempest.* Both are so exquisitely right in the general design and in the polished execution of every detail. Bradman on Saturday was as audacious as Macartney in the second innings of the Lord's Test of 1926. His cutting was as safe and brilliant as that of Duleepsinhji on the previous day. He played the ball on the leg side as deftly as Hendren had, and Woolley for all his advantage in height was not so very much the more powerful off-driver. Bradman's innings began, so to speak,

....

* A small but terrifying lady then appearing in St John Ervine's *The First Mrs Fraser*, where her leading man was the Yorkshire cricket follower Henry Ainley. She had earlier created the role of Judith Bliss in Noel Coward's *Hay Fever*, and was in due course made DBE.

in the middle, for he had no need to play himself in. He was still in the middle of it when stumps were drawn, for he had not begun to lift the ball off the ground as they do who propose to get on or get out when it makes no difference which of their alternative objects they achieve. He has, in fact, played the first part of an extremely steady innings, treating each ball sent down to him strictly on its merits as he discerns them. And yet he has scored 155 runs in 2½ hours.

Bradman went in at 3.30 p.m., and reached 50 (out of 66) in 45 minutes, his fastest in a Test match. 54 at tea, he reached 100 (out of 152) in 105 minutes. At the close his 155 not out had taken him 165 minutes — Croome was inaccurate on this point — and been scored off 171 balls.

If one were to begin particularising his strokes there would be no end to this account, but one of them must be specially noted. Hammond was put on at the Pavilion end to bowl defensively, and was doing his job quite well. Naturally he had a defensive field, with only one man in the slips. He sent down a fast, good-length ball which broke back viciously at the top of the off and middle stumps. Bradman met it with an orthodox-looking back stroke which had the effect of a late cut. The ball flew, and clearly was meant to fly, wide of the solitary slip and fine enough to beat the deep third-man. White, who was so successful in slowing down the scoring in Australia, could do nothing with him. He chasséed out to the pitch of the good-length balls, and altered the direction of them as well as their length to suit his purpose, so that he could drive them where the fieldsmen were not.

Bradman had applied himself to the White problem. Since being dropped for the Second Test of 1928–9, he had now encountered the slow left-arm bowler in four matches against England. His run rate per 100 balls was, successively, 26, 38, 59 — and now at Lord's, 76.

The crowd twice paid him unusual but well-deserved compliments. They gave Tate one of the loudest rounds of applause heard when he succeeded in bowling a maiden over to him. And once when he shaped to cut at a dangerous ball from that bowler some 2,000 people appealed for the expected catch at the wicket, and were badly scored off when he checked his stroke.

Woodfull very wisely did not quicken the pace of his scoring materially, though he also walked in, One, Two, Three! to drive the slow bowlers. Just when he seemed certain to carry his bat he walked a little too straight down the pitch to an off-ball from Robins and missed it. Duckworth gathered it rather clumsily, but fortunately for him Woodfull had given himself up for lost, and the wicket was broken in time.

ENGLAND
1st innings (concluded)

J.C. White	not out	23
Duckworth	c Oldfield b Wall	18
Extras		10
Total		425

AUSTRALIA BOWLING

	O	M	R	W
Wall	29.4	2	118	3
Fairfax	31	6	101	4
Grimmett	33	4	105	2
Hornibrook	26	6	62	1
McCabe	9	1	29	0

AUSTRALIA
1st innings

W.M. Woodfull	st Duckworth b Robins	155
W.H. Ponsford	c Hammond b White	81
D.G. Bradman	not out	155
A.F. Kippax	not out	7
Extras	(b 1, lb 5)	6
Total	(2 wkts)	404

Fall of wickets: 1–162, 2–393.

Third Day

1 July 1930. As a result of the third day's play in the Test match at Lord's, England, with eight wickets to fall in their second innings, are still 206 runs behind. Australia, by scoring 729 runs before the innings was declared closed with six wickets down, made the highest score which has ever been made in a Test match, the previous best being the 636 by England at Sydney in the tour of 1928–29.

The course of the game yesterday proceeded according to plan, W.M. Woodfull's plan. His men supported him so loyally that he was able to declare at tea-time, and set the English team to save the match if they could. Play began punctually at 11 o'clock, and at 12.15 D. Bradman, attempting to play a leg-glance off Hammond, snicked the ball past short slip's right hand. That was the only incident of note which had occurred, and it becomes noteworthy merely because it was the first time that Bradman had omitted to strike the ball with the exact part of the bat which he intended to apply to it. A.P.F. Chapman saw no reason to try any eccentric expedients at the start of the day, especially as a new ball could be claimed when a run or two had been made. He deputed G.O. Allen (Pavilion end) and Tate to open the bowling. Tate had obviously recovered some of the optimism which was missing on Saturday. But Allen, it must regretfully be admitted again showed that it is hardly fair to bring a man into a Test match when he has for some time had no opportunity of breathing the atmosphere of first-class cricket. It is easy to be wise after the event, as many were yesterday at Lord's and elsewhere. But when the team was chosen Allen, presuming him to be fit, well, and in form, was as good a substitute for Larwood as could be found. His selection was admittedly a gamble, because it was not known that he was in form. Any other available bowler of pace might have increased the margin of safety for Australia as well as for England.

Allen was soon taken off, and Tate changed ends. Tate bowled excellently well, bringing the ball quickly off the pitch, and using the wind, which had backed towards the South, to make the ball swing away. But neither Bradman nor A.F. Kippax took any liberties with him. R.W.V. Robins was expensive, though he seemed more comfortable in his run-up to the crease, and once beat Kippax with a quick leg-break. But he could not avoid dropping the ball short at intervals, and

anything like a long-hop was properly punished by both batsmen. Very soon J.C. White took his place, and one noticed with some sinking of heart that Chapman showed no intention of standing at silly mid-off for him. The inference was that for this turn something of guile, possibly a deceptive trick of flight, was lacking from White's bowling.* Without his silly mid-off his value as a defensive, or offensive, bowler, diminishes considerably.

Both batsmen played him in the right way by running him down with three quick steps, and driving him with straight bats. Chapman at extra-cover and White at mid-off [someone nodded, Robins fielded at mid-off for White] stopped everything within reach, and timed their efforts so well that the hardest hits seemed to have been made with a soft ball. But every now and again one got through, and every now and again their threat to run in made White pitch short, and that meant four runs between long-off and long-leg. Bradman was the more efficient and frequent hooker of the two batsmen. In every other department Kippax was his equal in efficiency, his superior in grace. Since Hammond lost something of the stylishness which distinguished him in his freshman's year, we have seen no such graceful attitudes as those into which Kippax flows in making his strokes.

No wicket fell before the luncheon interval [Australia were then 544 for two]. Indeed there never seemed any strong probability that one would fall, and about half-past 12 Chapman began to concentrate on checking the pace of the scoring in order to postpone to the latest possible hour the now inevitable declaration. He found his most trustworthy agent in Hammond, who bowled with most commendable accuracy to a rather curiously set field. Occasionally Bradman found opportunities to show that his dab past slip off the good-length breakback was no accident,

* In the 1928–9 series White, bowling interminably, had conceded only 31 runs per 100 balls, compared with 51 at Lord's, by pitching two feet short of his English length on the faster Australian wickets.

and of course the occasional loose ball got all that it asked for. Tate also put in a long and useful spell of defensive bowling. But the two could not be kept on indefinitely on a hot day, and their reliefs were expensive.

We had visions of a third new ball being required to take the third wicket, and we were tolerably certain that Bradman would achieve the object, which was obviously in his mind, of cutting the late R.E. Foster's record of 287. But Bradman at long last made a mistake, and by the mercy of providence the resulting catch went to Chapman at extra-cover. Bradman did not quite get to the pitch of an off ball and apparently hit it very hard, and only just within reach of the fieldsman's right hand. But there was less pace on the ball than the stroke had indicated, and Chapman had to take it at the extreme of his telescopic reach and *also at the second intention.* How long Bradman batted and how many 4's he hit are matters of little moment [five hours 20 minutes, 25 4's]. He had played only one stroke otherwise than as he had intended, and his intentions had always been of copybook correctness. That might be a description of an innings by W.G. Grace himself.

Kippax went soon afterwards, clean bowled in cutting at a ball that hit his middle stump. It was undoubtedly a cut because he withdrew his left foot towards square-leg to give himself room in which to make it. Every one must regret that so polished a batsman, having got so near to his 100 in a Lord's Test Match, should fail to make it on what may be his only opportunity to earn the distinction. But when all is said he did take a liberty. After that the quality of the batting deteriorated, but the rate of scoring increased. V.Y. Richardson and S.J. McCabe hit out at everything, caring little whether the ball went in the air or not, and when they were out W.A. Oldfield scored quite as fast as either of them by more orthodox methods.

The appearance of the score-sheet and the bowling analysis suggests that runs were cheap. It is true that the bowling opposed to the Australians disappointed the expectations of the optimistic supporters of English cricket, if any there are. But the most crabbed critic will find little to complain of in the English fielding, and when those who took part in the match tell their grandchildren all about it they will conclude their reminiscences by saying: "And blessed if I don't think that fellow Chapman's fielding was the best thing of the whole lot."

Once during the earlier part of the afternoon Tate had made a ball fly up at the Nursery end in a way suggesting that the wicket might be beginning to break. But no further evidence to this effect was forthcoming. And when Hobbs and Woolley started England's second innings the ball seemed to come on quite comfortably to the centre of their bats. At first Hobbs, placing his strokes masterly, scored the faster. But Woolley

BRADMAN Cricket's greatest man of destiny. A Yorkshire life member; Companion of the Order of Australia.

received a short ball now and again, which he hooked severely for 4. He might, however, have been caught by Oldfield when he cut at a long hop from Wall which rose shoulder high.

"Trouble began when Grimmett came on as first change," is a phrase kept permanently in type in the offices of all respectable newspapers. It must be used once more, for, coming on at the Nursery end as soon as the shine was off the ball, he got two immensely valuable wickets. Hobbs must have made a complete miscalculation, for he walked in front to play a half-volley to leg, and was bowled round his pads. He could hardly believe it: Woolley also had to be informed that he was out. He stepped a long way back to turn a shortish ball to leg, hit it to the boundary and carefully swung his left leg, the dangerous one, clear of his wicket, but his right foot must have slipped, for the heel touched the leg stump and dislodged a bail. Hammond started sketchily against Grimmett, but has made a couple of his own off-drives at the other end.

K.S. Duleepsinhji so far has played better than he did at the beginning of his first innings. But Grimmett almost had him with that infernal top-spinner which threatens to break and skids on fast and low. The batsman just got the edge of his bat down in time.

Anything may happen today, except an English victory. The weather may take a hand in the game, for there is rain about. In fact, the only certain thing is that the Australians will put every ounce of body into their out-cricket.

Fourth Day

2 July 1930. The score-sheet of the second Test Match at Lord's yesterday evening showed that Australia had beaten England by seven wickets. If the figures could be taken at their face value they would also indicate that England, after having a record score made against them on the second and third days, made a most creditable attempt on the fourth to draw the match.

Indeed, there was a moment when cricketers of

AUSTRALIA
1st innings

W.M. Woodfull	st Duckworth b Robins	155
W.H. Ponsford	c Hammond b White	81
D.G. Bradman	c Chapman b White	254
A.F. Kippax	b White	83
S.J. McCabe	c Woolley b Hammond	44
V.Y. Richardson	c Hobbs b Tate	30
W.A. Oldfield	not out	43
A.G. Fairfax	not out	20
Extras	(b 6, lb 8, w 5)	19
Total	(6 wkts dec.)	729

Fall of wickets: 1–162, 2–393, 3–585, 4–588, 5–643, 6–672.

ENGLAND BOWLING

	O	M	R	W
Allen	34	7	115	0
Tate	64	16	148	1
White	51	7	158	3
Robins	42	1	172	1
Hammond	35	8	82	0
Woolley	6	0	35	0

ENGLAND
2nd innings

Hobbs	b Grimmett	19
Woolley	hit wkt b Grimmett	28
Hammond	not out	20
K.S. Duleepsinhji	not out	27
Extras	(b 4)	4
Total	(2 wkts)	98

Fall of wickets: 1–45, 2–58.

uncomfortably long experience, sitting in the pavilion, began to ask one another whether they were destined to see the history of the 1882 Oval match repeat itself. Then England, put in to make just about the same number as the Australians required yesterday, had 50* on the board before a wicket fell, and were beaten by seven runs. Then the wicket was sticky and Spofforth could make the ball do anything but talk. Yesterday the whole of the stickiness was provided by W.M. Woodfull, for the pitch remained hard and true to the end. Woodfull's defence, his confidence and sound judgment, were of immense value to his side when the three wickets were cheaply obtained, and the whole English XI was fighting, as its captain had fought throughout the match.

....

* Not exactly: 50 was reached with two wickets down.

And A.P.F. Chapman was directly responsible for the enthusiasm which inspired them.

It is true that he had no hand in the fall of the first wicket. But he took the second as surely as if he had himself bowled the middle stump out of the ground. Tate was bowling quite nicely from the Pavilion end, but not so dangerously as he can. D. Bradman cut at a ball wide on the off-side, and timed his stroke exactly. Now we have noticed when watching this young gentleman play his remarkable first innings that a salient feature of his batting was the way he makes the ball run. Often the pace at which it reached the boundary was quite out of proportion to the amount of physical exertion expended in starting it. There is no doubt about the pace on the ball which Bradman cut to Chapman. Very few of the company present saw it after it left the bat until it was tossed triumphantly in the air. Then one realised that one had seen Chapman stoop as if to pick something off his toes. Verily and indeed the man has the worth of a good change bowler in him.

At the other end to Tate R.W.V. Robins was for a while inspired to greatness. He avoided the error of pitching short, and made the leg stump his target. Even when Woodfull was opposed to him there always seemed a chance that some incident favourable to England would happen. But in the end he lost his length. Three expensive overs made the Australians quite safe, and by five o'clock they had won a victory which none may begin to pretend was undeserved. They were definitely superior on this occasion in batting and bowling. Neither side could claim very much advantage in ground fielding. The one department of the game in which England showed the better form was the catching.

It is tempting for many reasons to say why there is no need for the Selection Committee to panic, and make wholesale alterations in the team for the Leeds Test Match. One of the reasons is that discussion of another subject postpones description of England's batting in the second innings. This is an unsavoury task. A total of 375 looks quite respectable, but the truth is that the compiling of it induced much more amusement than respect in the minds of intelligent spectators. There is a convention of Country House Cricket, and there is the convention of the Test Match. The stand between Chapman and Allen which produced 125 runs in about an hour and a half conformed to all the unwritten rules governing play on private grounds. Allen batted extremely well — for a fast bowler. At intervals a casual visitor to Lord's might have been excused for guessing that Chapman was the fast bowler of the side. Between those intervals he hit Grimmett with splendid power and played the faster bowling masterly. But an uncompromising regard for truth compels the admission that the intervals were sufficiently frequent to account for the dismissal of a whole side on its unlucky day. However, we have by now reconciled ourselves to the fact that Chapman has lost something of the stylishness which characterized his centuries for Cambridge against Oxford, and for the Gentlemen again the Players, and marked him as the legitimate successor to Woolley.

What was really depressing was that his predecessors in the batting order were dominated by Grimmett, and in their shorter spells of bowling by Fairfax and Hornibrook. K.S. Duleepsinhji was more nearly master of his fate than any other. Hammond was curiously at fault in timing his strokes. He would run in to drive Grimmett, hit up a cloud of dust, and kill the ball by hammering it into the ground. Hendren raised high hopes by running in to the slow bowler and driving him through the covers to the Mound stand, as fine a stroke as any seen in the match. Then he did the thing against which his life for two years has been one continuous protest. He became leaden footed, and over-reached himself to push a slow leg-break down silly mid-off's throat. K.S. Duleepsinhji, as a matter of course, made some delightful strokes, notably two off-drives at Grimmett's expense, which lofted the ball just rightly over the in-fielders. But Hornibrook [slow-medium left-arm] bowled exceptionally well to him, and twice beat both him and Oldfield with balls that broke back sharply. Hammond's timing was just beginning to improve when he was caught at forward short-leg by Fairfax.

It was a dismal moment when England's captain came in, and his opening efforts to play Grimmett increased the gloom. Immediately he had a slap, as the bowler intended he should, at a wide off-ball and put it up gently between cover and extra-cover. Grimmett left it to Richardson, and Richardson had already started the wrong way in anticipation of a better stroke.* Very soon afterwards Hornibrook again beat K.S. Duleepsinhji with a ball which swung in from the off and broke back from the pitch. K.S. Duleepsinhji played just well enough to touch it, and this time Oldfield was all there.

There followed the stand between Chapman and Allen, to which allusion has been made. One felt, as one did not feel when Woodfull, Ponsford, Bradman, and Kippax were batting during the Australians' first innings, that it could not last. Probably it would have ended earlier had Woodfull been able to make use of Fairfax, who, apparently, had jarred himself when he fell in catching Hammond.

It was Grimmett who got the wicket just when it was badly wanted. His quick oncomer found Allen in front of his wicket. Fairfax when he did come on got Chapman well caught at the wicket. The end was now in sight, but it might have been considerably delayed if Robins had not run out White, or alternatively if White, knowing his partner's predilections, had backed up more readily.

The concluding act of the drama has already been described. It did something to soothe our wounded national vanity.

HEADINGLEY 1930

Two weeks after Chapman had won the toss at Lord's, Woodfull did so at Headingley. Changes had

. . . .
* Other accounts have it that Richardson and Ponsford in the covers left the catch to each other.

been made: Australia had replaced Ponsford and Fairfax (both unfit) with A.A. Jackson and E.L. à Beckett; England dropped Woolley, Hendren, Allen, Robins and White, restoring Sutcliffe, Larwood and R. Tyldesley from the victorious Trent Bridge side, and including Leyland and Geary; *The Times* sent R.B. Vincent in place of A.C.M. Croome.

On 11 July 1930 *The Times* was in a predicament. To which game should it accord priority — a Test match at Leeds or the Eton and Harrow annual extravaganza at Lord's, where the hyphenated stakes were taken care of by Harrow's Mr R.D. Stewart-Brown and Eton's Mr J.C. Atkinson-Clark. With a sharp nudge from Bradman, *The Times* compromised: more column inches to Eton and Harrow (assuming a review of the dresses counts as a species of leg-byes) but the Test match removed from "Sporting Intelligence" to the main news page. Opposite the main news page were the leading articles: *Iron and Steel Facts*, which may or may not have excited interest; *Turks, Kurds and Persians*, which presumably did to Turks, Kurds and Persians living in the south-east of England; and...As readers of *The Times* always turn first to the leading articles:

ENGLAND V. BRADMAN

12 July 1930. On August 27 D. G. BRADMAN will reach the ripe age of 22. The number of runs he will have made by that time is mercifully still unknown. His first two scores on English turf were 236 and 185 not out; and early in the season, with 252 and 191 against the bowlers of Surrey and Hampshire, he joined the select band of English batsmen — only four in all — who have made 1,000 runs off their own bat before May was over. After that he was fairly quiet till he came to the Test Matches, in which he has scored 131 in the second innings at Nottingham, 254 in the first innings at Lord's, and now, in his first and still unfinished innings at Leeds, 309 out of 458. His total for the season is exactly 2,000. In the three Test Matches alone he has already made more

ENGLAND v. AUSTRALIA
Lord's, 27, 28, 30 June, 1 July 1930

ENGLAND
1st innings

J.B. Hobbs	c Oldfield b Fairfax	1
F.E. Woolley	c Wall b Fairfax	41
W.R. Hammond	b Grimmett	38
K.S. Duleepsinhji	c Bradman b Grimmett	173
E. Hendren	c McCabe b Fairfax	48
A.P.F. Chapman	c Oldfield b Wall	11
G.O. Allen	b Fairfax	3
M.W. Tate	c McCabe b Wall	54
R.W.V. Robins	c Oldfield b Hornibrook	5
J.C. White	not out	23
G. Duckworth	c Oldfield b Wall	18
Extras	(b 2, lb 7, nb 1)	10
Total		425

2nd innings

J.B. Hobbs	b Grimmett	19
F.E. Woolley	hit wkt b Grimmett	28
W.R. Hammond	c Fairfax b Grimmett	32
K.S. Duleepsinhji	c Oldfield b Hornibrook	48
E. Hendren	c Richardson b Grimmett	9
A.P.F. Chapman	c Oldfield b Fairfax	121
G.O. Allen	lbw b Grimmett	57
M.W. Tate	c Ponsford b Grimmett	10
R.W.V. Robins	not out	11
J.C. White	run out	10
G. Duckworth	lbw b Fairfax	0
Extras	(b 16, lb 13, w 1)	30
Total		375

Fall of wickets: 1–13, 2–53, 3–105, 4–209, 5–236, 6–239, 7–337, 8–363, 9–387, 10–425.

Second innings: 1–45, 2–58, 3–129, 4–141, 5–147, 6–272, 7–329, 8–354, 9–372, 10–375.

AUSTRALIA BOWLING (6-ball overs)

	O	M	R	W	O	M	R	W
Wall	29.4	2	118	3	25	2	80	0
Fairfax	31	3	101	4	12.4	2	37	2
Grimmett	33	4	105	2	53	13	167	6
Hornibrook	26	6	62	1	22	6	49	1
McCabe	9	1	29	0	3	1	11	0
Bradman					1	0	1	0

AUSTRALIA
1st innings

W.M. Woodfull	st Duckworth b Robins	155
W.H. Ponsford	c Hammond b White	81
D.G. Bradman	c Chapman b White	254
A.F. Kippax	b White	83
S.J. McCabe	c Woolley b Hammond	44
V.Y. Richardson	c Hobbs b Tate	30
W.A. Oldfield	not out	43
A.G. Fairfax	not out	20
C.V. Grimmett		
P.M. Hornibrook	did not bat	
T.W. Wall		
Extras	(b 6, lb 8, w 5)	19
Total	(6 wkts dec.)	729

2nd innings

W.M. Woodfull	not out	26
W.H. Ponsford	b Robins	14
D.G. Bradman	c Chapman b Tate	1
A.F. Kippax	c Duckworth b Robins	3
S.J. McCabe	not out	25
Extras	(b 1, lb 2)	3
Total	(3 wkts)	72

Fall of wickets: 1–162, 2–393, 3–585, 4–588, 5–643, 6–672.

Second innings: 1–16, 2–17, 3–22.

ENGLAND BOWLING (6-ball overs)

	O	M	R	W	O	M	R	W
Allen	34	7	115	0				
Tate	64	16	148	1	13	6	21	1
White	51	7	158	3	2	0	8	0
Robins	42	1	172	1	9	1	34	2
Hammond	35		82	1	4.2	1	6	0

AUSTRALIA WON BY 7 WICKETS

runs than any Australian batsman has made before in a completed rubber, and has easily outdone all previous Test Match records with the bat. He does not merely break records; he smashes them. In the first innings at Lord's, and again yesterday at Leeds, the play resolved itself in each case into a duel between England's bowlers and fielders on the one side and one young Australian on the other; and no one has any doubt as to who had the best of it. Apart from all questions of style and grace, the object of the batsman in the game of cricket is to make runs. Without as a rule troubling, like ordinary mortals, to play himself in, DON BRADMAN sets about the bowling directly he gets to the wicket, and goes on making them all the time. The most ardent advocate of brighter cricket could ask no more of him, except, perhaps, that he should occasionally — say rather oftener than once in a hundred or so — put a ball in the air. At his present rate of scoring it may take him a year or two before, like the holder of the one record that is still left for him to beat, he has a century of centuries to his credit. But that is for the future. For the moment it is enough that at Leeds, to quote our Special Correspondent, he "pulverized" the English bowling by a display of batsmanship which, for ease of scoring, combined with absolute security, was beyond all criticism.

One of the most cherished myths of English cricket is that Chapman retained attacking fields throughout Bradman's innings at Headingley in 1930. As Geary soon bowled without any slip at all, and at one time had a man behind him on the boundary as well as a long-on and a long-off, and as Larwood was forced to remove two of his slips — one to deep in the covers, and the other to deep mid-wicket, the myth is without foundation.

BRADMAN 309 NOT OUT

By R.B. Vincent

12 July 1930. The Australians early today [11 July] had reason to fear that the luck of the Leeds ground, notoriously antipathetic to England, had at last turned against them, for it was announced that Ponsford, in addition to Fairfax, would be compelled by illness to stand down from the team. They obtained, however, some measure of comfort by obtaining the first use of a pitch which although it played yesterday even easier than that at Lord's had done on the first day, is so covered with bare patches that it is impossible to believe that it can last four days. The use they made of their advantage of winning the toss was to score

AUSTRALIA

W.M. Woodfull	b Hammond	50
A.A. Jackson	c Larwood b Tate	1
D.G. Bradman	not out	309
A.F. Kippax	c Chapman b Tate	77
S.J. McCabe	not out	12
Extras	(b 1, lb 8)	9
Total	(3 wkts)	458

Fall of wickets: 1–2, 2–194, 3–423.

To bat: V.Y. Richardson, E.L. á Beckett, W.A. Oldfield, C.V. Grimmett, T.W. Wall, P.M. Hornibrook.

ENGLAND: J.B. Hobbs, H. Sutcliffe, W.R. Hammond, K.S. Duleepsinhji, M. Leyland, A.P.F. Chapman, M.W. Tate, G. Geary, H. Larwood, G. Duckworth, R. Tyldesley.

458 runs for the loss of only three wickets, and so must surely at least have placed themselves clear of any danger of being beaten.

But whatever may happen during the next three days this has been Bradman's match, for by scoring 309 not out he has made the highest individual score which has ever been made in a Test Match, so, at long last, beating the 287 made by R.E. Foster at Sydney during the tour of 1903–1904. That he would achieve this feat before the end of this tour was expected by all who have seen him play. He came near to it at Lord's, and in every game of importance he has shown a sureness of scoring power to which there has seemed no limit. How high he ranks among the greatest batsmen the world has ever known is not yet established, but at the moment, and at his age, his promise has been exceeded by none. It is idle to compare him with his great predecessors, Victor Trumper, who was no doubt more graceful, or C. Macartney, who was more impertinently shattering, but for sheer and continual efficiency his performances are truly astounding. To-day he pulverized the English bowling not with the abandon of Macartney, who, like Bradman, also scored 100 runs before luncheon on the same ground, but by a display of batsmanship which in ease of scoring combined with absolute security could not be surpassed. To mention the strokes from which he scored most of his runs is to go through the whole range of strokes known to a modern batsman. Once or twice he demonstrated an idea which is not generally understood, but at no time did he take anything approaching a risk, and he cannot have hit the ball in the air more than three times during the day. It was in fact an innings so glorious that it well might be classed as incomparable, and how the Yorkshiremen loved it.

On a pitch of such easy pace and against a batsman of such superb technique, supported as he was by Woodfull and Kippax, no bowler of the present generation could have been expected to do wonders, but it must be admitted that on the whole the English bowling was colourless and undistinguished. Apart from a poor over by Tyldesley during his first spell and some full pitches later in the day from Leyland, no complaint can be made of the accuracy of the bowling, but there was a complete absence of sting in it, and only Hammond at one time gave the impression that it was worth keeping a bowler on for another over because of the threat of a wicket falling. Larwood came off the pitch no faster than was comfortable to the batsmen and scarcely ever made the ball come back. Tate only once or twice could get the ball past the bat, and Geary could do little more than keep the runs down by an astute placing of his field. Altogether Duckworth must have had the quietest day behind the stumps that he has had for a very long time. The splendid fielding of many members of the team was spoiled by the inability of one or two to get down to the ball, but Chapman had an easier task in spreading his men out than he had had in the first two matches, and he made things easier for himself by declining to allow Hammond and Hobbs to remain anchored in their habitual positions.

Larwood started the bowling with a fairly strong wind blowing from the direction of mid-on, and he had K.S. Duleepsinhji, Hammond, and Geary respectively at first, second, and third slip. Sutcliffe was at deep fine-leg and Leyland at third man. For Tate Duleepsinhji was dropped back to third man and Leyland trotted across to deep square-leg. Off the fifth ball of Tate's first over the unlucky Jackson was caught at forward short leg, but the crowd had then to wait from 20 minutes to 12 until five minutes past 3 before the next wicket fell, by which time the score had been taken from two to 194, and still with the imperturbable Bradman grinding out the runs. Woodfull played just such an innings as is expected of a workmanlike No. 1 batsman. His own rate of scoring may have been slow, but the real value of his batting lay in the fact that he made things seem so simple for his illustrious partner. Woodfull early in his innings certainly did edge one ball from Larwood through the slips, but otherwise never offered the bowler the least glimmer of hope.

Bradman, without in any sense forcing the pace or taking any liberties, at once took runs whenever they were offered. He scored 11 runs in one over from Larwood, which included a beautiful stroke past cover-point in which he lay right back to place the ball through the opening and a stroke off his legs to the on boundary. Geary came on at Tate's end at 30, and during a fairly long spell he did contrive to keep Bradman reasonably quiet, and Tate, going on at the other end, was granted his one solitary excuse for scratching the back of his head when he barely missed Woodfull's off bail. Tyldesley was tried in place of Geary at 48, but even his three out-fieldsmen could not prevent full pitches from being hit for 4, and Geary had to be brought on again at the other end to steady the game. Bradman greeted him with the first really impudent stroke he had so far played, an amazing hook only just wide of mid-on from a ball outside the off stump. This he followed with a square cut, also for 4, and at 1 o'clock the English bowlers bore every appearance of hoping that a batsman would get out, rather than of suspecting that they would get him out. Hammond was given a trial, but he did not bowl so well then as he did in the afternoon, and Bradman reached his 100 out of 128 runs scored from the bat when he had been in for only 85 minutes, and that without ever suggesting that he was in a hurry. At the luncheon interval the total was 136, of which Woodfull's share, though only 29, had been of the greatest value.

Both Bradman and Woodfull hit Geary, who started the bowling after the interval, square for 4 and so Hobbs was moved back from cover-point to the boundary, a defensive move which was indicative of what was to follow. Bradman played one superb late cut off Larwood, but in the same over he played the first bad stroke of his innings and was lucky to see the ball sail in the air safe out of reach of second and third slip.

Hammond, having relieved Larwood, produced a spell of sustained attacking bowling at the end of which he had the satisfaction of getting a ball through more quickly than Woodfull expected and so at last a wicket fell when the spectators had become prepared to see the same pair together for the rest of the day. The arrival of Kippax, however, was not much encouragement to the bowlers. He was twice late in one over from Larwood, but, that little trouble once over, he settled down to play with the ease which Bradman had been showing. Things looked rather desperate for England before the tea interval, when Tyldesley and Leyland, neither of whom showed the least sign of taking a wicket, were kept on for half an hour, but by this time Bradman had eased down a little, reserving, perhaps, his energy for his great achievement later in the day.

Bradman scored his 200 out of 268 on the board, but two minutes later he should have been caught off a skier by Tate at mid-on, but Tate was curiously slow in starting to make the catch. Kippax also had an escape when he had scored 24, but this was a very hard chance, high up to Leyland at mid-off, and England had no manner of consolation until a wicket fell in the only way one was likely to fall — a glorious catch by Chapman at backward point dismissing Kippax, who is as good a No. 4 as his captain is a No. 1. Just before this Bradman had made his record-breaking stroke, and no ground in the world could have offered him such sincere and prolonged congratulations as did the crowd at Leeds.

AUSTRALIA 566 (D.G. Bradman 334; M.W. Tate 5 for 124), ENGLAND 391 (W.R. Hammond 113; C.V. Grimmett 5 for 135) and 95 for 3.

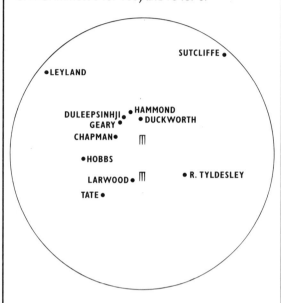

Larwood's field for Bradman, Headingley 1930. Larwood bowled 147 balls at Bradman in 1930 (108 in 1928–9), conceded 137 runs (72 in 1928–9) and dismissed him at the Oval. A photograph shows Duckworth—the catcher—and Duleep at second slip as politely inquisitive. Hammond at first slip is patently bored. Ian Peebles, the gully fielder, wrote long afterwards that Bradman had withdrawn his bat

Also on the main news page: *The Simla Debate, Wild Scenes in Bombay* and *Public Works Bill.* The match was drawn, over five hours being lost to rain.

INCIDENTAL INNINGS, 1934

In successive innings Bradman had scored 65 against Leicestershire, 0 against Cambridge University, 5 against the MCC, 37 against Oxford University and 0 against Hampshire.

By R.B. Vincent

28 May 1934. A century in a cricket match very often means little more than the perfunctory applause of the crowd and the formal uplift of the

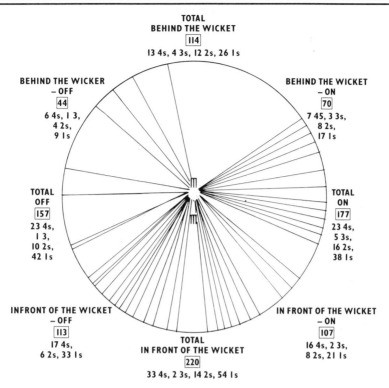

TOTAL
BEHIND THE WICKET
114
13 4s, 4 3s, 12 2s, 26 1s

BEHIND THE WICKER
– OFF
44
6 4s, 1 3,
4 2s,
9 1s

BEHIND THE WICKET
– ON
70
7 45, 3 3s,
8 2s,
17 1s

TOTAL
OFF
157
23 4s,
1 3,
10 2s,
42 1s

TOTAL
ON
177
23 4s,
5 3s,
16 2s,
38 1s

INFRONT OF THE WICKET
– OFF
113
17 4s,
6 2s, 33 1s

IN FRONT OF THE WICKET
– ON
107
16 4s, 2 3s,
8 2s, 21 1s

TOTAL
IN FRONT OF THE WICKET
220
33 4s, 2 3s, 14 2s, 54 1s

Bradman at Headingley, 1930, c G. Duckworth b M.W. Tate 334, made out of 506 in 6 hours 23 minutes (52.32 runs per hour, 74.55 runs per 100 balls). Only boundaries are shown. Bowlers off whom Bradman scored his 334:

	Balls	Runs	Fours
H. Larwood	70	84	14
M.W. Tate	125	93	13
G. Geary	88	56	8
W.R. Hammond	37	21	2
R. Tyldesley	90	53	6
M. Leyland	38	27	3
	448	334	46

batsman's cap, but there were two made at Lord's on Saturday in the match between Middlesex and the Australians which deserved more than ordinary respect. Middlesex, striving hard, scored 258 runs, of which Hendren made 115, and when the Australians went in Bradman had scored 100 of their total of 135 for two wickets.

Not for the obvious reason that Bradman was playing on the other side — it is the fashion now to despise anything well done by one born in this country — but because of its immense merit, the onlooker could but declare the Australian's to be the greater achievement of the two. It was com-

monly agreed that no one could expect to have a better return for his money all this summer through. He reached his century in the last over of the day, beautifully nursed by Darling, who himself was playing a great innings, and he had been batting for only 70 minutes against bowling which might well have been allowed to look reasonably good against any other batsman in the world.

Bradman has had a bad spell lately, but he is now a greater cricketer than he was in 1930. A more certain run-maker he could not be expected to be, but there is a self-pleasure, relieved of anxiety, in his batsmanship which now makes him every bit as dear to an English crowd as were Macartney and Trumper...

The beginning of the Australian innings at a quarter-past 5 was as thrilling as their start recently at Southampton. [When A.E.G. Baring took the first three Australian wickets for six runs — W.M. Woodfull 2, W.A. Brown 0, Bradman 0; the tourists recovering to total 433.] J. Smith, bowling from the Nursery end, with the second ball of the innings had Woodfull leg-before-wicket, and with only nine runs scored he did exactly the same to Ponsford. Bradman, for all the great things he did later in the day, did his utmost by nibbling at the ball to get out in his first over to Smith.

A despairing Bradman turned to Hendren in the slips and asked "What can I do, Pat?", the answer coming "Give her a go, Don."

Then he hit Judge twice past cover-point, hooked him twice for four, and generally began to make a nuisance of himself.

When Robins came on at the Pavilion end, it was sheer murder, and it was not long before the bowling quite naturally began to look a little loose. H.J. Enthoven himself bowled as steadily as anyone, and I.A.R. Peebles, when he first went on, was good, but Bradman, stepping back, hit balls of all lengths anywhere he chose. A smart single in the last over of the day and he had scored a century which no one who saw it will ever forget.

An Australian publication suggests the order of Bradman's 19 boundaries was as shown below. The 11th was the most unusual: "Smith dropped one short, and as it flew, Bradman stooped and smashed it to the leg boundary as though he was making an overhead shot at tennis."

Bradman's century was timed at 77 minutes, his boundaries being hit within the space of 70 minutes or so. This was the innings which persuaded the Hon. R.H. Lyttelton to have a second glass of port after dinner. On Monday Bradman added 60 runs in 47 minutes — his 160 included one six, one five, and 27 fours — before being brilliantly caught by J. Hulme off Peebles in front of the pavilion. "After he retired Sir Donald ranked this innings as probably the most attractive of his career from a spectator's point of view" (Irving Rosenwater).

MIDDLESEX: 258 (E. Hendren 115, R.W.V. Robins 65) and 114 (C.V. Grimmett 5 for 27) lost to the AUSTRALIANS 345 (D.G. Bradman 160, A.F. Kippax 56) and 29 for none by ten wickets.

17 July 1934. Bradman delighted a large crowd at Sheffield with what must undoubtedly be one of the greatest batting exhibitions of his career.

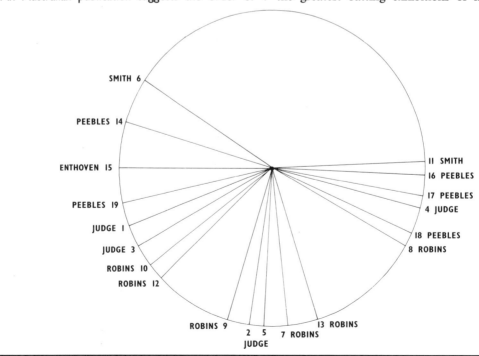

Against Yorkshire's strongest attack [W.E. Bowes, T.F. Smailes, G.G. Macaulay, H. Verity and C. Turner] Bradman made 140 runs, but the size of his score was not the most important part of his innings. Its greatness lay in the manner and speed with which those runs were made. Bradman employed every conceivable kind of stroke, with the result that it was humanly impossible to set a field in any way to block his scoring strokes. Bradman's first 50 runs, which included five 4's, were made in the reasonable time of 75 minutes. Indeed, he advanced his score from 40 to 50 with singles, but then the massacre began. His second 50 runs, in which he hit one 6 and ten 4's, took him a mere 23 minutes, and his final 40 runs, which included one 6 and seven 4's, were scored in 20 minutes. In all, Bradman was at the wicket for three minutes under two hours.

Bradman at first was strangely quiet, but he did not hesitate to deal severely with a short, bumping ball from Bowes, to the imminent danger of two short-leg fieldsmen...Bradman eventually on-drove Macaulay for a single to reach his 50, and then proceeded to massacre the bowling. Boundary hits followed each other with an almost monotonous regularity, and there was a gasp of astonishment from the crowd when Bradman at last condescended to run a single. Bradman completed his 100 with two more singles, and then continued his succession of 4's. Suddenly, to the evident relief of the fielding side, Bradman hit across a straight ball from Leyland* and was bowled.

Bradman's scoring strokes in this Sheffield innings were thus:

111411124314131142411111111111
50 in 74 minutes

444164444444111
50 in 26 minutes/100 in 100 minutes

442164412444
40 in 20 minutes/140 in 120 minutes

. . . .

* The successful bowler summed up his triumph: "Bradman, tired out, bowled Leyland."

YORKSHIRE 340 (A.B. Sellers 104) and 157 (A. Wood 59) drew with the AUSTRALIANS 348 (W.M. Woodfull 54, D.G. Bradman 140; W.E. Bowes 7 for 100) and 28 for one wicket.

209 FOR TWO AT LUNCH

10 September 1934. The Australians drew an enormous crowd on Saturday to the last match of the Scarborough Festival, in which they were playing Mr H.D.H. Leveson-Gower's XI. They gave a most convincing display of forcing cricket. Play was limited to 10 minutes under five hours, during which the Australians scored no fewer than 442 runs for the loss of five wickets.

An attack which included Farnes, Nichols, Bowes, Verity and Townsend [among *Wisden's* Cricketers of the Year in, respectively 1939, 1934, 1932, 1932 and 1934] seemed formidable enough to trouble any team, and had catches been held these bowlers would have done a great deal more than merely worry the batsmen, but with his score at 15 Bradman, who in his innings of 132 completely demoralized the bowling, was missed by Wyatt in the gully...For a few overs Farnes, who throughout the day bowled magnificently, made the ball kick awkwardly, and Brown, who opened the innings with Ponsford, soon chopped a rising ball into his wicket, but then came the great Bradman, cheered all the way from the pavilion to the wicket, to play one of those delightful innings which are unique to Bradman when he is in one of his lighter moods.

For the next hour and a half Ponsford was forgotten. Indeed, nothing but Bradman's masterly display mattered. To describe his strokes would be impossible. He hit the ball in every conceivable kind of way to every conceivable corner of the field. His first 50 runs, which included eight 4's, were scored in 40 minutes. Then came two more 4's and a single and Bradman took a rest. Indeed, for five minutes he allowed Ponsford to do all the scoring, but Verity was brought on to bowl and off started Bradman again. Twelve runs were taken off Verity's first over and, occasionally condescending to run a single, Bradman scored his second 50 runs, including 10 4's, in another 40 minutes. He reached his century with a 4 to long-leg off Verity's bowling, and the next ball was hit in the same direction for 6. Two more boundary hits and a single followed and in all that over counted 19 runs to Bradman. In the next 10 minutes he hit up 32 runs and then jumped out to Verity once too often and was stumped.

McCabe was in difficulties straight away but managed to complete his century in two hours and 20 minutes.

AUSTRALIANS 489 (D.G. Bradman 132, S.J. McCabe 124, W.H. Ponsford 92, A.G. Chipperfield 53; K. Farnes 5 for 132) beat LEVESON-GOWER's XI 223 (M.S. Nichols 75) and 218 (L.O'B. Fleetwood-Smith 6 for 90) by an innings and 48 runs.

The Times covered the 1946–7 tour of Australia with a Special Correspondent, paying the *Manchester Guardian* £500 for the services of cricket's supreme stylist. In mid-December the sides assembled at Sydney for the second Test.

By Neville Cardus

14 December 1946. At half past 11 Hammond and Bradman walked on to the field to look at the wicket which lay stretched there, a perfect oblong rather suggestive of a polished coffin ready to serve as a repository for some poor bowler's hopes if not his mortal bones. The sky was an immensity of blue, a single cloud on it would have been a pollution. The sun shone so profusely everywhere that any kind of shade seemed a remarkable invention of man and against nature. Hammond this time won the toss without a single show of emotion, and at noon the Australian players entered the arena, cricketers moving in Nebuchadnezzar's furnace, while the crowd assembled humming with anticipation, and the Hill gathered in strength, overhauling its catechism and vocabulary.

Early in 1947 a letter appeared in *The Times* from the paper's former drama critic.

MEREDITH AT MELBOURNE

From Mr Charles Morgan
Sir, May a faithful reader of cricket reports be allowed to thank you and your Special Correspondent at Melbourne for the best he has read these 40 years? Who shall dare to say now that George Meredith is forgotten?

"Naturally the England players were now men uplifted [Bradman had been dismissed]: Mercury bubbled in the blood...The issue was here a very ache of intensity; the arms of the deities above were stretching far beyond their reach as Miller went out of his ground to Wright..." And might not this be a fitting end to *The Tragic Comedians:* "A great match, even if much greater than the players in it."?

Your obedient servant,
CHARLES MORGAN
January 8, 1947

A leg injury heavily strapped and also suffering from gastritis, Bradman made 234 in the second Test at Sydney, sharing in a fifth-wicket partnership of 405 with S.G. Barnes (234).

Fourth Day

17 December 1946, Sydney. Bradman limped and Barnes, after a blow on the hand, walked down the wicket to show the bruise to Bradman. There were other consultations between them, but whether medical or strategical must remain a matter of conjecture. Another relieving point of the cricket before luncheon, and, indeed, throughout Australia's innings, was the agile, expert, and enthusiastic wicket-keeping of Evans. He was excellent, if not of the rarest lustre. Bradman, of course, made a huge score amid tremendous acclamation, in spite of all the rumours and talk of his state of health. And, apart from some preliminary faltering against Wright, he played with a calm, impressive deliberation.

As a batsman supposedly an invalid, he must be likened to those rich men who, though given up by their doctors, continue to enjoy their poor health to an old age, causing annoyance to expectant relations. Greatness answers criticism by ways of its own. If Bradman today is a ghost of the Bradman of 16 years ago we must not do him wrong, being, if not majestical, at least commanding at every one of his appearances. This will be, indeed, a hard ghost to lay.

Bradman, it seems necessary to remind ourselves, is a cricketing genius and therefore not subject to those physical impediments with which merely talented folk cannot cope. This was an example of adaptation; many times Bradman must to-day have had to conquer an old lust, an old remembered sensation of a crashing drive at the very sight of a half volley. In this innings experience and judgment and a critical understanding of what and what not to attempt were the dominating qualities. To say the truth, apart from his limp I could discern little amiss with Bradman once the game's position was reasonably favourable for Australia. If he did not pull or hook or pounce on the bowling as of old, he played much as he wished and he exceeded Barnes's rate of scoring because his range of strokes is so wide that he can get runs at leisure by ones and twos. He still has many centuries in him which he will give to Australia and the world whenever he chooses, or whenever the situation demands.

Bradman still had 20 centuries in him in first-class cricket — in 54 innings. After his 234 at Sydney, his 59 innings averaged 102.11; his remaining 21 Test innings averaged 92.62, and included six hundreds.

WILLIAM HAROLD PONSFORD
Victoria

Ponsford persuaded many bowlers they were better off tackling Bradman. He was the first of the monolithic scorers, always playing within his own capabilities, which were awe-inspiring. Further words of introduction are superfluous.

A RECORD SCORE

VICTORIA

W.M. Woodfull	c Ratcliffe b Andrews	133
W.H. Ponsford	b Morgan	352
H.L. Hendry	c Morgan b Mailey	100
J.S. Ryder	c Kippax b Andrews	295
H.S.B. Love	st Ratcliffe b Mailey	6
S. King	st Ratcliffe b Mailey	7
A.E.V. Hartkopf	c McGuirk b Mailey	61
A.E. Liddicut	b McGuirk	36
J.L. Ellis	run out	63
F.L. Morton	run out	0
D.J. Blackie	not out	27
Sundries		27
Total		1,107

Fall of wickets: 1–375, 2–594, 3–614, 4–631, 5–657, 6–834, 7–915, 8–1,043, 9–1,046, 10–1,107.

BOWLING (8-ball overs)

	O	M	R	W
R. McNamee	24	2	124	0
H. McGuirk	26	1	130	1
A.A. Mailey	64	0	362	4
N. Campbell	11	0	89	0
N.E. Phillips	11.7	0	64	0
G. Morgan	26	0	137	1
T.J.E. Andrews	21	2	148	2
A.F. Kippax	7	0	26	0

28 December 1926, Melbourne. Continuing their first innings in the Sheffield Shield match against New South Wales here today, Victoria, who at the close of play overnight had scored 573 for one wicket, batted all day and were all dismissed for 1,107, so beating the world's aggregate score "record" in first class cricket of 1,059 made by Victoria against Tasmania on the same ground in February 1923 [when Ponsford made 429].

Ponsford's magnificent innings was brought to a close for 352, his hits including thirty-six 4's. Hendry scored 100 in an hour and 53 minutes by attractive cricket, while Ryder batted brilliantly for a splendid 295. He was batting for four hours and five minutes, and hit six 6's and thirty-three 4's, the chief feature of his innings being his forceful driving...Victoria's innings lasted altogether ten hours and 33 minutes [104 runs an hour]. Mailey was the most successful bowler.

Victoria won this game by an innings and 656 runs.

The background to Headingly 1934 must be noted. Ponsford, twice, and Bradman, once, had topped 400 in a first-class innings, yet playing together in the same Australian side against England on nine occasions they had formed a partnership only twice with trifles of 81 and 32. On 20 July 1934 England were bowled out for 200 by Grimmett, O'Reilly and Chipperfield on what R.E.S. Wyatt termed a "Featherbed". At the close the

AUSTRALIA

W.A. Brown	b Bowes	15
W.H. Ponsford	not out	22
W.A. Oldfield	c Ames b Bowes	0
W.M. Woodfull	b Bowes	0
Extras		2
Total	(3 wkts)	39

perils of sending in nightwatchmen, eminent or otherwise, had been made apparent.

A day later the balance had been restored.

By R.B. Vincent

23 July 1934. The crowd started the day hopefully talkative, both to the players and to each other; they rewarded Bradman with loud cheers when he started his innings brilliantly; they relapsed into a rather dour gloom when both Ponsford and Bradman lowered their rate of scoring [to 51 runs an hour before lunch] and settled down to kill the heart of the bowlers; and then they rose in their enthusiasm after tea when runs were coming at a great pace here, there, and everywhere. Some few had left in disgust at the tea interval, but those who stayed gave of their fullest admiration to Ponsford, for even if that terrible Bradman had made 271 excellent runs, it was by common consent Ponsford's day.

No one can fail to be an admirer of Ponsford as a stroke player — who will ever forget his innings at the Oval in 1930? [110, one occasion when he mastered Larwood] — but on Saturday for sheer workmanship he excelled himself. Winding himself up with the appearance sometimes of entwining himself with that huge bat of his he met the ball consistently full in the middle of the blade. His attacking strokes were made with such judgment that he could find a hole on a densely packed off-side field, and his defensive strokes, with men waiting almost under his green cap cocked over his left ear, were played with an utterly dead bat. It was a superb display of the type which the big occasion demands, and so, too, was that of Bradman, who has been up to these tricks before in a Test Match at Leeds.

The pitch during the period between the luncheon and tea intervals seemed to be getting faster and faster, while the bowlers became more and more innocuous. Ponsford in particular had seconds to spare when playing Bowes, who when he bowled to Bradman had no one in the slips, merely Hammond in the gulley, and the off-side boundary ominously girdled with fieldsmen.

Again the modern myth that pre-war bowlers always attacked Bradman with close-set fields is shattered.

...If the runs had come easily before tea [71 an hour since lunch] they flew off the bat afterwards [84 an hour], and it was soon after 5 o'clock that the record partnership of 323 between Hobbs and Rhodes was broken...At last when Ponsford and Bradman had added 388 in five and a half hours Ponsford, forcing a ball from Verity away to square-leg, touched his wicket and a bail fell off. He himself had been in for six hours and a quarter and had hit 19 4's. It was a magnificent innings, and just to keep the fielding side amused McCabe then came in for the last 35 minutes, during which Bradman hit two 6's, one an on-drive off Verity, and the second a terrific pull off Hopwood. It is a dismal outlook indeed for England.

AUSTRALIA

W.A. Brown	b Bowes	15
W.H. Ponsford	hit wkt b Verity	181
W.A. Oldfield	c Ames b Bowes	0
W.M. Woodfull	b Bowes	0
D.G. Bradman	not out	271
S.J. McCabe	not out	18
Extras	(b 1, lb 8)	9
Total	(4 wkts)	494

Fall of wickets: 1–37, 2–39, 3–39, 4–427.

Rain saved England from defeat.

ENGLAND 200 and 229 for 6, AUSTRALIA 584 (W.H. Ponsford 181, D.G. Bradman 304).

Ponsford's last Test — he retired at the close of the 1934 tour — saw him at well below his best form. However, he did have the satisfaction of heading the Australian averages with 94.83 to Bradman's 94.75.

18 August 1934

AUSTRALIA

W.A. Brown	b Clark	10
W.H. Ponsford	not out	205
D.G. Bradman	c Ames b Bowes	244
S.J. McCabe	not out	1
Extras	(b 1, lb 8, w 2, nb 4)	15
Total	(2 wkts)	475

To bat:
W.M. Woodfull, A.F. Kippax, A.G. Chipperfield,
W.A. Oldfield, C.V. Grimmett, H.I. Ebeling and
W.J. O'Reilly.

Fall of wickets: 1–21, 2–472.

ENGLAND BOWLING

	O	M	R	W
Bowes	21	1	110	1
Allen	13	1	109	0
Clark	27	7	78	1
Hammond	9	0	36	0
Verity	23	3	79	0
Wyatt	4	0	28	0
Leyland	3	0	20	0

ENGLAND: C.F. Walters, H. Sutcliffe, F.E. Woolley,
W.R. Hammond, R.E.S. Wyatt, M. Leyland,
L.E.G. Ames, G.O. Allen, H. Verity, E.W. Clark,
W.E. Bowes.

Umpires: F. Chester and F. Walden

By R.B. Vincent

20 August 1934. The Australians having won the toss in the last Test Match at the Oval on Saturday behaved very much as was expected of them, the score at the close of play being 475 for two wickets. What we have seen already is only the beginning of their innings, only an introduction to the match and the more serious business which is to follow later — perhaps much later — so it is horrible to imagine in what state of mind they will be who of their own free choice watch this monstrosity to its termination. Perhaps those who were at the Oval on this first day have tasted the cream of the match.

There was nothing very remarkable in the fact that Ponsford and Bradman by scoring 451 runs for the second wicket broke every kind of record for a partnership in Test Match cricket. They had already established the previous record at Leeds in the last match, when they had made 388, and another 63 runs was very little to a pair of batsmen for whom the English captain and his bowlers must by now have a fierce distaste. But Bradman's own innings was one of the best and the most enjoyable that he has yet played in a Test Match in this country. His batting is so often placed in one of two categories, 1934 or 1930: on Saturday he treated his admirers — and who of that crowd of 22,000 was not an admirer of Bradman? — to a blend of the two methods. The terrible efficiency of 1930 was there, and so, too, was the joy of scoring runs cheerfully which he has shown us in this year. I do not believe that mortal man could provide a display of batting more wholly satisfying than this most recent achievement in an already glorious career.

No batsman is really worth the name unless he takes some risks — even in a match which may last for a month — and on Saturday Bradman was not afraid to chance his arm, but in his case a stroke which to others might seem adventurous comes to look quite normal, so brilliant is his technique, so amazingly fast is his footwork. His defensive strokes in particular continually threaten to pierce the field until the adjective defensive is entirely inappropriate. He prefers to drive the ball off his back foot and as late as possible, but on Saturday he frequently came out with the full-blooded drive with the left foot well out in the manner illustrated when the camera first took photographs of cricketers in action.

While all this was going on there was Ponsford at the other end. I have admired Ponsford's batting on many occasions; on Saturday I must say I was a little disappointed in him. He is still there with 205 runs under his number on the board; he has made a perfect nuisance of himself to the bowlers, from time to time flashing out the most brilliant strokes; but for all that, he was most uncertain to the faster bowlers, more especially when the ball was pitched on the leg-side or the least bit short. Much of his ducking to balls which rose little more than stump high was absurd, which, conversely, makes one admire the mental adjustment of a man who, obviously disliking fast bowling, can stay in all day to score more than 200 runs.

On England's side of the picture there is little as yet over which to grow enthusiastic. There was a general air of uncertainty in the placing of the field which suggested a raw team, the fielding itself, even when allowance is made for the roughness of the ground, was far below what is expected in a Test Match, and too many catches were missed. Certainly the chances which Ponsford gave were none of them easy ones, but it is not too much to ask for one catch in four to be held. As for the bowlers, they were slaving on a pitch which might have broken the heart of Tom Richardson, and no available contemporary fast bowlers could have kept up a better pace than did Allen and Clark. Bowes occasionally relapsed into medium pace, never at any time being really dangerous. There was a period in the game when Clark might well have been given another fieldsman on the leg side, but that is getting too near to a controversial subject.

Everything and everybody was bright and jolly when Bowes bowled the first over of the match from the Vauxhall end to Ponsford, who made a most inelegant thrust at the last ball, which passed wide of the off stump. Woodfull wisely and unselfishly had written his own name down fifth on the batting order, and Brown in his first over to Bowes twice deflected the ball to long-leg, where Wyatt on each occasion saved the boundary. Allen was the other opening bowler, and one rather wondered why Clark had not been given the new ball with the wind blowing across the ground from the west side. Both bowled to two slips, two gullies, and two rather indeterminate men close in on the leg side.

Ponsford's start was more than shaky, for he was most reluctant to stand his ground, but 20 runs had been scored before Clark came on at the Vauxhall end. The fifth ball of his first over was

the perfection of a fast left-handed bowler's art: it went with his arm and then came back from the middle and leg to hit the middle and off stumps, Brown, who had shaped to play the ball, being utterly beaten.

That occurred at noon, and it was 20 minutes past six, the crowd already trickling out of the ground, before the next wicket fell. Bradman started his scoring with a 4 past second slip off Bowes, who had now come on at the Pavilion end, and, soon after, he drove the same bowler past extra-cover-point, which was followed by a glorious cross-batted bang straight up against the pavilion railings. Clark, although he had been bothering Ponsford, who was crouching and glaring under the huge peak of his cap, just could not make the ball rise sufficiently viciously for a catch, and for a short time he tried bowling over the wicket, which had no effect at all.

Bowes had bowled softly, and one longed for just a shade more of hostility in the bowling when Hammond was put on at 48, Allen soon coming on again at the other end. Allen bowled definitely well this time, as he did later in the afternoon, but Ponsford drove him with a full flourish of the bat once past cover-point, which he followed with a snick between first and second slips. Bradman had forced Hammond away to the leg boundary, Verity coming on at the Pavilion end at 85 with the effect of giving Ponsford some relief from the fast bowlers.

Ponsford once drove Allen straight for 4 all run, but he had two escapes soon afterwards. In each case he played a ball from Allen round to backward short-leg, and there was a chance for Wyatt to make a catch, the second being the easier of the two. Bradman sent the 100 up with 1 drive past extra-cover off Verity. Clark had another try at the Vauxhall end, and the umpires whipped the bails off just when Bowes was preparing for one more over before luncheon, when the score was 123, Ponsford then being 66 and Bradman 43.

Bowes and Clark started the bowling after the interval, with Verity fielding half way down and just clear of the pitch on the leg side when Bradman was batting. Ponsford again had a narrow squeak at 70, when Woolley got his right hand high up to a ball from Bowes, who was being unmercifully treated by Bradman. Clark offered two no-balls in one over to Ponsford, each of which was hit for 4, and Allen came on for one

over before Hammond was given another trial. Bradman by this time was running through his full repertoire of strokes; he lay back to hit Hammond past mid-off, and cut him late to the boundary, so sending the 200 up in five minutes under the three hours.

The new ball, which was given to Clark and Bowes, delayed both batsmen in reaching their centuries, but it was Allen, when he came on at the Vauxhall end to bowl the best series of overs seen during the day, who was the most troublesome. Still there remained that gap on the leg side between forward short-leg and mid-on, which if only it had been filled might have meant a wicket. Ponsford reached his 100 first, after he had been in for three hours. Bradman followed soon after, and almost immediately was beaten by a good ball from Clark. Ponsford had his next "life" at 113, when he hit a ball from Verity hard to Wyatt at mid-off, and, two runs later, he might have been caught low down by Woolley at second slip off Allen.

At last after tea Clark was given something like a suitable arrangement of fieldsmen on the leg side, but Ponsford's anxiety had by now largely abated and the ball was more composedly tucked away. Clark gave the crowd, who had been appreciative, but quiet, all day, except when a battery of searchlights was flung across the ground to stop people outside from taking photographs, something to make a noise about when he gratuitously gave away four overthrows by flinging the ball from mid-off at the stumps, and Bradman made them cheer again when he drove Verity to the off and hit him hard and high in the air to leg. But, to tell the truth, now that Allen's last spell of energy was spent, it was sheer massacre.

Several suggestions were made by the crowd as to who should bowl, and in the end Wyatt did try a few overs himself, and he allowed Leyland, who found it hard to pitch the ball on the ground, to be on long enough to experiment on a variation of

PONSFORD   "He always suggested the old advertisement for Michelin tyres." — Robertson-Glasgow.

round-the-wicket and over-the-wicket bowling. The sun was throwing longer shadows; the scoreboard was rattling round, and there was a heated argument as to whether there was room for a fourth figure to be inserted in the space allotted for the total, when suddenly Bradman, in trying to hook a short ball from Bowes, hit it with the bottom and edge of his bat and was caught at the wicket.

There was still another 10 minutes left for play, during which one was left wondering whether in fact Bradman had indeed gone. To-day it will be the turn of the Australian batsmen.

The Ponsford–Bradman partnership of 451 lasted 316 minutes: 85.63 runs an hour. More than half a century later it will not be considered sadistic to mention certain details.

The maximum shade temperature at the Oval on Saturday, 18 August 1934 was 80°F. After lunch, while Ponsford jogged at 37 runs an hour, Bradman averaged 53 runs an hour — though after tea, when his score was 150, Bradman accelerated to 65 runs an hour. If, during the partnership, Bradman had progressed at no more than Ponsford's rate, the stand would have been only 401; on the other hand, had Ponsford rivalled Bradman's rate, the stand would have been 501. In 1934 a new ball became available to the fielding side every 200 runs, that is, England had

three new balls during the course of the day. Ray Robinson, *Between Wickets* (1958), had this relevant point: "Probably the greatest compliment Bradman ever paid Ponsford was an indirect one. On the night after their 451 partnership, Don mentioned that he thought Bill should have taken the greater part of the bowling with the new ball at 400!"

Had the present ruling existed in 1934, the third new ball of the Australian innings would have been available to England with the score 700 for nine.

After the opening day, the fifth Test became a more rational business:

Day 2: Australia 701, England 90 for none.
Day 3: Australia 701 and 186 for two, England 321.
Day 4: Australia 701 and 327, England 321 and 145.

AUSTRALIA 701 (W.H. Ponsford 266, D.G. Bradman 244) and 327 (Bradman 77, S.J. McCabe 70; W.E. Bowes 5 for 55, E.W. Clark 5 for 98) beat ENGLAND 321 (C.F. Walters 64, M. Leyland 110) and 145 (C.V. Grimmett 5 for 64) by 562 runs.

McCabe, as usual, opened the bowling in England's second innings and was taken off with figures of 5–3–5–2. He was not supposed to take wickets; doubtless Grimmett at cover was letting Woodfull know what he thought of such nonsense.

HEDLEY VERITY
Yorkshire

Verity, arguably the greatest English bowler of the pre-1939 decade, made his county championship debut for Yorkshire on 31 May 1930, against Leicestershire at Hull, his match analysis 39–15–60–8. He was already 25 years old, the bowler he would replace at the end of the season, Wilfred Rhodes, 52. They were different in method: whereas Rhodes by this time had lost his spin and relied on flight (in 1930 he bowled 554 overs in the Championship, conceding only a run and a half an over), Verity was slow–medium in pace and brought the ball down from a great height. For the record, he and Rhodes bowled together in only three championship matches: Rhodes 60–20–113–6 and Verity 108.4–36–206–24.

On 18 May 1931 — his twenty-sixth birthday — Verity bowled in his nineteenth Championship innings, against Warwickshire at Headingley. So far his wickets totalled a mere 64; now he was a host unto himself as he spun out the opposition: 18.4–6–36–10. The following year, also at Headingley, and in his seventy-eighth innings, he again took all ten wickets — against Nottinghamshire. On both occasions the bowler at the other end was G.G. Macaulay, who, if not a great off-spinner in his slower guise, was certainly a very good one. The same superb Yorkshire close fielders supported Macaulay and Verity and the pitch was a finger-spinner's dream at either end. Yet the respective figures of the bowlers present a challenge to theorists: even bearing in mind the effect of the 1935 lbw law, when did the ball breaking away from a right-handed batsman become less dangerous than the one breaking in to him? One automatically thinks of the 1956 Old Trafford Test.

Left-hander's leg-break

		O	M	R	W
1931	Verity	18.4	6	36	10
1932	Verity	19.4	16	10	10
1956	Lock	14	3	37	1
	Lock	55	30	69	0

Off-break

		O	M	R	W
1931	Macaulay	23	9	34	0
1932	Macaulay	18	11	20	0
1956	Laker	16.4	4	37	9
1956	Laker	51.2	23	53	10

Rhodes last played for England in 1930 at Kingston; had Verity survived the Second World War, and emulated Rhodes as veteran tormentor of batsmen, he would have been available for the Old Trafford Test of 1956. In which case it is safe to assert Laker's haul of wickets would have been fewer than 19.

VERITY'S REMARKABLE RECORD

By Dudley Carew

13 July 1932. The match between Yorkshire and Nottinghamshire at Leeds, although it had sufficient excitement in itself, will be remembered always for the bowling of Verity. At luncheon yesterday Nottinghamshire, who led by 71 runs on the first innings, had scored 38 runs for no wicket, but they were all out for 67 runs, and Verity had not only done the hat trick, but had come out with the extraordinary analysis of:

O.	M.	R.	W.
19.4	16	10	10

Bowlers have taken 10 wickets in one innings many times before, but never at such a fantastically small cost as Verity took his yesterday. The result of the match, thanks to Verity's astonishing achievement, was an easy win for Yorkshire by 10 wickets, with nearly an hour to spare.

Yorkshire declared at their overnight total of 163 runs for nine wickets and so seemed to put the future conduct of the match in Nottinghamshire's hands — they might choose to force the pace and declare in time to give themselves a reasonable chance of getting Yorkshire out, or they might concentrate on making sure of the first-innings points. Defeat at the time seemed out of the question.

The rain on the previous evening held up play until 12.30, and the hour's cricket before luncheon, during which Keeton and Shipston scored 38 runs together, suggested that the first-innings points were Nottinghamshire's objective. Keeton started off by hooking two short balls in Bowes's first over for a 4 and a 3, but this violence was not kept up, and later on Verity bowled seven maiden overs in succession. Both Keeton and Shipston had scored 18 runs at the interval, and the manner of their batting afterwards suggested that Nottinghamshire were definitely reconciled to their gain of five points.

With the total at 44, however, Verity, who before luncheon had only one slip and now had two, got Keeton caught by Macaulay, his original first slip. This reinforcement of the slips argued a certain increase in the difficulties of the pitch, and the batting of Walker at the beginning of his innings against both Verity and Macaulay, who was bowling round the wicket to two slips and two short-legs, confirmed the impression that the ball was turning more quickly. At 47 Shipston touched a ball of Verity's with the edge of his bat, and was caught at the wicket, and A.W. Carr was out before he had scored in almost exactly the same way he had been in the first innings, only this time Barber took the catch in front of the sight-screen instead of at long-off.

The pitch was now definitely difficult, and at 63 Verity took his fourth wicket when Walker played a perfectly correct stroke, found the spin too much for him, and was well caught low down with his right hand by Macaulay at first slip. Harris, playing in much the same way, was caught at second slip off the next ball, and Verity then proceeded to perform the hat-trick by getting G.V. Gunn, l.-b.-w. with a good-length ball which came straight through. One run later, at 64, A. Staples provided Verity with his seventh successive wicket, and Larwood, hitting out, was beautifully caught by Sutcliffe running back from extra cover-point.

Verity now had the chance of doing the hat trick twice in one innings. As a matter of fact Lilley scored three very lucky runs off the ball that might have given it to him, but Verity's bowling had changed the match right round, and Nottinghamshire, and not Yorkshire, were now in danger of defeat. Although Verity missed doing the hat trick twice he got rid of Voce and S. Staples with two successive balls in the same over as Lilley scored his three runs, but, unluckily for him, Nottinghamshire had no twelfth man to bat for them. Since luncheon Verity's analysis read:

O.	M.	R.	W.
12.4	9	10	10

Certainly the pitch became increasingly difficult, but, while Verity could not have accomplished his astounding success without its aid, it was only an accessory after the fact to his flight and length, which continually made the batsmen play the strokes they did not wish to after the ball had pitched. The turf and his finger spin did the rest.

Nottinghamshire lost 10 wickets for 29 runs after luncheon, and Yorkshire were left with 139 runs to win and with nearly 2¾ hours to spare. Holmes and Sutcliffe started off by scoring 50 runs in 40 mins. The pitch was by no means perfect, but they hit the loose ball hard, and at tea time 81 runs were on the board, of which Holmes had scored 43 and Sutcliffe 30. After tea the batsmen made light of the bowling again, and the runs were obtained in 100 minutes without loss, Holmes having nine 4's in a delightful 77. He also completed his 1,000 runs during his innings. This was the seventy-second time that the Yorkshire opening pair have put on 100 runs for the first wicket.

```
 .  .     .  .     .  .     .  .     .  .     .  .     .  .
 . M .    . M .    . M .    . M .    . M .    . M .    . M .
 .  .     .  .     .  .     .  .     .  .     .  .     .  .

LUNCH

 .  .     .  .     .  .     .  .     W  .     .  .     .  W
 . M .    . M .    .        . M .    . M .    .  .     . M .
 .  .     .  .     2  .     .  .     .  .     .  I     .  .

 W  .     .  .     3  I     .  W     .  .     3  W
 . M .    . M .    .  .     W M .    . M W     .
 .  .     .  .     .  .     W  .     .  W      W
```

                        IN 52 BALLS 10 WICKETS FOR 9 RUNS

                        IN 37 BALLS 9 WICKETS FOR 7 RUNS

                        IN 15 BALLS 7 WICKETS FOR 3 RUNS

VERITY AT LORD'S, 1934

The Lord's Test seemed destined to be a draw until the weekend rain gave Verity the chance to take 14 wickets for 80 on the third day. England had started well, endured a partial collapse, then recovered to 293 for five on Friday; by the end of Saturday, Australia had made 192 for two, some 248 behind England's score. Talking points were many — the admirable style of C.F. Walters and W.A. Brown, the

wonder of being able to play as wicketkeeper as grand a batsman as Ames and the absurdity of Chipperfield's leg-breaks being more successful than those of Grimmett and O'Reilly — but they centred on one man.

Bradman was sickening for something. His batting at Lord's, as at Trent Bridge, was feverishly brilliant: understandable in a Trumper but not in Bradman, whose first three Test innings in 1934 totalled 90 runs from 107 balls. History would show that Bradman was sickening both for a large score — and this was delayed for a month — and the illness which proved wellnigh fatal at the end of the tour.

ENGLAND WIN IN AN INNINGS

By R.B. Vincent

26 June 1934. England beat Australia in the second Test Match at Lord's yesterday by an innings and 38 runs, a remarkable result at 6 o'clock on the third day of the match, even if rain had fallen heavily during the week-end. The King, who watched the play in the morning, went on to the field at half-past 12, when the two teams were presented to him.

Obviously England had the luck of the game which came from winning the toss, but at no time yesterday did Australia have to bat on a wicket appreciably more difficult than that on which England was striving to save the game in the fourth innings at Trent Bridge. So far as these games have gone each side has had its opportunity, well and truly taken. No two opinions will agree on the exact state of the pitch at Lord's yesterday. It was inclined to pop in the morning; after an hour's play it became easier; and in the afternoon, playing appreciably faster, it took spin much more to the bowler's fancy. Certainly it was never anything approaching to a sticky wicket, and Verity, the great and undisputed hero of the match, had all the time to make the Australian batsmen believe that it was just a little more unkind than in fact it really was.

Helped as he was by a queer lack of confidence among the Australians, to whom the very sight of sawdust may suggest unknown horrors, Verity's achievement must be written down as one of the greatest in the whole story of Test Match cricket. In the first innings he took seven wickets for 61 runs in 36 overs, and in the second innings eight wickets for 43 runs in 22 overs. Only one bowler before has taken 15 wickets in a match between England and Australia, W. Rhodes at Melbourne in the tour of 1903–1904.

For the greater part of the day yesterday he bowled from the Pavilion end with three slips to the right-handed batsmen and three short-legs to Darling and Bromley, and during all this time one saw only one ball which was pitched not of the length he meant. Continually he made the batsman play to the ball, whether going with his arm, or coming back to offer a catch to Hammond at third slip and Hendren at silly mid-off. It was indeed a great bowling performance, a left-handed bowler taking just the slight chance that was offered him.

It may sound unkind to the Australians, and

YORKSHIRE v. NOTTINGHAMSHIRE
Headingley, 9, 11 and 12 July 1932

NOTTINGHAMSHIRE

1st innings

W.W. Keeton	b Rhodes	9
F.W. Shipston	b Macaulay	8
W. Walker	c Barber b Bowes	36
Mr. A.W. Carr	c Barber b Verity	0
A. Staples	b Macaulay	3
C.B. Harris	lbw b Leyland	35
G.V. Gunn	b Verity	31
B. Lilley	not out	46
H. Larwood	b Leyland	48
W. Voce	b Leyland	0
S.J. Staples	b Leyland	0
Extras	(b 8, lb 6, w 2, nb 2)	18
Total		234

2nd innings

W.W. Keeton	c Macaulay b Verity	21
F.W. Shipston	c Wood b Verity	21
W. Walker	c Macaulay b Verity	11
Mr. A.W. Carr	c Barber b Verity	0
A. Staples	c Macaulay b Verity	7
C.B. Harris	c Holmes b Verity	0
G.V. Gunn	lbw b Verity	0
B. Lilley	not out	3
H. Larwood	c Sutcliffe b Verity	0
W. Voce	c Holmes b Verity	0
S.J. Staples	st Wood b Verity	0
Extras	(b 3, nb 1)	4
Total		67

YORKSHIRE

1st innings

P. Holmes	b Larwood	65
H. Sutcliffe	c Voce b Larwood	0
A. Mitchell	run out	24
M. Leyland	b Voce	5
W. Barber	c & b Larwood	34
Mr A.B. Sellers	b A. Staples	0
A. Wood	b Larwood	0
A.C. Rhodes	c A. Staples b Voce	3
H. Verity	b Larwood	12
G.G. Macaulay	not out	8
W.E. Bowes	not out	1
Extras	(b 5, lb 5)	10
Total	(9 wkts dec.)	163

2nd innings

P. Holmes	not out	77
H. Sutcliffe	not out	54
Extras	(b 4, lb 4)	8
Total	(0 wkt)	139

NOTTINGHAMSHIRE BOWLING

	O	M	R	W	O	M	R	W
Larwood	22	4	73	5	3	0	14	0
Voce	22	2	52	2	10	0	43	0
S.J. Staples	7	2	8	0	18.4	5	37	0
A. Staples	11	3	20	1	6	1	25	0
Harris					3	0	12	0

Umpires: H.G. Baldwin and W. Reeves

YORKSHIRE BOWLING

	O	M	R	W	O	M	R	W
Bowes	31	9	55	1	5	0	19	0
Rhodes	28	8	49	1				
Verity	41	13	64	2	19.4	16	10	10
Macaulay	24	10	34	2	23	9	34	0
Leyland	8.2	3	14	4				

YORKSHIRE WON BY 10 WICKETS

perhaps a trifle ungenerous to Verity, but, if the truth must be told, the batting was a little feeble. Woodfull in the second innings, by putting the whole of his body between the pitch of the ball and the stumps, did his noble utmost to keep one end intact, and Chipperfield played two gallant innings, but the Australians themselves would be the first to try to forget some of the meagre strokes that were offered. No one who saw it can ever forget the crude manner in which the great Bradman gave his wicket away when so much depended upon him. For all that, bad strokes or not, it was a great victory for England, and now all is again to be played for.

The match was continued in the morning, only after the players had taken up their position with the score at 192 for two wickets, and had ambled back to the Pavilion before a ball had been bowled because of bad light. Ten minutes and out they came again, with Bowes bowling from the Nursery end and Verity at the other. Bowes, it should be said, bowled well and ill in turns; when he was good he looked likely to take a wicket, more than once being able to bring the ball back up the hill. He had periods all through the match, however, when he became slower than medium and shorter than ordinary. Verity can always make the ball stand up, and it was therefore not surprising to see him pack the slips, with Hammond moved first from short to second, and then second to third slip. The first wicket fell when Brown, who had played so well on Saturday evening, waved his bat at a ball well outside the off-stump from Bowes, and was caught at the wicket, three wickets then being down for 203 runs.

Thoughts of a follow-on at once flew round the ground, and I must at once plead guilty having said during the Test Match at Nottingham that in a four-day match a side 200 runs behind could be sent in again. This law of cricket applies only to matches in Australia. We knew at this moment that it was only 150 runs, and we were encouraged to believe that even so England could do it when Darling, attempting a hook, was caught at backward short-leg, the score then being only 204

and 87 runs more wanted to save the follow-on. One run later McCabe was caught at seconod slip off Verity, the nastiest ball that Verity bowled all day, quick off the pitch and spinning away from leg to the off-stump.

When bowling to Bromley Verity looked for catches close in on the leg-side, but Bromley took four runs between the fieldsmen, and Geary, who seemed handicapped by a bad leg, came on in place of Bowes. With the score at 218 Bromley was out as Verity had intended he should be, caught at short-leg off a ball which jumped up a little. Oldfield, in the beginning of his innings, was lucky in playing the ball somehow and somewhere just clear of Verity's cluster of slips, and when he played out to the ball one could not help feeling that the deeper fieldsmen were just a few yards too deep, several strokes landing the ball first bounce into their hands. With a definite bite in the pitch R.E.S. Wyatt tried Leyland at the Nursery end, but his length was irregular, three full-pitches in two overs being unhelpful to the occasion. Just at this moment, when Oldfield by driving Leyland to the sight screen insisted on a deep fieldsman, there was an impression that England was a bowler short. Hammond, who next to Verity was the best of England's bowlers, had a spell from the Pavilion end and Verity was tried at the other.

Chipperfield had some awkward moments from Verity, but he was the most likely to hold out, once hitting Hammond straight to the boundary. Another spell of Geary meant little, and 40 runs had been added for the wicket before Oldfield, playing forward, was well caught, high up, at second slip. The threat of a follow-on was once more upon the Australians, and it was only delayed by Grimmett's streaking two 4's through the slips off Bowes before he was bowled. At the luncheon interval Australia, with only two wickets to fall, still wanted 18 more runs.

O'Reilly afterwards did his utmost to allow Chipperfield to make the runs, but at 284 he let loose at a well-pitched-up ball, missed it, and was bowled. Wall, without a run added, was leg-

ENGLAND v. AUSTRALIA
Lord's, 22, 23 and 25 June 1934

ENGLAND

C.F. Walters	c Bromley b O'Reilly	82
H. Sutcliffe	lbw b Chipperfield	20
W.R. Hammond	c & b Chipperfield	2
E. Hendren	c McCabe b Wall	13
R.E.S. Wyatt	c Oldfield b Chipperfield	33
M. Leyland	b Wall	109
L.E.G. Ames	c Oldfield b McCabe	120
G. Geary	c Chipperfield b Wall	9
H. Verity	st Oldfield b Grimmett	29
K. Farnes	b Wall	1
W.E. Bowes	not out	10
Extras	(lb 12)	12
Total		440

Fall of wickets: 1–70, 2–78, 3–99, 4–130, 5–182, 6–311, 7–359, 8–409, 9–410, 10–440.

AUSTRALIA BOWLING

	O	M	R	W
Wall	49	7	108	4
McCabe	18	3	38	1
Grimmett	53.3	13	102	1
O'Reilly	38	15	70	1
Chipperfield	34	10	91	3
Darling	6	2	19	0

Umpires: F. Chester and J. Hardstaff, Sr

ENGLAND WON BY AN INNINGS AND 38 RUNS

AUSTRALIA

1st innings

W.M. Woodfull	b Bowes	22
W.A. Brown	c Ames b Bowes	105
D.G. Bradman	c & b Verity	36
S.J. McCabe	c Hammond b Verity	34
L.S. Darling	c Sutcliffe b Verity	0
A.G. Chipperfield	not out	37
E.H. Bromley	c Geary b Verity	4
W.A. Oldfield	c Sutcliffe b Verity	23
C.V. Grimmett	b Bowes	9
W.J. O'Reilly	b Verity	4
T.W. Wall	lbw b Verity	0
Extras	(b 1, lb 9)	10
Total		284

2nd innings

W.M. Woodfull	c Hammond b Verity	43
W.A. Brown	c Walters b Bowes	2
D.G. Bradman	c Ames b Verity	13
S.J. McCabe	c Hendren b Verity	19
L.S. Darling	b Hammond	10
A.G. Chipperfield	c Geary b Verity	14
E.H. Bromley	c & b Verity	1
W.A. Oldfield	lbw b Verity	0
C.V. Grimmett	c Hammond b Verity	0
W.J. O'Reilly	not out	8
T.W. Wall	c Hendren b Verity	1
Extras	(b 6, nb 1)	7
Total		118

Fall of wickets: 1–68, 2–141, 3–203, 4–204, 5–205, 6–218, 7–258, 8–273, 9–284, 10–284.

Second innings: 1–10, 2–43, 3–57, 4–94, 5–94, 6–95, 7–95, 8–95, 9–112, 10–118.

ENGLAND BOWLING

	O	M	R	W	O	M	R	W
Farnes	12	3	43	0	4	2	6	0
Bowes	31	5	98	3	14	4	24	1
Geary	22	4	56	0				
Verity	36	15	61	7	22.3	8	43	8
Hammond	4	1	6	0	13	0	38	1
Leyland	4	1	10	0				

before-wicket, and so Australia followed on 156 runs behind.

The second innings was begun at a quarter to 3, Wyatt starting his bowling with Bowes, from the Nursery end, and K. Farnes, who was not very comfortable on an injured foot. England's captain knew when he sent Australia in again that he had only half a bowling side, but he no doubt felt that if wickets were to fall it were better that they

were Australian wickets, and his trust in Verity was profound. Only 10 runs had been scored when Brown was caught on the leg side trying to hook Bowes, who, as in the first innings, had started well.

Woodfull's anxiety was shown when McCabe came in to bat next in place of Bradman, and it was not long before Wyatt showed the full force of his attack by putting Verity on at the Pavilion end with Hammond at the other to relieve a patently tiring Bowes. McCabe twice in one over from Verity was lucky to escape being caught in the slips, and Woodfull once put the edge of his bat at the last moment to a ball from Hammond which might have hit his middle stump, but which went for four runs.

Verity, even when bowling to McCabe, was now well on top, and the turn of the game came when McCabe drove a ball hard at Hendren at silly mid-off. The catch was held, and the bottom was knocked out of Australia's batting. Bradman, rather in the manner of the Bradman of 1930, played some workmanlike strokes until, with the score at 57, he suddenly perpetrated the worst stroke he has ever made in his life. He slashed, crooked bat, against the break to Verity, and, skying the ball, was caught by the wicket-keeper. Darling was all but bowled by the first ball he received from Verity, who by now was merely

waiting for wickets, and at 94 the Australians suffered their final blow when Woodfull, playing back to a leg-break, was caught at extra slip. He had not made many impressive strokes, but so long as he was there Australia was alive.

Darling at 94 was bowled by Hammond, who most certainly had deserved a wicket, and one run later Verity took a good catch off his own bowling, high and to the right, to get rid of Bromley. Then the cheering broke out full-hearted, and the wickets fell accordingly. Oldfield, who might have been a nuisance, was leg-before-wicket; Grimmett, who also can be tiresome, was caught at third slip from the first ball he had; and Chipperfield, who had had a nasty blow from Hammond, was caught at first slip.

Verity was bowling to batsmen whom he knew he could get out, and the end came when Hendren, rolling on his back, caught Wall close in under his bat.

STANLEY JOSEPH McCABE
New South Wales

TRENT BRIDGE, 1938

When Hammond declared England's innings closed at 658 for eight wickets at 3.15 p.m. on the second afternoon of the first Test at Trent Bridge two results could be discounted: an England defeat and an Australian victory. In the event the pitch won: the first day saw 422 for four wickets, the second 374 for seven, the third 375 for eight and the fourth 325 for five. But dominating the game was an innings by McCabe, of which it can safely be said that nothing greater has ever been witnessed, at least in England. When play began on Monday, 13 June, Australia were 138 for three: Fingleton, Brown and Bradman out, McCabe 19 not out, scored in 35 minutes.

By Dudley Carew

14 June 1938. Whatever happens in this Test match of records at Trent Bridge the name of S.J. McCabe must imperishably be associated with it. Figures are often uninformative, but sometimes they have a way of speaking the truth with utter clarity and conviction, and yesterday McCabe actually scored 213 runs out of 273 in three hours and three-quarters [actually three hours 20 minutes]. In all he made 232 and hit one 6 and 30 4's [34 to be exact]. Considering the pace at which he went and the risks which he most laudably and legitimately took in the interests of his side, the mis-hits were astonishingly few and there was not a chance in the whole course of the great and historic innings.

The Australians went in again shortly before 4 o'clock, needing 247 runs to save the innings defeat. J.H. Fingleton and W.A. Brown scored 89 runs for the first wicket, and when stumps were drawn D.G. Bradman was not out, the score was 102 for one wicket, and there was the feeling of a draw in the air.

It was obvious that the first hour yesterday morning was going to be of great importance, and the crowd, when play was begun, seemed even bigger than it had been on Saturday morning, and it was not long before the gates were closed. W.R. Hammond opened the bowling with K. Farnes, who had two slips and a gully, and Wright, who had one slip and a forward short-leg. England got the quick wicket they wanted, but it was not the important one, as it was F.A. Ward [the night-watchman], and not McCabe, whom Farnes bowled.

This happened after only six runs had been added to the overnight score of 138, and seven runs later they suffered a really formidable casualty in the person of A.L. Hassett. Hassett went out to drive Wright through the covers, did not get his left leg quite far enough across, and the ball flew off the edge of the bat to Hammond at first slip.

The rest of the morning was dominated by McCabe. His side were struggling for their lives, and the English bowling and fielding were re-inforced with a proper hostility and confidence. The out-cricket was altogether more formidable and better organized than that of Australia had been, but never for a moment did McCabe play like a member of a losing side. His batting was cool, upright, and aggressive enough to earn him 83 runs off his own bat before luncheon.

Once he mistimed an on-drive and lifted the ball, but generally the ball came off the bat as he

McCABE   Australian classical master whose three immortal innings graced Sydney, Johannesburg and Nottingham.

intended it to. He placed Sinfield down to the boundary at fine-leg and a cut for 3 off the same bowler got him his 50. When Hammond came on he forced successive balls off his legs to the boundary, both strong handsome shots, brought up the 200 by hooking Farnes, and in the same over he played a lovely forcing shot off his back foot through the covers. Shortly before this, however, he had lost C.L. Badcock. Wright had been bowling his leg-breaks at something not far from medium in pace, and bowling them with a most commendable accuracy, and when Badcock had made nine he produced a devastating googly which

completely deceived Badcock, who tried to cut it, and which came in to hit the top of the off-stump.

Hammond did not take the new ball, and Verity did not appear until the time was five minutes past 1. He could make nothing of the pitch, and did not look as dangerous as either Sinfield or Wright. McCabe duly reached his 100 and added two runs before luncheon, when the score was 261 and B.A. Barnett's contribution a highly important 20. It was a little grim to reflect that at lunch-time on the third day only 14 wickets had fallen.

The weather afterwards was hot and sultry, and McCabe, who, goodness knows, had been severe enough on the bowling before luncheon, became brutal to it afterwards. He soon lost Barnett, but the fall of the wicket seemed to encourage him to take the game into his hands. His attack was terrific in its power and virility, and at the end of an hour an England team which had looked assured of victory wilted, and wilted not without cause. The 4's came faster than an agitated pencil could note them down. Three of them came in one over off Farnes, and then the unfortunate Wright felt the full force of his wrath. Two successive balls were driven straight and handsomely to the boundary, and the fact that neither W.J. O'Reilly nor E.L. McCormick could help him very much mattered not at all.

Nine wickets were down for 334, but such was his attack in the next 20 minutes or so that the England bowling began to look as though it would find Fleetwood-Smith's wicket, let alone McCabe's, difficult to take. Wright played his part well, taking the Australians' innings as a whole, and the fact that he lost his length under the lash of McCabe's driving, cutting, and hook-ing should not unduly upset him — McCabe, as he was yesterday, would have upset greater bowlers. Three times in one over McCabe dis-missed the ball superbly to various parts of the field, and then he scored 16 runs off four succes-sive balls from Wright, first an on-drive, then a full-pitch — full-pitches in this match have not been conspicuous by their absence — pulled

round to square-leg to give him his 200, then that shot off the right foot through the covers, and finally a hook off a long-hop.

When he eventually lifted a ball from Verity to extra cover-point he could retire with the know-ledge that if his side were to save the match that devastating 75 minutes after luncheon would be mainly responsible. The pitch had already had well over 1,000 runs scored on it, but it still looked as though it could supply a good many more.

The Australians followed on 247 runs behind, and although in a normal match the outlook would be distinctly gloomy Test Matches are not normal matches, pitches are miraculous. 247 was a good deal less than they must have anticipated when the fifth wicket fell, and above all the England bowling had experienced McCabe. Farnes and Hammond again opened the England bowling and Fingleton and Brown countered it and the subsequent bowling changes with sense and composure. It would have been the blackest of ingratitude to McCabe had they thrown away by recklessness what the good McCabe had done by his brilliance, and yet they were stupidly barracked. When will the vast gulf that divides caution when it is necessary and caution when it is not be recognized by crowds?

Figures did indeed speak the truth about McCabe's innings.

1. His 232 was scored at a run a minute.
2. On the second day he made 213 of 263 runs from the bat — 81 per cent.
3. He scored his last 100 runs in 55 minutes.
4. At the fall of the ninth wicket, he and Fleetwood-Smith (who went in at No. 10 for Victoria only when H. Ironmonger was also playing) added 77 in 28 minutes — Fleetwood-Smith surviving 18 balls.
5. The record books state that after reaching 200 in 225 minutes, McCabe added a further 32 in five minutes. If this sounds unlikely, it must be remem-bered that McCabe hit 16 of his 34 fours during the tenth wicket partnership.

ENGLAND v. AUSTRALIA
Trent Bridge, 10, 11, 13, 14 June 1938

ENGLAND

L. Hutton	lbw b Fleetwood-Smith	100
C.J. Barnett	b McCormick	126
W.J. Edrich	b O'Reilly	5
W.R. Hammond	b O'Reilly	26
E. Paynter	not out	216
D.C.S. Compton	c Badcock b Fleetwood-Smith	102
L.E.G. Ames	b Fleetwood-Smith	46
H. Verity	b Fleetwood-Smith	3
R.A. Sinfield	lbw b O'Reilly	6
D.V.P. Wright	not out	1
Extras	(b 1, lb 22, nb 4)	27
Total	(8 wkts dec.)	658

K. Farnes did not bat.

Fall of wickets: 1–219, 2–240, 3–244, 4–281, 5–487, 6–577, 7–597, 8–626.

AUSTRALIA BOWLING

	O	M	R	W
McCormick	32	4	108	1
O'Reilly	56	11	164	3
McCabe	21	5	64	0
Fleetwood-Smith	49	9	153	4
Ward	30	2	142	0

Umpires: F. Chester and E. Robinson

MATCH DRAWN

AUSTRALIA

1st innings

J.H. Fingleton	b Wright	9
W.A. Brown	c Ames b Farnes	48
D.G. Bradman	c Ames b Sinfield	51
S.J. McCabe	c Compton b Verity	232
F. Ward	b Farnes	2
A.L. Hassett	c Hammond b Wright	1
C.L. Badcock	b Wright	9
B.A. Barnett	c Wright b Farnes	22
W.J. O'Reilly	c Paynter b Farnes	9
E.L. McCormick	b Wright	2
L.O'B. Fleetwood-Smith	not out	5
Extras	(b 10, lb 10, w 1)	21
Total		411

2nd innings

J.H. Fingleton	c Hammond b Edrich	40
W.A. Brown	c Paynter b Verity	133
D.G. Bradman	not out	144
S.J. McCabe	c Hammond b Verity	39
A.L. Hassett	c Compton b Verity	2
C.L. Badcock	b Wright	5
B.A. Barnett	lbw b Sinfield	31
F. Ward	not out	7
Extras	(b 5, lb 16, nb 5)	26
Total	(6 wkts dec.)	427

Fall of wickets: 1–34, 2–111, 3–134, 4–144, 5–151, 6–194, 7–263, 8–319, 9–334, 10–411.

Second innings: 1–89, 2–259, 3–331, 4–337, 5–369, 6–417.

ENGLAND BOWLING

	O	M	R	W	O	M	R	W
Farnes	37	11	106	4	24	2	78	0
Hammond	19	6	44	0	12	6	15	0
Sinfield	28	8	51	1	35	8	72	1
Wright	39	6	153	4	37	8	85	1
Verity	7.3	0	36	1	62	27	102	3
Edrich					13	2	39	1
Barnett					1	0	10	0

A batsman and a bowler paid tribute to McCabe's innings. Bradman said simply: "If I could play an innings like that I'd be a proud man, Stan." S.F. Barnes turned to Neville Cardus:

Barnes: The finest innings I have seen.
Cardus: Think again, you saw Trumper.
Barnes: I can only repeat it is the greatest I ever saw.
Cardus: I'd have liked to see you out there bowling to McCabe.
Barnes: I don't think I could have kept him quiet.

Only three Australians played in the Tests at Sydney 1932, Johannesburg 1935 and Trent Bridge 1938 — McCabe, Fingleton and W.J. O'Reilly.

By Jack Fingleton

26 August 1968. For the legion of his friends and admirers in this country, it was sad news that Stanley Joseph McCabe had died.

McCabe, like Sir Donald Bradman and W.J. O'Reilly, two immortal contemporaries of his cricketing time, came from what is known in Australia as "the bush". McCabe hailed from the south-western New South Wales town of Grenfell a prosperous sheep and wheat-growing area. Like the other two, he learnt his cricket on the true surface of a concrete pitch.

McCabe like Bradman at that period, who came from Bowral, then settled in Sydney to work and to foster his cricketing prospects, but unlike Bradman he had no meteoric rise to fame. He rose there steadily. He was, at 20, the surprise choice in W.M. Woodfull's 1930 team to England; McCabe was the youngest in the team and he had not previously hit a first-class century.

McCabe was a successful if not unduly prominent member of that side in which Bradman dominated the series, making scores of 131, 254, 334 and 232. There was also Ponsford. McCabe, like some of his fellows, was engulfed by the Bradman dynasty, but he surged to immortality in 1932–33 in Australia, when, in Sydney, against the devastating bodyline bowling of Larwood and Voce, under the direction of Jardine, he hit an incredible 187 not out. On a sunny Saturday morning, he sent the Sydney crowd into ecstasies of joy and disbelief as he flayed both Larwood and Voce on the leg side.

McCabe's heroics of that innings, in many minds, dispelled the Australian contentions that bodyline was unsporting and hampered stroke play. McCabe, however, was first to admit that things went his way. Neither he nor any other Australian ever again attacked Jardine's methods with such brilliancy.

McCabe had 137 against England at Old Trafford in 1934; he hit 112 against England in Melbourne in 1936 and he hit 232 against England at Trent Bridge in 1938. On tour, he hit 149 against South Africa at Durban in 1935–36 and made 189 not out against South Africa at Johannesburg. His Trent Bridge and Johannesburg innings ranked with the Sydney one against England as three of the greatest of all Test time.

One hesitates to say which of McCabe's three innings was his greatest. That at Johannesburg, another one of sheer bowling massacre, was played on a broken pitch in the dark light of a pending storm. McCabe so demoralized the Springboks that the South African captain, Herbert Wade, appealed successfully against the light from the field. Yet, in retrospect, and considering the opposition, possibly McCabe's Sydney innings was his greatest.

McCabe was a classical batsman of easy and graceful movement. His footwork was impeccable. He once said he learnt more about footwork in an innings at the Oval by Jack Hobbs (McCabe was fielding in the covers) than he did in the rest of his career. McCabe was a master of the pull, which he played to any ball a fraction short, and a drive in all its directions.

That, in a sense, was McCabe the batsman, who was also a good slip-field and fair medium paced bowler. His manner and character never changed. He abhorred humbug. He was the warmest and most loyal of friends and there was neither deceit nor conceit in his nature.

DENIS CHARLES SCOTT COMPTON
Middlesex

Compton should be discussed only by those who never saw him; any who came under his spell are apt to attribute to him qualities possessed by no mortal man. He was a great batsman who caused even the bowlers he put to the sword to enjoy the game more than their figures suggested they should. A grand romantic, he retired from regular cricket before the age of 40; his knee injury persuaded many to curse the very mention of football. As an outside-left at Highbury, Compton was doubtless a star; as the spirit of happy adventure at Lord's, or anywhere else in the world, he was unique.

He made his Championship debut for Middlesex a week after his 18th birthday in 1936. Tate's pace off the pitch saw G.O. Allen utter the customary advice — "Play forward!" Compton, at No. 11, did just that, 14 runs accruing until he was lbw to J.H. Parks. Elevated three places in the order, he next faced Larwood and Voce; the former was still good enough to finish the season with 119 wickets at 12.97 runs each — the most effective bowler in England: Compton 26 not out. Clark, Northamptonshire's fast left-arm destroyer of any who flinched, found Compton coming in at 21 for five. "He stood up to Clark like a veteran," his runs 87. There followed an innings of 53 against the Essex of Farnes and Nichols. The youth clearly liked fast bowling; 87 and 96 against Kent (both scores made in less than two hours) was his answer to Freeman. Dudley Carew of *The Times* said everything: "He is an astonishingly mature cricketer for his age, not only

in defence but in the even more important matter of picking out the ball to hit and hitting it in the right way. He has style, he has discretion, and he has the strokes." Carew then said more: "This match has shown him as such a good batsman that figures are a mere irrelevance." P.F. Warner declared Compton to be the best young batsman to come out since Hammond.*

On 17 July 1937 Middlesex began a match with Gloucestershire at Lord's. At the close Gloucestershire had been dismissed for 200 (C.J. Barnett 83), Middlesex replying with 225 for six.

By R.B. Vincent

19 July 1937. ...Compton was magnificent; he played all the bowling, and this Gloucestershire bowling is in variety and employment good, with ease and hostility, making all the strokes which are demanded of a batsman. He is anything but a one-stroke batsman, and if he seemed at times to take liberties, they were no more than the chances of a man who has faith in himself and understands that there are unguarded parts of the field to which the ball can be hit with impunity.

20 July 1937. When play was begun in the morning Middlesex were already 25 runs ahead with

....
* Who, aged 18, had played twice against Armstrong's 1921 Australians, and made 1, 0 and 1.

four wickets yet to fall. They lost Muncer with only two runs added, but thereafter Compton took entire charge of the proceedings. Sims did at one time score five runs all from one blow, four of them coming from an overthrow which was zealous but wild. Compton scored 50 out of the first 58 runs in 40 minutes. He made most of his runs with superb drives: even Hammond could

not persuade him to play anything but a forcing stroke. His timing, too, was so good that he found for himself gaps in the field, well placed as it was. He scored 71 runs in an hour, easily gained against a bowling side who still had hopes that their batsmen would not be left too much to do in their second innings. Then, with the score at 319 he was caught at deep mid-off after as pleasurable an innings as could have been desired. He had hit 22 4's.

GLOUCESTERSHIRE 200 (C.J. Barnett 83; C.I.J. Smith 5 for 59) and 204 (B.O. Allen 57) lost to MIDDLESEX 352 (D.C.S. Compton 177: C. Tyler 5 for 110) and 36 for 2 by 8 wickets.

Three months after his nineteenth birthday, Compton made his debut for England, against New Zealand at the Oval. His 65 delighted all, his method of departure (run out) greatly regretted. A straight drive by his partner, J. Hardstaff, was deflected from the bowler's hand with Compton out of his ground. Post-war run-outs with Compton at the crease were not unknown, his preliminary call — as one wit suggested — being a mere opening of negotiations. But as Compton himself said with disarming gravity, "I do run myself out as often as I do the man at the other end."

Trent Bridge 1938 was McCabe's match. Four England batsmen scored hundreds in a total of 658 for eight declared: Hutton 100, Barnett 126, Paynter 216 not out and Compton 102. The last-named joined Paynter at 281 for four on the first day, and was 69 at the close (422 for four). The ghost of A.C.M. Croome seemed to be inhabiting the press box for *The Times:*

By Dudley Carew

11 June 1938. Compton batted with the assurance of a man who remembered cricket as it was played under the leadership of W.G. Grace at Crystal Palace.

COMPTON   No batsman has taunted cover point as charmingly as Compton, often from yards down the wicket.

13 June 1938. The contrast between Paynter and Compton was marked. Paynter looked utilitarian and post-War; he is a fine man for doing the honest work of getting runs. Compton, on the other hand, looked an artist, and the instincts of the great cricketers who played in the days when the war meant the Boer War moved in his strokes. He cut McCabe for 4 handsomely and showed an off-drive which was technically perfect. When he played his defensive strokes, too, he played them as though he had been reading text-books.

Compton soon went ahead of Paynter, but they were both running neck and neck in the nineties and then O'Reilly came on and Paynter in his first over cut him square to the boundary and then hooked him for another 4, which gave him his hundred. The over altogether cost O'Reilly 14 runs. Compton was not long in following him — it was that delectable cut of his which brought him safely home'— and then was out hitting at Fleetwood-Smith and being caught by C.L. Badcock deep at square-leg. It was a lovely and memorable innings, and it had taken him only two and a quarter hours.

Lovely and memorable perhaps; Hammond spoke sternly on the iniquity of getting out for 102 in a Test against Australia.

The second Test at Lord's saw Compton reach new heights: England, with a first-innings lead of 72, were 76 for five when he joined Paynter.

By R.B. Vincent

29 June 1938. . . . Then followed a stand between Paynter and Compton,* fine cricketers both of them, which put new heart into England and must have worried Bradman. Fleetwood-Smith was brought on for a short spell, but he was too untidy in his length to be economical, and even McCabe, a model of accuracy, was twice driven in front of the wicket to the boundary by Compton...Things were improving from England's

. . . .

* Wearing a cap: this information for the late middle-aged.

point of view when Paynter, attempting a second run of a stroke to fine leg, had his wicket thrown down [128 for six]. At this stage of the game, when a stolen run was of little importance and when a wicket meant everything to Australia, it was a stupid thing to have done. Ames was no sooner in than he received the blow on his finger [which broke it], but he struggled on until the luncheon interval, Compton doing all the scoring. Compton during this time definitely established himself as a Test Match player of class. His batting is so compact, the blade so straight both in his forward and defensive play, and his short-armed hook, which he used freely to McCormick, is played with intense power. Some of his off-side strokes came as a delightful relief in a game which had been made up to a great extent of pushes to leg.

Aided by some lusty blows from Wellard (38), Compton's 76 not out enabled Hammond to declare at 3.20 p.m., thus setting Australia an impossible target of 315 in 165 minutes.

When war came in 1939 Compton was three months past his twenty-first birthday. He had played 12 Test innings, average 52; the two seasons 1938–9 had him play 61 innings in the County Championship, average 56.44. He had most certainly arrived.

A GREAT GAME

Middlesex won the Championship in 1947, the runs and hundreds from their first four batsmen: J.D. Robertson 2,214 (11), S.M. Brown 1,709 (3), W.J. Edrich 2,257 (8), D.C.S. Compton 2,033 (11), whose respective averages of 65, 40, 77 and 96 combined to make 278 — runs made at some speed. The bowling was mainly in the hands of L.H. Gray and Edrich with the new ball, before the spinning trio of J.A. Young (left-arm), J. Sims (googly) and Compton took over. A wicket every 50 balls from this quintet, and the two-thirds to one-third ratio of spin to pace, meant that Middlesex were apt to dismiss an opposition twice in eight and one-half hours.

In mid-August Middlesex played Kent at Lord's, the first day producing 434 runs for 13 wickets, the second 322 runs for 12 wickets and the third 419 runs for 13 wickets. In the home side's first innings, Wright bowled Compton for 16 with a perfectly pitched leg-break.

By R.B. Vincent

16 August 1947. The whole summer season will offer no better game of cricket than that which Kent won over Middlesex at Lord's yesterday, with but five minutes to spare, by 75 runs. Nor will there be seen a grander innings than that played by D. Compton.

This indeed was county cricket at its very best, and if Middlesex still stay four points behind Gloucestershire in the championship it would be a poor heart and a broken voice that did not respond to the excitement of the last half-hour's play at Lord's yesterday. Such was the opinion of a distinguished American visitor who watched the pangs of Kent's triumph.

Kent, when play started in the morning, had already a lead of 298 runs with five wickets still in hand. Their position was sufficiently established, with G.F. Anson secure and Evans bordering on the brilliant — lucky as he may have been to have escaped the chance of a catch in the slips when he had made but 20. The declaration came in time to allow Middlesex half an hour's batting before luncheon needing 397 runs to win at a rate of 100 an hour.

With Brown bowled off his pads and Robertson leg before wicket to the first ball after the interval two wickets were down for 28 runs; and, what was much more to the point, Wright was again bowling to a length. So the answer lay in whether Edrich and Compton could first break the bowling and then score from it quickly enough to win the match. When at 88 Edrich was brilliantly caught by the bowler off a hard enough drive the game had reached a new and uncomfortable phase for Middlesex.

R.W.V. Robins, severe on this occasion,

helped Compton to take the score to 135 before he was bowled, and there followed a partnership between F.G. Mann and Compton which first stemmed Kent's hopes and then actually offered Middlesex some prospect of victory. Compton played every manner of stroke least expected by the bowler. With three men close in on the leg side and three more spread on the boundary he yet found every manner of means, moving his feet even as the ball left the bowler's hand, to place or strike the ball to every part of the field.

It was truly a great performance against so adept a bowler as Wright and, with Mann equally ready to accept the challenge, there was every possibility of Middlesex winning the game, for such rate of scoring cannot be reckoned by so many runs in so many minutes. Middlesex have a measure of time quite of their own.

The score had been taken to 296 when Compton nodded, hitting a ball into the hands of cover point, and 10 runs later Mann, hastening his stroke, was bowled. So then Kent were on top, and there they stayed, even if they did leave it a little late.

KENT 301 (L.J. Todd 62, A.E. Fagg 66, B.H. Valentine 61) and 324 for 8 declared (L.E.G. Ames 69, Valentine 92, G.F. Anson 51, T.G. Evans 56) beat MIDDLESEX 229 (J.D. Robertson 110; D.V.P. Wright 7 for 92) and 321 (D.C.S. Compton 168, F.G. Mann 57) by 75 runs.

	Overs	Seam	Spin
Kent 1st innings	91	30	61
Middlesex 1st innings	81	18	63
Kent 2nd innings	118	34	84
Middlesex 2nd innings	81	18	63
	371	100	271

1947 was also the year of Compton's mastery over the South African bowlers. His scores in the Tests were 65 and 163, 208, 115 and 6, 30, 53 and 113 — that last innings being played at the Oval.

By R.B. Vincent

20 August 1947. ....Compton, a batsman of such versatility that a record of his strokes played would be as fantastic to the reader as it was to the bowlers and a well-set field. He favoured to start with a series of blows to good-length balls which passed cover-point as the flight of fancy. Later he showed the stroke with the roll of the wrist which deflected the ball to long leg, and always took delight in a movement backwards and a thump away to long-on. Robertson, polished batsman that he is, could be no more than onlooker to all this — so, for a matter of fact, had many admiring fieldsmen to be, for the ball was over and over again placed wide of their grasp.

In 1948, against Bradman's all-conquering side, Compton scored 184 in the second innings at Trent Bridge before treading on his wicket while trying to evade a bouncer from Miller; and, after deflecting a no-ball from Lindwall onto his temple, 145 not out at Old Trafford. Both innings merited chapters, both were confined to the inevitable post-war *précis*.

Then, in 1950–51, he failed repeatedly for F.R. Brown's team in Australia. Ironically, had his form displayed in 1948 and 1950–51 been reversed, England would merely have been beaten more convincingly in the former series, though probably have won the latter. Thereafter Compton was still a great batsman but never one who could rely on the early footwork. However, there were occasions when his genius seemed wholly restored.

THE COMPTON OF OLD

By John Woodcock

3 July 1954. The Pakistan bowlers were slain at Trent Bridge yesterday as no Test match bowlers have been slain since the era of Bradman, and their executioner was Compton, who in his hundredth Test innings and in his most irrepressible way put together the eighth highest score in the history of Test cricket. No higher Test match innings than Compton's has been played since Hutton made 364 in sharpest contrast against Australia at the Oval in 1938.

But only on paper can Compton's effort compare with the great innings of the past, for Pakistan, to whom one's sympathies go out, followed their faint-hearted batting on Thursday with bowling which languished beneath accepted standards. In 290 minutes England added 437 runs, and took their lead to a mountainous 401. In the last hour Pakistan reduced this to 342, thanks to a brilliant little innings by Hanif.

Pakistan, in ony their second venture against England, were unlucky in two respects. In the first place, on a pitch which gave them no glimmer of hope Fazal, the mainspring of their attack, was handicapped by a slightly strained muscle which forced him to reduce by half his run and his pace. In the second place they struck the Compton of his greatest days, and in these forbidding circumstances they dropped him when he had made but 20. Poor Imtiaz behind the wickets was the unfortunate culprit, and if ever there was a punishment out of proportion to the crime it was surely his yesterday. For the four hours following the offence he had to watch Compton plundering his countrymen with all his old and famous genius.

There came the familiar mannerisms, the daring sorties down the pitch, the incredible lateness of stroke, the uncanny improvisation, the uncertainty between wickets, and the effortless drives timed to beat the fieldsmen in the small arc in front of the wicket between cover point and wide mid-on.

By half-past two Compton had reduced Pakistan to complete impotence. The bowlers lay at his feet, baffled as to where to pitch the ball; the fielders had been turned to stone, and the strokes flowed from his bat like a river in spate.

It was at Nottingham for Australia, in 1938, that S.J. McCabe made 232 in less than four hours. This was one of the most glorious innings played on the ground, and one with which Compton's yesterday in a less orthodox way, and against far less testing bowling, was comparable in devastating and memorable stroke play.

Compton was not the day's only reveller. Simpson, without quite regathering the threads as he left them on Thursday night, reached the 100 which he had fashioned then so readily and with such charm, and Graveney played a beautiful innings full of the airs and graces of batsmanship. But let the day's figures tell their story, and let them not slip from a right context, in which the ball never lifted above the height of the stumps, in which much of the fielding if not demoralized was slow, and in which only three fit bowlers figure, one of whom, Kardar, was out of practice, and another, Khalid, only 16.

The day was only a few minutes old when Compton, through a cold, almost autumnal haze, began twiddling his bat in his hands as he likes to, and hitting the ball away with great confidence. From the Pakistan viewpoint his bat must have looked ominously wide and have sounded ominously sweet. Twenty-eight came in the first half-hour, and at five past 12 Compton hit a full pitch away to the mid-wicket boundary and hooked a long hop for 4 to put England ahead. It was strange that Kardar persevered with Khan for an hour and with Fazal for 90 minutes while the new ball approached. Neither was fresh when it became available.

Simpson, after completing his fourth Test match hundred in three hours 20 minutes with a most gracious cover drive, had hit all across Khalid and been bowled, and Graveney had at once begun to play as though he had been batting for as long as Simpson. He looked yesterday a very handsome player, fully worthy of his England cap. All his elegant, powerful strokes came into use, and before luncheon he made Compton's performance seem even sober.

After luncheon all this was changed, and Compton became the one central and dominating figure, his momentum and irresistibility rising. His partnership with Graveney, who finally drove Kardar with tremendous power chest high to extra cover, reached 154 in 85 delightful minutes, 84 of them to Graveney; 59 came in half an hour following the new ball at a quarter past two, and after batting for two hours and three-quarters Compton reached his sixteenth Test match cen-

tury — only D.G. Bradman, W.R. Hammond, and Hutton have scored more.

He proceeded really to let loose, as much as to say: "Now I'll show you a few strokes," and his next 187 runs came in 125 amazing minutes, the last 137 of them in 75 minutes. There were strokes that have a place only in Compton's repertoire, and the ball was to him the size of the moon. Inevitably there were chances, too, but the fielding became rather ragged and disconnected, and at times Compton threw his bat at everything as if keen to get out.

But with his injured knee standing up wonderfully well to the strain he could not, and with Bailey batting as though against Australia in a crisis it was five minutes to 5 before he did. Then Khalid bowled him when he had added 192 with Bailey, who had scored 27 of them, and when Compton had hit 33 4's and a 6. Twenty-five minutes later Sheppard put a merciful end to the sufferings of Pakistan.

PAKISTAN 157 and 59 for no wicket, ENGLAND 558 for 6 declared (R.T. Simpson 101, D.C.S. Compton 278, T.W. Graveney 84). PAKISTAN 157 and 272 (Hanif Mohammed 51, Maqsood Ahmed 69) lost to ENGLAND 558 for 6 declared by an innings and 129 runs.

In 1956 the Selectors (G.O. Allen, W. Wooller, L.E.G. Ames and C. Washbrook) persuaded the youngest of their number, the 41-year-old Washbrook, to play in the Headingley Test. He obliged with a fine innings of 98. For the Oval match Compton was recalled to bat, if necessary, on one leg.

COMPTON'S GREAT INNINGS

England won the toss and lost P.E. Richardson, M.C. Cowdrey and the Rev. D.S. Sheppard for 66 runs.

By John Woodcock

24 August 1956. Compton's performance came straight out of a story book. He went in when

England earlier in the day had also been struggling hard, and Australia were out for his blood. He might have been thinking of those who felt he should not have returned. Certainly no one could have been sure that he would justify his selection, and one wonders if he has ever experienced anything much more nerve racking.

But his eye still seemed wonderfully quick and dependable, and gradually he got the feel of a Test match again. Slowly, too, he realized that with care and discipline he could still do most of the things that once made him the scourge of bowlers. And he proceeded to play an innings which increased considerably in value after he was out. It was a triumph as much of character as skill, and when eventually he fell at 94 everyone must have shed a silent tear.

...Australia had been for the moment on top when Compton rolled in to see what he could do about it. He seemed keen to get there, as though embarrassed by his reception, and the clock was put back as Miller greeted him with a really quick one down the leg side. Ten minutes later he was still not off the mark, but three singles, a sweep for 4 off Benaud, and then a cover drive gave him the start he wanted. Presently he was twiddling his bat, with his hair out of place, in much the old way, and May now warmed to his task with two lovely cover drives and a force to the square leg boundary.

The pattern of the afternoon was established. Except for an hour's bowling by Benaud, Johnson relied on his seamers. May contented himself with an occasional aristocratic stroke, Compton gathered ones and twos, attempting rather more as his confidence grew, and after 57 minutes the partnership was worth 50. Now and then the bat was beaten outside the off-stump and Compton, when he was 43, was very nearly bowled playing no stroke to Lindwall. But, generally, it was delightful batting, mature and controlled, and by tea the attack was with England.

Compton had overtaken May and completed 50 in 110 minutes, and during the early evening the initiative moved more firmly towards England. May passed his fifth 50 of the summer against Australia in two hours, and the partnership realized 100 in 144 minutes. Compton was now thoroughly enjoying himself, and the crowd were enjoying him. There were more of those confidential asides to the players and umpires in which he loves to indulge. May was less intimate, more statuesque, and Australia's bowling was made to look more amiable than it probably was. The pitch, apart from an occasional ball that bounced higher than expected, was now placid, and England's batting was a joy to watch.

For a long while there were only two alarms. Compton, when he had made 69, was dropped at slip by Archer off Miller, trying to drive and hitting perhaps slightly across the line. The ball travelled fast and Archer got both hands to it above his head. This was just before the new ball was taken at 179, and 16 runs later when Lindwall was bowling with it Compton only just cleared Craig at mid-wicket with an onside push.

As six o'clock came and went, and a quarter past approached, it seemed that Australia had failed to take their chance. Compton, as weary as he obviously was, was full of familiar mannerisms and he still found the energy for some vivid strokes. It looked for all the world as though he and May, who was now playing for the morrow, would see out the day. The landslide was started off by a fine low catch at leg slip by Davidson off R.G. Archer which sent back Compton. The latter's passing was not altogether surprising for he was by then lame and tired...

Compton was out at 222 for four, the close-of-play score 223 for seven.

ENGLAND 247 (P.B.H. May 83 not out, D.C.S. Compton 94; R.G. Archer 5 for 53) and 182 for 3 declared (D.S. Sheppard 62) drew with AUSTRALIA 202 (K.R. Miller 61) and 27 for 5.

On this occasion Laker's match figures were 50–26–88–7.

COMPTON ROLLS BACK THE YEARS

By Kenneth Gregory

2 July 1957. For 10 memorable minutes at Lord's yesterday, Compton rolled back the years to his vintage summer of 1947 and gave as dazzling an exhibition of stroke play as one could wish to see...When he entered, warmly welcomed by a small crowd, just before one o'clock, he announced his mood with an impudent late cut. He then pushed Tattersall square off his legs for two, pulled Wharton savagely for four, and avoided the next ball which rose quickly in masterly style. A slash over gully having suggested fallibility, Compton next checked his forward stroke after Tattersall had beaten him through the air, and then advanced down the wicket to that bowler, his drive leaving even so active a fieldsman as Statham at extra cover motionless.

A near squatter from Wharton found his reactions sufficiently in command to produce a decisive dab, and then down the wicket he went again for another superb extra cover drive. A further turn of the wrists followed a moment later by a lofted pull, and Washbrook paid Compton the compliment of bringing back Statham. A fierce maiden over compelled Compton to observe the proprieties, and then his middle stump was knocked yards out of the ground by a ball which found him unable to move in time. As he left for the pavilion Compton grinned appreciatively at the bowler and Statham bowed low.

Neville Cardus was one of Compton's warmest admirers; a few sentences written in the Adelaide of February 1947 are offered as epilogue.

When the day began the heat was such a swamp of sweat and humidity that it would be appropriate if I were to address this message "from darkest Australia". [As Cardus sweltered, England was snowbound; when a train got stuck for four hours just outside Redhill, its driver tried, unsuccessfully, to chip ice from the line with a piece of wood.]

Compton, though quiet and for a long time only decorative, played forward defensive strokes as easefully and lightly as though batting on a lawn with flower beds near and not to be broken rudely.

A dazzling attempt [by Tallon] at stumping an inch from the bails caused Compton to squirm as though electricity-generated, but his right foot did not go over the line.

...another champagne drive of Compton's, this time through the covers from a ball of Dooland's so replete with spin that as it flashed to the fence the ball gathered the momentum of a stone thrown on ice.

After tea Compton's innings threatened an effortless, even a magnanimous plundering of the attack. His drives were delightful. Though of hammered power, the strength in them was lissome and young. All the wrinkles of yesterday were forgotten. It came as a shock to see him return a ball to Lindwall impulsively. As he realised what he had done Compton smote his person with his bat...

At Adelaide in 1947 Compton made a hundred in each innings; but, as Dudley Carew had written years before, Compton was such a good batsman that figures were a mere irrelevance.

KEITH ROSS MILLER
Victoria and New South Wales

The war was over — in Europe since 7 May, in the Far East since 14 August. Lord's would therefore celebrate in the only way possible with a match between England and the Dominions. Prior to this, five unofficial Tests had been played, England v. Australia, with two wins to each side and the other game drawn. The "visitors'" star turned out to be one Flying Officer K.R. Miller, RAAF, who, aged just 20, had some years earlier made 108 for Victoria against the South Australia of Grimmett. "Don't get on to the back foot against that infernal top spinner," seemed to be the answer. In command of England during the summer of 1945 was Squadron Leader W.R. Hammond.

Not all cricket correspondents were present at Lord's for the England v. Dominions game. Neville Cardus was in Australia broadcasting on music and putting the finishing touches to his *Autobiography*, Major E.W. Swanton, R.A, was readjusting himself:

A few days after the Japanese surrender our camp at Kanburi began to assemble frequently for news bulletins. Emissaries, we heard, were flying hither and thither, instructions and encouragement were being relayed from Governments to POWs; the air was heavy with the most momentous happenings. Moreover, many of those present had had no news of the outside world for months, or longer; yet, no item commanded so much attention as the Test Match at Manchester.

I had, by then, already taken my first walk for three and a half years as a free man. We found ourselves in a Thai village on the edge of the jungle. In the little café our hosts politely turned on the English programme. Yes, we were at Old Trafford, and a gentleman called Cristofani was getting a hundred...

The date was 22 August, D.R. Cristofani had reached 100 in 105 minutes from the bowling of W.E. Phillipson, R. Pollard, George Pope and D.V.P. Wright, and if Major Swanton was hearing the commentary from Old Trafford live, then he must have been listening at 3.15 p.m. Double British Summer Time, for it was approximately at that hour that Cristofani reached his hundred.

By R.B. Vincent

First Day

27 August 1945. A splendid innings by M.P. Donnelly, the New Zealand left-handed batsman, was in the main responsible for the Dominions presenting a score of 307 in the first innings of their three-day match against England at Lord's on Saturday. At the close of play England had lost three wickets for 28 runs.

A.L. Hassett, to whom the spectators at Lord's would have been pleased to give tribute towards the end of the season, was unfortunately unable to play because of illness, leaving the Dominion side to be captained by the adaptable L.N. Constantine.

D.R. Fell and H.S. Craig started the day's batting, chiefly to the bowling of W.E. Phillipson, on a wicket which obviously was to give little encouragement to the bowlers. Craig made many pleasant strokes with a nice flexibility of wrist, and the score had been taken easily to 37 before D.V.P. Wright, in the first of his spells from the Nursery end, had him caught at the wicket, and the words "caught Griffith" inevitably brought to memory recent happenings at Old Trafford.* Not so long afterwards J. Pettiford was bowled in trying to hook a ball to which he got only the inside edge of his bat. This brought in K.R. Miller, careful at first to play forward to smother any spin which the pitch might offer, and at luncheon, after a brief delay of a quarter of an hour during rain, the score stood at 90 for three, Craig having given a catch to J.G.W. Davies at cover-point, the last man in the world to whom to give such an opportunity.

Soon after the interval Miller was out, as he has been twice before, to E. Hollies, and England were spared the anxiety of more trouble when Constantine was caught at mid-off. Half the side was then out for 109, and the stage was set up for magnificent partnership of recovery between Donnelly and C.G. Pepper. Donnelly for a period showed the defensive stroke, which he plays correctly, but he gradually warmed to the pleasure of attacking Hollies, and short balls from Phillipson went to the boundary on either side of the wicket. Pepper, playing to the pitch of the ball, did his part nobly enough, and together they added 120 runs in 100 minutes before W.R. Hammond snapped a catch from Pepper in the slips with an ease which is all his own. After that it was Donnelly, who scored 19 runs in one over off Hollies, all the way until he was out to a well-

. . . .

* In the recent England v. Australia "Victory Test" at Old Trafford, Vincent had watched S.C. Griffith and had written "more alert and intelligent wicketkeeping has seldom been seen for many a long year".

judged catch running back by the bowler. He had been in for just over three hours and had hit two 6s and 18 4s.

England had scored but eight runs when J.D. Robertson misjudged Constantine's slower ball, and with L.B. Fishlock out soon afterward, England's batting order was altered — always a dangerous move at the end of a day. As it was, only Phillipson's wicket was lost.

THE DOMINIONS 307 (H.S. Craig 56, M.P. Donnelly 133, C.G. Pepper 51; D.V.P. Wright 5 for 90), ENGLAND 28 for 3.

Second Day

28 August 1945. A true report of a cricket match should be factual, a record of events as they were presented to the observer by the players, but there come the rare occasions when one cricketer dominates everything that has occurred during the day.

Just such a spectacle was presented to those who were at Lord's yesterday to see W.R. Hammond bat with a power and majesty which could never have been excelled by his predecessors, for all must grant him his place over a long period of years as one of the greatest of batsmen. The match was between England and the Dominions, a suitable ending to this year's big cricket, and when play was continued on the second day yesterday England, with three wickets down, were 279 runs behind.

S.C. Griffith, who had been sent in on Saturday night when wickets were tumbling, played his part nobly yesterday morning, but even so the score board read dismally 52 for four when he was out. There then entered Hammond, and one could clearly sense the anxiety felt by the attacking side whether this was to be the deciding moment of the game. Hammond played one streaky stroke through the slips off R.G. Williams, but from then on he dictated the run of the play. James Langridge stayed in long enough to show some nice strokes before, with the score at 78, he missed a full pitch, and at 96, with six men out, H. Gimblett was caught at deep mid-off.

How well W.J. Edrich, who came in next, acquitted himself cannot be measured in the runs he scored, for he stayed in during a most critical time while Hammond, over after over, was killing the bowling. Hammond was particularly severe on D.R. Cristofani, and there were times when no place in the Pavilion was safe from the fury of his off-drives, the luncheon interval arriving with the score at 152, of which Hammond had then made 57. No sooner were they out again than Hammond drove another ball into the Pavilion, with Edrich still modestly curtailing his own hitting powers. Hammond's selection of the suitable ball to hit — and hit it he did terrifically hard — and his perfectly shaped defensive strokes which, with his sense of timing, often found runs were those of the man who can make all other batsmen look second class.

The new ball, after Pepper and Cristofani had spun the old one to their bone, had no effect on either Hammond or Edrich, until at last Hammond, tired as well he might be, leant out to a ball and was stumped. The partnership had added 177 runs, and Hammond himself had been in while 221 were added. That he hit three 6's and ten 4's is merely incidental to a display which was true glory to watch.

After this England's innings petered out, with Edrich having nursed the bowling before he tried to hit the ball into the Edgware Road only to be quietly caught in the slips.

The Dominions, when they went in again after all this, found that their batsmen had a lead of only 20 runs to play with, an advantage which

MILLER   Here the ageing magnifico; as batsman, bowler or fielder, the most exciting cricketer of his generation.

was increased quietly by D.R. Fell and H. Craig until at 49 Fell was clean bowled playing back to a ball which he must afterwards have wished he had attacked. Seven runs later England were rid of an awkward customer in J. Pettiford, who was bowled by a leg-break, but there was K.R. Miller to follow and to score so quickly that the Dominions well regained their advantage. Craig was caught by the vigilant Hammond at short slip, yet the bowlers in the last three-quarters of an hour could find no flight or spin to prevent Miller from sweeping the ball to leg or forcing away balls of quite reasonable length to the off, once treating himself, in the manner of Hammond, to a full-blooded blow over the long-on boundary. And so a grand day's cricket, which was watched by a crowd of nearly 20,000, ended with the Dominions 165 runs ahead with seven wickets yet to fall.

THE DOMINIONS 307 and 145 for 3 (K.R. Miller 61 not out), ENGLAND 287 (W.R. Hammond 121).

Third Day

29 August 1945. The Dominions beat England with only 10 minutes left for play at Lord's yesterday by 45 runs in a match which will be long remembered by those who were lucky enough to see it.

Such fierce hitting as that of K.R. Miller, with 6's at one time more common than the mere 4's, such perfection of batsmanship as that of W.R. Hammond in each innings, and so close a finish after it all, was seldom to be seen at any time in the greatest days of cricket. In one respect only did the game, played for the most part in sunshine before large crowds, leave an unhappy memory. Those who now are privileged to sit in the front of the pavilion at Lord's committed a breach of manners when they failed to rise to their feet to acclaim Hammond, a tribute which was more than well earned.

When play was continued in the morning with the Dominions already 165 runs ahead with seven wickets yet to fall in their second innings, the tempo of the game was at once set by Miller. He immediately set about Hollies, first landing a ball into the Pavilion and then with a fuller stroke driving it high into the gallery. Throughout the battery that was to come Wright bowled well from the Nursery end, keeping Miller reasonably quiet, but once at the other end Miller seemed intent on demolishing the pavilion. Donnelly was bowled by a ball pitched well up to him at 200, and Pepper was out nine runs later, but when Langridge came on three 6's were struck off him in his first over, two by Miller and one by Constantine. One began to wonder whether Lord's was a big enough ground for such terrific hitting, which in the opinion of one who has known the ground for over 60 years has never been seen before. Miller during the first 75 minutes of play yesterday had struck 100 runs, and there was a time when Hammond to guard the boundary to the bowling of Davies had to dispense with a slip field. At last Miller, who had been in for two hours and three-quarters and who had hit seven 6's and thirteen 4's, was caught at extra cover-point, and an innings which will certainly be remembered for all time by those who saw it came to an end. Thereafter the wickets fell fairly quickly, the whole side being out at a quarter past two.

England's rate of scoring to win the match need not have been alarming, but they could not afford to lose a wicket, especially that of so good a left-handed batsman as Fishlock, so wantonly as when, with only 25 runs scored, he was run out off a no-ball. Gimblett had started well enough with a slash through the covers off Williams, who not long after retired with a strain. The purpose of England's captain was clear when he sent Edrich in at the fall of the first wicket, and things were going well until at 42 Gimblett was bowled by a googly.

The time was then 10 minutes to three and there entered Hammond to join Edrich in a partnership which was obviously one way or the other to have a deciding influence on the game. Hammond's attitude was one of extreme composure, with no hurry or flurry, and in Edrich he had an efficient and quiet supporter. The first 100 runs had been scored in 80 minutes, during which time Hammond had already treated himself to a 6, now a fashionable enough stroke, and both the clock and the bowlers were being mastered when, with the score at 128, Edrich flashed with a flat bat at one of those balls which Ellis bowls obliquely across the wicket. Hammond, on the other hand, played that ball always with his right leg well behind the line of the ball and his bat immaculately straight.

The score at the end of England's second hour of batting was 150, a fair enough rate with the knowledge that the pace is always likely to increase at the end of an innings, if the batsmen have established a winning position. Hammond, with some help from Robertson and Langridge, gave them that hope so long as he was in. No contrivance of bowling could shake his determination, master at that moment as he was of the situation. Suddenly the time arrived, as it does so often in cricket, when the game turned, Hammond for once misjudging the flight of a ball to be stumped. In matches of first-class importance

ENGLAND v. THE DOMINIONS
Lord's, 25, 27, 28 August 1945

THE DOMINIONS
1st innings

D.R.Fell	c Griffiths b Wright	12
H.S. Craig	c Davies b Phillipson	56
J. Pettiford	b Davies	1
K.R. Miller	lbw b Hollies	26
M.P. Donnelly	c & b Hollies	133
L.N. Constantine	c Hollies b Wright	5
C.G. Pepper	c Hammond b Wright	51
D.R. Cristofani	lbw b Edrich	6
R.G. Williams	lbw b Wright	11
R.S. Ellis	b Wright	0
C.D. Bremner	not out	1
Extras	(lb 3, w 2)	5
Total		307

2nd innings

D.R.Fell	b Davies	28
H.S. Craig	c Hammond b Davies	32
J. Pettiford	b Wright	6
K.R. Miller	c Langridge b Wright	185
M.P. Donnelly	b Wright	29
L.N. Constantine	c Fishlock b Hollies	40
C.G. Pepper	c Robertson b Hollies	1
D.R. Cristofani	b Wright	5
R.G. Williams	c Hammond b Wright	0
R.S. Ellis	st Griffiths b Hollies	0
C.D. Bremner	not out	0
Extras	(b 6, lb 8, nb 1)	10
Total		336

ENGLAND BOWLING

	O	M	R	W	O	M	R	W
Phillipson	16	2	40	1	2	1	1	0
Edrich	9	1	19	1	3	0	13	0
Wright	30	2	90	5	30.1	6	105	5
Hollies	20.2	3	86	2	29	8	115	3
Langridge	6	1	24	0	8	0	57	0
Davies	22	9	43	1	13	3	35	2

ENGLAND
1st innings

L.B. Fishlock	c Pettiford b Ellis	12
J.D. Robertson	lbw b Constantine	4
James Langridge	lbw b Cristofani	28
W.E. Phillipson	b Pepper	0
S.C. Griffith	c Bremner b Williams	15
W.R. Hammond	st Bremner b Pepper	121
H. Gimblett	c Pettiford b Cristofani	11
W.J. Edrich	c Pepper b Cristofani	78
J.G.W. Davies	lbw b Pepper	1
D.V.P. Wright	lbw b Pepper	0
E. Hollies	not out	0
Extras	(b 7, lb 6, w 2, nb 2)	17
Total		287

2nd innings

L.B. Fishlock	run out	7
J.D. Robertson	c Fell b Pettiford	5
James Langridge	b Pepper	15
W.E. Phillipson	run out	14
S.C. Griffith	c Pepper b Pettiford	36
W.R. Hammond	st Bremner b Cristofani	102
H. Gimblett	b Pepper	30
W.J. Edrich	c Pepper b Ellis	31
J.G.W. Davies	b Pepper	56
D.V.P. Wright	b Cristofani	0
E. Hollies	not out	0
Extras	(b 6, lb 5, nb 4)	15
Total		311

THE DOMINIONS BOWLING

	O	M	R	W	O	M	R	W
Miller	1	0	2	0	5	0	28	0
Williams	22	4	49	1	2	0	11	0
Ellis	4	3	4	1	22	4	54	1
Cristofani	23	4	82	3	21.3	1	64	2
Constantine	15	2	53	1	6	0	27	0
Pettiford	5	0	23	0	14	3	45	2
Pepper	18	3	57	4	33	13	67	3

THE DOMINIONS WON BY 45 RUNS

Hobbs has made a century in each innings six times; this was the seventh occasion on which Hammond has achieved that remarkable feat.

Soon afterwards Langridge was out and it was left to those two fine products of Cambridge, Griffith and Davies, to make a fight of what seemed to be a dead match. Seasoned in good cricket, and quite undaunted by any such occasion, they played the bowling on its merits to add 85 runs before Griffith was seventh man out with three quarters of an hour left for play and 74 runs more wanted to win. Davies stuck to his work nobly, but there was nothing to follow, and 10 minutes before time the last wicket fell.

Legend has it that the author and subject of the following eulogy were apt to whistle and hum themes from Beethoven to test the other's knowledge. The innings in question was 141 not out.

By Neville Cardus

4 February 1947, Adelaide. In two hours and a half Keith Miller made a glorious century. He was a young eagle among crows and daws, but then they clipped his wings. In more prosaic and technical language Yardley, by bowling at his leg-stump to an appropriately placed field, cramped his strokes and possibly exposed limitations in his onside method. He was obliged to spend two hours over making his last 40 runs. It is hard to believe he hit only nine 4's. But these facts of utility are for the statisticians of the game, and were duly noted by Mr Ferguson. It was not necessary to look at the scoring board at all to gauge the essential quality of his cricket; indeed the solid wall of a score board could not possibly catch the reflection of batsmanship so brilliant and swift in movement and so magnificently masculine in easeful, concealed strength.

For long his strokes were nearly all alive and hard, and they were all 4's in the estimation of the accountancy of the game's true genius. Even his defensive shots were positive, struck with a bat of lovely swing and curve of wrists, adding lustré as

well as direction. To a quick ball just short of a length, the kind which usually can only be resisted as though by some blunt instrument, he played far forward with the piercing aim of an arrow, the left leg and the bat thrust out thrillingly, the body inclined and vital with the stab of aggression. It is not usual to see this classic forward action in a modern Australian player; it is a stroke out of Debrett's, lordly and pedigreed. His late cut, too, is a gleam or flash from the golden age; and his attitude to cricket is almost as obsolete as chivalry. Only as a last resort does he play defensively, and he does so with reluctance, tossing the mane of his black hair backwards like a young horse chafing on the bit.

In the first half hour of the morning he scored 40. The first ball bowled by Wright, a no-ball, was swept for six to square leg, and there was little effort though the sweep of the stroke was dramatically opportunist. For once in a way we could feel a difference of light and shade at one end of the wicket. Johnson reached 50 and was a good craftsman, but he was divested of presence, and every other batsman suffered equal obliteration. When Yardley first bowled, Miller thrust straight for four a ball never destined to be plundered, and another ball of much potential power of penetration by Bedser was likewise treated; the bat was straight and the right foot a living stanchion.

A massacre of the English attack seemed certain, if such a bloodthirsty word can be applied to batsmanship of such patrician manners. But Yardley now bowled on the leg stump; Hammond was at fine leg and there was a long leg as well as a man at forward short leg. So accurately did Yardley aim, so tight was his length, that even Miller was shorn both of runs and strokes. After scoring 67 in 75 minutes he had to be content with another 22 in 80 minutes, by which time the tail had arrived, and now he pranced and charged at everything. This, of course, was good and necessary bowling policy for England as a cricket team engaged in a Test match, but also it was as though a Kreisler had been deprived of his Strad and given a one-string fiddle instead.

MARTIN PATERSON DONNELLY
Wellington and Warwickshire

The University match of 1946 was memorable only for the batting of Donnelly, who played the second of his great innings at Lord's, the first having been for the Dominions v. England the previous year. Cambridge were the more immature side, only one man having passed his 26th birthday, whereas Oxford had six. D.H. Macindoe, the Oxford captain, had appeared in the University match of 1937 at a time when Donnelly was winning golden opinions with the New Zealand tourists.

The Cambridge bowlers were not disgraced at Lord's in 1946, twelve Oxford batsmen in the match (including Donnelly in the second innings) being dismissed for 108 runs. But the batting had little to offer, 286 runs from 1,007 balls suggesting acceptance of the inevitable. The match figures of three Oxford bowlers said everything: Macindoe 55–29–82–3, B.H. Travers (another medium-pacer) 38.5–20–57–6 and the slow left-arm J.N. Bartlett 35–20–28–7.

By R.B. Vincent

8 July 1946. The University cricket match which was begun at Lord's on Saturday surely recaptured some of its former dignity, for even if the teams bore signs of the effect of the years lost during the war, there was a marked indication of a revival of interest in the game among followers of cricket in general.

The day's play, during which Cambridge scored 201 and Oxford 99 for three wickets, was never very thrilling, but it has at least left the issue for the moment reasonably open, though Cambridge are yet to rid themselves of the fearsome Donnelly. Among those who watched the game was the Mackinnon of Mackinnon who played for Cambridge 76 years ago. [He died on 17 February 1947 in his 99th year.]

Cambridge's start on the most perfect of wickets was shocking. First Lacy-Scott swished at a ball on the off side to be caught in the slips; Bodkin, the captain, missed a straight ball and was leg-before-wicket; and when Willatt was caught at short leg three wickets were down for 13 miserable runs. If Macindoe is no longer quite the bowler we remember before the war, he was making some pace off the pitch and on the whole kept a tidy length. Mischler and Shuttleworth, the former with some well-placed strokes to leg, slowly dragged their side out of immediate horror before Bloy had Shuttleworth caught at the wicket. Cambridge lost yet another wicket soon after luncheon, when Mischler hit intemperately against the break, five men then being out for 98 runs.

With Pepper and Conradi in together it seemed that Cambridge had a period of grace offered to them when they might offensively have recovered much of the lost ground. Yet the batsmen continued to allow fieldsmen to be set unnaturally close to the bat, with no one to guard the deep, and the bowler once having to run after a ball which had unexpectedly been driven straight. Still the score had crept to 125 before Conradi misdirected a blow at a short ball, and at long last when Trapnell joined Pepper a belated intention was shown to attack the bowling. During this time the fielding of Donnelly at cover-point was continually to be admired. It would be difficult to estimate how many runs he saved.

Pepper at 156 was clean bowled, leaving Trapnell heroically enough on the search for chances of scoring. It was the left-handed Bartlett who finished off the innings by tempting Trapnell once too often to brave the cow shot and then taking the last two wickets. Looking back on the innings as a whole, one had a feeling that Cambridge had at one time blindly ignored an invitation by their opponents to put themselves on much better terms. They were, in fact, not sufficiently experienced for the occasion.

Cambridge, when their turn came to attack the Oxford batsmen, also started off with a cluster of fieldsmen in the slips, and the ball was pitched too wide to insist on it being played. With Rumbold static and obdurate, Sale got along with the business of run-making, 36 being on the board when suddenly Griffiths surprised Rumbold with a straight ball, and at 47 the dangerous Maudsley was bowled by Trapnell, who at that time was bowling better than anyone had done during the day.

So there entered Donnelly to provide a double left-handed combination against Mills when he came on with his leg-breaks. Mills did once beat Donnelly on the forward stroke, but though the wicket-keeper whipped off the bails the back foot had not been dragged over the crease. It was Trapnell who at 70 had Sale caught at second slip, and thereafter Donnelly was obviously content to wait until to-day to continue an innings which may make all the difference to the match.

Close: CAMBRIDGE 201 (N.M. Mischler 42, B.M.W. Trapnell 41; J.N. Bartlett 4 for 12), OXFORD 99 for 3 (R. Sale 42, M.P. Donnelly 29 not out).

Second Day

10 July 1946. Oxford at Lord's yesterday brushed aside for a time any further suggestion that Cambridge could challenge their expected all-round superiority, nobly as the less experienced and younger Cambridge side had played out their game, and at the close of play, which was prolonged until 7.30, with seven wickets still in hand, they wanted only 11 runs to win.

The early part of the day unquestionably belonged to Donnelly, a batsman in any company of outstanding class. His strokes are so perfectly timed, with never that sign of the sliced blow so common to the left-hander, and his placing of the ball is so exquisite that one may be allowed to believe that the best of the University bowlers — even S.M.J. Woods — would have had difficulty in keeping him in order.

The Cambridge bowlers in the morning, faced, as they must have felt, by an awkward proposition, did well enough so long as this terrible Donnelly could be kept to the non-striking end. The score was taken from 99 to 120 before Bloy was bowled by Bodkin, a left-handed bowler of some pace who well might have used himself more continually, but still Donnelly was scoring runs from off-drives which demanded a ring of fieldsmen. Nor did Griffiths, who has bowled well in this match, subdue him with the new ball, the straight and full blade of the bat driving it away with ease to the off boundary. He made 71 runs in the hour yesterday morning, and was advancing with never the sign of a hurry to a score which might have surpassed the highest ever made in a university match when suddenly he played a trifle late to a ball of reasonable length.

The rest of Oxford's innings was tentative, though prolonged, and Cambridge were allowed use of the wicket rather surprisingly only 60 runs behind. Their start this time was nearly as disastrous as it had been in the first innings. Their opening batsmen looked strangely uncomfortable to Macindoe and to Travers, who unaccountably made the ball rise from the pitch. The result was that Willatt was caught at short-leg, Bodkin caught in the gully, and, with Lacy-Scott out to another jumper, three wickets were down and Cambridge had gleaned but 27 runs.

Runs were coming again until Bartlett, who can flight the ball, had Shuttleworth leg-before-wicket, and when he bowled Pepper half the side was out for 62, only one run on balance on the two days' play. The position was too bad for Conradi, a left-handed batsman of ideas, to endure, yet in the end Oxford had only 68 runs to make to win in the fourth innings. They lost two wickets for 25 runs and, greatly more than that, Donnelly followed at once to be caught in the slips. In spite of the gracious extension of time Oxford were never quite able to finish the game off yesterday.

At 57 for 3 wickets at the close, Oxford soon won on the third day.

CAMBRIDGE UNIVERSITY 201 and 127 (J.N. Bartlett 3 for 16) lost to OXFORD UNIVERSITY 261 (M.P. Donnelly 142; W.H. Griffiths 5 for 84) and 69 for 4 wickets by 6 wickets.

In retrospect, the most interesting event on the first day was reported in an adjoining column of *The Times*. Two old Cambridge Blues, J.G.W. Davies and B.H. Valentine, both made hundreds as Kent romped to 487 at Colchester, Essex obliging with 153 overs.

LORD'S, 1947

The summer of 1947 was one of continuous sunshine (or so one remembers, but wrongly), of spinners, the visiting South Africans and Compton and Edrich. As every schoolboy knows how many runs and hundreds the former made, let us link them together for posterity: 7,355 runs and 30 hundreds. Meanwhile in the Parks at Oxford Donnelly reigned supreme, as he would on 16 July at Lord's.

By R.B. Vincent

17 July 1947. The match between the Gentlemen and Players regained a great measure of its former glory at Lord's yesterday. Two teams worthy of contemporary English cricket had been invited to play, and the public were quick to realize that this was indeed a game of cricket to be watched.

Test matches and trial games were forgotten for a moment and grandly the cricketers answered to the occasion. If a great proportion of the onlookers left the ground in the evening acclaiming the batsmanship of M.P. Donnelly, an equal number must have remembered one spell of bowling by Wright to the apparently invincible Edrich. And so at the end of a day of enjoyment the Players had scored 67 for two wickets in reply to the Gentlemen's first innings total of 302.

Some may decry the quality of our bowlers; others may suggest that they will be encouraged in their art by having a more comforting ball with which to bowl. Certainly Butler and Gladwin yesterday disclosed no tremendous possibilities, but they pegged manfully at their work — one of the greatest qualities of a bowler.

The Gentlemen had what should have been a nice advantage by winning the toss on a wicket which could in no way be unfriendly to them, but they had an unpleasant shock when Pawson, with only seven runs on the board, moved his bat a little negligently to a ball outside the off stump and was caught at the wicket. Willatt was so uncertain to the ball going away from him on the leg side that Ames, the Players' captain, moved himself from first slip to a more anticipatory position.

Edrich, after a short period of decent exploration, advanced to the attack, checked in the matter of run-getting by some fast fielding by his friend Compton in the region of long-on. He found his opportunity, however, to lie back to thump the ball past cover-point, until Wright bowled him a series of overs, drawing him out and as often as not deceiving him with spin. Willatt, patiently batting, had just struck Walsh, bowling left-handed over the wicket, to the off boundary when he was bowled by a ball coming in to him more sharply than he had expected, and at the luncheon interval the score stood at 63.

A period afterwards, with Edrich still tamed by Wright, soon took life when Donnelly, never hurrying, but always sure whether he would force the ball off his back foot or play out to it, scurried the rate of scoring. When he had made 39 he should have been caught off his glove from a ball from Wright; yet for a time, with Edrich now in full flow, 86 runs were added in an hour's play.

At last, after some previous appeals, Wright had Edrich, as he had always intended to do, leg-before-wicket. The score then stood at 155, and 15 runs later R.T. Simpson was caught in the slips. N.W.D. Yardley greeted the occasion by hitting the first ball he received for 4, and there was every sign of a long partnership when he played a stroke of no known pattern and was bowled. Still there was Donnelly, an analysis of whose strokes, though pleasant, must be proscribed by space. He had a feeling of the exact pace of the wicket and a precise knowledge of what ball to expect. His drives to the off were framed as if he had asked a bowler in the nets to give him just such a ball, and anything short of a length was sent with a short-armed blow, final and counting four runs. His runs in the circumstances were all that mattered, and the other distinguished Gentlemen must excuse the recorder if not sufficient attention is paid to their exploits.

The score sheet was unusual. Edrich and Donnelly between them made 241, seven other Gentlemen 19. To put it another way, the highest Test innings of R.T. Simpson, N.W.D. Yardley, T.E. Bailey, F.R. Brown and S.C. Griffith would one day be 156 not out, 99, 134 not out, 79 and 140. For the Gentlemen at Lord's in 1947 they made 4, 9, 0, 0 and 2. Donnelly made his 162 out of 243, and hit 26 fours.

THE GENTLEMEN 302 (W.J. Edrich 79, M.P. Donnelly 162 not out) and 209 drew with THE PLAYERS 334 for 8 declared (C. Washbrook 101, D.G.W. Fletcher 77) and 3 for none. There was some rain and much bad light.

SIR LEONARD HUTTON
Yorkshire

Hutton achieved a perfection of style equalled by few batsmen; his greatness could be appreciated even when he was not scoring. He was, among opening batsmen, the legitimate successor to Hobbs, but their careers were different. Hutton played for Yorkshire when he was 17, Hobbs made his debut for Surrey at 22 — Hutton retired through ill-health before he was 40, Hobbs batted on into cricketing old age. When Hutton retired he had played seven fewer innings than Hobbs at the same age and had scored 5,000 runs more.

One Hutton record (for which he was not responsible) will probably never be rivalled: in five successive England v. Australia series, *The Times* employed five correspondents to appraise Hutton as batsman and, finally, as captain: 1946–7 Neville Cardus; 1948 R.B. Vincent; 1950–51 R.C. Robertson-Glasgow; 1953 Geoffrey Green; and 1954–5 John Woodcock.

In the Second Test at Sydney in 1946–7, Hutton played his greatest innings — 37.

By Neville Cardus

18 December 1946, Sydney. England's innings began with a radiance of stroke play by Hutton which elevated a match mainly of mass production and utility to the realms of fine art. He survived an appeal for leg before first ball [from Miller], then in swift and most easeful sequence he rippled the sunlit field by stylish drives to the on off the pads, quick and wonderfully late. The curve of his body over and into the hits was lovely. Then Miller bumped short stuff at him and once he narrowly escaped being caught at the wicket while ducking. A forcing hit from the back foot off a ball of good length from Miller bruised the fence; in less than half an hour Hutton achieved six boundaries, each an adornment and honour to cricket, and England's score sped to 49. Upon the heavy care-worn face of modern Test matches this glorious batsmanship came as a visitation and flush of the rarefied spirit of those who die young because the gods love them. And in the last over before luncheon the cruellest bolt of mischief brought Hutton down to the prosaic earth; he attempted another forcing back stroke off Miller, and, after hitting the ball, lost grip of his bat with one hand and the uncontrolled swing of it broke his wicket. This was a crying shame, challenging justice and philosophy. But art, so we tried to console ourselves, is not a matter of numbers and duration, and this innings by Hutton will be remembered.

The Brisbane Test of December 1950 was the first between England and Australia for which an available Bradman had not been chosen since Sydney just 22 years previously. The MCC tour of 1950–51 was also the first to see a cricket correspondent of *The Times* sent to Australia, though most newspapers had taken the hint from the body-line season and had done so in 1936–7. Accordingly, R.B. Vincent travelled with the cricketers on the *Stratheden*, his fellow journalists including R.C. Robertson-Glasgow of *The Observer*. "Beau" Vincent — his given names were Richard Beaumont — and "Crusoe" were firm friends, the latter seeing Vincent's writing as reflecting "the soul of cricket; its dignity and humour; its old age and perpetual youth; and he has a unique gift of transferring to print, without loss to either side, the inconsequent wisdom of conversation".

However, Vincent's spiritual home was Lord's — Manchester was far distant; he reported from Perth and Adelaide in October, and attended an Iverson press conference at Melbourne in November. Iverson was Australia's new mystery bowler who performed with a folded-down finger grip. "For the googly," Vincent assured *Times* readers, "he points his index finger towards long leg; for the top spinner he points it straight at the stumps; for the leg spinner, which he has only learnt in the past eighteen months, he points it towards third man." Which seemed not to have helped those members of the MCC party who took *The Times* airmail edition. Vincent

The First Test

First Day

AUSTRALIA
1st innings

J. Moroney	c Hutton b Bailey	0
A.R. Morris	lbw b Bedser	25
R.N. Harvey	c Evans b Bedser	74
K.R. Miller	c McIntyre b Wright	15
A.L. Hassett	b Bedser	8
S.J.E. Loxton	c Evans b Brown	24
R.R. Lindwall	c Bedser b Bailey	41
D. Tallon	c Simpson b Brown	5
I.W. Johnson	c Simpson b Bailey	23
W.A. Johnston	c Hutton b Bedser	1
J. Iverson	not out	1
Extras	(b 5, lb 3, nb 3)	11
Total		228

Fall of wickets: 1–0, 2–69, 3–116, 4–118, 5–129, 6–156, 7–172, 8–219, 9–226, 10–228.

ENGLAND BOWLING (8-ball overs)

	O	M	R	W
Bailey	12	4	28	3
Bedser	16.5	4	45	4
Wright	16	0	81	1
Brown	11	0	63	2

watched Miller make 214 out of a New South Wales score of 509 for three at Sydney, and then collapsed, so leaving the joys of country cricket at Newcastle and Lismore to Reuter. By the end of November, *The Times* had a Special Correspondent — Robertson-Glasgow — in Brisbane, Vincent retiring from the paper.

Robertston-Glasgow summed up his own writing: "I had always laughed when playing cricket [for Oxford University, Somerset and the Gentlemen], except when slip fielders showed signs of lumbago, and I saw no reason to stop laughing when I wrote about it." A scholar of Charterhouse, and later of Corpus Christi College, Oxford, "Crusoe" was a classicist.

Because Sir Leonard Hutton enjoyed Robertson-Glasgow's writing, he is here invited to share his own triumphs, and those of Bedser, with an at times anarchic view of the games in which both appeared.

By R.C. Robertson-Glasgow

1 December 1950, Brisbane. During a day's cricket of the utmost interest to an enthusiastic and impartial crowd numbering 15,000 Australia were dismissed by England in the first Test match here for 228. Washbrook and Simpson then went forth to bat when less than a quarter of an hour remained. But the light from a sun rarely free from cloud was failing fast and the 13 cricketers and two umpires withdrew till the morrow.

It would be as unfair to the batsmen as to the bowlers not to say that this was England's day. How far England's bowlers were helped by a pitch so recently considered innocent can hardly be assessed till it has received the speed of Lindwall and Miller, the variety of Johnston, and the wiles of Iverson and Johnson. Again rain is prowling around, but the weather prophets in Brisbane have long ago gone out of serious business.

Yet this much is certain, that F.R. Brown and his men played as a team of happy unity and strong purpose, which went far towards regaining the confidence of the doubters and confirming the adherence of the faithful. It was, indeed, a team performance. There was the morning Bedser, solid and dependable; the afternoon Bedser, a bowler not far inferior to Tate in speed from the pitch and accuracy of direction. There was the close backward leg catch by Hutton off Bailey which sent back Moroney in the first over. There was Bailey's bowling with the new ball late in the afternoon, at its best just when it seemed that Lindwall and Johnson might revive the dying innings. There was the interest in Wright's spin. How dimly do Wright's bowling figures mirror his value. There were Brown's two wickets, both taken when the batsmen were waxing troublesome, and there was Evans's wicketkeeping, aggressive and sure, at once radiating and reflecting optimism. There was, too, Harvey's great innings. He came in and at once batted as if there were 300 on the board and he had not heard that this was a Test match.

The spectators at the start had hardly settled to their seats when Moroney, who had dropped his bat while cleaving his way through the photographers — an evil omen? — was returning to the pavilion. When Harvey came in Morris at once sensed his partner's zeal and manoeuvred to give it full play like a master who knows the moves and delights to see them executed by a pupil. Morris watched while Harvey flowed with strokes. Only for one over did Harvey falter, when Wright, displacing Bailey, beat him with a googly, then with a topspinner that nearly had him l.-b.-w. But truculence never quite grew to domination, and lunch, at 69 for one, came with the bowling just holding its own.

Soon after lunch Morris was l.-b.-w., trying to hook Bedser, and from that blow the Australian innings only spasmodically recovered. Miller just leaned forward for a straight 4 off Bedser, but he was perplexed by Wright and once he turned round as if to bless the bails for their smallness. Then he was found in two minds over a shortish ball and spooned an easy catch to the sprightly McIntyre at close mid-on. Harvey did not long survive his gay companion, for Evans brilliantly ended a brilliant innings with a catch on the leg side of the wicket. He also whipped off the bails "just to show 'em." Neat Hassett, who had been, as it were, quietly prospecting, received a ball from Bedser to which he knew no answer. It came from leg to off and knocked back the off stump. That was 129 for 5.

So Loxton and Lindwall, a sturdy pair, came together. Loxton could not quite decide on policy, but Lindwall determined on obstinacy. Just before tea Evans made the second of his two remarkable catches. Brown found a teasing length with his leg-spinners. Loxton snicked one wide and hard. The ball bounced to the right from Evans's gloves, but before it reached the ground he had plunged like Nijinsky and caught it. After tea, Brown and Wright bowled for the half-hour or so before the new ball was due, and Brown, at 172, persuaded Tallon into an indiscretion and Simpson held a good catch at deep square-leg. Johnson, though never quite happy, made some strong drives.

Then came Bailey and Bedser for their final effort, Johnson mistimed a drive and was neatly caught at mid-off. Johnston mixed comedy with atrocity. The gallant Lindwall edged an outswinger into Bedser's capacious hands at second slip, and Iverson, with his antique bat, was soon left unattended by Johnston, who sliced a stroke more severely than any dub on the golf course.

There was no play on Saturday, 2 December, due to rain. Memories went back to 1936–7, when Australia made 58 (one man absent) in their second innings at Brisbane, followed by 80 (one man absent) in their first at Sydney, and England's 76 for 9 declared in their first innings at Melbourne. All after rain.

4 December 1950, Brisbane. Edward Lear and Hogarth should have returned to life to describe the second day's cricket in the first Test match at Brisbane, and had these two grown weary with laughter or tears, their places could conveniently have been taken by Rabelais and Phil May. If the Marx Brothers had seen it, they would surely by now be considering a film called "A Day at the Test."

Second Day

ENGLAND

1st innings

R.T. Simpson	b Johnston	12
C. Washbrook	c Hassett b Johnson	19
T.G. Evans	c Iverson b Johnston	16
D.C.S. Compton	c Lindwall b Johnston	3
J.G. Dewes	c Loxton b Miller	1
L. Hutton	not out	8
A.J. McIntyre	b Johnston	1
F.R. Brown	c Tallon b Miller	4
T.E. Bailey	not out	1
Extras	(b 2, nb 1)	3
Total	(7 wkts dec.)	68

Fall of wickets: 1–28, 2–49, 3–52, 4–52, 5–56, 6–57, 7–67.

AUSTRALIA BOWLING (8-ball overs)

	O	M	R	W
Lindwall	1	0	1	0
Johnston	11.2	1	35	5
Miller	10	1	29	2

AUSTRALIA

2nd innings

J. Moroney	lbw b Bailey	0
A.R. Morris	c Bailey b Bedser	0
R.N. Harvey	c Simpson b Bedser	12
K.R. Miller	c Simpson b Bailey	8
A.L. Hassett	lbw b Bailey	3
S.J.E. Loxton	c Bailey b Bedser	0
R.R. Lindwall	not out	0
I.W. Johnson	lbw b Bailey	8
Extras	(nb 1)	1
Total	(7 wkts dec.)	32

Fall of wickets:
1–0, 2–0, 3–0, 4–12, 5–19, 6–31, 7–32.

ENGLAND BOWLING

	O	M	R	W
Bailey	7	2	22	4
Bedser	6.5	2	9	3

ENGLAND

2nd innings

R.T. Simpson	b Lindwall	0
C. Washbrook	c Loxton b Lindwall	6
J.G. Dewes	b Miller	9
A.V. Bedser	c Harvey b Iverson	0
T.E. Bailey	c Johnston b Iverson	7
A.J. McIntyre	run out	7
T.G. Evans	not out	0
Extras	(nb 1)	1
Total	(6 wkts)	30

Fall of wickets: 1–0, 2–16, 3–22, 4–23, 5–23, 6–30.

AUSTRALIA BOWLING

	O	M	R	W
Lindwall	5	3	11	2
Johnston	3	0	9	0
Miller	4	3	1	1
Iverson	3	1	8	2

Friday was drama. To-day was low comedy and the clowns, as it has ever been, were the victims as well as the playgivers. Compton or Chaplin, Grimaldi or Moroney, what's in a name?

Here, rightly speaking, is the time table. At 1 p.m. England went in to bat for the first time. At 3.20 p.m. Brown declared at 68 for seven wickets and tea was taken. After it, Australia went in to bat for the second time with a lead of 160. At 4.40 Hassett declared with the total 32 for seven wickets. At 5.55 bad light ended the play with England's second innings' score standing at 30 for six wickets. So England, with Evans, Hutton, Compton, Brown, and Wright, so to speak, in hand, need another 163 to win and they have a possible three days in which to do it. If the night and morrow be fine the pitch could recover a medium of sanity and the task would verge on the reasonable. If not, only unearthly skill can avail.

Let none begrudge Australia her position of command. Luck and games are good companions. But it should be recorded that so far in this match England has bowled and fielded rather better than Australia and has batted at best no worse. Indeed, the pitch is the victorious villain.

Fears as to its future conduct were expressed in a previous report and it proved to be "all and more than all the fancy painted." It was truculent, riotous. It sometimes made a fool even of the bowler. The bowlers of medium and fast-medium pace managed it best: Bedser and Johnston and

Bailey. Miller, except for the ball with which he bowled Dewes in England's second innings, used off-spin from round the wicket and never looked as difficult as these three.

Lindwall yorked Simpson at the very start of that second innings, but the pitch was, as a whole, not so amenable to his speed for all its control. Iverson's mysterious off-spin brought him two wickets late in the day, but his victims fell because of a sudden carelessness rather than any venom in the ball. Through all the farce and tragedy the feeling persisted that art was being mocked except for half an hour or so when Hutton was batting in the firt innings. Then for a space the slapstick stopped. He looked like a fencing champion somehow embroiled in a jug and bottle fight.

Processions, except for that which the Lord Mayor annually provides, rarely profit by detailed descrption. But the spectators, rightly hilarious after Saturday's disappointment, applauded the comings and goings with impartial excitement. Washbrook and Simpson, with only a flickering smile from fortune, scored 28 between 1 o'clock and lunch by the most skilful and courageous batting yet seen in the match.

Directly after lunch Washbrook was caught at silly mid-off. All the day the sillier positions in the field were densely populated. Evans was typically and briefly gay and once sharpened Moroney at cover-point with a stroke which sent the ball in and out of cupped hands with much resonance. Simpson was bowled by a good one that chanced not to kick. Compton ran out to drive and scored three over the slips, then was caught at wide slip with his left forearm in front of his head. Dewes was neatly taken at slip and McIntyre was too late in the stroke. Hutton, as already mentioned, insisted on being Hutton. Brown swished fatally, snicked, and soon after declared the innings closed.

Within the short and appointed time the same sort of thing was being done even less successfully by batsmen in green caps. The first three went for nought. Moroney was l.-b.-w. without perceptible motion of bat or foot. Morris was out to a

wonderful catch low to the right by Bailey at first slip, and Loxton to an easier catch rather wider. Hasset was l.-b.-w. in rather the Moroney manner. Johnson, after some defiance, went in the same sort of way. Miller joined Harvey and hit two cracking 4's to the off and then was out to an admirably judged catch at very deep cover-point. Harvey gave Simpson an easier catch and Lindwall was now free to open the bowling for the second time in the day.

The heavy roller had been used and for a short time the pitch looked less vicious. The first ball was a fast yorker and hit Simpson's stumps. Dewes and Washbrook gave a fair imitation of comfort till Washbrook mistimed a hook and was easily caught at short-leg. Dewes went at 22 and Bedser, the next research student, appealed against the light which to the view of some was becoming as dim as England's hopes. The appeal was not upheld. Bailey batted with solid determination. Bedser soon deserted him. Bailey then lifted a ball to long-leg. McIntyre hit his first ball from Iverson to the leg boundary and his second nearly as hard. But he tried a fourth run. Tallon seized Johnston's return and threw down the

---

Third Day

ENGLAND
2nd innings (continued)

T.G. Evans	c Loxton b Johnston	5
L. Hutton	not out	62
D.C.S. Compton	c Loxton b Johnston	0
F.R. Brown	c Loxton b Iverson	17
D.V.P. Wright	c Lindwall b Iverson	2
Extras	(b 6, nb 1)	7
Total		122

Fall of wickets: 7–46, 8–46, 9–77, 10–122.

AUSTRALIA BOWLING

	O	M	R	W
Lindwall	7	3	21	2
Johnston	11	2	30	2
Miller	7	3	21	1
Iverson	13	3	43	4

Umpires: A.N. Barlow and H. Elphinston

AUSTRALIA WON BY 70 RUNS

wicket. Hutton was half-way to the pitch before he found the fielders walking in.

And that, as the ancient Greek messengers delighted to say, is all the trouble for the moment.

5 December 1950, Brisbane. Australia won the Test match here by 70 runs, the match ending just before luncheon on the third day of play, when the gallant and obstructive Wright, who had helped Hutton to add 45 runs and resisted many a bait, hooked a short ball into Lindwall's hands at backward square-leg.

The result had been foreshadowed on the crazy day before. It is not comfortable for a visiting critic to have to write that England batted, bowled, and even fielded better than Australia in losing a match. But thus it was. The weather and its legatee, the pitch, won. This cannot prevent congratulations to our old friends and enemies and wonderful hosts. But it would be straining obsequiousness to pretend that, as yet, Australia is anything like the team which two years ago humbled England at Lord's and the Oval. They miss the batting or Sir Donald Bradman and S.G. Barnes, the former's inevitability and the latter's truculence. The balance of power may yet alter.

But England surprised even herself on the first day and went down on the third with flags flying and the spectators cheering every stroke by Hutton. Like the Tuscans by the Tiber they could not forbear. For here was greatness unmistakable. Hutton stood there and drove Lindwall at his ardent fastest. Drove him like flaming fire. And there, ranged in a line deep on the off side, were Miller, Harvey and Hassett. Deep not just only for tactical reasons, but because it wasn't wise to come too close. Iverson's spin and guile Hutton more than answered with all that he has of footwork, experience, and intuition. None that saw this innings will ever forget it. It contained one false stroke, a square cut that travelled in the air for two runs.

So to the morning, which dawned in a sky fair but still treacherous. There was a light skitter of rain soon after Hutton and Evans reached the wicket, but it was soon evident that the pitch had simmered down from viciousness to occasional truculence. Left-handed Johnston bowled a few balls on it at customary fast-medium pace, was glided for 4 by Evans, and changed to his slower spinning method. At the south end Iverson bowled and was soon cut square by Hutton to the boundary, but Johnston then struck two deadly blows. At 47 he had Evans caught at short leg. The sight of Compton coming in raised our spirits and charmed away our fears, but alas, for once, he started with a weak stroke and there was Loxton again jubilant at short leg.

So, just after a quarter past 12, Brown walked to the wicket with strong and purposeful gait, and was loudly cheered on his way. He was sometimes in perplexity to Iverson, but he rode the deceptions rather as a genial assistant is not laughed down on the conjurer's platform. Johnston's bowling, he met firmly and with apt use of the old-fashioned forward stroke. Once Johnston, with extraordinary agility, nearly caught and bowled him low with the right hand. The spectators grew more excited. But not Hutton. With cool and level command he kept the bowling of Iverson when he could, and at the very deathbed of a Test match he played like a master, showing the pupils in a free and sunny hour. Johnston began to look almost easy, and soon after he had been driven by Brown to the long-on boundary, Hassett, whose captaincy remained shrewd and calm, brought on Miller. Miller used his fast-medium method from over the wicket. But it was Iverson who broke the partnership, causing Brown to play forward just too soon, and so give an easy catch to Loxton at short leg.

That was at 77 for nine, and 10 minutes to one. Wright, who not only knows the primary strokes, but can play them, defended with studious serenity. Once he snicked a ball from Iverson into the top of his pads and enjoyed a sort of game of round the mulberry bush with wicketkeeper Tallon, to the amusement of nearly all. Then came the last phase and Hutton's crowning glory. The arrival of the total 100 and Hutton's 50 were scarcely noticed in the splendour of Hutton's strokes. When England needed 86 to win he hooked a riser from Miller and Lindwall, at full length and long leg, got a hand to the ball. The records may call it a chance if they like. At 1.26 Hassett gave Iverson a turn at what is locally called the Vulture Road end. An ill-omened bird? Anyhow, with the last ball before lunch Iverson successfully tempted Wright. And Hutton passed from a sight to a memory.

"Crusoe's" enjoyment of the tour continued. The second Test at Melbourne was a low-scoring game, neither side able to reach 200.

1 January 1951, Sydney. To fly from the nearly unbearable agonies of the Melbourne Test match to the almost baroque entertainment of MCC versus New South Wales at Sydney was a strain, an emotional adjustment. It was as if the curtain had fallen on *East Lynne* to rise after a flurried intermission on the *Comedy of Errors*, for the great A.R. Morris, in the course of scoring 60 in the hour and a half before lunch, was visibly missed four times...It was a little like a fielding practice that goes wrong. Indeed, Morris recalled that other clown of Shakespeare, Barnadine, who expressed himself too lazy to be executed.

Dates here become irrelevant, only "Crusoe's" style mattered. Early in the third Test:

When the total was 19 the ball, possibly because it was being bounced too severely in childhood, lost its shape and there was the strange sight of two admirable umpires, Elphinstone and Barlow, kneeling opposite each other and organizing another ball by banging it on the turf. A rare and interesting rite.

After Harvey had snicked Bedser between gully and slips, he twice missed overbold hooks at Warr:

Harvey has the advantage gained by the stroke player. He causes the man who should catch the snick to be elsewhere and deeper...Loxton had been at sea. But Tallon seemed to be playing in some dimension undreamed of even by Einstein. Brown passed the ball around and over Tallon's bat. But the stumps themselves seemed to side-step.

...At 32 Iverson had the great Hutton, who played half-cock to what he must have thought was a googly. It was the topspinner. It lifted and snicked his bat. Tallon grabbed at the ball and only hit it on to Johnson's left hand at slip, thence the ball bounced and was almost in the grass when Tallon leapt round and held it with right arm at full stretch. He might have been Nijinsky — or Evans.

The fourth Test at Adelaide was lost by England, so making the score for post-1945 games: Australia 11, England 0. At the close of the second day Hutton was 56 not out. Thereafter:

The Australian bowling was adequate except when directed at Hutton. He was the master. For the second time within six months he carried his bat through an England innings. He added exactly 100 runs to his overnight score. To-day he gave one chance late in the day to deep mid-off, pleasure to thousands, and honour to the art of batting. His judgment of length was extraordinary. Iverson's off-spinners he would watch almost on to the stumps and deflect them for runs to leg. Then suddenly scorning the suggestion of subservience he would jump out and drive him clean through the covers.

Lindwall and Miller he played easily; only Johnston, the shrewdest of the Australian bowlers, extracted Hutton's deepest resources of shrewdness. In all he batted for six hours and 10 minutes and hit 11 4's. The Australian team clapped him all the way in and the crowd rose to him.

Evans's batting had suggested a kettle that wishes vainly to come to the boil. He knew that defensive assistance to Hutton was needed and for some 40 minutes his impatience expressed itself only in some fanciful ideas of running between the wickets...Hutton looked on like a tolerant headmaster at the silliness of a junior, but when Evans hit a good length ball straight into the hands of extra-cover the head master sat down in the crease and shook his head sadly, even though he had just reached his 100 with a single to leg off Lindwall.

Fifth Test

At the close on the second day England were 218 for six — Hutton 79, R.T. Simpson 80 not out) in reply to Australia's 217.

Third Day

27 February 1951, Melbourne. Great batting by Simpson, the Lancastrian sense and resolution of Tattersall in Simpson's support, and Bedser bowling at his best have given England a clear chance of winning the fifth Test match here. With two days left Australia lead by only 26, and in their second innings have lost the wickets of Morris, Burke, Harvey, and Miller...

Simpson had scored 92 [England 246 for nine] when Tattersall joined him and suitable expressions of sympathy were being prepared by critics and spectators. Iverson surrounded Tattersall with eight close fielders, including Tallon, like turnkeys of old taking the likeness of a prisoner. Iverson is a leg-spinner to the left-hander, and twice he shaved the stumps vertically and laterally. So Simpson really began. In one over from Miller he hooked a 4, cut a 2, and deflected a 3 and reached his 100 in four hours and three-quarters. Tattersall joined in with a sort of leg glide for 2 off Miller and Johnston was called upon by Hassett.

The excitement and the scoring quickened. Johnston spread his field, but Simpson, now looking like a master showing strokes to the boys, pierced that field almost at will. Tattersall was seldom allowed more than two balls an over, and these he would play with phlegmatic accuracy.

All the world loves a last-wicket stand and the crowd roared applause at the skill and the control of the scene. Just before luncheon Johnson had a turn with his off spinners and Lindwall was brought back from unwanted exertions in the deeper field. Lindwall tried Simpson with some wider bowling on the off, but Simpson chased it and drove it past cover-point. So to luncheon — England 303 for nine, Simpson 143, and Tattersall 6.

After luncheon Miller was cut for 4 by Simpson and snicked for 4 by Tattersall. With another 4 past extra-cover off Johnson Simpson reached 150. And now questions were being asked about record last-wicket stands. But Miller, with an extra fast ball, knocked Tattersall's stumps anyhow and England led by 103. The tenth wicket had added 74. In less than an hour and three-quarters Simpson had scored 76. His 156 not out, the same score as Hutton had made at Adelaide, took in all 5½ hours. Patience and stroke-play in happy marriage.

At 20 minutes to 3 Morris and Burke started Australia's second innings. Bedser began with a swinging full toss which had Evans prone on the leg side, but at once it was plain that his speed from the pitch was even greater than usual. After that one "sighter" he wasted nothing. At the pavilion end Bailey, whose ankle is unsound, bowled with a shortened run and Morris twice hit him for 2 past cover-point. Then, to the third ball of Bedser's second over, Morris tried a surely presumptuous hook and was lbw. Hassett was cheered to the wicket, but from Bedser's seventh ball, which moved late and sharp from leg, he saw Burke neatly caught at first slip. That was at total six.

Harvey was next, and he would not be suppressed. Attack is his glory and strength, and, unaltered by a false stroke or two at the start, he began to raise the spirits of the spectators. At 25 came Hassett's chance at slip off Bedser. At 32 Wright came on for Bailey, and from his faster ball he appealed for lbw against Hassett, who surely survived by the narrowest margin.

Tea came at 65 for two. After tea Wright bowled for 75 minutes from the pavilion end at his best — no bowler more various than he. Harvey again swept him to the leg boundary and reached 50 in 90 minutes. Then, as so many have done, he hooked at Wright once too often and was lbw to a ball that nipped through fast and rather low. Miller was next and was at once asked by a spectator to "hit a six," a natural, but not wholly opportune, request. Brown now came on for Bedser, fancying his chance of again having Miller caught and bowled. He was right. Miller again played forward just too soon and Brown scooped up a right-handed catch from near the grass. The total was 89.

Now for this last hour England needed the loan of Lindwall and Miller. Hassett and Hole stuck it out. Hole had times of perplexity against Wright, but the much-needed wicket did not fall. Hassett, looking even smaller than usual, did what he was set to do. Tattersall came on for Brown and Bedser, then Bailey for Wright. Bailey tested Hole with an almost headhigh full toss. So a great day's cricket ended. To-morrow's could be even greater.

Close: AUSTRALIA 217 and 129 for 4 (A.L. Hassett 44 not out, R.N. Harvey 52), ENGLAND 320 (R.T. Simpson 156 not out).

Fourth Day

28 February 1951, Melbourne. Shortly before 5 o'clock this afternoon Hutton turned a ball from Hassett to leg for a single and England had won the fifth Test match against Australia by eight wickets. So victory came after 13 years. It was a resounding victory won against chivalrous, but tough, opponents by a team of cricketers who, if late in the series, answered both the leadership of a true captain and their own latent powers.

Luck did not unduly help either side. The pitch remained good to the end. To the end, too, if we allow for the pleasing comedy of the last six balls from Hassett, the Australians strained spirit and sinew in defence of their invincibility. Their fielding was superb and when Washbrook was out at the total of 32 and only 65 runs were needed still, we were half ready to believe that Iverson would suddenly reveal some further freak of spin, or that Lindwall and Miller would rise to demoniac strength and unearthly brilliance and snatch victory from England at the last. But whatever fantasies may have clouded or illumined the minds of the spectators, there was one man out in the middle, Hutton, who stood no nonsense from sceptic or bowler.

As is the way of greatness, he controlled and commanded without fuss. Early in the innings he hit Lindwall for a sizzling 4 past cover. Then, when Iverson came on, he knew and showed himself to be the master. Praise, too, to Simpson. Late, but not quite too late, he found his own high artistry of stroke-play, put away the pedestrian accuracy of the mere workman, and turned a position of doubt to one of lively hope.

So much for the batting. In the bowling Bedser once more showed that he is the best of his kind in the world to-day. Throughout the match, indeed throughout the series, no Australian batsman wholly mastered his late swerve either way, his accuracy of direction, and his stinging pace from the pitch. His was a double task to quell runs and to take wickets, and he achieved it. Wright also, that variable genius, had his share in the victory. He ended both Harvey and Hassett when each was set and happy. As an old Yorkshire player once remarked: "Any fool can bowl batsman when he's made nowt."

In the morning when Hassett and Hole continued from a total of 129 for 4, Brown was faced with a tactical problem, mild perhaps in retrospect, but real enough when every Australian run was a drag on hope. Should he or Bedser bowl during seven overs before the new ball was due? Bedser has no dislike of work or of a ball of moderate age, but this part-rended ball had apparently grown senile early. So Brown took it and in the first two overs by him and Wright singles came with an ease that was alarming or reassuring according to party.

Hole did once glide Wright in the air not far from Bailey's outstretched hand, and Hassett did have some trouble with Wright's googly. But the googly on the middle-and-leg is ever the spinner's second best, and it was a beautifully pitched leg-break which, at 142, beat Hassett's back-stroke and hit his middle and off stumps. Wright, a man of quiet temper, jumped in triumph. That was the second ball of an over. The seventh Johnson ballooned to very deep mid-on, and Brown never looked as if he would not catch it.

So Lindwall joined Hole and Bedser came on at the Richmond end for Brown. He harassed Lindwall, who was almost caught by Sheppard diving to the right at short-leg. Suddenly Wright lost accuracy, and Hole, who now carried the Australian innings and hopes with debonair courage, cracked him thrice in one over to the boundary — two hooks, then a late cut off the faster ball. Forty minutes before luncheon Bedser took the new ball and Bailey succeeded Wright. Drinks, irrelevant to most, were brought out. Then Bedser had a duel with Hole. Evans missed a chance of stumping on the leg side, and Hole made an uppish stroke wide of the slips, then a beautiful drive for 4 past mid-off. Soon after Hole reached his 50. Lindwall, never so convincing in his more sedentary mood, edged Bedser for 4 between the slips, who rearranged themselves with postdated care.

At the pavilion end Bailey lapsed into eccentricity with two overhead full tosses, then he cooled himself down to a more methodical attack at the leg-stump with three close leg fielders. Hole was quietened and when he did try a drive Bailey almost caught and bowled him with a goalkeeper's fling to the right. Then Bedser, as if tired of other people's oddities and luck, bowled Lindwall, who was framing vaguely for a cut. That was 192 for seven and Tallon walked in very slowly with head cocked a little to the side as one who hears the deadly approach of the tumbril. He scored one run to leg. And so to lunch — 193 for seven and Australia only 90 ahead. Hole had then scored 61.

After lunch the air was heavily humid and a slight mist as of autumn come too soon hung over the scene. Bailey tried no more ballistic experiments and bowled Hole with a fast and well-pitched-up ball. Hole will surely be seen with the next Australian team in England. He batted for two hours and 40 minutes. And now Bedser who had taken the first two wickets, took the last two also. He pierced Johnston's airy defence and caused an outswinger to whizz from the edge of Iverson's antique bat* into Compton's hands at second slip. No nonsense about it. He had taken 30 wickets in the five Tests.

After use of the light roller Hutton and Washbrook went out to face Lindwall (pavilion end) and Miller just before a quarter to three. Lindwall went through more unlimbering exercises than usual and some prophesied an attack of much height as well as speed. But it was speed only, and in the very first over Hutton drove a 4 off Lindwall like the crack of a pistol. Miller once passed Hutton with a beauty, but Hutton did not mean to play any game with time and 17 runs were on the board, 16 to Hutton, when after two overs each, Lindwall and Miller were succeeded by Iverson and Johnston, the latter using his slower method. Washbrook, never happy to Iverson, swatted away in a whole over without effecting anything except complicated fusion of himself with Tallon, who kept wicket in quite his old style. Hutton, by contrast, interpreted Iverson as flowingly as a scholar translates a once puzzling passage. At the other end Washbrook hit Johnston square to the off boundary. Then he cocked up the easiest of catches to short-leg. Sixty-three to win when Simpson came in and rain now threatening.

Simpson began with a few deflections, then attacked, hooking Johnston violently for 4 past short-leg's head. Twenty minutes before tea Johnson bowled an over of convenience to let Iverson and Johnston change ends. Harvey's fielding at cover-point was a sight to see. Still

....

* Iverson was supposed to pick up any piece of wood handy before leaving the dressing room. His batting average for the five Tests of 1950–51 was 0.75, leaving one to wonder if—had he continued in cricket—he might eventually have challenged H. Ironmonger's 2.62.

Hutton batted with a free certainty, and the issue must now be sure. But at 62 Simpson drove Iverson to Harvey's right and ran. Harvey, who had once already thrown down the bowler's wicket, did so again and Simpson was far run out. Now the spectators began to cheer nearly everything, and Compton came in. He turned Iverson to leg for 1, and so to tea with 31 needed for victory. Hutton had scored 40 out of 64.

Afterwards some thought that Hassett might bring on Lindwall and Miller again for a last fling.

But he kept on Iverson and Johnston. A light rain now fell. In 2's and singles the runs came and Hutton reached his 50 — 16 to win. When 8 were needed Hole came on for Iverson; with 4 to win Hassett took the ball from Johnston. With humorous care he called long-leg in closer. A run to Compton, a run to Hutton, another to Compton. Then Hutton, with ironical precision, pushed a single to leg and all was over. And soon the two captains, Hassett and Brown, were making speeches on demand to the cheering throng.

AUSTRALIA v. ENGLAND
Melbourne, 23, 24, 26–8 February 1951

AUSTRALIA

1st innings

J. Burke	c Tattersall b Bedser	11
A.R. Morris	lbw b Brown	50
A.L. Hassett	c Hutton b Brown	92
R.N. Harvey	c Evans b Brown	1
K.R. Miller	c & b Brown	7
G.B. Hole	b Bedser	18
I.W. Johnson	lbw b Bedser	1
R.R. Lindwall	c Compton b Bedser	21
D. Tallon	c Hutton b Bedser	1
W.A. Johnston	not out	12
J. Iverson	c Washbrook b Brown	0
Extras	(b 2, lb 1)	3
Total		217

2nd innings

J. Burke	c Hutton b Bedser	1
A.R. Morris	lbw b Bedser	4
A.L. Hassett	b Wright	48
R.N. Harvey	lbw b Wright	52
K.R. Miller	c & b Brown	0
G.B. Hole	b Bailey	63
I.W. Johnson	c Brown b Wright	0
R.R. Lindwall	b Bedser	14
D. Tallon	not out	2
W.A. Johnston	b Bedser	1
J. Iverson	c Compton b Bedser	0
Extras	(b 2, lb 8, w 1, nb 1)	12
Total		197

Fall of wickets: 1–23, 2–111, 3–115, 4–123, 5–156, 6–166, 7–184, 8–187, 9–216, 10–217.

Second innings: 1–5, 2–6, 3–88, 4–89, 5–142, 6–142, 7–192, 8–196, 9–197, 10–197.

ENGLAND BOWLING (8-ball overs)

	O	M	R	W	O	M	R	W
Bedser	22	5	46	5	20.3	4	59	5
Bailey	9	1	29	0	15	3	32	1
Brown	18	4	49	5	9	1	32	1
Wright	9	1	50	0	15	2	56	3
Tattersall	11	3	40	0	5	2	6	0

ENGLAND

1st innings

L. Hutton	b Hole	79
C. Washbrook	c Tallon b Miller	27
R.T. Simpson	not out	156
D.C.S. Compton	c Miller b Lindwall	11
D.S. Sheppard	c Tallon b Miller	1
F.R. Brown	b Lindwall	6
T.G. Evans	b Miller	1
A.V. Bedser	b Lindwall	11
T.E. Bailey	c Johnson b Iverson	5
D.V.P. Wright	lbw b Iverson	3
R. Tattersall	b Miller	10
Extras	(b 9, lb 1)	10
Total		320

2nd innings

L. Hutton	not out	60
C. Washbrook	c Lindwall b Johnston	7
R.T. Simpson	run out	15
D.C.S. Compton	not out	11
Extras	(lb 2)	2
Total	(2 wkts)	95

Fall of wickets: 1–40, 2–171, 3–204, 4–205, 5–212, 6–213, 7–228, 8–236, 9–246, 10–320.

Second innings: 1–32, 2–62.

AUSTRALIA BOWLING

	O	M	R	W	O	M	R	W
Lindwall	21	1	77	3	2	0	12	0
Miller	21.7	5	76	4	2	0	5	0
Johnston	12	1	55	0	11	3	36	1
Iverson	20	4	52	2	12	2	32	0
Johnson	11	1	40	0	1	0	1	0
Hole	5	0	10	1	1	0	3	0
Hassett					0.6	0	4	0

Umpires: A.N. Barlow and H. Elphinston

ENGLAND WON BY 8 WICKETS

RAYMOND RUSSELL LINDWALL

New South Wales and Queensland

Lindwall, to those born between 1920 and 1940, was the greatest of fast bowlers. Which poses the legitimate question: was he a fast bowler in the sense that Tom Richardson was? At times his pace was fast–medium; then a wicket fell and the casual onlooker (except there were no casual onlookers when Lindwall was bowling) suspected a delivery of blistering speed or one held back. Lindwall, in short, was capable of bowling very fast; otherwise, the comparison must be with, say, Grimmett. A master of length and variations, Lindwall thought batsmen out.

As a boy he had watched Larwood at Sydney. In due course Lindwall's approach to the wicket resembled Larwood's — thirteen strides which began easily, then accelerated almost imperceptibly. At the long delivery stride Lindwall was moving at top speed, the left shoulder pointing, the back arched. If the right arm was not as high as Larwood's, there was the compensation of the ball tending to skid through. At first an out-swing bowler, a season in the Lancashire League where the slips did not include McCool and Miller saw him perfect the in-swinger. He was then the complete bowler, to the end of his career the most compelling of all to watch. His main 1948 adversaries in England were Hutton, Washbrook, W.J. Edrich and Compton — an impressive quartet by any standards.

Lindwall was also a good enough batsman to score two Test hundreds, once at Melbourne sharing in an eighty-wicket partnership of 154 with Tallon — the rate 106 runs an hour. Perhaps because he had been born in a certain age, or perhaps due to professional pride, Lindwall did not bowl bouncers at tail-enders.

THE OVAL, 1948

By R.B. Vincent

16 August 1948. Australia dismissed England on the first day of the fifth Test match at the Oval on Saturday for 52 runs, and at the close of play had in their turn scored 153 for the loss of only two wickets. This was the lowest total ever made by England against Australia in this country, the previous lowest being one of 53 at Lord's in 1888.

It is quite easy to say that England's batting was deplorable. It certainly was; but it is more to the point to say that Australia's bowling, catching, and ground fielding were superb. Australia have produced many sides which have roused one to great admiration by the force of their out-cricket; on this occasion, in Bradman's last Test match, they touched the heights of combined hostility in attack.

Yardley, having won the toss with the pitch deemed sufficiently recovered from rain for a start to be made at noon, simply had to bat first. And to be sure the pitch played tamely enough to justify his decision. Yet so accurately and persistently did the bowlers of pace, Lindwall, Miller, and Johnston, acquit themselves that

Bradman never even had to think of using his spin bowler, Ring. The first wicket fell when Dewes, with the score at two, was out to a ball from Miller which swung and beat him from the pitch. That was a poor enough start, to be followed by two catastrophic raps, and they were both wickets taken by Australia rather than wickets thrown away by England. Edrich thought he saw a chance of hitting away to leg a ball a shade shorter than the ones he had been given before. He hit the ball firmly enough, but Hassett held the catch close to the square leg umpire. Compton, having once had his bat knocked out of his hand and not certain whether to retrieve it or run as the ball had flown over slip's head, could have been run out had Hassett returned the ball from third man to the bowler's end. He declined to take so gratuitous an advantage. That did not help much for the score had risen only to 17 when Compton was the second man to be caught brilliantly near the square leg umpire, and that also off a hard enough blow.

Hutton, in the meantime, was batting with assurance enough, yet never suggesting anything very startling in the nature of a challenging attacking stroke. Crapp was caught at the wicket playing no sort of stroke, and in 90 minutes before luncheon only 29 runs had been scored and four men were out. England, however, could take what comfort they could find in that Yardley was still in with Hutton.

That comfort was soon upset when, with only six runs added, Yardley was bowled by that faster ball which Lindwall reserves for the express purpose of hitting the stumps. After that there was little more to do than to watch a succession of England's batsmen formally take guard and appropriately get bowled. Still Hutton, standing in a Sahara of sawdust, batted on and just before the end treated himself to an off drive which flew in the air and actually reached the boundary. He just failed to carry his bat through the innings, being last man out, magnificently caught low down at the wicket from what looked to be a perfectly shaped glide. England's innings, if such it can be called, lasted for two hours and 25 minutes, and Lindwall's analysis of six wickets for 20 runs in 16 overs and one ball was something to talk about.

When Australia started their innings the sun was shining, and there was some hope that the pitch might do something to save the collective face of England's batsmen. Barnes and Morris soon showed that nothing of the sort was to be allowed to happen. Each in his own way played as certainly as could be. Barnes, always on the alert, had once to play his stroke a trifle more hurriedly than he was prepared to do, but the bat was always there. Watkins, who started the bowling from the Pavilion end, was not a success as a medium paced left handed bowler. Australian batsmen pay respect to accurate bowling, but Watkins lacked both length and direction and he was accordingly hit unceremoniously by both batsmen. Bedser bowled steadily but that was not enough, and it took Morris and Barnes only an hour to pass England's total and they continued on their way scoring at an even rate and with the utmost ease, some of Morris's strokes to the off side being beautiful to watch.

A spell by Young from the Pavilion end had done little but slightly check the rate of scoring, and it was not until Hollies came on that a wicket fell. With the score at 117 he enticed Barnes just for that once to grope for the ball and to be caught at the wicket. So with the Pavilion standing to their feet and the English team standing in midfield ready to acclaim him with three cheers in came Bradman, to be out to the second ball he received, beaten and bowled by a googly. The day then passed with Morris and Hassett batting away, and Australia already 101 runs ahead.

Close: ENGLAND 52 (R.R. Lindwall 6 for 20), AUSTRALIA 153 for 2 (S.G. Barnes 61, A.R. Morris 77 not out).

Second Day

17 August 1948. England, after their dismal start on Saturday in the Test match at the Oval, made

a fair measure of recovery yesterday and it can at least be said that the match is still alive.

To dismiss Australia for 389 runs on a pitch of perfect pace was in itself an achievement, for this, judged by modern standards, was no excessive total, and at the close of play, although still 283 runs behind with one wicket already fallen, there was an air of challenge in the batting of Hutton and Edrich which, if supported, may yet make Australia fight all the way.

Bedser and Edrich, when they started the bowling in the morning on a pitch which the week-end had left neutral in pace, had a hard task before them. Morris is so quick on his feet that he can afford to walk across his stumps with the certitude that he is in the exact position to play the ball as late as he requires — so late, in fact, that he can treat himself to a chop off the off-stump which can be taken either as a defensive stroke to the turning ball or a deflection to score one run down to third man. Equally so in his attacking strokes to the off-side he finds time to cover the ground and to strike the ball at the last possible moment away through the most carefully placed field. He is, in fact, a batsman of genius, but of a genius born to the soundest principles batsmanship.

When Hollies, who throughout the innings had insisted on careful attention, came on Morris reached his century with a perfectly timed stroke to the off-side for three runs, and when Young came on at the Pavilion end he greeted him at once with an off-drive bang to the boundary. Even so, only 43 runs had been scored in the first hour of play, Hassett, the inscrutable, being content to watch the display of Morris while for his part playing with an almost deadly nonchalant bat. Young in his first spell had done little to suggest the disruption of the partnership, but when he came on again he at once had Hassett leg-before-wicket, and so three Australians were out for 226.

...With the arrival of Tallon, another batsman who has plenty of ideas of scoring, the total had risen to 359 [for seven wickets] and then at last Morris was out — run out — the only way that one could see that he ever would be out. Tallon played a ball down to deep backward-point, Morris ran and Simpson, the substitute, had the ball back to Evans to enforce the penalty for a run which was never there. Morris, whose innings had combined exquisite stroke play with perfect judgment, had batted for six hours and three-quarters, and had hit 16 fours. Those are facts; the true value of his innings can be best judged by those who had to bowl to him. The humble spectator felt that this is a young man who will cause England's bowlers a deal of trouble for years to come.

Close: ENGLAND 52 and 54 for 1, AUSTRALIA 389 (A.R. Morris 196; W.E. Hollies 5 for 131).

Third Day

18 August 1948. Heavy rain at 4 o'clock at the Oval yesterday — when England, still 159 runs behind in their second innings with only three wickets to fall, were faced with a summary defeat in the fifth Test match — has for a moment delayed the issue.

The weather will surely relent sufficiently during the next two days to allow Australia their deserved victory. When that is achieved will be the time to pay due tribute to Bradman's splendid team.

For the moment one can but record a short day's play, remarkable mainly for the batsmanship of Hutton, a Test match batsman of true value in any epoch, and the sustained, insistent attack of this Australian team. One must go back many years to the time of Richardson and Lockwood, later through that period when Macdonald and Gregory skittled batsmen out, with Larwood of pace and accuracy, to find a peer to Lindwall. He surely is one of the great fast bowlers of all time, perfect in action — you must stand square to the wicket to see the full joy of his follow-through — wise in the exact moment to loose off that frightfully fast ball, and above all continually accurate in length. If this English summer has allowed us nothing else it has granted the sight of Lindwall bowling.

England were 283 runs behind when Hutton and Edrich batted to Lindwall, from the Vauxhall end, and Johnston, and there was a nasty shock when Edrich was bowled by a glorious ball, that of a true fast bowler, which whipped back to hit the stumps. The score was then 64, but Bradman, apparently not quite satisfied, brought Ring on in place of Lindwall. Bradman's captaincy has a reason in it which only the cultured observer can follow. Ring had not bowled in the first innings — he had not been needed — and on this occasion if he was inclined to pitch his leg break to the off stump, so allowing too many balls to be left alone, he was always bowling to a length. Compton was strangely uneasy for so distinguished a batsman. He was uneasy and uncertain in the reach of his forward stroke, and one had to wait some time before at last he followed the ball with the full blade of his bat to score four runs away to long leg.

Hutton was certainty itself, yet only 29 runs had been scored in the first hour of play. Hutton was peppering the off side with drives of good timing, but not quite well enough placed to pass four Australians standing and alert all in a row from point to mid-off. At luncheon the score had risen, soundly from Hutton and a shade uncertainly from Compton, to 121, with the Australian bowlers menacingly in charge of the situation.

Compton was out soon after the interval to a catch at second slip, a hopeful grab at the ball which stuck. Then, as a variety, Bradman put Loxton on to bowl as fast past the bat as Lindwall had done. Hutton found the chance to reach his 50 with a beautifully timed off-drive off Loxton, and so Bradman once more brought on Ring. Crapp was never happy to Miller, who bowled every kind of ball, fast, medium, even slow, delayed from the back of his hand, and once made Crapp duck his head and be hit on his cap to one which could have risen little above bail high. Ring once did drop a ball a shade short of a length — this Hutton hit, full to the leg boundary for four, but with the score at 153 he was caught at the wicket to a ball of perfect length from Miller to which he played back just too late.

Crapp was utterly bowled, and half the side was out for 164, with Watkins three runs later caught with ease by Hassett at deepish mid-on. Evans had struck Ring away to the off, and he had turned a ball from Lindwall away to leg before he had a straight and fast ball which hit his stumps. The light was then very bad, and it did seem a little hard on Evans that it was not until he had been dismissed that the umpires decided a halt should be called. In fact the rain followed so persistently that had it come one over earlier Evans might have still been not out.

Close: ENGLAND 52 and 178 for 7 (L. Hutton 64), AUSTRALIA 389.

Fourth Day

19 August 1948. Twenty minutes of play at the Oval yesterday was sufficient for England's last three wickets to fall and so present Australia with a handsome victory in the fifth and last Test match by an innings and 149 runs.

England's last moments of anguish were imposed by Johnston who, when only three runs had been added to Tuesday's total of 178, bowled Bedser with his slower ball.

Yardley made a final gesture of defiance, hooking a ball from Johnston for three and then putting Lindwall, who just previously had nearly decapitated England's captain, for two to the leg side. In the end Yardley was caught in the slips from a stroke which was intended to send the ball away to the leg boundary. With Hollies caught at mid-on first ball all was over, leaving Johnston two years to wait for the first ball in the first Test match in Australia with the opportunity of completing a long interrupted hat-trick.

So from the particular to the general. Australia, in spite of having lost the toss on four occasions, have this season won four of the five Test matches, the other having been left drawn. It is indisputably a fine and telling record, and has loosened many tongues in argument as to the exact merit of this Australian team when compared with its other illustrious predecessors. That it is a fine side there can be no shadow of doubt, even when one must grant some poverty in the present standard of the teams which have been called upon to represent this country...

This then is Bradman's last Test match in this country, suitably recognized yesterday at the Oval by speeches, cheers, and general acknowledgment of a great cricket career. Whether, as was said, he is the greatest cricketer of all time will not be accepted by those who must retain that honour for "W. G." Let us say that he is the greatest of the present age, and can rank with Trumper, Ranji, Macartney, and Hobbs. Surely that is in all conscience sufficient praise. Let us, too, give him all credit for his captaincy, alert and yet at the same time composed; and to the support of a side which has always been ready to produce that little piece of extra effort required at a particular moment. The batting of Barnes, quick footed and watchful, with the occasional telling scoring stroke, is best appreciated by England's bowlers who have had the task of trying to disturb him.

But it is young Morris who has struck the note of grandeur, which the years to come must swell. And there has been Hassett, as welcome and popular a cricketer on every ground in this country as ever Australia sent to us. That air of detachment, while in effect taking the fullest share in the conduct of the game, belongs to Hassett, and Hassett alone. In truth a charming cricketer, and let us hope that when Australia visit us again he will captain the side. Miller we knew too, grand in his natural flair and boyish exuberance, severe in attack, both when batting and bowling, and always on the move. We have also seen young Harvey — remembered in particular for his innings in the Leeds Test match and placed in the note-book for future reference with three lines emphatically under his name.

Let us turn to the bowlers — not forgetting that many of them are batsmen as well. To begin with, Australia had the tremendous advantage of being able to start with two fast bowlers, with another for first change. Lindwall it must be who will be acclaimed as the foundation of Australia's attack and the terror of England's batsmen. His control of pace — three of fast medium pace and then one of scorching velocity — was always bowled to the length he wished and continually aimed at the stumps. It has been a sight to see. Fortunately he conquered a tendency to bowl a no-ball, and if it has been suggested that every now and then he pitched the ball purposedly a shade short, well, it has been done before and will be done again by bowlers who have the necessary pace to allow that licence.

If this Australian team had no spin bowler comparable to Mailey, Grimmett, or O'Reilly, they were able so to work the changes of their fast and medium paced bowlers, with Toshack always a danger as a left-hander, to prevent a threat of any combination of batsmen establishing themselves with an immoderate sense of certitude. To support this attack they have had a magnificent wicket-keeper in Tallon and, most important of all, a field always placed for the exact purpose of each ball bowled.

ENGLAND v. AUSTRALIA
The Oval, 14, 16–18 August 1948

ENGLAND

1st innings

L. Hutton	c Tallon b Lindwall	30
J.G. Dewes	b Miller	1
W.J. Edrich	c Hassett b Johnston	3
D.C.S. Compton	c Morris b Lindwall	4
J.F. Crapp	c Tallon b Miller	0
N.W.D. Yardley	b Lindwall	7
A.J. Watkins	lbw b Johnston	0
T.G. Evans	b Lindwall	1
A.V. Bedser	b Lindwall	0
J.A. Young	b Lindwall	0
W.E. Hollies	not out	0
Extras	(b 6)	6
Total		52

2nd innings

L. Hutton	c Tallon b Miller	64
J.G. Dewes	b Lindwall	10
W.J. Edrich	b Lindwall	28
D.C.S. Compton	c Lindwall b Johnston	39
J.F. Crapp	b Miller	9
N.W.D. Yardley	c Miller b Johnston	9
A.J. Watkins	c Hassett b Ring	2
T.G. Evans	b Lindwall	8
A.V. Bedser	b Johnston	0
J.A. Young	not out	3
W.E. Hollies	c Morris b Johnston	0
Extras	(b 9, lb 4, nb 3)	16
Total		188

Fall of wickets: 1–2, 2–10, 3–17, 4–23, 5–35, 6–42, 7–45, 8–45, 9–47, 10–52.

Second innings: 1–20, 2–64, 3–125, 4–153, 5–164, 6–167, 7–178, 8–181, 9–188, 10–188.

AUSTRALIA BOWLING

	O	M	R	W	O	M	R	W
Lindwall	16.1	5	20	6	25	3	50	3
Miller	8	5	5	2	15	6	22	2
Johnston	16	4	20	2	27.3	12	40	4
Loxton	2	1	1	0	10	2	16	0
Ring					28	13	44	1

AUSTRALIA

S.G. Barnes	c Evans b Hollies	61
A.R. Morris	run out	196
D.G. Bradman	b Hollies	0
A.L. Hassett	lbw b Young	37
K.R. Miller	st Evans b Hollies	5
R.N. Harvey	c Young b Hollies	17
S.J.E. Loxton	c Evans b Edrich	15
R.R. Lindwall	c Edrich b Young	9
D. Tallon	c Crapp b Hollies	31
D.T. Ring	c Crapp b Bedser	9
W.A. Johnston	not out	0
Extras	(b 4, lb 2, nb 3)	9
Total		389

Fall of wickets: 1–117, 2–117, 3–226, 4–243, 5–265, 6–304, 7–332, 8–359, 9–389, 10–389.

ENGLAND BOWLING

	O	M	R	W
Bedser	31.2	9	61	1
Watkins	4	1	19	0
Young	51	16	118	2
Hollies	56	14	131	5
Compton	2	0	6	0
Edrich	9	1	38	1
Yardley	5	1	7	0

Umpires: H.G. Baldwin and D. Davies

AUSTRALIA WON BY AN INNINGS AND 149 RUNS

JAMES CHARLES LAKER
Surrey and Essex

Laker was the supreme English off-spinner of his time — some would say of all time. He twice reduced a cricket match to the realms of absurdity, on the first occasion at Bradford.

By R.B. Vincent

1 June 1950. A remarkable bowling performance by J. Laker was the outstanding feature of the first day's play in the Test Match trial at Bradford yesterday. England's captain won the toss and decided that sunshine in the morning after some recent rain warranted sending The Rest in to bat. How nobly he was supported by Laker is shown by an analysis of 14 overs, 12 maidens, 2 runs, 8 wickets, astonishing figures in such a game, and yet it is impossible to believe that the miserable total of 27 could not have been improved by what is assumed to be the second best eleven available in this country. England, when their turn came, were all out for 229, and then The Rest again lost two wickets cheaply before the close.

That the pitch took spin and accepted it greedily enough to make the ball turn sharply, more especially at the end to which Laker was bowling was evident so soon as he went on and he was helped with his off-break by a slight fall in the ground. Both Bailey and A. Bedser at the beginning of the innings had made the ball rise sharply and the spectators were quick to sniff trouble in store for the batsmen. Yardley's intimate knowledge of the Park Avenue wicket had stood him in good stead.

The first wicket to fall was a gift to Bailey, for Sheppard gratuitously walked in front of his stumps, offered no stroke, and was out lbw. Bailey had started with two slips and two gullies, but soon moved one of his slips across to the leg side with a chance of a ball popping up to a

ENGLAND V. THE REST
31 May 1950

THE REST

D. Kenyon	c Evans b Laker	7
D.S. Sheppard	lbw b Bailey	4
G.H.G. Doggart	c Bailey b Laker	2
P.B.H. May	c Hutton b Laker	0
D.B. Carr	c Bailey b Laker	0
E.A. Bedser	lbw b Laker	3*
R.T. Spooner	b Laker	0
R.O. Jenkins	not out	0
R. Berry	b Laker	0
F.S. Trueman	st Evans b Bedser (A.V.)	1
H.L. Jackson	c & b Laker	5
Extras	(b 3, lb 1, w 1)	5
Total		27

ENGLAND BOWLING

	O	M	R	W
Bailey	6	4	3	1
Bedser (A.V.)	9	3	12	1
Laker	14	12	2	8
Hollies	7	5	5	0

....

* Laker always insisted that he gave this county colleague a single to get off the mark.

hurried stroke. Kenyon was playing with some sureness, but the score had been taken only from seven to 10 when on came Laker. With the second ball of his first over he had Doggart caught by the most forward of his three short-legs, and the fifth ball of that over May, playing forward edged into the hands of fine short-leg. The score remained at 10, and so it still was when Carr, trying to hook a ball which certainly was not short enough to justify the stroke, was caught off a skier at mid-wicket.

Four crack batsmen out for 10 runs was amazing, and the fifth wicket fell when Evans dived wide to the leg side to hold a catch which ended Kenyon's innings with the score no higher than 18. Hollies, when he came on at the other end to Laker, could not produce the same amount of spin. With the score at 19 E. Bedser was bamboozled, and in his next over Laker took two more wickets, first bowling Spooner with a gem of a ball which went through everything that could have been in the way, and then utterly beating Berry. To vary the progress of the match Bedser took the next wicket when Evans stumped Trueman brilliantly from a ball on the leg side, but Laker was in at the death when he held a splendid catch off his own bowling to finish off the innings just when luncheon was being served up.

The remainder of the match took a day to complete, ENGLAND 229 (L. Hutton 85, J.G. Dewes 54; R. Berry 5 for 73) beating THE REST 27 and 113 (W.E. Hollies 6 for 28) by an innings and 89 runs.

The Laker summer of 1956 began at the Oval in May for Surrey against the Australians. He bowled for four and a half hours in their first innings to achieve figures of 46–18–88–10. The First Test was drawn, the Second won by Australia and the Third by England, by which time Laker had taken 32 Australian wickets in all matches at 12.31 runs each, conceding a run and a half an over — a wicket every 44 balls.

England won the toss at Old Trafford and batted until ten minutes after lunch on the second day reaching a score of 459.

OLD TRAFFORD, 1956

By John Woodcock

28 July, 1956. One of the most amazing batting collapses in the 80 years of Test cricket took place in the fourth match between England and Australia at Old Trafford yesterday and as a result it is virtually certain that for the next 18 months the Ashes will be in England's keeping. Only unyielding rain can save Australia now from overwhelming defeat, for last night they were 322 runs behind England with nine second innings wickets to fall, having been bowled out once for 84 and made to follow on in face of England's total of 459.

At four minutes to four Australia's score was 48 for no wicket and McDonald and Burke, if they were not exactly making light of the bowling of Laker and Lock, at least were suggesting that England would have to work hard for victory. Eighty minutes later Australia's first innings was over. They had capitulated to the spin of Laker whose off-breaks they had found unplayable. His remarkable figures are eloquent enough. In his last nine overs he had taken nine wickets for 16 runs, and after he had claimed a victim, seven in all, with every third ball he bowled.

There has never been anything like it before and the Australians came one by one to the slaughter convinced, it seemed, before they took strike that they had not long to live. All 10 wickets tumbled while 36 runs were being made and the villain of the piece, one felt, was not only the pitch. Nor was Laker's brilliant exploitation of it wholly responsible for what happened. Psychology played its part; for the batsmen, once the storm had broken, made little effort to seek an answer to England's spin, and in thinking there was not one they were wrong.

It was a nasty wicket certainly; but had not England scored freely on it? And the fact, too, that Lock bowled 22 overs for only one wicket and that between them Lock and Laker toiled for 18 overs before they struck at all shows that it was far from impossible. The ball turned, sometimes more quickly than another, but generally it came through at an even height. A side of well organized English batsmen accustomed to the ball deviating might have made 250 against Laker and Lock. Several Huttons, Mays and Baileys might have made more. But Australia, although they have had lessons on their tour, knew not what it was all about and this, the fact that England were crushing them in such conditions must have taken some of the gilt from England's gingerbread.

There is no doubt that this is a bad pitch for a five day Test match and the Australians may even feel that it is an unfair one. Yet in one's own mind one is sure that the groundsman did not know what, as it were, was coming out of the hat. It so happens that when it comes to spinning a way to victory Australia are left far behind, and yesterday morning when Benaud made an occasional ball bite, one knew that Laker and Lock would in all likelihood have the winning of the match in their power. Statham and Bailey had no chance of doing much and when Australia began their first innings, these two bowled only as a formality.

After 40 minutes Laker replaced Bailey and Lock Statham, but not until they changed ends half an hour later was the innings hurled into confusion. Then the disasters came thick and fast, and one must recall them as they occurred. At 48 McDonald, pushing forward to Laker, was caught off the inside edge of his bat at backward short-leg, and three balls later Harvey was bowled by what was to him a beastly leg-break. At this moment of crisis young Craig came out to bat in his first Test innings against England and the crowd received him more warmly than anyone else so far during the match.

But Craig needed more than the moral support of cricket lovers and understanding mothers, and although he looked, as he always does, neat and full of talent this was more than he could cope with. He was undefeated, it is true, at tea, but he was leg before playing back to an off break in the

second over afterwards. Before that, Burke, pushing forward at Lock, had been caught by Cowdrey low to his right at slip, and at the same score Mackay, his bat dangling like a lifeless pendulum, was caught in the gully. Oakman stooped in the manner of a giraffe for this low catch and he did the same four minutes later to catch Miller in Laker's leg trap.

A drive for 6 by Miller had been a lone defiant stroke. Indeed this and a cover shot by Archer stood like standards in Australia's surrender. But Archer soon flung his bat wildly at Laker, Benaud was caught on the boundary, and, to finish things off, Laker bowled Maddocks and Johnson in the same over. Laker returned happy in his triumph, Johnson was a picture of dejection and he must have had the sympathy of many.

AUSTRALIA

1st innings

C.C. McDonald	c Lock b Laker	32
J. Burke	c Cowdrey b Lock	22
R.N. Harvey	b Laker	0
I.D. Craig	lbw b Laker	8
K.R. Miller	c Oakman b Laker	6
K. Mackay	c Oakman b Laker	0
R.G. Archer	st Evans b Laker	6
R. Benaud	c Statham b Laker	0
R.R. Lindwall	not out	6
L. Maddocks	b Laker	4
I.W. Johnson	b Laker	0
Extras		0
Total		84

2nd innings

C.C. McDonald	retired hurt	11
J. Burke	not out	33
R.N. Harvey	c Cowdrey b Laker	0
I.D. Craig	not out	8
Extras	(lb 1)	1
Total	(1 wkt)	53

Fall of wickets: 1–48, 2–48, 3–62, 4–62, 5–62, 6–73, 7–73, 8–78, 9–84, 10–84.

Second innings: 1–28

ENGLAND BOWLING

	O	M	R	W	O	M	R	W
Statham	6	3	6	0	3	0	11	0
Bailey	4	3	4	0	3	1	11	0
Laker	16.4	4	37	9	8	2	17	1
Lock	14	3	37	1	8	3	13	0

The wicket had not suddenly deteriorated as the course of the innings might suggest. Rather had Australia's spirit been broken by Laker and in 10 minutes they were out there struggling again. They did so in fact with some success, for in the 55 minutes left they lost only Harvey. McDonald had just retired with temporary knee trouble and Harvey hammered his first ball, a full pitch from Laker, straight to Cowdrey standing 20 yards out in the direction of mid-wicket. Poor Harvey tossed his bat in the air; he had completed a pair of spectacles all in four balls and within an hour. Perhaps this is a record of some sort. But the record that mattered was Laker's and now he stands to break some more today.

Third and Fourth Days

Rain permitted only 45 minutes play on the third day (Australia 59 for two; Burke out at 55), and an hour's play on the fourth (Australia 84 for two). John Woodcock ruminated the while on Friday's play: "It was hysterical batting, sans spirit, sans skill, sans everything, in the face of some fine off-break bowling."

A final Woodcock thought reads ironically today: "A touring side to be complete should be equipped for any contingency, and if Australia come to England without genuine spin they are asking for trouble." That was in 1956; more recently, since the retirement of Gibbs, West Indies have not been so equipped.

1 August, 1956. England won the fourth Test match against Australia at Old Trafford yesterday by an innings and 170 runs, so retaining the Ashes, and Laker made the achievement possible by taking all 10 wickets in Australia's second innings. Either feat is notable enough; but when one leads to the other a mockery is made of all laws of probability. Last Friday Laker captured nine wickets in Australia's first innings and his remarkable tally of 19 wickets for 90 runs must always make this one of the most memorable games of cricket ever played. Indeed, it is unlikely that Laker's performance will ever be equalled. Cobden's match and Fowler's match and many others

LAKER   Over after over, hour after hour, and day after day, he bewildered the Australians in 1956.

have their own place in history. This one will always be remembered as Laker's match for the way in which his off-breaks paralysed Australia.

There are many tedious records which have singularly little meaning, but those which the 34-year-old Laker surpassed yesterday were all of considerable significance. In the first place he became the first bowler ever to take 19 wickets in any first-class match, let alone a Test match. In Test matches S.F. Barnes headed the list with 17 for 159 against South Africa in 1913. Against Australia, H. Verity and W. Rhodes both took 15 in a match, and for Australia F.R. Spofforth took 14 in 1882. But Laker's crop leaves all these far behind and now with 39 wickets in the series, he has equalled the number established by A.V. Bedser as a record against Australia in 1953. At the Oval, Laker will almost certainly exceed Bedser's total and the whole affair, which is already stranger than fiction, is made even more incredible by the fact that Laker also bowled out the Australians on his own for Surrey in May.

Now he has enabled England to hold the Ashes on three successive occasions for the first time since five matches in a series became the rule in 1897. It is also the first time since 1905 that England won two matches at home in one summer against Australia. And to make Laker's achievement all the more extraordinary is the fact that Lock, who is generally so irresistible when the ball is turning, plugged away for 69 overs in the match for one wicket. That to some extent is a comment on the state of the pitch. Lock did not bowl particularly well, nor did things go his way, and Laker bowled magnificently. But the pitch was very far from being a travesty.

This match will always be talked about as much as any of the 171 played between England and Australia before, not only because of Laker's analysis but also because there arose on the second day a widespread controversy over the condition of the pitch. Then the ball spun from dry turf. Yesterday it did so after persistent rain and the batsmen's task grew progressively harder. Yet for a long while it seemed that the grass would not dry sufficiently or quickly enough for England to win and as nothing was foregone the play was full of tension. One knew that the turn would not have to be ridiculously awkward for England's purpose and during the long partnership between Craig and McDonald the batting was so

good that the art was made to seem perfectly feasible. As soon as Craig was out, it was made at times to look impossible. In reality it was somewhere between the two when the game finally hurried to its conclusion.

McDonald's innings was a triumph for his fighting spirit. He is no great technician, but once he is entrenched he is as stubborn as they come. To score runs he waited for a chance to cut. For the rest of the time he played forward or back in a way too open to please the purists, but he was wonderfully watchful and there could have been no better example of unyielding concentration. Craig, who was his partner for so long, played an innings of almost equal value. He could hardly have had a fiercer baptism in Test matches against England, but the experience of it will always stand him in good stead.

Craig is still only 21, yet he had a long time in the wilderness awaiting a chance to show his skill. Now his patience and perseverence in the face of

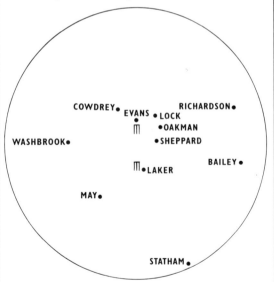

Laker's field at Old Trafford, 1956. In five Tests Laker took 46 wickets, average 9.60 (37 balls/wkt, 25 runs/100 balls)

38 right-handers	*8 left-handers*
6 bowled playing back	2 bowled
8 lbw playing back	6 caught—3 slip, 1 cover,
3 bowled not playing back	1 mid-off, 1 mid-on
2 stumped	
19 caught—12 by short-legs,	
7 deep on on-side	

all manner of disappointments have been re-warded and there are many series ahead for England to appreciate his beautiful method. Two hall-marks of class are stamped on his play. In the first place he has plenty of time in which to make his strokes, in the second his judgment of length is extremely sound, and not until Laker dislodged him yesterday did England start striding towards victory.

Play was begun only 10 minutes late, although it had rained heavily through the night until 5 o'clock, and before luncheon the pitch was too saturated to be of any use to anyone. May explored every move. He began with Bailey, who was inclined to bowl too short, and later he gave Oakman a turn. Statham, too, tried with the new ball to hammer some life from the pitch. But of course the attack was based primarily on Laker and Lock, and what they wanted most of all was some sunshine to dry the turf. There was a stiff wind, which sent the many lowering clouds scudding over the ground, but that was not enough, and towards the end of the morning some blue sky began to appear. And with it the pitch perked up and the ball showed signs of misbehaving.

At luncheon McDonald and Craig were still together. They had then added only 59, but the important thing was that they had each been batting for more than four hours. Ahead of them stretched another four and only 15 minutes of these had ticked away when Laker struck his first blow. Craig, still showing a full sense of duty after 259 minutes, played back where he might have been better advised to go forward, and was leg-before. Several other Australians were to do the same and the departure of Craig revealed a hollow middle to Australia's innings. Mackay splashed about in deep water until he sank pushing forward at Laker and being caught off the edge of the bat at second slip. Miller undermined himself, by choosing to take everything he could on the pads. One has never seen him so completely dispossessed and he was out at 130 lunging myopically at a ball he might have made into a full pitch. Archer at once was caught by the

middle of three backward short legs playing back to Laker and the day was not yet half run. The sun, too, was now blessing the scene, the threat of showers was fading and as Laker's spin quickened it seemed that there might be a collapse of the kind that had been witnessed on Friday.

Perhaps if Benaud had fallen at once there would have been, for Mackay, Miller, and Archer had not scored a run between them and between 25 past two and five to three four wickets had gone for 16 runs. But McDonald stood immensely determined amid this crumbling world, and now Benaud stayed with him until tea. That was for 80 minutes, and it began to seem again as though England might be thwarted. Benaud carried gamesmanship almost to an extreme by asking for guard in every over, and slowly and deliberately taking a botanical interest in the pitch after every ball. It is fair enough to repair each divot mark which the ball makes, but Benaud's way of doing it irritated the crowd, just as his admirable powers of resistance must have worried England.

When the final two hours of the evening started, whichever side was to win still had a long way to go. Someone was going to be denied and the likelihood that it would be Australia increased when McDonald's monumental vigil of 337 minutes was ended by the second ball after tea. He pushed forward at an off-break and Oakman at backward short leg took his fifth catch of the match. The next two balls from Laker must have settled any doubts that had been sown in English minds. Both of them turned viciously and now it was only a matter of time and a question of whether Laker could take the last three wickets himself.

This was suddenly a fabulous possibility, and three-quarters of an hour later it was an accomplished deed. First Benaud was forced back on to his stumps and bowled by a generously flighted off-break, then Lindwall was snapped up in the leg trap, and finally Maddocks was trapped leg-before. Australia were beaten, the crowd flooded the ground, there were smiles and handshakes, and the hero jogged off as though nothing very much had happened. Close behind him was May, who could feel justly proud at having led England to the Ashes at his first attempt. His splendid efforts must not be overlooked, but this now was Laker's hour, and here to end with and for all time are his figures. In Australia's second innings he took 10 for 53, in the match 19 for 90 in 68 overs, and yesterday eight for 26 in 36 faultless overs. Surely there may never again be anything like it.

ENGLAND V. AUSTRALIA
Old Trafford, 26–30 July 1956

ENGLAND

P.E. Richardson	c Maddocks b Benaud	104
M.C. Cowdrey	c Maddocks b Lindwall	80
Rev D.S. Sheppard	b Archer	113
P.B.H. May	c Archer b Benaud	43
T.E. Bailey	b Johnson	20
Washbrook	lbw b Johnson	6
Oakman	c Archer b Johnson	10
Evans	st Maddocks b Johnson	47
Laker	run out	3
Lock	not out	25
Statham	c Maddocks b Lindwall	0
Extras	(b 2, lb 5, w1)	8
Total		459

Fall of wickets: 1–174, 2–195, 3–288, 4–321, 5–327, 6–339, 7–401, 8–417, 9–458, 10–459.

AUSTRALIA BOWLING

	O	M	R	W
Lindwall	21.3	6	63	2
Miller	21	6	41	0
Archer	22	6	73	1
Johnson	47	10	151	4
Benaud	47	17	123	2

AUSTRALIA
1st innings

C.C. McDonald	c Lock b Laker	32
J. Burke	c Cowdrey b Lock	22
R.N. Harvey	b Laker	0
I.D. Craig	lbw b Laker	8
K.R. Miller	c Oakman b Laker	6
K. Mackay	c Oakman b Laker	0
R.G. Archer	st Evans b Laker	6
R. Benaud	c Statham b Laker	0
R.R. Lindwall	not out	6
L. Maddocks	b Laker	4
I.W. Johnson	b Laker	0
Extras		0
Total		84

AUSTRALIA
2nd innings

C.C. McDonald	c Oakman b Laker	89
J. Burke	c Lock b Laker	33
R.N. Harvey	c Cowdrey b Laker	0
I.D. Craig	lbw b Laker	38
K.R. Miller	b Laker	0
K. Mackay	c Oakman b Laker	0
R.G. Archer	c Oakman b Laker	0
R. Benaud	b Laker	18
R.R. Lindwall	c Lock b Laker	8
L. Maddocks	lbw b Laker	2
I.W. Johnson	not out	1
Extras	(b 12, lb 4)	16
Total		205

Fall of wickets: 1–48, 2–48, 3–62, 4–62, 5–62, 6–73, 7–73, 8–78, 9–84, 10–84.

Second innings: 1–28, 2–55, 3–114, 4–124, 5–130, 6–130, 7–181, 8–198, 9–203, 10–205.

ENGLAND BOWLING

	O	M	R	W	O	M	R	W
Statham	6	3	6	0	16	9	15	0
Bailey	4	3	4	0	20	8	31	0
Laker	16.4	4	37	9	51.2	23	53	10
Lock	14	3	37	1	55	30	69	0
Oakman					8	3	21	0

Umpires: F.S. Lee and E. Davies

ENGLAND WON BY AN INNINGS AND 170 RUNS

ALEX VICTOR BEDSER
Surrey

Bedser took his first wicket for Surrey less than ten weeks before his 28th birthday: such was the effect of the Second World War on his career. After a mere 32 wickets in the County Championship he played for England; in the three-match series of 1946 against India his 24 wickets averaged 12.41. Thereafter this great bowler was the basis of his country's attack for many years. Described as medium-pace, he was, of course, much faster, though he liked to have the wicketkeeper standing up as Strudwick and Duckworth did for Tate. However, his most famous delivery — the one which started on the off stump, swung late to the leg, and then came back to hit middle and off, so accounting for Bradman at Adelaide in 1946–7 — did have Evans standing back.

Prior to the Tests of 1953, Bedser had appeared 42 times for England, the other opening bowlers numbering 15 (including F.R. Brown on one occasion when Bailey was injured). Bedser had taken 182 wickets, the others 101. Before Trueman's sensational debut against India in 1952 the score was Bedser 162, others 72. From which we may conclude that Bedser, like Tate, was not a lucky bowler.

TRENT BRIDGE, 1953

By Geoffrey Green

12 June, 1953. When one writes that the siege of Nottingham has begun it is as good a way as any other of describing the opening of the first Test match at Trent Bridge yesterday. On a grey day, broken now and then by the lightest of drizzles and bad light that finally put a summary end to the proceedings at 6 o'clock, Australia could muster no more than 157 runs for three wickets in a playing time of four hours and a half. And this after winning the toss on a docile pitch full of runs for those who wanted to collect them.

Thus England at this moment may be said to have come out of the opening round of the struggle with their heads reasonably high. None more so than Bedser, who in a truly great exhibition of bowling stood astride the scene like the giant that he is. Even if he had had no claim to the scalps of Hole, Morris and Harvey, the rest of his achievement in the conditions would alone have entitled him to the highest praise, for to bowl 25 overs against Australia for a mere 26 runs is in itself a feat to remember well. He bowled only one loose ball all day, and this Morris dispatched to the long leg boundary. Two other 4's were conceded by him, one from a no-ball, the other off the inside edge of Miller's bat, perilously close to the off stump, and in all there were only 16 scoring strokes off his superb length from beginning to end. It was a great effort, supported by the more prosaic qualities of Wardle and Bailey, that pinned Australia down.

England, in fact, won their point with only four bowlers, for their policy was revealed the moment they decided to exclude Statham for a batsman. In effect, the day was carried through with three bowlers and a half, for Tattersall came little into the picture with his rolled off-spin, for which there was little response, and when he did he was comparatively expensive against the left-handed Morris. Morris, indeed, once caused almost an earth tremor by helping himself to three boundaries in a single over. All this was fine enough in its way. But had it not been for Bedser the day would have been as dreary as the leaden skies that hung low over the crowded scene.

Four hours and a half for 157 runs; Hassett, precise and neat, almost that same span for 67; Morris, spending three hours and a quarter over his 67! What a picture it conjures up. Can one wonder at the restiveness that began to spread like a rash around the ground when, by mid-afternoon, the Australian total had yet not reached three-figure proportions. It is a story as gloomy as some Russian novel. But there it is. This is a five-day Test match in the modern idiom, when the Dr Jekyll becomes the Mr Hyde. Players lose their identity as the strange malady descends with its burden. Fancy even a batsman of the cavalier spirit of Miller descending to a watchful automaton taking over an hour for 19 runs.

So, standing back from the struggle as one would do to assess a painting, one can see it in its true perspective. Here, already begun, is a battle of attrition. England, packed with batting, have set out to contain their opponents with a limited attack. Australia have answered by digging in after a disturbing and early disaster when Bedser's seventh ball of the day, a late in-swinger, hummed past Hole's forward stroke to knock back the middle stump. Against a defensive field, set astutely by Hutton to Wardle and Tattersall, and to Bailey, when the last named was performing as a stock bowler, the Australian stroke play was never severe enough — nor indeed was the intention ever really apparent — to break through the ring. That the left-handed Wardle during his morning and afternoon spells, each of an hour, never employed a slip or any other fielder in an offensive position is

in itself commentary enough. The same applied also to Tattersall when he shared the attack for a part of the afternoon.

So the day painfully unwound itself after that first shout of exaltation when Hole went. By lunch time, taken 10 minutes early because of a drizzle, Australia were no more than 54 for one as Morris and Hassett plodded forward. Each was once beaten by Bedser's late swing, but these were the only ripples on a smooth surface. Somewhere just before half-past three the 100 went up as Morris and Hassett, at times visibly in pain with his forearm, reached their fifties. One could sympathize with the ironical applause of an audience whose patience had been well tried, and further tested by a gentle fret that took away another 40 minutes of play before tea, with Australia 123 for one. Not that there was much to be missed in truth.

But the new ball immediately afterwards brought in a last crowded hour. Morris was trapped leg before on his weakness on the leg stump, once again to become Bedser's victim, and when Harvey, the one man who might have brought brightness to the shadows, was held by Compton at short fine leg — how nearly he dropped it! — there was a positive upsurge of emotion. Australia 128 for three and the great Harvey, unhappily meeting the shine, out for nought.

But that was the end of the excitement, though Miller, struggling against the receding light of the

AUSTRALIA
1st innings

G.B. Hole	b Bedser	0
A.R. Morris	lbw b Bedser	67
A.L. Hassett	not out	67
R.N. Harvey	c Compton b Bedser	0
K.R. Miller	not out	19
Extras	(b 2, lb 1, nb 1)	4
Total	(3 wkts)	157

Fall of wickets: 1–2, 2–124, 3–128.

ENGLAND BOWLING (to date)

	O	M	R	W
Bedser	25	12	26	3
Bailey	28	7	55	0
Wardle	29	14	34	0
Tattersall	10	1	38	0

evening, was beaten three times in one of Bailey's overs. Miller, chosen for Australia though not fully fit, may yet find something of his genius as Hassett moves on towards the goal he has set himself. But rain stands in the air and the best laid plans of both sides, negative or otherwise, may yet be upset.

Second Day

13 June, 1953. The siege of Nottingham yesterday became Alice in Wonderland at Trent Bridge. How else is one to explain a Test match which so completely changed its character, with England gaining an apparent initial advantage with her limited attack and then losing it with her strengthened batting?

Who, for instance, would have dared foretell at 20 minutes past one, with a giant scoreboard showing Hassett past his century and Miller past 50 and the total 237 for three, that Australia would never reach 250? Or that within two hours and a half of that miracle the same wave of disaster would have enveloped the cream of England's batsmen as Kenyon, Simpson, Compton, Graveney, Hutton, and May were back in the cold shadows of the pavilion? Thus England, facing a total of 249, were 92 for six when bad light for the second day in succession cut short the struggle a moment before 6 o'clock.

If the struggle, so watchful and evasive at the start, yesterday burst into full life, let it not be thought that the infamous Nottingham pitch itself caused the upheaval. Its character, indeed, remained largely unaffected by the rain of the previous night, except that perhaps towards the close of yesterday's sensations Hill did manage to turn a ball or two quickly as he pitched in the rough. No, what caused events really to turn a violent somersault was magnificently controlled swing bowling in a heavy, damp atmosphere with the new ball, first by Bedser, finely seconded by Bailey, and later by the devastating Lindwall, all of it supported by catching of the highest grade.

So the issue has at last been joined. It was joined, one repeats, at that moment of 20 minutes past one when Miller, clearly champing under the oppressive chains of self-discipline, finally swept at Wardle's accurate length to give Bailey a well-judged high running catch on the leg side. Thus was ended a fourth wicket partnership of 109 in nearly three hours. That in fact was the breaking point of the tactical, defensive struggle between Hutton and Hassett.

From the moment that Bailey took the new ball in his hands at 244 for four it became difficult to chase the thread of events. But this much at least stood out clear and resplendent. Bedser, this day, again bowled for England as he can seldom have bowled before, emerging with the final figures of seven for 55 and thus, in one giant, exciting sweep, equalling S.F. Barne's distinction of 189 wickets in Test cricket.

Cold figures can only tell the facts. They cannot disclose the heart, but cold figures show that between a quarter past two and five minutes to three Australia tumbled from 244 for four to 249 all out. It was enough to make any Englishman see visions and dream dreams.

It all began as Evans dived acrobatically low to his left, snatching Benaud's too finely judged glance to Bailey's very first delivery with the new ball. It was a wonderful catch, and all that was needed to rouse the deepest creative energies of Bedser from the pavilion end. In the very next over the Surrey giant pitched a fizzer on Hassett's leg stump and hit the top of the off, the sort of ball that alone was capable of dislodging Australia's captain.

So Hassett went, having discharged his duty faithfully after six hours and a half at the crease. His innings may have lacked the higher graces, but it was untroubled and it was his answer to Hutton. Certainly it has now assumed a special significance, together with the watchful part played by Morris and Miller, in the light of after events. In all the sudden destruction that so quickly followed, as Tallon, Lindwall, Hill, and Davidson fell before the whirlwind, Bedser ended with four wickets for two runs in 27 balls, and Bailey two for 2.

With the river Trent at his back Lindwall, too, soon caught the tide. In his fourth over a fast in-swinger was glided by Kenyon high to Hill's right at short fine leg — one of the steel band of eight fieldsmen ringing the bat. In the very same over his second ball, also an in-swinger, to Simpson, beat the batsman's back stroke to gain an lbw decision.

In Lindwall's next over Compton, playing that forward stroke of his that usually leaves cover point groping to the left, now did not quite find the true length as the ball swung away late. In a flash Morris had dived forward in the gully to hold a lightning catch just off the ground. Thus, at the same desperate score of 17 three of England's champions had gone. It was bowling and catching in the grand manner, magnificently wrought, swift and breathless.

Now England were in the fire. But Hutton, serene and classical in style, with Graveney at his side, spanned the last half-hour to tea when the score had crept up to 41, just as Hill with his top spin, relieved Johnston. Nor was there relief later as lbw appeals against both batsmen sprung excitedly from the lips of Lindwall, Hill and then even the left-handed Davidson, once he had taken over from Lindwall at the end of his great spell of bowling that had covered an hour and a half.

But England were by no means out of the wood at Lindwall's retirement. Certainly Hutton, striking Hill beautifully through the covers, and Graveney added 59 runs in just over the hour to upset the normal pace of things. But between 5 and 6 o'clock as the light receded rapidly, England lost three more wickets.

First Graveney, glancing loosely at Hill, allowed Benaud to make another sharp and great diving catch at close fine leg. When Hutton, the master himself, the one man apparently able to stand above the storm, then drove slightly late at Davidson, there was Benaud to take yet one more swift catch in the gully. Hutton's 43 runs stood alone in the match for grace and quality. Certainly they showed their value in a sad score of 82 for five.

May fought on gallantly through three-quarters of an hour of severe examination in the poorest of visibility, while an appeal against the light by Bailey was turned down. But no sooner was May finally out to Hill, snapped up by Tallon off the edge of a forward stroke, than the umpires closed the proceedings after only two balls had been bowled at Evans in the sepulchral gloom. It was a puzzling climax indeed as the cinders of a strange day were being raked out.

AUSTRALIA

1st innings

G.B. Hole	b Bedser	0
A.R. Morris	lbw b Bedser	67
A.L. Hassett	b Bedser	115
R.N. Harvey	c Compton b Bedser	0
K.R. Miller	c Bailey b Wardle	55
R. Benaud	c Evans b Bailey	3
A.K. Davidson	b Bedser	4
D. Tallon	b Bedser	0
R.R. Lindwall	c Evans b Bailey	0
J.C. Hill	b Bedser	0
Extras	(b 2, lb 2, nb 1)	5
Total		249

Fall of wickets: 1–2, 2–124, 3–128, 4–237, 5–244, 6–244, 7–246, 8–247, 9–248, 10–249.

ENGLAND BOWLING

	O	M	R	W
Bedser	38.3	16	55	7
Bailey	44	14	75	2
Wardle	35	16	55	1
Tattersall	23	5	59	0

ENGLAND

1st innings

L. Hutton	c Benaud b Davidson	43
D. Kenyon	c Hill b Lindwall	8
R.T. Simpson	lbw b Lindwall	0
D.C.S. Compton	c Morris b Lindwall	0
T.W. Graveney	c Benaud b Hill	22
P.B.H. May	c Tallon b Hill	9
T.E. Bailey	not out	2
T.G. Evans	not out	0
Extras	(b 5, lb 3)	8
Total	(6 wkts)	92

Fall of wickets: 1–17, 2–17, 3–17, 4–76, 5–82, 6–92.

AUSTRALIA BOWLING (to date)

	O	M	R	W
Lindwall	12	1	35	3
Johnston	8	3	14	0
Hill	14	7	24	2
Davidson	8	4	11	1

Third Day

16 June 1953. England this day expects every batsman to do his duty at Trent Bridge. The signal is hoist and the aim clear. Kenyon alone is gone with 42 scored, but Hutton and his lieutenants remain, left with 187 runs to gather for a famous Test match victory over Australia.

The task may prove to be a mountain or a molehill. Yet so far the Nottingham pitch, its character blackened by Australian totals of 249 and 123 and an England innings of 144, has really been its benign self: and 48 overs must still be bowled before Lindwall can use the new ball once more. But the threat of rain, which was falling again last evening, remains, possibly to alter the whole picture. The Trent Bridge scene is alive and expectant. It awaits an end none dare foretell.

Saturday, as Friday, was three-dimensional. Events stood out exciting and clear as the balance of a remarkable match was swung once more by the wonderful bowling of Bedser. Whatever happens, his superhuman efforts will never be forgotten. When Australia went to the crease again, one over before luncheon, with a comfortable first-innings lead of 105, the same question was heard on every side: "Can he do it again?" The afternoon and the man gave up their answer, and that first faint flicker of hope spurted into a consuming fire as Australia was stripped of her authority.

Bedser indeed even surpassed his figures of Friday, though the intrinsic quality of his performance was perhaps not quite on the same exalted level, for the Australian batting, Morris apart, now curiously lacked its traditional application. Yet the fact remains that by taking another seven wickets to gain the almost unbelievable match analysis of 14 for 99 — this on a pitch that offered little material help — Bedser has turned away, momentarily at least, the finger of defeat that was so close upon England's shoulder. In doing so he passed S.F. Barnes's record of 189 Test match wickets, and now only C.V. Grimmett, the Australian is ahead of him with 216.

But if the lion's share of the praise is Bedser's,

two other factors must not be overlooked as the game hangs so delicately balanced. First, England's out-cricket of Saturday, finely controlled by Hutton, certainly equalled that of Australia earlier. Not the flimsiest of chances was let slip, Simpson in particular snatching out of the thin air at deep square leg a one-handed running catch from Tallon just before tea, the like of which takes place usually in imagination. Next, one would add the batting of Bailey and Wardle in the morning, as England struggled to repair some of the damage begun overnight by Lindwall. Indeed, when it all comes to be weighed up at the end Bailey and Wardle may find a place of honour beside Bedser and Hutton. Similarly, should the scales finally tip towards Australia, Morris's great and lonely innings of Saturday afternoon may yet prove to have been the decisive ounce in the desperate battle.

Bailey and Wardle, in fact, almost alone were instrumental in England reaching finally a total of 144 before Lindwall finished off the innings with the new ball just before luncheon. In all Bailey, utterly composed, got his head down well to hold up Australia for an hour and a half before a quick top spinner from Hill ended him. Wardle, too, was no less admirable in his unbeaten knock of an hour. It was a characteristic effort, built on a mixture of Yorkshire grit and unorthodox attacking strokes of his own left-handed variety. He brought character and humour to the dark picture, too. Bless a man who rubs his chest when hit on the toe by a fast full toss, thus stripping the mask of convention from a Test match, however desperate!

So, at 25 minutes past one, Morris and Hole came to face Bedser once more, their partnership in effect already worth 105 runs. One noticed, incidentally, that Hassett — unlike Hutton later in the evening — called only for the light hand-roller as the prelude to his side's second innings. In the light of after events and the small spot that Bedser for a short time found at the Trent Bridge end — Hassett himself was its one victim — this may have proved a wrong decision. But pitches and rollers are deep mysteries. At all events things soon began to hum in the afternoon, as Australia openly set out to go quickly for consolidation.

The easy and graceful way in which Morris disclosed his left-handed strokes as he punished Bailey stood out in sharp contrast with his methods of last Thursday. Australia may yet regret the runs they wasted then, just as Morris's innings now shone out as a beacon from the disasters that so soon began to flow.

Bedser, with the pavilion his background, again was the executioner, destroying all but the inspired Morris. First he hit Hole's off stump behind an attempted forcing stroke to the off. That was at half-past two, with the total 28. An hour later the scoreboard showed 68 for five, with Morris 50 not out. The atmosphere was electric as the packed assembly, living every ball, itself touched the very heartbeat of the quickening tussle.

After Hole there came the diminutive Hassett. Outwardly he remained calm, but soon he was troubled and then dispatched by Bedser as England's giant pounded the ball up off an indefinable spot. Hutton took the simple catch in the leg trap from the shoulder of the bat. Harvey, the menace, soon had his fangs drawn, finely caught off a hook, also close in Bedser's leg trap, by Graveney, who had been moved there astutely by Hutton. The great Miller, surprised by a full pitch, tossed his head in disgust as he hit the ball straight to Kenyon at mid-wicket. When Benaud at once lost his leg stump Australia, half the side gone, once more were bowed before Bedser. Only Morris, past 50 and resplendent in stroke play, had stood up to the storm as the Surrey man at last put on his sweater, having taken wickets in his fourth, seventh, ninth, 11th, and 12th overs for 28 runs.

But where Bedser left off Tattersall took over. A clever ball, going with the arm perhaps, found the important leg stump of Morris to end a distinguished innings. His 60 runs out of a position that showed 81 for 6 speak their own volumes. England were over the hump, and by a quarter to five, with sure, deep catching, had bought the last wickets as Davidson, Tallon, Lindwall, and Hill tried to hit their way out of the

net. In two and a quarter hours and 39 overs Australia had been put out for 123, and there was Bedser receiving yet a second tremendous ovation as he ran up the pavilion steps.

England's target at last was revealed — 229 to win with time to spare. But the late evening had first to be spanned, a period as tense as any in a match already full of drama. First Lindwall's violent lbw appeal against Hutton with his second ball drew no answer. Then, with the over incomplete, Hutton won his appeal against the light to gain 15 minutes' grace. So, with Lindwall on the attack, the final hour unwound itself desperately until bad light again relieved England of a last quarter of an hour's examination. In all this Hutton was sure. But Kenyon, a mixture of solid and airy strokes, followed Miller's demise by hitting a full pitch from Hill straight at mid-on. And now Hutton and Simpson start again on the last journey. There is more than one way to Parnassus.

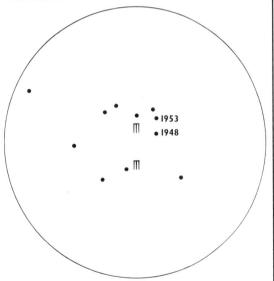

Bedser's field at Trent Bridge, 1948 and 1953, or, as he prefers to say, the initial field placings: "I would point out that my field was never static. I moved the fielding position in accordance with how the ball was behaving, and how certain batsmen played." (Placing of short-legs in 1948 and 1953 varied according to player and how much the ball was swinging.) There is a famous photograph of a Bradman dismissal at Trent Bridge in 1948. Hutton, just behind square, is taking the catch: two other short-legs are in front of the wicket. Bradman's feet are well wide of the off stump.

Of England's 42 for one wicket at the close, Hutton had scored 10 and Simpson 8. Rain prevented any play on the fourth day, and until the final two hours of the fifth day, during which time Hutton and Simpson added a further 78 runs.

ENGLAND v. AUSTRALIA
Trent Bridge, 11–13, 15, 16 June 1953

AUSTRALIA

1st innings

G.B. Hole	b Bedser	0
A.R. Morris	lbw b Bedser	67
A.L. Hassett	b Bedser	115
R.N. Harvey	c Compton b Bedser	0
K.R. Miller	c Bailey b Wardle	55
R. Benaud	c Evans b Bailey	3
A.K. Davidson	b Bedser	4
D. Tallon	b Bedser	0
R.R. Lindwall	c Evans b Bailey	0
J.C. Hill	b Bedser	0
W.A. Johnston	not out	0
Extras	(b 2, lb 2, nb 1)	5
Total		249

2nd innings

G.B. Hole	b Bedser	5
A.R. Morris	b Tattersall	60
A.L. Hassett	c Hutton b Bedser	5
R.N. Harvey	c Graveney b Bedser	2
K.R. Miller	c Kenyon b Bedser	5
R. Benaud	b Bedser	0
A.K. Davidson	c Graveney b Tattersall	6
D. Tallon	c Simpson b Tattersall	15
R.R. Lindwall	c Tattersall b Bedser	12
J.C. Hill	c Tattersall b Bedser	4
W.A. Johnston	not out	4
Extras	(lb 5)	5
Total		123

Fall of wickets: 1–2, 2–124, 3–128, 4–237, 5–244, 6–244, 7–246, 8–247, 9–248, 10–249.

Second innings: 1–28, 2–44, 3–50, 4–64, 5–68, 6–81, 7–92, 8–106, 9–115, 10–123.

ENGLAND BOWLING

	O	M	R	W	O	M	R	W
Bedser	38.3	16	55	7	17.2	7	44	7
Bailey	44	14	75	2	5	1	28	0
Wardle	35	16	55	1	12	3	24	0
Tattersall	23	5	59	0	5	0	22	3

ENGLAND

1st innings

L. Hutton	c Benaud b Davidson	43
D. Kenyon	c Hill b Lindwall	8
R.T. Simpson	lbw b Lindwall	0
D.C.S. Compton	c Morris b Lindwall	0
T.W. Graveney	c Benaud b Hill	22
P.B.H. May	c Tallon b Hill	9
T.E. Bailey	lbw b Hill	13
T.G. Evans	c Tallon b Davidson	8
J.H. Wardle	not out	29
A.V. Bedser	lbw b Lindwall	2
R. Tattersall	b Lindwall	2
Extras	(b 5, lb 3)	8
Total		144

2nd innings

L. Hutton	not out	60
D. Kenyon	c Hassett b Hill	16
R.T. Simpson	not out	28
Extras	(b 8, lb 4, w 2, nb 2)	16
Total	(1 wkt)	120

Fall of wickets: 1–17, 2–17, 3–17, 4–76, 5–82, 6–92, 7–107, 8–121, 9–136, 10–144.

Second innings: 1–26.

AUSTRALIA BOWLING

	O	M	R	W	O	M	R	W
Lindwall	20.4	2	57	2	16	4	37	0
Johnston	18	7	22	0	18	9	14	0
Hill	19	8	35	3	12	3	26	1
Davidson	15	7	22	2	5	1	7	0
Benaud					5	0	15	0
Morris					2	0	5	0

Umpires: D. Davies and Harold Elliott

MATCH DRAWN

FAZAL MAHMOOD
Northern India, Punjab and Lahore

Fazal Mahmood was the principal agent in Pakistan's unique achievement — a Test victory on their first tour of England. Indeed, his 12 wickets for 99 runs at the Oval evoked memories of Spofforth's 14 for 90 on the same ground in 1882. Bowling at just over medium-pace with a movement from leg, Fazal was unfortunate to miss selection for the 1946 All-India party in England.

Readers with a sense of the macabre may take delight in Fazal's figures in nine Tests against India in 1954–5 and 1960–61: 385.5 overs, 153 maidens, 570 runs, 24 wickets, 23.75 average. Fazal conceded a mere 1.4 runs per over in nine draws.

By John Woodcock

13 August 1954. Strange as it may seem, Pakistan probably spent last night listening and hoping for the sound of rain, for in a tricky wicket this morning seems to lie their only chance of extending England after the happenings of the first day of the fourth Test match at the Oval. The pattern then was the same as it has been for most of the series, namely a delay for rain and a desperate struggle for runs by Pakistan, which produced a total of 133 in just under 3½, England knocked one run off this score before stumps were drawn.

Poor Pakistan. They won the toss, and that was a promising start...But they squandered their good fortune, and the sad truth is that their innings seemed vulnerable at once.

Hanif, their strength and stay, was lost in the first over before a run had been scored, leg-before-wicket hooking at a long hop from Statham, and for almost two hours and a half after that England's three fast bowlers were in complete charge. It was a quarter past 5 before a spinner was tried, and by then the score was 82 for eight wickets.

One has come to expect nothing but good and accurate bowling from Statham, and just that was forthcoming. From Loader and Tyson there was something less accurate, but at times equally penetrating. The former's greatest merit yesterday lay in his subtle changes of pace, for his direction was not all it might have been, and when it came to demolishing the tail he could not do it. Tyson, on the other hand, after a wild first over, bowled straighter than when last one saw him, and through the air he was certainly extremely quick. It is easily possible to imagine him coming off the Perth wicket fearsomely fast in a few weeks' time.

Tyson bowled 13.4 overs in four short spells, the last of which was of only four balls and the first of four overs, for which he was given the new ball in preference to Loader, had its dramatic moments. Evans stood as far back as he can ever have done, and Tyson ran from well towards Vauxhall, but not a single ball of his opening over was straight, although Alimuddin slashed at one and gave a technical chance to third slip. His next over, however, was much better, and off the third and fourth balls of his third over he bowled Alimuddin and Maqsood, both of whom played late and tentative strokes. That was 10 for three, and after 50 minutes, with the score at 26, Waqar, who had already nearly fallen — played on to Statham — was bowled in Loader's second over, driving at a ball of full length with his head in the air.

There followed the first partnership of any consequence, Imtiaz and Kardar adding 25 in half an hour, and while they were together there was just a chance that the innings might be saved. But Imtiaz's favourite stroke, the hook, was his undoing when Tyson came back for his second spell. He flailed at a bouncer, and Evans, springing towards the leg slips, made a most spectacular catch. At the same score Wazir, before he had faced a ball, was smartly run out by Simpson fielding at short leg, and Fazal gave Evans a further chance to show his agility with a catch off the inside edge of the bat. [At tea the score was 59 for 7].

...It transpired, however, that the end was not so near as Kardar must have feared, for the last three wickets more than doubled the score, and when finally the last man was out there was time for only an over apiece by Fazal and Mahmud in the gloomiest light before half past 6.

...It is interesting that England's bowlers averaged only 15 overs an hour for the 205 minutes of Pakistan's innings.*

Close: PAKISTAN 133, ENGLAND 1 for no wicket.

Rain prevented any play on Friday, 13 August.

Third Day

16 August, 1954. Pakistan are 66 runs ahead of England with six second innings wickets to fall in the final Test match at the Oval. This position

. . . .

* The following winter in Australia, again under the captaincy of Hutton, England once bowled 54 8-ball overs in five hours, i.e. about 14.2 6-ball overs an hour. By the standards of the 1980s this was most commendable.

was reached on Saturday after much absorbing and fluctuating play watched by a fine crowd which basked content beneath the sun. Here at last was the traditional summer scene — the emerald grass, the glistening flannels, the myriad shirtsleeves round the ground, the spontaneous cheers and the happy buzz of conversation.

Fourteen wickets fell in 305 minutes for 192 runs, and, of course, the whole tenor and progress of the day revolved around the behaviour of the pitch. To begin with it was so wet that, in spite of the warm morning air, and although no rain had fallen since Friday's dreadful downpour, play was not possible until a quarter past 12. As it dried out, however, its temper became frayed, and for a while only the great as well as the lucky could survive. That, at least, was the impression which England's batsmen gave, and that they lived until teatime was due to the talents of Compton and May and perhaps as well to the inexperience of Pakistan's slow bowlers, accurate as these were. Between innings the heavy roller cooled some of the fire in the grass and it never again flared up quite as it had done.

One could not suppress the feeling as the covers were rolled on at the end of play that England had scarcely earned their position of advantage. About their batting there had seemed a lack of real purpose and determination, nor had they bowled with the greatest aggression and imagination. The need for Bedser was pronounced. McConnon, especially, did nothing on the day to raise any hopes that he will be a thorn in Australia's side, and had Pakistan batted on Thursday as they could and should have done and scored something over 200, England would still be well in the wood. As it is they should achieve whatever is asked of them in the fourth innings, unless there is more rain or by then the whole top of the wicket has been chipped away.

If there were shortcomings in England's performance there was, as well, much that was good, and no day in the present series of Test matches has been so evenly contested. Pakistan were soon fired by the idea that for a change they had

England on the run, and their first innings lead of three looked at times like being much more substantial. A close attacking field was placed and in Mahmud's second over Simpson, pushing forward "unsuspectingly", could not escape the first lifter of the day, Kardar taking a comfortable catch in the gully. Hutton, who had watched a ball drop from his pads on to his stumps without doing any damage, and May now added 20 in 10 minutes, 18 of them brilliantly in two overs in which they took several calculated risks to try to shift the moral balance and knock the bowlers off a length.

Fazal and Mahmud, to their credit, kept their accuracy and, indeed, until luncheon, bowled faultlessly. The enduring Fazal was still bowling when the innings closed, a spell of four hours broken only by luncheon, and perhaps it was not surprising that he could not still control his direction when, in mid-afternoon with the wicket at its worst, compelling the batsmen to play was the first essential. Hutton and May after their short assault were forced to return to defence, and when Hutton next took a liberty he was out. He swung at Fazal, the ball soared off the top edge high over the slips, and Imtiaz took a catch running back towards the boundary.

May and Compton played through splendidly until luncheon, the former making one matchless cover drive off Fazal, but with the 50 passed at half past two the pitch took a turn for the worse. At 56 May edged a horrible ball to gully, where Kardar held a good right-handed catch. Graveney had a short nightmare of an innings during which he hardly made contact before snicking a forward stroke to second slip; and Evans's play seemed to be a confession that he had virtually no chance of staying in.

Fazal was in command; the ball was rearing and turning, and suddenly at 69 for five, the beginning of the huge English tail* was easily

. . . .

* England's normal buffer state before the tail, T.E. Bailey, was on duty at Weston-super-Mare, where he appeared at 12.30 and reached his 100 soon after 6 p.m. His calls, so men said, could be heard on the old pier, a goodly distance from Clarence Park.

showing. But, in fact, except for Statham, the last five batsmen all played with some skill and resolution while watching a remarkable display by Compton at the other end.

Compton batted for 2 hours 20 minutes. For most of this time he concentrated on defence and played superbly, and his runs, when they came, were usually the result of improvization. His antics sometimes led him into trouble; he was badly dropped twice, at 34 and again at 38, and towards the end of his innings he hit at most things as though feeling that this was the right procedure and if it failed then little would be lost for Pakistan would be in before the pitch eased. In the end England had much to thank him for, just as Pakistan owed a great deal to Fazal and Mahmud.

Pakistan were left with five minutes under two hours batting before the close, and not for the first time they began with a masterly little innings by Hanif. Statham and Loader bowled five overs between them before Hutton put his trust in his spinners, and Hanif, who undoubtedly has a spark of genius about his batting, scored the first 19 runs, 15 of them off Statham with flashing hits to leg, and four with a magnificent square cut off Loader. He did not score again, however, and 20 minutes later he was caught at slip reaching forward to a sharply turning leg break. That was the beginning of trouble for Pakistan, and in the struggle that followed Shujauddin, who had gone in first with Hanif, was also caught at slip, Maqsood was taken at mid-wicket, and the dogged Waqar smartly thrown out by Hutton. A couple less wickets gone and the star of Pakistan would now be high.

Close: PAKISTAN 133 and 63 for 4, ENGLAND 130 (D.C.S. Compton 53; Fazal Mahmood 6 for 53).

Fourth Day

17 August 1954. England enter the last day's play at the Oval needing 43 runs to beat Pakistan in the fourth Test match, and the batsmen left to do or die are Wardle, Tyson, Statham, Loader and McConnon, the last of whom is suffering from the effects of a dislocated finger. The position is fraught with excitement — one would need uncommon faith to fancy England's chances — and if this morning does bring one of the most unexpected results in the history of Test cricket England will have themselves to blame. Most of their cricket yesterday was thoroughly poor — in batting, bowling and fielding — and that is something which one reports with a heavy heart on the eve of an Australian tour.

In the general disappointment at England's performance one must not forget to praise Pakistan for a splendid recovery. In the first 40 minutes yesterday they seemed to shatter their last hopes of victory, for, at the end of that time, they were but 85 runs ahead, with only their last three batsmen remaining. In the end, however, these three doubled the score, and managed to leave England 168 to win with 155 minutes yesterday and all to-day in which to get them.

It seemed, and should have been, a straightforward enough task. The wicket was true; the outfield was faster than at any time during the match, and one's only fear was of the length of England's tail, for which the selectors, rather than the batsmen themselves were to blame. And surely, in any case, the chance of Pakistan penetrating as far as the tail was remote. Indeed, there was reason to hope that England would get the match over and done with before nightfall.

That was how one felt about it when Hutton and Simpson came out at 25 minutes to 4 to begin their task, with another huge crowd revelling in the sunshine. Nor at teatime, taken 50 minutes later, had one changed one's opinion, although Fazal by then had captured the great Hutton's wicket at 15 when the latter, having been drawn forward to a leg cutter, gave Imtiaz a catch behind the wicket. The score was 49 for one, and May had made some brilliant strokes off the back foot. By 5 o'clock he and Simpson had added 51 in as many minutes, and even for an hour after

the latter had driven a half-volley straight back at Zulfiqar there seemed no cause for worry.

Victory yesterday became, it is true, less and less likely, for Pakistan were concentrating only on defence. With 35 minutes left and just before May was out, England needed 59 with eight wickets in hand and there was no sign of the storm which suddenly burst. It was caused originally, perhaps, by the desire of the English batsmen to make haste. It was aggravated by Fazal's very fine bowling and by England's inept batting.

First, at 109 May, after reaching 50 in 75 minutes, mistimed a stroke off the back foot and gave Kardar at extra cover a simple catch. Evans, who now came in to try to force victory before the close, was at once frustrated by Pakistan taking drinks, and almost as soon as he was able to get to work Fazal bowled him. England now turned to defence, but at 10 minutes past 6 Shuja got past Graveney, and the possibility of a sensational result was there for all to see. The Pakistanis, after all their misfortunes of the summer, were in a high state of flutter. If they could somehow account for Compton, who has so often stood as England's last reliable prop, they could win, and this they did with five minutes left, when he pushed out at a beautiful ball from Fazal and was caught by the unfailing Imtiaz.

Pakistan looked as though they could hardly believe their good fortune. Within half an hour England had lost their last four reliable batsmen for 11 runs, and the game had turned an astonishing somersault.

Close: PAKISTAN 133 and 164 (J.H. Wardle 7 for 56), ENGLAND 130 and 125 for 6 (P.B.H. May 53).

Fifth Day

18 August, 1954. The young cricketers from Pakistan had their finest hour, and England one of their less glorious, at the Oval yesterday when the fourth and final Test match was won and lost there by 24 runs. Pakistan gained a victory which carried with it a sharing of the rubber and England suffered a defeat which came as a rather un-welcome awakening within a month of sailing for Australia.

Some may say that the full strength of England was not in the field, some that the losers had the worst of the wicket, but first and foremost all should acknowledge a performance of great merit by Pakistan, and one upon which they are to be congratulated most warmly. By seizing their chance with both hands and winning this Test match on English soil on their first tour they have achieved in less than four months what it took Australia two years, South Africa 28 years, and West Indies 22 years to achieve, and what to this day has eluded New Zealand and India.

Pakistan's particular hero was Fazal, who brought his tally of wickets in the match to 12, and who throughout the series has established himself as a bowler of medium pace fit to rank near our own Bedser. Next to Fazal one would put Wazir and Zulfiqar, whose ninth wicket part-nership of 58, when all seemed lost, gave birth to the recovery from which victory sprang. Kardar, when suddenly he saw the heel of Achilles ex-posed, captained his side in every respect as astutely as he has done all summer, and there was an alert response from those under him.

Much of England's play, from the moment that Wazir and Zulfiqar came together on Mon-day morning, was almost too bad to be true. The bowling of Loader and Tyson became lifeless and inaccurate; the fielding became casual: and the inadequacy of the batting on a good wicket is reflected in the scorebook. May and Simpson played well, but they got themselves out, and Compton's 29 would have been nearly 50 had he made the most of the loose balls he received. Graveney failed in the crisis as he had in the first innings, and the tail proved to be no shorter than one had feared. Nor, should Bailey by some mischance be out of action, and if five bowlers are played as they surely must be, will it be any shorter in Australia.

The odds, when play started yesterday with England's last four wickets needing 43 runs, seemed to be slightly in Pakistan's favour, and one simply hoped that England would put up a fight. Their main chance rested with Wardle, who has made a good many runs against Pakistan this year. Given the opportunity he could have won the match off his own bat in 10 minutes, but Kardar sensibly chose Mahmud to bowl with Fazal, and speed does not suit Wardle's book so well as spin. The result was that Wardle was prevented from using the long handle and never flourished.

There was an impartial cheer for anything of note from the small crowd, and the sense of strain in the middle was soon shown in an injudicious single. Then at 129 Wardle was dropped at sec-ond slip off Mahmud, a none too difficult catch as slip catches go, and presently the same batsman survived two leg-before appeals from Fazal. After 25 minutes only six had been scored, but by then Tyson seemed to be finding his feet, and Pakistan badly needed a wicket. It came just on noon, when Tyson felt speculatively for an outswinger from Fazal and gave Imtiaz his seventh catch of the match. Loader now came in ninth instead of his usual eleventh, and at once forced a 4 to long-on, followed by a quick single which took the score to 138.

With 30 needed from three wickets it was anyone's game, and yet within a quarter of an hour the end had come. At 138 Wardle was caught round the corner turning Fazal off his legs, and Loader, hitting out desperately, immediately sent a steepling catch to cover-point, where Waqar, after an agony of suspense, held it and threw it aloft. There remained only some missing and snicking, a run out escape, and then a fatal call by McConnon, who under-estimated Hanif's quick-ness and accuracy of throw from cover-point to the bowler's end. Hanif hit the stumps, umpire Davies adjudicated, and Pakistan who had come to learn, had come and conquered.

ENGLAND v. PAKISTAN
The Oval, 12–14, 16, 17 August 1954

PAKISTAN
1st innings

Hanif Mohammed	lbw b Statham	0
Alimuddin	b Tyson	10
Waqar Hassan	b Loader	7
Maqsood Ahmed	b Tyson	0
Imtiaz Ahmed	c Evans b Tyson	23
A.H. Kardar	c Evans b Statham	36
Wazir Mohammed	run out	0
Fazal Mahmood	c Evans b Loader	0
Shujuaddin	not out	16
Zulfiqar Ahmed	c Compton b Loader	16
Mahmood Hussain	b Tyson	23
Extras	(nb 2)	2
Total		133

2nd innings

Hanif Mohammed	c Graveney b Wardle	19
Shujuaddin	c May b Wardle	12
Waqar Hassan	run out	9
Maqsood Ahmed	c Wardle b McConnon	4
Imtiaz Ahmed	c Wardle b Tyson	12
A.H. Kardar	c & b Wardle	17
Alimuddin	lbw b Wardle	0
Wazir Mohammed	not out	42
Fazal Mahmood	b Wardle	6
Zulfiqar Ahmed	c May b Wardle	34
Mahmood Hussain	c Statham b Wardle	6
Extras	(b 3)	3
Total		164

Fall of wickets: 1–0, 2–10, 3–10, 4–26, 5–51, 6–51, 7–51, 8–77, 9–106, 10–133.

Second innings: 1–19, 2–38, 3–43, 4–52, 5–63, 6–73, 7–76, 8–82, 9–140, 10–164.

ENGLAND BOWLING

	O	M	R	W	O	M	R	W
Statham	11	5	26	2	18	7	37	0
Tyson	13.4	3	35	4	9	2	22	1
Loader	18	5	35	3	16	8	26	0
McConnon	9	2	35	0	14	5	20	1
Wardle					35	16	56	7

ENGLAND
1st innings

L. Hutton	c Imtiaz b Fazal	14
R.T. Simpson	c Kardar b Hussain	2
P.B.H. May	c Kardar b Fazal	26
D.C.S. Compton	c Imtiaz b Fazal	53
T.W. Graveney	c Hanif b Fazal	1
T.G. Evans	c Maqsood b Hussain	0
J.H. Wardle	c Imtiaz b Fazal	8
F.H. Tyson	c Imtiaz b Fazal	3
J.E. McConnon	c Fazal b Hussain	11
J.B. Statham	c Shuja b Hussain	1
P.J. Loader	not out	8
Extras	(lb 1, w1, nb1)	3
Total		130

2nd innings

L. Hutton	c Imtiaz b Fazal	5
R.T. Simpson	c & b Zulfiqar	27
P.B.H. May	c Kardar b Fazal	53
D.C.S. Compton	c Imtiaz b Fazal	29
T.W. Graveney	lbw b Shuja	0
T.G. Evans	b Fazal	3
J.H. Wardle	c Shuja b Fazal	9
F.H. Tyson	c Imtiaz b Fazal	3
P.J. Loader	c Waqar b Hussain	5
J.E. McConnon	run out	2
J.B. Statham	not out	2
Extras	(lb 2, nb 3)	5
Total		143

Fall of wickets: 1–6, 2–26, 3–56, 4–63, 5–69, 6–92, 7–106, 8–115, 9–116, 10–130.

Second innings: 1–15, 2–66, 3–109, 4–115, 5–116, 6–121, 7–131, 8–138, 9–138, 10–143.

PAKISTAN BOWLING

	O	M	R	W	O	M	R	W
Fazal	30	16	53	6	30	11	46	6
Hussain	21.3	6	58	4	14	4	32	1
Zulfiqar	5	2	8	0	14	2	35	1
Shuja	3	0	8	0	10	1	25	1

Umpires: F.S. Lee and D. Davies

PAKISTAN WON BY 24 RUNS

MICHAEL COLIN COWDREY
Kent

Cowdrey began his cricketing life as a child prodigy, then by degrees dwindled into a great batsman. Some said he was even better than he looked but that was to misjudge the nature of the man. Because Cowdrey regarded cricket as a civilized pastime, he tended to correct the shortcomings of bowlers rather than emphasize them. To score over 40,000 first-class runs a man must be acquisitive, yet Cowdrey never seemed greedy in the manner of a Bradman or a Boycott. The possessor of an immaculate technique, he batted as though he wished to establish Canterbury in high summer in all parts of the globe. He gave rare pleasure to connoisseurs everywhere, not perhaps the compliment today that it would have been fifty years ago. The difference between Cowdrey in a Test match and Cowdrey in the Fathers' match was one of degree and not of kind.

In mid-century Sir Pelham Warner wrote a foreword to *Public Schools Cricket, 1901–1950* (edited by W.N. Roe), and ventured to select two teams, one from the seventeen schools which had been most represented in the Public Schools XI or Southern Schools v. The Rest, the other from those left over. The pleasure of writing them down cannot be resisted.

The 17 Schools
D.J. Knight (Malvern)
R.A. Young (Repton), wkt
K.S. Duleepsinhji (Cheltenham)
K.L. Hutchings (Tonbridge)
D.R. Jardine (Winchester), capt.
A.P.F. Chapman (Uppingham)
G.O. Allen (Eton)
J.N. Crawford (Repton)
T.E. Bailey (Dulwich)
J.C. Clay (Winchester)
N.A. Knox (Dulwich)
The Rest
R.E.S. Wyatt (Coventry)
R.T. Simpson (Nottingham)
W.J. Edrich (Norwich)
W.R. Hammond (Cirencester)
G.T.S. Stevens (UCS)
F.R. Foster (Solihull)
J.W.H.T. Douglas (Felsted)
P.G.H. Fender (St Paul's), capt.
J.C. White (Taunton)
W.H.V. Levett (Brighton), wkt
K. Farnes (Romford)

As M.C. Cowdrey and P.B.H. May both qualify for the 17 Schools, the reader may decide for himself who shall be omitted to secure their inclusion, before choosing a team from both lists.

THE SCHOOLS AT LORD'S

By R.B. Vincent

30 July 1946. Clifton and Tonbridge yesterday started what can only be loosely termed as the schools' fortnight at Lord's, and at the close of play Tonbridge, with all their wickets in hand in their second innings, were still 45 runs behind.

Youthful prodigies are often uncertain quantities, but it would surely seem that in M.C. Cowdrey Tonbridge have produced a boy, now only 13½ years old, of quite exceptional promise. A leg-break bowler, he has gradually crept his way up the batting order until yesterday, in the match of matches, he went in first wicket down to score 75 of his side's total. Patently here is a cricketer of intelligence supported by confidence.

The Clifton captain, having won the toss, sent Tonbridge in to bat and had to wait until 40 runs were on the board before Bowler was deceived by the straighter ball of Exton, who fancies the off-spinner to the fashionable leg-side trap. So long as Kemp was in there was method in the Tonbridge batting, but thereafter too much of the over hopeful cross bat. During what might have been a cataclysm of wickets this young Cowdrey batted with the temperate hostility of one accustomed to seasons of school matches. Already he has the footwork and the wrists of a gifted batsman — but too much must never be written of so young a player. It may be true, however, that none so young, so small, and so efficient since E.M. Dowson*, has been seen in school cricket.

The last man out, he was called on early in Clifton's innings to bowl against the wind, a little more than he could do. In the meantime Penny and Crawford, batsmen both of the good schoolboy standard, took Clifton's score to 79 against bowling at times a trifle irregular before Penny was caught at short-leg. Crawford, not afraid to play out to the pitch of the ball, was building up the score and with only three wickets down for 136 Clifton were heading for a long lead on the first innings. The Tonbridge captain wisely had given Cowdrey only short spells of bowling, but in one of these he took three wickets quickly with spin bowling, which is rare enough to-day, and,

....

* E.M. Dowson won his colours at Harrow aged just over 15. He appeared at Lord's against Eton 1895–99 and Oxford 1900–3.

well as M.L. Green played, the back of Clifton's strength was broken.

In the Tonbridge second innings

Cowdrey batted, as one acute observer remarked, like a professional seen through the wrong end of a telescope. Never in a hurry, certain of himself whether to lay forward or back, and always ready to sweep the ball away to leg, he amply confirmed the high opinion which had been formed of him on the first day.

TONBRIDGE 156 (M.C. Cowdrey 75; R.N. Exton 6 for 64, T.S. Penny 4 for 32) and 175 (D.S. Kemp 44, D.K. Horton 51, Cowdrey 44; Exton 8 for 61) beat CLIFTON 214 (P.M. Crawford 57, M.L. Green 56, M.F. Bishop 44 not out; P.N. Kirch 4 for 20) and 115 (Bishop 45 not out; Cowdrey 5 for 59) by two runs.

Cowdrey's match analysis was 37–5–117–8.

One's only regret is that Cowdrey did *not* — as he points out with some gravity — wear short trousers in the above match. Had he done so, there would have been sartorial comparisons with the 13-year-old Bradman who, batting for Bowral at Moss Vale, scored 37 not out wearing short white knickerbockers.

By John Woodcock

31 December 1955, Melbourne. England are suffering from the effects of a disastrous start in the third Test march, which was begun here to-day, and that 41 for four wickets was increased to a total of 191 just before 6 o'clock was due to a great innings by Cowdrey. The day belonged as much to him as to Australia, but it will need another supreme effort in the field if England's losses are to be retrieved.

There were two villains, Miller and the pitch, and the volatile one exploited the mischievous other to produce a destructive and brilliant piece of bowling. Miller professes not to like bowling, probably, one feels, with his tongue in his cheek,

COWDREY   Out of his ground to kill off spin; Lock lurking for any stroke made in no-man's land.

and it was generally thought that after his knee trouble he was unlikely to bowl unless things were running badly for Australia. But not a bit of it. He bowled as he always does, like a man who was born to bowl, with abounding verve and dash, and within 37 balls he got rid of Edrich, Hutton, and Compton for five runs. No two successive balls were alike, many were spitefully fast, and almost all were to a full length.

At the other end was Lindwall, who for an hour while the pitch was malicious was little less fierce a proposition. The ball was not moving alarmingly in the air, but for about a dozen overs it kept lifting horribly. All along one knew that the dampness would soon go, and that if only England could fight through resolutely and reasonably unscathed until luncheon all should be comparatively calm afterwards. It was easy to see, by the way they threw everything into their

effort, that Miller and Lindwall knew this too, and England could not resist them.

May and Compton were caught off their gloves off balls that reared sharply at them. Hutton always looked out of sorts and Edrich was soon gone. Thus it was left to the rest to salve what they could from the wreckage, and Cowdrey, with the help first of Bailey and then of Evans, did a magnificent job.

That Cowdrey is soon going to rank as a Test match player of the very first magnitude seems as certain as anything can be in cricket. Yet he will play few finer innings than he did to-day. For the fifth time in five Test innings he came in at a time of crisis, the score being 21 for two, and he quickly lost Hutton and Compton.

A century against Australia is the ambition of every cricketer; to get one in a crisis out of 158 runs and before nearly 70,000 people at Melbourne at the age of 22 makes it a great achievement. J.W. Hearne was only 20 when he made 114 on the same ground in 1911, and Cowdrey is the youngest MCC century maker in Australia since then, being a few months younger than the Nawab of Pataudi when the latter made 102 at Sydney in 1932. Bradman, incidentally, was 21 when he made his first Test match 100 in England. One will not soon forget the ovation which Cowdrey had when, with his score at 97, he turned Archer for 3.

It was a lovely day, with a few white clouds sailing by, when Hutton won the toss and smiled his delight. The pitch had a brown, arid look about it, and although Melbourne wickets are invariably lively before luncheon on the first day, Hutton could have had no qualms about his decision. The English outlook seemed most hopeful. England entered the match without Bedser, whose dismissal for an unsuccessful spinner seems precipitate and hard to reconcile. They opened with Edrich, who had scored 20 runs in his five previous innings in that position on this tour.

The first over from Lindwall was misleading, four byes off the first ball giving Maddocks an unfortunate start to his Test career and seven runs coming off the rest.

In the second over, however, two balls climbed steeply off the pitch, and in the third one's suspicions that it was lively were confirmed when two balls lifted at Hutton, who fended them off only just in front of backward short leg and gully. The importance of the period before luncheon was at once obvious, and, almost as soon, Australia had more than countered the losing of the toss. In the fourth over Edrich glanced Miller to the middle of three backward short legs, where Lindwall held a neat catch by his ankles. Hutton took seven off two full pitches in the next over before May fell to the last ball, which kicked odiously off a good length and travelled to gully as a gentle offering.

Cowdrey began with his only edgy stroke, a 4 between third slip and gully off Lindwall, and then, in the eighth over of the day, Hutton probed forward at Miller and edged a low catch to first slip. Compton got a generous reception and started confidently enough with a 3 through the covers, one of only two scoring strokes off Miller in his nine overs before luncheon, but after 50 minutes he was out just as May had been, only off the bowling of Miller and not Lindwall. Neither batsman was truly behind the line of the ball, but they were both very unlucky. Poor Compton was caught off his thumb, and an X-ray was necessary to see that no bone was broken. Had it been, his own and England's cup would have been full.

As it was, at 41 for four the innings was dreadfully broken and now, as at Brisbane when they came together at 25 for four, Cowdrey and Bailey began their rescue work. At Brisbane they added 82, today 74, and when, half an hour before tea, Bailey was eventually caught the pitch had become so utterly placid that there seemed little reason why the pair should not have gone on for a considerable time. Bailey mishooked a long hop on to his pad, whence it lobbed to Maddocks — a luckless end which was not deserved after he had batted well through the worst.

When this misfortune came Cowdrey had been becalmed for 40 minutes, and he remained so for another 20. It was the one time in his innings when he was not master of the bowling, and during it he scored only four runs. After luncheon he had gone easily to his 50, made out of 69 in 100 minutes, and in the overs before tea he crashed three handsome boundaries off Johnson and Johnston to make his score 68.

Cowdrey began the evening by driving and sweeping Johnston majestically for two 4's in the same over and then driving Lindwall for another, and with Evans showing welcome discretion together with some good leg-side strokes, the score was soon jogging along, 35 coming in 40 minutes. Cowdrey was the figure to watch in the centre of the great arena as he neared his 100, and he overshadowed Miller, who came on for two bustling overs, his only others apart from his devastating spell. At 169 Cowdrey lost Evans, but within 10 minutes he had retaliated by scoring the 10 runs he needed for his 100. A delicious late cut off Johnson, then off Archer a terrific straight drive for his fifteenth 4 and at 179 his 3 to leg.

He was out rather unusually 10 minutes later, padding up outside the off stump to a prodigious off-break and being bowled behind his legs. He had batted for 227 minutes and once he was gone the tail folded up in the last half-hour to Archer. But Tyson and Statham stayed just long enough to realize that the pitch will have to become more spirited again in the morning if they are to pluck the brand from the burning.

THE SKILL AND CHARACTER OF COWDREY

By A.G. Moyes

England's cricket veterans failed rather badly here to-day and it was left to the team's baby to lead them and show them a way to better things. The pitch before luncheon had some life, as in former years, with the ball occasionally lifting rather abruptly and causing May and Compton to be caught off their gloves, but Cowdrey faced similar hazards and conquered because he was behind and over the ball, showing superior technique to the others.

His was a lovely innings, full of delightfully timed strokes, but his execution was no more perfect than his grand temperament for the desperate situation. Coming in when Edrich and May were out for 21 and losing Hutton eight runs later, he played masterly, assured cricket, was never in trouble and it is many years since England sent such a gifted youngster to this country.

Bailey did a fine job of digging in his toes, while Evans, for the first time on the tour, showed something of the batting skill which once was his. Perhaps May had to fail after four centuries in successive matches, but his strokes were not good and the same applied to Hutton, who more than once was not behind the ball outside the off stump

and finally fell to a slip catch. It was a disappointing total indeed, but after all England made only 154 at Sydney and then won. However, this pitch will be very docile to-morrow.

Ranking with Cowdrey in assessing the day's honours comes Miller, whose bowling before lunch of nine overs, eight maidens, for five runs and three wickets must live in history as one of the most remarkable ever seen. Recently removed from the casualty list and ordered to bowl in short spells only, he went from noon to half past one, always menacing and hostile, and often venomous, his right arm a whip of war.

Once again England omitted Bedser and one heard everywhere the opinion expressed that if they had decided to do that they might have omitted him from the original 12, thus saving this great player the indignity of final exclusion. Surely he deserved better treatment. Let us finish with Cowdrey. Almost everything that is great in

ENGLAND
1st innings

L. Hutton	c Hole b Miller	12
W.J. Edrich	c Lindwall b Miller	4
P.B.H. May	c Benaud b Lindwall	0
M.C. Cowdrey	b Johnson	102
D.C.S. Compton	c Harvey b Miller	4
T.E. Bailey	c Maddocks b Johnston	30
T.G. Evans	lbw b Archer	20
J.H. Wardle	b Archer	0
F.H. Tyson	b Archer	6
J.B. Statham	b Archer	3
R. Appleyard	not out	1
Extras	(b 9)	9
Total		191

Fall of wickets: 1–14, 2–21, 3–29, 4–41, 5–115, 6–169, 7–181, 8–181, 9–190, 10–191.

AUSTRALIA BOWLING

	O	M	R	W
Lindwall	13	0	59	1
Miller	11	8	14	3
Archer	13.6	4	33	4
Benaud	7	0	30	0
Johnston	12	6	26	1
Johnson	11	3	20	1

AUSTRALIA: L. Favell, A.R. Morris, K.R. Miller, R.N. Harvey, G.B. Hole, R. Benaud, R.G. Archer, L. Maddocks, R.R. Lindwall, I.W. Johnson, W.A. Johnston.
Umpires: M.J. McInnes and C. Hoy.

cricket has been done by youth. The lad with the significant initials proved this again to-day.

The supreme effort mentioned by John Woodcock at the start of his despatch was duly forthcoming, no Australian batsman in either innings reaching 50, and only Maddocks (47 in the first innings) making more than 33 against the fast bowling of Tyson and Statham.

ENGLAND 191 (M.C. Cowdrey 102) and 279 (P.B.H. May 91; W.A. Johnston 5 for 25) beat AUSTRALIA 231 (J.B. Statham 5 for 60) and 111 (F.H. Tyson 7 for 27) by 128 runs.

The match figures of the two England fast bowlers were:

Tyson 33.3–3–95–9
Statham 27.3–1–98–7

A CANTERBURY TALE

I.M. Chappell's Australians batted throughout the first day at Canterbury for 415 for eight wickets. Declaring overnight, they dismissed Kent for 202 on the second day, before making 112 for three, so leading by 325 runs.

By Alan Gibson

28 June 1975. Just after 6 o'clock yesterday with nine overs yet to play, Kent won the match, an unexpected but jubilated outcome. Cowdrey had won it for them. Plump, brown, benign, is the way we usually think of Cowdrey nowadays. It is reported that he cannot be sure of a regular place in the Kent XI and is thinking of going to Sussex for a year or ten. I suspect that his secret plan is to score another 100 centuries for Sussex. After all, Hobbs scored almost that many after he was 40, and Cowdrey is only 42, hardly more than a well developed boy really. As he came running triumphantly in after what must have been one of the most satisfying innings of his life, he looked

less like the familiar archideaconal personage than a skipping lamb finding another spring.

The Australians batted for another half hour in the morning, and declared with a lead of 353. Play was to continue until six, and so Kent had about 350 minutes to score the runs. This seemed only a theoretical consideration, especially as Julien was injured and unable to bat, and Elms was limping, and would need a runner, as he did in the first innings.

Luckhurst and Johnson made a useful start, but both were out before luncheon and soon afterwards Woolmer, going well, was hit painfully on the arm by Lillee. He made a plucky try to carry on, but had to retire. Ealham was out first ball. Kent were 116 for three, or 116 for five and a half, more probably. The Australians thought they had won, understandably. The pitch was still a good one but they were down to the middle of the order and grandpa was bound to make a mistake soon.

Chappell bowled his spinners for most of the afternoon, a sensible enough policy. Several times Higgs had Cowdrey in trouble and was always the likeliest man to get him out. But we began to notice that the runs were piling and Cowdrey had found a valuable partner in Nicholls. Cowdrey 50, cheers. Hundred partnership, cheers. Kent 226 for three at tea, they ought to save it now — and then the dawning thought: goodness they might win!

The same thought had obviously reached the Australians. Lillee came on after tea with a fast spell, and two close short legs for Nicholls, the left-hander. He had Nicholls caught at the wicket at 242 and Shepherd leg before at 246.

There was an unexpectedly good innings by Rowe, and when he was out, caught at the wicket off Gilmour, Woolmer returned: more, louder cheers. His partnership with Cowdrey took Kent through with scarcely a tremor.

I don't know whether the Australians minded being beaten. Tests are the only matches that matter on tour, was the doctrine laid down by M.A. Noble in 1909. But the result cannot much have encouraged them, and correspondingly it will have encouraged English cricketers. The dreaded men are not unbeatable. The benefit of this match for the Australians was that several of their young men — Higgs, Robinson, Hurst, Turner — had a chance to acclimatize themselves to the disciplines of the three-day game.

And what shall I say about Cowdrey? That he cut, that he drove, that he hooked, that he glanced? All these things he did. It was a memorable innings. But I shall reserve my full discussion of Cowdrey's batting until he retires, which is likely to be around 1984.

AUSTRALIANS 415 for 8 declared (A. Turner 156, R.B. McCosker 58, K.D. Walters 50) and 140 for 3 declared (R.M. Laird 63 not out), KENT 202.

KENT

2nd innings

B.W. Luckhurst	lbw b Hurst	40
G.W. Johnson	b Gilmour	11
R.A. Woolmer	not out	71
M.C. Cowdrey	not out	151
A.G.E. Ealham	c McCosker b Lillee	0
D. Nicholls	c Robinson b Lillee	39
J.N. Shepherd	lbw b Lillee	2
C.J.C. Rowe	c Robinson b Gilmour	30
Extras		10
Total	(6 wkts)	354

Fall of wickets: 1–39, 2–77, 3–116, 4–242, 5–246, 6–295.

B.D. Julien, R.B. Elms and D.L. Underwood did not bat.

AUSTRALIANS BOWLING

	O	M	R	W
Lillee	22	3	95	3
Gilmour	21.5	2	92	2
Hurst	13	0	48	1
Higgs	12	0	67	0
Mallett	13	3	42	0

AUSTRALIANS: R.B. McCosker, A. Turner, I.M. Chappell, R.M. Laird, K.D. Walters, R.D. Robinson, G. Gilmour, D.K. Lillee, A.A. Mallett, A.G. Hurst, J.D. Higgs.

KENT WON BY 4 WICKETS

PETER BARKER HOWARD MAY
Surrey

A CAPTAIN'S MASTERPIECE

On 3 June 1957 West Indies were playing England at Edgbaston and bowled 135 overs. The following day, there being a ten-minute interval between two innings, West Indies and England between them bowled only 133 overs. The explanation may be stated simply: West Indies had gone into the field with only one fast bowler, Gilchrist, who had broken down, while England, although including Statham, Trueman and Bailey, had in their ranks Lock and Laker. The year 1957 represented a kind of no-man's land in West Indies cricket: it was half-way between two outstanding sides — Goddard's of 1950 and Worrell's of 1963. In 1957 the West Indies attack was basically Ramadhin, who, sages said, should be played as an off-spinner but who certainly turned the other way as well. When play began at Edgbaston on 3 June 1957 Ramadhin's haul of Test wickets in England totalled 35, average 19.60; thereafter he took 5 wickets, average 93. Two captains helped to destroy him — his own, J.D.C. Goddard, who clearly overbowled him at Edgbaston, and England's, P.B.H. May, who played one of the greatest of all innings by a leader of his country's side.

By the close of play on the third day — Saturday, 1 June — England's plight was desperate. Their first innings 186 had been dwarfed by West Indies 474, the latter honoured by a superb hundred in his first West Indies v. England match by O.G. Smith, who was killed two years later in a road accident. England batted

again on the Saturday and made 102 for two wickets.

By John Woodcock

3 June 1957. If England save the first Test match against West Indies at Edgbaston it will be to everyone's surprise. With two days left for play they need 186 runs to avoid an innings defeat and Richardson and Insole are both out in their second innings.

There still are, of course, means of escape. May, for instance, who was batting beautifully on Saturday evening, might make a large score, and Close and Cowdrey remain intact. Bailey, too, if he takes root might last until eternity, and then it would be a question of someone staying with him. Again it could rain and West Indies be thwarted thus. Yet the chances are that Ramadhin will have settled the matter by to-night. If so, England's batsmen must hope to have learnt something from their experience. Already in their second innings they have played Ramadhin more confidently and this will not be a barren Test match for them if, at the end of it, they have asserted some sort of authority over him.

ENGLAND
Second innings

P.E. Richardson	c sub b Ramadhin	34
D.B. Close	not out	34
D.J. Insole	b Ramadhin	0
P.B.H. May	not out	21

| Extras | (b 12, lb 1) | | | 13 |
| Total | (2 wkts) | | | 102 |

Fall of wickets: 1–63, 2–65.

WEST INDIES BOWLING

	O	M	R	W
Gilchrist	11	0	34	0
Atkinson	8	3	8	0
Ramadhin	21	6	33	2
Sobers	10	4	14	0

Fourth Day

4 June 1957. England fought a great fight at Edgbaston yesterday and confounded all the pessimists who, on Saturday night, had given up as lost the first Test match against West Indies. A memorable innings of 193 by May, a tremendously dogged one of 78 by Cowdrey, and a record unbroken partnership of 265 between the two have even given England a chance of victory. Perhaps one should repeat that England may even win, for they are now 90 runs ahead with seven wickets in hand and the pitch is dusting up. What a somersault that is for the match to have turned!

Cowdrey and May against Ramadhin. It was a battle royal, and the two batsmen, in winning it, displayed rare character and skill. May's must be ranked among the finest innings ever played by an England captain. Someone was going to have to pay for his failures in South Africa, and it is the West Indies he has chosen at a time when only a great effort could save his side. Cowdrey did all that was asked of him, and Ramadhin, incredible as it may seem after last Thursday's performance, bowled 48 overs without a single wicket. Goddard must have wished for Valentine to keep Ramadhin company, but Valentine was musing at the ringside, and now the scoreboard shows an England total of 378 for three. Only one batsman out in six hours' play: it was a return to the old days.

...A mountainous task faced England when the day began: a deficit of 186 runs; two second innings wickets already gone; 12 hours left for play; and the awful prospect of Ramadhin wheeling away for over after over as the day burnt itself through. The odds, had there been a call-over on the ground at 11 o'clock, must have been long against England saving the game. More to the point seemed to be the time at which they would expire, and when, after 20 minutes, Close was swallowed up at slip by Weekes off Gilchrist, England's chances became only more remote.

Close had begun the day by clipping Atkinson through the covers. Twice he did so in four balls, and the second time the stroke flew at catching height within a few feet of a fielder. The danger, one felt, was that he would play too much like a man trying to score the fastest hundred of the year, without due care and attention in fact, and it was indeed a reckless stroke to a wide ball which brought his end. So England were down to seven wickets, and there were thoughts of a tea-time train to London. The door now, it seemed, was shut, if not bolted, in England's face. Yet slowly, very slowly, May and Cowdrey began to prise it open again and let in a breath of hope.

...The score was 113 for three when Ramadhin first went through that quick, businesslike approach to the wicket. That was a five minutes to 12, and he had no rest before luncheon. Afterwards West Indies took the new ball and it was three o'clock before Ramadhin returned at the pavilion end. At 10 to four he switched again, and he was given 10 minutes leave before tea. Through the evening he bowled for all but half an hour, and so far as one can remember he perpetrated only two full pitches. Cowdrey was so surprised that he mishit the first; the second flashed for 4 past cover point.

When Ramadhin pitched short the ball made such pace off the turf that considerable care was needed in dispatching it. Gradually, of course, he showed signs of wear, but he has an economical action and his accuracy over so long a period was remarkable. May and Cowdrey could afford no lapse of concentration, and as they grafted on one thought of that taut match at Sydney in December of 1954 when the two of them came together with England face to face with defeat. Not until yesterday had they shared a comparable partnership, and now, as then, the atmosphere was just as tense.

In Australia they prepared the way for a famous victory. Yesterday they gave England at least a chance of another, and it was interesting to mark the contrast between the two. In Australia both were at much the same stage in their development. In maturity and skill there was little to choose between them. Now May was more masterful, more assured, and a long time seldom passed without him playing a stroke of exquisite beauty. Cowdrey contented himself with second fiddle. He had less of the bowling and he had to work harder for his runs. For instance, it took him an hour to move from 40 to 50, and by nightfall he had made no more than 78 out of a partnership of 265.

MAY   Fast bowling hammered from the back foot, though perhaps his greatest glory was through mid-wicket.

From time to time the large crowd gasped as one batsman or the other had a narrow escape. May several times was fortunate in the short leg area with strokes which he lifted unintentionally. There was an occasional snick through the slips, and not many overs from Ramadhin went by without a surreptitious appeal for leg-before. The inscrutable Ramadhin would half turn his head, raise his eyebrows and look questioningly at the umpire out of the corner of his eye. But the gentlemen in white coats must have seemed to him like Russian diplomats at their most obstinate as they vetoed his requests. Generally the batsmen were right forward on the front foot.

Statistics tell the story as England's fourth wicket pulled the innings round. May and Cowdrey were some while becoming properly acquainted, and for a long time Ramadhin's every over was greeted with grave apprehension. But the luck ran for England, as it had done for the West Indies through a vital phase on Friday afternoon, and the rate of scoring grew as West Indies were worn down.

At a quarter past one May reached his 50 with one of his favourite on-drives for 4, and when the players retired for luncheon England were 176 for three. The afternoon was dotted with milestones. The hundred partnership was raised after 145 minutes, and May went to his sixth Test century with a characteristic stroke wide of mid-on off Ramadhin, his eleventh four in 250 minutes', batting. The stand was worth 150 shortly before 4 o'clock, and a moment later Cowdrey's personal 50 was hoisted. It was a small proportion of the runs, but none the less significant for that.

By tea-time England were 279, May having scored exactly 100 runs during the day, and by 20 minutes to five the scores were level. Englishmen then began to build castles in the air. Could it possibly go on? Could England even leave themselves a winning chance to-day? Or would someone suddenly have a rush of blood to the head? In fact the partnership continued to flourish. A short single saw up the 300, another both took the partnership to 200 and gave May his 150, and still Cowdrey plodded modestly along.

Still, too, England were fortunate in that the ball when it was in the air did not go to hand, and West Indies suffered another loss when Gilchrist had to leave the field with a sprained ankle. By then they were in need of three substitutes and looking rather sorry for themselves. May took advantage of it with a 6 over mid-wicket off Atkinson and a murderous 4 in the same direction within a couple of balls. Once he was all but caught and bowled by Smith, diving to his right, but at once he took a fresh guard as though to assure everyone of his determination not to let it happen again.

As the day died away the pattern was firmly established. At one end there was Cowdrey, in a cap, pushing massively forward, his bat and pad tightly locked together. At the other, May was bare-headed, master of the situation, his bat as clean and white as when he started, his manner as composed. West Indies were resigned now to waiting for to-day, their supporters in the crowd were silent, and Ramadhin at the last was sent empty away. What an extraordinary game cricket is.

ENGLAND

Second innings

P.E. Richardson	c sub b Ramadhin	34
D.B. Close	c Weekes b Gilchrist	42
D.J. Insole	b Ramadhin	0
P.B.H. May	not out	193
M.C. Cowdrey	not out	78
Extras	(b 23, lb 8)	31
Total	(3 wkts)	378

Fall of wickets: 1–63, 2–65, 3–113.

WEST INDIES BOWLING

	O	M	R	W
Gilchrist	26	2	67	1
Atkinson	47	19	93	0
Ramadhin	69	26	107	2
Sobers	18	4	30	0
Smith	19	3	38	0
Goddard	6	2	12	0

Fifth Day

5 June 1957. The first Test match between England and West Indies ended in a draw at Edgbaston yesterday after pursuing an extraordinary course. Had England won, as they desperately nearly did, it would have come to be known in future years as one of the most remarkable matches ever played. As it was they were baulked by three wickets after West Indies, left in mid-afternoon to make 296 to win in 160 minutes, had staggered to 72 for seven on a pitch frayed by constant wear. At the last it was the clock that beat England as Lock and Laker strove to make the kill. And yet, perhaps, on reflection a draw was the fairest result of all.

Above all this strange game will be remembered for the remorseless partnership between May and Cowdrey which snatched England from the very jaws of defeat. It seemed hardly conceivable that anything could happen to dwarf Ramadhin's devastating bowling on Thursday. And when West Indies followed with an innings of 474 the match, to all intents and purposes, was over. England could only hope to salve a degree of prestige from the wreckage and to find some of the answers to Ramadhin when they batted a second time. But no game is ever lost till it is won, and yesterday evening it was West Indies who were thankful when time was called.

In the long story of Test cricket there have been only two larger partnerships than that of 411 which May and Cowdrey now shared. One, of 451, was between Bradman and Ponsford at the Oval in 1934, and that will surprise no one. The other was between Mankad and Roy 18 months ago in a Test match between India and New Zealand at Madras. But never before has there been such a stand at such a dire time. On and on the two Englishmen went, calm and cultured in all they did until at the last they were doing much as they pleased. Misfortune placed its hand firmly on West Indies when it robbed them of their two opening bowlers, Gilchrist and Worrell. But Ramadhin still had to be denied for 76 overs, and nothing can detract from the performance of May and Cowdrey. It was wonderful in every sense.

...Poor West Indies! There was a new ball available to them at the start of the day, and, with

Worrell and Gilchrist out of action they had no one to use it. So Ramadhin and Atkinson toiled away throughout the morning. Goddard resorted at once to a defensive field which was surprising. It meant that England were granted the initiative, and they never let it go. Once Ramadhin beat Cowdrey and a stumping appeal was dismissed. Occasionally, too, May was in doubt to Ramadhin. Yet now the magician had lost his magic. The spring had gone out of his run, the poison had left his fingers, nor was he quite so mechanically accurate, and small wonder, for already he had bowled more overs than any man before him in an innings of a Test match.

...By luncheon England were 467 for three, the monumental partnership was worth 354, and Cowdrey was in full bloom. He went from 100 to 116 with four classic boundaries. At last he could afford to relax, and when the afternoon arrived May felt able to do the same. The timing of the declaration was what must have been exercising May now, and one's fear was always that he might err on the side of caution. That is his tendency, and yesterday he waited until twenty past three before indicating to Goddard that he had had enough.

By then May was toying with the bowling. He had given a hard chance to Smith at mid-wicket in the first over of the afternoon, and when he was 278 he hooked Smith off the meat of the bat to Alexander, one of the three substitutes who made a brave effort to hold the ball. Another substitute, Asgarali, eventually took the catch which brought the great stand to an end. Since luncheon one landmark after another had been passed. Up went the 500 at twenty-five to three, followed five minutes later by Cowdrey's 150 which occupied 500 minutes and included 16 fours. His third 50 had been scored in less than an hour, and the fact that yesterday he outpaced May will give some idea of how brilliantly he played.

May's innings, of course, was one of superlatives and England's recovery will always have a place in history. As for their total, it was the highest ever made in a match between the two countries here in England. And May's own score of 285 not out — his highest in first class cricket, and the best ever score by an England captain — has been exceeded only eight times in Test cricket. One hoped he might declare when Cowdrey was caught at long-on. England then were 236 ahead, and the chances of a West Indian victory were as remote as was the possibility of an English revival when Cowdrey joined May at 10 minutes to 12 on Monday morning. But May batted on for a further half an hour, passing his 250 in the process with an immense 6 off Atkinson. He added 59 with Evans and batted in all for 555 minutes, hitting two 6's and 25 4's. As he left the field the whole crowd rose to him and he was cheered out of sight. A moment later Smith, with a broad grin on his face, bowed his way in as his side's only wicket-taker of the day. And the steel calypso band cheerfully struck up to encourage the West Indies in the task that lay ahead of them.

MAY ELEGANT NOT ONLY IN STYLE BUT IN MANNER

By Alan Gibson

2 January 1980. Fifty years ago, on New Year's Eve, Peter May was born. Early in his life it became clear that he was going to be good at cricket. He was captain of Charterhouse in 1947, scored hundreds against both Eton and Harrow, and for the Public Schools against the Combined Services. He went on to Cambridge, after his national service (he made his first-class appearance for Combined Services — and had played for Berkshire — he was born at Reading — in 1946).

For Cambridge he scored nearly 3,000 runs in three seasons, at an average of more than 60. In 1950 he played for Surrey, winning his county cap, and in a Test trial. In 1951 he played for England, against South Africa, and scored a century in his first Test innings. He played in all

ENGLAND v. WEST INDIES
Edgbaston, 30, 31 May, 1, 3, 4, June, 1957

ENGLAND
1st innings

P.E. Richardson	c Walcott b Ramadhin	47
D.B. Close	c Kanhai b Gilchrist	15
D.J. Insole	b Ramadhin	20
P.B.H. May	c Weekes b Ramadhin	30
M.C. Cowdrey	c Gilchrist b Ramadhin	4
T.E. Bailey	b Ramadhin	1
G.A.R. Lock	b Ramadhin	0
T.G. Evans	b Gilchrist	14
J.C. Laker	b Ramadhin	7
F.S. Trueman	not out	29
J.B. Statham	b Atkinson	13
Extras	(b 3, lb 3)	6
Total		186

2nd innings

P.E. Richardson	c sub b Ramadhin	34
D.B. Close	c Weekes b Gilchrist	42
D.J. Insole	b Ramadhin	0
P.B.H. May	not out	285
M.C. Cowdrey	c sub b Smith	154
T.G. Evans	not out	29
Extras	(b 23, lb 16)	39
Total	(4 wkts, dec.)	583

Fall of wickets: 1–32, 2–61, 3–104, 4–115, 5–116, 6–118, 7–121, 8–130, 9–180, 10–186.

Second innings: 1–63, 2–65, 3–113, 4–524.

WEST INDIES BOWLING

	O	M	R	W	O	M	R	W
Worrell	9	1	27	0				
Gilchrist	27	4	74	2	26	2	67	1
Ramadhin	31	16	49	7	98	35	179	2
Atkinson	12.4	3	30	1	72	29	137	0
Sobers					30	4	77	0
Smith					26	4	72	1
Goddard					6	2	12	0

WEST INDIES
1st innings

B. Pairaudeau	b Trueman	1
R.B. Kanhai	lbw b Statham	42
C.L. Walcott	c Evans b Laker	90
E.D. Weekes	b Trueman	9
G.S. Sobers	c Bailey b Statham	53
O.G. Smith	lbw b Laker	161
F.M. Worrell	b Statham	81
J.D.C. Goddard	c Lock b Laker	24
D. Atkinson	c Statham b Laker	1
S. Ramadhin	not out	5
R. Gilchrist	run out	0
Extras	(b 1, lb 6)	7
Total		474

2nd innings

B. Pairaudeau	b Trueman	7
R.B. Kanhai	c Close b Trueman	1
C.L. Walcott	c Lock b Laker	1
E.D. Weekes	c Trueman b Lock	33
G.S. Sobers	c Cowdrey b Lock	14
O.G. Smith	lbw b Laker	5
F.M. Worrell	c May b Lock	0
J.D.C. Goddard	not out	0
D. Atkinson	not out	4
Extras	(b 7)	7
Total	(7 wkts)	72

Fall of wickets: 1–4, 2–83, 3–120, 4–183, 5–197, 6–387, 7–466, 8–469, 9–474, 10–474.

Second innings: 1–1, 2–9, 3–25, 4–27, 5–43, 6–65, 7–68.

ENGLAND BOWLING

	O	M	R	W	O	M	R	W
Statham	39	4	114	3	2	0	6	0
Trueman	30	4	99	2	5	3	7	2
Bailey	34	11	80	0				
Laker	54	17	119	4	24	20	13	2
Lock	34.4	15	55	0	27	19	31	3
Close					2	1	8	0

Umpires: C.S. Elliott and E. Davies

MATCH DRAWN

four Tests against India in 1952, and did well. There was something exceptional in the making.

In 1953 there was a mild setback. He played against Australia only in the first Test and the last. He failed in the first, in which he batted at No. 6. He was always happier, even when young, with the responsibility of batting No 3 or 4. When he came back for the last Test, the decisive one, at

No. 3, he scored 39 and 37, both innings of much consequence in the context.

Thereafter, except for injury or illness (of which he had rather more than his share) he was always an England player. Before his early retirement in 1963, he had played in 66 Tests, in 41 of which he was captain. The number of captaincies is a record, although we should not make too much of it, because so many more Tests were being played. He averaged 47 in Tests, and 51 in first-class cricket — 27,500 runs, 85 centuries.

I put the figures in because they deserve it, but you may be thinking, especially those of you who did not see him, or only saw him when you were very young, "Yes, we know all that, we know he was one of the great English batsmen, but how would you describe his play?'

The word that occurs to me is *elegance*. "Elegant but not ostentatious", as Johnson said of Addison's prose. May, even if he was beaten, never looked uncouth. People who were there tell me that this was true even on the 1958–59 tour of Australia, when English batsmen were constantly reduced to inelegant attitudes by the "dubious actions" of the bowlers — rather as Australians had been, a quarter of a century earlier, on the "bodyline" tour.

May's style was the kind we call classical. The upright stance, the backlift, the immediate judgment of length and adjustment of feet, the pounce to the overpitched spinner, the quick step back, almost to the stumps, for the cut: these were the things we had always associated with the Edwardians, the amateur batsmen of the golden age. May of Charterhouse made a fit companion for MacLaren and Jackson of Harrow, Fry of Repton, Foster of Malvern. At least he would have done, had he not been a couple of generations late.

You might say that, although not the least of the apostles, he was one born out of due time (you could say much the same of Cowdrey of Tonbridge, who came along a little later). Yet in another sense he was very much a man of his time. Only rarely, in Test cricket, did he display all his stroke-making gifts. Yet he had a mastery of concentration which none of the Edwardians had, except Jackson. He had greater patience than any of them but then he could afford it, since he did not have to face the challenge of three-day Tests.

He was often seen at his best for Surrey, when Surridge was captain. Surridge was a man who hated draws. As an England captain, and an England batsman, May crammed himself into

the mould of his predecessor, Hutton, who was an even more beautiful batsman and an equally wise captain, but became increasingly cautious in both aspects. I have always thought that May was appointed to the England captaincy too soon. Another couple of years without the responsibility might have given him the confidence to be a little more adventurous. Also, we might not have lost him as early as we did.

May was elegant not only in style but in manner, not only in his cricket but his character. He came to the front at a time when pressures on top class cricketers were intensifying, although they were not so terrifying as those of today (of course the rewards were correspondingly less). A captain's lot was a particularly difficult one, with the press almost dictatorial in demands for constant attempts to pry into private life.

The more brash among them sometimes thought May remote, although he was always polite and tactful. When the 1958–9 side returned from Australia, he was immediately asked for his views on throwing. He replied that Englishmen should look forward to seeing Norman O'Neill, one of the best throwers (from the deep) that he had ever seen. His field manners were what we expected (rightly or wrongly) from the old-style amateur. There was one unfortunate mix-up about the use of a runner in the West Indies, when May was in the wrong, but it was no more than a misunderstanding, and May, although it was not generally known until he returned, prematurely, to England soon afterwards, was unwell.

Of his many great innings, the one that comes most readily to my mind was in the first Test against the West Indies in 1957. It was, in its earlier part, a defensive innings, but the circumstances demanded that. The West Indies bowled England out for 186, and scored 474. England had conferences and interviews, and lost three for 113 in the second innings, when May and Cowdrey came together. The next wicket, Cowdrey's fell at 524. He had made 154. May went on to 285 not out, until he declared at 583 for 4. E.W. Swanton wrote that "the concentration, the restraint, the technical excellence of these two innings could not be overpraised. Never have two young cricketers built such a monument to patience and determination". I did not see the match, but I would bet that they were, both of them, *elegant* innings.

May came in for some criticisms because he did not declare earlier, and certainly the weary West Indies' score at the end, 72 for seven, suggested that he might have done. But it was not unreasonable to feel that he had saved a match that looked hopelessly lost, and that would do for now. The West Indies were never the same side again that season.

I am afraid our sage and beloved Cricket Correspondent is not enjoying himself too much at present in Australia. I dare say, as he wilts beneath the barrage of ballyhoo (how inadequate a word that has become) he reflects on better days and better manners, and that his tours with May are often in his thoughts. And I dare say that May, from his ripe and rounded middle age (although remember that Woolley, Hobbs, and Rhodes, to take three, all played first-class cricket when they were older) feels relief to be well away from it, despite the monetary attractions. Of all leading English cricketers, at least since the first war, he would have looked the most incongruous in this setting. So perhaps he was not, after all, a man born out of due time.

FREDERICK SEWARDS TRUEMAN
Yorkshire

Trueman retired from first-class cricket more than twenty years ago. Since then he has said all there is to say on the achievements of F.S. Trueman. In 1963 at Edgbaston he bowled against one of the finest of West Indies sides.

By John Woodcock

10 July 1963. It was not another epic struggle but a massacre instead. Left to make 309 to win at 66 runs an hour, West Indies were bowled out in 124 minutes for 91. Soon after three o'clock the match was over, the series level, and England were being led off the field by Trueman with another resounding feat to his name.

In the final reckoning West Indies had shown, perhaps, a lack of resolution. The ball had swung, prodigiously at times; it had moved readily off the seam. Yet behind it all was Trueman's superlative bowling. In 14.3 overs he took seven wickets for 44 runs, the last six of them in 24 balls at the cost of a snick for four by Gibbs.

When at Sydney in January, Davidson decided the third Test match in Australia's favour he gave as great an exhibition of fast bowling as I had ever thought to see. Yesterday Trueman equalled it for venom and variety. With his hair escaping in dark and wild curls, and his run a thing of gathering strength, he took control of the game. Every ball was charged with danger and I felt at the end that, had he needed to, he could have bowled the same side out again.

Under a hot sun and on thankless wickets Trueman is no longer the force he was. In England when there is moisture in the turf he is as good, if not better than ever. For some years he has looked forward to the day when he could take a yard or two off his run and rely not so much on his speed as on the many other facets of his bowling. This was the Trueman we saw now. He bowled with his brain as much as with his muscle. Beneath a clouded sky he moved the ball with late and vicious swing; off the seam it cut like a rattlesnake, this way and that. I have no doubt that Hall and Griffith watched with admiration, hoping that they too will one day bowl so well.

As for the West Indian batsmen, they were the victims also of their own dispositions. They sought to play their strokes before getting a sight of the ball. It was splendid that they should, in this way, accept the challenge of Dexter's declaration. They could have chosen, with a lead in the series, to play quietly for a draw. Had they done so from the start they would probably have achieved it. Instead, they fired away with abandon and before they knew where they were they had been holed through the sides.

For all but three overs Trueman was supported by Shackleton, whose nagging length made the West Indians fret the more. It was Shackleton

TRUEMAN   A pigeon-toed Greek sculpture.

who took the first wicket in his first over, Carew being leg-before trying to tuck one away to the onside. In Trueman's second over Hunte was well caught low down at second slip. The ball before he had snicked for four, in much the same direction. England sensed their chance and made like tigers for the kill.

There was never a sense of permanence about any of the batsmen. Kanhai, a brilliant and unfettered performer, began to play shots at Trueman that would have held an element of chance even at Georgetown when he had been batting for most of a day. He was still there at luncheon, having had some narrow escapes and played a number of breathtaking strokes. But by then Butcher had been bowled by Dexter's second ball. I remember Marshall, the Hampshire cavalier, telling me a year or two ago that the best ball he had received in the whole of one season was bowled to him by Dexter. So, now, Dexter confounded Butcher with an evil breakback. As he did so he leapt like a salmon at a weir.

At the start of the afternoon West Indies needed 254 to win. They had seven wickets left and there was three hours and a half remaining. When Sobers and Kanhai began at once to throw the bat it was clear that they were playing with fire. As two of the most dynamic and gifted batsmen in the world it was in their power to win the match. But with three good wickets gone already there was little margin for error. In the event, Sobers was soon magnificently caught by Sharpe. Sobers slashed at a shortish ball from Shackleton, which lifted just a little, and in one action Sharpe both protected his face and held the catch. This alone would have been a justification of Sharpe's selection, irrespective of the runs he scored.

At 64 for four West Indies were in obvious danger. Kanhai, however, was undeterred. At 78 he mistimed a violent hook at a bouncer from Trueman and spooned a gentle catch to Lock at backward short leg. Spectacular, rash, foolhardy, daring — Kanhai's innings was all these things. His dismissal seemed an unnecessary waste and Worrell, as he passed him outside the

pavilion gate, answered a penitent look with an admonitory one.

Within half an hour the match was finished. Only Solomon and Worrell were left to stand against the tide, and Worrell fell to a questionable decision. Trueman was bowling so superbly now, with two or three balls in an over getting past the bat, that I doubt whether Worrell could, anyway, have resisted him for long. It was sad, however, that he should go as he did. The appeal for a catch at the wicket was loud and widespread: Worrell, when he was given out by umpire Gray, made it clear with a gesture that he thought the ball had brushed against his arm. It seemed, on Worrell's part, an act not of irritation but of sheer despair. The West Indians, I know, are not happy with the umpiring of the last two Test matches and this was the culmination of their disappointment.

Like a tornado Trueman swept through the tail. The heart had gone out of the West Indians by now; the will to fight had been destroyed; the end was a release from their suffering. Murray was caught at the wicket off a lifting outswinger; the two fast bowlers Hall and Griffith, fell in the same over; and last of all, Solomon was caught by Parks. Solomon had batted for 48 minutes. He must have felt in this time like the inhabitants of Tristan da Cunha when their island home erupted. He was powerless to intervene as Trueman rumbled through the innings.

The match had been played in conditions which are traditionally suitable to English cricketers. Their bowlers especially had used the grassy wicket as experience has taught them. With two hours 40 minutes to spare they had won a game which, at the weekend, had seemed destined to be drawn. But West Indians suffer these lapses from time to time. Temperament and technique, which enable them one day to be the game's most attractive batsmen, can let them down the next. Yesterday any side with Trueman in it, bowling as he was, would have been hard to hold. In the last two Test matches he has taken 23 wickets, and in his Test career he has taken 275, which is 32 more than the next man. Now, in one of his more memorable outings, he has restored the balance of the series.

England had batted for 70 minutes during the morning before closing their innings. Sharpe and Lock allowed them to choose the moment of declaration. These two added 89 for the ninth wicket, which accords them the satisfaction of a record for England against West Indies. They made 52 of these yesterday with Lock showing Sharpe the way. Lock's 56 was his highest score for England. It helped to alter the complexion of the match, leaving West Indies with a task in their fourth innings which would have been formidable even on a firm wicket and a fast outfield. Lock treats batting as though it was a matter of life and death; so, for England, it was, when he came at 189 for eight.

Sharpe continued where he left off Monday evening. In this innings he was like a man whose memory had returned. His batting had about it a strength of purpose not to be expected from someone appearing in his first Test match. For almost four hours he sustained the innings when England could ill afford to lose him.

Even under Worrell's persuasive and restraining influence the West Indians are not the masters of their moods. Few cricketers are, come to that. Yesterday they looked strangely listless in the field. Though they had a new ball with which to start the morning they took no advantage of it. Griffith was tired from his exertions of the previous day. Hall, whose strength is his speed, found the pitch too slow. In the end it was Gibbs who bowled Lock, with Dexter making signals of aggression from the pavilion. By lunchtime Carew, Hunte and Butcher were out. The axe and the block were in position. In less than an hour afterwards the execution was complete.

CAPTAIN OF YORKSHIRE

By midsummer 1968 there was trouble brewing in Yorkshire, with the members of the committee and two sub-committees meeting in secret session.

ENGLAND v. WEST INDIES
Edgbaston, 4–6, 8, 9 July 1963

ENGLAND
1st innings
216 (D.B. Close 55; G.S. Sobers 5 for 60)

2nd innings
278 for 9 dec. (E.R. Dexter 57, P.J. Sharpe 85 not out, G.A.R. Lock 56)

WEST INDIES
1st innings

C.C. Hunte	b Trueman	18
M.C. Carew	c & b Trueman	40
R.B. Kanhai	c Lock b Shackleton	32
B.F. Butcher	lbw b Dexter	15
J.S. Solomon	lbw b Dexter	0
G.S. Sobers	b Trueman	19
F.M. Worrell	b Dexter	1
D.L. Murray	not out	20
W.W. Hall	c Sharpe b Dexter	28
C.C. Griffith	lbw b Trueman	5
L.R. Gibbs	b Trueman	0
Extras	(lb 7, w 1)	8
Total		186

2nd innings

C.C. Hunte	c Barrington b Trueman	5
M.C. Carew	lbw b Shackleton	1
R.B. Kanhai	c Lock b Trueman	38
B.F. Butcher	b Dexter	14
J.S. Solomon	c Parks b Trueman	14
G.S. Sobers	c Sharpe b Shackleton	9
F.M. Worrell	c Parks b Trueman	0
D.L. Murray	c Parks b Trueman	3
W.W. Hall	b Trueman	0
C.C. Griffith	lbw b Trueman	0
L.R. Gibbs	not out	4
Extras	(lb 2, w 1)	3
Total		91

Fall of wickets: 1–42, 2–79, 3–108, 4–109, 5–128, 6–130, 7–130, 8–178, 9–186, 10–186.

Second innings: 1–2, 2–10, 3–38, 4–64, 5–78, 6–80, 7–86, 8–86, 9–86, 10–91.

ENGLAND BOWLING

	O	M	R	W	O	M	R	W
Trueman	26	5	75	5	14.3	2	44	7
Shackleton	21	9	60	1	17	4	37	2
Lock	2	1	5	0				
Dexter	20	5	38	4	3	1	7	1

Umpires: C.S. Elliott and L.H. Gray

ENGLAND WON BY 217 RUNS

However, when Lawry's Australians arrived at Sheffield, domestic differences were forgotten. In the absence of D.B. Close (injured) the county was led by Trueman. On the first day Yorkshire scored 271 for four wickets.

By Jack Fingleton

2 July 1968. It was Trueman's day at Bramall Lane. As Yorkshire's skipper, Trueman had the supreme satisfaction of asking Australia to follow on. As a bowler he took three wickets, as a fieldsman he took three catches and had one run out. Australia faces defeat.

Trueman [in his 38th year] is still a most useful cricketer and a good skipper to boot. He bowled with much of his old fire and zeal and his versatility was shown in a wonderful diving catch at second slip to dismiss Walters. Then again, when Lawry made a most horrible call which cost I.M. Chappell his wicket, Trueman pounced on the ball, and, running the opposite way, had it back to the stumps with a sideways jerk.

Lawry, Chappell and Connolly apart, the Australians batted atrociously. There was, in the first instance, a lack of common sense, a failure to put the head down, grit the teeth and fight back. The young Australians were warned that Yorkshire are always thorny at Bramall Lane, but the general reaction was "She'll be all right, mate." There was nothing much right about the Australian situation at the close.

It had happened before against Yorkshire. Rain saved us from defeat in 1938 [when at lunch on the third day Yorkshire needed only 67 to win with seven second-innings wickets in hand — and Sutcliffe not out]. The county beat Australia in 1893 here and in 1902 at Leeds, when Hirst took five for nine and Jackson five for 12 and the club cut the ball in half and presented it to the heroes. It was a pretty new ball. Only 23 had been scored from it.

There was nothing in the pitch to justify the Australian catastrophe. It had some pace and lift, but the Australians, as a team, had not the answer to the Yorkshire devil and dash.

The Australians always played as underdogs and I thought that I could well have been watching the English and not the Yorkshire team in action. It is a splendidly balanced side.

McKenzie hit back for the Australians in the morning, regaining some bowling reputation that was lost on Saturday. He had 12 for three off 21 balls at one stage.

Illingworth batted splendidly, hitting Gleeson for a six; Taylor got 14 in eight minutes yesterday after getting 10 in 80 minutes on Saturday. Trueman called his men in at 355 for nine, the biggest score yet against Australia, beating England's 351 for seven at Lord's last week, and Sussex's 330, the previous best by a county against Australia.

Trueman gave Lawry his biggest fright of the tour when he bowled a full-toss "beamer" first ball. He also gave Redpath one the same over, but pinked instead his own wicketkeeper, Binks, on the right forearm.

The Australians quickly had four boundaries off Trueman. One felt the flush was too vivid to be healthy, and so it proved. Redpath erred at playing Trueman down the leg side, where Binks took a good tumbling catch, and Walters sparred and was taken in the great manner by Trueman.

Before Redpath went he survived the closest call when Lawry asked him for a dangerous run and Taylor uprooted the middle stump. The umpire, Spencer, said not out. The spectators said plenty for the rest of the day.

The mud and rain caused two breaks after luncheon. Lawry batted supremely but his calling was another matter. Chappell, fighting well, was nowhere near home for a call which justified half a run at the most. Lawry got a nasty one at last off the bowler's roughage — Spencer once severely cautioned Hutton for his run-through — and Connolly alone of the remainder showed fight.

Hutton bowled well as did Illingworth and Hutton also took a splendid running catch. He also lifted Lawry's leg stump near the finish with a delicious late swinging yorker.

The Australians have all today to redeem themselves. For the second time in a week

Australia have followed on.* And to rub it in, Taylor, of Yorkshire, won the throwing competition with a throw of 110 yards.

Close: YORKSHIRE 355 for 9 declared (G. Boycott 85, P.J. Sharpe 56, R. Illingworth 69 not out), AUSTRALIANS 148 (W.M. Lawry 58) and 15 for one.

3 July 1968. Not a single excuse can be made for the Australians' defeat by an innings and 69 runs. If ever there was a clear-cut victory this was it, and in hastening to congratulate a side which played splendidly from the first ball on Saturday, one does so as a member of the 1938 Australian team who were saved from certain defeat by the weather. This is the first time Lawry's team has been beaten, although they were morally beaten by England at Lord's last week.

They should give every Australian side that comes to Bramall Lane a brochure on how to play cricket against Yorkshire. It is difficult to impress upon young men making their first visit here that this is not just another county game. Bramall Lane bristles with belligerency from the beginning and another plain fact is that there is never any nonsense about Yorkshire cricket. Every run against Yorkshire has to be earned, every wicket has to be won.

It is, in truth, just like Test cricket and I must add that this closely-knit Yorkshire team on the field, at least, whatever their alleged disagreements are elsewhere and the way they function as a machine makes one think that they could worthily represent England. Such is the value of teamwork.

"Never mind, Lawry", a spectator called out to the harassed Lawry on Monday, "You'll have it easier against Cowdrey and England next week."

Yorkshire, true to their nature, gave "nowt" away. They play three seamers and two tight spinners. At a social gathering the preceding evening, Trueman told me his side would win for

. . . .
* In the Lord's Test Australia made 78 and 127 for four in reply to England's 351 for seven, declared.

certain. Never an over-modest man, Trueman said: "We get bonus if we beat you. Yorkshiremen can smell brass from long way off. You've got no chance."

And so it proved. Australia's only hope of salvage was the weather. It poured at 10.30 and it looked like night. Thirty minutes later the sun shone and the game began twenty minutes late. The light during the day was good to dull to duller and the Australian appeal in mid-afternoon was more in the nature of despair.

The pitch remained good, yielding not undue encouragement to Illingworth and Wilson. Redpath might have been hardly done by when umpire Aspinall raised his finger to Hutton's sole appeal for leg before. It was more the posterior than the leg.

Walters settled in admirably and fought every inch of the way to lunch. Chappell, unfortunately run out in the first innings, was again a most determined opponent. At luncheon the Australians were 105 for three, Walters a splendid 46, replete with many delicious strokes and sound defence. Chappell was 15. Sheahan who had two superb square cuts off Hutton, had his middle stump uprooted by the old warrior, Trueman. The ball came back with venom from the off.

The Australians slipped into the abyss after lunch when Walters reached, instead of going across the pitch, to Trueman. Chappell alone fought on. The rest of the Australians were pitifully unequal to the task. Illingworth teased them with spin, length and change of pace. It was grand stuff for the happy spectators. Binks did an able job, Hutton took another good running catch and the end came amid the encircling gloom — for the Australians.

One man remains to be saluted — Freddie Trueman. He has been a bonny fighter all these years. He led Yorkshire in this game from the front, taking wickets, taking catches, and captaining his side with rare generalship. Here, I also thought, was one who could have led England with distinction. He knows the moves, he is a canny thinker; but then, in all countries, bowlers are strangely believed not to possess the where-withal to lead their national teams. It is an odd belief.

YORKSHIRE 355 for 9 declared, beat the AUS-TRALIANS 148 and 138 (K.D. Walters 62) by an innings and 69 runs.

VALE

11 November 1968. Frederick Sewards Trueman, now in his thirty-eight year, has announced his retirement from first-class cricket. "Time marches on", he said. It takes with it a character who has enriched the game and a fast bowler of monumental achievement.

Trueman holds the record bag of Test wickets. Between 1952 and 1965 he took 307 in 67 appearances for England. These are figures which tell well enough of a wonderful natural talent.

He was born with a rhythm for bowling and a strong physique which assured him of cricketing success. But what marked him out from other cricketers, apart from his ability, was his temperament, which was forthright, and his sense of humour, which was basic.

His best years were from 1958 until 1964, though right from the start he was attended by success. His first series for England was in 1952, when he took 29 wickets in 119.4 overs and put the Indians to flight.

In 1953 he had a part in England's at last regaining the Ashes, and in 1955 he established a partnership with Brian Statham which became as famous and as fecund as that between Larwood and Voce or Lindwall and Miller. Both Trueman and Statham were superb fielders, and the years

of their prime coincided with a period of English ascendancy.

But it was Trueman's personality as much as his prowess that made him star quality. Wherever he appeared — from Bradford to Brisbane, via Bridgetown and Bombay — he was cheered on sight.

Of England's fast bowlers since the war, Tyson, for a short time, was the fastest, Statham the most accurate, and Trueman the most volatile. He emerged from the coal face, as it were, of a mining village—rough hewn and with a strong disinclination to compromise his character. Because of this he blotted his copybook in the West Indies in 1953–54 and was left out of MCC teams to Australia in 1954–55 and South Africa in 1956–57.

I am reluctant to believe that characters are many fewer now than they were; but it may be a long time before another comes along of Trueman's calibre. Last year he took only 66 wickets, so that he is wise to give up before his powers fail and to accept a lucrative offer from the International Cavaliers.

Undoubtedly, Trueman goes down as one of the greatest of all fast bowlers. Sometimes with spectacular success he wielded a bat like a pick-axe, and had he put his mind to it he could have made many more runs than he did.

Because of who and what he is, many of the best cricket stories are attributed now to Fred. That is a compliment in itself. But here, as an example, is an authentic specimen.

During the MCC tour to Australia in 1962–63, at a civic reception in Perth, a bishop mounted the platform. Trueman to David Sheppard, wearing a dog collar for the occasion: "Is that your senior pro?" This, for once, is an unexpurgated version.

SIR GARFIELD ST AUBRUN SOBERS
Barbados, South Australia and Nottinghamshire

In 1950 Neville Cardus broadcast a talk on his World XI of the century. Emphasizing that it would play three-day games, and casting Hammond in the role of 12th man — "if only to see the expression on Wally's face as he carried out the drinks" — Cardus produced this order: Hobbs, Trumper, Bradman, Macartney, F.S. Jackson (captain), Faulkner, Miller, Rhodes, Oldfield, Larwood, Barnes. Twenty years later Cardus was handed his list and asked to make any alterations which the passing of time could possibly have made necessary. "I don't suppose Don would object to taking over the captaincy." So saying, Cardus crossed out "Jackson", and inserted "Sobers".

Sobers made his Test debut at Kingston against England in March 1954 at the age of 17 years 245 days. Played as a bowler, he took four wickets for 75 runs and batted at No. 9. Fifteen Tests followed, during which he went in everywhere and anywhere: as opener four times, No. 3 six times, Nos 4, 5 and 7 once each and at No. 6 twice. After sixteen Tests he had played 28 innings with an average of 34.25. Then on 26 February 1958 West Indies met Pakistan at Kingston in the third match of a series. At 274 for four on the opening day, Pakistan were out for 328 on the second, West Indies replying with 147 for one — Hunte 100 not out, Sobers 20 not out. A day later West Indies were 504 for one: Hunte 242, Sobers 228.

3 March 1958, Kingston, Jamaica. G. Sobers, the 21-year-old West Indies batsman, beat Sir Leonard Hutton's world record Test score with 365 not out in the third Test against Pakistan here on Saturday. Sir Leonard hit 364 for England against Australia at the Oval in 1938 when he was 22. Sobers batted for 10 hours and eight minutes compared with Hutton's 13 hours and 20 minutes.

The position, in fact, could hardly have been more favourable for record breaking. Sir Leonard Hutton's score, of course, was also compiled in ideal circumstances. England had won the toss, the pitch was one of "Bosser" Martin's specials, and the passage of time was incidental. Yet Australia, under Bradman, were the opponents then. Hanif, for his part, was always fighting an anxious rearguard action. Had he got out at any time for close on three days, his side would probably have lost; but he grafted on and West Indies were denied.

Now Sobers has taken the opportunity of making a famous niche for himself. Only eight batsmen, Bradman, Ponsford, and MacLaren among them, have played higher innings in first-class cricket; and he joins the select company of Headley, Weekes, Walcott and Worrell as the only West Indians ever to exceed 300.

It is, in its way, an immense achievement by a player of glittering promise, and one hopes that in accomplishing it Sobers did not compromise his true character and merely fall a prey to records. For that to happen to such an exciting and enthusiastic cricketer would be sad indeed.

Pakistan have only three recognized bowlers to call on in this match as the result of injuries to Mahmood Hussain (pulled thigh muscle) and Nasimul Ghani (broken thumb) early in the West Indies innings. Both will be out for the rest of the tour. In addition, Kardar has a broken finger on his bowling hand. The tourists have cabled home asking for a spin bowler to join them at British Guiana. Meantime, West Indies have declared at 790 for three in reply to Pakistan's 328. The match will continue to-morrow and on Tuesday.

WEST INDIES v. PAKISTAN
Kingston, 26–8 February, 1, 3, 4 March, 1958

PAKISTAN
1st innings
328 (Imtiaz Ahmed 122, Saeed Ahmed 52,
Wallis Mathias 77; E. Atkinson 5 for 42)

2nd innings
288 (A.H. Kardar 57, Wazir Mohammed 106)

WEST INDIES

C.C. Hunte	run out	260
R.B. Kanhai	c Imtiaz b Fazal	25
G.S. Sobers	not out	365
E.D. Weekes	c Hanif b Fazal	39
C.L. Walcott	not out	88
Extras	(b 1, lb 8, w 4)	13
Total	(3 wkts. dec.)	790

O.G. Smith, F.C.M. Alexander, L.R. Gibbs, E. Atkinson, R. Gilchrist, T. Dewdney did not bat.

Fall of wickets: 1–87, 2–533, 3–602.

PAKISTAN BOWLING

	O	M	R	W
M. Hussain	0.5	0	2	0
Fazal Mahmood	85.1	20	247	2
Khan Mohammed	54	5	259	0
Nasim-Ul-Ghani	14	3	39	0
A.H. Kardar	37	2	141	0
Wallis Mathias	4	0	20	0
Alim-Ud-Din	4	0	34	0
Hanif Mohammed	2	0	11	0
Saeed Ahmed	6	0	24	0

WEST INDIES WON BY AN INNINGS AND 174 RUNS

SOBERS BOWLS...

The unfairness of allowing Sobers to bowl and bat in the same match was made manifest at Lord's in June 1970. While no one suggested that Sobers was a more devastating bowler than the W.A. Johnston of 1948, or the A.K. Davidson of a decade later, or a finer left-hand batsman than A.R. Morris, R.N. Harvey or M.P. Donnelly at the peak of their powers (and had Sobers been born in Surrey, the competence of Laker's short-leg fielders would scarcely have been diminished had he been substituted for Lock), the magnoperative genius of Sobers was a little too much.

By John Woodcock

18 June 1970. With the exception of Ray Illingworth, who played a captain's innings of 63, England's batting against the Rest of the World at Lord's yesterday was too bad to be true. At lunch time, on an admittedly lively wicket, they were 44 for 7, and the ghost of W.G. was reported to have been seen calling for a large brandy at the Long Room bar.*

To have watched English batsmanship reduced to such a level was sad indeed. And by the time England came on to bowl, in the late afternoon, the wicket had shed some of its early life.

Had England fielded first, the Rest might have been the ones to struggle. Instead, by the close of play they had achieved already an invincible position.

Sobers bowled beautifully to take six for 21 in 20 overs. He did the damage mostly with the ball that he runs away to the slips, and in this he was helped by Barlow, Kanhai and Engineer. Engineer held four catches behind the wicket and missed two; at slip, Barlow, as usual, dropped nothing, while Kanhai caught one out of two.

Gibbs fielded brilliantly in the gully, and Richards and Lloyd each held on to chances which they could well have missed. If a side are to

* At last Woodcock acknowledged the ghost of A.C.M. Croome.

be called a World XI, it is as well that they should play like one, as they did now.

On this evidence, the enjoyment of the series will come from seeing the best cricketers in the game exhibiting their skills. And as a testing ground, the games will help the England selectors in sorting out their countless problems. Yesterday, none of England's batsmen did himself the slightest bit of good. They were embarrassed, I imagine, by their abject failure.

Having flashed the first ball of the match over the heads of the slips for four, Jones was soon caught at the wicket off Procter. When Luckhurst flicked Sobers to short leg he had spent 45 minutes searching vainly for the middle of his bat. Denness, his county partner, survived for 70 minutes without finding the chance to play any of the delightful strokes he has.

D'Oliveira made little contact for 20 minutes before being caught at the wicket; Sharpe, out of form for Yorkshire, was soon caught at slip off one that lifted; and so was Knott. Snow, number 10 for Sussex but number eight for England, was also gone by lunch.

Afterwards, Illingworth batted astonishingly well. His driving and forcing put the others to shame. Underwood, playing forward where the batsmen had played back, helped in an eighth wicket partnership of 50 in 40 minutes, and for the ninth wicket Illingworth and Ward added 31.

Compared with Sobers and Procter, the rest of the bowling was mercifully mild; and in England's next innings we may hope that Gibbs will at least be needed.

Of England's total of 127, no more than 30 came in front of the wicket. While South Africa's opening pair, Richards and Barlow, were making 69 in 17 overs, it was a different story. The ball was flying less by now, and no one swung it as Sobers had. Even so, Ward and Snow were in no mood to spare themselves and they brought from Richards the real stuff of batsmanship.

For him and Barlow it was interesting, but not intimidating, to know what they would have been up against had South Africa been playing England.

Hereabouts, England's consolation came from a lovely catch by Sharpe, taken low down at slip, and from the sight of D'Oliveira taking his sixth wicket of the season. But the day's memory was of that foresaken English batting.

Brian Statham, who is now employed by Guinness, the sponsors of the match, was in evidence at lunchtime. His reply to the assertion that he would have enjoyed himself "out there this morning" was as pertinent as his bowling. Always a man of few words, he said simply: "Against that lot, yes."

Close: ENGLAND 127 (R. Illingworth 63: G.S. Sobers 6 for 21), REST OF THE WORLD 115 for 2 (E.J. Barlow 50 not out).

SOBERS BATS...

Second Day

20 June 1970. Gary Sobers was at it again yesterday. He followed that devilishly good piece of bowling on Wednesday by making 147 not out and putting the English bowlers to flight. There were some 12,000 people to watch the great man in action.

The prelude to Sobers's 22nd Test 100 was one by Barlow. Graeme Pollock, too, made 55, if with less than his usual mastery; and Sobers's partner in an unbroken partnership of 177 for the seventh wicket was Intikhab. This is an eleven composed of batsmen who pledge themselves to hit the ball, and as such everyone in the country remotely interested in cricket should try to see them play. It is a pity only that there is no one here to stake a claim on Australia's behalf.

I have seldom seen Sobers bat with more relish, or hit the ball harder than he did yesterday. Only Bradman, with 29, has made more Test hundreds than Sobers, though Hammond and Cowdrey are on the same mark. If Sobers had been treating this merely as an exhibition he would be out by now. Instead he played quietly through the final overs of the evening as though his appetite had been whetted for today. So far he has hit 25 fours and one six.

Up to a point England did quite well. Half an hour before tea they had six men out for 298, on a pitch which was a great deal more placid than on Wednesday. The bowling was done mostly by Snow, Ward and Shuttleworth, and the best of these was Ward. In his later spells Snow was cruelly punished, and Shuttleworth rather lacked direction. So long are the runs of these three that England's over rate was inevitably slow, and Illingworth was reluctant to quicken it up by the earlier use of himself and Underwood.

Illingworth allowed D'Oliveira a long spell before giving Underwood a chance, and not until after luncheon did he bowl himself. To give D'Oliveira his due, he required careful watching; yet in the light of his record over the last two years it is hard to see him as a Test match bowler. In 1969 he was 125th in the national averages with 14 wickets at 43 apiece. How strange, then, that by the time Underwood was called upon D'Oliveira had already had 13 overs and Barlow had made 98.

SOBERS Indisputably the greatest cricketer of the twentieth century.

In the field England made one costly mistake. This was when Luckhurst, on the long leg boundary, dropped Sobers off Shuttleworth. The catch looked easier than it was, though for such a splendid fielder as Luckhurst it was still easy enough. This was incidentally one of only two chances which England had on a day when Sharpe at slip, so far as I can remember, never touched the ball.

Barlow's was a remarkable innings for someone who had played virtually no cricket since March. Unlike Pollock and Richards, who live by the light of nature, Barlow's strength is his determination. He fairly bristles with it, and it had come in useful on Wednesday evening, when he was looking for a footing. Yesterday in a stand of 131 with Pollock, he was the more convincing partner. The fact that Pollock is recovering from influenza may have had something to do with this, and he too, of course, is short of cricket.

For Pollock the innings amounted to a long net, which in the ordinary way is a form of practice he moves heaven and earth to avoid. In the first hour he made 13 to Barlow's 39; by lunchtime the Rest were 215 for two, the morning having yielded 100 runs. For the four South Africans in the Rest side, there is the added incentive of knowing that by their performances, South Africa's cricket is being measured — by the West Indians not least.

By the afternoon, Barlow and Pollock were all set to show it off at its best; but no sooner had they begun to do so than both were out. Pollock, having just hit one glorious stroke through the covers, was bowled by Underwood, attempting another. And two balls later Barlow hooked a long hop to short midwicket, where Underwood, diving to his right, held an unexpectedly brilliant catch.

The rest of the day was dominated by Sobers, well though Intikhab played. He made a careful start, with no more than a dozen runs in his first hour. Lloyd, likewise, played as though with every intention of staying at Sobers's shoulder. When the new ball was taken at 285 for four, these two were together, the groundwork done.

But at 293 Lloyd chopped Ward into his stumps, and at 298 Ward bowled Engineer. That, for England, was the last glimmer of hope on another sobering day.

Close: ENGLAND 127, REST OF THE WORLD 478 for 6 (E.J. Barlow 119, R.G. Pollock 55, G.S. Sobers 147 not out, Intikhab Alam 56 not out).

Third Day

22 June 1970. Any doubt as to whether or not it is right for the present cricket matches between England and the Rest of the World to be ranked as an official Test series has, to my mind, been resolved. The determination of the players has already justified the recognition of the games.

When England played the Rest of the World at football, there were no doubt those who considered it wrong to reward the players with a full cap. Richie Benaud feels the same way now. Yet England are being put to the test as they never were last year by New Zealand or West Indies, nor will be in 1971 by India and Pakistan. To the England team, their individual performances are vital.

D'Oliveira's second innings of 78 was characteristic. No sooner is his Test career in jeopardy than his temperament and a straight-forward batting technique save him for another day. That could well be so now, though he is obviously overplaced at No. 4.

The same sort of thing can be said of Illingworth. Simply as a spinner I would rather see Pocock or Wilson, partly because of their age. And as a captain, Cowdrey is no inferior to Illingworth. Indeed, on tour he is to be preferred. Yet at Lord's last year, against West Indies, it was Illingworth who helped to save England with a hundred: and in the present match his batting has been distinctly useful.

Like D'Oliveira, Illingworth has a hardy temperament; but with an eye on the future there is hardly room for them both. There seems to me no reason why the selectors should not decide this week on their captain in Australia; and if Cowdrey is their answer, then Illingworth, for all his competence, may have to go.

Close: ENGLAND 127 and 228 for 5 (B.W. Luckhurst 67, B.L. d'Oliveira 78), REST OF THE WORLD 546 (G.S. Sobers 183, Intikhab Alam 61).

Fourth Day

23 June 1970. Ray Illingworth did all he could to save England by making 94 yesterday. It was the innings of a fighter, played for a cause that was already lost. Knott made Illingworth a dogged partner, and so long as these two were together the Rest were made to work for their success. Which was really all that one could ask.

The irony is, of course, that had England been playing a moderate Indian side at Lord's on Saturday, winning hands down, the ground would have been full to overflowing. As it was, there were fewer than 15,000 there to watch the best cricketers in the world in glorious weather. The regulars who stayed away made a curious decision, the Saturday at Lord's being an occasion which only their absence can diminish.

It would be wrong to judge the state of English cricket by what has happened so far in this match. Had England, rather than the Rest, been bowling last Wednesday morning, it might have made a vast difference. No one, it is true, would have been likely to bowl as well as Sobers; but there was much more in the wicket then than there has been ever since.

England, too, will be able to field a stronger side in the remaining matches. Colin Cowdrey should be back, whether or not as captain. Edrich may be fit again and, all being well, Boycott will soon follow Cowdrey into form. I would, in fact, back him to do so in a Test match more confidently than for Yorkshire.

Here at Lord's, Jones has missed his chance. His fielding is hardly up to it, and he was out to the first ball of England's second innings, flashing unimpressively at Procter. Sharpe is another

whose days seem to be numbered, especially if Cowdrey is available to field at slip; and Denness and Shuttleworth may be struggling for survival. It was unfortunate for Shuttleworth to be chosen for his first Test match at a time when he was not happy with his bowling.

Luckhurst with a resolute innings of 67 on Saturday, has done enough to be retained. He is a game fighter, rather in the old mould of "hungry" cricketers.

As he showed on a notable occasion at Georgetown, Knott enjoys having his back to the wall. He moves eagerly into line, and being a wicketkeeper he reads the spinners well. By the time he was leg-before to Gibbs, trying to hit a full toss to square leg, he had batted for three hours and helped to give point to the day.

But the difference between that desperate struggle for survival in West Indies, when Knott and Cowdrey stood firm for so long, was the difference between war and peace. At Georgetown the noise was incessant, the tension unbearable. Yesterday it was all agreeably relaxed. Technically, too, there was a difference, this being the change in the leg before law which now discourages the batsman from padding up. Snow, for instance, was obliged to play with his bat yesterday, which he did for an hour. In West Indies, to the indignation of their bowlers, he kept kicking the ball away.

As on Wednesday, Illingworth batted uncommonly well. Until this match his best first-class score of the season had been 41; but you would never have known it. In the two hours of the morning he was beaten no more than two or three times, and he was in no real trouble until Sobers resorted to his chinamen and googlies. These were never Illingworth's favourite dish, and it was not long now before he was caught at slip off the googly. It is, of course, greatly to Illingworth's credit that in both innings he played better than the batting specialists. His reward for this is the England captaincy in the second Test match on Thursday week.

During the morning England advanced from

228 for five to 293 for five, and by lunchtime those who had come to Lord's were not regretting it. But 25 minutes afterwards Knott was out, and 10 runs later Illingworth yielded to Sobers.

The Rest continued right to the end to do their stuff in the grand manner. England's last three wickets all fell to the leg spinner, Intikhab, one of them to a googly and another to a stumping. In view of the fact that India and Pakistan no longer play Test matches against each other it was good to see Intikhab and Engineer teaming up in this way. The harmony of the Rest side, bound by the bond of cricket, was in fact an impressive feature of a successful match.

To each member of the winning side the victory was worth something in the region of £300 — thanks partly to the sponsorship of Guinness and the virtuosity of Sobers. So frequent are the signs of Sobers's genius that his performance here, devastating as it was, was not necessarily his best. What it showed, however, beyond a shadow of doubt, was the extent to which he has been restored by a winter in Barbados. While he was there his reluctance to play cricket, compared with his readiness to play golf, was not to everyone's liking. But it seems to have been just what he needed. In the second Test match he will lead the same side.

ENGLAND v. REST OF THE WORLD
Lord's, 17, 19, 20, 22 June 1970

ENGLAND
1st innings

B.W. Luckhurst	c Richards b Sobers	1
A. Jones	c Engineer b Procter	5
M.H. Denness	c Barlow b McKenzie	13
B.L. d'Oliveira	c Engineer b Sobers	0
P.J. Sharpe	c Barlow b Sobers	4
R. Illingworth	c Engineer b Sobers	63
A.P.E. Knott	c Kanhai b Sobers	2
J.A. Snow	c Engineer b Sobers	2
D.L. Underwood	c Lloyd b Barlow	19
A. Ward	c Sobers b McKenzie	11
K. Shuttleworth	not out	1
Extras	(lb 5, nb 1)	6
Total		127

2nd innings

B.W. Luckhurst	c Engineer b Intikhab	67
A. Jones	c Engineer b Procter	0
M.H. Denness	c Sobers b Intikhab	24
B.L. d'Oliveira	c Lloyd b Intikhab	78
P.J. Sharpe	b Sobers	2
R. Illingworth	c Barlow b Sobers	94
A.P.E. Knott	lbw b Gibbs	39
J.A. Snow	b Intikhab	10
D.L. Underwood	c Kanhai b Intikhab	7
A. Ward	st Engineer b Intikhab	0
K. Shuttleworth	not out	0
Extras	(b 4, lb 8, nb 6)	18
Total		339

Fall of wickets: 1–5, 2–17, 3–23, 4–23, 5–29, 6–31, 7–44, 8–94, 9–125, 10–127.

Second innings: 1–0, 2–39, 3–140, 4–148, 5–196, 6–313, 7–323, 8–334, 9–338, 10–339.

REST OF THE WORLD BOWLING (6-ball overs)

	O	M	R	W	O	M	R	W
McKenzie	16.1	3	43	2	15	8	25	0
Procter	13	6	20	1	15	4	36	1
Sobers	20	11	21	6	31	13	43	2
Barlow	4	0	26	1	7	2	10	0
Intikhab	2	0	11	0	54	24	113	6
Gibbs					51	17	91	1

REST OF THE WORLD

B.A. Richards	c Sharpe b Ward	35
E.J. Barlow	c Underwood b Illingworth	119
R.B. Kanhai	c Knott b d'Oliveira	21
R.G. Pollock	b Underwood	55
C.H. Lloyd	b Ward	20
G.S. Sobers	c Underwood b Snow	183
F.M. Engineer	b Ward	2
Intikhab Alam	b Ward	61
M.J. Procter	b Snow	26
G.D. McKenzie	c Snow b Underwood	0
L.R. Gibbs	not out	2
Extras	(b 10, lb 5, nb 7)	22
Total		546

Fall of wickets: 1–69, 2–106, 3–237, 4–237, 5–293, 6–298, 7–496, 8–537, 9–544, 10–546.

ENGLAND BOWLING

	O	M	R	W
Snow	27	7	109	2
Ward	33	4	121	4
Shuttleworth	21	2	85	0
d'Oliveira	18	5	45	1
Underwood	25.5	8	81	2
Illingworth	30	8	83	1

Umpires: J.S. Buller and A.E. Fagg

REST OF THE WORLD WON BY AN INNINGS AND 80 RUNS

The 1970 Tests between England and The Rest of the World followed the cancellation of the South African tour, the subject of an article by Irving Rosenwater in the 1971 *Wisden*, pp. 128–41. The relevant dates at the conclusion of hostilities — for such they were — would seem to be:

> *21 May:* The Home Secretary (Mr L.J. Callaghan) receives the chairman (Mr M.J.C. Allom) and secretary (Mr S.C. Griffith) of the Cricket Council, requesting the tour be cancelled "on the grounds of broad public policy". The Home Secretary's letter to the Chairman of the Cricket Council "amounted to a government directive, and faced with a formal request of this kind, the Cricket Council had little choice but to agree. They bowed to *force majeure*. Not even a vote was taken" (Rosenwater, p. 141).

> *22 May:* South African tour cancelled.
> *17 June:* Start of Lord's Test between England and The Rest of the World.
> *18 June:* General Election. Labour defeated.

For the record here are the fourteen players chosen by the South African selectors and those who represented The Rest of the World:

South Africa
Dr Ali Bacher (Transvaal), captain
E.J. Barlow (Western Province)
B.A. Richards (Natal)
R.G. Pollock (Eastern Province)
B.L. Irvine (Transvaal)
J.D. Lindsay (N.E. Transvaal)
H.R. Lance (Transvaal)
M.J. Procter (Western Province)
P.M. Pollock (Eastern Province)
P.H.J. Trimborn (Natal)
A.J. Traicos (Rhodesia)
A.M. Short (Natal)
G.L.G. Watson (Transvaal)
G.A. Chevalier (Western Province)
Manager: J.B. Plimsoll

The Rest of The World
G.S. Sobers (West Indies), captain
E.J. Barlow (South Africa)
F.M. Engineer (India)
L.R. Gibbs (West Indies)
Intikhab Alam (Pakistan)
R.B. Kanhai (West Indies)
C.A. Lloyd (West Indies)
G.D. McKenzie (Australia)
D.L. Murray (West Indies)
Mushtaq Mohammed (Pakistan)
P.M. Pollock (South Africa)
R.G. Pollock (South Africa)
M.J. Procter (South Africa)
B.A. Richards (South Africa)
Manager: F.R. Brown

SOBERS GIVES NOTICE OF RETIREMENT

By John Woodcock

17 August 1974. Only for another three weeks will it be possible to watch Gary Sobers, arguably the greatest cricketer of all time, playing the game which has brought him such fame and which he has played so gracefully for over 20 years. He gave notice yesterday of his intention to retire at the end of the present season.

Nottinghamshire have eight matches left, three of them on Sundays, in which to take a last look at Sobers, and I advise those who can to do so. I say that for two reasons: first, because he will be really trying and secondly, because we shall seldom see his like again. Already this month he has made the fastest championship 100 of the year, in 83 minutes, for Nottinghamshire against Derbyshire.

Sobers is 38. He played his first first-class match, for Barbados against the Indians, in 1953. Chosen as a slow bowler, he sent down 89 overs in the match, at the age of 16. His first Test match was against England the next year, since when his all round record in Test cricket has surpassed anything ever achieved before. He has scored

8,032 runs in Test matches, including 26 hundreds, and taken 235 Test wickets and 110 Test catches. He played an innings of 254 at Melbourne which Don Bradman described as the best ever seen in Australia and one of the most perfect ever played. He could equally well have bowled an opening spell with the new ball to strike terror into the hearts of the best batsmen in the game.

It is this incredible versatility that has made Sobers pre-eminent in the game. I have heard famous and greatly gifted cricketers saying of him that it was simply not fair for one man to be so impossibly good at so many things. He has been as likely to win a Test match with a breathtaking catch in the leg trap as with a brilliant throw from cover point; as likely to turn another with a spell of orthodox, left arm spin, as he did only last February in Port of Spain, as with a dozen overs of chinamen and googlies or a couple of fast inswingers; as capable of a long defensive innings as an attacking tour de force.

As a captain, in Test and other cricket, he was never prepared sufficiently to involve himself with the whole running of a side, both on and off the field, to be particularly successful.

He saw his job, I think, as starting at 11.30, or whenever he led his side on to the field, and finishing when the day's play was done. Dedication was not in him. I suppose it never needed to be. Without trying, or without appearing to try, he was better than anyone else, and he has always considered that life is for the living. I have not often passed more than a few moments with Sobers without him laughing about something. He had the rare gift to go with his wonderful talent of being able to see that cricket is a game for the playing and not a war for the fighting.

At the end of MCC's tour to West Indies in 1967–68, Colin Cowdrey, who had led England through a hectic series to a narrow victory, said that if he had at that moment to choose one word to apply to Sobers it would not be his agility or his temperament or his eyesight or his footwork, or even his virtuosity, but his sportsmanship. In victory and defeat he was the same person, born in a humble Barbadian home, the son of a seaman, but with a remarkable way of getting the game in perspective. While others around were working themselves into a frenzy, Sobers was sharing a joke with the opposition, fortified by the thought that, win or lose, it was not going to be the end of the world.

There were times when his own players felt that he batted too low at No. 6, always his favourite place in the order. Often the effort was made to persuade him to go in higher, but even in his prime he rarely did. This suited England, of course. Deflating as it was, after taking the fourth wicket of an innings, to see Sobers walking out to bat, he would undoubtedly have made even more runs than he did had he batted higher up. Then, though, he would have had less time to study the racing form and that would never have done.

Away from cricket, Sobers has always been happiest either at the races or on the golf course. There was never a rest day last winter, during the Test series against West Indies, when he was not looking for 36 holes of golf. Out of the clubhouse window of the new Barbados Golf and Country Club, on the rest day at Bridgetown, I saw a file of golfers and caddies in the distance walking down a path from the 15th green to the 16th tee. Leading them was Sobers, with his unmistakable walk — sparing one leg because of the knee which has given him so much trouble but still extraordinarily feline and keen to get to the next hole, although it was his second round of the day.

He had played in the morning with David Marsh, a former British Walker Cup captain, who said of Sobers that he was a lovely hitter of the ball, long off the tee and with a good touch. In his retirement he will play a lot of golf and have a chance, he hopes, to put something back into cricket. Not that after such generous a career he is in its debt.

SIR FRANK MORTIMER MAGLINNE WORRELL
Barbados and Jamaica

Worrell batted with such luminosity during the West Indies' tour of England in 1950 — could even Kippax or Duleepsinhji have cut so charmingly? — that the remainder of his career might well have been an anti-climax. Artists of his calibre are apt to slide from the pinnacle, repeating their masterpieces but rarely. No post-war batsman has afforded the same pleasure that Worrell did at his best, which is not necessarily to say Worrell was the greatest, simply that a man who can wield a bat like a wand may bemuse onlookers. Sceptics may demur, but Worrell could drive and hook as though with a wand.

At the age of 36, he took a West Indies side to Australia. Worrell was a black man, the first to lead his country. He was the possessor of an ice-cold brain; he moulded some rare individual talents into an outstanding team. There is nothing more to say of Worrell save that having narrowly lost the series in Australia, his men were given a motorcade farewell. Today England and Australia play for the Ashes, Australia and West Indies for the F.M. Worrell Trophy.

THE BRISBANE TEST

By Michael Davie

9 December 1960, Brisbane. The Australian attack was given the most spectacular thrashing of the last decade here today, on the opening day of the first Test match between Australia and the West Indies.

The Australian selectors this morning left out Martin, the left-handed spinner, from the 12 they had named earlier so that the Australian bowling, as to its five principal performers, was precisely the same as it was two years ago here against MCC: Davidson and Meckiff, Mackay as first change, and Benaud and Kline. MCC, it will be recalled, were dismissed in their first innings, which occupied most of a day, for 134 and in their second for 198 — and Bailey, in that innings, made 68 in seven hours and 38 minutes. Today, under not dissimilar conditions, the West Indies in six hours made 359 for seven wickets.

Some MCC batsmen two years ago claimed that on the easy-paced Brisbane wicket the ball did not come through quickly enough to make stroke-play feasible. The same line of thought seems not to have occurred to the West Indians. In their first 250 runs, scored in the startling time of 229 minutes, there were no less than 35 boundaries.

The West Indians were, of course, lucky. They decided to pack their team with batsmen, at the expense of a fast bowler, and the outcome might have been very different against this strong Australian batting side had they lost the toss. However, they won it, and on a day of good batting conditions — a little sultry in the morning but thereafter warm and pleasant, with the wicket at the easiest it is likely to be during the match — they took their opportunity superbly. Their confidence improved with every hour that went by, and Australia will have to bat in their second innings on a pitch that is virtually certain to wear.

Primarily it was the day of Sobers and Worrell. Their partnership began at noon, when it seemed as if the recklessness of their earlier batsmen, all of whom were out to poor strokes, might have thrown away the advantage of winning the toss. At ten past three, when Sobers was out, they had taken the score from 65 for three to 239 for four.

Neither batsman at any time looked less than a great player. Sobers, in particular, hit the ball with extraordinary power. Once he drove Davidson so hard to McDonald, fielding three-quarters of the way to the boundary at long off, that the ball bounced off the wretched McDonald's hands and arms and shot 15 yards in the air before it cracked against the rails. McDonald put his hands in his armpits and danced with pain.

Before the game, Sobers had convinced himself that he was in a bad patch, and some Australian critics, remembering how easily Benaud had removed him in the New South Wales match, were inclined to doubt his capacity to handle a leg-spinner of Benaud's class. But there was nothing better in Sobers's innings to-day than his playing of Benaud. He used his feet, was always precisely behind the line of the ball and lashed anything the slightest bit loose to the boundary. He struck Benaud for three crashing fours in succession and he twice straight drove him with such viciousness that even Benaud, who is frightened of nothing, thought it wiser not to put his hands to the ball.

Sobers was utterly dominant. He reached his 50 in 57 minutes, and his 100 in 125 minutes, with 15 boundaries, and was out finally for 132. Worrell, meanwhile, was content to play a secondary role, but he always looked dignified and calm, with the demeanour of a master watching his best pupil.

The Australian plan, it appeared, was for Davidson, knowing the West Indian weakness for driving the wider ball outside the off stump, to use the crease as much as he could and bowl diagonally across the wicket to the right-handers. The strategy worked admirably with Smith,

Hunte and Kanhai, who were all out trying to score off balls moving away from them to the off.

But Worrell refused to be tempted. When he did go for the off drive he got right over the ball and smacked it straight through the covers as if he were illustrating a textbook. Davidson had him in the end as he leaned forward and was beaten in the air. But by then he had made 65.

These two great batsmen on their form to-day would probably have dominated any bowlers. They demonstrated, nevertheless, that the Australian attack at present has only two top-class bowlers, Davidson and Benaud. For all the hammering these two took they never lost their accuracy or thoughtfulness. But by half past five tonight, when Kline and Simpson were bowling, the attack looked no better than county standard.

...The Australian catching was immaculate, but their ground fielding, understandably, was sometimes untidy. All in all they looked a more vulnerable side in the field than they have looked for a long time.

Close: WEST INDIES 359 for 7 (G.S. Sobers 132, F.M. Worrell 65, J.S. Solomon 65).

Second Day

10 December 1960, Brisbane. After two days play in the first Test match between West Indies and Australia, the Australians are a slightly dishevelled side. They are already in the undignified situation of having to hope for a draw.

Technically, the second day's play was as interesting as the first, though less spectacular. It produced the astonishing sight of the Australians being unable to prevent the West Indies' ninth wicket putting on 86 runs in 69 minutes; it supplied further evidence of the decline of Meckiff; it raised the general cricketing conundrum of what a captain should do when his side contains only one effective fast bowler; and it offered the first sight of Australia's new opener, Simpson, trying to confirm his claim to the gap left by the retirement of Burke.

Benaud, since he took over the Australian captaincy, has not had a worse morning in 14 Test matches than he had yesterday. It was plainly of the greatest importance that the West Indies innings, 359 for seven overnight, should be quickly guillotined, particularly since the wicket is confidently expected to help spinners in Australia's fourth innings. Instead Benaud was plagued by a captain's nightmare, the bad batsman who is unpredictable in his shots and who refuses to get out.

Hall, the batsman in question, established himself yesterday as the comedy lead of the tour. He is 6ft. 2in., perfectly built and gangling, wears a tiny, plum-coloured cap, keeps his shirt open to the waist and displays round his neck a golden cross. Like Trueman he takes himself very seriously as a batsman. He spins his bat before he takes his stance and he concludes each stroke with a wristy flourish which he elaborates with extra touches when he misses the ball.

While he and Alexander were taking the West Indian score past 400 and Benaud's analysis up to 93 for no wickets, the Australians were nearer humiliation than an Australian Test side has been for a long time. Hall and Alexander hit Meckiff for 39 off three overs. Once again he bowled with scrupulously legal action and once again it appeared unlikely that he is now the fast bowler Australia needs to partner Davidson.

The disadvantages of having only one good fast bowler in a side were underlined when West Indies fielded. Having omitted Watson, Hall's usual partner, they opened the bowling with Worrell. But Worrell's medium pace achieved nothing except to play in the Australian openers and allow them to get their breath back after being buffeted by the violence of Hall. Both Benaud and Worrell must now be questioning the convention which requires two fast bowlers be given the new ball. The Australian use of Meckiff for the second new ball gave the West Indies nearly 40 runs, and West Indies' use of Worrell helped the Australians off to a sound start.

Finally to Simpson. He is a smallish, neat man of 24, whose father was a professional footballer in Scotland. He played against MCC on the last tour here in the second Test match but had an unhappy game. Since then he has made a lot of runs in Sheffield Shield matches and has spent a season in the Lancashire League.

On the whole he came out of yesterday's Test reasonably well, though he went so slowly that he was heckled by the crowd. Both the Test match atmosphere and the pace of Hall seemed to make him nervous; he has not yet learnt how to move out of the way of bumpers and once or twice risked serious injury. He plays the ball well off his legs and is workmanlike rather than good to watch.

Like Simpson, the other Australian batsmen made heavy weather of the task of chasing the large West Indian total. McDonald played a characteristically brave but chancy innings; Harvey was unrecognizable; and O'Neill took 89 minutes for 28 not out.

Close: WEST INDIES 453 (F.C.M. Alexander 60, W.W.Hall 50; A.K. Davidson 5 for 135), AUSTRALIA 196 for 3 (C.C. McDonald 57, R.B. Simpson 92).

Third Day

12 December 1960, Brisbane. West Indies here today missed the best opportunity of winning a Test match that Australia can reasonably be expected to give them in the current series. When they went out to field this morning in the hard, brilliant light of a Queensland summer's day Australia were 257 runs behind them on first innings with seven wickets to fall. By the end of the day their advantage had been squandered.

To beat the Australians in a Test match you have to make the most of such chances as they and Providence supply. But West Indies dropped catches, bowled worse at the very times when they should have bowled as never before in their lives, and the captaincy of Worrell at critical moments was hard to follow. They seemed to take the field almost resigned to the Australians making a lot of runs. There was an unexpected piece of captaincy at the very start, for with the new ball due Worrell kept on Valentine and Hall for a quarter of an hour with the old one while the batsmen were allowed to sample the light and pace of the pitch.

West Indies wasted the new ball again, even as they had wasted it at the opening of the Australian innings. Hall today was lethargic as well as inaccurate — his first spell of five overs produced 37 runs — and Worrell was little above medium pace. It was not easy to see why Sobers, the best of the West Indies bowlers on Saturday, was barely allowed a sight of the new ball this morning. There was a further instance of inexplicable captaincy when, after Favell was run out, Mackay came in half an hour before lunch. Hall at that point had enjoyed a forty-minute rest, yet Worrell allowed a quarter of an hour to slip by before Hall unleashed a ball at the new batsman.

Before lunch, besides, the West Indies dropped two important catches, both off O'Neill. He gave a chance to Sobers at first slip when he was 47 and another to Alexander at the wicket soon afterwards. Thus by the interval the Australians had moved forward to 306 for four and were clearly on the way to a big total. West Indies had lost their chance. They got back into the game again after tea when, in 40 minutes, they dismissed five Australians for 36 runs; but by then the damage had been done.

For Australia, O'Neill played an initially patchy but ultimately impressive innings. With Harvey he is now Australia's unquestioned star. He has filled out in the past two years and must now, at the age of 23, weigh over 14 stone. He looks thick-set, solid and strong and has the forearms of a weight-lifter. His 181 could not compare with Sobers's century last Friday. Sobers's batting was remarkable; when he hit the ball it was hard to understand where the power of his shots were coming from. All technique was hidden. O'Neill, on the other hand, visibly applied the rules of correct batsmanship. It was the innings of an athletic and capable young man, keen, unsophisticated, straightfoward. Sobers on Friday was impassive and outwardly

detached. O'Neill's application showed in every line of his face. He battled.

Before lunch O'Neill had his two lives and was content to take runs as they came. After lunch he cut loose, thrashed the West Indies for 40 in 40 minutes and showed some of the talent that caused him, when he first came to general attention four years ago, to be talked about as a future Bradman or Macartney. Technically it is hard to fault him, except that he is sometimes a dangerous runner. He put on 84 with Favell, 103 with Mackay and 88 with Davidson. At five o'clock he was still batting with as much determination and energy as he had shown in the early morning.

Close: WEST INDIES 453 and 0 for no wicket, AUSTRALIA 505 (N.C. O'Neill 181).

Fourth Day

13 December 1960, Brisbane. At close of play on the fourth day of the first Test match all the signs were that Australia are poised for victory. With one wicket standing in their second innings, the West Indies are 207 ahead, but with the wicket, as yet, taking spin without viciousness, this total — in what will probably be not far short of six hours' batting — seems a relatively undemanding task for so strong a batting side as Australia.

The West Indian hope tonight must be that Hall, who made 50 in the first innings and is now in for the last wicket with Valentine, will strike a few blows tomorrow. It is conceivable, though not likely, that every run could count at the end of the day.

It was an absorbing day's cricket and indeed this match throughout has been packed with interest. Unlike other days of the match, which have been hot and sunny, today was cloudy with thunderstorms prowling around the horizon. One of them had broken during the night, yielding two inches of water, but the wicket was unaffected and the outfield had soaked up every drop without trace. Unlike other days, too, today produced a genuine, old-fashioned Test match atmosphere:

a fight for runs; maiden overs; and batsmen endlessly pushing forward.

Throughout the six hours of play the probabilities of the outcome swung to and fro like a metronome. The West Indies began their second innings 52 runs behind. At 100 for two before luncheon it seemed possible that they would be able to set Australia something around 275 to get in their last innings. The same sort of thing seemed possible again at tea time. Had they been able to do so, the outlook for the West Indies tonight might have been very different.

The start of the West Indies innings was of the exhilarating, carefree type that has come to be expected of them on this tour. They are as aware as anyone else that Davidson is a great bowler, but that does not prevent them from laying into him from the opening over. Smith again failed as an opener when he hit a catch to O'Neill in the covers (it transpired that Smith was suffering from tonsillitis), but Hunte and Kanhai went rocketing onwards to 50 in 40 minutes off 65 balls.

Hunte cut uppishly and was caught in the slips. Half an hour later Sobers, who seemed to be sleep-walking today, got a beauty from Davidson which must have swung late. Sobers hit over the top of it and was bowled, as one Sydney evening paper writer told his readers, lock, stock and barrel.

The West Indies were now the equivalent, subtracting the Australian lead, of 62 for three — and fighting. At luncheon they were 119 for three with the match in the balance. The afternoon was Test cricket at its best. With infinite care, like men dismantling a bomb, Worrell and Solomon took the score from 127 for four, when Kanhai was out, to 204 for four.

Kanhai played the kind of stroke that no West Indian at that stage of the game should have found physically possible. As if the warning of the first innings had not been enough for him, he again tried to drive a ball from Davidson that was swinging away outside the off stump, and was caught at the wicket.

Worrell and Solomon, however, were taking no risks of that sort. Worrell in particular batted

magnificently. He has had an exceptionally consistent tour so far, with an average of over 70, and today he conducted himself, in a critical situation, with all the experience and technical dexterity at his command.

Worrell is the world's most imperturbable batsman. He never pulls his cap or fiddles with his pads; he remains in all circumstances perfectly calm, dignified and polite. Once today he smiled when he was in the middle of coming down on top of a Davidson yorker. If he could distribute some of his composure to his men, he could have a much more effective team under his command. . .

After tea the West Indies slumped. They lost five wickets in two hours for 55 runs. It was the new ball that did the damage. Davidson forced Worrell back on his heels, Worrell got an inside edge, and Grout took a brilliant catch. Thereafter Solomon and his new partner, Alexander, were in the position of trying to save the game rather than win it.

The scoring rate dropped still farther, the ground was silent, and crossword puzzles were produced while the West Indies, in the hour after Worrell's dismissal, scratched together 20 runs. Then Alexander, who had taken over an hour for five, tried to sweep a faster ball from Benaud which kept low and bowled him to give Benaud his first wicket of the match. The Australians were now well and truly through.

Close: WEST INDIES 453 and 259 for 9 (R.B. Kanhai 54, F.M. Worrell 65), AUSTRALIA 505.

Fifth Day

14 December 1960, Brisbane. The first Test match between Australia and the West Indies ended here at four minutes past six tonight with the first tie and the most sensational finish in the history of Test cricket.

After the game, with sweat pouring off his brow, the Australian captain, Benaud, said that this had been "the greatest cricket match I have ever played in and the finish could only be described as fantastic". The West Indies captain, Worrell, took the same view: "I have never played in a game like it before." And to Sir Donald Bradman it was "the greatest Test match of all time."

Overnight the West Indies had been 207 runs ahead with one wicket standing, and this morning and afternoon there was much palpitating cricket as they finished their innings and Australia set out after a total of 233. But it was at the tea interval that the tension really began to mount.

At tea the game could scarcely have been more evenly balanced. Australia, 109 for six, needed 124 to win in exactly two hours. The wicket was the colour of pale straw, scarred with black patches around the crease: though anything but easy, there were still runs in it.

The Australians, plainly and characteristically, decided to go for the runs. Valentine bowled to Benaud and Benaud hit him high over mid-on's head for four. Hall, who had wrecked the start of Australia's innings with a fine, sustained spell of fast bowling (his figures were 12–3–38–4) came back for his second spell and Davidson clipped him easily into the covers. Ramadhin replaced Valentine and with his first ball baffled Davidson completely. But, the Australians kept on the attack, driving firmly and running quick singles.

At five o'clock, with an hour to go, Australia needed 61 with the new ball between them and victory. Davidson picked Ramadhin off his stumps and hit him a colossal blow in the air to the mid-wicket boundary to put up his 50. If he were not the best new ball bowler in the game, Davidson would be in the Australian side for his batting. When Worrell now took himself off and put on Sobers to bowl his left arm tweakers over the wicket, it seemed to be the critical moment to the entire match. Benaud seemed to think so too, for he watched Sobers on to the bat with deepest concentration before he swung him out to mid-wicket for four off the last ball. The Australians were keeping in exact step with the clock.

Davidson drove Ramadhin straight for four and swung him round to the fine leg boundary to bring up the 100 partnership in 95 minutes. Forty-three minutes to play and 40 wanted. The West Indies fielding hereabouts was magnificent and so was the Australian running of safe, quick singles. Benaud hit Ramadhin straight for one run and Australia had reached 200. With half an hour to go, with Hall taking the new ball and the crowd alight with excitement, Australia needed 27, still with four wickets intact.

Benaud hit Hall in the air not far short of Hunte at square leg, and Davidson hooked him first bounce to the midwicket boundary. With 20 minutes left and 19 runs to get Worrell brought back Sobers at the other end bowling his faster ones, but Benaud, looking now more sallow than ever, drove him to mid-on for four. Benaud had his 50 in just over two hours. With 15 minutes left Australia needed 10, and then nine in 10 minutes after Hall had bowled a long over for one run.

At last, with seven minutes left, Benaud pushed Sobers to mid-wicket for one quick single too many. Solomon hit the stumps and Davidson who had made 80, was run out. Six minutes left, seven runs to win and three wickets remain. Grout was hit on the leg and the whole crowd seemed to appeal. But he was not out and he then took a single to mid-on. So, as the last over of the match started, Australia needed six to win and Grout faced Hall. Grout was hit in the stomach and Benaud dashed through for a run when the ball dropped at Grout's feet. Benaud swung at the next ball with all the power at his command, got a touch, and Alexander caught it: the crowd went through the roof. Six balls to go, five runs to get and two wickets to fall.

Meckiff kept Hall out on his first ball and gave a nervous smile. The next one went through to the wicketkeeper, who threw it to Hall, and if Hall had hit the wicket when they took another quick single, Meckiff would have been out. Four balls to go and four to get. Grout struck the next ball high and straight up in the air; everyone rushed forward and Hall, knocking Kanhai out of the way, got under it and, to roars of ecstasy, dropped it while the batsmen went through. Three balls left for the three runs wanted.

Meckiff got hold of the next ball and it soared out towards the midwicket fence looking like six and the end of the match. But Hunte cut it off on the bounce as the batsmen, running like men possessed, went through for a third run and now Grout was run out by a foot. The sides were level with two balls to go.

In came Kline, looking pale and drawn. He took guard and not a bird moved. He lashed out like a man in a nightmare fighting off phantoms: the ball flew to midwicket, there was a flurry of desperate fieldsmen, Solomon flung at the wicket and to an incredulous shout of joy and anguish, scattered the stumps. The umpire's finger shot up and Meckiff was out. It was a tie. Four wickets had fallen in 13 balls, three of them run out, and three of them in seven balls.

The day had started with an hilarious stand between Hall and Valentine who kept out Davidson and Benaud in full cry for nearly 40 minutes to add another 25 runs to the West Indies overnight score of 259 for nine. The time they took was as important as the runs they made, for they left Australia 233 to win in 312 minutes, or a rate of 45 an hour. Even so, it had seemed well within Australia's power to get them with time to spare.

But the Australians got off to a bad start. Simpson, who showed little sign of liking Hall in the first innings and was even less comfortable in the second, when Hall was bowling up to his reputation, tried to pull the sixth ball of the fast bowler's second over and was caught by the forward of three short legs. Harvey took a four off his first ball and then played back, got an outside edge and Sobers dived unbelievably to pick up the ball an inch from the ground in his right hand. He dislocated a finger doing so and left the field grimacing with pain to have it strapped.

At luncheon Australia were 28 for two. Then, a quarter of an hour after the interval, O'Neill was caught at the wicket off Hall and Australia seemed on the run. They were 49 for three. Favell was nearly out to the next one, and from the next

ball of the new over McDonald played forward to what seemed a straightforward ball from Worrell and was clean bowled. The West Indies were then right on top. When a quarter of an hour later Favell turned Hall straight into Solomon's hands at short leg and Australia were 57 for five it seemed all over.

The next wicket went to Ramadhin. He came on at three o'clock, just about the time Australia needed 150 in even time with Mackay getting dug in. His first ball to Mackay was a googly. Mackay, wholly baffled, followed it to give a catch to slip which, agonizingly, was dropped. But this affected Mackay's temperament and it was not surprising shortly afterwards when Ramadhin got one to turn a little more sharply to hit the leg stump.

That brought together Benaud with Davidson for a stand of a lifetime. But it nearly never began, for the second ball Benaud got from Ramadhin he never saw and he could scarcely believe his luck when he found it had somehow missed the stumps. Then both batsmen began to settle down and Benaud off-drove Valentine just before the tea interval to bring up the Australian 100 in 175 minutes.

Until that interval, and its extraordinary sequel, it had scarcely seemed possible that Australia could win the match. Subsequently it seemed impossible they should lose. There seems every likelihood, indeed, that historians of the game will decide that this was not only the first tie in Test cricket but one in which, of all Tests, the expectation of victory most frequently oscillated between two teams. The second Test match of the series, which starts in Melbourne on December 30, should fill that airless and mammoth stadium.

SIR FRANK WORRELL

14 March 1967. Sir Frank Worrell, the great West Indian cricketer, died yesterday in Kingston, Jamaica, at the age of 42. His death will come as a profound shock to cricket lovers around the world for it is little more than three

AUSTRALIA v. WEST INDIES
Brisbane, 9, 10, 12–14 December 1960

WEST INDIES
1st innings

C.C. Hunte	c Benaud b Davidson	24
C. Smith	c Grout b Davidson	7
R.B. Kanhai	c Grout b Davidson	15
G.S. Sobers	c Kline b Meckiff	132
F.M. Worrell	c Grout b Davidson	65
J.S. Solomon	hit wkt b Simpson	65
P. Lashley	c Grout b Kline	19
F.C.M. Alexander	c Davidson b Kline	60
S. Ramadhin	c Harvey b Davidson	12
W.W. Hall	st Grout b Kline	50
A.L. Valentine	not out	0
Extras	(lb 3, w 1)	4
Total		453

2nd innings

C.C. Hunte	c Simpson b Mackay	39
C. Smith	c O'Neill b Davidson	6
R.B. Kanhai	c Grout b Davidson	54
G.S. Sobers	b Davidson	14
F.M. Worrell	c Grout b Davidson	65
J.S. Solomon	lbw b Simpson	47
P. Lashley	b Davidson	0
F.C.M. Alexander	b Benaud	5
S. Ramadhin	c Harvey b Simpson	6
W.W. Hall	b Davidson	18
A.L. Valentine	not out	7
Extras	(b 14, lb 7, w 2)	23
Total		284

Fall of wickets: 1–23, 2–42, 3–65, 4–239, 5–243, 6–283, 7–347, 8–366, 9–452, 10–453.

Second innings: 1–13, 2–88, 3–114, 4–127, 5–210, 6–210, 7–241, 8–250, 9–253, 10–284.

AUSTRALIA BOWLING (8-ball overs)

	O	M	R	W	O	M	R	W
Davidson	30	2	135	5	24.6	4	87	6
Meckiff	18	0	129	1	4	1	19	0
Mackay	3	0	15	0	21	7	52	1
Benaud	24	3	93	0	31	6	69	1
Simpson	8	0	25	1	7	2	18	2
Kline	17.6	6	52	3	4	0	14	0
O'Neill					1	0	2	0

AUSTRALIA
1st innings

C.C. McDonald	c Hunte b Sobers	57
R.B. Simpson	b Ramadhin	92
R.N. Harvey	b Valentine	15
N.C. O'Neill	c Valentine b Hall	181
L. Favell	run out	45
K.D. Mackay	b Sobers	35
A.K. Davidson	c Alexander b Hall	44
R. Benaud	lbw b Hall	10
A.T.W. Grout	lbw b Hall	4
I. Meckiff	run out	4
L.F. Kline	not out	3
Extras	(b 2, lb 8, nb 4, w 1)	15
Total		505

2nd innings

C.C. McDonald	b Worrell	16
R.B. Simpson	c sub b Hall	0
R.N. Harvey	c Sobers b Hall	5
N.C. O'Neill	c Alexander b Hall	26
L. Favell	c Solomon b Hall	7
K.D. Mackay	b Ramadhin	28
A.K. Davidson	run out	80
R. Benaud	c Alexander b Hall	52
A.T.W. Grout	run out	2
I. Meckiff	run out	2
L.F. Kline	not out	0
Extras	(b 2, lb 9, nb 3)	14
Total		232

Fall of wickets: 1–84, 2–138, 3–194, 4–278, 5–381, 6–469, 7–484, 8–489, 9–496, 10–505.

Second innings: 1–1, 2–7, 3–49, 4–49, 5–57, 6–92, 7–226, 8–228, 9–232, 10–232.

WEST INDIES BOWLING

	O	M	R	W	O	M	R	W
Hall	29.3	1	140	4	17.7	3	65	5
Worrell	30	0	93	0	16	3	41	1
Sobers	32	0	115	2	8	0	30	0
Valentine	24	6	82	1	10	4	27	0
Ramadhin	15	1	60	1	17	3	57	1

Umpires: C. Hoy and C. Egar.

MATCH TIED

years since he ended his first class career as captain of the triumphant West Indian touring team in England. He was one of the finest all-rounders in the history of the game, but he will be remembered as much for his leadership as his play. It was he who moulded the West Indian Test team from a group of talented, entertaining but erratic individuals into what it has now become — probably the finest side in the world. In doing this he not only won personal fame but raised the status and dignity of the West Indian coloured cricketer.

Frank Mortimer Maglinne Worrell was born at Bridgetown on August 1, 1924. As nearly a natural cricketer as may be — for he was never coached and rarely practised — he was a leading figure in the remarkable upsurge of Barbadian cricket in the 1940s. He was an outstanding player from boyhood; at Combermere School he was primarily an orthodox slow left-arm bowler and as such — and a number eleven batsman — was first chosen for Barbados — when he was 17. A year later while still at school, sent in as "night watchman" he went on next morning to make 64 and to establish himself as a batsman. In the same West Indian season he scored 188, the first of his 40 centuries against Trinidad. In 1943–44 at 19, he made 308 not out in an unfinished partnership of 502 with John Goddard, a record for the fourth wicket which he and Walcott broke two years later with an unbroken 574, also against Trinidad. When world cricket recommenced after the Second World War, he and his fellow Barbardian batsmen, Walcott and Weekes, were the legendary "three Ws".

Worrell was the most orthodox of the three; his self-taught technique was so correct that he seemed incapable of a crooked stroke. Lithely built and superbly balanced, he was a stylist with an elegantly unhurried air, although his wide range of strokes, off front or back foot, was based on rapid movement into correct position. His cutting was delicate, his driving, for all its easy execution, powerful; he was strong on both sides of the wicket; and he combined ability to relax when not actually playing with the unremitting concentration of those who build long innings.

The demands of League cricket changed his bowling method from slow to fast-medium left arm; he exploited English conditions in sharp movement off the seam and his pace from the pitch was so hostile as at times to be little short of geniunely fast. Latterly his speed declined but to the end of his Test career his experience and control enabled him to seal up an end. He was a safe fieldsman and a clean catcher anywhere and latterly his fielding at silly mid-on was a considerable tactical asset for his bowlers.

As a young man he was markedly sensitive to criticism and some schoolday bitternesses rankled so deeply that, in 1947, he made his home in Jamaica. So it was as a Jamaican player that he established his Test place in the series of 1947–48 against England.

His performances brought him the offer which few West Indian cricketers have found it financially possible to resist and in 1948 he joined the Central Lancashire League club, Radcliffe. There, and subsequently with Norton and Church, he spent some dozen happy and successful years as a league professional. Meanwhile, he read first Optics and then Economics at Manchester University. He contrived, however, to take part in all the West Indies' Tests of that period except those of 1958–59 in India which coincided with the final terms before he took a B.A.(Admin.) degree. He made three tours of India with Commonwealth sides.

For the team of 1950, which was the first from the West Indies to win a Test, and a rubber, in England, he was top of the batting averages with 539 runs at 89.93 and made an important contribution to team-balance by his fast-medium bowling. At Trent Bridge after taking three important English wickets he scored 261, then the highest innings by a West Indian in a Test in England.

In the West Indian side which was beaten in Australia in 1951–52 he emerged as a genuine all rounder of Test standard. Apart from his technical ability, the quality of his temperament was strikingly apparent in Goddard's defeated and dispirited team of 1957 in England, when he made good the lack of an opening batsman and opened the bowling. He took seven English wickets in the innings at Headingley and finished second in the batting and first in the bowling averages for Tests.

It was now apparent that only internal politics could prevent him from captaining the West Indies. He himself wisely took little part in the occasionally acrimonious controversy which ended when he was asked to take the 1960–61 team to Australia; the first time a coloured West

Indian had been appointed to the captaincy of a touring side.

On that tour, which included the famous tied Test at Brisbane, cricket in Australia was raised to such heights of public esteem as it had not reached since the days of Bradman. Australian opinion was reflected in the institution of the "Worrell Trophy" for all future series between the two countries.

When he captained the touring side of 1963 to England, he was almost 39, a veteran by West Indian standards; indeed, all his famous contemporaries of the 1940s had retired from Test cricket. He himself was no longer the player he had been but, as batsman, bowler and fielder, he was still useful and he was one of the few men whose captaincy was so outstanding as to make a major contribution to a side's strength. He declared his purpose as not merely to win the Test series, but also to make such an impression as to bring West Indies to England again appreciably before the 1971 season of the Conference schedule. He achieved both his aims. The West Indies won the rubber three-one.

Worrell's captaincy was outstanding. Sharp in tactical perception, astute in attack and defence, quietly spoken, yet firm to the brink of ruthlessness, he outwitted his opponents and sustained his colleagues. As lately as 1957 a West Indian team had crumpled psychologically in face of defeat. Now, at one crisis after another, Worrell, with what sometimes seemed exaggerated calm, held them steady. His achievement may best be described as instilling in his players a professional attitude and stability which has endured. As in Australia, his side's cricket roused such immense public interest as achieved his second design. In the following winter the tour programme was revised, bringing another West Indian team to England in 1966.

By the time that decision was taken, Worrell had returned home to a magnificent public reception, the Post of Warden in the University of the West Indies at Kingston and a seat in the Jamaican Senate; a knighthood followed in the New Year Honours of 1964. In 1966 he was appointed Dean of Students for the branch of the University of the West Indies in Trinidad.

He was a non-smoker who kept enviably fit with a minimum of training. Convivial and conversational, he would talk gaily far into the night in his pleasant, slightly husky voice; he was quick and flexible in debate, fond of England and his many English friends, courteous in manner and he only rarely revealed the depth of his feeling on racial matters.

In 51 Test Matches he scored 3,860 runs at an average of 49.48 and took 69 wickets at 38.37.

He married Velda Brewster of Barbados in 1948; they had one daughter.

A Memorial Service for Sir Frank Worrell was held in Westminster Abbey on 7 April 1967. In his address, E.W. Swanton said "Yet just as England brought cricket to the West Indies she, in return I believe, has given us the ideal cricketer".

RICHIE BENAUD
New South Wales

Benaud won a place in his State side as a batsman, and in so far as he made 23 hundreds in first-class cricket, and averaged 36.50, he can hardly be dismissed as a failure. But his place in history has little to do with his batting, though this could be formidable, or even his fielding, which was superb. He was the last of the great Australian leg-spinners and an inspiring captain. Perhaps he was the leader of his country Keith Miller might have been earlier had that player been given the chance.

As a leg-spinner, Benaud was Grimmett's opposite — as *relatively* ineffective on the slower English pitches as Grimmett was on the faster ones of Australia. Yet his fame rests upon one series at home (where he had the advantage of Worrell as opposing captain) and one match in England. Suffice it to say that prior to England's second innings at Old Trafford in 1961, Benaud's 15 Test wickets at Trent Bridge, Lord's, Headingley, Old Trafford, Edgbaston and the Oval averaged 51 runs apiece.

BENAUD TRIUMPHANT AS CAPTAIN AND BOWLER

Australia had never been in command during the first four days of the 1961 Old Trafford Test:

First day:	Australia 124 for 4
Second day:	Australia 190
	England 187 for 3
Third day:	Australia 190 and 63 for 0
	England 367
Fourth day:	Australia 190 and 331 for 6
	England 367

Australia's lead was 154 runs with four second-innings wickets in hand.

By John Woodcock

2 August 1961. Australia made certain of retaining the Ashes at Old Trafford yesterday when they won the fourth Test match against England by 54 runs. It was for them one of their most famous and thrilling victories, made possible at the last by the daring and skill of their captain. For England it was a day that will become a dark and disappointing memory.

At five minutes to four England, needing 256 to win, had reached 150 for one with Dexter in full spate. There were still 105 minutes left. At 4.45 they were 171 for seven, and disaster had come down upon them when they seemed to have the match in hand. It was the second time in the day that they had been stopped in their tracks by an Australian counter-attack imaginative in conception and brilliant in execution. For some hours earlier, Davidson and Mackenzie had added 98 for Australia's last wicket to give the bowlers the ammunition they needed.

England's was a failure of temperament,

brought on by their inability to play spin bowling, particularly leg breaks, of the highest class. It may sound cynical, but it is true to say that England's pitiful collapse was true to form. Too often in the past few years they have been found wanting against Benaud, Ramadhin or Tayfield when there has been tension in the air.

For sheer excitement and palpitating changes of fortune the day will never be forgotten. Nor should the crushing anti-climax and England's deplorable batting be allowed to cloud the supreme merit of Australia's achievement. They began by hitting their way out of trouble with the greatest courage and even when England were advancing steadily through the afternoon they kept attacking.

In the 20 minutes before luncheon, England got away to a good start in their effort to score at 67 runs an hour for three hours and 50 minutes. Immediately afterwards, Benaud came on at the Stretford end, where later he was to decide the issue. As his partner he had first Davidson, then Simpson, and then Mackay. Finally, after he had taken six for 70 in 32 overs, and with Statham and Flavell together, he asked Davidson to finish the job.

For a long time the crowd cheered every run as England gathered speed. Pullar and Subba Row added 40 in 42 minutes before Pullar mishooked a long hop gently to midwicket. There followed the splendid phase for England, with Dexter in command. It was the plan that Subba Row should hold down an end and gather what runs he could without taking undue risks. He has a shrewd cricketing brain, as well as a calming influence upon others, and he played just the innings that was wanted from him.

So, too, of course, did Dexter, who came back to form with a resounding bang. Fifty were added in 48 minutes and when McKenzie replaced Davidson, Dexter hit him for 11 in an over. Drinks were taken at 3.15, to quench England's scoring rate as much as the fielders' thirsts. Dexter had been in for an hour before he made the semblance of a mistake, yet nothing would

BENAUD Stroke-maker, gully fielder and leg-break bowler, he gambled as a captain and won. Still talking.

divert Benaud from his determination to attack.

With the runs tumbling forth, he had Simpson bowling at one end and himself at the other. As Simpson was hit for 21 in four overs, most of them scored by Dexter, it must have seemed to some that Benaud was throwing the game away. What really he was doing was chancing all on England's fallibility against flighted spin.

Dexter reached his 50 in 63 minutes with his tenth four, a thundering shot through the covers. Another 50 came in half an hour, and with two hours left England, with nine wickets standing, needed only 132 to win. The equation a quarter of an hour later, immediately before Dexter left, was still more favourable to England, for Dexter by then had driven Mackay like a kicking horse for four, hooked him viciously to the pavilion and lifted him majestically for six. Hammond, Cowdrey, O'Neill, May, Miller — no one could have batted better than Dexter now, and with a single off Mackay he took England's score to 150 for one.

So there it was. Twenty minutes before tea England were on their way home, the sails billowing. And in shorter time than it takes to tell, they had run upon shoals and rocks and currents. Dexter's magnificent innings ended when he went to hit Benaud off the back foot for four. He had 15 boundaries to his name, every one of them of the purest pedigree. After a brief and smiling discussion with Subba Row, May was sent back second ball by Benaud. From round the wicket he had got this ball to pitch in the footmarks and bowl May behind his legs trying to sweep. Benaud leapt aloft like an astronaut becoming airborne.

Close's innings, which came next, is best talked about in whispers. One of the lessons of Dexter's innings had been the rewards there were for playing straight, a thing Close can do as well as most. As it was, he swung wildly at his first ball and continued to play as if out of his cricketing senses. The one and only time he tried to swing the bat through a true arc, he drove Benaud for a towering six. For the remainder of his innings he thrust his right leg down the pitch and aimed everything to leg. Needless to say, he was eventually caught, by O'Neill, placed carefully just behind the square leg umpire.

England's last chance of victory went with the last ball before tea, when Subba Row's long vigil was ended by a yorker from Benaud. In 20 minutes England had plunged to 163 for five, Benaud having taken the four wickets for nine runs in 19 balls. Looking through the glasses at the Australian side, they clearly could hardly believe their fortune. For one who has followed England round the world it was less surprising, and after tea England slipped quietly and ignominiously to defeat.

Murray was quickly caught at slip off Benaud, and Barrington was leg-before to Mackay. Runs were of no importance now, only time, and when Allen was superbly caught by Simpson, left-handed at slip, off Benaud, hope even of survival

was all but gone. Trueman lasted for 40 minutes before losing his head, and Flavell and Statham endured for 10 minutes of the 30 that were left when they were joined together.

Five years ago England were led off the field in this corresponding match by Laker, who looked as though nothing much had happened. It was their turn to have won the Ashes then. Yesterday, at 5.40, Benaud and Harvey walked off arm in arm to open the bottles of champagne. Less than two hours before, Benaud in the match had taken not a single wicket in 52 overs; his last four scores for Australia had been 0, 0, 2 and 1; and his reputation as a captain and a player was in jeopardy. Starting with Dexter's wicket, he then had figures of 6 for 30.

Benaud said afterwards that he knew by the middle of the afternoon that Australia could not save the game but that they might win it. His faith in his own ability, and his tactical appreciation, were wonderfully justified. England for their part had missed Cowdrey with the bat, just as they had missed him on Monday in the slips.

For the first time in this century Australia had come from far behind to beat their oldest enemy. For the first time since 1902 they had won at Old Trafford. They had been watched by record crowds paying record money. Seldom can a match have turned so complete a somersault in so short a time. Seldom can England have had greater cause for self reproach.

It had been from the start no day for the nervous. After 16 minutes, victory, it seemed, was in England's grasp. Allen, after opening with a wide, had Mackay caught at slip off his fourth ball. The first ball of Allen's third over had Benaud leg-before, playing back after his first movement had been forward. And five balls later Grout hoisted a catch to Statham in the covers.

As the England fielders gathered excitedly together they could hardly have thought to see the Australians rise to their feet again. They might have expected Mackay to be a thorn in their side, or Benaud, or even Grout. But Davidson was looking like an old, old man and the situation would surely be too much for young McKenzie.

But there followed an historic partnership. For the first time on the tour, Davidson rose to his full stature as a batsman. Shrugging off his aches and pains, he played the innings of his life. For its judgment and power and appearance his batting could have been no better. He gave a superb display of clean, crisp hitting, tempered by orthodox defence.

McKenzie played the secondary part like an experienced hand. Before he had scored, Statham twice shaved his stumps; once Dexter nearly had him leg-before; and once Trueman made the bails tremble. Yet generally speaking he met whatever came at him with the middle of the bat. The speed with which the picture changed defied belief.

It all began when May asked Close to bowl in place of Statham. Allen, who had taken his three wickets without the concession of a run, was being prevented by Davidson from bowling at McKenzie. May therefore decided, understandably enough, to confront him with spin from the other end, and this as it turned out was just what McKenzie wanted. In two overs Close bowled five full tosses and McKenzie found that even in Test matches they go sweetly off the bat.

After an hour Allen had bowled nine overs for two runs [his figures now 37–25–38–4]. In his tenth over Davidson suddenly cut loose. There was one flashing stroke off the back foot through ·the covers, one low straight drive, and two straight hits for six, making 20 in the over. Allen was removed at once and a quarter of an hour later the new ball became available. It was taken at 419 and still the stand continued, eating up the time if now less productive of runs.

McKenzie, when he was 25 and the score was 422, might have been caught by Dexter via bat and pad off Trueman. But even Statham and Trueman with the new ball were repulsed and eventually it was Flavell who ended Australia's innings. Davidson and McKenzie had added 98 in 102 minutes, the first 50 of them in only 39 minutes. It was the third best last-wicket partnership by an Australian pair against England. The other two, in 1903 and 1924, helped to lay the foundations to a stirring finish; now this one had set the stage for one of the most dramatic afternoon's cricket of this or any other age.

ENGLAND v. AUSTRALIA
Old Trafford, 27–31 July, 1 August 1961

AUSTRALIA
1st innings
190 (W.M. Lawry 74; J.B. Statham 5 for 53)

2nd innings
432 (Lawry 102, R.B. Simpson 51, N.C. O'Neill 67, A.K. Davidson 77 not out)

ENGLAND
1st innings
367 (G. Pullar 63, P.B.H. May 95, K.F. Barrington 78)

2nd innings

G. Pullar	c O'Neill b Davidson	26
R. Subba Row	b Benaud	49
E.R. Dexter	c Grout b Benaud	76
P.B.H. May	b Benaud	0
D.B. Close	c O'Neill b Benaud	8
K.F. Barrington	lbw b Mackay	5
J.T. Murray	c Simpson b Benaud	4
D.A. Allen	c Simpson b Benaud	10
F.S. Trueman	c Benaud b Simpson	8
J.B. Statham	b Davidson	8
J.A. Flavell	not out	0
Extras	(b 5, w 2)	7
Total		201

Fall of wickets: 1–40, 2–150, 3–150, 4–158, 5–163, 6–171, 7–171, 8–189, 9–193, 10–201.

AUSTRALIA BOWLING (6-ball overs)

	O	M	R	W
Davidson	14.4	1	50	2
McKenzie	4	1	20	0
Mackay	13	7	33	1
Benaud	32	11	70	6
Simpson	8	4	21	1

Umpires: John Langridge and W.E. Phillipson

AUSTRALIA WON BY 54 RUNS

ROBERT GRAEME POLLOCK
Eastern Province

BARRY ANDERSON RICHARDS
Natal, Hampshire and South Australia

INSPIRED POLLOCK RESCUES SOUTH AFRICA

By John Woodcock

6 August 1965. South Africa were rescued by one of the greatest and most gracious innings of recent times when the second Test match between England and South Africa was begun at Nottingham yesterday. It was played by R.G. Pollock, who made 125 between 12.20 and 3.20.

When the lissom figure of Pollock appeared from the Trent Bridge pavilion, South Africa were 16 for two, Cartwright having just taken the wickets of Lance and Lindsay in his third over. Forty minutes later they were 43 for four, with Barlow and Bland now out and Cartwright threatening total destruction. In these desperate circumstances Pollock set about the English bowling as though nothing would stop him. In 70 minutes after luncheon he scored 91 out of 102; in two hours 20 minutes he hit 21 fours, all but two of them off the meat of the bat.

It is the sure sign of greatness to stand alone, as Pollock did. He held dominion where others foundered. It was inspiration, as much as batting. The basic virtues were displayed to perfection: the top hand in control, the shoulder pointing the direction of the stroke, the ball timed not by effort so much as instinct. The majority of his boundaries came from strokes through the covers, off front foot or back: strokes that were effortless and fluent. Comparisons with F.E. Woolley were widespread, and inevitable.

I can think of no innings played against England since the war which was so critical and commanding; I can think of none more beautifully played. There were times when Bradman and Harvey did much as they pleased. The five great West Indian batsmen of the postwar era — Worrell, Weekes, Walcott, Kanhai and Sobers — have each had their irresistible days. Donnelly and Sutcliffe for New Zealand were batsmen of fine style and virtuosity.

Yet not since McCabe made 232 for Australia on this same ground in 1938 has a batsman held such sway over an English attack. Suddenly, Pollock charmed away routine, in a summer when one game of cricket has been too much like another.

Pollock apart, South Africa laboured for their runs on a pitch which allowed Cartwright what movement he wanted. England arrived at the ground with five fast or medium-paced bowlers at their disposal. Of these, Jones and Rumsey were omitted. Of those who were left, Larter and Snow each had a confident appeal for leg-before rejected, against Barlow and Lance respectively, before Cartwright took over. Snow bowled too much down the leg side to do himself justice. For Larter the pitch had too little bounce.

Cartwright's first two overs were maidens. In his third he had Lance leg-before with a ball which came back from the off and Lindsay caught at the wicket with the one that goes the other way. Barlow, after batting for almost an hour and a half, was caught at slip. Parks, as he dived for the snick, knocking the ball up for Cowdrey to catch. Bland was out unluckily. Playing defensively at Titmus he stunned the ball into the ground without realizing that it was spinning back towards Parks. The wicketkeeper swept the ball into the stumps with Bland discomposed and out of his crease.

For the remainder of the day everything was dwarfed by Pollock's glorious batting. When he scored a century in two hours in a Test match at Adelaide* the Australians could talk of little else. Yesterday his innings was fashioned in a crisis, though there was no knowing it from the way he played.

Cartwright was driven as in a county match he is never driven. When Titmus was hit for 12 in an over he was replaced by Barber, who was hit three times to mid-wicket for four. At the rate he was going in the first 70 minutes of the afternoon, Pollock would have reached a double hundred by tea had Cartwright not apprehended him. Pollock seemed surprised to be given out, caught at slip, thinking no doubt that the bat had made contact only with the ground. Had this been so, the ball could scarcely have been deflected to slip. The members, who had scarcely been able to believe their eyes, stood to Pollock, before sitting down to watch the last four South African wickets add another 91 runs.

South Africa's splendid recovery was complete when Boycott was caught low down at second slip at the second attempt off the second ball of England's innings, and when, in P.M. Pollock's second over, Barrington played on.

....

* John Woodcock missed this innings, patriotism decreeing he should be in Bombay where plague so debilitated England that for the Second Test of 1963–4 they fielded three batsmen (one unable to totter out), a batsman–wicketkeeper, J.M. Parks (who did not keep wicket), two all-rounders, four bowlers and a wicketkeeper, J.G. Binks, who scored 55. All five Tests were drawn; in the first three the Indian left-arm bowler, R.G. Nadkarni, achieved the restraining 98–68–60–4.

Van der Merwe had played an important part as Pollock's partner in a sixth-wicket partnership of 98, of which Pollock made all but 10. This began after Bacher had dragged a ball from Snow into his stumps in the second over after luncheon.

Van der Merwe made some stout blows on his own account. He was eventually sent back by

---

SOUTH AFRICA

1st innings

E.J. Barlow	c Cowdrey b Cartwright	19
H. Lance	lbw b Cartwright	7
J.D. Lindsay	c Parks b Cartwright	0
R.G. Pollock	c Cowdrey b Cartwright	125
K.C. Bland	st Parks b Titmus	1
A. Bacher	b Snow	12
P.L. van der Merwe	run out	38
R. Dumbrill	c Parfitt b Cartwright	30
J.T. Botten	c Parks b Larter	10
P.M. Pollock	c Larter b Cartwright	15
A.H. McKinnon	not out	8
Extras	(lb 4)	4
Total		269

Fall of wickets: 1–16, 2–16, 3–42, 4–43, 5–80, 6–178, 7–221, 8–242, 9–252, 10–269.

ENGLAND BOWLING

	O	M	R	W
Larter	17	6	25	1
Snow	22	6	63	1
Cartwright	31.3	9	94	6
Titmus	22	8	44	1
Barber	6	3	39	0

ENGLAND

1st innings

G. Boycott	c Lance b P.M. Pollock	0
R.W. Barber	not out	8
K.F. Barrington	b P.M. Pollock	1
F.J. Titmus	not out	4
Extras	(nb 3)	3
Total	(2 wkts)	16

Fall of wickets: 1–0, 2–8.

To bat: M.C. Cowdrey, P.H. Parfitt, M.J.K. Smith, J.M. Parks, T.W. Cartwright, J.A. Snow and J.D.F. Larter.

SOUTH AFRICA BOWLING

	O	M	R	W
P.M. Pollock	4	2	10	2
Botten	3	1	3	0
McKinnon	1	1	0	0

Umpires: C.S. Elliott and J.F. Crapp

Dumbrill and run out by the combined efforts of Parfitt (from cover point) and Smith (at the bowler's end); but Dumbrill stayed on to bat well himself. As we saw at Lord's, this South African tail has a tough streak in it. Botten batted for 40 minutes before Larter, Parks and the new ball accounted for him, and Cartwright had to be recalled before the innings was over.

At 80 for five, South Africa had been on the brink of collapse. By the close of play it was England who were fighting for their lives in the face of some fast and furious bowling by the other Pollock. In the last over, too, Titmus survived an appeal for leg-before from McKinnon that looked perilously close. These were the extremities of a day's cricket finer by far than one had thought possible on seeing the wicket on Wednesday afternoon. Skill had been rewarded.

SOUTH AFRICA 269 and 289 (E.J. Barlow 76, R.G. Pollock 59, A. Bacher 67; Larter 5 for 68) beat ENGLAND 240 (M.C. Cowdrey 105; P.M. Pollock 5 for 53) and 224 (P.H. Parfitt 86; P.M. Pollock 5 for 34) by 94 runs.

RICHARDS AND POLLOCK

By John Woodcock

5 February 1970, Durban. Some memorable batting by Barry Richards, who made 140 in three hours, and Graeme Pollock, who is 160 not out, reduced Australia's bowlers to a kind of resigned impotence when the second Test match between South Africa and Australia began here today. In glorious weather and on a wicket far removed from the meadow we had been promised, South Africa scored 368 for five.

When I say that Richards played, if anything, even better than Pollock, it may give an idea of the authority he exercised. Throughout his innings his abundant confidence seemed a greater danger to him than the Australian bowlers, and he was prevented from reaching his hundred before luncheon only by the defensive nature of Australia's fields.

Pollock's hundred was his fifth against Australia and his innings ended, for the time being, as it began — with some breathtaking strokes. During the hour in which he batted with Richards he made 53 out of 103 and in the last 35 minutes he scored 51.

As though to confound the prophets, and contrary to his own pronouncements, the groundsman had given the wicket a much needed shave since Wednesday afternoon. By doing so he denied the Australian seamers the movement they had hoped for and allowed us, after all, to see the game at its best. Thanks to Richards South Africa were 126 for two at luncheon and 229 for three an hour afterwards. In the two hours after that Australia forced themselves back into the game, and had Pollock been caught at the wicket off Gleeson when he was 104, South Africa would have been 300 for six. Lance, too, had a dreadful struggle, discovering whether there was a middle to his bat.

Whereas Richards was never beaten, Pollock played and missed half a dozen times. But once he had been reprieved, he gave the Australians a thrashing they will never forget. I have not seen mid-off and extra-cover come under such fire since one evening at Melbourne when Peter May cut loose against a new ball. Unless it was at Lord's in 1963 during Dexter's famous innings against the West Indies.

Richards batted from the start not as though he was beginning an innings but in the middle of one. He appeared never to have the slightest doubt in himself. From the way he batted there was no knowing that it was the first morning of a Test match. As he made 26 out of 30 in half-an-hour and 50 out of 67 in 80 minutes, a former South African batsman said that he had never seen an Australian side bowl so poorly. I preferred to think that I had seldom seen such batting — and in fact at the other end to Richards, the two hours of the morning yielded only 26 runs from the bat.

For 85 minutes Goddard acted as a foil to his brilliant young partner. When he hit a full toss from Gleeson low but straight to Lawry at silly mid-off, it had become a question of whether Richards could reach his hundred before luncheon. It was in the abortive rush to get him there that Bacher was out. Looking for a single, off the second ball of the last over of the morning, he was bowled round his legs by Connolly. It was an unselfish stroke and one which he would never have attempted in ordinary circumstances.

Had Richards reached his goal he would have become only the fourth batsman ever to make a hundred before luncheon on the first morning of a Test match, the others being Victor Trumper in 1902, Charlie Macartney in 1926, and Don Bradman in 1930. It was last done in any Test match, and on any morning, by Stan McCabe at Johannesburg in 1935–36.

While Richards and Graeme Pollock were together for the first hour of the afternoon, a crescendo was reached. Pollock was clearly not prepared to be outshone by Richards. Sometimes a tentative starter, he now made 14 in his first six balls and 25 in 20 minutes. Richards, meanwhile, swept past his hundred. Pollock's drives and forces were matched by Richards with drives and hooks. It is a measure of the batting by Richards, that, by and large, he looked sounder and more commanding than Pollock. I hardly see how anyone could have played much better. His judgment and placing were effortless and to Gleeson he moved confidently down the pitch to drive him either side of extra cover. In an hour after luncheon 103 runs had come, when Richards was bowled by Freeman hitting, almost for the first time, across the line. He had hit 24 fours and one six, an on-drive off Gleeson. Given the opportunity he will play many fine test innings. But I vow none will be better than this.

Close: SOUTH AFRICA 368 for 5 (B.A. Richards 140, R.G. Pollock 160 not out).

6 February 1970, Durban. Australia, by losing the wickets of four front rank batsmen as only four runs were scored, made one of the most disastrous starts imaginable today when they began their reply to a record South African total of 622 for nine wickets declared in the second Test here. From 44 for no wicket, Australia moved to 48 for four, with Barlow taking three wickets in 10 balls before bad light brought the close half-an-hour early.

Before this remarkable breakdown, Graeme Pollock had entranced us with a further display of his art, as he took his own score to 274, the highest individual score ever compiled by a South African in Test cricket.

The Australian collapse is quickly told. Lawry and Stackpole gathered runs steadily against the pace of Procter and Peter Pollock, who had only four overs apiece before Bacher brought on medium pace at each end. Barlow's first ball had Lawry leg-before, and in the same over Chappell was held by Gamsy as the batsman attempted to glance.

The wicketkeeper took another legside catch, this time off Goddard, to dismiss Stackpole as the total remained 44. Walters square-cut Barlow for one four before he gave a catch to gully. These slumps, of course, tend to happen after an arduous and dispiriting experience in the field and from every aspect Australians have had an unhappy time in this Test since the start. Now, already, they can at best only hope to save the game and the odds must clearly be against them achieving even this.

So long as Pollock was batting the record book was being re-written. The press contingent were among the victims. Peter van der Merwe and his brother-in-law John Waite, both writing on the present series, saw separate records surpassed by Pollock and Lance, who had added 200 for the sixth wicket, when Lance was stumped off Gleeson. The previous best for this wicket by a South African side was the 171 of Waite and Paul Winslow against England in 1955. Lance had been hopelessly out of form this year until he came up against the Australians in Johannesburg last week.

By luncheon Pollock had made 227, his fourth

double hundred and the highest score of his career. Afterwards he passed A.D. Nourse's 231, until now the highest score by a South African against Australia — Nourse was there to see him do it — and then with a straight drive for four off Stackpole he overtook Jackie McGlew, whose 255 not out against New Zealand at Wellington had stood for 17 years as the highest score by a South African in Test cricket.

A year ago the Australians were meting out to the West Indians just such a thrashing as they were receiving from the South Africans now. In the last four Test matches of that series, Australia made totals of 510, 547, 533 and 619. Yet here I was actually feeling sorry for them as they were driven from pillar to post by Pollock. No one looked like getting the ball past Pollock's bat, least of all that great trojan McKenzie.

Lawry called Chappell, his vice-captain, into regular consultation; in the field the Australians, though they never gave up trying, looked hot and uncomfortable. They never had more than one slip and they often had none. While Gleeson, and then Stackpole, bowled, the covers were heavily manned. It was splendid to see Pollock trying to pierce them and Chappell, Walters, Sheahan, Redpath and Lawry striving to stop him.

Pollock and Procter added 77 in 70 minutes, and Pollock was batting as though with his sights on another hundred, when holding back on a drive, he returned a low and gentle catch to Stackpole. It was somehow an unsuitable end to a wonderfully commanding innings. Pollock batted for just under seven hours and hit 43 fours to all corners of the ground. The outfield here is faster than I have ever seen it. There was no catching the ball once it was through the inner ring.

South Africa batted for another 80 minutes after Pollock was out for 63 more runs, and once they had achieved their highest total in Test cricket Bacher called the last pair in.

By then even these two were on the way to a record. But it was more than time to get the Australians to the crease. Of their bowlers, Connolly, Gleeson and Freeman had got the hundred

they did not want in the analyses, and about Gleeson's figures [51–9–160–3], there was a good old-fashioned ring. Shades of timeless Tests and suchlike things.

Close: SOUTH AFRICA 622 for 9 declared (B.A. Richards 140, R.G. Pollock 274, H.R. Lance 61), AUSTRALIA 48 for 4.

SOUTH AFRICA 622 for 9 declared beat AUSTRALIA 157 (A.P. Sheahan 62) and 336 (K.R. Stackpole 71, K.D. Walters 74, I.R. Redpath 74 not out) by an innings and 129 runs.

On 19 February 1970 the Third Test began at Johannesburg, South Africa again batting first. A

POLLOCK "At his best — mark you, only at his best — he reminds me of Woolley." — Neville Cardus.

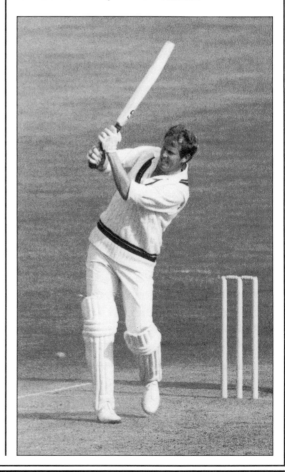

fierce storm took away 80 minutes of play, the close seeing South Africa 191 for five wickets — Richards 65, Pollock 52. John Woodcock reported that "Richards made 65 in 88 minutes of barefaced effrontery...Before he went in, Richards was described as being 'as nervous as a kitten'. Yet from the first over he threw his bat at the ball with a confidence I have never seen equalled at the start of a Test match."

One's memory was jogged: M.A. Noble, Australian captain-extraordinary and all-rounder, wrote in *The Game's the Thing*:

> Victor Trumper, unlike most other batsmen, never played himself in before trying to score. If he considered his first ball should be hit for four he hit it. On rare occasions he failed to time it properly and thus brought about his early downfall...One of his maxims used to be: "Spoil a bowler's length and you've got him." And a very sound maxim it is, for no kind of bowling is any use unless it is of good length...The outstanding feature of his batting was not so much that he made so many varied and beautiful strokes, but that he had the ability to get into the proper position which made those strokes possible.

The two sides moved to Port Elizabeth for the Fourth and final Test of the series.

DISDAIN FOR BOWLERS — RICHARDS' PROBLEM

By John Woodcock

9 March 1970, Port Elizabeth. After watching the series between South Africa and Australia, things will never be quite the same again. It has been like having doubts cast upon a faith, to see an Australian team so hopelessly confounded.

Yesterday in the fourth Test match their first innings came to an end with a succession of reckless strokes. Whereupon they were sent chasing round the ground without being able to do anything about it. While their bowlers were losing their length, their fielders were dropping their catches. The batsman to create the confusion and then benefit from it was Barry Richards.

In an innings of 126, he took his aggregate in his first Test series to 508 (72.4) and in the process made batting look simpler than he had any right to do.

It will be hard not to appear to be over-praising this brilliant young batsman. Against the Australian bowling he seems capable of playing an innings as near to perfection as he chooses. Such is his footwork, so quick his eye, wide his range of stroke, sound his method, deft his balance, instinctive his timing that he is spared the problems of the ordinary man.

Whether as he gets older — he is now 24 — and the pressures increase he will find batting more arduous remains to be seen. This can happen. Rather than becoming increasingly commanding a batsman develops inhibitions. Cowdrey is a case in point: he has seldom played again with quite the freedom of his first tour to Australia in 1954–55. At the moment the biggest problem of Richards is his own disdain for bowlers. That alone looked like getting him out yesterday.

He was dropped when he had scored 25 experimenting with a drive off Gleeson, and again at the wicket immediately after he had reached his 50. This time he was making room to hit a ball from Gleeson, which was straight and of a fairly full length, past cover point off the back foot. At 111, he was put down by Chappell at short midwicket, hooking at McKenzie. Chappell will hope that he never drops an easier catch than this and it was made no better for him by the fact that it would have provided McKenzie with his first wicket of the series.

The first ball of South Africa's innings, bowled by McKenzie, was a shade short of a length and lifted enough to exercise most batsmen. But Richards was in position almost before the ball had left the bowler's hand, and he played it with all the ease and time in the world. The Australians might have been excused for thinking that it was not fair. By mid-afternoon they were noticeably disheartened and whenever Richards, as though tired of his own mastery, gave them a chance to remove him they missed it.

It was off McKenzie that Richards played his two most splendid strokes. They were off successive balls, neither of them particularly short of a length. The first he crashed past cover point off the back foot, the second he hooked high into the stand for six, not at square leg but over mid-wicket. Between lunch and tea he made 85 runs; at 151 he reached the century in which he had never seemed particularly interested; and when he succeeded in getting himself out at 199, he had hit 16 fours and three sixes.

As a Hampshire man, I dearly hope that Richards can be persuaded to stay with the county for many years to come. Because of his age and ability, he represents the greatest cricketing asset they are likely to possess for a long time. Yesterday he had the glory to himself, though Gleeson bowled as admirably and unluckily as he invariably does. So far in the series Australia's fielders have dropped 13 catches off Gleeson's bowling. O tempora! O mores!

SOUTH AFRICA 311 (B.A. Richards 81, E.J. Barlow 73; A.N. Connolly 6 for 47) and 470 for 8 declared, (Richards 126, A. Bacher 73, B.L. Irvine 102, J.D. Lindsay 60) beat AUSTRALIA 212 (I.R. Redpath 55, A.P. Sheahan 67) and 246 (M.J. Procter 6 for 73) by 323 runs.

South Africa's overwhelming superiority was with both bat and ball. Their batsmen scored six individual hundreds to the Australians' none: the South African average runs per wicket from the bat was 38.67, the Australian was 20.60. Each in seven innings, Pollock averaged 73.85, Richards 72.57, Barlow 51.42 and B.L. Irvine 50.42; for Australia Redpath in eight innings (twice not out) averaged 47.16, no one else as many as 33.

The fast bowling of Procter (26 wickets, average 13.57) and P.M. Pollock (15 wickets, average 17.20) was the deciding factor, though the medium-pace A.N. Connolly's 20 wickets, average 26.10, for the

losers was also a memorable achievement. Barlow was the outstanding all-rounder with 360 runs, 11 wickets, average 23.36, and eight catches.

South Africa, certainly with their finest side ever, were henceforth banned from international cricket. The balance of power may be hinted at. From the Fourth Test at Adelaide in 1963–4 to the Fourth Test at Port Elizabeth in 1970, South Africa had beaten Australia eight times in eleven games, losing only once. During approximately the same period, Australia played England in 26 Tests, winning four and losing five; Australia won four Tests to West Indies' three in ten games; England won five Tests to West Indies' six in 18 games.

R.G. Pollock and Richards had chosen the wrong pastime; after South Africa's disappearance from Test cricket, their great golfing compatriot, Gary Player, was permitted to play in — and win — the Open, the US Masters and the US PGA.

GRAEME POLLOCK WITHOUT PEER

By John Woodcock

31 January 1970, Cape Town. Graeme Pollock, South Africa's greatest batsman and regarded by many as the best in the world, has no army of supporters or aircraft of his own, no fetish for fitness or yearning for retirement. He is just a mild, straightforward, easy-going fellow with a gift for batting, which it pleases him to use.

He enjoys living in Port Elizabeth, where he was brought up, because it's "away from the rat race". He is very much a home town boy. His father was editor of the *Port Elizabeth Herald* until he died last year; his wife is a Port Elizabeth girl and his young son is being nourished on Port Elizabeth air. When Graeme has some spare time from his new job as sales manager of a large group of clothing companies, he likes to round up two or three friends for a few frames of snooker at the club. It's a game with a tempo that suits him. Anything for the quiet life. In the field he likes to stand at slip. This involves a minimum of running and there is always someone close by with whom to discuss the less important matters of the day.

On the afternoon before a Test match when the teams are at practice you will see Eddie Barlow or Graeme's brother, Peter, or Trevor Goddard with their shirts clinging to their backs. Graeme will scarcely break out of a canter if he can help it. When last summer he was in England playing for the International Cavaliers, he and his wife rented a flat within a long iron shot of Lord's but it would never have occurred to him to go there for a net. He played for me in a village match in Hampshire and produced the perfect innings. In the evening he drank beer with the village side without the least embarrassment either to himself or them.

Graeme's grandfather was a Scottish Presbyterian minister. His own father had a year or two at Heriot's before the family came to South Africa to settle. The ability to play games is inherited though not until the present generation has it been so marked. Graeme and his elder brother, Peter, who is still South Africa's opening bowler, are the sons of a father who kept wicket for Orange Free State and a mother who played tennis for Natal.

Graeme could walk when he was eight months old and he was making centuries by the time he was nine years old. Just before he was 17 he became the youngest South African cricketer to score a first class 100 and just after he was 19 he scored a double 100 at an earlier age than any other South African. "For a long time," says his brother, "I thought he was sure to be found out. He was always so much better than the rest of us and we were all quite a bit older." But it has yet to happen. Graeme is still, at the age of 25, in a class of his own. But he is old enough now to worry about it. The more that is expected of him the more nervous he becomes. This is never evident but he assures me it is so.

He was at Grey High School in Port Elizabeth from the age of six to 16. The coach there at the time was George Cox, of Sussex, himself a true son of nature. Realizing that he had a rare talent in his hands Cox left well alone. I wish Graeme could have seen George on one of those days at Hove when his cap grew more faded in the sun and the shots he played were too brilliant to have come from any text book. A year after leaving school Graeme visited England with his parents and, at Cox's suggestion, he played half a dozen matches for Sussex second eleven.

By the time he was 18 he had decided to concentrate on cricket. It was not as rough a game as rugger, at which he excelled as a stand-off half, and it was less strenuous than tennis. Like Cliff Drysdale, with whom he played a lot of tennis, he had a two-handed backhand and at one time there was nothing to choose between them. By 1962 the New Zealanders were returning home from a tour to South Africa and saying that they had seen in Port Elizabeth the player of the future. And when the late Ron Roberts took a side to South Africa at the end of that year he came back with reports of a prodigy who had made 209 not out for Eastern Province.

A year later Graeme began his Test career. It was in Australia on a tour which started with his making nought and one against Western Australia in the first match. In the following week, after he had scored a century in 88 minutes against a combined eleven, Don Bradman said to him: "If you ever play an innings like that again I hope I'm there to see it." Well, he has been doing so ever since — the last of them was against the Australians at Port Elizabeth recently when he made 105 in 102 minutes. On that tour of Australia he treated Bradman to an innings of 175 at Adelaide (he and Barlow added 341 for South Africa's third wicket) and another of 122 at Sydney. On his only tour to England his 125 at Trent Bridge ranks among the finest innings of post-war cricket.

But if Bradman applauded Pollock's style of batting I am not sure that he can have approved of his view of records. In the Don's heyday there used to be a general exodus from shops and offices to watch him bat. If he was not out at lunch it was a safe bet that he would be there well into the afternoon if not the evening. When he made 309 in a single day against England at Leeds he described it as "a nice bit of practice for tomorrow". With Graeme Pollock it is different. Once past his 100 he is happy enough for someone else to take a turn.

As a captain he receives only moderately good notices. It may be that he is too phlegmatic for the job or not sufficiently dedicated, or perhaps because he has never really had to work at the game himself, he finds it difficult to comprehend the problems which lesser batsmen have to contend with. The most successful captains are not always the most talented and popular cricketers.

From his colleagues in the South African side come, quite independently, much the same observations... "Just a nice uncomplicated guy..." "If he were twice as ambitious they'd never get him out..." "Tricky to run with because he's always after the strike..." Bill Lawry, the Australian captain, is less enthusiastic — "A good bad ball player* — but he's always giving the bowler a chance." Richie Benaud on the other hand puts Graeme on a pedestal partly because of the caning he got from him in Australia. Bobby Simpson does the same and so I fancy does Gary Sobers.

When Sobers joined Nottinghamshire he was asked whether there was anyone else he'd particularly like the county to try to sign. The name Sobers gave was Pollock, who was approached and for a while thought seriously about it. What the struggling bowlers of other counties would have said I am not sure. I doubt whether the seam bowlers would have liked it, for they are Graeme's favourite dish. "Good fast bowlers and good spinners are a challenge. The easiest to attack are the medium pacers."

But Sobers and Pollock will never play for Nottinghamshire together. After one more visit to Australia in 1971, Graeme intends, though he

....

* Perhaps Lawry was saying by implication what he thought of his touring Australians' bowling in 1969–70.

will be only 28, to confine his cricket to South Africa. If so, South Africa's forthcoming tour to England may provide English cricket lovers with a last look at a splendid batsman. He is not the most elegant player of the day, as with his considerable height he might be, and he is certainly not the fittest. But with less fuss and effort than the rest he inflicts the greatest damage on a bowler's pride.

RICHARDS THE PRINCE

Richards meanwhile would play for South Australia in 1970–71 at an Australian dollar a run. He would cross the oceans as his contracts demanded: 1 March 1971 in Adelaide for South Australia, 3 April in Cape Town making a "guest" appearance for the Currie Cup winners Transvaal in the Republic Festival match, 28 April in the Parks at Oxford as opener for Hampshire. South Australia's investment was a wise one:

7	v. Western Australia	35	v. Queensland
44	not out	155	v. Queensland
224	v. MCC	13	
51	v. Victoria	178	v. New South Wales
42		105	v. Victoria
356	v. Western Australia	72	
146	v. MCC	55	v. New South Wales
23		32	retired hurt
16 innings	2 NO	1,538 runs	109.86 av.

The 356 against Western Australia found G.D. McKenzie, D.K. Lillee and G.A.R. Lock in opposition. Lillee may have been far from his glorious peak but he bowled successfully in the last two Tests against Illingworth's tourists. At Perth in November 1970 when Richards held sway, his figures were 18–1–117–0. On the first day Richards made 100 in 125 minutes, 200 in 208 minutes, 300 in 317 minutes — being 325 after 330 minutes at the close. Stylistically, his 224 against the MCC at Adelaide reminded Grimmett of McCabe, the batsman of whom Grimmett said to Jack Fingleton "I doubt if there is anyone who times a ball with such effortless ease. His footwork and technique are faultless."* Certainly over the next few years Richards' batting caused those reporting cricket for *The Times* to abandon themselves to superlatives before sinking into disbelieving ecstasy. Chronology is irrelevant.

By Peter Marson

7 July 1973. A hundred by Barry Richards had eluded me until yesterday, when he made two and a few more runs besides. As Henry Hall would say: "Here's to the next time." This really was a masterly performance and as near a faultless display of batsmanship as can be imagined. With an innings of 240 runs made in 274 minutes, Richards stroked his way to three sixes and 38 fours. His innings was well short of his highest score — 356 made for South Australia in 1970–71 — but easily his best in the county championship.

It is unlikely that any among a small band present yesterday at Coventry will forget so brilliant a passage in their cricketing experience, and that on an impeccable summer's day when so long as the West Countrymen celebrated, the sun's smile stayed broad and warm. While he was at the crease, Richards was Hampshire...He made his first hundred out of 178 in 140 minutes, his second out of 320 in 245 minutes, and of a host of glittering boundaries, the great majority had been driven in an arc of 90 degrees between square cover point and mid wicket. His innings exceeds that by Kanhai, the highest till now with 230 against Somerset, at Edgbaston in the middle of May, but when the multitude of facts and figures have been logged and locked away, Richards's elegance, style and skill will remain effervescent in the memory.

HAMPSHIRE 396 for 7 declared (B.A. Richards 240, C.G. Greenidge 56), WARWICKSHIRE 34 for one wicket.

Three years later Richards's father and mother

* *Cricket Crisis,* p.258.

arrived in England on holiday from Durban. On 29 May 1976 they were at Southampton for Hampshire's game with Kent; noting that his mother's birthday would coincide with the second day's play, Barry decided he would celebrate with a hundred. But when Hampshire won the toss, clearly a hundred for father must come first. It did.

By Peter Marson

1 June, 1976. Barry Richards is King! OK. That was the message written large at the county ground yesterday, and it was to the accompaniment of a royal salute of 19 fours, in a brilliant hundred, his second of the match. I have been witness to a century and more from this princely cricketer on numerous occasions, the best of which have been near ecstatic, but this present one, even by his own standards, was something to marvel at.

With Hampshire's score at 50 from 11 overs, Richards had made 40; at 100 from 22 overs he was 75, and when he stroked Hills to extra cover for a single he had hit his century out of 128 runs in 26 overs in 83 minutes.

Peter Marson wrote of "power, simplicity and ease" and left it at that.

HAMPSHIRE 307 (B.A. Richards 159) and 142 for 2 (Richards 108), KENT 309 (J.N. Shepherd 73, A.G.E. Ealham 51, D. Nicholls 50).

By Alan Gibson

1 September 1975. An innings of the utmost splendour by Richards eclipsed everything and everyone else yesterday at Bournemouth, and kept Hampshire at the top of the John Player League...Last year's champions put up a good fight for most of the match, but once Richards was well into his stride, they must have felt like some honest Trojan soldiers competing with Achilles, mortals struggling with the god-like.

Richards reached his hundred in 74 balls, with

scarcely a mishit. He hit, all told, five sixes — three in an over from Balderstone — and 12 fours, and yet scarcely ever seemed to strike the ball hard. Illingworth used six bowlers, but it did not matter what they did, or where he placed his field: it was all one. He himself bowled accurately on the leg stump with a strong leg field, but Richards still found the gaps, or stepped away and hit him into the open spaces. He was out just before the end, possibly fearing an over-exuberant welcome from the crowd. There are occasions now and then when a Sunday League match produces an innings which transcends the usual slap dash slog, and this was one of them.

THE RIGHT ELIXIR

By Richard Streeton

18 June 1971. All day yesterday there was vintage batsmanship to be admired at Southampton. But everything else was finally dwarfed by Barry Richards as he reached an undefeated 130, including 22 fours, in the last two hours and a half. Throughout, sunshine predominated over cloudy periods and the pitch emerged as an easier surface than had been expected.

For seven weeks those on the county championship circuit this summer have waited for Richards to tear an opposing attack to shreds in that devastating manner, which only he among the world's batsmen does nowadays with any regularity. He has been scoring runs but not with the ruthlessness and abandon that place him

apart. In the first innings he had chosen to bat in chains as he sought the right elixir. Now he tried the opposite formula and succeeded brilliantly in recapturing his most dazzling array of strokes. Graham's first two balls were savagely hooked and square cut to the boundary, and Richards's supremacy was established.

Figures must inevitably come into a description of an innings as magnificent as this. But they can never convey the scorching speed of the ball to the boundary all round the wicket from every conceivable shot. Every Kent bowler in turn was hooked, cut or driven, and if some fared a little less cruelly than others, it was only because Kent bowed to the inevitable and gradually stationed men all round the edge of the field. Richards reached 50 in 55 minutes with nine fours: his century came in 108 minutes with 19 fours; and amid all this splendour there was only one possible chance, a leg-side glance off Graham at 84 that the wicketkeeper might conceivably have held.

Even such a superlative performance as this has its peak, and this came when Richards took 21 off one over by Shepherd that included a no-ball. This lifted him from 63 to 84 with five fours and a single, the boundaries covering an arc from square leg round to cover point. Each time the Kent fieldsmen nearest was left flat-footed as the ball crossed the line.

John Woodcock said everything about the cricketer at his best on 11 September 1973: "Richards played as though from Olympus, the master of all he surveyed."

KENNETH COLIN BLAND
Eastern Province and Orange Free State

Bland, like Jessop before him, was one of cricket's great negative forces. With Jessop on the other side, few captains felt it safe to declare; when the ball was hit even remotely near Bland, wise batsmen took up their stance again and awaited the next delivery. Twice in the Lord's Test of 1965 Bland rocked England by making the highly unlikely seem, for him, the inevitable.

By John Woodcock

26 July 1965. England seemed after tea to be advancing to a comfortable lead, with Barrington moving purposefully to his hundred. Barrington's innings had been enriched with strokes. Now he tucked the ball away to midwicket for, as he thought, his ninety-second run; and Barrington is not a man to take chances with his running. Forward of the square leg umpire Bland was on patrol; he swooped to his left for the ball and threw down the bowler's wicket with Barrington inches from home. It was a marvellous piece of fielding and vital to the match.

27 July 1965. During the morning England's last four wickets added 51 runs in 95 minutes. Of these Titmus made 37, mainly with some good, meaty strokes through the covers. Bland placed a limit on England's innings with, if anything, an even better piece of fielding than that with which he ran out Barrington on Saturday.

A ball from Botten went some five or six yards round the corner off Titmus's pads, and Parks, the non-striker, called Titmus for the single that was there. Titmus seeing Bland at square leg and taking fright, sent Parks back, and Bland, pouncing on the ball and throwing on the turn hit the middle stump at the bowler's end.

In his last 10 Test matches, in Australia and South Africa, Bland ran nobody out. The batsmen dared not leave their crease when the ball was near him. He was more a deterrent than an instruction of destruction. Now, on successive cricketing days, the many long hours for which he has practised fielding on his own have been rewarded at Lord's before a large and appreciative audience.

MCC's tour of South Africa in 1964–5 was a subtle variation on that of 1930–31, when the series was decided by victory for one side in the First Test — for South Africa in 1930–31 and England in 1964–5. Thereafter attrition became the order of things. But whereas in 1930–31 South Africa sat on the splice at one up and four to play, in 1964–5 it failed to display much initiative when one down and four to play. In retrospect it can be seen that South Africa was halfway up the ladder to world supremacy: Barlow, Bland and P.M. Pollock had arrived, R.G. Pollock, though capable of greatness, had yet to reach his peak, B.A. Richards and M.J. Procter were in the wings.

The last day of the Second Test at Johannesburg found South Africa 146 for three, so requiring 68 runs to avoid an innings defeat.

By John Woodcock

29 December 1964, Johannesburg. England ran out of time in their efforts to win the second Test match against South Africa here today. They were thwarted partly by the weather and partly by a superb innings from Bland, who made 144 not out. Two hours and 10 minutes were lost at different times to rain and bad light.

To have lost the match South Africa would have needed to bat badly today. The pitch looked, if anything, to be rather easier than yesterday. It was a tribute to the groundsman's skill, providing as it did as interesting a Test match as we have seen for some time. If England had won it would have been their best performance on a good wicket since Australia were beaten at Melbourne two years ago.

The only South African wicket to fall before tea today was Pollock's. This was at 196 when South Africa still needed 18 runs to save an innings defeat. By the clock there was almost four hours left. An hour later, at 241 for five, the England side thought to a man that Varnals was caught off Allen by the most backward of the three short legs. Varnals stood his ground and the umpire turned down the appeal. It was a question whether the ball came off Varnal's pad or off his bat and pad.

Bland, for his part, batted without error. He is indeed a fine, upstanding cricketer, broad of shoulder, strong of heart, and sound of method. Of present day batsmen only Dexter could have matched the severity of Bland's hitting this afternoon. On this form he is one of the world's most compelling players. Today, too, like Dexter last Wednesday, he restrained himself when restraint was a virtue. Anyone standing in the way of Bland's drives or his forces off the back foot is made to pay for it with sore palms.

After the incident in which Varnals escaped with his wicket the pressure eased upon South Africa. For the next 55 minutes Varnals hung his head rather self-consciously at one end while Bland swept South Africa to safety. In steady, if

not heavy, rain Bland rode to his second Test match century. The other was against Australia at Sydney. Bland's first 50 took him two hours and a quarter. His last 75 runs were made in 80 minutes out of 96. England, it is true, suffered the disadvantage of a wet ball, but it was none the less a magnificent piece of batting...

In the hour and a quarter before luncheon, Pollock and Bland were in little trouble. Smith began with 10 overs from Allen and Titmus before taking the new ball as soon as it was due. Whether by accident or design, Pollock stayed away from Titmus's end and the nearest the two spinners came to a wicket was when Bland, hitting across the line at Titmus, survived a confident appeal for leg-before. In Titmus's next over Bland went down the pitch and pulled him stupendously for six. With the new ball both Price and Thomson were running across heavy ground. They left dark imprints behind them, though at the point of delivery the ground was as firm as ever.

Pollock had two close shaves when facing Price. Once he was nearly bowled by a high full toss which he seemed not to see. And then, when he was 51, a protective shot to a short ball was picked up on the half volley by Smith at short leg. This morning Pollock and Bland made a handsome pair. The scoring was slow. In 75 minutes only 41 runs were added. Yet, from South Africa's point of view, it was a promising partnership. Pollock looked much more himself than he had done before against this MCC attack, and Bland was in no way inferior to Pollock.

In Allen's second over of the afternoon Pollock was bowled pushing out to what to him was a leg break which turned. Bland at the time was 33. So far, in almost two hours today, he had scored 23. Of the last 140 runs his share was 111. He is a strapping fellow, with closely cropped hair and a slight stoop, and by three o'clock he was finding it all so easy that a draw was virtually inevitable. South Africa by then had a lead of 50 with five wickets left. The details thereafter were academic.

Five minutes before tea rain at last stopped play. When, an hour afterwards, it stopped, the players came out for a further 35 minutes in conditions that made bowling and fielding hazardous. The bowling was done for England by Boycott and Dexter, and at 3.20 Varnals was caught at the wicket off Dexter. At 5.20, with a possible 40 minutes remaining, Smith, who had been reluctant to resume for this last rather bizarre period, agreed with the batsmen to call it a day. Bland, with 17 fours and two sixes to his name, had given South African cricket the boost it needed.

ENGLAND 531 (R.W. Barber 97, E.R. Dexter 172, K.F. Barrington 121, P.H. Parfitt 52; P.M. Pollock 5 for 129) drew with SOUTH AFRICA 317 (E.J. Barlow 71, A.J. Pithey 85) and 336 for 6 (T.L. Goddard 50, R.G. Pollock 55, K.C. Bland 144 not out).

This 1964–5 MCC party played 17 first-class games, winning ten; the closest it got to defeat was in the penultimate game with an Invitation XI.

By John Woodcock

5 February 1965, Cape Town. Neither on the last tour to South Africa nor previously on this one has an MCC attack been so successfully handled as it was today. On a pitch which dried out to perfection a South African Invitation XI made 375 for seven, led by Bland with a resplendent innings of 116. From the younger generation of South African cricketers this was a splendid performance.

Bland came in when McPhun was bowled off his pads after half an hour. The bowlers had something to encourage them in the way of early moisture and resilience. It did not last, but it was there when Bland arrived, and Brown, bowling decidedly fast, was doing his best to exploit it.

Yet Bland took the initiative at once.

His one early stroke of luck was when, hooking at Brown, he got four over the wicketkeeper's head. Much later in his innings he was beaten on the forward stroke by Hobbs. These were his only mistakes.

Bland's main hits were five sixes and nine fours. The sixes were made up of three straight drives, two of them off Allen and one off Hobbs, and two hooks off Brown. His great strength enables him to drive for six almost without effort. His fitness allows him to play a strenuous innings on a day as hot as this without perspiring. His bat is so classically straight in defence and attack that when the ball is coming through truly, as it was now, it seems as though there is nothing that can go wrong.

Indeed, if I had to pick two batsmen in the world at the moment to play for my life, they would be Sobers and Bland. After batting 80 minutes today he was 81 not out and he had led Gamsy out of a maze of uncertainty.

Bland fancied nobody more than Allen, who was hit for 28 runs in four overs. I spend weeks in the year watching off-spinners and medium-paced bowlers being treated as though they were inviolable. I am told by the hour that there is nothing to be done about them. And when I see a striker as fine as Dexter tied down by off-breaks that do not turn — in the Test match here he made one scoring stroke in two hours against Bromfield — I fear that cricket has lost its heart and humour. Then along comes Bland, to cast the gloom aside and to display the glory of the drive.

Gamsy is a busy little player with a good cover drive and an inclination to use his feet. In this innings he was transformed by Bland's presence into something more than an acolyte. His contribution to a second wicket partnership of 188 in two hours and a quarter was 74, containing some good hooks and a couple of drives back over Hobbs's head.

By luncheon the South African XI were 133 for one off 33 overs. Smith, with customary caution, had not allowed Hobbs to bowl. Thus, when Hobbs came on he found Bland in full cry, yet he induced from Bland more respect than anyone. By 2 o'clock, when Bland completed a magnificent hundred in two hours, even Boycott was bowling in an effort to hold the flood. Twenty-five minutes later Bland, the striker, was sent back by Gamsy and thrown out by Hobbs fielding near the square leg umpire. This was one of several fine pieces of fielding by Hobbs.

The new ball, taken at 214 for two, accounted usefully for Gamsy and R.G. Pollock. Gamsy, hooking at Cartwright, was caught at the second attempt at backward short leg: Pollock, disturbed by some short-pitched bowling from Brown, was caught at slip off his glove. For the moment, at any rate, Bland's batting star is higher than Pollock's. In nine innings against Smith's side he has made 685 runs.

INVITATION XI 437 (D. Gamsy 88, K.C. Bland 116, P.L. van der Merwe 50, R. Muzzell 70, J.T. Botten 53; T.W. Cartwright 5 for 107) and 316 for 7 declared (Gamsy 55, Bland 67, R.G. Pollock 91, Muzzell 52 not out) drew with MCC 326 (G. Boycott 114, Cartwright 53 not out) and 205 for 7 (M.J.K. Smith 78 not out).

In MCC's second innings the seventh wicket fell at 100 before Smith and Cartwright survived for the last three hours.

It is perhaps relevant to point out that Bland was the senior member of several remarkable South African cricketers appearing, or about to appear at this time. Their ages at the close of MCC's tour were: Bland 26, Lindsay 25, Barlow 24, P.M. Pollock 23, B.A. Richards 19, M.J. Procter 18.

DENNIS KEITH LILLEE
Western Australia

Lillee was so recently a part of cricket — his career must have been more comprehensively televised than that of any other great bowler — that his stature may be assessed by John Woodcock. But since, with the passing of time, he will enter Australian mythology, and perhaps be acclaimed by admirers as the finest of fast bowlers from that country, a word of advice to those who scribble down world or national teams on the backs of envelopes may be in order. Never select a side for a span of more than 20 years.

Times readers were once treated to selectorial flights of fancy by Sir Home Gordon, a pundit-extraordinary born in 1871, and P.F. Warner, born in 1873. Here are their Australian XIs for the ages.

P.F. Warner's — 1919
J. Darling
V.T. Trumper
W.L. Murdoch
C.G. Macartney
C. Hill
M.A. Noble
C. Giffen
H. Trumble
C.T.B. Turner
J. McC. Blackham
F.R. Spofforth

Sir Home Gordon — 1956
P.S. McDonnell
V.T. Trumper
D.G. Bradman
C.G. Macartney
C. Hill
M.A. Noble
K.R. Miller
W.A. Oldfield
C.T.B. Turner
A.A. Mailey
F.R. Spofforth or R.R. Lindwall

Thirty-seven years separate the choice of these two sides but five, or possibly six, names are common to both. Turner, incidentally, had made his final Test appearance in 1894.

To reasonably modern eyes, neither of the above teams can compare with one Jack Fingleton chose at the end of 1948 to represent Australia, 1920–48:

W.H. Ponsford
A.R. Morris
D.G. Bradman
C.G. Macartney
S.J. McCabe
A.A. Jackson
K.R. Miller
J.M. Gregory
D. Tallon
C.V. Grimmett
W.J. O'Reilly

Meanwhile readers may guess the teams chosen by Sir Home Gordon in 1956 and by P.F. Warner in 1919 to play for England. Six names are common to both teams; Warner selected three bowlers each of whom generally took the new ball, Gordon selected three opening batsmen and four bowlers, each accustomed to open the attack.

By John Woodcock

28 December 1981. If there had to be reservations, however slight, about Geoffrey Boycott's stature as a batsman (not as an accumulator, but purely and simply as a great batsman) when he beat Garfield Sobers's Test record in Delhi last Thursday, there need be none about Dennis Lillee's as a craftsman with the ball. The 311 wickets which

LILLEE   In spite of his head band, the legitimate successor to Spofforth; the Demon whose mastery was consummate.

he has now taken, leaves him clear of Lance Gibbs (309) and Fred Trueman (307) with Derek Underwood, now on 286, and Ian Botham on 215, in perspiring pursuit. Being only 26, Botham, if he stays fit enough, may set the next target.

When Trueman was asked whether he thought his own total would ever be beaten, he said that if it were, whoever did it would be "bloody tired". Yet such is Lillee's natural rhythm and ability, that even at the age of 32, he looks to have plenty of bowling left in him.

Unlike any of the other great modern fast bowlers, he has succeeded in cutting down his pace to conserve energy, without losing his effectiveness. Trueman failed in this, despite his lavish talent, as indeed did Ray Lindwall, who bowled for Australia until he was 38, for the last season or two off a shortened run.

Lillee bears comparison with whichever fast bowler you care to think of. In appearance he is remarkably like the "Demon", Spofforth. Have a look at some of the photographs of the Australian sides of the 1870s and 1880s and Spofforth was clearly the Lillee of his day.

The time came, too, when Spofforth subordinated pace to accuracy and variation. For sheer speed, Lillee may never quite have equalled Thomson or Holding, or Roberts or Hall, or Larwood or Tyson, or perhaps Kortwright. But if not, it was a matter only of inches and until he changed his style he could be as savagely hostile as any of them.

The first Englishmen to see anything of Lillee were Ray Illingworth's side 11 years ago, when he opened the bowling for Western Australia. His captain then was Tony Lock; his first victim none other than Boycott. I remember how irritated one or two Australian watchers were that Lock gave Lillee only eight overs in MCC's first innings of 258 for 3 declared. In his first Test match, at Adelaide later that winter, Lillee took five for 84 in England's first innings.

In the years since then, he has overcome a serious back injury (stress fractures of the lower spine) which kept him out of the game from early in 1973 to late in 1974, and missed something like 20 Test matches between 1977 and 1979 through his connexion with World Series cricket, of which he was a founder member.

The way he had worked his way back to fitness came as a nasty shock to England's batsmen when they played against him at Brisbane in December 1974. Instead of finding him on the scrap heap, as they had hoped and rather expected, he established with Jeff Thomson (another unknown quantity when that tour started) one of the most devastating of all fast bowling partnerships.

In the Australian season of 1975–6, West Indies found Lillee and Thomson no less formidable a pair than England had.

For different reasons Trueman might also have played in a good many more Tests than he did. He was not, in fact, chosen to go either to Australia in 1954–5 or to South Africa in 1956–7, in spite of being in his prime at the time. Trueman's striking rate in his 67 appearances for England was 4.6 wickets per Test match as against Lillee's 5.4. The only fast bowler to have exceeded this figure of Lillee's was Tom Richardson, another tall, dark, moustachioed figure, who took 88 wickets in 14 Tests.

Lillee's action, like Richardson's and Spofforth's and Lindwall's and Trueman's, is of the classical kind — a model for an aspiring bowler. That, on occasions, he lets himself and the game down by behaving so absurdly badly, is the greatest pity. In most fast bowlers there is an irascible streak. It is an almost essential part of their make-up. One of the few exceptions was the benign and endearing Brian Statham.

Lillee, however, like John McEnroe, now the best tennis player in the world, does untold harm to the game he professes to love by defying the accepted codes of conduct. If, growing up in Australia, there is a generation of cricketers who think it clever to act like bush rangers, Lillee, a folk hero, must have much to do with it. For all that, it will be a very sad day when he is no longer to be seen bowling with supreme and irrepressible skill.

Such are the wonders of communication that it was possible to sit at home yesterday morning and listen to Lillee saying that he would need notice of the question as to which batsmen he has found it most difficult to bowl to, and to Trueman being hauled out of bed to congratulate his fellow-traveller — and to end Yorkshire's chequered year with a final dig at his fellow Yorkshiremen.

With so many Test matches being played these days — since the winding up of WSC in May, 1979, Lillee has played in no fewer than 26 — Lillee's record is no more likely to stand for ever than Boycott's. What will probably never recur is the remarkable coincidence whereby they both went ahead of all their rivals within four days of each other, Lillee on the very ground where, on New Year's Day, 1976, Gibbs passed Trueman's target.

ENGLAND

P.F. Warner's — 1919
W.G. Grace
J.B. Hobbs
K.S. Ranjitsinhji
F.S. Jackson
F.E. Woolley
A.G. Steel
A.A. Lilley
R. Peel
W.H. Lockwood
G.A. Lohmann
S.F. Barnes

Sir Home Gordon's — 1956
W.G. Grace
J.B. Hobbs
K.S. Ranjitsinhji
L. Hutton
F.E. Woolley
W. Rhodes
L.E.G. Ames or T.G. Evans
M.W. Tate
H. Larwood
G.A. Lohmann
S.F. Barnes

ISAAC VIVIAN ALEXANDER RICHARDS

Leeward Islands, Combined Islands, Somerset and Queensland

Richards may be considered the greatest of West Indies batsmen by those who have proved it to their satisfaction by feeding a few thousand details into their analytical means of proof. What support has Richards received from his batting companions? What is the calibre of the bowling pitted against him? How much has recent West Indies dominance of the game helped — or indeed, hindered him? How much has he suffered from a surfeit of cricket?

THE OVAL, 1976

By John Woodcock

13 August 1976. As inevitably as if his name was Bradman and the year was 1930 or 1934, Vivian Richards played another long innings against England when the fifth Test match started yesterday. By close of play he had made 200 out of a West Indian score of 373 for three. Fredericks scored 71, Rowe 70, and Lloyd and King, as well as Richards, are still to be dismissed.

If ever there was a day for winning the toss, this was it. England's one real chance seemed to lie in scoring some runs and then hoping to embarrass West Indies on a wearing pitch. Instead, Lloyd called right, for the fourth time out of five, and although England made an early break, they lacked the penetration that only truly fast bowling can provide on a pitch as slow as this and still

WEST INDIES

1st innings

R.C. Fredericks	c Balderstone b Miller	71
C.G. Greenidge	lbw b Willis	0
I.V.A. Richards	not out	200
L.G. Rowe	st Knott b Underwood	70
C.H. Lloyd	not out	15
Extras	(b 1, lb 10, nb 6)	17
Total	(3 wkts)	373

To bat: C.L. King, D.L. Murray, V.A. Holder, M.A. Holding, A.M.E. Roberts, W.W. Daniel.

Fall of wickets: 1–5, 2–159, 3–350.

ENGLAND BOWLING

	O	M	R	W
Willis	9	2	30	1
Selvey	10	0	45	0
Underwood	30	8	87	1
Woolmer	7	0	32	0
Miller	16	2	58	1
Balderstone	5	0	24	0
Greig	19	3	51	0
Willey	3	0	11	0
Steele	3	0	18	0

ENGLAND: R.A. Woolmer, D.L. Amiss, D.S. Steele, J.C. Balderstone, P. Willey, A.W. Greig, A.P.E. Knott, G. Miller, D.L. Underwood, R.G.D. Willis, M.W.W. Selvey.

Umpires: W.E. Alley and H.D. Bird

in good repair. Any self-respecting county side would have expected to make runs against this England attack in yesterday's conditions.

Richards's 100 was his 12th of the year, seven

of them in his last 10 Test matches. No one, I think, has scored seven Test hundreds in the same year before. Hammond once got six, so did Compton. Walcott scored five in one series, but Richards's seven, against Australia, India and England, is something new. Supremely well he played, too. There is not a shot he lacks, though yesterday, when no bouncers were bowled, he did not hook.

In the first Test match at Trent Bridge, when he was making 232, he played and missed any number of times. This time he was hardly beaten. He gave no chance until he was 166 and needed to take none either. Fredericks, also, did much as he pleased. Rowe, reduced to a skeleton by Thomson and Lillee in Australia last winter, found the English bowling exactly what his psychiatrist would have ordered.

His last seven scores against Australia were 7, 7, 15, 6 and 6. Once, after a particularly nasty ball from Thomson had got him out, he threw his bat across the West Indian dressing room and said: "Not even God could play those." Yesterday, he was back to his wristy best. By the evening England gave the impression of feeling as powerless as they looked.

Balderstone, who had held a wonderful catch to dismiss Fredericks, put down a percher from Richards, which was symptomatic of England's plight. Poor Underwood was the bowler. The only members of the England side not to bowl were Knott and Amiss. There is no reason on this evidence why West Indies, if they choose too, should not make 1,000 or why Richards should not beat Gary Sobers's record Test match score of 365. By the end his aggregate for the series of 738 put him in the top 10 for any series at any time.

On a pitch that is sure to take spin later in the match, West Indies have packed their side with speed. To discourage them, in future, from so discounting spin, I only hope that before next Tuesday evening Lloyd feels like giving his kingdom for Padmore. For England, Snow decided against playing, because of a slight strain, which left Selvey to open the bowling with Willis. It was another hot, cloudless day.

In the second over of the match Fredericks was missed at the wicket off Selvey. In the third, Greenidge was leg-before to Willis. The chance off Selvey was going straight to Greig at first slip when Knott dived across him and dropped it. England had a long wait for Frederick's next mistake. The ball that accounted for Greenidge came back at him off the pitch. At five for one, nearly five for two, England were not without hope, though it was soon fading.

Greig made an early change of bowling which took everyone by surprise, not least, I imagine, Willis. After four overs, Underwood was brought on in Willis's place, although Willis, having just taken Greenidge's wicket, had his tail up. Underwood had six overs in this spell and 10 were bowled before Willis came on again in place of Selvey.

The first hour brought 59 runs off 15 overs, the second 64 off 16 overs. By lunch Greig had tried six bowlers, which did not include himself. With his first ball in Test cricket Balderstone surprised Richards by turning one, Miller began with a tidy enough maiden. Selvey and Willis were comfortably played once the ball had lost its shine. Batting was made to seem absurdly easy almost throughout the partnership between Richards and Fredericks. It was ended, when it was worth 154, by a brilliant catch by Balderstone.

Spying a long hop from Miller, Fredericks picked a gap to the right of Balderstone in the covers. Although not renowned for his agility, Balderstone threw himself at the ball and held it one-handed. Had Knott caught Rowe soon afterwards off Underwood that, too, would have been a fine catch, taken off the under edge. At 215 Knott put another one down, this time off Greig, with Rowe, then 29, again the batsman. It was another nasty chance.

By tea England had used eight bowlers. In spite of these half chances at the wicket, no one posed much of a problem. Greig, bowling off-breaks for the first time since the second Test match, was tolerably accurate, Underwood looked anxious and Miller was not unpromising.

During the afternoon England bowled 36 overs and West Indies scored 127 runs.

Greig had been keeping Steele up his sleeve for the evening. When he came on Richards eased him through or over mid-wicket as he had everyone else. Past mid-wicket or through the covers was where Richards scored most of his 24 fours. When fatigue, or boredom, caused him to give mid-off a straight-forward chance, Balderstone dropped it. With Rowe he had added 191 when

WEST INDIES
1st innings

R.C. Fredericks	c Balderstone b Miller	71
C.G. Greenidge	lbw b Willis	0
I.V.A. Richards	b Greig	291
L.G. Rowe	st Knott b Underwood	70
C.H. Lloyd	c Knott b Greig	84
C.L. King	c Selvey b Balderstone	63
D.L. Murray	c & b Underwood	36
V.A. Holder	not out	13
M.A. Holding	b Underwood	32
Extras	(b 1, lb 17, nb 8)	27
Total	(8 wkts dec.)	687

A.M.E. Roberts and W.W. Daniel did not bat.

Fall of wickets: 1–5, 2–159, 3–350, 4–524, 5–547, 6–640, 7–642, 8–687.

ENGLAND BOWLING

	O	M	R	W
Willis	15	3	73	1
Selvey	15	0	67	0
Underwood	60.5	15	165	3
Woolmer	9	0	44	0
Miller	27	4	106	1
Balderstone	16	0	80	1
Greig	34	5	96	2
Willey	3	0	11	0
Steele	3	0	18	0

ENGLAND
1st innings

R.A. Woolmer	not out	6
D.L. Amiss	not out	22
Extras	(nb 6)	6
Total	(no wicket)	34

WEST INDIES BOWLING (to date)

	O	M	R	W
Roberts	5	0	19	0
Holding	4	3	3	0
Holder	3	2	6	0

Rowe went for a walk to Underwood and was stumped by Knott down the leg side.

The day ended with Lloyd and Richards quietly playing it out (Richards reached 200 with five minutes to go) and Knott as the holder of a world record. With the stumping of Rowe he passed Godfrey Evans's bag of 219 Test dismissals. Of Evans's 219, 173 were caught and 46 stumped. Of Knott's 220, 203 have been caught and only 17 stumped. Of the late Bert Oldfield's 132, as many as 52 were stumped. That is how much the game has changed.

When, eventually, England start their innings, they are likely to do so amid noises from the north country to the effect that Boycott is wanting to go to India with MCC — to return to Test cricket, in fact. If so, those who have borne the brunt against Thomson, Lillee, Roberts and Holding for the past two years will have to be careful not to be cynical. So, come to think of it, shall I.

Second Day

14 August 1976. By the time West Indies declared in the fifth Test match yesterday they had made 687 for eight, which is more than they had ever made against England. Of the seven higher totals made in Test cricket three were also at the Oval, in the thirties. Left with 50 minutes' batting England got a little bit closer to a draw, Amiss and Woolmer being still together when they went off to put their feet up.

Even Holding and Roberts found the pitch too slow to think it worth testing Amiss with the short stuff that unsettles him. Either that, or they like him too much. Four slips and a gully waited for the catch, but none came, and Amiss will go out again today to try to rehabilitate himself. It says much for Woolmer that there was far less doubt of his being able to look after himself. What strokes there were came mostly from Amiss; what anxiety, too.

Once England had failed to break through in the first hour of the day there was an inevitability about the West Indian innings, relieved only by

Richards's wonderful batting. England had the bowling only to hope and wait. Underwood, for example, took his second wicket in his fifty-eighth over. Out of the 183 overs which England bowled Willis and Selvey, their two faster bowlers, were given only 30 — an extraordinary statistic when one thinks of the extent to which English cricket is monopolized by medium pace.

Greig, with off-breaks, bowled as well as any-one. It was he who bowled Richards for 291 when Richards had the best chance he may ever get of surpassing Sobers's record Test score of 365. He looked disappointed enough at getting out to

RICHARDS The pirate of modern batsmen who worked his miracles with disdain; his on side play to be admired rather than copied.

suggest that he had his eye on Sobers's score. If they needed to win the match to win the series I doubt whether West Indies would have batted for as long as they did. As it was, they could hardly be blamed for so indulging themselves. It is nothing more than Australia used to do in Bradman's day — or than England did against West Indies when they made 849 at Kingston in 1930.

In a sense England were probably relieved that Lloyd continued the West Indian innings for as long as he did. Every minute of the evening in the field for England's opening batsmen meant a minute less to be negotiated in the middle at the end of two exhausting days. It was hot again and cloudless, and as on Thursday the gates were closed. The ground, so parched and hard, must have seemed bigger and bigger to the England fielders as the hours passed; no one excelled, none was disgraced.

As every captain knows, the surest way of incurring criticism is to lead a losing side. If Greig has any doubt about this he need only ask Clive Lloyd, or Denness for that matter. In the present match Greig more than once has tempted provid-ence. He did so first when he took Willis off immediately after he had taken Greenidge's wicket in the third over of the match. He did so again yesterday when he waited for 35 minutes before taking the new ball, which had been due by then for 26 overs. For most of the time he had his spinners bowling to a split field.

To stop a West Indian batsman, on as good a pitch as this, from whipping towards mid-wicket the ball that pitches on the off stump it is neces-sary to "make him come for it" — to give it width, in fact. By bowling mostly at the middle and leg England allowed West Indies to score probably 70 per cent of their runs on the leg side. Greig himself, yesterday afternoon, was the first bowler consistently to test a batsman's patience, as a result of which he picked up the wicket of Lloyd.

But, to be fair to Greig, the lack of quality in the English attack landed him with a job that would have tested the greatest of captains. Against better English bowling than this West

Indies scored just as fast at Lord's in 1973 when Illingworth was captain. When West Indies declared in that match, soon after tea on the second day, they had made 652 for eight. In the side that Greig is leading there is no great pace and no great spinner of the ball; any batsman worth his salt would have hoped to get runs at the Oval these last two days.

Richards made his so brilliantly and with such commanding ease that every batsman on the ground must have fancied his chance of going in and doing the same. Weekes, Worrell and Walcott never played any better than Richards. To say they played as well, when at their best, is praise enough. Worrell was more elegant, Walcott more powerful. Weekes was the most like Richards of the three, though I doubt whether he hit the ball as hard.

When, at last, 10 minutes into the afternoon, Richards was bowled by Greig, he had taken his aggregate for the series to 829, with an average of 118. Only Bradman (974 for Australia against England), Hammond (905 for England against Australia) and Neil Harvey (834 for Australia against South Africa) have made more than that in a Test series. Richards missed the second Test match, too.

Greig began the bowling yesterday with Miller and Underwood. After 11 overs, and 33 runs, he took the new ball, which was promptly hit for 60 in 11 overs. There was no holding Richards. His batting had everything: footwork, timing, virtuosity, balance, strength, concentration, and all the confidence in the world. None of the 12 higher scores made in Test cricket can have been more entertaining; most of them have been infinitely dull by comparison. Richards had batted for just under eight hours and hit 38 fours when he half made to drive Greig, changed his mind and was bowled between bat and pad.

Richards's batting was in a different class even to Lloyd's. The West Indian captain looked as interested in making 100 as in going in pursuit of England. He was most of the way there when driving at Greig, he was caught at the wicket. Which gives me a chance to correct my description yesterday of Rowe's dismissal. I gave Underwood no credit for a fine piece of bowling, being at the time in no position to see it. He beat him in the classical manner — outside the off-stump — and not down the leg side.

West Indies scored another 140 runs after Lloyd was out, at roughly a run a minute. After taking 70 minutes to make 12 King threw in several vivid strokes of his own. Murray, following Richards's Lord Mayor's Show, was mildly barracked; Holding with a final fling made 32 in 20 minutes; Underwood tired and sore, took two of the last three wickets; Balderstone, with the help of a catch by Selvey in front of the Vauxhall stand, took his first for England. When Holding was bowled Amiss, seeing Lloyd declare, knew the moment was at hand.

Vivian Richards started his remarkable run of scoring in the fourth Test against Australia starting on January 1, and his 291 at the Oval was the climax of an amazing eight months. His Test scores this year are: 44, 2, 30, 101, 50, 98, against Australia: 142, 130, 20, 177, 23, 64, against India: 232, 63, 4, 135, 66, 38 and 291 in England, stretching his own record for a calendar year to 1,710. His aggregate for this series is 829, average 118.42, the fourth highest in Test history and the best for a West Indian.

Above him are Bradman (974), Hammond (905) and Neil Harvey (834). His 291 yesterday was the highest innings by a West Indian in a Test in England and the 13th highest in all Tests.

WEST INDIES 687 for 8 declared (R.C. Fredericks 71, I.V.A. Richards 291, L.G. Rowe 70, C.H. Lloyd 84, C.L. King 63) and 182 for 0 declared (Fredericks 85 not out, C.G. Greenidge 85 not out) beat ENGLAND 435 (D.L. Amiss 203, A.P.E. Knott 50; M.A. Holding 8 for 92) and 203 (Knott 57; Holding 6 for 57) by 231 runs.

RICHARD JOHN HADLEE
Canterbury and Nottinghamshire

Hadlee astonished the cricket world in 1984 by performing the double of 1,000 runs and 100 wickets in an English season, the first time the feat had been accomplished for 17 years. Indeed, with the reduction in the number of first-class matches due to limited-overs cricket, *Wisden* decided that 1,000 runs and 75 wickets were the modern equivalent of the double, eventually reducing the target still further to 1,000 runs and 50 wickets.

The difference between cricket in the 1980s and in the first decade of the century is simply illustrated: Hadlee in 1984 completed his double in his 21st match on 27 August, George Hirst in 1906 in his 16th match on 28 June. As the latter's achievement was, and will remain, unique, Hadlee must be paid the compliment of comparison.

	Innings	NO	Runs	HS		Av.
Hirst	58	6	2,385	169		45.86
Hadlee	31	8	1,179	210 not out		51.26

	Overs	Mdns	Runs	Wkts	Av.	B/W
Hirst	1306.1	271	3,434	208	16.50	37
Hadlee	772.2	245	1,645	117	14.05	39

The history of the double between 1876 and 1967 shows 286 instances,* the mean 1,245 runs, average 31.80 and 117 wickets, average 20.40. A classification of all-rounders may be attempted by subtracting the bowling average from the batting average:

. . . .
* Excluding touring cricketers.

1876	W.G. Grace	43.37
1874	W.G. Grace	39.29
1920	J.W. Hearne	37.24
1984	R.J. Hadlee	37.21
1905	G.H. Hirst	34.01
1904	G.H. Hirst	33.27
1906	G.H. Hirst	32.34

Such was Hadlee's feat in 1984.

CRICKET ON A BLASTED HEATH

The England–New Zealand Tests of 1949 were like an enchanting outdoor production of *Much Ado About Nothing.* Thirty Tests between the two countries passed (twenty wins to England and ten draws), then in 1978 John Woodcock found himself in Wellington and quoting from *Macbeth* as a north wind unbalanced both bowlers and correspondents. Boycott, deputizing for an injured Brearley as captain, cast himself as the protagonist and, in the way of actor–managers, lingered long. Any spectator who had hibernated since 1949, and then flown south-eastwards in search of entertainment, would hardly have recognized events at Wellington as a game of cricket; certainly the twenty-two players on that ground would have turned up their noses at the mention of 1949 — "Cricket without aggro?" — and, if modern cricketers take refuge in jargon, "Not meaningful." Partly, even mainly, on account of the wicket at Wellington, cricket was no longer a spectator sport, rather a branch of *realpolitik* as England in their first innings advanced at 23.43 runs an hour from the 11.2 overs an hour bowled by New Zealand. A total of 555 runs from the bat off 254.4 overs, and gentlemen in England then in bed awoke, turned over and returned to sleep.

Third Day

By John Woodcock

12 February 1978, Wellington. England continued here today, against New Zealand, where they left off in Karachi, against Pakistan, by making batting look a formidably difficult science. Starting the day at 89 for two, in reply to New Zealand's first innings total of 228, they took another five hours and a quarter to make 215 all out. In the last 35 minutes New Zealand, in their second innings, scored 12 for no wicket, 10 of these being extras.

The wind eddied round the Basin Reserve and New Zealand bowled a telling length; the ball came through at uneven heights and paces, often moving about as well. It was neither the easiest day for batting nor as difficult a day as England made it look. Their batting can seldom have been weaker than it is at present — and the captain, for all his dedication and his distinction as a player, tends, I am afraid, to aggravate the problem. Boycott's 77 took him seven hours 22 minutes.

In three and a half Test matches in Pakistan and New Zealand, he has batted for 30 hours while making 406 runs — a rate, that is, of less than 14 runs an hour. The effect this has is to depress the other batsmen infinitely more than the opposing bowlers. Where England would be now without Boycott no one can say. They may still win what could become a close and exciting Test match. If so, the runs Boycott made yesterday and today could be seen as having decided it. Yet to score at the rate he does, never attempting an attacking stroke off anything but the rankest long hops, inspires the wrong people.

The pitch has become very dry. It bears enough dusty patches never to play particularly well. Although there are only two days left (tomorrow is a rest day) a result is on the cards. England certainly batted as though they thought so. Either that or they were batting to orders. Right from the start there were no strokes by which to remember the day. Taylor had scored eight in 70 minutes when he was caught and bowled, high up by Collinge: Randall, whose strength is to attack, made only four in three quarters of an hour before being brilliantly taken at second slip, low and right handed by Burgess. At lunch England were 126 for four, 37 runs having come off twenty three overs this morning.

Three times before Boycott was 40 the New Zealanders thought he was out — caught at the wicket in single figures, leg before in the teens and caught at second slip early this morning, off a glove, but New Zealand umpires are notoriously hard to satisfy. There is not much doubt that Wright was caught at the wicket off the first ball of the match or that Boycott was out at least once before eventually he was. That is the game out here, though, and it takes more than the odd alarm to stop Boycott soldiering on. This afternoon, when he was struck a nasty blow by Richard Hadlee trying, of all things, to hook a bouncer, he kept going, bruised and patched up but as obdurate as ever.

The new ball had been taken by then, and Roope had survived a start, in which, for the best part of an hour, he could scarcely lay the bat on the ball. For the fifth wicket he and Boycott had added 57 when Roope, who was starting to play well, was caught at the wicket off a flier from Richard Hadlee. This was a good, lively spell from the younger Hadlee, which lasted until tea.

In the third over afterwards Collinge, having replaced Hadlee, made the crowd's day when he had Boycott caught low down in the gully not quite on top of a ball he was steering in that direction. When Collinge had Rose caught at the wicket on Saturday evening, he became only the third New Zealander to take 100 Test wickets,

Taylor and Motz being the others. Boycott's progress today had been 10 runs in the first hour, 12 in the second, six (including a boundary) in the third and 12 in the fourth. If the ball did some unpredictable things that is still not my idea of Test cricket as Boycott should be playing it. In the course of his innings he passed Jack Hobb's test aggregate. Only Cowdrey, Hammond, Hutton, Barrington and Compton, among Englishmen, are above Boycott now.

Once Boycott was out the last four wickets fell for 27 runs in 65 minutes. Congdon managed to coax a couple of leg before decisions out of one of the umpires, which left him with the remarkable figures of two for 14 in 17.4 eight ball overs, bowled at the gentlest of paces, often to the most defensive of lines. Botham was caught at second slip and Old bowled by a ball that kept low. In the five overs that England had time to bowl after that, hardly a ball was straight. Having batted badly they bowled no better; but that, unlike the batting, is something we know they can remedy.

Close: NEW ZEALAND 228 (J.G. Wright 55; C.M. Old 6 for 54) and 12 for no wicket, ENGLAND 215 (G. Boycott 77).

Fourth and Fifth Days

14 February 1978, Wellington. New Zealand duly gained their first victory over England after 49 years of trying when they won the first Test match by 72 runs here this morning. After the resumption had been delayed by drizzle for threequarters of an hour, New Zealand took another 40 minutes to collect the last two England wickets.

Three thousand spectators were present to see sporting history made. Of the previous 47 Tests between the two countries England had won 23 and 24 had been drawn. Edmonds, first to go today, was caught at first slip off Richard Hadlee who, by claiming the last wicket as well, to another very good slip catch, finished the innings with six wickets for 26 runs.

On a rapidly disintegrating pitch 18 wickets fell

for 101 runs between lunchtime and the close of play yesterday.

At one end the pitch was in very poor shape, having been torn apart by bowlers' studs and all the traffic of a long match; at the other it was less worn but scarcely less treacherous. Starting their second innings immediately after tea England lost Boycott in the second over, bowled off his pads by Collinge when he made to play a full-length ball to leg. It was his first failure in 12 innings since returning to the England side last July, and it showed, of course, the extent to which England rely on him.

Taking seven hours twenty minutes to score 77, as Boycott did in the first innings before the pitch had gone to pieces, was carrying caution far too far; but this evening, without him, England were never in any sort of shape. Miller was out in Collinge's second over to a pig of a ball, caught at fourth slip off his glove; then Rose, playing no stroke to a rising ball from Richard Hadlee, was hit just below the right elbow. By now Hadlee and Collinge were making a formidable pair, Collinge pitching the ball well up and Hadlee bowling unpleasantly short and decidedly fast. I have no doubt that Hadlee felt there was a score to settle with Willis, who had himself bowled provocatively short.

Scenting victory, the crowd gave their bowlers loud and enthusiastic support. There is no more public test ground than the Basin Reserve; it is an island surrounded by traffic, with the boards that enclosed it being easily climbed. As England collapsed yesterday evening so the people poured over the fence to cheer their side on. At 18 Randall was leg before, playing across the line at Collinge, and Roope, having made no contact for 10 minutes, was caught at the wicket off a fine ball from Hadlee.

Only Botham was left after that with the power, and the nerve against fast bowling, to win the game for England. A straight drive, a hook and a square cut, all for four, raised hopes that he might be on the point of something spectacular, with Taylor as his sleeping partner; but, hooking at a ball from Hadlee that was not quite short enough for the purpose, Botham was caught near the square-leg umpire, the fielder having just been put there with that in view.

A good throw on the turn by Boock ran out Taylor, and there were still seven minutes left, with Rose only just back from an X-ray examin-ation, when Hendrick was eighth out. For the spectators — perhaps 10,000 of them — it would have made a wildly happy ending to a day of violent fluctuations had New Zealand won yester-day evening. The joy on the faces of such as Walter Hadlee, president of the New Zealand Cricket Council and father of Richard and Dayle,

NEW ZEALAND v. ENGLAND
Wellington, 10–12, 14, 15 February, 1978

NEW ZEALAND
1st innings

R.W. Anderson	c Taylor b Old	28
J.G. Wright	lbw b Botham	55
G.P. Howarth	c Botham b Old	13
M.G. Burgess	b Willis	9
B.E. Congdon	c Taylor b Old	44
J.M. Parker	c Rose b Willis	16
W.K. Lees	c Taylor b Old	1
R.J. Hadlee	not out	27
D.R. Hadlee	c Taylor b Old	1
R.O. Collinge	b Old	1
S.L. Boock	b Botham	4
Extras	(b 12, lb 3, w 1, nb 13)	29
Total		228

2nd innings

R.W. Anderson	lbw b Old	26
J.G. Wright	c Roope b Willis	19
G.P. Howarth	c Edmonds b Willis	21
M.G. Burgess	c Boycott b Botham	6
B.E. Congdon	c Roope b Willis	0
J.M. Parker	c Edmonds b Willis	4
W.K. Lees	lbw b Hendrick	11
R.J. Hadlee	c Boycott b Willis	2
D.R. Hadlee	c Roope b Botham	2
R.O. Collinge	c Edmonds b Hendrick	6
S.L. Boock	not out	0
Extras	(b 3, lb 8, w 2, nb 13)	26
Total		123

Fall of wickets: 1–42, 2–96, 3–114, 4–152, 5–191, 6–193, 7–194, 8–196, 9–208, 10–228.

Second innings: 1–54, 2–82, 3–93, 4–93, 5–98, 6–99, 7–104, 8–116, 9–123, 10–123.

ENGLAND BOWLING (6-ball overs)

	O	M	R	W	O	M	R	W
Willis	25	6	65	2	15	2	32	5
Hendrick	17	2	46	0	10	2	16	2
Old	30	11	54	6	9	2	32	1
Edmonds	3	1	7	0	1	0	4	0
Botham	13	2	27	2	9.3	3	13	2

ENGLAND
1st innings

B.C. Rose	c Lees b Collinge	21
G. Boycott	c Congdon b Collinge	77
G. Miller	b Boock	24
R.W. Taylor	c & b Collinge	8
D.W. Randall	c Burgess b Hadlee, R.	4
G.J.R. Roope	c Lees b Hadlee, R.	37
I.T. Botham	c Burgess b Hadlee, R.	7
C.M. Old	b Hadlee, R.	10
P.H. Edmonds	lbw b Congdon	4
M.J. Hendrick	lbw b Congdon	0
R.G.D. Willis	not out	6
Extras	(b 1, lb 3, nb 13)	17
Total		215

2nd innings

B.C. Rose	not out	5
G. Boycott	b Collinge	1
G. Miller	c Anderson b Collinge	4
D.W. Randall	lbw b Collinge	9
G.J.R. Roope	c Lees b Hadlee, R.	0
I.T. Botham	c Boock b Hadlee, R.	19
R.W. Taylor	run out	0
C.M. Old	lbw b Hadlee, R.	9
P.H. Edmonds	c Parker b Hadlee, R.	11
M.J. Hendrick	lbw b Hadlee, R.	0
R.G.D. Willis	c Howarth b Hadlee, R.	3
Extras	(nb 3)	3
Total		64

Fall of wickets: 1–39, 2–89, 3–108, 4–126, 5–183, 6–188, 7–203, 8–205, 9–205, 10–215.

Second innings: 1–2, 2–8, 3–18, 4–18, 5–38, 6–38, 7–53, 8–53, 9–63, 10–64.

NEW ZEALAND BOWLING

	O	M	R	W	O	M	R	W
Hadlee, R.J.	28	5	78	4	13.3	4	26	6
Collinge	18	5	42	3	13	5	35	3
Hadlee, D.R.	21	5	47	0	1	1	0	0
Boock	10	4	21	1				
Congdon	17.4	11	14	2				

Umpires: W.R.C. Gardiner and R.L. Monteith

NEW ZEALAND WON BY 72 RUNS

and John Reid, one of their great cricketers and now a Test selector, was splendid to behold.

In England's defence, batting had become horribly difficult, appreciably harder, I thought, than yesterday morning. Being bone dry the pitch was breaking up by the hour. It was of nothing like Test standard. Even so, a score of 53 for eight brooked no argument.

At lunch New Zealand were 75 for one, the only wicket to have fallen being Anderson's, leg before wicket to Old. In two hours thirty five minutes Wright had made 16 and there had been 16 extras: Anderson played more confidently than anyone else all day and Howarth, having given Wright an hour and threequarter's start, passed him off the last ball of the morning.

Not for the first time England had Willis to thank for suddenly transforming the game. In 43 balls this afternoon he took the wickets of Wright, Howarth, Congdon, Parker and Richard Hadlee for 11 runs; in two hours between lunch and tea New Zealand lost their last nine batsmen for 48. Bowling down the wind, which had swung round to the south and was less strong than on Sunday, Willis's success was due more to his lift than his pace.

The ball that was pitched short of a length endangered the ribs, and Willis spared no one. It was this as much as anything that caused Richard Hadlee to unleash a string of bouncers at the start of England's innings, one of which put Rose out of action.

There were two blinding catches by Roope at second slip, both low and diving to his right. I have never seen two better catches taken in quick succession by the same man, at slip or anywhere else. Howarth and Parker were both caught close up at short leg, trying to fend off rising balls, and Richard Hadlee skied a catch to extra cover. In support of Willis, Botham and Hendrick put in admirably steady spells, Botham having Burgess caught at mid-on and Dayle Hadlee at second slip, and Hendrick having Lees leg-before and Collinge very well caught, off another steeply-rising ball, by Edmonds, throwing himself forward at silly point. Having taken the field after lunch in a bad way, England left it for tea in high spirits, with no more runs to win than they should have been able to make. Two hours later they were dead, if not actually buried.

After the match England's captain met the press.

Speaking from behind a black eye, administered by Richard Hadlee when he missed an attempted hook in the first innings, Boycott said this afternoon that the better side had won. He thought both sets of bowlers had used the conditions well, and that England's batting was, "to some degree" a reflection of the standard of English batsmanship. "Character, defensive qualities and technique, as displayed by John Wright and myself" were what was needed, he said, to make runs on a pitch that was never easy. "You can't change the way people play", Boycott said. "You can only encourage people to play their own way and be available to advise them on points if the advice is wanted."

GEOFFREY BOYCOTT
Yorkshire

Boycott was a great batsman who played for Yorkshire. Yorkshire sacked Boycott in September 1986 because it had not won the Championship for 18 years. Admirers of Boycott claimed that this omission had nothing to do with their hero, Boycott detractors that he was wholly responsible. To non-Yorkshiremen there was another explanation.

LEADING PLAYERS OF THE YEAR DURING BOYCOTT'S CAREER

(Overseas in italics)

1962 (Boycott's debut)	1968 (Yorkshire's last Championship win)	1986 (Boycott's last season)
Batsmen		
R.T. Simpson	G. Boycott	*C.G. Greenidge*
T.W. Graveney	*B.A. Richards*	J.J. Whitaker
E.R. Dexter	*R.B. Kanhai*	*G.A. Hick*
M.C. Cowdrey	J.H. Edrich	A.J. Lamb
P.B.H. May	*G.S. Sobers*	*B.M. McMillan*
J.H. Edrich	M.C. Cowdrey	R.J. Bailey
K.F. Barrington	R.M. Prideaux	*A.I. Kallicharran*
D.C. Morgan	K.W.R. Fletcher	M.W. Gatting
P.H. Parfitt	*F.S. Goldstein*	G. Boycott
M.J. Stewart	D.M. Green	*R.J. Hadlee*
Bowlers		
C. Cook	O.S. Wheatley	*M.D. Marshall*
D.A.D. Sydenham	D. Wilson	*R.J. Hadlee*
F.S. Trueman	R. Illingworth	J.H. Childs
L.J. Coldwell	D.L. Underwood	*S.T. Clarke*
P.J. Loader	K. Higgs	*A.H. Gray*
J.C. Laker	T.W. Cartwright	*T.M. Alderman*

1962	1968	1986
J.D.F. Larter	*B.L. d'Oliveira*	*M.A. Holding*
H.L. Jackson	A.G. Nicholson	J. Simmons
O.S. Wheatley	J.S.E. Price	P.W. Jarvis
H.J. Rhodes	N. Gifford	*P.B. Clift*

It never seems to have struck Yorkshiremen during the Boycott-inspired strife that the county's greatest sides — those of the early 1900s, the early and mid-1920s, and the 1930s — would have had a far harder task had they been competing under modern conditions. Lord Hawke's men might well have finished second to Sussex if Fry and Ranji with the bat had been supported by, say, the great Australia off-spinner Hugh Trumble with the ball, particularly in a wet season. Derbyshire in the 1930s were a formidable bowling combination: would Yorkshire necessarily have triumphed had Derbyshire included George Headley?

When Boycott was dismissed by his county in 1986 Sir Leonard Hutton said "He must be the best five-day player there has ever been." To which a former Yorkshire captain, J.R. Burnett, added: "Unless it was on a sticky wicket, if he got a hundred in a normal county match it would make it very difficult for Yorkshire to win the game, because at his normal rate it takes him around 80 overs and that is too slow." In other words, Boycott insisted on playing Test cricket for his county. Here we might insert a note whose irony Boycott will enjoy. Herbert Sutcliffe never played in a five-day Test. Of his 33 Tests in England, 24 were three-day and six four-day affairs; the other three — the Oval games of 1926, 1930 and 1934 — were to be played to a finish but in the event only one (1930) lasted beyond four days, and that was over before tea on the fifth day. It may be argued that the transition from county to Test cricket, and back, should present few problems to a great batsman; in the case of Boycott, it was a dominant factor. Having tasted nectar for slow scoring on the summit, he was reluctant to quicken his pace in the valleys where he was rewarded with orange squash.

It was widely believed that Boycott absented himself from England sides in the mid-1970s because he had not been appointed captain. This encourages the question: could Boycott have run a departmental store? When in 1948 there was some controversy over the appointment of a solicitor, Sir Arthur fforde, to be headmaster of Rugby School, C.B. Fry wrote a letter to *The Times:* "A really successful headmaster [or captain of England] could have run a departmental store, a battleship, or a brigade with success." The thought of Boycott running a brigade horrifies; he was a born supreme commander whom mere generals could not answer back. Boycott as captain of England — a dedicated autocrat in charge of cricketers conditioned by the welfare state — may have experienced problems. Though the genial George Hirst was a fine coach at Eton, Wilfred Rhodes failed at Harrow, where (or so it was said) he would confound a batsman with his flight and then wander down the pitch and illustrate how Jack Hobbs would have played the stroke.

However, a Boycott deprived of the England captaincy at least united Yorkshire. It was bad enough that the job should go, successively, to a Scot, a South African and one born in Harrow; that

BOYCOTT The most controversial great cricketer of his time; forcibly retired at forty-five, he gloried in his own cause.

Denness, Greig and Brearley played for Kent, Sussex and Middlesex...

Boycott made the mistake of playing a virtuoso innings early in his career. Less than two years after this Gillette Cup final masterpiece, he appeared in a Test against India at Headingley, where his lack of enterprise did not meet with approval.

YORKSHIRE EXPLODE ALL MANNER OF MYTHS

By John Woodcock

*6 September 1965.*Things could scarcely have gone worse for Surrey than they did in the Gillette Cup final at Lord's on Saturday. Having chosen to field they allowed Yorkshire, off their quota of 60 overs, to reach 317 for four, which is the largest score ever made in the one-day knock-out competition; Surrey themselves were bowled out for 142. Even in their palmiest days, Yorkshire were never more convincing.

It would be as well for a film of Yorkshire's innings to be circulated to all county cricketers — to be studied as a holiday task. It exploded all manner of myths. On a slow wicket and across a slow outfield, Yorkshire scored at the rate of five runs an over. In the ordinary way they might have been 60 for two at luncheon, and 245 all out at the end of the day, having scored at two runs an over and convinced themselves that it was impossible to do more.

Surrey stuffed their side with seam bowlers, partly to keep down the runs. Instead, the best bowling figures of the day went to Illingworth, who was the most accomplished spinner in the match. Sydenham, Gibson and Arnold were hit to all parts of the ground. Such batting as we saw from Yorkshire makes a charade of three-day championship cricket.

I believe that by playing as they did Yorkshire exposed not only themselves but all the other first class counties as well. In the future I shall never make it an excuse for Boycott that he is unfor-

tunately not endowed with strokes. His magnificent innings of 146, which is the highest ever played in the knock-out and which won him the award of the day, contained every shot in the book.

Cricketers tend to adjust their outlook according to the time at their disposal: a five-day Test match brings out the worst in them, and a one-day match the best. And in one-day cricket there are no averages to concern them. Averages, absorbing as they are, have a corrupting influence on 19 batsmen out of 20.

When Stewart chose to field he took the risk of finishing his own innings in poor light. He thought, no doubt, that on a slow wicket his seam bowlers would contain the batsmen with short-of-a-length bowling, and drive them to desperation. He reckoned, I expect, that by the time Surrey batted the outfield would have quickened up.

The match was due to begin at 10.45. That it started at 12.15, after Friday's torrential rain, was due to the new drains. The ground was virtually full. At one o'clock, in the twelfth over, Taylor was caught at second slip off Sydenham. Soon afterwards, when he was three, Close gave a hard chance between first and second slip which was Surrey's last opportunity of remaining in the game.

By luncheon Yorkshire had made 87 for one off 23 overs, with Boycott already tasting the pleasures of high living. I am told that in his early centuries for Yorkshire against Lancashire, Boycott played as he did now; since when he has been confined by the occupational inhibitions of the modern game.

By the time they were 109 for one with only half their overs gone, Yorkshire must have known that they would win. They went on plundering the bowling in a way that did the heart good. Trueman, sent in when Close's finely judged innings was ended, made 24 in 20 minutes. Hampshire following Trueman, at one time hit three sixes in three balls with glorious strokes.

At 4.15, with plenty of batting still to come, Yorkshire's allowance of overs expired. The whole ground had risen to Boycott by then for forgetting himself as he had. Someone closely associated with Yorkshire said to me not long ago that the best way for Yorkshire's opponents to beat them in the knock-out would be to keep Boycott in for the length of Yorkshire's innings, thereby reducing one end to a trickle. I agreed wholeheartedly. On Saturday Boycott confounded us both by releasing a torrent. May he do the same in Perth and in the eastern states!

There was never more than the remotest chance of Surrey making the runs they needed, even before Trueman settled the whole matter by taking the wickets of Edrich, Smith and Barrington in the same over. Some time later Illingworth, too, took three wickets in an over. Tindall played some good strokes after a shaky start, and with Long he made sure that by the time the match was over the shadow of the pavilion had reached the middle of the ground.

YORKSHIRE 317 for 4 (G. Boycott 146, D.B. Close 79) beat SURREY 142 in 40.4 overs (R.A.E. Tindall 57; R. Illingworth 5 for 29) by 175 runs.

On 8 June 1967 Boycott opened with J.H. Edrich for England in the Headingley Test with India. "Right from the start," wrote John Woodcock, "Boycott seemed resolved to be there at the finish — regardless of his responsibility as a public entertainer." Boycott was 25 at lunch, 75 at tea and 106 at the close. By this time India were reduced to three bowlers, Surti having gone off injured soon after lunch and Bedi at 3.50 p.m. During the day, while England scored 281 for three wickets, India bowled 114 overs.

On 9 June Boycott added 140 runs in three and a half hours, being undefeated with 246 when England declared at 550 for four wickets. Boycott was dropped for the next Test.

On Friday, 14 June 1974 the Yorkshire team settled into the Lansdown Grove Hotel, Bath (332 feet above sea level) in preparation for their game with Somerset. The following morning it was announced that the Yorkshire captain, G. Boycott, was confined to his room with influenza; P.J. Sharpe

would therefore lead the side. No further bulletins would be issued; Boycott was expected to take nourishment.

The Lansdown Cricket Club at Combe Park, Bath, has a distinguished history, among former members being Lord Hawke — like Boycott, a captain of Yorkshire — Mr Francis Popham, whose Wild Dayrell won the 1855 Derby after almost being nobbled on the eve of the race, the young John Simon, destined to become one of Britain's least distinguished Foreign Secretaries, and W.G. Grace. On Monday, 17 June 1974 Lansdown at last came by a worthy opening partner for Dr Grace.

Whether the cricket correspondent of *The Times* was on the Recreation Ground watching I.V.A. Richards make a century for Somerset or at Combe Park watching Boycott make one for Lansdown is not clear; as he strongly recommended Richards to the West Indies selectors, possibly the former.

BOYCOTT BACK IN SWING

By John Woodcock

18 June 1974. Better after his bout of 'flu and keen to get back to the wicket, Geoffrey Boycott found a game in Bath yesterday — for the Lansdown Club against Selwyn College, Cambridge. He made 108 before retiring, with the same satisfaction, I imagine, as a crack shot killing low pheasants.

He was lucky to find a wonderfully good pitch. It was here that Vivian Richards, now playing for Somerset, re-wrote the local record book last season. The ground is beautifully kept and fast scoring, and had the sight of Selwyn's left arm opening bowler, operating from over the wicket in the style adopted so successfully by Solkar, unnerved the Yorkshire captain, there was a hospital behind the bowler's arm.

But all was well. In one of the early overs Boycott hit the second, third, fourth and fifth balls for four and took a single off the last. Soon afterwards he had the ball changed, not because it was out of shape or swinging too much but because of the red marks it was leaving on the blade of his bat.

Little can Selwyn have thought, as they left for their West Country tour, that they would be called upon as cannon fodder for England's most prolific batsman. As improbable, you might say, as a side of clerics finding that their opponents in the Diocesan Cup have a certain Prebendary Trueman opening their attack.

Lansdown had their own Prebendary Trueman playing — the Reverend Peter Trembath — who confessed to praying that (a) he would not run Boycott out and (b) that Boycott would not run him out. Both prayers were answered, so proving the triumph of Methodism. However, it was a bad weekend for the White Rose, whatever its guise. Yorkshire lost to Somerset by seven wickets, Lansdown (182 for three, declared) lost to Selwyn College Cambridge (184 for nine) by one wicket.

BOYCOTT BACK TO CLAIM HIS KINGDOM

By John Woodcock

12 August, 1977. "Go to it, Geoff", the headline exhorted, in the local evening paper. A broadsheet it is, and Boycott's photograph took up most of the front page. Well, Geoff went to it all right, reaching the hundredth hundred of his career in the fourth Test match against Australia at Headingley yesterday, and so making the whole of Yorkshire deliriously happy. At close of play Boycott was 110 not out.

The climax came just before 6 o'clock when he drove Greg Chappell straight for four, and the hats went in the air. The day had been building up to that. Here he was, Yorkshire's one great player of the day, back in the England side after three years of self-imposed and self-conscious exile. Whatever the rights and wrongs of that, there could have been few people on the ground

yesterday who were not moved by the long struggle before them.

At lunch Boycott was 36; at tea, he was 79. With an hour to go he was 88. He had had his bad moments, being dropped once and survivng certainly one appeal for a catch at the wicket which the Australians thought was palpably out. It was a perfect day for cricket — warm, and blue, and just sufficiently breezy. From teatime onwards 25,000 people broke the silence only to cheer Boycott's every run. They crossed their fingers and sweated it out; for all I know, they said a tribal prayer.

When at last Boycott claimed his kingdom, the crowd, now standing, cheered and cheered and cheered. Those who invaded the ground to lay their hands on him will have to be forgiven. When Boycott emerged from underneath them, his cap was missing. By the time that had been returned and he had taken his final bow seven or eight minutes had been lost. Not that it was really lost. It was too famous an occasion for that, and one made more emotional by the fact that, in Yorkshire at any rate, the man is a martyr.

Boycott is the 18th batsman to score a century of centuries, and the first to make the one hundredth of them in a Test match. After this, he can forget his grievances. Yesterday was a personal triumph such as few cricketers enjoy. This was his 645th first class innings. Only Bradman (295), Compton (552) and Hutton (619) have taken fewer innings to reach the landmark. Sutcliffe, the other Yorkshire opening batsman, besides Hutton, to get there, took 700 innings. W.G. Grace took 1,113; Cowdrey, who got there two years ago, took 1,035; Edrich, who made it only last month, took 945. Sutcliffe went on to make 149 hundreds, Hutton to make 129, Hobbs to make 197; Boycott could well have another 50 in him.

By 11 o'clock the gates were closed — just after Brearley had won the toss for England. Nowhere in the world is there a better place for batting than Headingley, on such a morning as this. You can name all the great run-getting grounds, such as

Adelaide and Kingston, and Cape Town and Karachi, and Kanpur, but on none of them is the light better than it was now, the temperature more suitable, the outfield faster or the pitch more accommodating. It was a wretched toss to lose for a side already two matches down in the series.

Yet England lost Brearley in the first over of the match, caught at the wicket off a fine ball from Thomson that moved from leg to off. From the way he turned his back on the appeal, Brearley must have disagreed with the decision. That his was the only wicket to fall before lunch was due partly to Woolmer's knack of playing and missing outside the off stump. Though less often than it often does on the first morning of a match, the ball still moved about.

While Woolmer and Boycott were adding 82 for the second wicket, Boycott looked the sounder and Woolmer the more fluent. Not many runs were scored in front of the wicket. Those that were came mostly from cover drives by Woolmer. When Boycott was 22, and the score 48, he survived a difficult chance to Marsh, diving low to his right, off Walker; when he was 26, a boisterous appeal for a catch at the wicket off Pascoe was turned down on the grounds that the ball had brushed Boycott's forearm.

At lunch, England had scored 76 for one off 28 overs. In the fourth over of the afternoon Woolmer, found out again outside the off stump, was caught low down at first slip, Chappell making the catch look much easier than it was. It was not until Randall had taken three fours to third man that Chappell placed a fielder there for the first time in the day. Just as his brother did, when he was Australia's captain, Greg Chappell believes in keeping his slips and gullies intact for as long as he reasonably can. To break them up must seem like conceding the initiative.

When Randall was leg-before, though, aiming at midwicket, Australia were doing well. Three or four times, too, they might have picked Greig up early on. It was 20 minutes or so before the ball began to go where Greig intended. Some imper-

ious drives came to nothing. Then he hooked Chappell for six, just over long leg's head, and drove both Thomson and Pascoe for four. Boycott, meanwhile, kept plodding along, taking infinite care not only in the production of his strokes, but in checking his guard, clearing out his block, and making sure that nowhere was there a buckle loose. To watch Boycott was to see the perfectionist at work.

When Bright bowled only his second over of the day, at 167 for three, Boycott hit two of the first three balls for four. Off the last ball of the over all those fielders near the bat claimed a legside catch to Marsh, an appeal which grew more passionate the clearer it became that umpire Alley was unmoved. The scene ended with Bright having an admonitory finger wagged at him by Alley. At tea, England were 185 for three.

Afterwards, as the clouds built up, the ball began to move about again, especially for Walker. Walker will bowl no better on another

ENGLAND

1st innings

J.M. Brearley	c Marsh b Thomson	0
G. Boycott	not out	110
R.A. Woolmer	c Chappell b Thomson	37
D.W. Randall	lbw b Pascoe	20
A.W. Greig	b Thomson	43
G.R.J. Roope	not out	19
Extras	(b 1, lb 3, w 2, nb 17)	23
Total	(4 wkts)	252

Fall of wickets: 1–0, 2–82, 3–105, 4–201.

AUSTRALIA BOWLING (to date)

	O	M	R	W
Thomson	21	4	78	3
Walker	27	12	59	0
Pascoe	20	7	48	1
Walters	3	0	5	0
Bright	6	3	14	0
Chappell	10	2	25	0

AUSTRALIA: R.B. McCosker, I.C. Davis, G.S. Chappell, D.W. Hookes, K.D. Walters, R.D. Robinson, R.W. Marsh, R.J. Bright, M.H.N. Walker, J.R. Thomson and L.S. Pascoe.

Umpires: W.L. Budd and W.E. Alley

Test day than he did now, and yet finish with five wickets. When he came off, with Boycott in the nineties, he was given a reception which suggested that that was what he had done. Greig had been bowled by then, driving hugely at Thomson. Boycott's partner, therefore, when he went to his hundred was Roope, always a fidgety starter, and yesterday a lucky one. Half a dozen times Walker must have beaten him. But he avoided running Boycott out, thank goodness. Had Roope done that we might not have had a crowning to report, but a riot.

STUMPED

25 September 1986, leading article. If our society has seemed a divided one for the last quarter of a century, the fault must lie with Yorkshire County Cricket Club and its most celebrated player. It has not been an issue of the Red Rose versus the White, the haves and the have-nots, or the North against the South. It has been a case of whether every decent Englishman (or woman) has been for Geoffrey Boycott or against him.

Bear that in mind and his dismissal this week by the county he has always been proud to call his own should cultivate a wistful tear or two. Whatever the rights and wrongs of it, summers will never seem quite the same again.

That he is at least partly to blame for the controversy which has always clouded his illustrious career is beyond question. He has in his time refused to play for England — apparently piqued at not being appointed captain — has disqualified himself less directly by playing a winter's cricket in South Africa and, on one notorious occasion in India, has walked away from a match pleading sickness, only to be subsequently discovered quietly playing golf. It has not been the kind of conduct to endear him to the England selectors.

But Boycott has been still less popular with his fellow players. He has been accused of dullness at the crease and dourness away from it, of playing for himself rather than for his team, of a selfish dedication to his cricketing career, and of being unacceptably professional.

At 45 years of age, however, he remains a rare cricketer. To be sacked by his county after topping its batting averages again (he averaged over 50 this season) seems a curious way to go. Is he really that unplayable? Industry, politics, finance are worlds peopled (if not entirely) by extremely "professional" persons, whose contributions to the nation's well-being go unquestioned. Moreover, to dismiss Boycott on the grounds that he is blocking the path of advancement for younger promising players is an explanation which makes little sense outside Yorkshire. Nor is it easy to understand why he should be penalized for making runs slowly, when at least he makes plenty of them.

This nation's cricket grounds have surely not seen the last of Geoffrey Boycott, which must mean that we have not heard the last of him either. This is a happy thought on which to end. Whatever one may have thought of this enigmatic cricketer, the last 24 years would have been the poorer without him. To be stumped by his own county side must make him feel rather hard done by.

IAN TERRENCE BOTHAM
Somerset and Worcestershire

Botham at his peak was many things to those who saw and marvelled: Superman, Batman, the ultimate Rambo, a throwback to the heroes of *Boy's Own Paper*, the product of an age which glorified in the cult of the televized individual, an arrogant exhibitionist capable of listening if his leader possessed an ice-cold brain, a champion walker who strode the length of Britain in aid of charity before tackling the Alps with an elephant which clearly thought that if Botham insisted on taking his pet along, at least he should carry it. (This was never suggested to Botham.) "Alone I did it," said Coriolanus in a different context, and if Botham did not often echo these thoughts aloud it was because he was probably otherwise engaged contemplating the sartorial splendour of his then agent, Mr Tim Hudson.

Botham at lower than Test level presented problems. Walter Hammond was the great Gloucestershire and England cricketer, Botham the great England cricketer who sometimes played for Somerset. (The effect of Test calls on county clubs has altered the meaning of the Championship: in 17 seasons Hobbs missed 32 Surrey matches, in 12 seasons Hammond 57 Gloucestershire matches, in the nine years 1977–85 Botham was unavailable, only rarely due to injury, for 106 Somerset matches.) In golfing terms, Somerset welcomed Botham as club professional only to find he was a renowned tournament player who, in any one year, took more wickets for England than he did for his county. The 1985 season saw Botham fourth in the batting aver-

ages, his record for Somerset in eleven games:

17 innings	5 not out	1,211 runs	100.91 av.

in spite of which Somerset finished bottom. This same year Botham hit 80 sixes, scored a hundred off 50 balls in 49 minutes against Warwickshire and two further hundreds against Glamorgan and Hampshire, both off 76 balls. He reached his 1,000 runs in 1,010* minutes, three-quarters of the runs coming from fours and sixes. It was the stuff of mythology.

In terms of glory, certain years are for ever associated with certain players: 1902 with Trumper, 1930 with Bradman: 1981 was Botham. To fashion one immortal innings may hint of skill and good fortune, to fashion another less than a month later suggests an appetite for greatness. To spend the intervening game bowling the other side out is an assertion of omnipotence, as though McCabe had batted two of his masterpieces in one series and between times had grabbed the ball from O'Reilly to bowl like Spofforth. Not only unlikely but impossible — yet Botham did it. He was the reincarnation of Cuchulainn, the Irish hero suggested by Andrew Lang as the originator of cricket. Cuchulainn, armed with a club (an apt description of Botham's bat), defended a hole in the ground into which his adversary tried to pitch a ball.

. . . .

* Students of the absurd may note that Botham reached his 1,000 runs (26 July) in 16 hours 50 minutes—seven hours ten minutes less than it had taken Bradman (31 May) in 1930. Bradman had hit one six—off a no-ball.

In 1981 only eleven Australians were permitted to take the field at the same time against Botham, though the number was irrelevant when he proceeded to hit sixes.

The Botham saga of 1981 must be summed up before being described in some detail.

By John Woodcock

25 September 1981. Little did I think, as I drove away from Lord's after the second Test match, that when the cricket season ended it would rank as one of the best for many years. It had rained for most of May over much of the country; because they dropped their catches, England had lost to Australia at Trent Bridge; Lord's had been a poor, over-cautious match; Botham had just stepped down from the captaincy, his form as uncertain as his future; 12 Test matches had passed since England had won.

Our hopes for something better came suddenly to rest with Mike Brearley. Even before Botham got the second of his two ducks at Lord's, Alec Bedser and his co-selectors had decided to send for Brearley. They had thought of Fletcher, considered Boycott, toyed with the idea of Knight and opted in the end for Brearley, who was in good form with the bat and by common consent was the best captain in the country.

Brearley had led England, between 1977 and 1980, with a good understanding of the job, albeit mostly against less than the strongest opposition. When Australia had their Packer players back in Australia in 1979–80, England had been whitewashed, but the players favoured Brearley's return, and by the time of the last Test match, barely seven weeks after the disillusionment of Lord's, his reputation as an outstanding captain was secure. Like Bradman, Benaud, Ian Chappell and Worrell, of postwar Test skippers, Brearley has a gift for handling sides.

Botham's wonderful achievements against Australia this summer owed almost as much to Brearley as Brearley's record owes to Botham. Whether England's revival is continued will

BOTHAM   The superb physique bore this for years. He restored genuis to English cricket, his success often preposterous.

depend to no small extent upon how Botham fares under Fletcher and, after that, under Fletcher's successor. Although Botham is reluctant to admit it, England could not have won at Headingley and Edgbaston with him as captain — simply because, in the tight and dramatic situations which arose, it would have been asking too much of him to get the strategy right.

So to Bedser for bringing Brearley back, to Brearley for reviving Botham, and to Botham for his tours de force, English cricket is profoundly indebted. They saved the season from being completely dominated by overseas players.

The leading batsmen were Zaheer Abbas (av. 88.69), Javed Miandad, A.J. Lamb, I.V.A. Richards, C.E.B. Rice, P.N. Kirsten and G.M. Turner; the bowlers R.J. Hadlee, S.T. Clarke and J. Garner.

Trevor Bailey thought the Australian batting in the

six-Test series of 1981 the worst he had seen from any of their sides. Certainly the 32 least successful innings played by the specialist batsmen T.M. Chappell, Dyson, Hughes, Wood and Yallop averaged 5.00 runs each. However, 27 innings by Boycott, Brearley, Gatting, Gooch, Gower, Parker and Woolmer averaged 6.85 runs each. 1981 was a series largely dominated by pitches.

What was indisputable was the quality, on paper and often in fact, of the Australia trio, Lillee, Lawson and Alderman; when fit, they challenged comparison with Lindwall, Miller and Johnston of Bradman's 1948 side.

Third Test

By the close on the third day at Headingley, England were 174 (I.T. Botham 50) and, following on, seven for one wicket in reply to Australia's 401 for nine wickets declared (J. Dyson 102, K.J. Hughes 89, G.N. Yallop 58; I.T. Botham 6 for 93).

"The only break in the clouds for England has come from Botham's return to better form," wrote John Woodcock. "...On Saturday he scored a 50, only his second in his last 22 Test innings but made with his old gusto."

Fourth Day

BOTHAM BATS LIKE JESSOP TO KEEP GAME ALIVE

By John Woodcock

21 July 1981. The third Test match contained a most joyous surprise at Headingley yesterday. England were heading for an innings defeat when, against all the signs, they took their score from 135 for seven to 351 for nine in only 35 overs, Botham making 145 not out with as magnificent a display of attacking batsmanship as can ever have graced the ground.

When Dilley joined Botham, Lillee and Alderman, with Lawson relieving each of them in turn, had been working their way through England's second innings as inexorably as they did through the first. Boycott had had to be dug out, as you would expect, and Willey had played a few good strokes before falling into a trap [caught at fly-slip]. But England still needed another 92 runs to make Australia bat again when Dilley came shuffling to the wicket.

The way, after that, the ball rocketed to the boundary, not from one end but from both, was in startling contrast to everything, that had gone before. Botham was already under way, playing much as he had on Saturday but with a shade more discretion. His previous highest Test score was also at Headingley*. That, too, was a superb innings, played, though, not against a rampaging Australian side but against India's medium pace.

What, yesterday, was unforeseen and unforeseeable was the way Dilley batted. In West Indies last winter he scored 11 runs in his seven innings, a total that never looked like being many more. Now, when the ball was pitched up to him, he hit it for four, more often than not through the covers. Until Botham cut loose, Dilley outscored him; once Botham had done so he bestrode the field. He went from 36 to 100 with 14 fours, a six and two singles. It was a marvellous piece of savagery, acknowledged, when he reached his seventh Test century, with a standing ovation. By close of play he had batted for three hours and a half and hit 26 fours and one six, a straight drive off Alderman made from down the pitch.

When he came in, the crowd gathered round the pavilion to cheer him as though he had won the match for England, rather than having given them what amounts to an outside chance of victory. Whoever wins, to have Botham looking himself again makes the remainder of the summer and the rest of the series an altogether more cheerful prospect.

....

* 137 in 1979, an innings which included five sixes and sixteen fours, and lasted two and three-quarter hours.

Close: AUSTRALIA 401 for 9 declared, ENGLAND 174 and 351 for 9 (I.T.Botham 145 not out, G.R. Dilley 56).

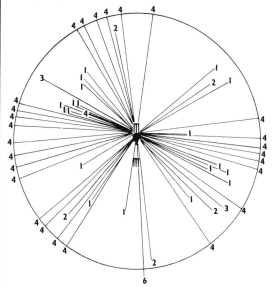

Botham at Headingley, 1981, 149 not out scored in 219 minutes from 148 balls. Balls not scored off, 94: balls scored off, 54 (one six, 27 fours (one overthrow four), two threes, five twos, 19 singles)

Fifth Day

ENGLAND AWAKE TO A NEW JERUSALEM

22 July 1981. England's victory in the third Test match at Headingley yesterday was greeted by the kind of scenes reserved for great sporting occasions. After Australia, needing only 130 to win, had been bowled out for 111, the crowd massed in front of the pavilion, cheering their heroes and waving the Union Jacks they were saving for the Royal wedding.

. . .If Botham's unforgettable innings made the recovery possible, it was Willis who crowned it with a marvellous piece of bowling after Australia had got to within only 74 runs of their target with nine wickets standing. When play started yester-day morning the chances seemed to be that Willis

was playing in his last Test match. He had bowled below his best in England's first innings and it was not until his second spell now, after he had changed ends, that he caught the wind.

That was where Brearley came in. His return to the England side had not only released Botham to play his game unhampered by the burden of captaincy; it meant that England, with so few runs to play with, were under the command of a supreme tactician. To everyone on the ground, except those who wanted Australia to win, it was a great reassurance to see Brearley handling the situation with calm and understanding.

After England's last wicket had added only another five runs at the start of the day, Brearley opened the bowling with Botham and Dilley, England's third different new ball partnership of the match. His reason for this was partly psycho-logical: Botham and Dilley having shared such a decisive partnership with the bat, it was worth seeing whether they could repeat it with the ball.

In the event Dilley, though he was to hold a great catch later in the innings, was taken off after two unimpressive overs. Although in his second over Botham had Wood caught at the wicket he looked hardly in the mood to move another mountain.

That Willis was the man to do this, at the age of 32, and with knees that have often had to be supported by sticks, was a mark of rare courage. He had started with five rather laboured overs from the Football Stand End. At 48 for one, half an hour before lunch, Brearley gave him the breeze, the decision which launched him on his devastating spell.

It was noticeable even in his first over from the Kirkstall Lane End that Willis was bowling faster than in his earlier spell; not only that, he was making the ball lift as well. At 56, he got one to rear almost geometrically at Chappell, who cocked it up for Taylor, running forward, to take the catch. At 58, in the last over before lunch, Hughes and Yallop both went without scoring, Hughes beautifully caught at second slip by Botham, diving to his left, and Yallop also out to a very good catch. Gatting, standing his ground at short leg and reacting quickly to Yallop's desperate attempt to keep down another kicking delivery, threw himself forward for the ball.

Whereas at the start of the day the skies were clear, by now the clouds were rolling in, causing the ball to move about rather more, even to bounce more steeply. To keep his hands warm for

the slip catch that could have gone his way, Brearley was constantly blowing into them.

With Yallop's departure, off the fifth ball of an over, lunch was taken. I harboured a fear that during the interval Willis might stiffen up; but not a bit of it. Brearley had him on again straight away afterwards, bowling as furiously and well as I have ever seen him. When in making a super-

ENGLAND v. AUSTRALIA
Headingley, 16–18, 20, 21 July 1981

AUSTRALIA

1st innings

J. Dyson	b Dilley	102
G.M. Wood	lbw b Botham	34
I.M. Chappell	c Taylor b Willey	27
K.J. Hughes	c & b Botham	89
R.J. Bright	b Dilley	7
G.N. Yallop	c Taylor b Botham	58
A.R. Border	lbw b Botham	8
R.W. Marsh	b Botham	28
G.F. Lawson	c Taylor b Botham	13
D.K. Lillee	not out	3
T.M. Alderman	did not bat	
Extras	(b 4, lb 13, w 3, nb 12)	32
Total	(9 wkts dec.)	401

2nd innings

J. Dyson	c Taylor b Willis	34
G.M. Wood	c Taylor b Botham	10
T.M. Chappell	c Taylor b Willis	8
K.J. Hughes	c Botham b Willis	0
G.N. Yallop	c Gatting b Willis	0
A.R. Border	b Old	0
R.W. Marsh	c Dilley b Willis	4
R.J. Bright	b Willis	19
G.F. Lawson	c Taylor b Willis	1
D.K. Lillee	c Gatting b Willis	17
T.M. Alderman	not out	0
Extras	(lb 3, w 1, nb 14)	18
Total		111

ENGLAND

1st innings

G.A. Gooch	lbw b Alderman	2
G. Boycott	b Lawson	12
J.M. Brearley	c Marsh b Alderman	10
D.I. Gower	c Marsh b Lawson	24
M.W. Gatting	lbw b Lillee	15
P. Willey	b Lawson	8
I.T. Botham	c Marsh b Lillee	50
R.W. Taylor	c Marsh b Lillee	5
G.R. Dilley	c & b Lillee	13
C.M. Old	c Border b Alderman	0
R.G.D. Willis	not out	1
Extras	(b 6, lb 11, w 6, nb 11)	34
Total		174

2nd innings

G.A. Gooch	c Alderman b Lillee	0
G. Boycott	lbw b Alderman	46
J.M. Brearley	c Alderman b Lillee	14
D.I. Gower	c Border b Alderman	9
M.W. Gatting	lbw b Alderman	1
P. Willey	c Dyson b Lillee	33
I.T. Botham	not out	149
R.W. Taylor	c Bright b Alderman	1
G.R. Dilley	b Alderman	56
C.M. Old	b Lawson	29
R.G.D. Willis	c Border b Alderman	2
Extras	(b 5, lb 3, w 3, nb 5)	16
Total		356

Fall of wickets: 1–55, 2–149, 3–196, 4–220, 5–332, 6–354, 7–357, 8–396, 9–401.

Second innings: 1–13, 2–56, 3–58, 4–58, 5–65, 6–68, 7–74, 8–75, 9–110, 10–111.

Fall of wickets: 1–12, 2–40, 3–42, 4–84, 5–87, 6–112, 7–148, 8–166, 9–167, 10–174.

Second innings: 1–0, 2–18, 3–37, 4–41, 5–105, 6–133, 7–135, 8–252, 9–319, 10–356.

ENGLAND BOWLING (6-ball overs)

	O	M	R	W	O	M	R	W
Willis	30	8	72	0	15.1	3	43	8
Old	43	14	91	0	9	1	21	1
Dilley	27	4	78	2	2	0	11	0
Botham	38.2	11	95	6	7	3	14	1
Willey	13	2	31	1	3	1	4	0
Boycott	3	2	2	0				

AUSTRALIA BOWLING (6-ball overs)

	O	M	R	W	O	M	R	W
Lillee	18.5	7	49	4	25	6	94	3
Alderman	19	4	59	3	35.3	6	135	6
Lawson	13	3	32	3	23	4	96	1
Bright					4	0	15	0

ENGLAND WON BY 18 RUNS

human effort he was occasionally no-balled, Brearley told him not to bother, bowl your fastest, he said, and keep digging it in.

After Old had knocked out Border's leg stump, a vital contribution, Willis did the rest. At 68 he had Dyson caught at the wicket, hooking, as important a wicket as any in view of the skill and resolution with which Dyson had played.

At 74 Marsh, a dangerous customer, hooked him to long leg where Dilley, only a yard in front of the crowd, judged to perfection a high and horrible catch. At 75 Lawson gave Taylor his 1,271st first class wicket, a new wicket-keeping record, though in all the excitement few knew it.

There followed a partnership between Bright and Lillee which rekindled Australia's fading hopes. Taking their lives in their hands, they added 35 in four overs before another fine catch, this time by Gatting, accounted for Lillee. Running in from mid-on, Gatting dived forward for a mis-timed hook. The ball was a long time in the air and Gatting had a lot of ground to cover.

With only 20 needed and Lillee and Bright going as well as they were, Lillee's wicket was a vast relief. There was only Alderman to be dealt with now and to finish things off Brearley brought back Botham in place of Old. Botham would have done it, too, had Old, at third slip, not dropped Alderman twice in the over. As it was in the next over Willis yorked Bright and the match was won.

Fourth Test

BOTHAM YET AGAIN A MAN POSSESSED

By John Woodcock

3 August 1981. For the second time in a fortnight England's cricketers staged an astonishing recovery to beat Australia at Edgbaston yesterday. At Headingley on July 21 they won the third Test match by 18 runs after bowling Australia out in their second innings for 111; yesterday they won the fourth by 29 runs, dismissing Australia for 121 when they needed only 151 to win.

Once again Ian Botham was in the very thick of the action. When Australia must still have been fancying their chances of pulling it off — they reached 100 for four in the sort of glorious sunshine they are accustomed to in Sydney and Perth — Botham came on and took their last five wickets for one run in 26 balls. Bowling like a man possessed, he gave England a lead of two matches to one in a series which they seemed only recently to be on the point of losing.

When Border was out at 105, Australia required 46 to win with five wickets in hand.

...Within threequarters of an hour it was all over. Marsh, having hit his first ball from Emburey for four, became the first of Botham's victims, his middle stump knocked out as he aimed through mid-wicket. Next ball, Bright was leg-before to one that kept low. Lillee denied Botham his hat-trick more by luck than judgment, being beaten all ends up by his first ball.

So long as Kent, an accomplished player but one who was weaned on the spurious pressures of World Series Cricket, was there, there was still a batsman left to try to conduct the Australian operation. But at 120 he lost Lillee, Taylor catching him at the second attempt and far away in front of second slip. With only Hogg and Alderman to help him now, Kent decided that there was nothing for it but to throw the bat. In doing so he was bowled off his pads by Botham, who, with the last ball of the same over, bowled Alderman and grabbed a handful of stumps as souvenirs.

ENGLAND 189 (T.M. Alderman 5 for 42) and 219 (R.J. Bright 5 for 68) beat AUSTRALIA 258 and 121 (I.T. Botham 5 for 11) by 29 runs.

Fifth Test

The Old Trafford Test was played on a pitch described by the Australian captain Hughes as "a real beauty". Brearley won the toss and batted, though John Woodcock "had hoped to see England in the field, not least because it is such an ordeal having to watch them bat".

At the close on the first day England were 175 for nine wickets made off 74 overs, Tavaré's 69 occupying four and three-quarter hours. The second day was even more eccentric after Allott, 52 not out, and Willis had added 56 for England's last wicket, Australia succumbing in 30.2 overs for 130 runs. At the close England, in the persons of Boycott and Tavaré, had increased the lead to 171 with nine wickets in hand.

On Saturday afternoon Cuchulainn reached for his club and marched to the middle. The following appeared on the front page of *The Times*.

WAS BOTHAM'S INNINGS THE GREATEST EVER?

By John Woodcock

17 August 1981. Ian Botham's innings was, of its kind, perhaps the greatest ever played and the chart details its progress. It began just before half past two in the fifth Test match at Old Trafford on Saturday afternoon, when England, in their second innings, were 104 for five after starting the day at 70 for one. With a relentless display of tight fielding and accurate bowling, Australia had recovered from an apparently hopeless position to one from which they could well win.

In 34 overs, Boycott, Gower, Gatting and Brearley had fallen to Alderman and Lillee, while a mere 34 runs were being scored. Although still in, and batting with the utmost resolution, Tavaré, England's No. 3, had made only nine runs in the two hours of the morning, and another two in the first 20 minutes of the afternoon. The light was grey, the pitch not unhelpful to the faster bowlers.

When Botham walked out to bat he left an England dressing room in which few could bring themselves to watch the play. There is nothing worse for England cricketers than to see a hard won advantage against Australia being gradually whittled away. Contrasting with England's abject surrender was Australia's uncontrollable joy.

The cheers which greeted Botham were of desperate encouragement, the position scarcely less fraught than at Headingley where he made his historic 149 not out. His 118 on Saturday was an even finer innings. It was more calculated for one thing, and less chancy.

At Headingley, he played a wonderful, unforgettable slog, but it was also a lucky one. On Saturday, with a full sense of responsibility, he played himself in. If Brearley said anything to him as they passed on the pavilion steps, other than the customary "Good luck", it might simply have been: "Now, take your time" — and to the Australians it must have been increasingly worrying the way he did so.

Off his first 32 balls Botham scored five runs. With a new ball available in only 17 overs from the time he took guard, Bright was soon bowling at one end and Whitney at the other. When Alderman did take the new ball, immediately it was due, Botham had made 28 from 53 balls. At the other end, Tavaré was taking good care of himself, not scoring much but relieving Botham of the anxiety of seeing a partner in distress. Of the 149 they added together, Tavaré's share was 28.

Botham had been in for 65 minutes when the new ball was taken. At 150 for five, one or two of the England side were to be seen watching the cricket again. Tavaré, wrapped in his cocoon, had completed the slowest half century ever made in a Test match in England. Then, suddenly, the floodgates opened.

Rather than finishing off the England innings, as they were expected to do, Lillee and Alderman took a dreadful hammering. Lillee had already bowled 14 overs in the day and Alderman 16. If they had lost their edge, it would not have mattered had it not been for Botham.

When, 13 overs later, Botham was caught at the wicket, he had made another 90 runs in 49 balls. Off Alderman's first over with the new ball he took seven; off Lillee's, 19. In the remaining nine overs in which he received a ball he made six and 10 off

Alderman, five, six and 13 off Lillee, eight and seven off Bright and one and eight off Whitney. I refuse to believe that a cricket ball has ever been hit with greater power or rarer splendour.

Where England's earlier batsmen, apart from Tavaré, had found survival impossible, Botham made the boundaries seem far too short and the wicket far too good. When Lillee bowled bouncers to him he hooked them off his eyebrows for six. When Alderman tried one it was pulled to mid-wicket for six. The crowd became a mass of dancing people and waving flags. Never before in Anglo-Australian Tests has anyone hit six sixes in an innings. Having reached his hundred with one, a sweep off Bright, Botham drove Bright over the sight screen for another. He also hit 13 fours.

The fastest hundred in Test cricket, in terms of balls received, was by the West Indian, Roy Fredericks, at Perth in 1975. It took him 71 balls. In 1902 the mighty Jessop scored 102 against Australia at the Oval in 75 balls. On Saturday, with the Ashes in the balance, Botham's hundred took 86 balls (one fewer than at Headingley), though he went from five to 118 in 70 balls.

It was an innings that could have been played in the first place only by a man of astonishing power. Botham's attack on the new ball was a mixture of crude strength and classical orthodoxy.

At Trent Bridge in 1938, while Stan McCabe was scoring 232, Bradman called from the balcony to those in the dressing room: "Come out here, you may never see the like of this again."

So it was on Saturday. Botham, as McCabe occasionally did, is able to scale heights beyond the reach of ordinary men.

The remainder of the game was summed up in the scorecard, Australia making a splendid fight in their second innings when Yallop batted finely and Border, despite a fractured finger in his bottom hand, lasted for five minutes under seven hours.

Tavaré occupied the crease for four hours 45 minutes and seven hours 15 minutes in his innings of 69 and 78, his 147 runs in 720 minutes beating such previous records as B. Mitchell's 149 runs in 575 minutes for South Africa v. England at Edgbaston 1929 and D.J. McGlew's 119 runs in 555 minutes for South Africa v. England at Trent Bridge, 1955.

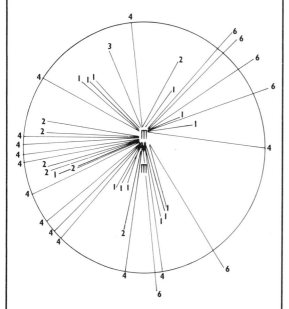

Botham at Old Trafford, 1981, c Marsh b Whitney 118 scored in 122 minutes from 102 balls. Balls not scored off, 62: balls scored off, 40 (six sixes, 13 fours, one three, seven twos, 13 singles)

ENGLAND v. AUSTRALIA
Old Trafford, 13–17 August 1981

ENGLAND

1st innings

G. Boycott	c Marsh b Alderman	10
G.A. Gooch	lbw b Lillee	10
C.J. Tavaré	c Alderman b Whitney	69
D.I. Gower	c Yallop b Whitney	23
J.M. Brearley	lbw b Alderman	2
M.W. Gatting	c Border b Lillee	32
I.T. Botham	c Bright b Lillee	0
A.P.E. Knott	c Border b Alderman	13
J.E. Emburey	c Border b Alderman	1
P.J.W. Allott	not out	52
R.G.D. Willis	c Hughes b Lillee	11
Extras	(lb 6, w 2)	8
Total		231

2nd innings

G. Boycott	lbw b Alderman	37
G.A. Gooch	b Alderman	5
C.J. Tavaré	c Kent b Alderman	78
D.I. Gower	c Bright b Lillee	1
M.W. Gatting	lbw b Alderman	11
J.M. Brearley	c Marsh b Alderman	3
I.T. Botham	c Marsh b Whitney	118
A.P.E. Knott	c Dyson b Lillee	59
J.E. Emburey	c Kent b Whitney	57
P.J.W. Allott	c Hughes b Bright	14
R.G.D. Willis	not out	5
Extras	(b 1, lb 12, nb 3)	16
Total		404

Fall of wickets: 1–19, 2–25, 3–57, 4–62, 5–109, 6–109, 7–131, 8–132, 9–175, 10–231.

Second innings: 1–7, 2–79, 3–80, 4–98, 5–104, 6–253, 7–282, 8–356, 9–396, 10–404.

AUSTRALIA

1st innings

G.M. Wood	lbw b Allott	19
J. Dyson	c Botham b Willis	0
K.J. Hughes	lbw b Willis	4
G.N. Yallop	c Botham b Willis	0
M.F. Kent	c Knott b Emburey	52
A.R. Border	c Gower b Botham	11
R.W. Marsh	c Botham b Willis	1
R.J. Bright	c Knott b Botham	22
D.K. Lillee	c Gooch b Botham	13
M.J. Whitney	b Allott	0
T.M. Alderman	not out	2
Extras	(nb 6)	6
Total		130

2nd innings

G.M. Wood	c Knott b Allott	6
J. Dyson	run out	5
K.J. Hughes	lbw b Botham	43
G.N. Yallop	b Emburey	114
A.R. Border	not out	123
M.F. Kent	c Brearley b Emburey	2
R.W. Marsh	c Knott b Willis	47
R.J. Bright	c Knott b Willis	5
D.K. Lillee	c Botham b Allott	28
T.M. Alderman	lbw b Botham	0
M.J. Whitney	c Gatting b Willis	0
Extras	(lb 9, w 2, nb 18)	29
Total		402

Fall of wickets: 1–20, 2–24, 3–24, 4–24, 5–58, 6–59, 7–104, 8–125, 9–126, 10–130.

Second innings: 1–7, 2–24, 3–119, 4–198, 5–206, 6–296, 7–322, 8–373, 9–378, 10–402.

AUSTRALIA BOWLING (6-ball overs)

	O	M	R	W	O	M	R	W
Lillee	24.1	8	55	4	46	13	137	2
Alderman	29	5	88	4	52	19	109	5
Whitney	17	3	50	2	27	6	74	2
Bright	16	6	30	0	26.4	11	68	1

ENGLAND BOWLING

	O	M	R	W	O	M	R	W
Willis	14	0	63	4	30.5	2	96	3
Allott	6	1	17	2	17	3	71	2
Botham	6.2	1	28	3	36	16	86	2
Emburey	4	0	16	1	49	9	107	2
Gatting					3	1	13	0

Umpires: D.J. Constant and K.E. Palmer

ENGLAND WON BY 103 RUNS

INDEX OF TEST CRICKETERS

INDEX OF CORRESPONDENTS

PICTURE ACKNOWLEDGE- MENTS

Endpapers, Patrick Eagar and BBC Hulton Picture Library; pp. 10, 25, 28, 32, 48 BBC Hulton Picture Library; p. 60 A. Wilkes & Son; p. 73 The Keystone Collection; pp. 86, 107, 124, 129 BBC Hulton Picture Library; Photos Ltd; pp. 137–8 The Keystone Collection; pp. 144, 158, 175, 192, 202 BBC Hulton Picture Library; p. 207 P.A. Reuter; pp. 216, 237, 244, 263, 270, 277, 286, 303, 310, 322, 327, 335, 342 BBC Hulton Picture Library.